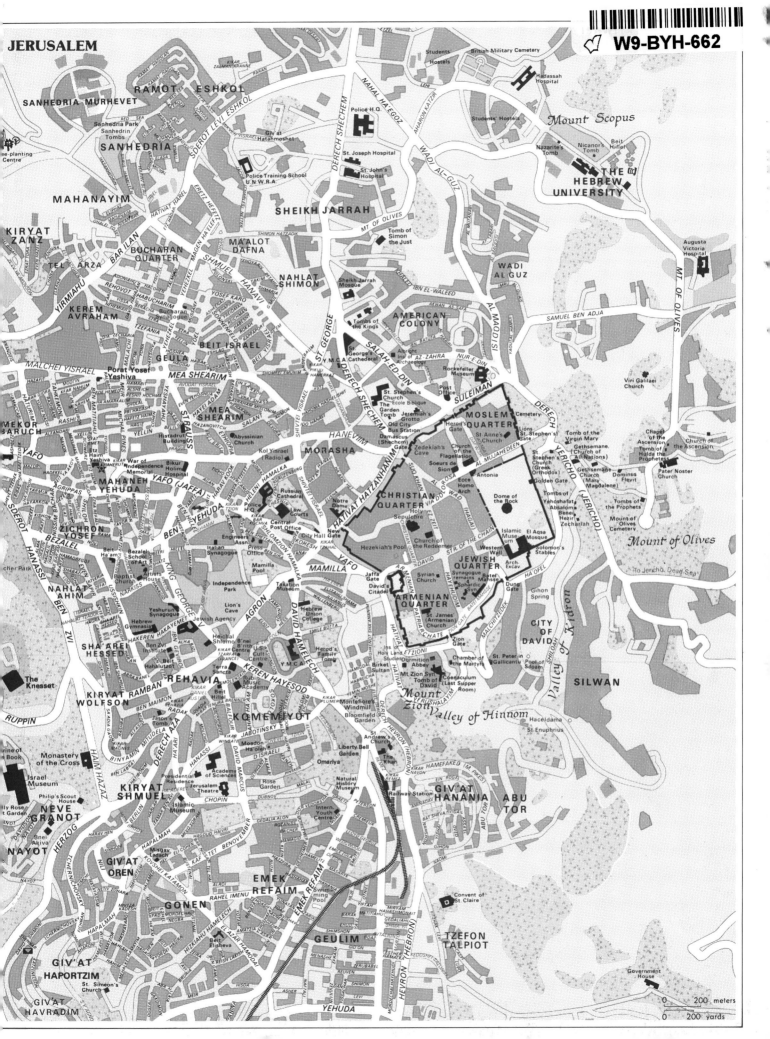

ZONDERVAN NIV

ATLAS OF

THE BIBLE

PREMIER
REFERENCE
SERIES

ZONDERVAN NIV
ATLAS OF
THE BIBLE

CARL G. RASMUSSEN

MAPS BY CARTA, JERUSALEM

ZondervanPublishingHouse

Grand Rapids, Michigan

A Division of HarperCollinsPublishers

CARL RASMUSSEN is professor of Old Testament at Bethel College, St. Paul, Minnesota, and adjunct professor at the Institute of Holy Land Studies in Jerusalem. He was for seven years dean of the Institute of Holy Land Studies in Jerusalem. His love for and intimate knowledge of the lands of the Bible are in evidence throughout the text of this atlas.

Zondervan NIV Atlas of the Bible
Text: Copyright © 1989 by Carl G Rasmussen.
Maps: Copyright © 1989 by Carta, Jerusalem

Published simultaneously in the United Kingdom by
Marshall-Pickering under the title
The NIV Atlas of the Bible

Requests for information should be addressed to:
ZondervanPublishingHouse
Grand Rapids, Michigan 49530

Library of Congress Cataloging-in-Publication Data

Rasmussen, Carl.
    The Zondervan NIV Atlas of the Bible / by Carl Rasmussen
        p.   cm.
        ISBN: 0-310-25160-5
    1. Bible–Geography.   2. Bible—History of Biblical events.   3. Bible—History of contemporary events.   I. Carta
(Firm).   II. Title.   III. Title: NIV atlas of the Bible.
    BS630.R37   1989
    220.9'1—dc20
                                                                                                    89-8506
                                                                                                    CIP

Picture Credits: Photographs pages 14, 30, 206, 207 (both), p. 208 (all six) – Zev Radovan; pages 2, 11, 109, 117 – Seffy Ben-Yoseph; page 67 – Judith Hadley; pages 22, 56, 63 – from *Picturesque Palestine—Sinai and Egypt*, ed. Sir Charles Wilson; drawings pages 82, 84, 139 – Carta; all other photographs are by the author, Carl G Rasmussen.

The quotation from the Merneptah Stele on page 106 is taken from James B. Pritchard, ed., *Ancient Near Eastern Texts Relating to the Old Testament*, 3rd ed. with Supplement, copyright © 1969 by Princeton University Press. Used by permission.

Designed by Carta, The Israel Map and Publishing Company Ltd.
This edition is printed on acid-free paper and meets the American National Standards Institute Z39.48 standard.

Printed in the United States of America

04 / ❖ Q/ 18 17 16

ERRATA

Page 84, Map "Isaac and Jacob"
Mari should be southeast (1 inch east, 3/4 inch south) of the location indicated on the map.

Page 114, Map "David and Saul"
The Jabbok is the river directly to the north of the river currently marked "Jabbok."

Page 125, Map "The Divided Kingdom and Shishak's Invasion"
The dot for Dan should be green instead of black.

Page 181, Map "Paul's First Missionary Journey"
The Orontes river continues north to Antioch and from there west to the Mediterranean Sea.

Preface

In 1967 my wife and I undertook a journey that changed the course of our lives. In that year we traveled to Jerusalem, where we enrolled as students at the Institute of Holy Land Studies. It was during that time that I developed my interest in the historical geography of the Bible, an interest that intensified during my graduate studies in the United States. But it was during my seven-year tenure (1973–80) as dean of the Institute of Holy Land Studies that I became keenly aware of the extraordinary usefulness of historical geography as a tool for the interpretation of Scripture. Upon returning to the United States to assume a teaching position at Bethel College (Minn.), this conviction deepened as I had the opportunity to teach college and seminary students as well as numerous adult Sunday school classes and forums, and to see these students gain confidence in their understanding of the historical aspects of their faith. Indeed, an understanding of the geographical dimension of history opens up new vistas for students of all texts—both sacred and nonsacred.

My work in the historical geography of the Bible has been aided by many, but it is with deep appreciation and thanksgiving that I remember the late Dr. G. Douglas Young and his successors at the Institute of Holy Land Studies for making a study center available for Christian students in Jerusalem. Particular thanks also go to Prof. Anson Rainey, my teacher and later my colleague in Jerusalem, who has so generously shared his wealth of knowledge with me as well as with his other students, and to my friend James Monson, also of Jerusalem, whose enthusiasm and expertise have influenced me as well as countless other students and teachers. In the actual production of this book, Ms. Judith Hadley of Cambridge, and Daryl and Wendy (Youngblood) Morrissey have read the manuscript in whole or in part and have made many helpful suggestions. However, the views presented in this book are my own and in some instances diverge significantly from those of my friends mentioned above.

The writing of this book has taken place over a number of years, and the staff at Zondervan Publishing House—Dr. Stanley Gundry, Ed van der Maas, Gerard Terpstra, Ginny Vander Jagt, Jan Ortiz, and Ruth van der Maas—have been very encouraging and patient during the process. In Jerusalem, I have had the good fortune to work with the fine people at Carta Map Company—Messrs. Emmanuel and Shay Hausman, Lorraine Kessel, Avraham Cohen, Amnon Shmaya, Yosef Valency, and Shula Hod—and their hospitality, suggestions, and creative and technical competence have been much appreciated. In addition I wish to thank the regents of Bethel College for two sabbatical leaves of absence which have helped so much to see the book to completion, and the Christian College Consortium for their generous grant which helped defray the expense of studying in Jerusalem. The staffs at the Institute of Holy Land Studies and Tantur Ecumenical Institute have also been very hospitable during my frequent stays in Jerusalem.

It has been a special pleasure to share the joys of the land of the Bible with my wife Mary and more recently with three intrepid trekkers, John, Peter, and Andrew. It is because of her encouragement and attention to our family while I was off working on this project in Israel or in the States that I have been able to complete this book. It is to her, with deep gratitude and love, that this book is dedicated, with the hope that the reader will come to share our love for the land, the people, and the God of the Bible.

Contents

Preface 5
Abbreviations 8
Introduction 9

GEOGRAPHICAL SECTION

Introduction to the Middle East as a Whole 12
The Geography of Israel and Jordan 16
The Five Major Longitudinal Zones 16
Introduction to the Five Zones 16
Coastal Plain 16
Central Mountain Range 18
The Rift Valley 19
Transjordanian Mountains 22
The Eastern Desert 23
Weather Patterns 24
The Dry Season—Summer 24
The Rainy Season—Winter 24
The Transitional Seasons 26
Major Natural Routes—Roads 27
Roads and Modes of Travel 27
The International North-South Route 27
The International Transjordanian Route 28
Interregional and Local Routes 28
Geographical Regions of Israel and Jordan 29
Bashan 29
Huleh Valley 31
Upper Galilee 32
Plain of Acco 32
Lower Galilee 33
Sea of Galilee 35
Jezreel Valley 36
Mount Carmel 36
Sharon Plain 38
Hill Country of Manasseh 39
Hill Country of Ephraim 40
Hill Country of Benjamin 41
Hill Country of Judah 42
Judean Wilderness 42
Dead Sea 44
Philistine Plain 46
Shephelah 47
Negev 49
The "Arabah" South of the Dead Sea 51
Gilead 52
Jordan Valley 52
Moab 55
Edom 55

The Geography of Egypt 57
The Geography of Syria and Lebanon 62
The Geography of Mesopotamia 65

HISTORICAL SECTION

The Pre-Patriarchal Period   70
    Garden of Eden   70
    Table of Nations   71
    Mesopotamia During the Early Bronze Age   73
    Egypt During the Early Bronze Age   73
    Palestine During the Early Bronze Age   74

The Patriarchs and the Egyptian Sojourn   76

Exodus and Conquest   86
    The Exodus from Egypt   86
    The Conquest of Canaan   92

Settlement in the Land of Canaan   96
    Allotment of the Land   96
        Judah   96
        Ephraim   96
        Manasseh   97
        Benjamin   98
        Simeon   98
        Zebulun   98
        Issachar   99
        Asher   99
        Naphtali   100
        Dan   100
        Reuben, Gad, and Manasseh   101
        Levitical Cities   102
        Cities of Refuge   103
    The Period of the Judges   104

Transition to the Monarchy: Samuel and Saul   110

The United Monarchy: David and Solomon   116

The Divided Kingdom   124

Judah Alone   134

Exile and Return   140

The Arrival of the Greeks   147

The Maccabean Revolt and Hasmonean Dynasty   153

Early Roman Rule in Palestine   160

The Life of Christ   166

The Expansion of the Church in Palestine   174

The Journeys of Paul   180
    The Early Life of Saul   180
    Paul's First Missionary Journey   180
    Paul's Second Missionary Journey   183
    Paul's Third Missionary Journey   184
    Paul's Journey to Rome   186

Jerusalem   188

The Disciplines of Historical Geography   201

APPENDICES

    Notes   209
    Bibliography   215
    Timeline of Biblical History   216
    Glossary of Terms   218
    Index of Scripture References   219
    Index of Persons   222
    Gazetteer and Index   224

Abbreviations

ANEP	Pritchard, J. B., ed. *Ancient Near East in Pictures Relating to the Old Testament.* Second edition. Princeton: Princeton University Press, 1969.
ANET	Pritchard, J. B., ed. *Ancient Near Eastern Texts Relating to the Old Testament.* Third edition. Princeton: Princeton University Press, 1969.
BA	*Biblical Archaeologist*
BAR	*Biblical Archaeology Review*
BASOR	*Bulletin of the American Schools of Oriental Research*
C	Celsius
c., ca.	*circa,* about
ch., chs.	chapter(s)
d.	died
e.g.	for example
EAEHL	Avi-Yonah, M., and Stern, E., eds. *Encyclopedia of Archaeological Excavations in the Holy Land,* 4 vols. Jerusalem: Massada Press, 1975–1978.
EB	Early Bronze Age
ed., eds.	editor(s)
esp.	especially
et al.	and others
F	Fahrenheit
fn., fns.	footnote(s)
ft.	foot, feet
H.	Horbat
ha.	hectare(s)
IDB	Buttrick, G. A., et al., eds. *Interpreter's Dictionary of the Bible,* 4 vols. New York: Abingdon, 1962.
IDBS	Crim, K., et al., eds. *The Interpreter's Dictionary of the Bible: Supplementary Volume.* Nashville: Abingdon, 1976.
IEJ	*Israel Exploration Journal*
in.	inch(es)
J.	Jebel
JBL	*Journal of Biblical Literature*
Jos.*Antiq.*	Josephus: *The Antiquities of the Jews*

Jos.*Apion*	Josephus: *Against Apion*
Jos.*Life*	Josephus: *Life*
Jos.*War*	Josephus: *The Jewish War*
Kh.	Khirbet
KJV	King James Version
km.	kilometer(s)
L.	lake
LB	Late Bronze Age
LXX	Septuagint
m.	meter(s)
MB	Middle Bronze Age
MBA	Aharoni, Y., and Avi-Yonah, M. *The Macmillan Bible Atlas.* Revised edition. New York: Macmillan, 1977.
mi.	mile(s)
mm.	millimeters
MT	Masoretic text
Mt(s).	Mountain(s)
N.	Nahr/Nahal
NASB	New American Standard Bible
NBD	Douglas, J. D., and Hillyer, N., eds. *New Bible Dictionary.* Second edition. Wheaton: Tyndale, 1982.
NEB	New English Bible
NIV	New International Version of the Bible
NT	New Testament
OT	Old Testament
p., pp.	page(s)
par., pars.	paragraph(s)
PEQ	*Palestine Exploration Quarterly*
R.	river
RSV	Revised Standard Version
sq.	square
T.	Tell (Arabic)/Tel (Hebrew)
TA	*Tel Aviv*
V.	valley
v., vv.	verse(s)
W.	Wadi
ZPEB	Tenney, M. C., ed. *Zondervan Pictorial Encyclopedia of the Bible.* 5 vols. Grand Rapids: Zondervan, 1975.

Introduction

When one thinks of the Middle East, many different mental images come to mind. Some envision oil wells dotting the barren landscapes of Saudi Arabia, Iran, and Iraq. Others recall pictures of fighting in the streets of some Middle Eastern capital, or desert battles involving tanks and aircraft. Images of mosques and minarets, of bazaars, of camels and deserts flash into mind. For some, pictures of Jews returning to Palestine, establishing the State of Israel, and making the desert bloom are dominant. Yet, for many, the Near East remains somewhat enigmatic and remote. However, for both Christians and Jews, the Near East is of special interest, since both Christianity and Judaism believe that God has acted in and through the lives of individuals and nations in this area in such a way that those special events and peoples are believed to have continuing worldwide significance.

This atlas has been written in the belief that once one has a basic understanding of the geography of the Middle East one has a much better chance of coming to grips with the flow of historical events that occurred there. This is not to say that the physical environment dictated the events of history, but on the other hand, it should be recognized that historical events were oftentimes greatly influenced by the geographical environment in which they occurred. Thus Part One of this atlas begins with a geographical description of the Middle East as a whole—studying its major regions. Since most biblical events occurred in the area that is now occupied by the modern states of Israel and Jordan, special attention is given to the geography of those countries. To aid in the geographical understanding of the regions of the Middle East, the cartographers at Carta have prepared special "block maps" that illustrate the topography of the regions in a very vivid fashion. These maps have been supplemented with charts, diagrams, and pictures in an effort to enable the reader to enter into the world of the Bible.

The second part of the atlas is historical in nature and focuses on events beginning in the third millennium B.C. and continuing up to the fall of Jerusalem in A.D. 70. Although this book is not intended to be a history of Israel, biblical and extrabiblical texts that lend themselves to geographical illustration have been emphasized. Because of the interplay of time and space in historical events, chronological considerations need to be dealt with, and the rather standard dates found in the *Encyclopedia of Archaeological Excavations in*
the Holy Land have been used for archaeological periods and for the kings of Egypt, Assyria, etc. However, dates for the Judean and Israelite kings follow those developed by E. Thiele (see the Bibliography). The dates for Israel's early history—the patriarchs, the exodus from Egypt, the conquest of Canaan, and the period of the Judges—follow a plain reading of the biblical text and in the mind of this author fit quite well with known extrabiblical chronologies. The author is well aware of alternate chronological schemes, but an atlas is not the place to discuss all these in detail. The interested reader will find references to some of the relevant literature in the endnotes of the appropriate chapters. A general chronological chart is located in the appendixes, but more detailed charts are presented at the beginning of each chapter to aid in the understanding of that specific period. A separate chapter is devoted to Jerusalem; it reflects an analysis of the most recent topographical, archaeological, and historical studies with regard to this, the most important of biblical cities. The second part of the atlas concludes with an essay on "The Disciplines of Historical Geography."

The third part of the atlas consists of a number of appendices, which include endnotes for the various chapters, a bibliography of selected important works dealing with the geography and history of the Bible, a glossary of terms, a chronological chart, an index of Scripture references, an index of persons, as well as a gazetteer and index. The latter contains notes on biblical site identifications. In general, the reader can consult the standard Bible encyclopedias and dictionaries for more detailed treatments of various geographic names or the works of P. Abel, Y. Aharoni, M. Avi-Yonah, Z. Kallai, and others. The interested nonspecialist reader is also encouraged to consult popular periodicals such as *The Biblical Archaeology Review* and the *Biblical Archaeologist* in order to keep abreast of the most recent archaeological discoveries relating to the history, archaeology, and geography of the Bible.

In the map-making process one has to choose which existing antiquity site is to be identified with a given biblical site so that dots can be placed on the maps. Site identification is not an exact science, and the reader is invited to consult the essay on "The Disciplines of Historical Geography" to become familiar with some of the complexities of this process. In this endeavor we are all dependent on the work of others, and this atlas is no exception. Pioneering research in the identification of biblical sites has been carried out by many, but the contributions of E. Robinson, Abel, Aharoni, Avi-Yonah, and Kallai are of special significance (see the Bibliography for their works). The vast majority of site identifications adopted in this atlas are based upon their works, but a number of modifications have been made in light of more recent studies.

The spelling of biblical names follows the pattern set in the New International Version of the Bible. Arabic and Hebrew place names have been transliterated in English characters, and usually these transliterated names sound reasonably close to their Arabic and Hebrew counterparts. Those familiar with either language should not have any difficulty in locating the exact Arabic and Hebrew words if they desire to do so. When quoting from the Bible the NIV has been used save where specific exceptions are noted. When extrabiblical texts are cited, reference is made to the standard English translation of these texts, *Ancient Near Eastern Texts Relating to the Old Testament* (= *ANET*). When the reader is referred to the works of the first-century A.D. Jewish historian Josephus, first the older (''Whiston'') reference is given, followed in brackets by the appropriate reference to the now-standard Loeb Classical Series edition.

This atlas with its numerous maps and diagrams contains an immense amount of information and myriads of details. The author, cartographers, and editors have done everything in their power to avoid inaccuracies and inconsistencies and to eliminate errors. However, some may remain, and both the author and the publisher will be grateful for any corrections submitted by readers of this atlas.

I hope that, just as this book has grown out of my classroom and field experiences with college and seminary students as well as with adult study groups, students of the Bible will find it useful both in their personal study of the Bible and in the classroom. In addition, I trust that travelers to the Holy Land will find the geographical section of the book especially helpful as they prepare themselves for a once-in-a-lifetime experience in the land(s) of the Bible, and that the book as a whole will serve them in good stead before, during, and after their travels to the Middle East.

The countryside near Emmaus in the Valley of Aijalon, from the Hill Country of Judah.

Geographical Section

Introduction to the Middle East as a Whole

The stage on which the major events of Old Testament history took place includes all the major countries shown on page 13, as well as some of the smaller Arab states that are situated in the southern and eastern portions of the Arabian Peninsula. This large land mass is bounded on the west by the Nile River and the Mediterranean Sea, on the north by the Amanus and Ararat Mountains, and on the east by the Zagros Mountains and the Persian Gulf. To the south, the Nafud Desert and the southern tip of Sinai form a rather amorphous boundary. By the beginning of the New Testament era, particularly during the apostolic period, the western horizon of the biblical world had expanded to include Greece, Italy, and even Spain.

Much of the Middle East, in its more limited Old Testament sense, is desert. Large portions of modern-day Syria, Iraq, Jordan, and Saudi Arabia include desert wastes such as the Syrian Desert, the Nafud, the Arabian Desert, and the Ruba al-Khali. These huge deserts cover some 487,000 square miles (1,261,330 sq. km.), or about half of the total area of these countries, and this figure does not even include the desert wastelands of the Negev, Sinai, and Egypt.

Besides the huge deserts in the region, the seas and gulfs that help outline the Middle East on the south, east, and west have greatly influenced life in the area. The most important of these bodies of water is the Mediterranean Sea, for it is from it, from the west, that life-giving rains come to the Middle East (except for the monsoon rains in southern Saudi Arabia, which are produced by a different cycle). In very real terms, much of what has occurred in the Middle East can be summed up as a struggle between the influences of the desert and of the Mediterranean Sea. This is true of its geology, climate, flora, fauna, farming, herding, and the movements of ethnic groups. For example, during certain periods the dominant ethnic influences have been from the sea—note the arrival and the historical significance of the Philistines, Greeks, and Romans—while during other periods the major ethnic influences have been from the tribes located in or on the fringes of the desert, such as the Amalekites, Moabites, Edomites, Israelites, and Ammonites. The interaction of these diverse groups was sometimes peaceful but often violent. In either case, this interaction was played out on many different levels and can be pictured as a struggle between the desert and the sea, or the desert and the sown.

Climatically, the year in the Middle East can be divided into two major periods: the dry season (the summer months) and the wet season (the winter months). The amount of rainfall the various regions of the Middle East receive during the winter months varies widely, but generally speaking the northern areas receive more rainfall than the southern ones, higher elevations receive more rain than areas of low elevation, and the regions closer to the Mediterranean receive more rain than those distant from the sea. These winter rains nourish the grain crops that grow throughout the area in places where the total rainfall is more than 12 inches (300 mm.) annually. In addition, flocks of sheep and goats feed on the winter grasses that cover regions that generally receive more than 8 inches (200 mm.) of rain.

Normally, springs, wells, and cisterns supply many of the inhabitants of the Middle East with drinking water throughout the year. The other significant sources for fresh water, apart from rain water, are the great rivers of the Middle East—the Nile of Egypt and the Tigris and Euphrates of modern-day Syria and Iraq. Some of the earliest civilizations developed along the banks of these rivers, where the people could irrigate their crops with river water. Of these great civilizations, the Bible mentions the mighty powers of Assyria and Babylonia, whose heartlands were along the Tigris and Euphrates, and, of course, the perennially powerful Egypt.

One can find the region where the majority of people have lived in the Near East since earliest historical times (ca. 3000 B.C.) by highlighting on a map the areas watered by the Nile, the Tigris, and the Euphrates, as well as those regions that receive over 12 inches (300 mm.) of rainfall annually. This area, in which adequate water supplies make the growing of agricultural products possible, is roughly the shape of a crescent with one point in the Nile River, the other in the Persian Gulf. Its arc passes through Syria, Lebanon, and Israel, hovering over the desolate Syrian Desert to the south. In this area, aptly named the "Fertile Crescent," civilizations have risen and fallen throughout the millennia.

Generally, enough wheat and barley were grown in each of the populated areas of the Fertile Crescent to supply the local population, and some countries (Egypt, for example) were able to export grain to neighboring as well as distant lands during certain periods. Although most of the countries produced sufficient food supplies, many of them lacked other raw materials necessary for daily life. For example, the Mesopotamian region needed timber, building stones, copper, iron, tin, gold, and silver. Egypt, too, lacked local

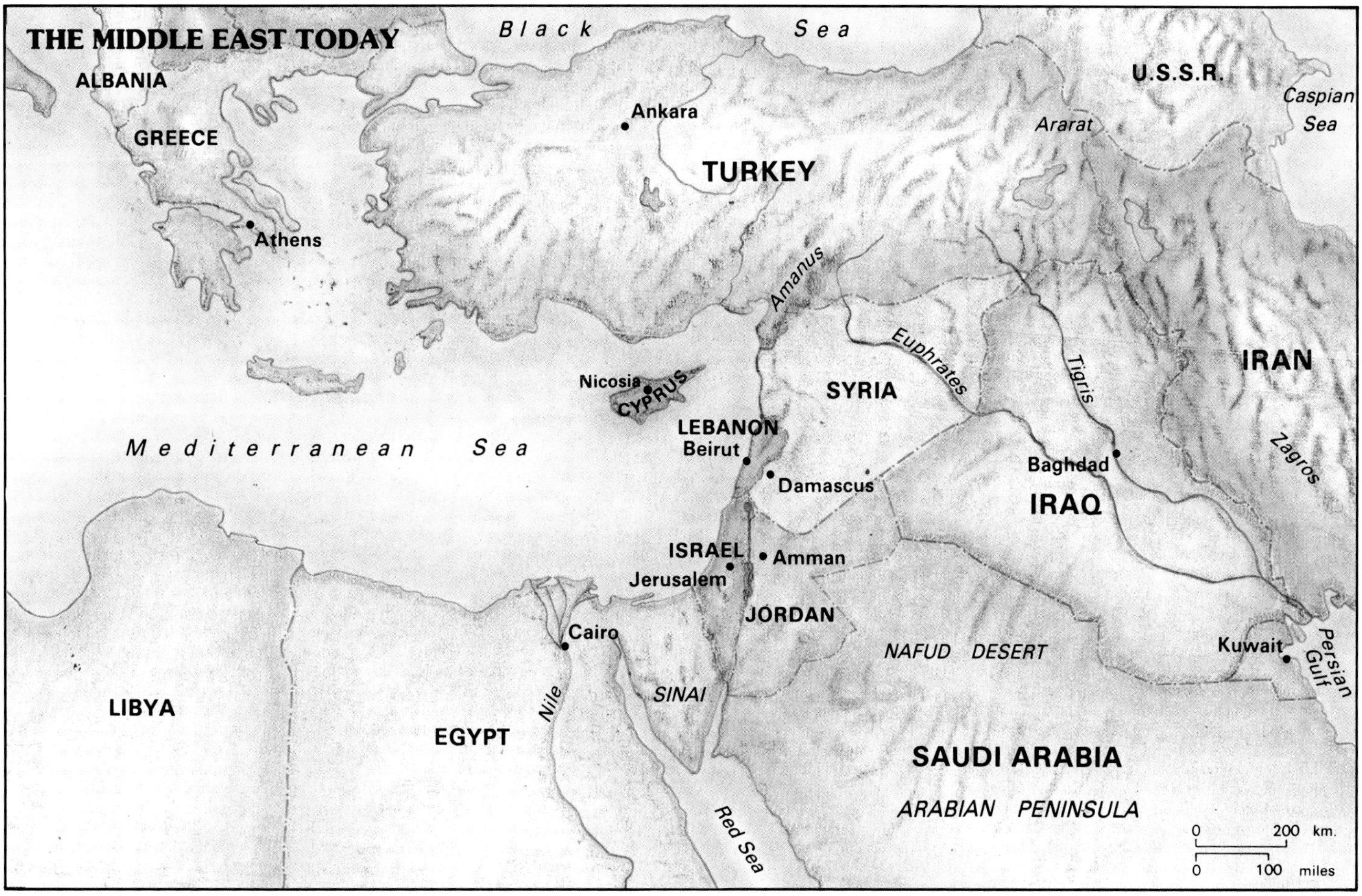
THE MIDDLE EAST TODAY
Black Sea
ALBANIA
GREECE
Athens
Ankara
TURKEY
U.S.S.R.
Ararat
Caspian Sea
Amanus
Euphrates
Tigris
IRAN
Nicosia
CYPRUS
SYRIA
LEBANON
Beirut
Damascus
Mediterranean Sea
Baghdad
IRAQ
Zagros
ISRAEL
Amman
Jerusalem
JORDAN
Cairo
NAFUD DESERT
Kuwait
Persian Gulf
SINAI
Nile
LIBYA
EGYPT
SAUDI ARABIA
ARABIAN PENINSULA
Red Sea
0 200 km.
0 100 miles

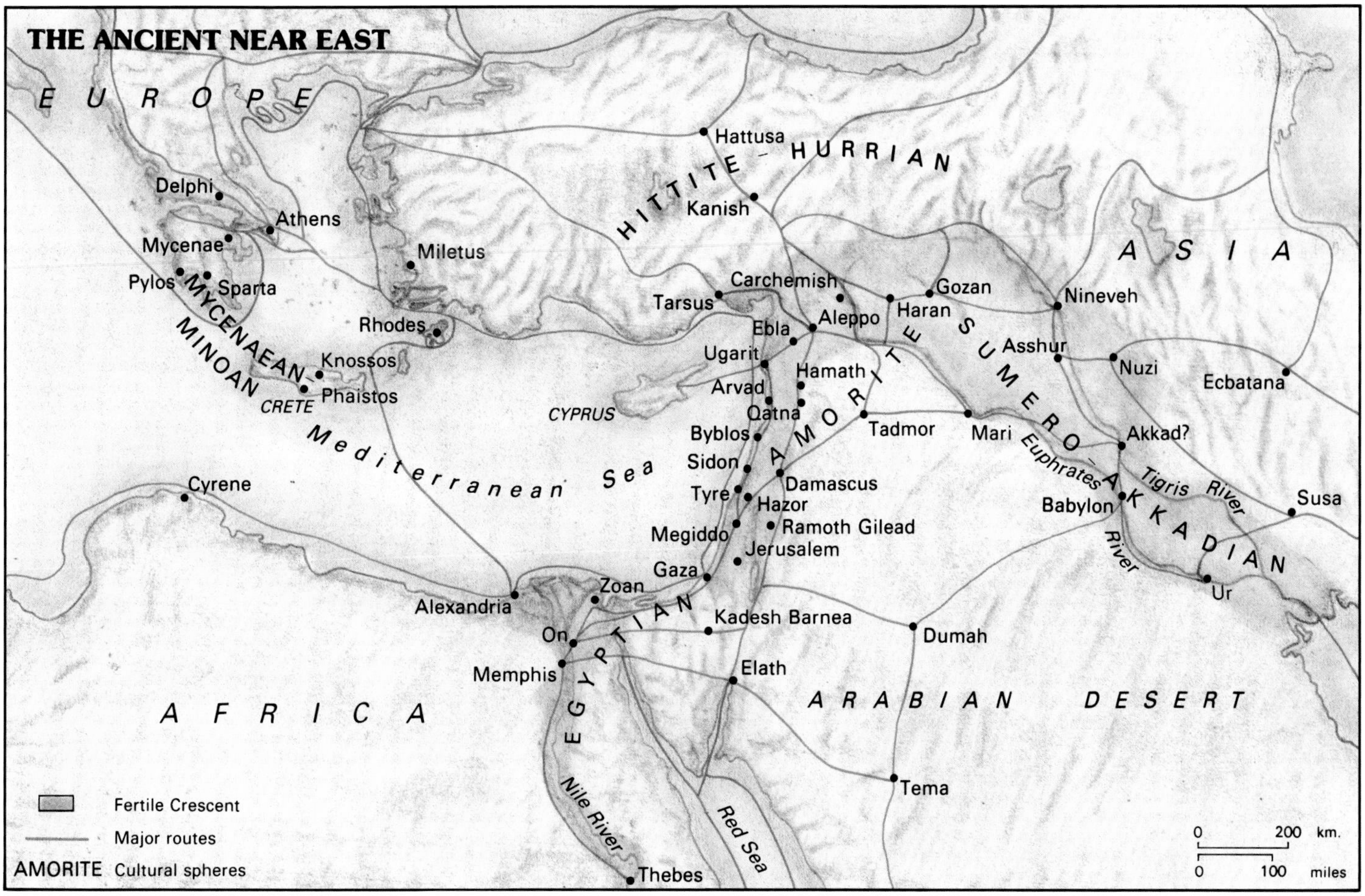
THE ANCIENT NEAR EAST
EUROPE
Hattusa
HITTITE - HURRIAN
Kanish
Delphi
Athens
Mycenae
Miletus
Pylos
Sparta
MYCENAEAN
MINOAN
ASIA
Carchemish
Gozan
Nineveh
Tarsus
Haran
Aleppo
Rhodes
Ebla
Asshur
Nuzi
Ecbatana
Knossos
Ugarit
Hamath
Phaistos
CRETE
Arvad
Qatna
CYPRUS
AMORITE
SUMERO-AKKADIAN
Byblos
Tadmor
Mari
Akkad?
Mediterranean Sea
Sidon
Euphrates River
Tigris River
Tyre
Damascus
Cyrene
Hazor
Babylon
Susa
Megiddo
Ramoth Gilead
Jerusalem
Gaza
Ur
Zoan
Alexandria
EGYPTIAN
Kadesh Barnea
On
Dumah
Memphis
Elath
AFRICA
ARABIAN DESERT
Tema
Nile River
Red Sea
Thebes
Fertile Crescent
Major routes
AMORITE Cultural spheres
0 200 km.
0 100 miles

supplies of timber, copper, and iron. Some of these raw materials were available from countries within the Fertile Crescent (e.g., timber from Lebanon and Syria), but other products, including gold, silver, copper, tin, and iron, were in short supply and were often imported from outside the region. Thus, as these raw materials entered the Fertile Crescent and foodstuffs and finished products such as textiles left it, a network of routes developed that connected the various countries with one another.

Although there were many ways to travel from one city to another, travelers tended to follow well-established routes in order to avoid areas that would impede their progress, such as swamps, rivers, flooded or muddy areas, regions that were too sandy or too rocky, places inhabited by hostile tribes or governments, forested regions, and routes that included long, difficult climbs up and down mountains and hills. In addition, long-distance travel over great desert expanses was normally avoided because of the lack of water and the hostility of dangerous tribes. One of the major international routes ran approximately 1,770 miles (2850 km.) from Ur in southern Mesopotamia to Thebes in southern Egypt. Along the way it passed through great urban centers such as Babylon, Mari, Tadmor, Aleppo, Ebla, Damascus, Hazor, and Gaza. It does not appear that this road as a whole had a name, but it was made up of shorter segments that ran from city to city, and in all probability these shorter stretches had special names. For example, the portion of this road that ran eastward from Egypt across northern Sinai into southern Canaan/Philistia was known as "the way of the land of the Philistines" (Exod 13:17 RSV). This name is a typical example of the ancient custom of labeling roads as "the way to/of X" (where X = a geographical place name). Other portions of this major international route certainly also had names, but they are rarely preserved in the historical sources.[1]

Although an "international route" may bring to mind images of concrete and asphalt highways crisscrossing a continent or country, it should be remembered that "roads" in the ancient world were, until late in the Roman period (ca. A.D. 200), usually unpaved dirt paths. These dirt roads were cleared of stones and kept relatively free of weeds and fallen trees, and in some cases they were graded. In the earliest times the most common mode of transportation was walking, while donkeys were used as pack animals. Under these conditions, a caravan normally moved at the rate of two or three miles per hour. Sometime during the second millennium B.C., camels began to be used on the desert paths. These animals, which on average could carry 400 pounds (180 kg.) of cargo, eventually began to be used on other routes as well. During early times ox-drawn carts were also used for transporting bulky items, but due to the poor condition of the roads the use of carts and carriages for transporting goods and people over long distances did not come into general use until the roads were upgraded during the Roman period.

An international route brought mixed blessings to the inhabitants of the population centers that lay along it. On the one hand, those centers had immediate access to the goods that the traveling merchants were carrying, and the inhabitants of the centers could gain added revenue by imposing tolls and by providing services (food, shelter, protection, etc.) to the caravans. On the other hand, the people traveling in these caravans exposed those centers to new external influences—religious, political, economic, etc.—that were not always welcomed. In addition, some of the mighty armies of the great powers of antiquity—the Egyptians, Assyrians, Babylonians, Persians, Greeks, and Romans—passed along these same international routes, bringing with them death, destruction, and deportation.

A glance at the map on page 13 shows that the major routes that connected the continents of Europe, Asia, and Africa passed through the region of Israel and Syria. It was in this area that God placed the descendants of Abraham, that they might live in obedience to his covenant. There they were tested to see if they would keep themselves free from pagan influences, if they would be a light to the nations around them, and if they would trust in God rather than chariots, for their ultimate security. They were told that obedience to God's commands would bring blessing and prosperity, while disobedience would bring punishment. Thus the drama of the biblical story develops: How would Israel respond to God's gracious acts and attendant commands?

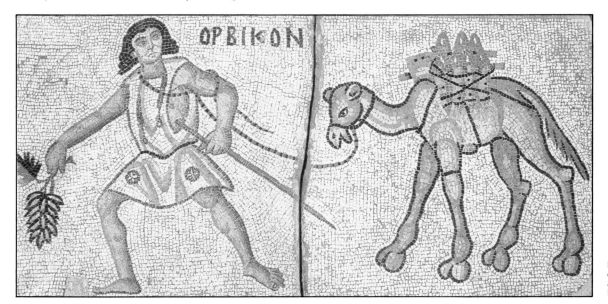

Detail of a man leading a caravan of camels. From a Byzantine church in the Negev.

COMPARATIVE SIZES OF MIDDLE EAST COUNTRIES

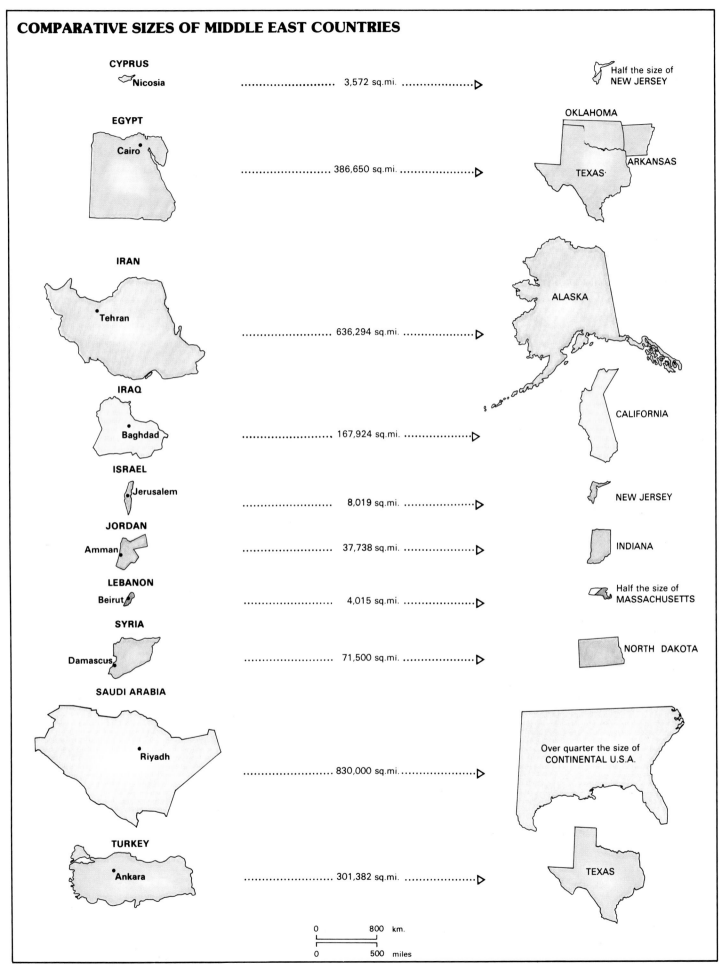

CYPRUS
Nicosia

.... 3,572 sq.mi. ....▷

Half the size of
NEW JERSEY

EGYPT
Cairo

.... 386,650 sq.mi. ....▷

OKLAHOMA
ARKANSAS
TEXAS

IRAN
Tehran

.... 636,294 sq.mi. ....▷

ALASKA

IRAQ
Baghdad

.... 167,924 sq.mi. ....▷

CALIFORNIA

ISRAEL
Jerusalem

.... 8,019 sq.mi. ....▷

NEW JERSEY

JORDAN
Amman

.... 37,738 sq.mi. ....▷

INDIANA

LEBANON
Beirut

.... 4,015 sq.mi. ....▷

Half the size of
MASSACHUSETTS

SYRIA
Damascus

.... 71,500 sq.mi. ....▷

NORTH DAKOTA

SAUDI ARABIA
Riyadh

.... 830,000 sq.mi. ....▷

Over quarter the size of
CONTINENTAL U.S.A.

TURKEY
Ankara

.... 301,382 sq.mi. ....▷

TEXAS

0   800   km.
0   500   miles

15

The Geography of Israel and Jordan

The Five Major Longitudinal Zones

The land of Israel is situated at the southeastern corner of the Mediterranean at approximately the same latitude as southern Georgia, Dallas, and San Diego. The proximity of Israel to the Mediterranean Sea and the Arabian Desert has greatly influenced her topography, climate, flora, fauna, and human history. Throughout the ages, the desert and the sea have vied with one another for control of the land.

The stability of Israel's permanent western boundary, the Mediterranean Sea, stands in contrast to the fluctuations of her eastern border. At times the edge of the eastern desert served as the boundary, while during other periods Israel's territory ended at the Jordan River. This variability is reflected in the fact that, although the Jordan River formed the traditional eastern boundary of the land of Canaan (e.g., Num 34:12; map p. 91), the Israelite tribes settling east of the Jordan in Gilead considered themselves part of Israel in spit of the fact that the "land of the Gilead" was outside the "land of Canaan" (Josh 22; map p. 91).

The classical boundary description of the heartland of Israel was summed up in the phrase "from Dan to Beer-sheba" (Judges 20:21; 1 Sam 3:10). However, to the south, Judah was allotted territory as far as the Kadesh Barnea/Desert of Zin area, and during periods of strength she extended her rule even farther south, down to Elath on the Red Sea (1 Kings 9:26; 2 Kings 14:22; 2 Chron 26:2). Only on rare occasions was Israel able to extend her rule as far north as Damascus, even though that region was included in the traditional descriptions of the "land of Canaan" (Num 34:7–11; Josh 13:4–5; map p. 91). It seems that Israel was not able to control the Phoenician coast to the northwest, except possibly during the days of David (2 Sam 24:7).

This geographical section will deal with the territory from Mount Hermon in the north to Elath in the south and from the Mediterranean Sea to the Arabian Desert, since most events of biblical history took place within this area. A grasp of the physical stage on which the events of redemptive history occurred can bring those events to life and make it easier to understand and interpret both the records of the events and the message of the prophets and the psalmists who lived and ministered to God's people.

Coastal Plain

Five major longitudinal zones can be distinguished as one moves from west to east: the coastal plain, the central mountain range, the Rift Valley, the Transjordanian mountains, and the eastern desert. The coastal plain stretches from Rosh HaNiqra in the north to the Nahal Besor, south of Gaza, a distance of approximately 120 miles (193 km.). Because it is close to the Mediterranean Sea, this zone receives 25 to 16 inches (640 to 400 mm.) of rain per year; the northern sections receive considerably more rain than the southern. Powerful springs, such as the one at Aphek, provided water, but more commonly the people of the region used wells to tap the water table, which lies just below the surface.

The coastal plain can be divided into four subregions. The Plain of Acco is located in the north, extending from Rosh HaNiqra to Mount Carmel. From the tip of Mount Carmel, the Coast of Dor runs south to the Nahal Tanninim. From there the plain widens and the Sharon Plain extends south to the Nahal Yarkon. And in the south, the Philistine Plain stretches from the Nahal Yarkon to the Nahal Besor. In many of these coastal areas elevations rise from sea level in the west to some 600 feet (180 m.) in the east, before reaching the more pronounced rise in elevation to the central mountain range. The coastal plain consists mainly of low, rolling hills covered with fertile alluvial soils. In the northern sections of the plain several low, narrow kurkar (fossilized dune sandstone) ridges run parallel with the coast close to the shoreline. In the south, narrow strips of sand dunes are more prominent. Because of the absence of major topographical obstacles, the coastal plain became the most natural route for north-south travel between Babylonia/Assyria/Syria and Egypt. Even so, travelers had to be careful to avoid the sand dunes, large rivers such as the Nahal Yarkon, and the low-lying areas that became swampy during the winter months. They also had to be sure that their route passed near adequate supplies of drinking water and that they chose the most appropriate track through Mount Carmel.

One of the most noticeable features of the coastline of Israel is that it is relatively unbroken by any major promontories that could provide natural harbors, except in the Mount Carmel–Acco region. Because it lacked natural harbors, Israel never developed into a seafaring nation as did Phoenicia, its neighbor to the north. Acco, slightly sheltered

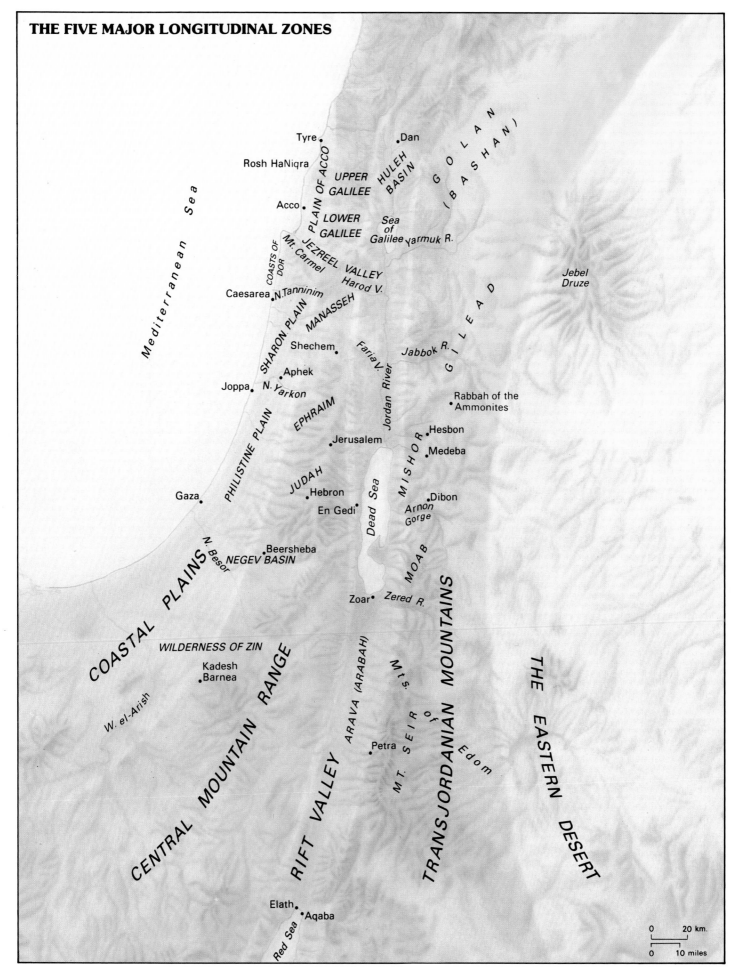

THE FIVE MAJOR LONGITUDINAL ZONES

Mediterranean Sea

Tyre
Rosh HaNiqra
PLAIN OF ACCO
UPPER GALILEE
Dan
HULEH BASIN
GOLAN (BASHAN)
Acco
LOWER GALILEE
Sea of Galilee
JEZREEL VALLEY
COASTS OF DOR
Mt. Carmel
Harod V.
Yarmuk R.
Caesarea
N.Tanninim
MANASSEH
SHARON PLAIN
Shechem
Faria V.
Jabbok R.
GILEAD
Jebel Druze
Joppa
Aphek
N. Yarkon
EPHRAIM
Jordan River
Rabbah of the Ammonites
Hesbon
Jerusalem
MISHOR
Medeba
JUDAH
Gaza
PHILISTINE PLAIN
Hebron
En Gedi
Dead Sea
Dibon
Arnon Gorge
MOAB
N. Besor
Beersheba
NEGEV BASIN
Zoar
Zered R.
COASTAL PLAINS
WILDERNESS OF ZIN
Kadesh Barnea
W. el-Arish
CENTRAL MOUNTAIN RANGE
RIFT VALLEY
ARAVA (ARABAH)
Petra
Mts. of Seir
MT. SEIR
Edom
TRANSJORDANIAN MOUNTAINS
THE EASTERN DESERT
Elath
Aqaba
Red Sea

0   20 km.
0   10 miles

by a small promontory, was Israel's major port throughout antiquity, while Joppa, which had little natural protection, was of less significance. Eventually such seacoast cities as Aczib, Dor, Caesarea, Ashdod, Ashkelon, and Gaza also served as harbors, but only Caesarea ever rivaled the Phoenician cities of Tyre, Sidon, and Byblos.

In portions of the coastal plain, grain crops flourished in the winter and spring months while flocks grazed there during the remainder of the year. But to the international powers of antiquity, such as Egypt and Babylonia, the road that passed through the coastal plain that was of prime importance for their commercial and military activities. For the local inhabitants this was a mixed blessing; in times of peace they gained income by servicing the caravans, but during times of war the populace suffered as armies swept through the territory, consuming their recently harvested crops and taking their wives and children captive.

Central Mountain Range

The second major longitudinal zone is the central mountain range, which runs from Galilee in the north to the Negev Highlands in the south. This range, rising in places to more than 3,000 feet (915 m.), is severed in an east-west direction by the Jezreel Valley in the north and the Negev Basin in the south; in these two places east-west traffic can flow with relative ease.

The central mountain range is composed primarily of harder limestones of the Cenomanian-Turonian-Eocene types. These limestones usually erode in such a way that deep V-shaped valleys are formed. Such a valley—usually dry during the summer months but sometimes flowing with water during the winter—is called a *wadi* in Arabic and a *nahal* in Hebrew. The watershed, or central spine of the mountains, runs basically north-south; these deep wadis therefore run off the range roughly to the east and west, draining into the Rift Valley and the Mediterranean Sea. Travel along the bottoms of these deep wadis is very difficult because of boulders and occasional cliffs. Travel across the wadis is almost impossible; one would have to descend several hundred feet down an irregular slope, cross the wadi, and then climb up several hundred feet on the opposite side. Yet this unusual type of route seems to have been taken by Jonathan and his armor-bearer as they approached the Philistine camp at Micmash (1 Sam 13:23–14:14; map p. 112). Because of the difficulty in traveling either in or across the wadis, the roads in the central mountains have generally tended to follow the ridges. Indeed, one of the routes used most often in Bible times was the road that ran along the north-south watershed ridge between Shechem and Hebron, passing Shiloh, Bethel, Ramah, Gibeah, Jerusalem, and Bethlehem along the way (map p. 105).

In the mountain regions between Galilee in the north and Hebron in the south, the western slopes in particular receive considerable amounts of rainfall (20 to 40 in. [500 to 1000 mm.]). The abundant rain, along with the fertile terra rossa

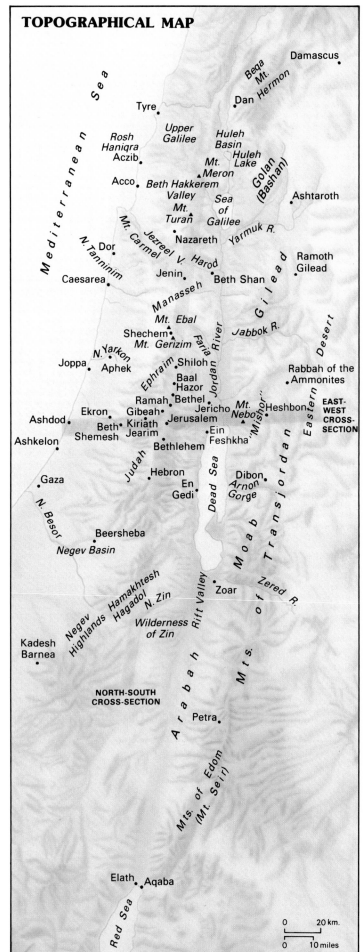

TOPOGRAPHICAL MAP

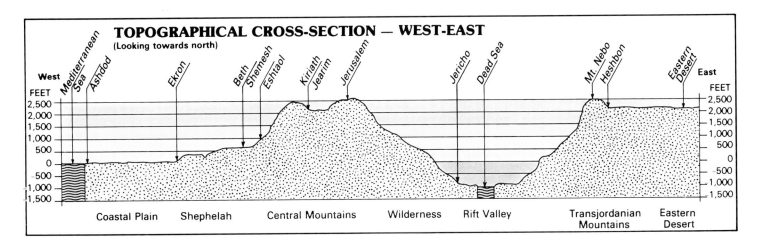

TOPOGRAPHICAL CROSS-SECTION — WEST-EAST
(Looking towards north)

West / East

Mediterranean Sea, Ashdod, Ekron, Beth Shemesh, Eshtaol, Kiriath Jearim, Jerusalem, Jericho, Dead Sea, Mt. Nebo, Heshbon, Eastern Desert

FEET: 2,500 / 2,000 / 1,500 / 1,000 / 500 / 0 / -500 / -1,000 / -1,500

Coastal Plain   Shephelah   Central Mountains   Wilderness   Rift Valley   Transjordanian Mountains   Eastern Desert

and rendzina soils formed from the rock, insure the fertility of the area. Here—largely on hillside terraces that are partially formed by the natural bedding of the limestone—fields of wheat, groves of olive trees, and vineyards flourish (Deut 8:8; Ps 147:14; Hab 3:17–19). Using the numerous stones that they remove from their small fields, the farmers build walls along the terrace edges and then plant their crops in these narrow strips of land, 50 to 100 ft. (15 to 30 m.) wide. The landscape from Galilee to Judah is characterized by this kind of terrace farming.

In the hills, because the upper layers of limestone are quite porous, much of the winter rain water seeps into the ground. It continues to seep down until it reaches an impermeable layer, where it begins to flow laterally. Eventually the water reaches the ground surface on the edge of a hillside or near the bottom of a valley where it flows out as a spring. At times, settlements developed close to these fresh-water springs. But because these small settlements were often located on the wadi's slopes and terraces, where the springs were, they were somewhat difficult to defend against attack from above.

By about 1400 B.C., the construction of cisterns solved the problem of being completely dependent on natural water sources such as springs and wells. Hewn out of the limestone and lined with plaster to prevent leakage, the cisterns collected the water from the winter rains for year-round use. Soon these bell-shaped caverns became commonplace in the hill country. Because the opening at the top was small, little sunlight entered the cavity, and the growth of algae in the standing water was thus retarded. Of course, spring water ("living water") and well water were preferred to stagnant cistern water (John 4:1–26). A cracked cistern, from which the water had drained away into the porous limestone, was useless (Jer 2:12–13).

It was in the central mountain range that the Israelites first settled—in Galilee, Manasseh, Ephraim, and Judah. Because the international powers of antiquity were primarily interested in controlling the coastal plain, the location of the Israelite villages and farmsteads in the mountains provided the people with considerable security. Only during periods when they considered their power to be great did the Israelites move out into the coastal plain and attempt to control it (e.g., during the days of Solomon, Uzziah, and Josiah; maps pp. 120, 128); but this almost always resulted in conflict with one or more of the great powers, and in each instance Israel was eventually forced back into her hill-country heartland. The remoteness, security, and provincialism of the central mountains contrast sharply with the openness, insecurity, and more cosmopolitan nature of the coastal plain.

The Rift Valley

The third major zone in Israel is the prominent north-south depression that stretches from Dan to Elath. This depression is part of the Rift Valley system that extends for 3,700 miles

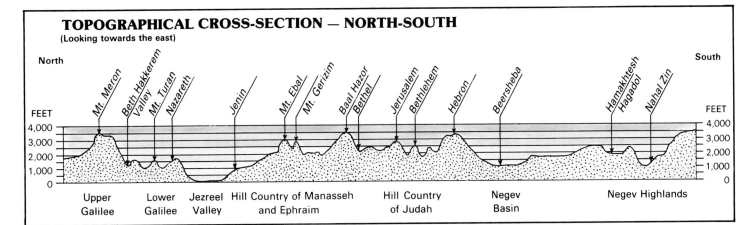

TOPOGRAPHICAL CROSS-SECTION — NORTH-SOUTH
(Looking towards the east)

North / South

Mt. Meron, Beth Hakkerem Valley, Mt. Turan, Nazareth, Jenin, Mt. Ebal, Mt. Gerizim, Baal Hazor, Bethel, Jerusalem, Bethlehem, Hebron, Beersheba, Hamakhtesh Hagadol, Nahal Zin

FEET: 4,000 / 3,000 / 2,000 / 1,000 / 0

Upper Galilee   Lower Galilee   Jezreel Valley   Hill Country of Manasseh and Ephraim   Hill Country of Judah   Negev Basin   Negev Highlands

(5950 km.) from southern Turkey into Africa. North of Israel the system continues in a northeasterly direction into the Lebanese Beqa; to the south it runs through the Red Sea and down into Africa.

In Israel proper, this depression runs from Dan in the north to the southern tip of the Dead Sea, a distance of 150 miles (240 km.), and then continues south-southwest as far as Elath, a distance of 110 miles (175 km.). The various sections of the Rift Valley are diverse in character; a considerable amount of rain falls in the northern section (24 in. [610 mm.] at Dan), whereas in the south the rainfall is negligible (2 in. [50 mm.] at the south end of the Dead Sea). The valley receives runoff water from the mountains to the west and east along its entire length.

The northernmost section of the Rift Valley, called the Huleh Basin, covers a 20-by-5-mile (32-by-8-km.) area. The basin has a Mediterranean type of climate and receives about 24 inches (600 mm.) of rain each year. The springs at the foot of Mount Hermon, which are fed by the melting snows, form the headwaters of the Jordan River. As the Jordan flows through the basin, it is restrained by a natural basalt dam; its waters collect behind this dam, forming the Huleh Lake, known in antiquity as Lake Semechonitis. Until very recent times, this lake and the marshes it created forced people to live around the edges of the basin. A branch of the International Highway between Damascus and Egypt ran along its western perimeter.

The Jordan, after passing through the Huleh Basin, enters the north end of the Sea of Galilee. This most famous of biblical lakes lies 690 feet (210 m.) below sea level and measures 13 by 7.5 miles (21 by 12 km.). The temperate Mediterranean climate makes the nearby region a very desirable place to live. The sea itself is a major source of fish for the inhabitants of the region, and a number of small but fertile plains along its shoreline have been intensively cultivated throughout history.

The Jordan River flows out of the southeast corner of the Sea of Galilee as it begins its descent to the Dead Sea. The actual distance between the Sea of Galilee and the Dead Sea is 65 miles (105 km.), but the length of the Jordan as it winds

its way between these points is 135 miles (215 km.). Along the way the Jordan receives water from the Yarmuk and Jabbok rivers on the east and the Harod and Faria valleys on the west. The Yarmuk is the major tributary; it doubles the amount of water flowing in the Jordan. Until modern times, when the Israelis and Jordanians began diverting water for commercial purposes, the Jordan averaged 100 feet (30 m.) in width with a depth of 3 to 10 feet (1 to 3 m.), although after heavy rains in the late winter and spring its width could swell to almost a mile (1.6 km.) in places.

The Rift Valley between the Sea of Galilee and the Dead Sea can be divided into three north-south longitudinal sections. The whole valley, which is bounded on the east and west by the mountains of Transjordan and Cisjordan, is called the *Ghor* in Arabic. The valley varies in width from 3.5 miles (5.6 km.) at its narrowest point to 14 miles (22.5 km.) near Jericho; its average width is 7.5 miles (12 km.). The bed of the Jordan River and its immediate vicinity is called the *Zor* in Arabic. The width of the Zor varies from 600 feet to a mile (180 m. to 1.6 km.). This area is very lush, teeming with all kinds of plant and animal life. In the Bible it is referred to as "the thicket" (NIV; e.g., Jer 12:5; 49:19; 50:44). On both sides of the Zor is the *Qattara,* a bleak area of chalky, salty marls, where very little grows.

South of Beth Shan the climate rapidly changes from a Mediterranean to a steppe/desert-like climate. It is in general very difficult to establish permanent settlements in the steppe/desert area, except where springs are available, as at Jericho, or where perennial wadis such as the Jabbok or Faria flow. During the summer months the temperatures are very hot: the average daily high at Jericho during August is 102° F (39° C).

The Jordan River completes its course by flowing into the Dead Sea—the lowest spot on the surface of the earth (1,310 ft. [400 m.] below sea level). In the Bible it is called the "Salt Sea" because of its high mineral content. This sea, which does not have any outlet, measures 47 by 11 miles (76 by 18 km.) and is divided into two major sections: the deeper northern two-thirds and the shallower southern third. Steep cliffs border the sea on the east and the west. Rainfall is

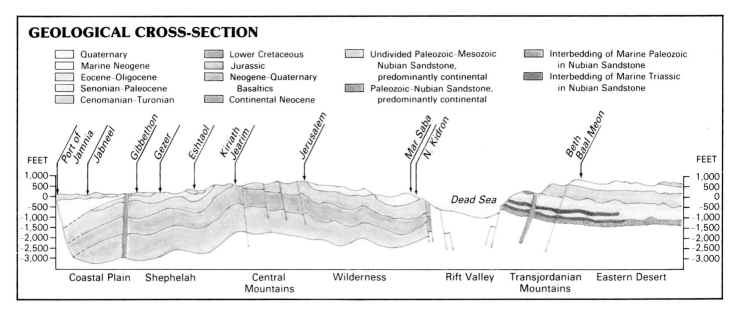

GEOLOGICAL CROSS-SECTION

Quaternary
Marine Neogene
Eocene-Oligocene
Senonian-Paleocene
Cenomanian-Turonian

Lower Cretaceous
Jurassic
Neogene-Quaternary
Basaltics
Continental Neocene

Undivided Paleozoic-Mesozoic
Nubian Sandstone,
predominantly continental
Paleozoic-Nubian Sandstone,
predominantly continental

Interbedding of Marine Paleozoic
in Nubian Sandstone
Interbedding of Marine Triassic
in Nubian Sandstone

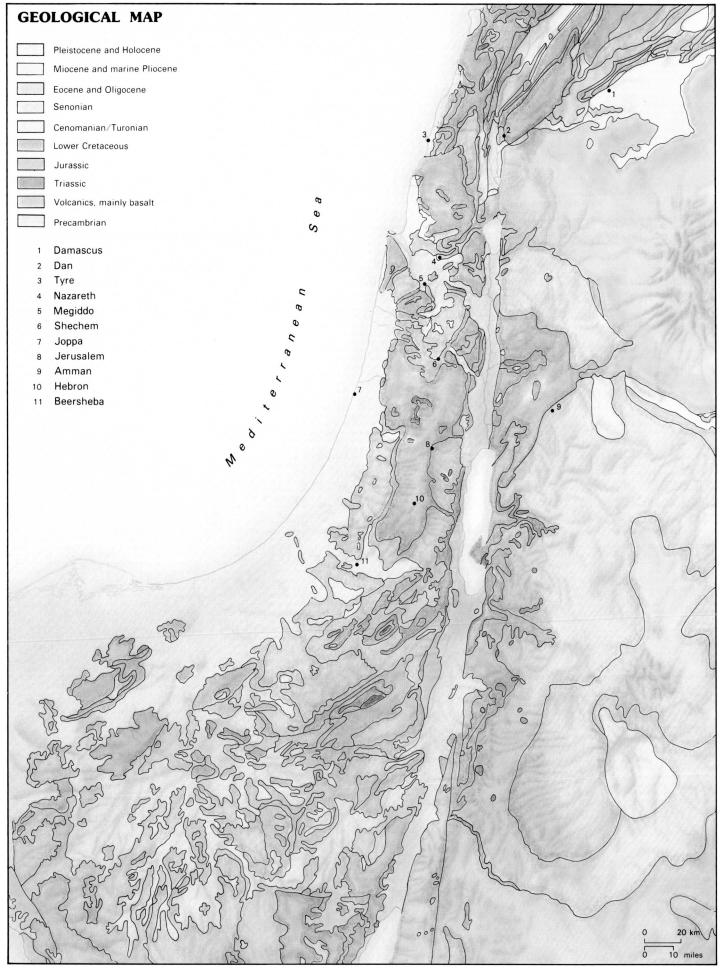

GEOLOGICAL MAP

Pleistocene and Holocene

Miocene and marine Pliocene

Eocene and Oligocene

Senonian

Cenomanian/Turonian

Lower Cretaceous

Jurassic

Triassic

Volcanics, mainly basalt

Precambrian

1 Damascus
2 Dan
3 Tyre
4 Nazareth
5 Megiddo
6 Shechem
7 Joppa
8 Jerusalem
9 Amman
10 Hebron
11 Beersheba

Mediterranean Sea

0   20 km

0   10 miles

sporadic; the southern portion of the sea receives only 2 inches (50 mm.) per year. Temperatures are high, especially during the summer months. Only where there are springs (e.g., Ein Feshkha, En Gedi, Zoar) or perennial rivers (e.g., Arnon, Zered) can settlements develop. Because of the steep cliffs and desert conditions, there was never much travel that passed through this area.

South of the Dead Sea, the Rift Valley continues 110 miles (177 km.) to the shores of the Red Sea. This region is called the ''Arava'' or ''Arabah'' on modern Israeli maps, although the biblical ''Arabah'' was primarily north of the Dead Sea (e.g., Deut 3:17; Josh 11:2; 2 Sam 2:29). The valley rises from 1,310 feet (400 m.) below sea level at the surface of the Dead Sea to 1,165 feet (355 m.) above sea level at a point 50 miles (80 km.) north of Elath before descending to the Red Sea. The whole length of the ''Arava'' is a desolate desert region, hemmed in on the east by the towering mountains of Edom and on the west by the Highlands of the Negev. In ancient times the region was practically devoid of settlements, save for an occasional fort built to guard the caravan routes that crossed from Edom to the Negev and the route that joined Elath with Mediterranean ports such as Gaza.

Elath marks the extreme southern boundary of Israel. At various times the Israelites used the port at Elath or the caravan route that led to southern Arabia to maintain contact with exotic countries such as Ophir and Sheba. This southern extension of the Rift Valley thus was the gateway to Arabia, Africa, and India.

Transjordanian Mountains

To the east of the Rift Valley rise the towering mountains of Transjordan, stretching from Mount Hermon in the north to the Gulf of Aqaba (Gulf of Elath) in the south. While the western slopes of these mountains are often quite steep, the eastern slopes descend gradually into the Arabian Desert. The eastern boundary of this region lies approximately along the line of the old Hejaz railroad, which ran between Damascus in Syria and Mecca in Saudi Arabia.

The northernmost section of this region is called the

Spring on the border of the land of Edom with the rugged mountains of Edom in the background.

Bashan. It includes the Golan and reaches from the foot of Mount Hermon to the Yarmuk River. Extinct volcanic cones dot the landscape, and the rich soil is derived from volcanic debris. This area is relatively high in elevation and thus receives a considerable amount of rainfall and even some snow. Travel in the Bashan is somewhat difficult during the winter months because of muddy conditions. During certain historical periods one of the branches of the International Highway skirted its northern boundary, just to the south of Mount Hermon, connecting Dan with Damascus.

To the south of the Bashan is the region of Gilead, which stretches from the Yarmuk River in the north to an imaginary east-west line drawn through the north end of the Dead Sea. On the east, the desert is only 25 to 30 miles (40 to 48 km.) from the Jordan Valley. The major river, which divides Gilead into two almost equal parts, is the Jabbok. Gilead is composed primarily of the harder Cenomanian limestones, and its western portion is characterized by deep V-shaped valleys, much like the Hill Country of Judah. Topography and sufficient amounts of rainfall make it a good area for wheat, olives, and grapes.

The area to the south of Gilead, reaching to the Zered Valley, was the old tribal territory of the Moabites. It too is bisected by a river, the magnificent Arnon, which flows into the Dead Sea. To the north of the Arnon is a plateau area called the *Mishor,* which in some places reaches elevations of 2,100 feet (640 m.). This tableland was allotted to the Israelite tribes of Reuben and Gad and became a point of dispute between Moab and Israel. The cities of Heshbon, Medeba, and Dibon dominated the region.

To the south of the Mishor, elevations rise to 3,600 feet (1100 m.). This area between the Arnon and the Zered was the heartland of Moab. Various types of limestone and, further east, chalk predominate in this region, whereas along the western cliffs that face the Dead Sea the lower layers of multicolored Nubian sandstone are exposed. Because some layers of the sandstone are relatively impervious to water, numerous springs dot the landscape. Although some grain crops are grown in this area, agriculturally it is not as productive as Gilead to the north, for as one moves south the amount of rainfall begins to decrease. Mesha, one of the ancient kings of Moab, was famous for the sheep that he raised and supplied to Israel (2 Kings 3:4).

South of the Zered Valley the mountains of Edom extend to Aqaba, some of them reaching elevations of 4,500 feet (1370 m.). Along the western crest of this ridge there is sufficient rainfall for growing wheat and barley, but at lower elevations the amount of rainfall decreases rapidly. In biblical times one of the names for the region was Mount Seir, "The Hairy One," probably because of the scrub forests that covered the mountains. Again, hard limestone and chalk dominate the surface of the landscape, but because the steep western slopes, composed of Nubian sandstone, have a red appearance in the late afternoon sun, the name "Edom" (Heb. for "red") is very appropriate for this area. The most famous city of this remote region is Petra, capital city of the Nabateans (ca. 200 B.C. to A.D. 200), the people who eventually replaced the Old Testament Edomites.

Roads in the Transjordanian mountains, like those in the central mountain range, avoided the deep valleys wherever possible. The major road was the Transjordanian Highway, which connected Damascus (and hence Assyria and Babylonia) with the countries located in present-day Saudi Arabia. This highway went through such important cities as Ashtaroth, Ramoth Gilead, Rabbah of the Ammonites, and Heshbon. The southern portion of the highway, near Heshbon, was called the "King's Highway" (Num 21:22), although this name was evidently used for another road as well (Num 20:17). In any case, the Transjordanian Highway was second in importance only to the main International Coastal Highway, which connected Gaza and Damascus.

The Eastern Desert

The fifth and final longitudinal zone is the great desert expanse east of the Transjordanian mountains. In the north, the great volcanic mountains and the lava flows of the Jebel Druze make this an inhospitable region, although its high elevation ensures adequate rainfall to grow crops. But elsewhere in this zone rainfall is negligible, and thus the barren desert stretches eastward some 450 miles (725 km.) to the Euphrates River.

Out of this desert came many peoples desiring the greener farmland of the Fertile Crescent. At various points in history these groups included the Amorites, the Arameans, the Nabateans, and ultimately the Arabs, all of whom pushed into the settled regions in the continuing struggle between the desert and the sown, between the desert and the Mediterranean Sea.

ISRAEL AND JORDAN — CALIFORNIA

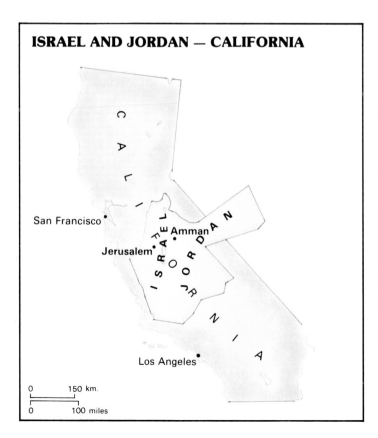

San Francisco

Jerusalem • Amman

Los Angeles

0   150 km.

0   100 miles

Weather Patterns

Israel's year is divided into two major seasons: the rainy season (mid-October through April) and the dry season (mid-June through mid-September). These seasons are separated by the transitional months.

The Dry Season—Summer

In contrast to the variable climatic conditions experienced in many parts of North America, conditions in Israel during the summer months are relatively stable. Warm days and cooler nights are the rule, and it almost never rains. In Jerusalem, for example, the average August daytime high temperature is 86° F (30° C), the nighttime average low is 64° F (18° C).

Summer days are relatively cloudless; indeed, Israel is one of the sunniest countries in the world. On a typical summer day, temperatures begin to climb immediately after sunrise. Within a short time a cooling sea breeze begins to blow in from the west. After passing through the coastal plain it reaches Jerusalem in the mountains at about noon, and its cooling effect prevents the temperature from rising significantly during the afternoon hours. But the breeze usually does not reach Transjordan until mid to late afternoon, so temperatures there continue to climb through most of the day.

The summer months see grapes, figs, pomegranates, melons, and other crops ripening and being tended by the farmers. The summer dew and deep root systems bring needed moisture to these crops. Most of the fruits are harvested in August and September. During the summer, the shepherds move their flocks of sheep and goats westward, allowing them to feed on the stubble of the wheat and barley fields that were harvested in the spring. Because the soil is dry during the summer months, travel is fairly easy. In biblical times, caravans and armies moved easily through most parts of the country, the armies helping themselves to the plentiful supplies of grain at the expense of the local populace.

The Rainy Season—Winter

The rainy season, extending from mid-October through April, is characterized by occasional rain storms that roll in off the Mediterranean Sea, normally bringing three days of rain followed by several days of dry weather (although deviations from this norm are frequent). During January the mean daily temperature in Jerusalem is 50° F (10° C; see map p. 25 for temperatures in other cities). For this reason, Jerusalem receives snow only once or twice each year, and even then the snow rarely remains on the ground more than a

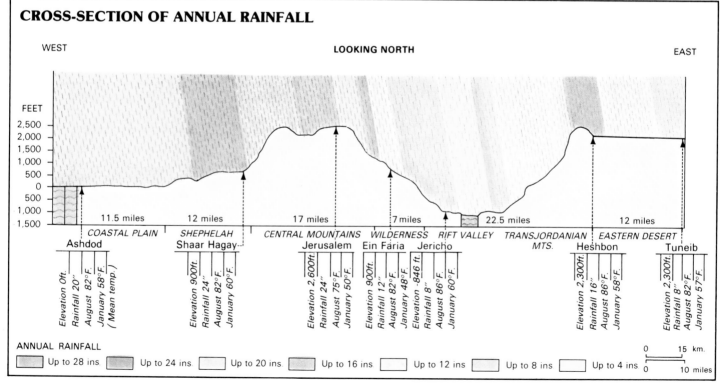

CROSS-SECTION OF ANNUAL RAINFALL

WEST — LOOKING NORTH — EAST

FEET
2,500
2,000
1,500
1,000
500
0
500
1,000
1,500

| COASTAL PLAIN | SHEPHELAH | CENTRAL MOUNTAINS | WILDERNESS | RIFT VALLEY | TRANSJORDANIAN MTS. | EASTERN DESERT |

11.5 miles | 12 miles | 17 miles | 7 miles | 22.5 miles | 12 miles

Ashdod — Shaar Hagay — Jerusalem — Ein Faria — Jericho — Heshbon — Tuneib

Ashdod: Elevation 0 ft. / Rainfall 20" / August 82° F. / January 58° F. (Mean temp.)

Shaar Hagay: Elevation 900 ft. / Rainfall 24" / August 82° F. / January 60° F.

Jerusalem: Elevation 2,600 ft. / Rainfall 24" / August 75° F. / January 50° F.

Ein Faria: Elevation 900 ft. / Rainfall 12" / August 82° F. / January 48° F.

Jericho: Elevation -846 ft. / Rainfall 8" / August 86° F. / January 60° F.

Heshbon: Elevation 2,300 ft. / Rainfall 16" / August 86° F. / January 58° F.

Tuneib: Elevation 2,300 ft. / Rainfall 8" / August 82° F. / January 57° F.

ANNUAL RAINFALL

Up to 28 ins. | Up to 24 ins. | Up to 20 ins. | Up to 16 ins. | Up to 12 ins. | Up to 8 ins. | Up to 4 ins.

0   15 km.
0   10 miles

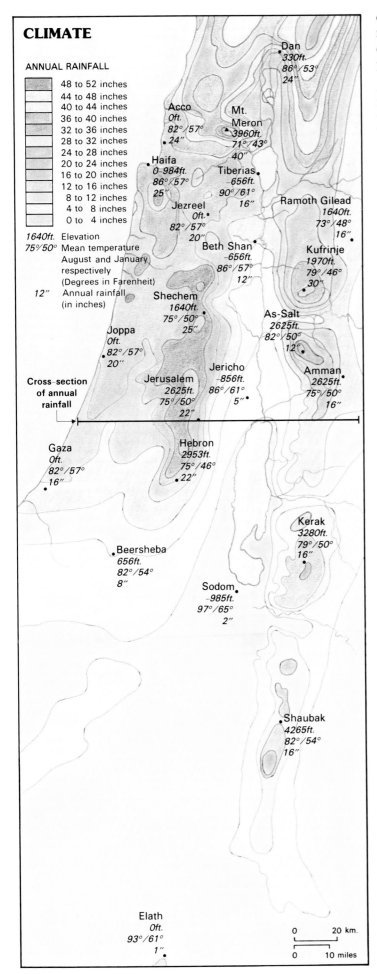

CLIMATE

ANNUAL RAINFALL

- 48 to 52 inches
- 44 to 48 inches
- 40 to 44 inches
- 36 to 40 inches
- 32 to 36 inches
- 28 to 32 inches
- 24 to 28 inches
- 20 to 24 inches
- 16 to 20 inches
- 12 to 16 inches
- 8 to 12 inches
- 4 to 8 inches
- 0 to 4 inches

1640ft. Elevation
75°/50° Mean temperature August and January respectively (Degrees in Farenheit)
12" Annual rainfall (in inches)

Cross-section of annual rainfall

Dan
330ft.
86°/53°
24"

Acco
0ft.
82°/57°
24"

Mt. Meron
3960ft.
71°/43°
40"

Haifa
0-984ft.
86°/57°
25"

Tiberias
-656ft.
90°/61°
16"

Jezreel
0ft.
82°/57°
20"

Ramoth Gilead
1640ft.
73°/48°
16"

Beth Shan
-656ft.
86°/57°
12"

Kufrinje
1970ft.
79°/46°
30"

Shechem
1640ft.
75°/50°
25"

As-Salt
2625ft.
82°/50°
12"

Joppa
0ft.
82°/57°
20"

Jericho
-856ft.
86°/61°
5"

Jerusalem
2625ft.
75°/50°
22"

Amman
2625ft.
75°/50°
16"

Gaza
0ft.
82°/57°
16"

Hebron
2953ft.
75°/46°
22"

Kerak
3280ft.
79°/50°
16"

Beersheba
656ft.
82°/54°
8"

Sodom
-985ft.
97°/65°
2"

Shaubak
4265ft.
82°/54°
16"

Elath
0ft.
93°/61°
1"

0   20 km.
0   10 miles

---

day. However, cold temperatures, combined with wind and rain, make life a bit uncomfortable in the hilly regions—a discomfort the people gladly bear because of the life-giving power of the rains.

During a typical year a farmer plows his field and plants his grain crops after the "autumn rains" of October through December have softened the hard, sun-baked soil. The grain crops grow from December through February, when 75 percent of the rain falls, and they continue to ripen during March and April, as the rains begin to taper off. These "spring rains" are important for producing bumper crops. The Bible actually refers to the three parts of the rainy season in Deuteronomy 11:14: "Then I will send rain [Heb. *māṭār*; Dec.–Feb.] on your land in its season, both autumn [Heb. *yôreh*; Oct.–Dec.] and spring rains [Heb. *malqôsh*; March–April], so that you may gather in your grain, new wine and oil" (cf. also Jer 5:24; Hos 6:3). Because Israel is situated between arid and wet climatic zones, the amount of rainfall throughout the country varies considerably (Amos 4:6–8). The general principles that describe this variation usually work in combination. They are as follows:

1. The amount of rainfall decreases as one moves from north to south (note the decrease in the amounts for the cities in the Rift Valley from Dan to Elath).

2. The amount of rainfall decreases as one moves from west to east, away from the Mediterranean Sea (note the sites in the Jezreel and Harod valleys).

3. The amount of rainfall increases with the elevation (cf. the amounts for cities in the mountains with those of cities at lower elevations).

4. The amount of rainfall is greater on the windward (Mediterranean) side of the mountains than on the leeward side (cf. the amounts for Shaar HaGay and Ein Faria, located at the same elevation, on the diagram on p. 24).

Most of the land north of Beersheba receives sufficient rain to grow grain (i.e., more than 12 inches [300 mm.] per year). But in those regions where the total annual average is only 12 to 16 inches (300 to 400 mm.), the growth of grain crops is by no means assured, for a variation of only 4 to 6 inches (100 to 150 mm.) can spell disaster. In addition, farmers throughout the country face numerous uncertainties:

1. The *beginning* of the rainy season is sometimes delayed until December, resulting in a shorter growing season.

2. The *end* of the rainy season can come as early as March, again causing a shortening of the growing season.

3. The *total amount* of rainfall in a given locality can, and often does, deviate considerably from the listed mean.

4. The *distribution* of rainfall in a given season can vary considerably. For example, in some years, parts of the country can go without rain for four or five consecutive weeks during the months of January and February, usually the rainiest months of the year. A prolonged dry spell such as this can seriously affect crop yield.

One of these negative factors, or several working in combination, can seriously retard the growth of crops. In a good year the farmer can sow and "reap a hundredfold" (Gen 26:12), but a series of drought years can be devastating and, in the past, could drive people from the land (Gen 12:10).

The Israelites knew that it was Yahweh, the Lord, who had his eyes on the land continually, from the beginning of the year to its end, and that their obedience to his commandments would bring blessing, while disobedience would usher in drought and disaster (Deut 11:8–17). But given the uncertainties about the amount and distribution of the rainfall, it is no wonder that some Israelites were drawn to participate in the worship of Baal, the Canaanite storm god, who was believed to bring fertility to the land.

The Transitional Seasons

The first transitional season lasts from early May through mid-June. The temperatures gradually rise, and the season is punctuated by a series of hot, dry, dusty days during which the winds blow in from the eastern and southern deserts. On these days, which are called, by the names of the winds, *hamsin, sirocco,* or *sharav,* the temperature often rises 25° F (14° C) above normal, and the relative humidity can drop by as much as 40 percent. Hamsin conditions can be very enervating to both humans and beasts, and they completely dry up the beautiful flowers and grasses that covered the landscape during the winter months (Isa 40:7–8). The positive effect of these winds, however, is that the hot, dry weather aids the ripening of the grains by "setting" them before the harvest. It is during this season that first the barley and then the wheat harvest takes place.

The second transitional season, from mid-September to mid-October, marks the end of the stable, dry, summer conditions. It is the time of the fruit harvest, and farmers begin to look anxiously for the onset of the rainy season—note the prayers for rain in the Jewish rituals associated with the last day of the Feast of Tabernacles. In the fall, travel on the Mediterranean becomes dangerous (Acts 27:9), and it remains so throughout the winter months.

Remnant of a Roman milestone — a typical feature found along major highways.

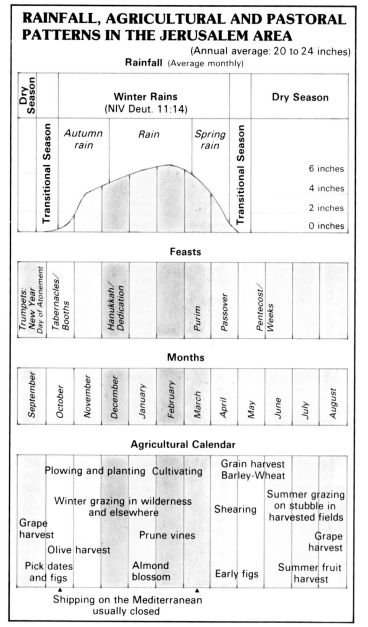

Major Natural Routes

Roads and Modes of Travel

The roads that developed in the ancient land of Israel can be divided into three major categories: international routes, interregional routes, and local routes. One of the uses of the international and interregional roads was commercial. The roads were used for the transportation of scarce supplies, such as certain foodstuffs, copper, iron, tin, gold, silver, incense, dyes, and pottery (bulkier items such as timber and stones were usually shipped on boats and rafts).

In addition, these roads served as thoroughfares for military expeditions, for itinerant tradesmen such as smiths, for the migration of peoples, for the conveyance of governmental and commercial messages, and for the travel of pilgrims to holy places. Those who controlled the the roads, whether brigands or a more permanent central government, could derive considerable income from the traffic on them. The central government could collect tolls from passing caravans, sell food and lodging, and "offer" the services of military escorts that could be hired by the caravans to "insure" their safe passage through "dangerous" territory.

Those living along the international routes were exposed to new intellectual, cultural, linguistic, and religious influences, and this inevitably led to a degree of assimilation. For example, the ease of travel in and out of Samaria, when compared with the remoteness of the Hill Country of Judah, helps to explain the openness of the former to non-Israelite religious and cultural influences. This, in turn, eventually led to the deportation of the Northern Kingdom some 130 years before the captivity of Judah (see pp. 124–34). Similarly, during the Persian and Greco-Roman periods, increased exposure to international influences led to a rapidly accelerated process of assimilation.

Besides walking, early modes of transportation included donkeys, solid-wheeled carts, and chariots. Camels eventually began to be used to carry heavy loads, especially in caravans. Horses were used in the second and first millennia B.C. to draw chariots and to serve in cavalry units; during the Persian period (538–332 B.C.) and later, their use for everyday travel became more common. In New Testament times all these means of transportation were used, and the improvement of the road system increased the use of carts and chariots. Travel during the dry summer season was preferred to attempting to negotiate the muddy, rain-soaked terrain in the winter months. The spring and summer seasons were "the time when kings go off to war" (2 Sam 11:1) because the roads were dry and the newly harvested grain was available to feed their troops.

By the time Abraham arrived in the land of Canaan (ca. 2000 B.C.), the lines of communication within the country were already well established. In Old Testament times, roads between urban areas were prepared but not paved. Basic "road building" operations included the removal of stones from the path, the clearing of trees and bushes, the maintaining of shallow fords in the river beds, and possibly the construction of trails along steep slopes. By New Testament times the Romans had developed advanced road-building techniques, and it is probable that the construction of a rather well-developed road system had already begun in Syria and Judah. Roman road-building techniques included the preparation of the roadbed by leveling the ground and cutting rocks, the use of curbing to mark the edge of the roads, attention to drainage problems, and the laying of paving stones.

The International North-South Route

The most important international route through Israel connected Egypt with its rivals/allies to the north and east (Syrians, Assyrians, Babylonians, Persians, Hittites, Hurrians, etc.). This international route is sometimes called "The Way of the Sea" (Isa 9:1) or the "Via Maris." These are slight misnomers because only portions of this route ran to, or along, the sea coast. It seems that although portions of it were named in ancient times (e.g., the portion leading from Egypt across Sinai to the Philistine coast was called the "way of [to] the land of Philistines," Exod 13:17 RSV), the whole route did not have one special name. It seems best not to use "The Way of the Sea" (= "Via Maris"), for it is not even certain that this term ever referred to a portion of this International Highway (see above, p. 14). After crossing northern Sinai, this route proceeded from Gaza through the Philistine and Sharon Plains to the area of the city of Yaham, avoiding such obstacles as sand dunes, low-lying muddy spots, the Yarkon River, and the swamps of the Sharon Plain. In order to proceed from Yaham to the Jezreel Valley a traveler had to follow one of the passes that led through Mount Carmel, such as the one that ran from Aruna to Megiddo.

The route northward along the coast led from Megiddo to Hannathon to Acco and from there north to Tyre and Sidon. Several options were available for travel from Megiddo to Damascus, from where one could proceed to Turkey or to the Euphrates River. A major road led southeast from Megiddo to the Beth Shan area. From there it went north to the southern shore of the Sea of Galilee, where it turned northeastward, ascended the valleys of the Yarmuk and Raqqad rivers (or the hills just north of them), and ultimately arrived in the Ashtaroth–Karnaim area, where it joined the Transjordanian Highway. Another route continued eastward from the Beth Shan area, forded the Jordan River, and ascended one of the ridges that led up to the Highlands of Gilead. After arriving at Ramoth Gilead, one could proceed directly northward to Damascus.

Another road took travelers from Megiddo to Hazor by heading northeast from Megiddo, skirting the slopes of Mount Tabor, continuing through the Arbel Pass, and heading north past Kinnereth to arrive at Hazor. During the Roman period and later, a road led east from Hazor, crossed the Jordan River in the area of the Bridge of Jacob's Daughters, and then ascended the Golan Heights on the way to Damascus. Alternatively, one could head north from Hazor to Dan and from there head east to Damascus, skirting the southern slopes of Mount Hermon. In addition, an important branch of the International Route led directly north-northeast from Dan up into and through the Lebanese Beqa toward cities such as Lebo Hamath, Kedesh, Hamath, and Aleppo.

The International Transjordanian Route

The other International Route, not quite as important as the preceding, led south from Damascus and traveled the entire length of Transjordan. One branch of this route ran east of the watershed of the Transjordanian mountains. It passed through important cities such as Karnaim, Ashtaroth, Ramoth Gilead, Rabbah of the Ammonites, Heshbon, Aroer, Kir in Moab, and Bozrah. Along this route there were good supplies of water, but one had to cross, often with difficulty, wadis such as the Yarmuk, Jabbok, Arnon, and Zered. The eastern branch of this route ran along the edge of the desert. It avoided the deep wadis, but it did not pass through as many important commercial centers, nor did it have as much water available, and the caravans traveling along it were subject to raids by desert tribes. These two branches met at Rabbah, the capital of the Ammonites, and then split again as they continued southward. Eventually, in the Bozrah region, the traveler could proceed westward and strike out across the Negev and Sinai toward Egypt or head south-southeast and follow the caravan routes into the Arabian desert. The Transjordanian Highway was especially important for the conveyance of luxury goods such as gold, frankincense, and myrrh from southern Arabia to the Near Eastern commercial center of Damascus.

Interregional and Local Routes

Many of the interregional and local roads are discussed below in the regional sections. However, for biblical studies the interregional route that ran from Beersheba in the south to Shechem in the north—via Hebron, Bethlehem, Jerusalem, Gibeah, Ramah, Bethel/Ai, and Shiloh—is of extreme importance. This route appears again and again in the biblical text. Some people call it the "Route of the Patriarchs" because Abraham, Isaac, and Jacob traveled its length, while others refer to it as the "Ridge Route," for in many places it "tiptoes" along the watershed of the Judean and Ephraim mountains. Even when it is not specifically mentioned, it often furnishes the backdrop for many events recorded in the Bible.

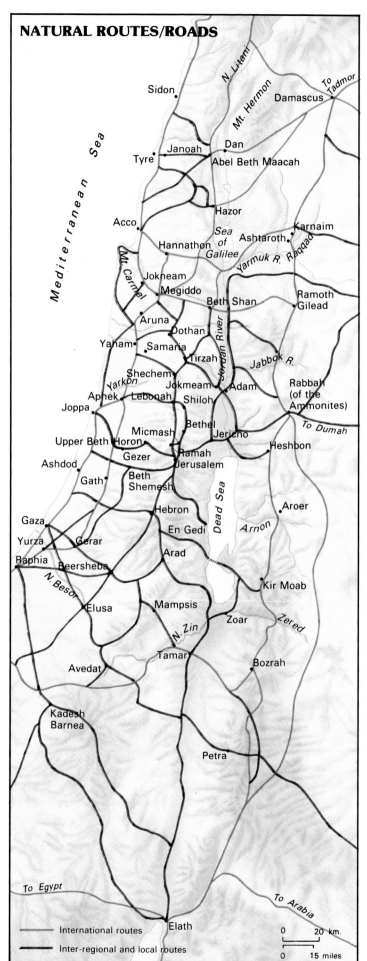

NATURAL ROUTES/ROADS

International routes

Inter-regional and local routes

0   20 km.

0   15 miles

Geographic Regions of Israel and Jordan

Bashan

Bashan is a high plateau region located in the northeastern corner of Israel. Measuring some 37 miles (60 km.) east-west by 56 miles (90 km.) north-south, it is bounded on the west by the Rift Valley, on the north by Mount Hermon, and on the east by Mount Bashan, while on the south it eventually merges into Gilead. Running down its center in a north-south direction are several rows of extinct volcanoes whose conical shapes break up the relatively flat terrain. The name Bashan, which originally seems to have referred to the fertility of the region, is used sixty times in the Old Testament (NIV).

The area north of the Yarmuk River is composed of volcanic soils, rocks, and mountains, while south of the Yarmuk the land consists of softer, chalky limestone formations. The general slope of northern Bashan is from the north-northeast downward to the south-southwest. This northern portion is divided into an eastern and a western section by the Nahal Raqqad. The western section receives close to 40 inches (1000 mm.) of precipitation per year; this, combined with the fertility of the volcanic soil, makes it a rich agricultural area. In Old Testament times the semi-independent states of Geshur and Maacah were located in the southern and northern portions of this western section respectively (see maps pp. 103, 117). The fertility of the region was well known, for the biblical writers repeatedly speak of the fatness of the animals that grazed there and of the oak forests that covered portions of the landscape (see,

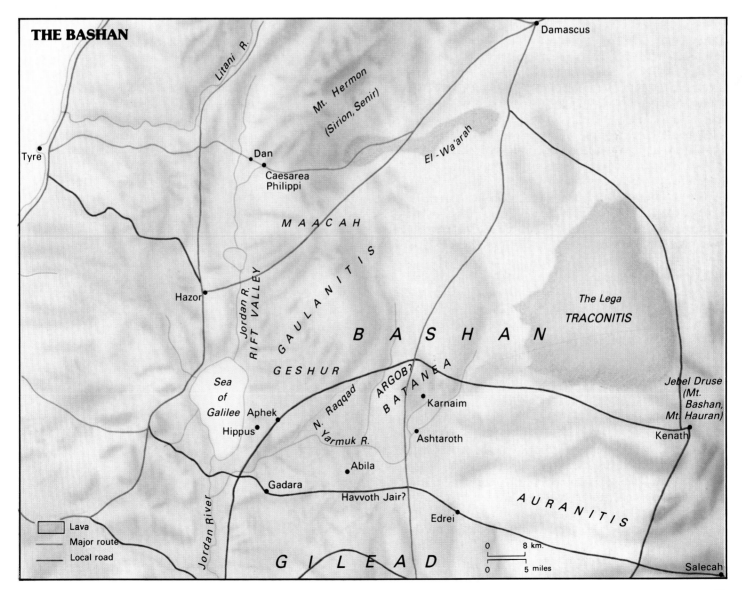

THE BASHAN

Damascus

Litani R.

Mt. Hermon
(Sirion, Senir)

El - Wa'arah

Tyre

Dan

Caesarea
Philippi

MAACAH

Hazor

Jordan R.

RIFT VALLEY

GAULANITIS

BASHAN

The Lega
TRACONITIS

GESHUR

N. Raqqad

ARGOB?

BATANEA

Sea
of
Galilee

Aphek

Karnaim

Jebel Druse
(Mt.
Bashan,
Mt. Hauran)

Hippus

Yarmuk R.

Ashtaroth

Kenath

Abila

Gadara

Havvoth Jair?

AURANITIS

Edrei

Lava
Major route
Local road

0   8 km.
0   5 miles

G I L E A D

Salecah

e.g., Ezek 27:6; 39:18). In New Testament times this area west of the Nahal Raqqad was known as Gaulanitis. It became an important producer of wheat in the Roman Empire, in spite of the fact that in certain regions there are basalt boulders that make plowing difficult.

To the east of the Nahal Raqqad rainfall is not as abundant, and although the average of 12 to 24 inches (300 to 600 mm.) per year occasionally results in bumper crops of wheat, droughts can strike the region in other years. It is probable that in the Old Testament period this territory was called the district of Argob (cf. Deut 3:13–14; 1 Kings 4:13); in the New Testament era it was known as Batanea. This area, open to invading armies from the north (see, e.g., Gen 14), is said to have been a region with "sixty large walled cities with bronze gate bars" (1 Kings 4:13).

On the northern edge of Bashan, Mount Hermon (also called Sirion and Senir, Deut 3:9) rises to an elevation of 9,232 feet (2814 m.), towering over the surrounding area. Its peaks, snow-covered for more than six months of the year and sometimes visible from over 100 miles (160 km.) away, receive more than 60 inches (1500 mm.) of precipitation annually. This moisture, much of which seeps into the hard limestone foundations of the mountain, reappears as powerful springs that feed the Jordan River as well as the Damascus Oasis. It was near Caesarea Philippi, located at the southern foot of Mount Hermon, that Peter made his great confession regarding Jesus' messiahship (Matt 16:13–20; Mark 8:27–30). Six days later Jesus was transfigured in the presence of Peter, James, and John—probably somewhere on Mount Hermon (Matt 17:1–13; Mark 9:2–13). To the east of Mount Hermon the prominent lava flow called the el-Wa´arah forms the remaining portion of Bashan's northern border. Because it is difficult to travel across the el-Wa´arah, the roads heading south from Damascus were diverted to the east or west of the outflow.

On the east, Bashan is separated from the desert by more volcanic flows and by mountains. The northernmost flow, the Leja ("Refuge"), was known in New Testament times as Traconitis, the "Torn Land." This remote and desolate area was under the control of Philip the tetrarch (Luke 3:1). To the east of the Leja is the even more desolate es-Safa, and to the south of the Leja rises the massive Jebel Druze, also known as Mount Bashan and Mount Hauran. Because of its high elevation (ca. 5,800 ft. [1770 m.]) it receives good amounts of rain each year, in spite of its easterly location. The roughness of the territory, however, precludes the growing of much wheat; this volcanic mountain area evidently was primarily used for grazing and for obtaining forest products (see, e.g., Ezek 27:6; 39:18).

South of the Yarmuk River the plateau region continues for some 18 miles (30 km.) as it gradually blends into the Gilead region. This area was possibly the Old Testament "Havvoth Jair," which is variously described as being "in Bashan" (Josh 13:30) and "in Gilead" (1 Kings 4:13). This territory was captured by Israel but remained a source of dispute between Israel and its neighbors to the northeast—Geshur and Aram (Syria) (1 Chron 2:23).

The chief cities of Bashan were Ashtaroth and Edrei, the capital cities of King Og (e.g., Josh 12:4; 13:12). Later in the Old Testament period, nearby Karnaim replaced the formerly prominent Ashtaroth. Salecah seems to have been the easternmost limit of Israelite interest in the region. During the Hellenistic and Roman periods (332 B.C.–A.D. 324) the area was heavily populated by Jewish settlers but was also well known for its Greco-Roman cities (including Gadara, Abila, Hippus, Raphana, and Caesarea Philippi).

Not only was Bashan rich in agriculture, but during the Roman period and afterward it also served as a thoroughfare for the main International Highway. One very important highway branch, used in both Old and New Testament times, skirted the southern end of the Sea of Galilee and either ascended the western scarp of Bashan, just to the north of the Yarmuk River, or followed the Yarmuk and the Raqqad valleys on up toward Damascus. Aphek was one of the cities guarding this route, and it was here that Israel fought the Arameans (Syrians) on several occasions (1 Kings 20:26, 30; 2 Kings 13:17; see maps pp. 126, 129). This road probably formed part of the Roman "grain route" by which grain from Bashan was shipped via Lower Galilee to the Mediterranean port of Ptolemais (OT Acco). Other branches of the International Highway led from Hazor and Dan to Damascus, crossing Bashan along the way. In addition, the important Transjordanian Highway headed directly south from Damascus through Bashan or, more specifically, through the district of Argob/Batanea, avoiding the el-Wa´arah, the Leja, and Mount Bashan as it passed by Ashtaroth and Edrei on its southerly course. During most of the year travel through the area was not difficult so long as the caravans avoided the various basalt outflows and boulder-strewn areas. In the winter months, however, the snow and the mud must have slowed the speed of the caravans.

The southern area of Bashan bordered by the Yarmuk River.

Huleh Valley

The Huleh Valley is the northernmost section of the Rift Valley system in Israel. It stretches from the north shore of the Sea of Galilee up to Dan, a distance of 23 miles (37 km.). It is bounded on the west by the steep scarp of eastern Upper Galilee, which in places rises 1,600 feet (490 m.) above the valley floor. On the east, the approach to Bashan is much more gradual, while north of the Dan/Abel Beth Maacah region the land rises into the Lebanese Beqa.

The portion of the valley southeast of Hazor is a "plug" of basalt that flowed down from Bashan and filled the Rift Valley all the way to the Sea of Galilee. The waters of the Jordan River collected to the north of this blockage, forming a medium-sized lake. Eventually the river carved its way through this basalt barrier on its way down to the Sea of Galilee. Here the Jordan drops some 900 feet (275 m.) over a distance of only 10 miles (16 km.), making this the steepest gradient of the river.

Behind this basalt barrier a small lake (Huleh Lake, 5 sq. mi. [13 sq. km.]) and swamp lands (12 sq. mi. [31 sq. km.]) remained until recently; the area was drained by the Israelis in 1958. Josephus' name for the Huleh Lake was Lake Semechonitis (e.g., *War* 3.10.7 [515]). Cane and papyrus grew in the lake and the swamp land. In addition, fowl, animals, and fish abounded in the region.

The southern portion of the Huleh Valley receives about 16 inches (400 mm.) of rain each year, the northern portion almost 25 inches (630 mm.). At the foot of Mount Hermon a number of springs contribute to the five rivers that combine to form the headwaters of the Jordan, adding to the lushness of the region.

Because of the lake and swamps, the major settlements of the area—Dan, Abel Beth Maacah, and Hazor—were located along the higher fringes of the valley. This area was

UPPER GALILEE AND THE HULEH VALLEY

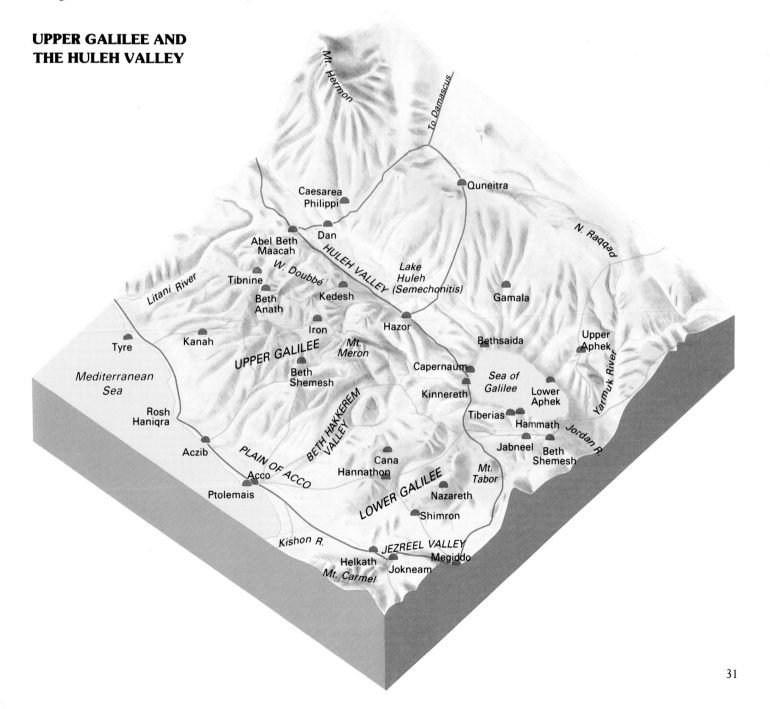

quite exposed to outside influences because the major International Highway from Egypt into the Lebanese Beqa ran alongside of it. In addition, during the intertestamental period and later, a branch of this important route passed just south of the Huleh Basin on its way to Damascus. Thus, during times of invasion from the north or the northeast, this region usually was the first to feel the brunt of the attack (see, e.g., 1 Kings 15, 2 Kings 15, and map p. 129).

Upper Galilee

The name Galilee is used only six times in the Old Testament but appears sixty-four times in the New Testament, primarily in connection with the ministry of Jesus. The origin of the term is somewhat obscure, but it seems to mean "region" or "district." In the Old Testament period the region was referred to as "Galilee of the Gentiles" (Isa 9:1), but by the New Testament era it had a large Jewish population.

Galilee is divided into two major regions by a fault line that runs from Acco eastward toward the north end of the Sea of Galilee. A valley, today called the Bet Hakkerem Valley, marks this fault and serves as the dividing line between the two parts. Upper Galilee, so called because its elevation is much higher than that of Lower Galilee, is located to the north of the Bet Hakkerem Valley. A steep rock scarp rises some 1,500 feet (460 m.) out of the valley, making the transition between the two regions quite dramatic. The eastern boundary of Upper Galilee is clearly defined by the steep north-south scarp that descends rapidly into the Huleh Valley. On the west, Upper Galilee drops off into the Plain of Acco and in one place, at Rosh HaNiqra, actually reaches the Mediterranean Sea. The northern boundary of Upper Galilee is uncertain. Some Israeli geographers suggest that the Litani River forms its natural northern limit, while others place the northern limit along the fault line that runs from Rosh HaNiqra northeast toward Tibnine.[1]

The whole region of Upper Galilee, but especially the central southern section, is an uplifted area dissected by numerous east-west and north-south fault lines. The eastern portion is composed of hard Eocene limestone interspersed with a few patches of basalt outcroppings; it is drained to the north by the Wadi Doubbe, which eventually joins the Litani River. The western section is composed mainly of hard Cenomanian and Turonian limestones and reaches a height of 3,963 feet (1208 m.) in the Mount Meron area; this is the highest elevation in all of Israel, with the exception of Mount Hermon. This western region tilts down toward the northwest, but eventually the streams turn westward and flow into the Mediterranean Sea.

In both the eastern and western sections good topsoil is available, and abundant rains (24 to 40 in. [600 to 1000 mm.] annually) assure the fertility of the region. The natural vegetation of the area most likely consisted of typical Mediterranean scrub forests, but settlers cut down the trees to plant crops. This transformation, which probably began with the arrival of the Israelite tribes, was basically completed by the beginning of the New Testament era, when most of the area was under intense cultivation.

Because of the dissected nature of the terrain, the major north-south roads ran around the eastern or western edges of Upper Galilee, bypassing this difficult area. There seems to have been, however, an east-west route that connected Damascus with the port city of Tyre. After crossing the northern end of the Huleh Valley, passing cities such as Dan and Abel Beth Maacah, it ascended the rocky scarp west of Abel Beth Maacah and continued on its way to Tyre along the ridges on the high ground of Upper Galilee, past villages such as Beth Anath and Kanah. Another interregional route led from Abel Beth Maacah up to Kedesh, and from there to Acco or Aczib via Iron and Beth Shemesh. These east-west routes must have been of some importance, for they connected the desert-oasis emporium of Damascus with the Mediterranean Sea.

In the Old Testament period the tribe of Asher settled in western Upper Galilee, while Naphtali was assigned its eastern portion. The northern limits of their settlements do not seem to have extended beyond the northern boundary of Upper Galilee. In New Testament times the area was predominantly Jewish, and most of it was under the control of Herod Antipas. Throughout history the high elevations and the ruggedness of the terrain have caused those living in the area to be somewhat isolated from international influences.

Plain of Acco

The Plain of Acco is situated to the west of Galilee and is bounded on the north by Rosh HaNiqra, on the west by the Mediterranean Sea, and on the south by Mount Carmel. The plain is divided into two parts. North of Acco, the plain is a narrow strip of land (12.5 by 3.7 mi. [ca. 20 by 6 km.]), filled with alluvial soil that has washed down from the hills of Upper Galilee. The wadis from the hills have cut through the kurkar (fossilized dune sandstone) ridges that run parallel to the coast and thus empty into the sea without difficulty. The shoreline is for the most part made up of a rough, abrasive kurkar platform, making it difficult to land boats in the area.

To the south of Acco, the plain is broader (9.3 by 6.2 mi. [15 by 10 km.]), and sand dunes extend inland from the coast. The dunes prevent the wadis from the hills of Lower Galilee from draining directly into the Mediterranean, so the plain area, except for the high ground close to the hills, is somewhat swampy. At the southern extremity of the plain, the Kishon River, coming from the Jezreel Valley, drains into Haifa Bay.

The city of Acco (Ptolemais) is located where the two sections of the Plain of Acco meet. Throughout most of its history Acco/Ptolemais served as the leading port for the whole of the land of Israel and Transjordan (note the roads leading to it; see map p. 33). In addition, a branch of the International Highway passed through the plain up the coast toward the cities of Tyre and Sidon, adding to the flow of traffic through the region. Although this area was assigned to

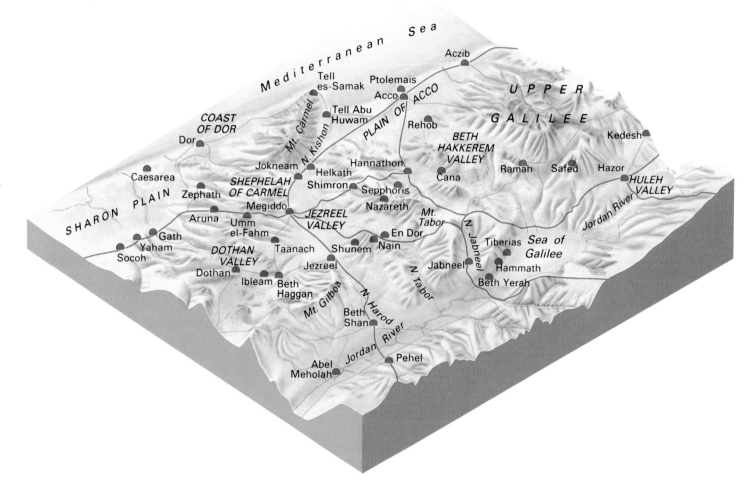

the tribe of Asher, the members of this tribe had great difficulty trying to overcome the Canaanites who lived on the plain (Judges 1:31–32), and the region was always open to outside influences coming from the Mediterranean. As a result, Acco/Ptolemais was either an independent city or under the control of a non-Israelite power during most of its history. It was at Ptolemais that the apostle Paul stopped on his way to Jerusalem at the end of his third missionary journey (Acts 21:7).

Lower Galilee

Lower Galilee, where none of the hills rise above 2,000 feet (610 m.), lies south of Upper Galilee. It is bounded on the east by the Rift Valley, on the south by the Harod and Jezreel valleys, and on the west by the Plain of Acco.

Lower Galilee can be divided into two rather distinct regions by drawing a north-south line through Mount Tabor. In the western section most of the hills are composed of hard Cenomanian limestone, except in the southwestern corner, where softer Eocene formations appear. This southwestern corner, with its low rolling hills and valleys, may be the area referred to as the "foothills" (Heb. *Shephelah* = "low-lands" RSV) of the "mountains of Israel" (Josh 11:16); they are structurally similar to the more frequently mentioned "western foothills" of Judah (also called Shephelah). The major relief lines in western Lower Galilee run in an east-west direction. A traveler going north or south through the area thus encounters a series of medium-sized ridges separated by broad fertile valleys. This topography causes the natural lines of communication to have an east-west rather than a north-south orientation. The area receives approximately 25 inches (630 mm.) of rain per year, and the rich alluvial soil adds to the fertility of the region. In ancient times the hills were covered with scrub forests, and the people tended to build their villages and roads on the hillsides in order to leave the valleys open for farming. In the winter, the broad valleys become partially flooded, making travel through them somewhat difficult; but they dry out in the spring and yield a good harvest of wheat and barley.

To readers of the Bible, the most familiar cities of western Lower Galilee are Nazareth and Cana. The former is situated on the southernmost ridge of western Lower Galilee, and from there one could look down on the caravans as they passed along the International Highway through the Jezreel Valley to the south, while on the northern side of the ridge one could see caravans making their way from Bashan to the port of Acco/Ptolemais. In the days of Jesus, Nazareth was a very small, out-of-the-way town situated in a chalky basin on the top of this ridge. Its association with Jesus has made it the large city that it is today. Cana was also a rather insignificant city, located on the southern slope of the Yodefat Range; all that remains of it today is the small, barren ruin of Khirbet Qana. It was here that Jesus performed his first recorded miracle: the turning of water into wine (John 2:1–11). From extrabiblical sources we know that in New Testament times there were numerous villages in western Lower Galilee, the most important of which was the capital Sepphoris, located 3.5 miles (5.5 km.) north-northwest of Nazareth.

In eastern Lower Galilee (the area east of the north-south Tabor line) the features of topographical relief run diagonally from northwest to southeast. Here again a series of ridges alternate with a series of valleys (such as the Nahal Jabneel and Nahal Tabor), which drain into the Rift Valley. The northeast slopes of the ridges are fairly steep; the southwest slopes descend more gradually into the valleys. The area is covered primarily with basalt stones and volcanic soil, making the landscape somewhat smoother in appearance than the other areas of Galilee. In eastern Lower Galilee the southern border reaches all the way to the Harod Valley and includes such famous mountain landmarks as the Hill of Moreh and Mount Tabor. The Hill of Moreh witnessed such events as Gideon's battle with the Midianites (Judges 7), Saul's meeting with the witch of Endor (1 Sam 28), Elisha's

raising of the son of the woman of Shunem (2 Kings 4), and Jesus' raising of the son of the widow of Nain (Luke 7). Deborah and Barak met the Canaanite forces at Mount Tabor (Judges 4, 5), and some consider this to be the site of the transfiguration of Jesus, although Mount Hermon is a more probable location (see above, p. 30).

The International Highway ran through eastern Lower Galilee in a northeasterly direction from Mount Tabor to the Horns of Hattin; from there it descended through the Arbel Pass to the northwestern shore of the Sea of Galilee and continued northward to Hazor. In Roman times the east-west grain road from Bashan, after passing south of the Sea of Galilee, ascended the Nahal Jabneel and then turned westward, continuing past Sepphoris and Hannathon on its way to Acco/Ptolemais.

In Old Testament times, Lower Galilee was only sparsely settled until the arrival of the Israelites (ca. 1400–1200 B.C.). Four of the tribes received their allotments in Lower Galilee: Issachar to the southeast of Mount Tabor, Naphtali to the northeast, Asher to the northwest, and Zebulun to the west (see map p. 99).

Because the terrain of Lower Galilee is much less rugged than that of Upper Galilee, Lower Galilee has been more accessible to outside influences throughout its history. One should also remember that although only a few villages are

SEA OF GALILEE

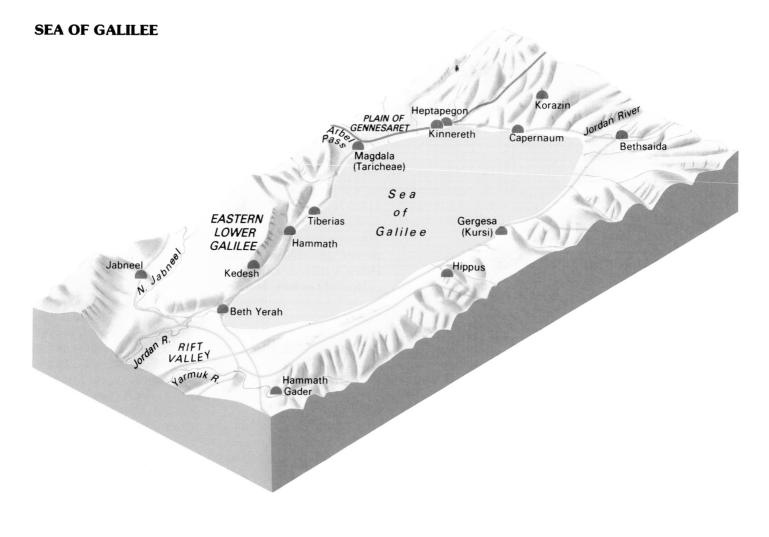

mentioned by name in the gospel accounts, a good portion of Jesus' early life was spent in the hills and valleys of Lower Galilee.

Sea of Galilee

The Sea of Galilee is located in the Rift Valley on the eastern border of Lower Galilee. The surface of the lake is approximately 1,280 feet (390 m.) below the surrounding hills and 690 feet (210 m.) below sea level. The sea measures 13 by 7.5 miles (21 by 12 km.) and has about 30 miles (48 km.) of shoreline. It is bounded on the north by the southern edge of the Huleh Valley, on the east by the hills of Bashan, on the west by the steep slopes of the hills of Lower Galilee, and on the south by the continuation of the Rift Valley. The fresh water of the Sea of Galilee has provided the inhabitants of the region with a good supply of fish throughout the ages.

In the Old Testament, the Sea of Galilee is mentioned only five times and is called the "Sea of Kinnereth." Tradition relates the name Kinnereth to the lyre-like shape of the lake, but the lake probably derived its name from the city of Kinnereth (Josh 19:35), located at its northwestern corner. This name, in modified form ("Lake of Gennesaret"), is used once in the gospel accounts. The names used in the New Testament are "Sea of Galilee" (five times), "Sea of

Tiberias" after the city of Tiberias (ca. A.D. 20; John 6:1; 21:1), and simply "the lake" (thirty-one times).

The sources of the lake include the Jordan River, which flows into the lake's northernmost point, and the fresh-water and saline springs that are found around and under the lake. In the northwest corner are seven salt springs, called Heptapegon, and along the lake's western shore just south of Tiberias are the hot mineral springs of Hammath (a Hebrew word meaning "hot"). Because of its lower elevation, the immediate vicinity of the lake receives less rain than the surrounding hills; Tiberias, for example, has an annual rainfall of only 16 inches (400 mm.). Yet, because of the rather steep hills that surround the sea, the wind rushing down the slopes can create sudden and violent storms on the lake. There is not much flat farmland along the shore of the lake, except for three small, very fertile plains on the northwestern, northeastern, and southern shores. The northwestern plain was known as the Plain of Gennesaret; Josephus writes of its extraordinary climate and produce, mentioning such diverse crops as walnuts, palm trees, figs, olives, and grapes (*War* 3.10.8 [3.516–21]). The plain in the Bethsaida region northeast of the lake is watered by several perennial streams and is equally fertile.

Although the Old Testament does not record much about the lake, it is known that the cities along its western shore were assigned to the tribe of Naphtali (see map p. 99). By the time of the New Testament the whole area was densely populated. To the east were cities such as Gergesa and Hippus that were associated with the Greco-Roman Decapolis, while on the western shore the major city was Tiberias, the city Herod Antipas had recently built and made the capital of Galilee. To the south of Tiberias were the hot springs of Hammath, to the north the commercial city of Magdala, or Taricheae (= "salted fish"?; Jos. *War* 3.9.7 [445]), where fish where processed for export. Along the shore of the northern third of the lake were cities in which Jesus ministered, including Gennesaret, Dalmanutha, Capernaum, Korazin, and Bethsaida.

Throughout the ages, paths have run around the edge of the lake, bypassing the swampy areas close to where the Jordan enters and exits the lake. Along the northwestern shore the International Highway, after descending from the hills of eastern Lower Galilee via the Arbel Pass to Magdala, crossed the Plain of Gennesaret and then ascended into the Huleh Valley as it proceeded northward to Hazor.

Most of the hills, boulders, and soils surrounding the lake derive from lava outflows. Houses in the area were primarily built of black basalt rock; because they had few windows and the people had only oil lamps for light, living in them must have been rather dismal. This may have been the physical backdrop to the description of the gloomy spiritual state of this region (Isa 9:1). The large basalt boulders in the area could be hand-tooled into quality household grinders, large commercial grinders with their millstones (Mark 9:42), olive presses, and other industrial implements. Thus in New Testament times the area's economic well-being depended on several sources: the presence of the capital of Galilee, Tiberias; the sick who came to the hot springs of Hammath and Hammath Gader for medicinal purposes; the fishing industry; the rich agricultural lands; the trade routes passing through the area; and the manufacture of basalt implements.

Southern end of the Sea of Galilee, looking eastwards.

Jezreel Valley

The term *Valley of Jezreel* is used only three times in Scripture; its Greek form, Esdraelon, occurs only in the extrabiblical literature of the Second Temple period. The valley evidently took its name from the Israelite settlement of Jezreel, situated at its eastern end. During the early years of Israel's residence in the land, most of the cities in the valley were under Canaanite control. An Israelite, when referring to the valley, would call it by the name of the Israelite village of Jezreel rather than by the name of one of the non-Israelite cities, such as Megiddo or Taanach, that were prominent in the valley.

Although there is some dispute as to the proper application of the name Jezreel Valley, the valley proper as understood in this discussion has a triangular, or arrowhead, shape. The points of the triangle are Helkath in the northwest, Mount Tabor in the northeast, and Beth Haggan in the southeast. The northern boundary line, which stretches 17 miles (27 km.) from Helkath to Mount Tabor, is formed by the southernmost ridge of western Lower Galilee, the Nazareth ridge. The southern boundary is formed by the Carmel range, which runs 20 miles (32 km.) from Helkath to Beth Haggan. The eastern boundary is less distinct; a good approximation is an imaginary line, 17 miles (27 km.) long, connecting Beth Haggan with Mount Tabor.

The valley itself is composed of rich alluvial soils that have washed down from the surrounding hills. The watershed to the east is the dividing line between the Jezreel and Harod Valleys. From the Mount Tabor and Mount Gilboa regions, the Kishon River drains the valley in a northwesterly direction, passing through the narrow exit at Helkath at an elevation of 80 feet (24 m.). Because of its gentle slope, the valley becomes quite muddy in winter; in ancient times travel across the valley was very difficult during the winter months. Most of the valley surface receives 20 inches (500 mm.) of rain annually, while the surrounding hills receive approximately 28 inches (700 mm.). It was probably during a winter rainstorm (with the ensuing muddy conditions) that the Canaanites abandoned their chariots, which were stuck in the mud, and fled on foot before the troops of Deborah and Barak, which were advancing from Mount Tabor (Judges 4:15; 5:20–21; Ps 83:9; map p. 107). Although the wet season caused problems for travelers, it enabled the inhabitants of the region to reap in spring and early summer bountiful harvests of wheat and barley, which "God had indeed sown" (Heb. *Yizreʿeʾl*, "God sows").

To the east of the watershed, beginning approximately at the city of Jezreel, a smaller, narrower valley, 11 by 3 miles (17.5 by 5 km.), descends into the Beth Shan region. Some geographers consider this alone to be the biblical Jezreel Valley, but here it will be called the Harod Valley, after the modern name of the nahal (Heb. for "valley") that descends along its length. This valley is bounded to the north by the southernmost basalt-soil slope of eastern Lower Galilee and to the south by the steep scarp of Mount Gilboa, which rises some 1,600 feet (490 m.) above the valley floor. Most of the valley is below sea level. Since it cuts through the under-ground water table, there are numerous springs that make this a fertile region in spite of the fact that Beth Shan receives only 12 inches (300 cm.) of rain annually.

Although the Jezreel and Harod valleys are important from an agricultural standpoint, they are of even greater strategic significance. The great north-south International Highway had to pass through the Jezreel Valley, while the easiest east-west route through the whole of Israel crossed both valleys. A traveler coming from the south along the International Highway, after having traveled through one of the Carmel passes, would be at either Jokneam, Megiddo, Taanach, or Beth Haggan. Most commonly he would arrive at the city of Megiddo and from there would cross the Jezreel Valley along the slightly higher ground formed by some basalt outcrops, proceeding in a northeasterly direction toward Mount Tabor. If he was going instead from Megiddo to the ports of Acco, Tyre, or Sidon, he could follow along the foot of the northern scarp of Mount Carmel, proceed through the narrow pass at Helkath (0.3 mi. [.5 km.] wide), and then, avoiding the sand dunes, head northward. Another route, possibly used as frequently as the preceding one, led directly north from Megiddo to Shimron. From there it continued through the low hills of western Lower Galilee to Hannathon, and from there westward to the Plain of Acco.

The other major route passing through this area connected Acco, via the cities of Megiddo and Jezreel, with Beth Shan. This east-west connecting route was of extreme importance, for from Beth Shan one could head northeastward to the southern end of the Sea of Galilee and from there ascend into Bashan and proceed on to Damascus, or one could head east from Beth Shan, ford the Jordan River, ascend the hills of Gilead, and eventually join the Transjordanian Highway at Ramoth Gilead.

It is evident that whoever controlled these valleys also controlled the major highways passing through the country. The tribes of Zebulun, Issachar, and Manasseh, which were allotted cities in and around the valley, had great difficulty in overcoming the Canaanites who lived there (Judges 1:27–28, 30); Israel probably did not gain actual control of the strategic valley strongholds until the days of David and Solomon (1 Kings 9:15). From the days of the Egyptian pharaoh Thutmose III (1486 B.C.) until the present, the Jezreel Valley has served as the stage on which the armies of the world have made their entrances and exits. Thus it is altogether fitting that this strategic location should be chosen as the setting of that great eschatological battle, the battle of Armageddon (Gr. form of Heb. *Har Mᵉgiddô*, "Mountain of Megiddo"; Rev 16:16).

Mount Carmel

To the south of the Jezreel Valley rise the towering rock scarps of Mount Carmel. The name *Carmel* means "plantation," "garden-land," and/or "garden-growth," and in Scripture the lushness of the vegetation on Mount Carmel became a symbol of great fertility (e.g., Song of Songs 7:5). Mount Carmel in a broad sense extends some 30 miles (48

Mount Carmel rising out of the Coastal Plain.

km.) along a line running from the Mediterranean Sea in the northwest to the Dothan Valley in the southeast.

Mount Carmel actually consists of three distinct geological regions. The northernmost of these is Mount Carmel proper. Composed primarily of hard Cenomanian-Turonian limestone formations with occasional patches of basalt, it rises to a height of 1,790 feet (546 m.) above sea level. Its northwestern tip dips into the Mediterranean Sea, and its western base runs parallel to the seashore for 20 miles (32 km.). On the north a very pronounced scarp rises some 1,500 feet (460 m.) above the floor of the Jezreel Valley. This rugged area, because of its elevation and its proximity to the sea, receives some 32 inches (800 mm.) of rain annually, along with a considerable amount of dew; in antiquity it was mostly covered with trees. Because of its massiveness and its steep slopes, particularly on the western and northeastern sides, travel across this portion of the mountain was practically impossible.

The second section of Mount Carmel, southeast of Mount Carmel proper, is called the Manasseh Region or the Shephelah (foothill) of Carmel. It is rectangular in shape and is composed of soft, chalky Eocene limestone. Because of its lower elevation (650 to 980 feet [200 to 300 m.]), less rain falls here than on Mount Carmel proper, and the chalky soil is not very fertile. Between these two sections is a Senonian chalk valley, or pass, through which traffic could flow from the Sharon Plain to Jokneam.

Further to the southeast is the third section of Mount Carmel, sometimes called the Umm el-Fahm region. This section, also rectangular in shape, is again made up of the harder Cenomanian-Turonian limestones. In some places it reaches elevations of 1,600 feet (490 m.). The soil is primarily rich terra rossa, and the annual rainfall (20 in. [500 mm.]) makes the region quite fertile. Between it and the Manasseh region to the northwest runs a second Senonian chalk pass, this one leading from the Sharon Plain to Megiddo. To the southeast of the Umm el-Fahm block lies another Senonian chalk area, namely the Dothan Valley, which separates this region from the hills of Manasseh; this valley forms the third important pass through the mountain. These strips of Senonian chalk that divide the Carmel Range, like other Senonian outcrops throughout the country, were frequently used as paths for roads because they are usually lower in elevation than the surrounding areas, are relatively free of boulders, and dry out quickly during the winter months.

Throughout antiquity the whole of Mount Carmel was probably covered with thick forests. In the biblical text we learn only of Elijah's and Elisha's associations with the mountain, although the cities bounding it on the northeast—Jokneam, Megiddo, and Taanach—are justly famous as Canaanite centers. Mount Carmel blocks the flow of north-south traffic from the Sharon Plain to the Jezreel Valley or to the Plain of Acco, so travelers, caravans, and armies throughout the ages had to use one of its three passes or attempt to go around the northwestern tip of the mountain. Thus if one could control the passes, one could control the flow of north-south traffic on the land bridge between the continents of Africa and Asia (recall Josiah's ill-fated attempt to prevent Pharaoh Neco from proceeding north by battling with him at Megiddo [2 Chron 35:22]).

SHARON, MANASSEH AND EPHRAIM

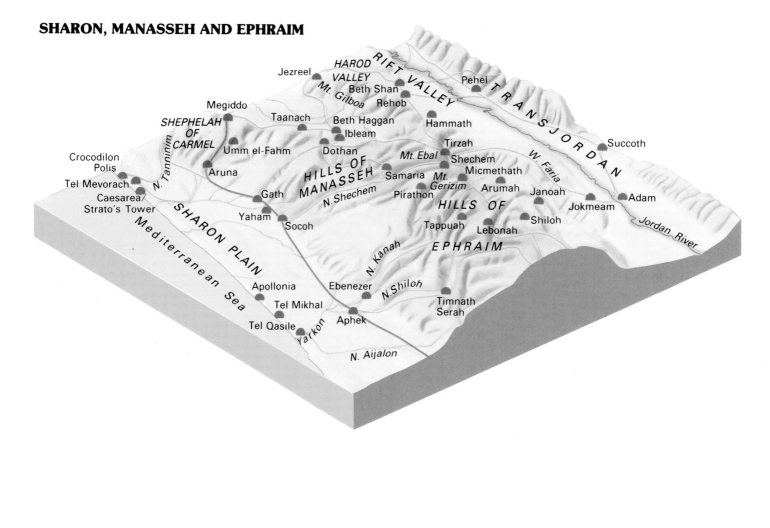

Sharon Plain

To the south of Mount Carmel is a section of the coastal plain called the Sharon, which is bounded on the north by the Nahal Tanninim (Crocodile River), on the east by the foothills of Ephraim and Manasseh, on the south by the Yarkon River, and on the west by the Mediterranean Sea. The Sharon measures 30 by 10 miles (48 by 16 km.) and is a flat area consisting of alluvial soils washed down from the hills and of deposits of Mousterian Red Sands. The areas where these latter deposits are found are well known today for the excellent citrus crops that grow there.

Along the western edge of the Sharon Plain three kurkar ridges run north-south, parallel to the seashore. One of these ridges in places forms the shoreline, while the other two are located slightly inland. The ridges block the westerly flow of the wadis, so that in ancient times the runoff water collected

behind these ridges, making the Sharon a very swampy area. It was not until Roman times that some outlets were cut through the ridges, and not until the twentieth century were the swamps completely drained.

In Old Testament times the Sharon was not used for agricultural purposes because of the swamps, the dense oak forests, and a thicket of scrub trees; indeed, it has been recently argued that the word Sharon indicates a "forest in the plain."[2] Evidently the Sharon was merely used as a place for the grazing of cattle during the Old Testament period (1 Chron 5:16; 27:29). The swampy conditions also forced the north-south International Highway to run along the eastern edge of the plain as it led northward from Aphek via cities such as Socoh, Yaham, and Gath, to Mount Carmel, avoiding the hills to the east and the swamps to the west. It was not until Herod the Great constructed Caesarea on the coast that any of the major highways ventured out into the plain itself.

To the north of the Sharon Plain is a thin strip of land measuring 20 by 2 miles (32 by 3.2 km.), tucked in between

Swamp near Roman dam in Sharon Plain, looking southwards.

the western slopes of Mount Carmel and the Mediterranean Sea. This northern extension of the Sharon Plain is sometimes called the Coast of Dor, after the chief Old Testament city located in the region. This strip of land provided a passageway around Mount Carmel that led from Tel Mevorach to Tell es-Samak. But due to the narrowness of the passage and the swamps in the region, this road was not used extensively in ancient times.

The coastline between Mount Carmel and the Yarkon River to the south is relatively smooth, and small natural harbors were found only at Athlit and Dor. Additional anchorages were developed at Crocodilon Polis, Strato's Tower, Apollonia, Tel Mikhal, and sites near the Yarkon. These anchorages could be used by vessels as they plied the coast; around 1100 B.C. the Tjekker, a tribe of the Sea Peoples, initiated maritime exploits originating from the city of Dor.[3] Not until Herod built the huge city of Caesarea (ca. 22–10 B.C.) did a city on this portion of the coastline serve as a major port. At that time some of the swamps were drained and portions of the land were put to agricultural use to serve as a hinterland for this new major urban center. Caesarea

was to become the governing center of the land for some 600 years (ca. A.D. 6–639).

Hill Country of Manasseh

To the east of the Sharon Plain rise the hills of Manasseh and Ephraim. These mountains are part of the massive Cisjordan range, which stretches from Mount Carmel and Mount Gilboa in the north to Beersheba in the south. Going from north to south, one passes through the old tribal territories of Manasseh, Ephraim, Benjamin, and Judah (see map p. 98). The geographical boundaries between these regions are sometimes almost imperceptible; but since each region does have its own distinctive character, they will be treated separately.

The Hill Country of Manasseh stretches from the Dothan Valley in the northwest and Mount Gilboa in the northeast to an imaginary east-west line drawn along the axis of the Kanah Ravine, extending from the Sharon Plain to the Rift Valley. The center of this territory is an uplifted area of Eocene limestone mountains, the southern tip of which culminates in the highest elevations in the whole region of Manasseh: Mount Ebal at 3,084 feet (940 m.) and Mount Gerizim at 2,891 feet (881 m.). This central area contains some large valleys, located at higher elevations, which receive 20 to 25 inches (500 to 630 mm.) of rain annually. At the northeastern edge of the central block is Mount Gilboa, which towers some 1,600 feet (490 m.) over the Harod Valley. Both the amount of rainfall on Mount Gilboa (ca. 16 in. [400 mm.] annually) and the number of dew nights fall considerably below those in the rest of the central region (compare David's words at the time of the death of Saul: "O mountains of Gilboa, May you have neither dew nor rain," 2 Sam 1:12).

To the east of the central core is an area composed primarily of Cenomanian limestone, with some outcroppings of Senonian and Eocene chalks closer to the Rift Valley. Near the Rift Valley the annual rainfall decreases (10 to 14 in. [250 to 350 mm.]), thus allowing only for marginal crops and grazing. The hills of eastern Manasseh are cut through by two parallel fault lines that outline the Wadi Faria. This wadi, from 0.3 to 1.9 miles (0.5 to 3 km.) wide and running in a northwest-southeast direction, begins in the Tirzah region (elevation 660 ft. [200 m.]) and leads down into the Rift Valley near the river ford at Adam (980 ft. [300 m.] below sea level). Because much of its course is below sea level, the wadi cuts through the underground water horizon and contains a number of important springs. The Wadi Faria has provided a convenient passageway between the Hill Country of Manasseh and the Transjordanian and Rift Valley regions. In addition, there is a thin ribbon-like "moat" of Senonian chalk that runs directly from Shechem toward Beth Shan, geologically separating central and eastern Manasseh. This "moat" provides an additional connecting link leading in and out of the region, as evidenced by the old Roman road that followed this track.

To the west of the uplifted central block are the lower chalk and limestone hills and valleys of western Manasseh. This area is not as rugged as the previous two and has relatively easy access routes into the hills via valleys such as the Nahal Shechem and the Dothan. Although the soil is not the most fertile, it is easily worked, and since the area is on the windward side of the mountains it receives a good amount of rainfall; it was therefore either tree covered or well cultivated throughout antiquity.

Of all the areas in the Cisjordanian mountains, the territory of Manasseh is most open to outside influences. Roads lead into the area via the Nahal Shechem, the Dothan Valley, the Wadi Faria, and the Shechem–Beth Shan "moat." Furthermore, one could cross from the Sharon Plain to the Rift Valley by following the zigzag route that led up the Nahal Shechem to Shechem, turning northeastward to Tirzah and from there heading southeastward down the Wadi Faria to the Rift Valley. This route joined the "watershed" or "ridge" route from the Jerusalem region at Shechem. Thus it is no wonder that Shechem, strategically located at this important road junction in a valley between Mount Ebal and Mount Gerizim, was for a long period of time both the

major city and the capital of the region. The move of the capital of the Northern Kingdom to Tirzah (see, e.g., 1 Kings 15:21, 33) seemed to reflect a more inward, defensive, conservative approach to international matters. But when the capital was finally moved to Samaria (1 Kings 16), located not far from the Sharon Plain on the western slopes of the mountains, the Northern Kingdom was open to the full force of cultural, religious, and political influences from the west (witness the arrival of Jezebel and her gods; 1 Kings 16:29–34). Samaria eventually became a great Greco-Roman city, and in time its name replaced Manasseh as the name of the region.

Hill Country of Ephraim

To the south of Manasseh are the hills that form the mountain heartland allotted to the tribe of Ephraim (see map p. 98). The Hill Country of Ephraim is bounded on the west by the Sharon Plain, on the east by the Rift Valley, on the north by the theoretical east-west line drawn along the Kanah Ravine (see above, pp. 39–40), and on the south by a theoretical east-west line through the city of Bethel. From north to south the Hill Country of Ephraim measures 15.5 miles (24 km.) and from east to west some 27 miles (43 km.). The area is composed entirely of hard Cenomanian and Turonian limestones. These limestones weather into the deep, V-shaped valleys that make the hills of Ephraim a rugged region: almost the entire area consists of very steep-sided, sometimes terraced, rocky hills, separated by dramatic, deep valleys (see above). The main wadi system is the Shiloh, which drains the whole central section of the region toward the Mediterranean Sea.

Elevations in the region range from 1,900 to 3,200 feet (580 to 975 m.); the highest peak is Baal Hazor (3,333 ft. [1016 m.]). The western slopes and central mountains receive abundant amounts of rainfall (20 to 28 in. [500 to 700 mm.]), while the eastern slopes receive less and less as one approaches the Rift Valley. The soil is fertile terra rossa; terrace farming is common, and vines, wheat, and other crops are grown on the small patches of arable land.

The major road through the area is the "Ridge Route" (see above, p. 28). This road, in the main, sticks close to the watershed and avoids the deep valleys to the east and west as it progresses from Jerusalem, via Bethel and Shiloh, to Shechem. Because the "wall-to-wall" limestone reaches from the coastal plain into the Rift Valley, approaches into the hills from either the west or the east are very difficult. This meant that Ephraim was normally spared from direct invasions and that it could serve as a place of retreat during times of political instability. The placement of the tabernacle at Shiloh during the period of the judges may have been motivated by the usefulness of the natural defenses of Ephraim. It is with good reason that one of the Levites was said to live in "a remote area in the hill country of Ephraim" (Judges 19:1), for certainly this was one of the most secluded places in the whole of the Cisjordanian mountain chain.

Hill Country of Benjamin

This region approximately coincides with the territory that once belonged to the tribe of Benjamin (see map p. 98). It stretches from Bethel in the north to Jerusalem in the south, a distance of 13.5 miles (21.7 km.). Its eastern border is the mountain's edge at the Rift Valley, its western boundary the western slopes of the hills descending into the coastal plain. From east to west it averages about 27 miles (43.5 km.) in width.

Most of eastern Benjamin is actually the northern extension of the chalky, dry Judean Wilderness (6 to 16 in. [150 to 400 mm.] of rain annually). It was used primarily as a place of refuge for the outcasts of society and as winter pasturage for sheep and goats. The central and western portions of Benjamin are composed of hard Cenomanian-Turonian limestone; the central section, through which the watershed runs, is a relatively high plateau (2,500 ft. [760 m.]). The "Benjamin Plateau" formed the core of Benjamin's tribal territory. It is circular in shape and is bounded on the south by Gibeah, on the east by Geba, on the north by Mizpah, and on the west by Gibeon. It receives about 25 inches (635 mm.) of rain annually. A number of springs are found in this area, as throughout the Cisjordanian mountains, and plastered cisterns were commonly used to collect rainwater. Settlements sprang up on the tops and slopes of the small limestone hills that dot the plateau. The hard limestone is relatively easy to work and was used in the construction of the walls of houses; the roofs were made of mud and plaster supported by timbers. The plateau's well-cultivated fields are blessed with fertile terra rossa soil. In Bible times, especially at the time of the arrival of the Israelites, the area was probably more densely covered with trees and forests than it is today.

To the south of Gibeah there is a second mountain plateau. It is elliptical in shape and is bounded on the south by Beth Hakkerem and on the west by the Waters of Nephtoah. The city of Jerusalem stands on the eastern edge of this plateau. This "Jerusalem Plateau" was shared by the tribes of Benjamin and Judah. The major internal route running from Hebron to Shechem, the "Ridge Route," ran across these two plateaus, passing close to the villages and sites of Beth Hakkerem, Gibeah, Ramah, Mizpah, and Bethel.

To the east and west of these plateaus are mountain ridges that extend perpendicularly to the central north-south mountain axis. These ridges, especially the western ones, are separated by deeply incised valleys through which travel is next to impossible. North-south travel through the whole region is very difficult if one leaves the plateaus or the watershed. Most east-west routes of any importance ascend into the mountains via one of the limestone ridges. A major interregional east-west road ran from Gezer on the coastal plain, through the Valley of Aijalon, up along the ridge on which Lower and Upper Beth Horon were located, via Gibeon, to Ramah, where it joined the Ridge Route. From there one could turn south to Jerusalem, north to Bethel, or continue through the wilderness down into the Rift Valley to Jericho. This route from the west was the major road to the capital city of Jerusalem, and throughout the ages those who have controlled Jerusalem have attempted to control this approach (see maps pp. 94 and 125 for several of the many military encounters along this road). The whole Benjamin Plateau was of strategic importance for the control of these internal routes. In fact, the Jerusalem and Benjamin plateaus were some of the "busiest" areas with regard to the flow of biblical events (see maps pp. 112, 126, et al.).

View of el-Jib (Biblical Gibeon), looking northwards, with Benjamin plateau beyond.

41

Hill Country of Judah

The tribe of Judah received the largest tribal allotment (Josh 15), which included all of the land stretching south from Jerusalem down to Israel's southern border with Sinai and from the Mediterranean Sea to the Rift Valley. However, the Philistines gained control of the coastal plain area, and the Negev was too dry to support a large population, so the majority of the Judeans settled in the Hill Country of Judah. This hill country is the final continuation of the central mountain spine that begins up at Mount Carmel and Mount Gilboa and disappears at the northern edge of the Negev Basin. The Hill Country of Judah stretches from Jerusalem 40 miles (64 km.) south to Khirbet Ira and is 11 to 14 miles (18 to 22.5 km.) wide; its western border is the Shephelah, its eastern border the Judean Wilderness (see below).

The Hill Country of Judah is composed of hard Cenomanian limestone and thus shares many characteristics with the Hill Country of Ephraim and that of Benjamin (see above, pp. 40–41). To the south of the Benjamin and Jerusalem plateaus the mountains begin to rise until they reach an elevation of 3,343 feet (1019 m.) just north of the Hebron area, at which point the hills begin their descent to 1,300 feet (400 m.) in the Khirbet Ira region. The central watershed that runs from Jerusalem to Hebron divides into two ridges at Hebron. One of these ridges continues almost due south via Carmel and Maon to Arad in the Negev, while the other proceeds southwest past Adoraim and Debir to Beersheba. The roads that ran along these two ridges provided important links between Judah and the trade routes of the Negev and the Red Sea.

Hebron is at the junction of the main Ridge Route and its two branches. It is the natural hub of the southern region of the Hill Country of Judah. Situated high in the hills, defended on all sides by the typical treacherous wadi systems, it protected Judah from the south. It also served as the spot where the central government in the hill country could make contact with the Bedouin and merchants of the Negev. At Hebron, produce from the hill country—wheat, barley, olives, grapes, pomegranates, and other fruits—could be exchanged for sheep, donkeys, camels, leather goods, and other products brought up from the desert regions to the south. It was to Hebron that the patriarchs gravitated, and it was at Hebron that David first established his kingdom (see, for example, map p. 77).

Because of the high elevation, the amount of rain in the area between Bethlehem and Hebron is high (20 to 28 in. [500 to 700 mm.]); south of Hebron, however, rainfall begins to drop off rapidly. During the winter months the Hill Country of Judah usually receives at least one snowfall, although the snow generally remains on the ground for only a day or two. Judah's higher elevations make it more difficult to grow olives there than in the Ephraim and Manasseh regions. Vineyards, on the other hand, are much more common in the Hill Country of Judah than in Ephraim and Manasseh. The terra rossa soil is farmed extensively on the small mountain plateaus and in the large valleys such as the Valley of Beracah ("Valley of Blessing"); the terraces on the steep wadi slopes were also cleared and farmed. Although the remote mountain territory between Shechem and Hebron was not of unusual economic, strategic, or political importance to the great powers of antiquity, yet it was there that some of the most significant events of redemptive history occurred. It was there that God settled, protected, and tested his ancient people Israel (see the Historical Section).

Judean Wilderness

The Judean Wilderness is a rectangular strip approximately 60 miles (96 km.) long and 10 miles (16 km.) wide, sandwiched between the crest of the hills of Judah and the Rift Valley. Its northern limit is close to the Wadi Auja, which enters the Rift Valley 5.5 miles (9 km.) north of Jericho. Its southern border is not well defined but reaches at least to an imaginary east-west line drawn through the southern end of the Dead Sea. The wilderness is primarily composed of Senonian rock formations, chalk, marl, and bands of flint.

The major topographical feature of the region is the steep descent from the Judean mountain ridge (2,500 to 3,000 ft. [760 to 915 m.] above sea level) to the surface of the Dead Sea (1,310 ft. [400 m.] below sea level). In some places this means a descent of 4,300 feet (1310 m.) over a horizontal distance of only 10 miles (16 km.). It is not a smooth incline but looks rather like a series of steps descending into the Rift Valley. The final "step" down is the most pronounced and consists of limestone cliffs 350 to 1,300 feet (100 to 400 m.) high, stretching along the length of the western shore of the Dead Sea.

As one moves east through the Judean Wilderness, the amount of rainfall drops off drastically. The 14 to 28 inches (350 to 700 mm.) of rainfall in the Hill Country of Judah decreases to less than 4 inches (100 mm.) near the shore of the Dead Sea. More than half of the wilderness area receives less than 8 inches (200 mm.) of rain per year. The scarcity of rain and the geology of the area make it impossible to grow crops here. The soils derived from the Senonian rock, chalk, and marl formations are infertile. In addition, when rain falls on these Senonian formations, they develop an impermeable upper layer that prevents the rainwater from soaking into the soil. The water instead rapidly runs off toward the Dead Sea. As a result, the Judean Wilderness is a desolate variegated landscape of plateaus, rounded hills, dramatic scarps, deep canyons, and cliffs. The only places where farming is possible in this inhospitable environment are along the western edge of the wilderness close to the watershed of the Judean mountains and in the Buqei'a. Because the wilderness was close to population centers such as Jerusalem and Hebron, all Judeans were well aware of its impact on their lives. It is no wonder that the messages of the prophets Amos and Jeremiah, who came from Tekoa and Anathoth (cities on the edge of the desert) respectively, reverberate with the imagery of the wilderness.

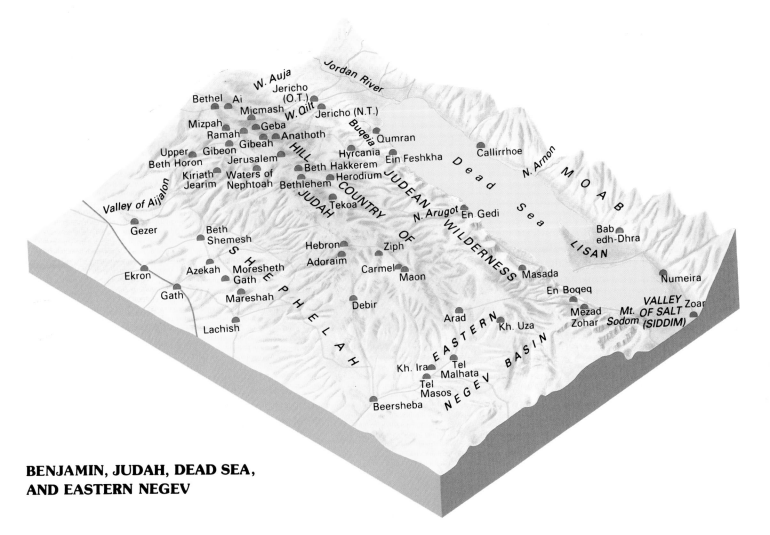

BENJAMIN, JUDAH, DEAD SEA, AND EASTERN NEGEV

In spite of these adverse conditions, an occasional acacia tree and a few dwarf bushes can be found in the bottom of the wadis. Only during the rainy winter months does some grass cover appear on the plateaus, but even then the meager greenery is basically confined to the northern slopes of the hills. It is during this "wet" season that the shepherds bring their sheep and goats into the wilderness to feed on the sparse vegetation.

The only major springs are located in the northern section of the Judean Wilderness, along the courses of the Wadi Auja and the Wadi Qilt; the central and southern sections are practically devoid of fresh-water supplies. Cisterns were hewn throughout the wilderness in an attempt to collect and store as much of the water from the winter rains as possible in order to insure a minimal supply of water. The Senonian rock formations are well suited for such storage systems. It is no wonder, then, that this rocky, chalky, dry, and desolate region is usually called the "wilderness" (Heb. *midbār*; NIV "desert") in the Bible, or also the "Jeshimon" (Heb. *yeshîmōn*), the "waste" or the "desert" place (1 Sam 23:19; 26:1, 3).

Throughout history, this relatively uninhabited wilderness served as a place of retreat and refuge. David fled from Saul into the wilderness (1 Sam 22:1–27:6). Herod the Great (37–4 B.C.) built a series of fortresses in the area—including the Herodium, Hyrcania, and Masada—which were to serve as retreats in case of trouble with his Jewish subjects or with his enemy the Egyptian queen Cleopatra (Jos. *War* 7.8.4 [295–303]). The Essenes went out into the solitude of the wilderness, to Qumran, to escape the religious establishment in Jerusalem and to "prepare the way of the Lord." John the Baptizer, while residing in the "Desert [= wilderness] of Judea," called the people of his day to a life of repentance (Matt. 3:1–12). Jesus experienced temptations while on a wilderness retreat (4:1–11).

The Judean Wilderness also served as the eastern defensive line of Judah. Any invaders from the east—from Moab, Edom, or the Arabian Desert—first had to cross the Dead Sea, scale the imposing cliffs along its western shore, and then march through a waterless wilderness before arriving at major population centers such as Jerusalem and Hebron.

The major roads through the Judean Wilderness all began at the large water sources located in the Rift Valley: the springs of Jericho, Ein Feshkha, and En Gedi. From Jericho at least three roads ascended into the hill country through the northern Judean Wilderness. The northernmost road followed the ridge just to the north of the Wadi Qilt into the Micmash–Ai–Bethel region. It is quite possible that Joshua led the invading Israelites into the hill country via this route (Josh 7–8). The middle road ascended to Jerusalem on a path slightly to the south of the Wadi Qilt system. This road roughly followed the line of the old border between the tribes of Benjamin and Judah (15:5–8; 18:16–19). Today, traces of the old Roman Road can be located along its path. In the days of Jesus, Jews traveling between Jerusalem and Perea in Transjordan made frequent use of this route; on occasion it was used by Jesus as he traveled from Jericho to Jerusalem (e.g., Matt 20:17–21:3). This road is also the setting of the parable of the Good Samaritan (Luke 10:30). The third route out of Jericho heads in a southwesterly direction and joins Jericho with Bethlehem.

In the central portion of the Judean Wilderness a road ran northwest from the spring of En Gedi up to the Tekoa-Bethlehem region. At En Gedi it ascended the steep cliffs (660 feet [200 m.] high) via a narrow, serpentine path that may be the biblical "Pass of Ziz" (2 Chron 20:16). The track then followed the ridge just to the north of the Nahal Arugot up to Tekoa. Remains of Israelite as well as Roman forts along its path have been found. This may have been the route followed by the Moabites, the Ammonites, and the Meunites who invaded Judah during the days of Jehoshaphat (872–848 B.C.; 2 Chron 20:1–30; see map p. 128).

In the southern section of the Judean Wilderness an important road led from the southern end of the Dead Sea into the Hebron area. The road ascended the cliffs along the western edge of the Rift Valley near Khirbet Uza where an Israelite fort guarded the approach. From there the road headed north via Arad and Carmel–Maon–Ziph to Hebron. The queen of Sheba may have used this route as she came from the Red Sea area to visit Solomon (1 Kings 10:1–13). In Roman times the road ascended the Rift Valley cliffs via the Nahal Zohar, passing the Roman fort Mezad Zohar in the valley. This route was of great importance for caravans coming from the Red Sea to Jerusalem, as well as for those that transported salt mined in the Mount Sodom region.

Dead Sea/Salt Sea

The largest inland body of water in Israel is the Dead Sea. It is located in one of the deepest sections of the Rift Valley; its surface is some 1,300 feet (400 m.) below the level of the Mediterranean Sea. Because of its position in the Rift Valley, which in the biblical period was known as the Arabah, it is also called the "Sea of the Arabah" (Deut 3:17; 4:49; Josh 3:16; 12:3; 2 Kings 14:25); and because its northern tip is due east of Jerusalem (only 15 miles [24 km.]), it is sometimes also called the "eastern sea" (Ezek 47:18; Joel 2:20; Zech 14:8).

The Dead Sea can be divided into two unequal sections by a tongue-shaped peninsula that protrudes into it from its eastern shore (= Lisan in Arabic, Lashon in Hebrew) The northern portion is 31 miles (50 km.) long, the southern section only 15.5 miles (25 km.). Its average width is close to 9.3 miles (15 km.). The northern section is the deeper of the two; soundings in the northeastern corner indicate that the bottom of the sea lies 1,300 feet (400 m.) below its surface. The southern end is quite shallow with a maximum depth of only 25 feet (7.5 m.).

However, there are considerable variations in the water level of the Dead Sea from year to year. In drought years the level can drop as much as 16 feet (5 m.), while in especially rainy years its level can rise a corresponding amount, adding 1 mile (1.6 km.) to the length of the sea. The now-dry basin at the south end of the sea gives evidence of this cycle of

contraction and expansion. In recent years the Israelis and the Jordanians have been using the waters of the upper Jordan and Yarmuk rivers for drinking and agricultural purposes, with the result that the amount of water entering the Dead Sea via its main source, the Jordan River, has been considerably reduced, so that the level of the sea has been dropping even more dramatically. Many recent maps still show a section of water 3 miles (4.8 km.) wide separating the Lisan from the western shore; however, today this is practically all dry ground. For other reasons also this area was either dry ground or at least shallow enough to be forded at various times throughout history. It is possible that the invaders from the east during the days of Jehoshaphat (872–848 B.C.) crossed the sea in this area (2 Chron 20:1–30), and there is some evidence that it was fordable during Roman times (63 B.C.–A.D. 324) as well as during other periods in history.

Fault escarpments to the west and east of the Dead Sea clearly outline its shore. On the west perpendicular cliffs, towering some 1,300 feet (400 m.) above the sea in spots, rise behind the narrow gravel-and-marl shoreline. In other areas the cliffs descend right into the sea, not even leaving space for a footpath along their base.

Along the eastern shore, the cliffs and mountains rise even more precipitously to elevations of 2,500 to 2,950 feet (760 to 900 m.). These cliffs consist of limestone formations on Nubian sandstone that is exposed in large areas. The mountains of Moab on the east side of the Dead Sea receive much more rainfall than the Judean Wilderness, so that several of the wadis that enter the Dead Sea from the east contain perennial springs. There has never been a north-south road along the eastern shore of the Dead Sea because the cliffs, like those along the western shore, often descend directly into the water.

In the south, the eastern shoreline is more expansive. There, jutting out into the sea, is the tongue-shaped Lisan, a very bleak and forbidding region composed of gravel, mud, and marl deposits that have weathered into formations like those of the badlands in the western United States. A basin at the south end of the sea, 13 miles (21 km.) in length, is covered with similar badland formations. This may be the area that in the Bible is called the "Valley of Salt" (2 Sam 8:13; 2 Kings 14:7; 1 Chron 18:12; 2 Chron 25:11) or the "Valley of Siddim" (Gen 14:3, 8, 10).

The region around the Dead Sea is very arid for several reasons: its low elevation, its position in the southern portion of the country on the lee side of the mountains, and its distance from the Mediterranean Sea. At the north end of the sea the rainfall averages 4 inches (100 mm.) per year, at the south end only 2 inches (50 mm.). Cloud cover in the area is minimal, and daytime temperatures can be very hot. In the summer, the average daily high temperature is 95° F (35° C), in the winter 68° F (20° C). Because the sea is bordered by cliffs on the east and west with open areas to the north and south, strong winds can develop during the late afternoon hours, causing whitecaps on the sea.

Due to these hot, dry conditions, there is a large amount of evaporation, which keeps the level of the sea relatively constant. Since there is no outlet, the evaporating water leaves behind most of its minerals. Hot sulphur springs, such as those of En Boqeq and Callirrhoe, and the natural salt deposits found in the vicinity also contribute to the exceptionally high mineral content of the sea—25 percent as compared to 5 percent for most oceans—that makes the water oily to the touch. The ancients were well aware of the sea's high mineral composition, naming it the "Salt Sea" (Gen 14:3; Num 34:3, 12; Deut 3:17; Josh 3:16; 12:3; 15:2, 5; 18:19). It was not until the modern era, however, that the sodium, magnesium, calcium, and potassium chlorides began to be mined by the Israelis and the Jordanians. The hot sulfur springs, incidentally, were known for their medicinal properties, and it was to Callirrhoe that Herod the Great retired in an attempt to be cured of his fatal illness (Jos. *War* 1.23.5 [656–58]).

Salt was a valuable commodity in ancient times, and there is evidence that Mount Sodom, located at the southwestern corner of the Dead Sea, was mined for this purpose. This narrow mountain consists of salt, gypsum, shales, sands, and marl. Rain water has weathered the rock into fantastic shapes, and from time to time explorers in the region have recognized "Lot's wife" among the salt formations (Gen 19:26)!

Another product that came directly from the sea and from the surrounding area was bitumen, a petroleum product that was used for the caulking of ships and for the making of medicines. The account of the battle between the five kings and the four kings in the days of Lot and Abraham mentions "tar [= bitumen] pits" in the "Valley of Siddim" (the Dead Sea area; Gen 14:10). Josephus later describes how in the Roman period the Dead Sea cast up "black masses of bitumen" that floated on the surface, "their shape and size resembling decapitated bulls," and how the laborers hauled this sticky material into their boats (e.g., Jos. *War* 4.8.4 [476–85]). Because of the presence of bitumen and sulfur springs, the sea was known to some classical writers as "Lake Asphaltitis."

There is little or no vegetation along most of the shoreline of the Dead Sea. Only a few tamarisk trees and other halophytic (salt-loving) plants grow along its banks. However, at oases such as En Gedi and Zoar, some vegetation is cultivated, including such luxury items as date palms and balsam trees. These types of plants flourish in the high-temperature, sweet-water environment of these oases.

Settlement of this desolate area has always been limited. During the middle of the Early Bronze Age (3150–2200 B.C.), large settlements were located at the southeastern end of the sea—at Bab edh-Dhra, Numeira, Zohar, Feifa, and Khana-zir (see map p. 75). During the period of the Judean monarchy (1000–586 B.C.), small settlements were established along the western shore of the Dead Sea, including such sites as Qumran and En Gedi. During the late Hellenistic and early Roman periods (ca. 152 B.C.–A.D. 70), small Jewish settlements were located along the western shore. The Essenes, who have become well known since the discovery of the Dead Sea scrolls, settled in the Qumran area. Farther south, Jews were living at the oasis of En Gedi, but it was Herod's great fortress of Masada, built on the top of a mesa-like rock, that dominated the southern landscape of the Dead Sea. Although living conditions around the Dead Sea were harsh, it was to places like Qumran, En Gedi, and Masada that the disenchanted or fearful would flee.

Oasis of En Gedi at western shore of Dead Sea.

Philistine Plain

South of the Sharon Plain and west of the Shephelah (see below) lies the southernmost section of the coastal plain within Israel proper. Bounded by the Yarkon River on the north, the Shephelah on the east, and the Nahal Besor and Nahal Gerar on the south, the Philistine Plain stretches some 50 miles (80 km.) along the shore of the Mediterranean Sea. It is wider in the south (25 mi. [40 km.]) than in the north (10 mi. [16 km.]).

The coastline itself is uninterrupted by any bays except for one formed by a small promontory near Joppa. The major features of the shoreline are dunes, wider in the south than in the north, and kurkar ridges, which are not as extensively

exposed here as they are along the northern coast. Further inland the landscape is relatively flat. The low, rolling hills are higher in the southern portion of the plain, where they rise to 330 to 500 feet (100 to 150 m.) east of Gaza, while in the northern part they rise to only 100 feet (30 m.) east of Joppa. In the north, the red sands of the Sharon Plain begin to disappear as they blend with the alluvial soils of the central portion of the Philistine Plain. In the south, the alluvial soils give way to the wind-blown loess soil that characterizes the Negev region of Israel (see below).

As is typical for the country, precipitation declines as one moves south, from 20 inches (510 mm.) annually at Joppa to less than 16 inches (400 mm.) at Gaza. Since grain is the major agricultural product grown on the plain, it is with good reason that the Philistines worshiped the grain god Dagon (1 Sam 5:2–5). The southern portion of the plain, near the coast, receives an extraordinary number of dew nights, 250

PHILISTIA, SHEPHELAH AND WESTERN JUDAH

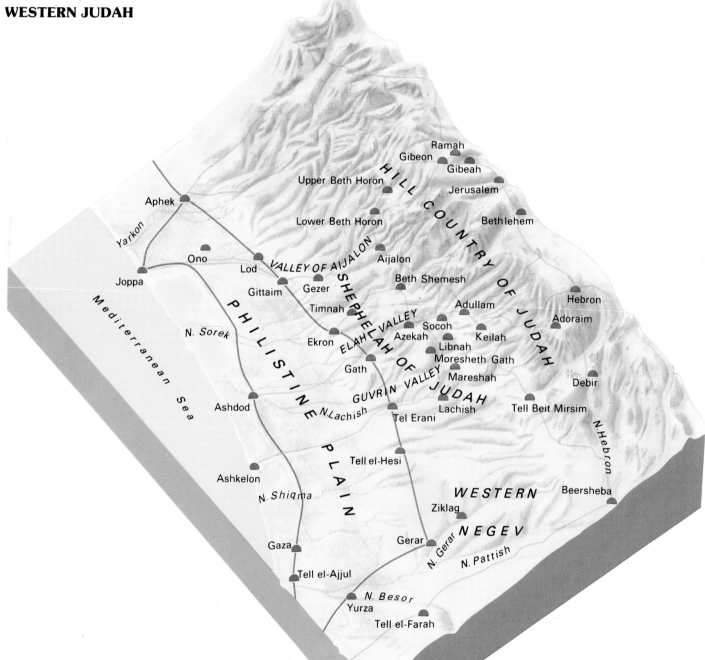

46

per year on the average, so that melon crops can be grown here during the rainless summer months.

After the grain crops were harvested in May–June, shepherds, who had been herding their flocks of sheep and goats in the Judean Desert or the Negev, probably brought them to the plain to feed on the stubble. It may very well be that the farmer and the shepherd often complemented each other's lifestyle and may often have been from the same family or tribe.

In the Philistine Plain, drinking water is available from wells dug in the wadi beds and from springs (cf. Abraham and Isaac's activities in this region, Gen 26:15–33). Excavations in the region have demonstrated that houses, city walls, and other structures were normally made of sun-dried mud brick, which eventually disintegrated. Subsequent rebuilding on top of the remnants of previous structures has produced numerous "tells" in the area. Travel in the region was relatively easy; the only obstacles were the sand dunes along the coast, the hills of the Shephelah to the east, and the low ground that could become muddy during the wet season. Two branches of the major International Highway ran through the Philistine Plain—one close to the coast via Gaza, Ashkelon, Ashdod, Joppa, and Aphek, the other inland via Tel Erani, Gath, Ekron, Gittaim, and Aphek. Both of these avoided the low, somewhat swampy area between the Nahal Aijalon and the Nahal Yarkon. In addition, the coastal branch, in order to avoid the Nahal Yarkon and the swamps of the Sharon Plain, had to swing eastward to join the inland branch at the strategically placed city of Aphek.

The northern portion of the Philistine Plain, between the Yarkon and the Aijalon, was called the "plain of Ono" (Neh 6:2) or the "Valley of the Craftsmen" (Neh 11:35). The former name was taken from one of the cities of the region; the latter may reflect the ancient memory that the Philistines of the area were blacksmiths, the craftsmen upon whom the Israelites were dependent during the reign of Saul (1 Sam 13:19–21). The chief city of the area, next to Aphek, was Joppa, which at various times during the biblical period served as the chief Judean port. It was from here that Solomon brought timbers to Jerusalem (2 Chron 2:16) and that Jonah departed from Israel (Jonah 1:3), and it was here that Peter visited the home of Simon the Tanner (Acts 9:43).

Philistia proper occupied the largest portion of the southern coastal plain, from the Nahal Aijalon to the Nahal Besor and Nahal Gerar. This territory with its five Philistine cities (Gaza, Ashkelon, Ashdod, Gath, and Ekron; see map p. 109), although assigned to the tribe of Judah (Josh 15:45–47), largely remained outside Israelite control. With the arrival of the Greeks, the name "Palestine," derived from "Philistine," came into use and eventually began to be used to refer to the whole of the land of Israel.[4]

The whole of the Philistine Plain was open to numerous outside influences. Throughout the ages, from the days of Thutmose III (1486 B.C.) to those of men such as Napoleon (A.D. 1799) and Allenby (A.D. 1918), the armies of the great international powers have marched up and down the coast, using it as a land bridge between Africa and Asia, while others, such as the Philistines and Crusaders, have used it as a beachhead as they attempted to establish themselves in the land.

Shephelah

The Shephelah is a transitional zone separating the Philistine Plain from the Hill Country of Judah. The Hebrew term *Shephēlâh* (used 20 times in the OT) is translated "(western) foothills" in the NIV. The term reflects the perspective of an Israelite standing in the Hill Country of Judah looking westward, *down* onto the lower foothills.

The Shephelah is approximately 27 miles (43 km.) long and 10 miles (16 km.) wide. It is composed primarily of soft Eocene chalks and limestones and is pockmarked with numerous caves. Its low rolling hills range from 300 to 1,200 feet (90 to 365 m.) in elevation—only about half the height of the "mountains" of the Hill Country of Judah to the west. The hills are covered by nari, a hard crusty rock about 3 to 5 feet (1 to 1.5 m.) thick. This crusty coating makes the surface of the hills useless for most agricultural purposes save for growing trees and bushes. In Bible times, scrub forests grew on these hills along with sycamore trees, which were cultivated for their figlike fruit. The area receives adequate amounts of rainfall, so grain and grapes can be grown in the relatively broad, alluvial valleys.

The villages, built with the local, mediocre limestones, clung to the hilltops and hillsides so as not to take up valuable farmland in the fertile valleys. The hills in this area do not form continuous ridges like those in the Hill Country of Judah. Thus the roads were laid out along the lower edges of the hills in order to avoid the valley floor, which could become muddy in the rainy season, as well as numerous ascents and descents. Water supplies for the inhabitants of the region included small springs, wells dug into the valley bottoms, and numerous cisterns.

In the northern two-thirds of the Shephelah there are five valleys that figure prominently in sacred history. The Aijalon Valley marks the northernmost limit of the Shephelah. The western approach to this broad chalk valley, now filled with rich alluvial soil, is guarded by the city of Gezer. The major road into the Hill Country of Judah and Benjamin passed eastward through this valley, avoiding the treacherous deep V-shaped valleys in Ephraim to the north as well as the 10-mile-wide (16 km.) band of hills and valleys of the Shephelah to the south. This road then ascended the continuous ridge on which stood Lower and Upper Beth Horon and eventually reached the hill country in the region of Gibeon. It was in the Aijalon Valley that the Lord, on behalf of Joshua and the Israelite army, "hurled large hailstones" down on the fleeing Amorites while the sun and the moon "stood still" (Josh 10:1–15; see map p. 94). It would be there, in the Valley of Aijalon, that the Philistines, the Egyptians, the Seleucids, the Romans, and many others would assemble to prepare to make their assaults into the Hill Country of Judah and Benjamin.

To the south of the Aijalon is the Sorek Valley, guarded on the west by the Philistine city of Timnah and on the east by Israelite Beth Shemesh. Many of the exploits of Samson took place in the Sorek (Judges 13–16; see map p. 107). And it was to Beth Shemesh that the Philistines sent the troublesome ark after having kept it in their territory for seven months (1 Sam 5:1–7:2; see map p. 111). An east-west road, not as important as the Aijalon–Beth Horon connection, passed through the Sorek to Beth Shemesh before ascending a limestone ridge to Kiriath Jearim on its way into the hills near Jerusalem.

The Elah Valley lies to the south of the Sorek; a road to the Bethlehem area ran through it. This valley, guarded on the west by the Philistine city of Gath and on the east by Azekah and Socoh, formed the stage on which the epic battle between David and Goliath took place (1 Sam 17; see map p. 113).

The Guvrin Valley to the south does not figure so prominently in biblical history, in spite of the fact that an important road to the Hebron area ran through it. The major city in the valley apparently was Mareshah, which became very important during the intertestamental period (then called Marisa). Micah the prophet came from the nearby city of Moresheth (Mic 1:1).

The fifth major valley is today called the Nahal Lachish, after the prominent biblical city Lachish, which lay along its course. This city, first conquered by Joshua (ca. 1400 B.C.; Josh 10:31–33; see map p. 94) and later by the Assyrian Sennacherib (701 B.C.; see map p. 134), was one of the last of the Judean cities to hold out against the invading Babylonian army (ca. 586 B.C.; Jer 34:7; see map p. 138). Lachish guarded an important interregional road that led up into the Hebron area via a ridge on which the city of Adoraim was located.

Throughout its history the Shephelah has served as a buffer zone between the provincial peoples living in the hill country and the usually more powerful, internationally oriented peoples of the coastal plain: between Hapiru and Egyptians (ca. 1400 B.C.), Israelites and Philistines (1200–700 B.C.), Judeans and Assyrians (701 B.C.), Judeans and Babylonians (586 B.C.), Arabs and Jews (A.D. 1948–67). Thus this seemingly placid and picturesque agricultural area has in fact served as a bloody battleground as peoples from the coastal plain tried to move into the hills and those living in the hills tried to expand their influence into the coastal plain.

Ancient pool in the Negev.

Negev

The term *Negev* is used 110 times in the Hebrew Bible, and its basic meaning can be either "dry" or "south." In 38 instances (NIV) it refers to a specific region located in the southern portion of the land of Israel. On maps of modern Israel the region bounded by Beersheba on the north, Elath on the south, the Rift Valley on the east, and Sinai on the west is referred to as the Negev. In the biblical text, however, the Negev, as a regional-geographical term, refers to a limited strip of land extending 10 miles (16 km.) north and 10 miles (16 km.) south of Beersheba and running east to west from the mountain ridge overlooking the Rift Valley to near the dunes along the Mediterranean Sea. The areas to the south of this region were called the "Desert of Zin" and the "Desert of Paran" (NIV). Notice that one could go *up*

(= north) from Kadesh Barnea into the "Negev" (Num 13:7, 22).

Topographically, the biblical Negev can be visualized as a double basin in the shape of an hourglass placed on its side, with Beersheba at the "waist" of the glass. To the north, east, and south of both basins is higher ground. The eastern basin, the administrative center of which was Arad, is drained by Nahal Beersheba, which flows west past Beersheba into the western basin, where it joins the Nahal Besor.

The soil of the Negev basin is a fine, wind-blown (aeolian) soil, called loess. When it rains, the surface of the loess soil becomes relatively impermeable, so that instead of seeping into the ground much of the water rapidly runs off into the wadis, creating miniature "badland" formations. The major water sources of the Negev were wells, which were usually dug in the bed of the wadis, often at the junction of two or more wadis, where water would tend to collect. For example, Beersheba, which can mean the "well of oath" or the "well of seven" (Gen 21:31; 26:33), was located at the

NEGEV AND THE ARABAH
SOUTH OF THE DEAD SEA

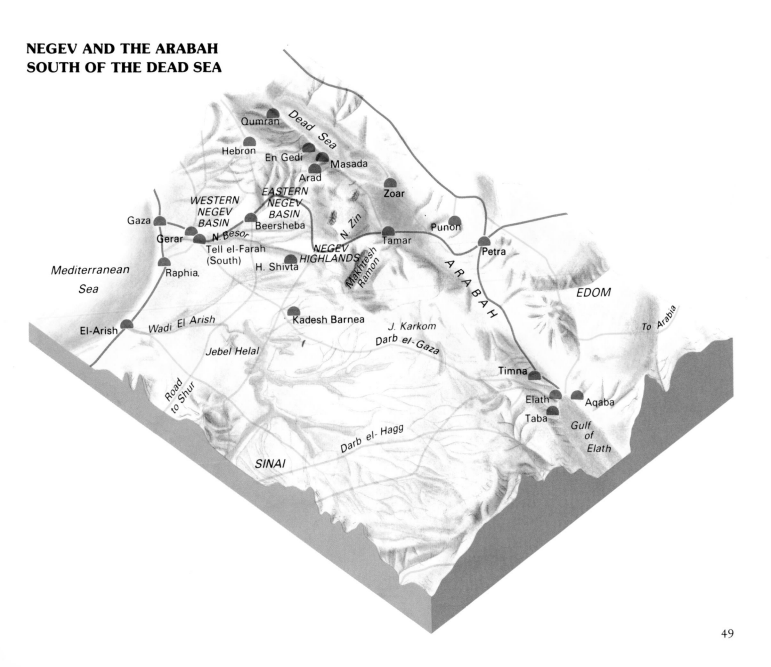

junction of the Nahal Hebron and the Nahal Beersheba. The biblical Negev is a transition zone that receives only 8 to 12 inches (200 to 300 mm.) of rain annually; however, deviations from this norm are very common. If the norm is reached, wheat and barley can be grown, but in only one of every three or four years is an adequate crop harvested. Thus the term *negev* is a very fitting one for this territory in that it is south of the heartland of Israel and considerably drier than most northern regions.

Besides being used for marginal agriculture, the Negev served for the pasturing of flocks of sheep and goats, as well as for the southern defense of Judah. City-forts, such as Beersheba and Arad, served as administrative, military, and religious centers. Of these, Beersheba normally was the southernmost outpost of the land of Israel, as reflected in the phrase "from Dan to Beersheba." Caravans traveling from Transjordan, Arabia, and the Gulf of Elath to a Mediterranean port such as Gaza were able to travel with ease across the low, rolling hills of the Negev.

To the south of the Negev is the area known as the Negev Highlands. This region, composed of limestone and chalk, contains a series of inland ridges that run parallel to the line

The Wilderness of Zin.

of the shore of the Mediterranean Sea—from the southwest to the northeast. Situated on three of these ridges, or anticlines, are three elliptical crater-like depressions called *makhteshim* in Hebrew (sing., *makhtesh*). Travel through any of these *makhteshim* is very difficult, for most of their sides are almost vertical cliffs. The highest elevation reached in the Negev Highlands is 3,395 feet (1035 m.) at Har Ramon. The Highlands are divided into northern and southern sections by the large, crescent-shaped Nahal Zin, which flows northeast into the Rift Valley.

The Negev Highlands constitute an arid region that receives only 4 to 8 inches (100 to 200 mm.) of rain each year. Agricultural products are extremely difficult to grow without costly irrigation techniques, and even grazing is difficult because of the scarcity of grass cover. However, caravans coming from Arabia via Transjordan or the Rift Valley had to cross this territory to take their wares to the port of Gaza. The various ridges and *makhteshim* lay across the caravan paths and proved to be formidable barriers to travel. The easiest route through the region ran from Tamar in the Rift Valley, up through the Nahal Zin, and from there northwest to Gaza. Roads sometimes ascended the various ridges (especially in the Roman and Byzantine periods), yet the track through the Nahal Zin, the modern "Way of the Sultan," served as the major connecting route.

South of the Negev Highlands rainfall decreases to only 1 or 2 inches (25 to 50 mm.) annually. The traveler going south encounters broad wadis such as the Paran and the Zenifim. Closer to Elath, sandstone and granite mountains, typical of southern Sinai and Transjordan, appear.

The "Arabah" South of the Dead Sea

The portion of the Rift Valley system that stretches 110 miles (175 km.) from the southern end of the Dead Sea to the tip of the Gulf of Elath on modern Israeli maps is called *Haarava*, "The Arabah." In the English Bible the Hebrew word *ʿarābâ(h)* is variously translated as "wasteland," "wilderness," and "desert land" (NIV; e.g., Job 24:5; Isa 35:1; Jer 51:43), but it is also used as a geographical term. In its latter sense, generally with the article ("the Arabah"), it appears twenty-eight times in the NIV and (with the possible exception of 1 Sam 23:24) refers to the area of the Rift Valley between the Sea of Galilee and the southern tip of the Dead Sea (see especially Deut 3:17 for an example of the common use of the term). Since the Dead Sea is occasionally called the "Sea of the Arabah" and because of the 1 Samuel passage above, it seems that the term may have referred to the entire Rift Valley, but due to the paucity of recorded historical events south of the Dead Sea there is no instance where the term is unambiguously used to refer to that area.

Following the modern Israeli usage, the Arabah, south of the Dead Sea, is composed of several sections. Extending 25 miles (40 km.) south of the Dead Sea is a severely dissected "badlands" area composed of Lisan marls and salt formations called the Sebkha, which at various times was covered by the Dead Sea (see above, p. 44). Farther south, gravel and rocks line the valley floor, and here the traveler sees the gravel delta of an occasional wadi. In the north and south the valley is hemmed in by mountain cliffs on the east and west, but it widens to 15 miles (24 km.) in the Punon region, where it loses some of its "Rift Valley" characteristics. Sixty-two miles (100 km.) south of the Dead Sea it even reaches an elevation of 1,160 feet (354 m.) above sea level before descending to the level of the Red Sea at the Gulf of Elath. Closer to Elath the slopes of the mountains east and west of the valley become more prominent, and at one point the valley narrows to a width of only 3.5 miles (5.5 km.).

The region of the Arabah receives between 1 and 2 inches (25 and 50 mm.) of rain each year; thus neither farming nor grazing is possible here. Although the area is basically devoid of vegetation, patches of halophytic (salt-loving) bushes and occasional acacia and broom trees are encountered, especially in the beds of the wadis. In biblical times the Arabah was used mainly as a highway. Since wells and springs are not numerous in this area, those who attempted to control the passage of caravans through the Arabah built small forts at these strategic watering points.

In biblical times the northeast extension of the Red Sea, the Gulf of Elath/Aqaba, was not used as extensively for shipping as one might expect, for the predominantly northern winds in the narrow gulf made the inbound trip difficult. In addition, coral reefs abound, currents are tricky, and fresh-water sources along the gulf's shores are rare. However, when ships did use the gulf, they were able to unload at Ezion Geber. The merchandise was then placed on camels or donkeys, and the overland caravans progressed up the Rift Valley to the Tamar region and from there headed northwest across the Negev.

The more popular trade route from the Far East was by sea to southern Arabia, where gold, frankincense, and myrrh could be added to the cargos brought in by ships. From there the caravans proceeded inland in a northwesterly direction via Yemen, Mecca, and Medina up to southern Edom. Caravans heading for Cisjordan may have descended into the Rift Valley at Elath and then headed north, or, more probably, they continued up the Transjordanian Highway to the Petra region, where they turned west, descended into the valley, and then continued on their way across the Negev to Gaza. If a caravan was headed for Egypt, it could descend into the Rift Valley at Elath and then continue across the middle of Sinai toward present-day Suez via the Darb el-Hagg, more recently used by Egyptians making pilgrimages to Mecca and Medina.

The only other major activity that took place in the Arabah was copper mining in the Timna region near Elath during the Chalcolithic, Late Bronze, and Roman periods and the occasional use of the copper mines near Punon, located in the Transjordanian mountains 33 miles (53 km.) south of the Dead Sea.

Many have considered the Arabah something of a frontier separating the Negev on the west from Edom on the east, yet there is some evidence that at times the Edomites spread from Transjordan into various portions of the Negev (Num 20:16; 34:3), as the Nabateans did after them. Indeed, some of the Judean-Edomite conflicts seemed to have been over the control of the trade routes through this area.

Gilead

Various forms of the word "Gilead" are used in the Scriptures a total of 110 times (NIV). Although on occasion it is used as a personal or tribal name, it is mainly used as a geographical term referring to the area of the country on the east side of the Jordan Valley between the Sea of Galilee on the north and the Dead Sea on the south. More precisely, this territory stretches from the southern edge of Bashan, approximately 18 miles (30 km.) south of the Yarmuk River (see p. 30), for 47 miles (76 km.) to near the latitude of Heshbon and the north end of the Dead Sea. Deuteronomy 3:10 indicates that the plateau (Heb. *mîshôr*) of Moab, as well as Bashan, was normally thought to be outside of Gilead proper. Northern Gilead is bounded on the east by steppe lands and lava flows and in the southeast by the edge of the Arabian Desert. Although even more precise boundary descriptions are possible, the Israelites often use the term "Gilead" to refer to all Israelite territory east of the Jordan River (e.g., see Josh 22 passim).

The heartland of Gilead is composed of an uplifted dome of hard Cenomanian limestone with stretches of Senonian formations to the north and the southeast. The Jabbok River divides this dome into two portions, the northernmost being the highest, reaching an elevation of 4,091 feet (1247 m.) at Jebel Umm ed-Daraj. Because of the high elevations, rainfall in both sections of Gilead is abundant, especially on the western side of the slopes, and olives, grains, and vines flourish. In biblical times the heights were covered with thick forests that ranked with those of Mount Carmel, Bashan, and Lebanon (e.g., Jer 22:6; 50:19). Gilead was famous for a balm extract that was used for medicinal or cosmetic purposes (e.g., Jer 8:22; 46:11; Gen 37:25). The dome area is structurally similar to the Hill Country of Judah, and thus the landscape is dissected by many steep-sided valleys, and plateau areas are not common. The major wadi of the region is the Jabbok, which begins near Rabbah (modern Amman), where it flows north and then heads west to join the Jordan River. In the western section of this steep-sided gorge, formations of Nubian sandstone have been exposed along its edges. Although narrow, the Jabbok is farmed along most of its length, and its descent from the hills of Gilead to Deir Alla (Plain of Succoth) in the Rift Valley is relatively easy. It is possible that the route that ran through this valley to Succoth, crossed the Jordan River, and continued up the Wadi Faria to Shechem, was the route used by Abraham and later by Jacob to enter the land of Canaan (Gen 12:5–6; 32:22–33:20). The major road through Gilead was a portion of the international north-south Transjordanian Highway that ran northward from Rabbah of the Ammonites past Ramoth Gilead to Ashtaroth in Bashan.

Historically, the northern portion of Gilead was allotted to half of the tribe of Manasseh, while the southern portion was allotted to Gad. The Ammonites seem to have been located on the southeastern fringes of the area at Rabbah, always ready to push into the dome area if possible. During New Testament times the southwestern portion of Gilead was known as part of Perea (see map p. 170), whereas the northern and eastern sections were associated with the cities of the Decapolis. Throughout history the region seems to have served as a place of retreat and refuge. David, for example, fled from Absalom to Mahanaim in Gilead, and Jeroboam I used Peniel (NIV) as his capital for a brief period of time, possibly in an attempt to escape the Egyptian Shishak (1 Kings 12:25; see below, p. 124).

Jordan Valley

Although the Jordan Valley stretches only some 65 miles (105 km.) from the Sea of Galilee to the Dead Sea, the actual length of the meandering river is approximately 135 miles (217 km.). The width of the river varies considerably from season to season and in various places, but at the Allenby Bridge, 7.5 miles (12 km.) north of the Dead Sea, its width fluctuates from 72 to 115 feet (22 to 35 m.). Early explorers report that at flood stage certain portions of the river reached a width of almost 1 mile (1.6 km.). The depth of the Jordan River at the Allenby Bridge varies from 4.3 to 13 feet (1.3 to 4 m.) from one season to another. During the winter and spring, especially from January through March, the highest water levels are reached. It has been found that the flooding is primarily due to the increased flow of the Yarmuk River, which drains portions of Bashan and Gilead. Schattner notes that the flow of the Yarmuk has been known to increase "from 50 m³/sec. to 1700 m³/sec."—a thirty-four-fold increase—in only two days![5]

In spite of the Jordan's meanderings, its gradient is relatively steep and the current is strong. Travel up and down the river by small boats is almost impossible because of the usually shallow but swift waters and the numerous rapids. The Lynch Expedition encountered some twenty-seven major rapids during their trip along the length of the Jordan in 1848.[6] There is no evidence from biblical times that any bridges were built across the Jordan, but the Medeba map indicates that by the sixth century A.D. at least, boats were used to ferry objects across the river. From the mention of "fords" in the Bible, it seems evident that these shallow areas were sought out as the most convenient points of crossing. Har-El notes some fifty-four fords, though this number must have fluctuated considerably through the centuries.[7] Swamps along the banks, swift currents, and muddy or very rocky bottoms can make the crossings treacherous as one wades, swims, or attempts to ride an animal across the stream.

The area of longitudinal strips of land bordering the river on each side is called the *Zor* in Arabic and is referred to in the Bible as the "thicket" (NIV; e.g., Jer 49:19; 50:44); the Hebrew *geʾôn hayyardēn* can be literally translated "the Pride of the Jordan." Each of the two strips of the Zor varies in width from 600 to 5,000 feet (180 to 1520 m.), and both were once covered with dense vegetation, including poplars, tamarisks, willows, cane, and reeds. On occasion, during times of flooding, some of the trees were almost completely covered with water. Wild animals—including lions, leopards, and jackals—were commonly found in this dense

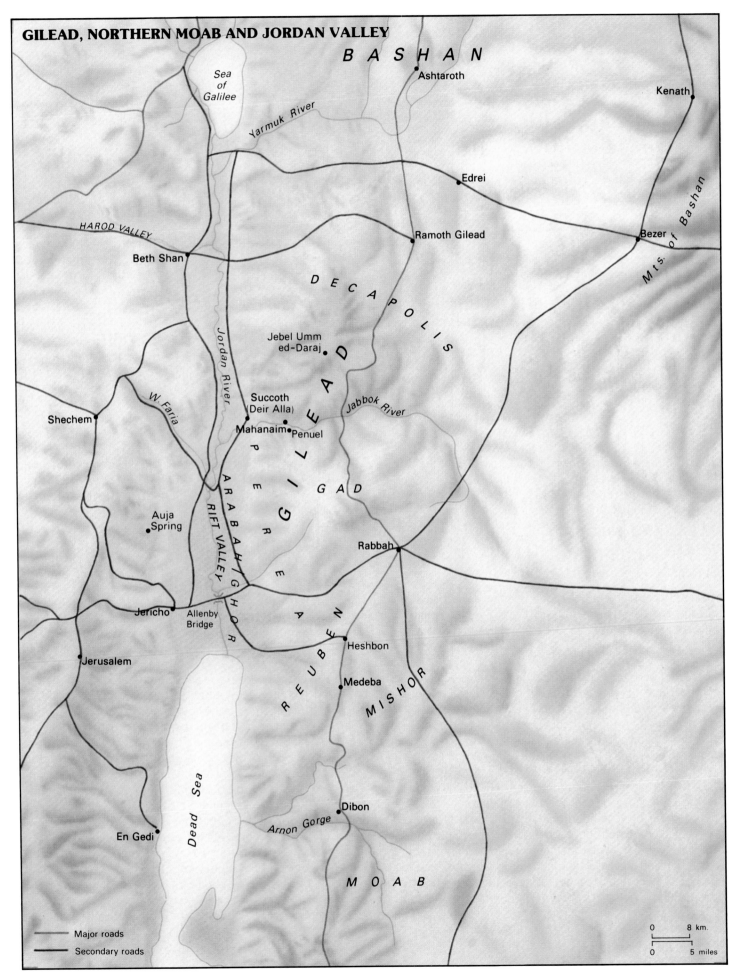

GILEAD, NORTHERN MOAB AND JORDAN VALLEY

B A S H A N

Ashtaroth

Kenath

Edrei

Yarmuk River

Ramoth Gilead

Bezer

*Sea
of
Galilee*

HAROD VALLEY

Beth Shan

D E C A P O L I S

Mts. of Bashan

Jordan River

Jebel Umm
ed-Daraj

W. Faria

Succoth
(Deir Alla)

Jabbok River

Shechem

Mahanaim•Penuel

G I L E A D

P E R E A

G A D

Auja
Spring

ARABAH/GHOR

RIFT VALLEY

Rabbah

Jericho

Allenby
Bridge

R E U B E N

Heshbon

Jerusalem

Medeba

M I S H O R

*Dead
Sea*

Dibon

Arnon Gorge

En Gedi

M O A B

—— Major roads

—— Secondary roads

| 0 | | 8 km. |
| 0 | | 5 miles |

53

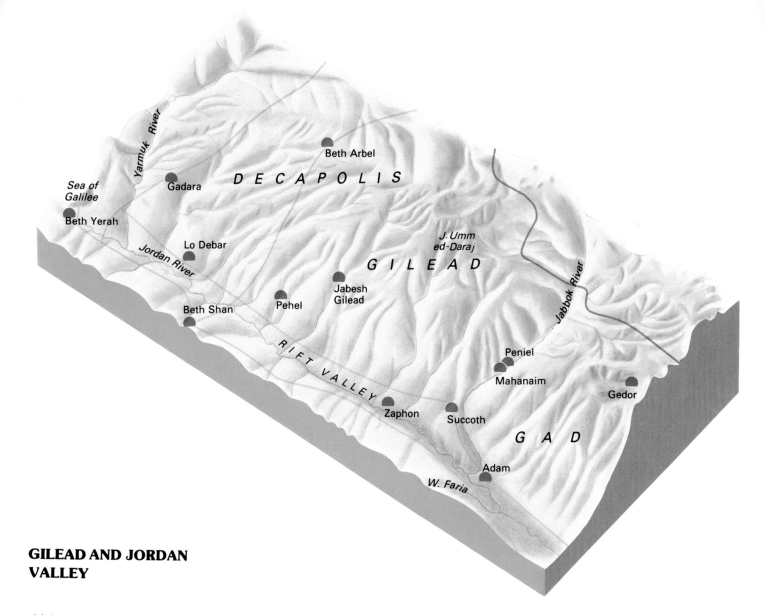

GILEAD AND JORDAN VALLEY

thicket. Because of the dangers associated with such wild-life, this region was generally avoided by humans and their domesticated animals, except when it was necessary to cross the river.

As one passes through the Zor, away from the river on either side, one comes to another longitudinal zone called the *Qattara* in Arabic. This region is composed of Lisan marl formations of clay and gypsum, which are impermeable to water. Runoff water in this area is considerable, and miniature "badland" formations abound. This type of terrain begins some 17 miles (27 km.) south of the Sea of Galilee and continues all the way down to the Dead Sea. The width of these two strips of the Qattara varies from 0.6 to 2 miles (1 to 3.2 km.). Because of the infertility of the soil, the region lacks a cover of vegetation, and thus the powers of erosion are magnified. From time to time large blocks of Lisan material can break away, the debris temporarily blocking the river. Earthquakes are common in the region, and on a number of occasions resulting blockages have stopped the flow of the river: in 1547, for 2 days; in 1906, for 10 hours; in 1927, for 27 hours (compare the crossing of the Israelites described in Joshua 3–4, esp. 3:16).

The major portion of the Jordan Valley is the area called the *Ghor* in Arabic (the biblical Arabah; see above, p. 51). It is bounded on the east by the hills of Gilead and on the west by the hills of Manasseh and Ephraim. It varies in width from 6.2 miles (10 km.) in the north to 2.5–3 miles (4–5 km.) in the middle, to 12.5 miles (20 km.) in the Jericho region. The northern section receives sufficient rainfall to grow crops, but as one progresses southward, the amount of rainfall drops off rapidly to only 4.6 inches (115 mm.) at the Allenby Bridge. Where there are springs (such as at Beth Shan, Auja, and Jericho), or perennial rivers (such as the Yarmuk, Jabbok, Harod, and Wadi Faria), it is possible to irrigate crops. Elsewhere scrub grass grew and was used for grazing flocks from January to March. Temperatures in the valley are warm during the winter and very hot in summer (Jericho's mean *low* in January is 50° F [10° C], its mean *high* in August is 102° F [39° C]!). Thus, although people did settle in the northern section of the valley or in the south at an oasis such as Jericho, the valley was not one of the most densely settled areas of the country.

Today the entire region of the Jordan Valley is being transformed into a rich agricultural area as the Israelis and Jordanians divert waters from the Jordan, Harod, Faria, and Yarmuk to irrigate their crops in this natural greenhouse. Thus conditions in the valley are somewhat different today from what they were in the ancient periods described above.

The name Moab is used most frequently in Scripture as a tribal name referring to the descendants of Lot (Gen 19:36–39); less frequently it indicates the territory where they settled. In the latter sense it refers to the region east of the Dead Sea—a region bounded on the north by Gilead, on the south by the Zered Valley, and on the east by the Arabian Desert. It measures some 56 miles (90 km.) from north to south and some 22 miles (35 km.) from east to west. Its eastern boundary is approximately the line of the Hejaz railway.

Moab is divided into northern and southern sections by the Arnon Gorge, which in places is 2,300 feet (700 m.) deep and, from rim to rim, almost 3 miles (5 km.) wide. On the south, between the Arnon and the Zered, is the old ancient core of Moab, which in the west consists of hard Cenomanian limestone resting on Nubian sandstone formations; the latter are the beautiful reddish cliffs that line the eastern shore of the Dead Sea. In eastern Moab areas of basalt are evident, but Senonian chalks and chert prevail. Elevations above 3,600 feet (1100 m.) are common, and at Jebel ed-Dabab, on the north bank of the Nahal Zered, an elevation of 4,282 feet (1305 m.) is reached. Rainfall approaches 16 inches (400 mm.) annually at these higher elevations.

The land stretching northward from the Arnon to the Heshbon region is called the "plateau" (NIV; Heb. *mîshôr*; see, e.g., Deut 3:10; Josh 13:9, 16), and it is considerably lower (2,300 feet [700 m.]) and less dissected than the region to the south of the Arnon. In one passage (1 Chron 5:16) it seems to be called Sharon, which probably means "forest in the plain," reflecting the fact that this area was at least partially forested in biblical times.[8] Because of the lower elevations, rainfall in the Mishor region approaches only 10 inches (250 mm.) annually. Throughout Moab the major agricultural crops were wheat and barley, and sheep breeding was a major source of revenue. Mesha, the king of Moab, is reported to have supplied the king of Israel with 100,000 lambs and the wool of 100,000 rams (2 Kings 3:4).

The Israelite tribes of Reuben and Gad were allotted cities in the plateau region (e.g., Num 32; Josh 13:15–28), but throughout history this territory was coveted by other nations as well, including the Amorites, the Ammonites from the northeast, and especially the Moabites from the south. It was the Moabites who usually fought with Israel for control of the region during the period of the divided monarchy (931–722 B.C.).

Two branches of the north-south International Transjordanian Highway ran through Moab. One branch ran just east of the western mountain ridge, passing through cities such as Rabbah, Medeba, Dibon, and Kir Hareseth. Along the way it had to descend into the deep gorges of the Arnon and the Zered, making the passage somewhat difficult. The second branch ran along the eastern edge of Moab near the desert frontier. Although geographical obstacles were not as great, caravans taking this route were exposed to raids from the tribes that often swept in off the desert.

The name Edom ("red") was used first as an alternate personal name for Esau (Gen 25:30) and then came to be used as a tribal name referring to his descendants (e.g., Gen 36:1–17; Num 20:14–20). These descendants, who probably absorbed portions of other tribal groups such as the Horites, eventually settled in the mountains east of the Rift Valley in the land between the latitudes of the southern end of the Dead Sea and the northern end of the Gulf of Elath/Aqaba, a distance of 110 miles (177 km.).

The land of Edom can be divided into three geographical sections. The northern area, which extends from the Zered Valley in the north to Punon, 25 miles (40 km.) to the south, seems to have been the heartland of Edom. The important city of Bozrah was located here. On the west, Nubian sandstone cliffs border the Arabah, while the high ground in the center is composed of hard Cenomanian limestone, which in turn gives way to chalk formations and the desert to the east.

The central section of Edom, stretching 50 miles (80 km.) from Punon in the north to Ras en-Naqb in the south, is a high mountain plateau region where elevations are above 4,900 feet (1490 m.); a high point of 5,696 feet (1736 m.) is reached 5 miles (8 km.) northeast of Petra. This high ground stretches 30 miles (48 km.) from north to south and then angles to the southeast into the desert for another 12 miles (19 km.). Because of the height of this middle area, the rainfall ranges from 6 to 10 inches (150 to 250 mm.) annually, and so some agriculture is possible. During the summer months, temperatures at these elevations often are cool; during the winter, snow can remain for days on the high mountain plateau while the lower surrounding areas receive little or no precipitation. To the west of the high plateau, the Nubian sandstone cliffs bordering the Arabah are even more prominent, and nestled in one of the steep-sided valleys is the famous rock-hewn city of Petra, which for a while was the Nabatean capital of the area.

The third region of Edom stretches 3 miles (5 km.) from Naqb Ishtar down to the latitude of the northern end of the Gulf of Elath/Aqaba. At the north end of this region the formations of Nubian sandstone head inland, to the southeast, whereas to the south of Gharandal granite mountains now mark the eastern edge of the Rift Valley. These granite peaks continue down the Gulf of Elath/Aqaba into Saudi Arabia. Between the granite and sandstone areas is the forbidding Wadi Hisma with its broad alluvial bottom (15 to 20 miles [24 to 32 km.] wide) dotted with massive sandstone mesas. Rainfall in the area is scant—less than 2 inches (50 mm.) annually.

Because of both the lack of rainfall and the dissected steep slopes of western Edom, the area was never well populated. In the northern and central sections, especially in the plateau area, the people were able to grow grain crops and raise sheep, goats, and camels. Up until modern times the higher regions of Edom were covered with forests, and this may have been one of the reasons why it was called "the hill

Entrance to the Valley of Petra.

country of Seir'' (e.g., Gen 36:9). Seir, ''the hairy one,'' may also be a reference to Esau, whose descendants were called Edomites.

The major factor contributing to the economy of Edom seems to have been its control of the caravan routes. The important north-south International Transjordanian Highway ran along the eastern edge of Edom, avoiding its rugged western slope and the high mountain plateaus. Near modern Ma'an this route divided into two branches. One headed southeast into Saudi Arabia, from where luxury items were imported that had originated in Arabia and even in India and Africa. The other branch headed southwest down to Elath at the head of the Red Sea. East-west routes connecting the Arabah with the Transjordanian Highway included, from north to south, (1) the road that ran up the Wadi Fidan, which passed Punon on its way up to Bozrah, (2) the road up the Wadi Musa, which led to Petra, and (3) a route that led into the mountains from the Arabah oasis of Gharandal. All these routes connected Edom with Egypt and/or the Mediterranean port of Gaza. Thus many of the much-sought-after luxury items had to pass through Edomite territory on their way from southern Arabia to the commercial centers in Egypt and to Damascus and the ports along the Mediterranean Sea. The people living in Edom at times were able to gain great wealth by controlling these caravan routes.

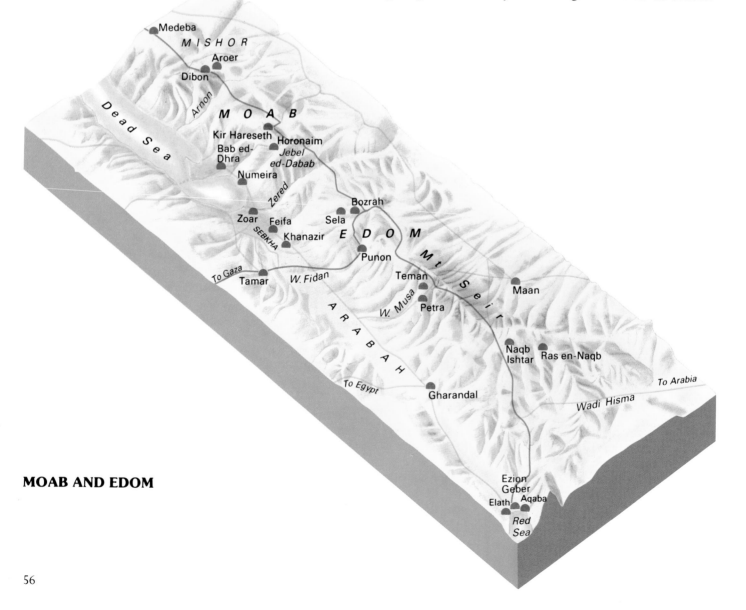

MOAB AND EDOM

The Geography of Egypt

Located in the northeastern corner of Africa, Egypt has been one of the great power centers of the Near East throughout historical times. The heartland of Egypt is basically a river oasis situated near the eastern edge of the Sahara Desert. Ninety-five percent of Egypt is stone, sand, and desert, while only 5 percent is rich agricultural land to which the life-giving Nile brings precious water and silt. Here along the Nile, on the "Black Land," lives 95 percent of the population of Egypt. As the Greek historian Herodotus wrote, "Egypt is a gift of the Nile."

The traditional boundaries of ancient Egypt were the Mediterranean Sea on the north, the Red Sea/Gulf of Suez on the east, the first cataract (= rapids) of the Nile near Aswan on the south, and a north-south line of oases that are about 120 miles west of the Nile. At various times Egypt attempted to control or exploit the resources of Sinai to the east, Nubia to the south, and Libya to the west, with varying degrees of success.

The northward flowing Nile, with its origins in Central Africa (the White Nile) and in the Ethiopian Highlands (the Blue Nile), is the longest river in the world (4,145 mi. [6670 km.]). The westerly source, the White Nile, supplies water year-round, while the more easterly Blue Nile provides an abundance of water during the months of June, July, and August—the monsoon season in the Ethiopian Highlands.

Egypt was divided into two major geographical regions. "Upper Egypt," which is upstream (i.e., south), stretches from the first cataract in the south to the beginning of the delta near Cairo, while "Lower Egypt" is the delta proper. In Upper Egypt the arable land along both sides of the Nile varies in width from six miles near Aswan to sixteen miles near Cairo in the north. In Upper Egypt the land is hemmed in on both sides by limestone cliffs, which in places (e.g.,

Canal near the Nile River bringing water to the fields.

Jebel el-Silsila) approach the riverbed itself. To the west is the foreboding Sahara Desert, the barrenness of which is only occasionally broken by an oasis. On the other side of the Nile, beyond the cliffs, is the Eastern Desert, an upward-sloping plateau of sand and stone culminating in the hills and mountains (4,000 to 7,000 ft. [1220 to 2130 m.]) that overlook and run parallel to the coast of the Red Sea and the Gulf of Suez. Although the Eastern Desert is desolate, at times the Egyptians worked the stone quarries and the gold, tin, and copper mines in the area. Several roads, the most important of which ran through the Wadi Hammamat, crossed the Eastern Desert, connecting the Nile Valley with the Red Sea and, hence, with eastern Africa, southern Arabia, and even India.

Life in Upper Egypt was regulated by the Nile. Prior to the construction of modern dams, which began in the nineteenth century and culminated with the building of the Aswan Dam in 1970, the Nile rose rather predictably between the fifteenth and eighteenth of June in the Aswan area. Depending upon the location, it would usually rise between 15 and 23 feet (4.6 and 7 m.) above its normal level. As it rose, it overflowed its banks and flooded the relatively flat fields nearby. The muddy flood waters covered the fields for several months, and as they began to recede in September/October, they leeched out unwanted salts and left behind a fresh layer of fertile silt.[1] The peasants planted their crops in the muddy soil during October/November and harvested from January through March.

Chief among the crops were wheat and barley. During certain periods Egypt served as the "breadbasket" for other parts of the world. In addition, vegetables, dates, and sesame were grown. Fish from the river were abundant, as were fowl—both species that were indigenous to Egypt and species that passed through the area on their biannual migration from Europe to Africa and back. In some areas grapes were cultivated, but the most common beverage was a barley beer rather than wine. Flax was grown and used to produce clothing, ropes, and sails, while papyrus was used for paper production and was exported.

The chief center of southern Upper Egypt was Thebes. Throughout the millennia palaces, tombs, and temples were constructed of limestone found in its vicinity. For the most part, the peasants lived in mud huts that were usually constructed on high ground so as not to be destroyed by the annual inundations. The Nile itself was the major "road," and barges and sailing ships were common modes of transportation. The current easily carried these vessels downstream, and they were able to sail upstream by making use of the prevailing north wind.

Southward travel by boat was interrupted by the first of six cataracts—places where the Nile crossed hard granite ridges that caused treacherous rapids. Located to the south of the first cataract were the lands of Nubia (from Egyptian *neb*,

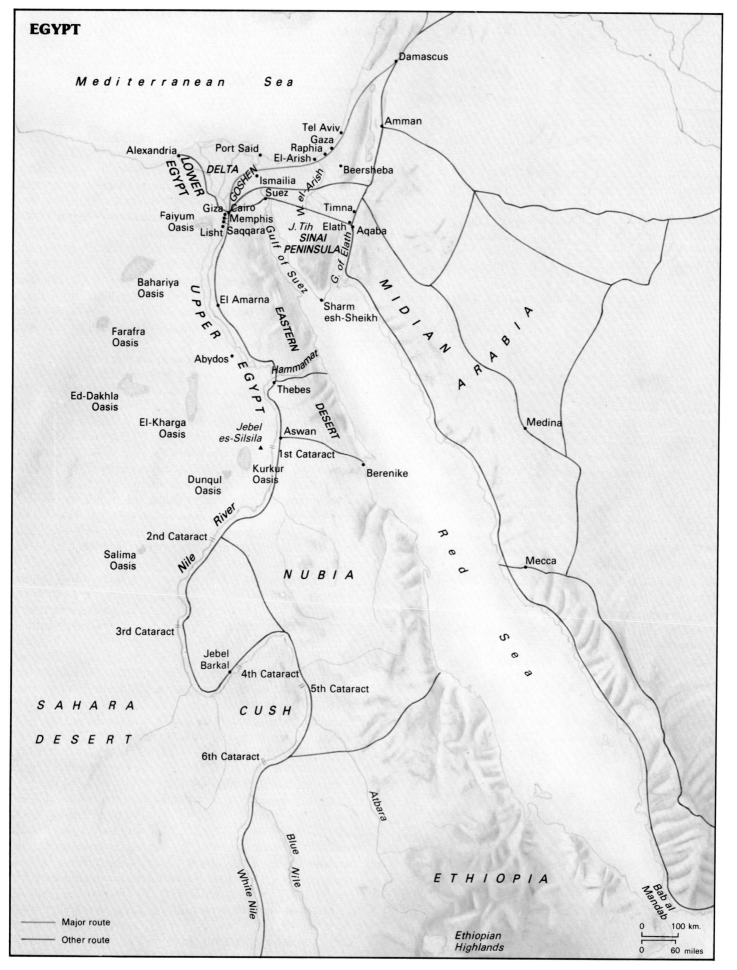

EGYPT

Mediterranean Sea

Damascus

Tel Aviv
Gaza
Raphia
El-Arish
Amman

Alexandria
Port Said
Beersheba

LOWER EGYPT
DELTA
GOSHEN
Ismailia
Suez

Giza Cairo
Memphis
Timna

Faiyum Oasis
Lisht Saqqara
J. Tih
Elath
Aqaba

SINAI PENINSULA

Gulf of Suez

Bahariya Oasis

UPPER

El Amarna

EASTERN

G. of Elath

MIDIAN

ARABIA

Farafra Oasis

Sharm esh-Sheikh

Ed-Dakhla Oasis

EGYPT

Abydos
Hammamat
Thebes

DESERT

El-Kharga Oasis

Jebel es-Silsila
Aswan
1st Cataract

Medina

Dunqul Oasis
Kurkur Oasis

Berenike

River

2nd Cataract

NUBIA

Red

Salima Oasis

Nile

Mecca

3rd Cataract

Sea

Jebel Barkal
4th Cataract
5th Cataract

SAHARA

CUSH

DESERT

6th Cataract

Atbara

Blue Nile

White Nile

ETHIOPIA

Bab al Mandab

Major route
Other route

0   100 km.

0   60 miles

Ethiopian Highlands

YEARLY CYCLE
IN ANCIENT EGYPT

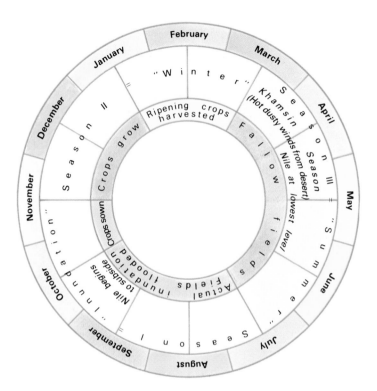

"gold," i.e., "the land of gold"), Cush, and eventually Ethiopia. At various times Egypt was able to exert control up to the second cataract and, on rare occasions, even to the fourth. Conversely, during periods of Egyptian weakness, the Ethiopians expanded northward into Upper Egypt (e.g., during the 24th Dynasty, ca. 720 B.C.).

The delta region north of modern Cairo is known as "Lower Egypt" (lower = lower in elevation, i.e., downstream). Roughly triangular in shape, it measures 100 miles (160 km.) north-south and 155 miles (250 km.) east-west, with a total area of close to 8,500 square miles (22000 sq. km.). Today, two main branches of the Nile make their way through the delta area to the Mediterranean Sea, but in the days of Herodotus (ca. 450 B.C.) there were seven branches of the Nile (as reported in Strabo, *Geog.* xvii.1.18). This low-lying area is well-supplied with fertile silt that has been washed down over the millennia and is crisscrossed by canals. Throughout the area, crops are grown in abundance. Wheat and barley, orchards, vineyards, and fig trees are plentiful. In ancient times the swamps provided some pasturage for cattle, and papyrus, sedge, and lotus plants were abundant. Animals such as the hippopotamus and crocodile were common. Ample supplies of fish, both from the Nile and the Mediterranean, were readily available, as were wild fowl, such as ducks and geese.

Although the coastal area of the delta receives close to 7 inches (175 mm.) of rainfall annually, irrigation has always

been the main technique used to water crops. The importance of the delta as a source of food supply can be seen in the fact that this area alone comprises 55 percent of the total arable land of Egypt north of the first cataract.

In the delta, settlements have always been located on the high ground between the canals, and although it is generally agreed that the delta was settled from earliest times, it is only from the second millennium B.C. onward that significant archaeological remains have been found. This state of affairs may be due to (1) silt covering earlier remains, (2) a rising water table, and (3) the effects of salt water on ancient monuments and villages.

Lines of communication are difficult to trace in the delta, but it seems that besides land transport, boat transport on the Nile and the adjacent canals was very important. For example, when Sinuhe (ca. 1950 B.C.) returned to Egypt from the land of Canaan, he boarded a ship in the eastern delta and traveled by boat to the town of Lisht (*ANET*, 21). The eastern delta was also the area the Bedouin from Sinai attempted to infiltrate to secure water for their flocks. And from here, the armies of the mighty pharaohs of the 18th and 19th dynasties (ca. 1500–1150 B.C.) launched their expeditions into Canaan and other countries of Asia. According to the biblical account, it was in the rich and fertile eastern delta, known as the "region of Goshen," that Jacob and his descendants settled and began their sojourn in Egypt (Gen 46–50; see Historical Section).

To the east of the delta lies the triangular Sinai Peninsula, with an area of 23,600 square miles (61100 sq. km.)—smaller than West Virginia. On the north it is bounded by the Mediterranean Sea as it stretches from Port Said on the west to Rafia or Gaza on the east. The western boundary is an imaginary north-south line, 80 miles (130 km.) long, that stretches from Port Said in the north to Suez in the south—basically following the path of the modern Suez Canal, which in turn is situated close to the line of the old easterly branch of the Nile and/or its major easterly canal. The southwest coast of Sinai borders on the Gulf of Suez, stretching 180 miles (290 km.) from Suez to Sinai's southern tip, Sharm esh-Sheikh. Sinai's southeastern side borders on the Gulf of Elath/Aqaba and is 120 miles (190 km.) long, but its eastern land boundary is more amorphous, although a line drawn from Elath/Aqaba to the Rafia-Gaza region—125 miles (200 km.) long—is a reasonable projection of this boundary.

The northern coastline of Sinai is composed primarily of sandy flats and some dunes, the latter extending from 25 to 60 miles (40 to 95 km.) inland. The water table is relatively close to the surface, and throughout the ages wells have been sunk in this area to supply the local inhabitants and travelers with fresh water. Through this area ran the major road connecting Asia with Africa. Recent explorations have shown that this route was in use from earliest historical times until the present. Not only did commercial caravans use it, but the great armies of the world have passed this way as well: the ancient Egyptian, Assyrian, Babylonian, Persian, Greek, and Roman armies, as well as modern British, Egyptian, and Israeli forces.

To the south, the dunes eventually give way to a series of mountains that are part of a chain that begins in the Negev to the northeast. Water supplies can be found in and near these

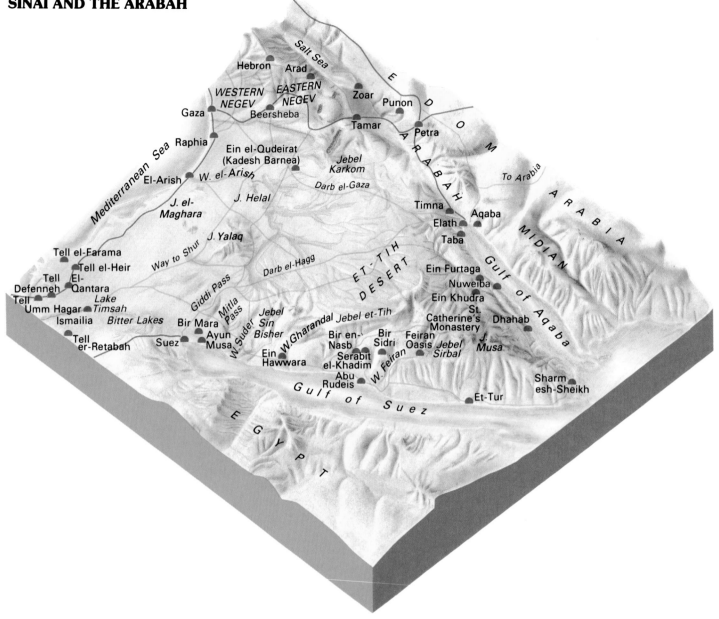

mountains, particularly in the northeast near Kadesh Bar-nea, where the most powerful spring of the peninsula is located. Fairly close to the line where the coastal region meets the foothills is an important route that connected Beersheba with what is today Ismailia. This may be the biblical "road to Shur" (Gen 16:7), which was used during patriarchal times for travel to Egypt. To the south of these mountains the broad, desolate, lifeless Tih region rises, culminating in the Jebel (Arabic for "Mount") Tih in the south. Most of northern Sinai is drained by the Wadi el-Arish ("Brook of Egypt"), which enters the Mediterranean Sea at el-Arish. A track called the Darb el-Hagg (the "Way of the Pilgrimage") connects Elath/Aqaba on the east with Suez on the west; it was of importance in more recent times—up to the late 1800s—as Egyptian Moslems used it on their pilgrimages to Mecca. During biblical times, this road connected Egypt with Midian (in Saudi Arabia) and provided the Egyptians with access to the copper mines at Timna, just north of Elath/Aqaba.

The southern tip of Sinai consists of dramatic, jagged granite peaks, some of which reach heights of over 8,600 feet (2600 m.). On the west a broad, flat plain, 10 to 15 miles (16 to 24 km.) wide, separates the mountains from the Gulf of Suez, while on the east the mountains often drop precipi-tously into the Gulf of Elath/Aqaba. Snow sometimes falls in this mountainous granite region, but the total amount of precipitation is minimal. The normal decrease in rainfall from north to south is operative in Sinai as in other regions of the Middle East (e.g., the Mediterranean coastal area receives ca. 8 inches [200 mm.] per year, the southern tip of Sinai 0.4 inches [10 mm.]). In the southern granite region, however, water collects in the wadis, and some oases are found around both springs and wells. The largest of these oases in southern Sinai is the Feiran Oasis, located at the foot of Jebel Sirbal.

Because of its rainfall deficiency and correspondingly rugged terrain, Sinai has never boasted a large population. A census in 1937 listed 18,000 inhabitants, of which only 2,500 lived in the south. Sinai's major importance has been as a land bridge between Africa and Asia. In modern times its mineral wealth has begun to be exploited, but in ancient times the Egyptians were primarily interested in mining the turquoise deposits in the Wadi Maghara and Serabit el-Khadim regions, for turquoise was in great demand for the production of rings, beads, necklaces, amulets, and scarabs. Although some deposits of copper are located in Sinai, it appears that the mines at Timna, just north of the northern tip of the Gulf of Elath/Aqaba, were the major sources of copper during certain periods. For students of the Bible, the events surrounding the giving of the Law at Mount Sinai are of prime importance (these will be discussed in the Historical Section).

The recorded history of Egypt began around 3100 B.C., when Upper and Lower Egypt were united into one country. As early as the third millennium B.C. the Egyptians had divided Upper Egypt into twenty-two nomes, or districts, and by the late first millennium B.C. twenty delta nomes were added to the total. During periods when the central government was relatively weak, the rulers of the nomes—the nomarchs—were often quite powerful.

Historians, following the lead of Manetho (an Egyptian priest who wrote ca. 282–245 B.C.), divide the line of kings into thirty or thirty-one "dynasties." Modern historians usually begin the 1st Dynasty at about 3100 B.C. and end the series with the Ptolemaic Dynasty (ca. 30 B.C.). In addition, Egyptologists and historians combine these dynasties into more comprehensive periods or eras:

DYNASTIES	PERIODS	APPROX. DATES
I–II	Early Dynastic	3100–2686
III–VIII	Old Kingdom	2683–2160
IX–XI	First Intermediate	2160–2040
XI–XIII	Middle Kingdom	2040–1633
XIV–XVII	Second Intermediate	1786–1558
XVIII–XX	New Kingdom	1558–1085
XXI–XXV	Third Intermediate	1085–656
XXVI	Saite Renaissance	664–525
XXVII–XXXI	Late Dynastic	525–330
	Conquest of Alexander	332
	Macedonian Domination	332–304
	Ptolemaic Dynasty	304–30
	Roman Conquest	30

More will be said about the significance of these and other periods at the appropriate places in the Historical Section of this atlas. Suffice it to say here that periods of strong central government (e.g., during the Old and Middle Kingdoms) were followed by periods of fragmentation, disorder, and political chaos (e.g., during the First and Second Intermediate Periods).

One of the first systems of writing was developed in Egypt. Although its origin is shrouded in the mist of antiquity, by the time of the 1st Dynasty (ca. 3100 B.C.) writing had been established in the country. For over three thousand years (until the fourth century A.D.), hieroglyphic writing was used in Egypt. The earliest form of the script made use of ideograms, or sense-signs, which represented a specific thing or idea, or something suggested by the thing (for example, a sun dish ☉ represented the sun; an outline of hills ᨏ, hilly or foreign lands; and writing and related words were represented by scribal tools—palette, water pot, and brush case). In addition, sound signs, or phonograms, soon came into use; here the pictures represented a sound or series of sounds (e.g., "r" from mouth ⬭, "pr" from the ideogram house ⬜). All together, a scribe needed to master some seven hundred characters.

The Egyptians referred to their language as the "words of the god" and considered it a gift of the god Thoth. The Egyptian priests were among the few who knew how to read and write (carve) the language when the Greeks took control of Egypt (ca. 332 B.C.), and thus the language came to be called hieroglyphics (Gr. *hieros*, "sacred," and *glyphein*, "to carve"). As early as the time of the Middle Kingdom, Egyptian scribes were using reed pens and papyrus to write a modified form of hieroglyphics called hieratic (Gr. "priestly") writing. Later, during the 25th Dynasty (ca. 700 B.C.), demotic (Gr. "popular"), a more rapid form of hieratic writing, came into use. The final phase of ancient Egyptian is Coptic, the script known from the third century A.D. onward. It makes use of the Greek alphabet plus seven special characters. This language is still read and spoken, particularly in the liturgy of the Coptic church.

A wealth of written material has been preserved from ancient Egypt, for almost every vertical surface of ancient temples, tombs, and buildings was covered with hieroglyphic inscriptions. In addition, the use of papyrus was very common, not only for literary texts, but also for economic, administrative, and personal documents. Because of Egypt's dry climate (only an inch [25 mm.] of rain per year from Cairo south), many monumental texts and documents on papyrus have been preserved. This rich and varied corpus includes religious material (such as the Pyramid and Coffin Texts, the Book of the Dead, Magical Papyri), scientific material (dealing with subjects such as medicine and mathematics), lexicographical material, legal texts, administrative documents, private letters, historical records, literary works, and poetry.

These texts shed an extraordinary amount of light on life in ancient Egypt, but many of them are not directly relevant to the study of biblical history or geography. Those that are most relevant can be grouped into a number of major categories.[2] For example, expedition journals or annals, providing descriptions of, for example, the expulsion of the Hyksos from Egypt or the conquest of Megiddo by Thutmose III, form one category of pertinent material. These annals, oftentimes found on the walls of temples or tombs, yield considerable information about Egyptian campaigns into western Asia. Other categories include topographical lists (such as Shishak's, providing data for historical geographers), literary papyri (e.g., the Tale of Sinuhe), administrative papyri, execration texts (texts invoking a curse), and correspondence archives (e.g., the el-Amarna letters, written in Akkadian). These and other Egyptian documents important for the understanding of biblical history and geography will be discussed at appropriate places in the Historical Section.

The Geography of Syria and Lebanon

The area shown below comprises primarily the modern states of Syria and Lebanon. It was not only an important area in its own right but also served as a crossroads that connected Babylonia and Assyria with Anatolia (modern Turkey) to the northwest, with the Mediterranean to the west, and with Palestine and Egypt to the southwest.

The region is bounded on the west by the Mediterranean Sea, on the north by the Amanus and Malatya mountains, on the east by a north-south line drawn through Jebel Sinjar, on the south by the Syrian Desert, and eventually on the southwest by Damascus and the Litani River. Often difficult to rule due to pressures from hostile desert and mountain tribes, it was not until the first millennium B.C. that the area was subdued and unified by the great empires of Assyria, Babylonia, Persia, and especially the Seleucids (see the Historical Section). It is difficult to find a single ancient name that refers to the whole region, although the area west and south of the Euphrates was called Amurru (the "West Land") and the "land beyond the River [Euphrates]" during the second and first millennia B.C.

Many varieties of landscape and lifestyle are found in this region. Grain crops can be grown north of an arc that runs from Damascus in the southwest, via Homs and Tiphsah, to Jebel Sinjar in the northeast. The land to the north and west of this rough line receives at least 10 inches (250 mm.) of rain annually, while rainfall drops off rapidly to the south of this arc. There lie the expanses of the Syrian steppe/desert where, along its northern and western fringes, nomads wander with their herds in search of winter grasses.

To the north and east of the Euphrates is a steppe area known today as the Jezirah, which in actuality is a westward extension of Assyria. This area is drained from north to south by the Habur and Balik rivers. The land between the Habur and the Euphrates may very well be the original "Aram Naharaim" (Gen 24:10; "the land between the two rivers"; Gr. *mesopotamia*). North of an east-west line drawn through Jebel Sinjar and Jebel el-Aziz, rainfall is adequate to grow grain crops in winter (over 12 inches [300 mm.]

SYRIA AND LEBANON

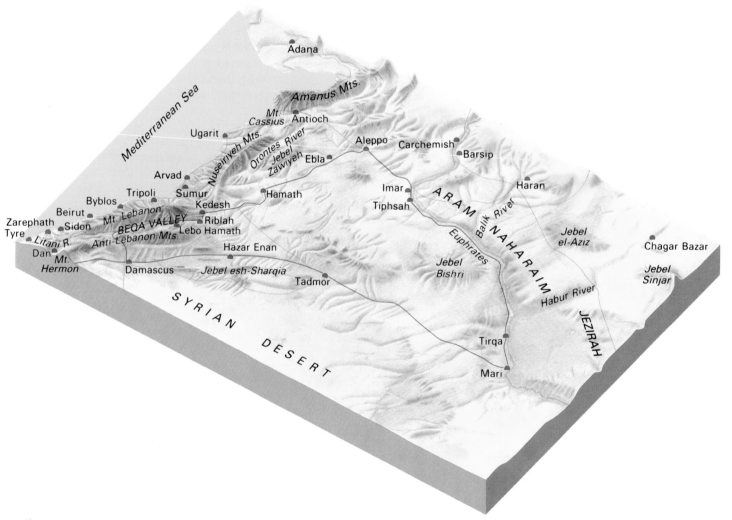

annually), and springs are plentiful. South of that line rainfall drops off, and the flat steppe land is mainly given over to grazing. Most of the major cities were either along or just north of this line. They include, from east to west, Chagar Bazar, Haran, and finally Carchemish, which was located on the bank of the Euphrates. The roads connecting Assyria, and even Babylonia, with Carchemish ran through this area, skirting Jebel Sinjar to the north or south. Carchemish was one of the key cities along this route, since from there caravans and/or armies could head northwest into Anatolia, westward to the Mediterranean, or southward into Syria, Israel, and Egypt.

To the south and west of the Euphrates is the area of Syria proper. This area can be conveniently divided into northern and southern portions by the "Homs-Palmyra [Tadmor] Depression [or corridor]."[1] This depression stretches westward from the bend of the Euphrates just southeast of Mari, through Tadmor and Homs, to the Nahr Kabir, which flows into the Mediterranean. When political conditions were relatively stable, and especially after the camel began to be used as a pack animal, this caravan route across the steppe/desert from Mari to Tadmor (ca. 145 mi. [235 km.]) became quite important. From Mari, bulk goods, especially lumber from Jebel Bishri and the Anti-Lebanon and Lebanon ranges, could be shipped down the Euphrates River. From Tadmor, caravans could continue almost due west along the depression, via Homs, to Mediterranean seaports near the Kabir River. In addition, a very important route ran southwest, along the edge of the desert, connecting Tadmor with Damascus, a distance of about 130 miles (210 km.), and hence with Israel, Egypt, and south Arabia. This road skirted the north flank of Jebel esh-Sharqia, making use of wells and springs along the way. Tadmor, later called Palmyra, was one of the great caravan cities of antiquity. The Bible mentions how Solomon built "Tadmor in the desert" as he attempted to gain control of the trade routes of the Levant (2 Chron 8:4, but compare 1 Kings 9:18, where the Hebrew has Tamar, but the Greek has Tadmor, as does the NIV). To the south of Tadmor and to the east of Jebel esh-Sharqia lies the tableland of the Syrian Desert, broken by rugged escarpments and bounded on the southwest by great, almost impassible basalt outflows. This area, with less than 8 inches (200 mm.) of rainfall, supports only pastoral nomads, who barely subsist here.

Situated in the southwest corner of this area is the magnificent oasis of Damascus. Receiving only 8 inches (200 mm.) of rain annually, the oasis is fed by the Barada River flowing down from the Anti-Lebanon range. Damascus was a key to Israel, for nearly all traffic entering or exiting Israel from the north had to pass through it. Because of this, the control of Damascus has been much disputed throughout history, yet rarely has Damascus been able to extend its control far in any direction, for it is hemmed in by mountains to the west and north and by desert and basalt outflows to the east and south. Here Israel's archenemies, the Arameans of Damascus, were headquartered.

Most of the area sandwiched between Damascus and the Mediterranean lies within the modern state of Lebanon. The southern boundary of this region is slightly to the south of the Litani River, and its northern boundary is at the Nahr Kabir at the western end of the Homs-Tadmor corridor. This river is actually the modern boundary between Lebanon and Syria. The region itself can be divided into four major longitudinal zones that run from the southwest to the northeast.

The "coastal plain" is at best very narrow, 5 to 10 miles (8 to 16 km.) wide, and in many places spurs of the Lebanon Mountains reach the shores of the Mediterranean, interrupting north-south travel along the coast. This area came to be known as Phoenicia. Its orientation has always been west-

In the grove of cedars, Lebanon. In the background is the snow-covered peak of Dahr el Kodib.

ward, toward the Mediterranean Sea. Great ports such as Tyre, Sidon, Beirut, Byblos, Tripoli, and Sumur alternately cooperated or vied with each other for control of shipping on the Mediterranean. The agricultural hinterland of each of these cities was very restricted, often necessitating trade with Israel and especially with Egypt for needed foodstuffs. In return they supplied much desired building timber to these and other countries throughout the millennia. Byblos, in fact, became a great distribution center, connecting Egypt with the remainder of the Mediterranean world. At certain times (e.g., during the Late Bronze Age, 1550–1200 B.C.), Byblos almost had the status of an Egyptian colony, as evidenced in the written documents from that period and by the many Egyptian artifacts found in excavations at Byblos (ancient Gebal). From Byblos, papyrus that had originated in Egypt was shipped all over the Mediterranean, and it should be remembered that the Phoenicians played a large role in the transmission of the alphabetic script westward to Greece at the end of the second millennium B.C.

Immediately inland from the coast are the majestic Mountains of Lebanon, rising in places to heights of over 10,000 feet (3000 m.). These mountains, composed of hard Cenomanian limestone, sandstone, and some Jurassic rock, receive over 40 inches (1000 mm.) of precipitation annually. For about six months of winter they are snow-covered, and this whiteness may have given rise to the name "Lebanon," which is related to a Hebrew root (*lbn*) meaning "white." Both the eastern and western slopes were tree-covered in antiquity, and it was here that the prized "cedars of Lebanon" grew. The trunks of these stately trees, along with those of cypresses and pines, were cut and used wherever long beams were necessary—for planks and masts of boats, for beams in palaces and temples, for paneling, etc. The western slopes of the mountains are dissected by deep, V-shaped wadis, and travel is very difficult. On the east, a steep escarpment drops off into the third longitudinal region, the Beqa ("Valley").

The long and narrow Beqa Valley stretches some 85 miles (140 km.) up to the area just south of Homs. On the west towers the escarpment of the Mountains of Lebanon, while on the east the Anti-Lebanon range rises. The north end of the Beqa is blocked by swamps and lakes that form behind a basalt outflow near Kedesh; the southern portion ends in a jumble of ridges and valleys. Most of the Beqa is above 3,000 feet (900 m.), but since it is on the lee side of the Lebanon range and slightly removed from the sea, it is in a partial rain shadow. Baalbek receives 16 inches (400 mm.) of precipitation annually, while the mountains to the west receive 40 inches (1000 mm.). In Beirut, on the coast, the average is 34 inches (850 mm.). In the Beqa, gardens flourish, as do olive and fruit trees, vines, and grains. Located near Baalbek is the north-south watershed of the valley; the Orontes drains the valley to the northeast, and the Litani drains it to the southwest. The latter river eventually turns due west and, after passing through a deep, steep, narrow gorge, flows into the Mediterranean 5 miles (8 km.) north of Tyre.

East-west travel through the Beqa was not too common, for the Lebanon and Anti-Lebanon ranges are very high and do not contain convenient passes. Southwest-to-northeast travel is also difficult due to ridges that intersect the valley and, in addition, the entrances at both ends of the valley are difficult—hills to the south, swamps to the north. Thus, the main International Route passed to the east of the Anti-Lebanon range through Damascus.

The Anti-Lebanon range stretches from Mount Hermon (9,232 ft., [2814 m.]) in the south approximately 85 miles (135 km.) to an area overlooking the Homs-Tadmor corridor. In most places precipitation reaches 40 inches (1000 mm.) annually, and a thick forest covered the rugged mountains during much of antiquity. From the slopes of the Anti-Lebanon the Barada River flows eastward, sustaining the oasis city of Damascus.

North of the Homs–Tadmor corridor, the major lines of relief are basically north-south. The narrow coastline, stretching 105 miles (170 km.) from the Nahr Kabir north to the Amanus Mountains, boasts a series of ports, including Arvad (an island anchorage), Tripoli, and Ugarit. Both Arvad and Tripoli served as ports for the western end of the route that ran through the Homs-Tadmor corridor, while Ugarit was connected via a pass to the northeast through the Nuseiriyeh Mountains with Aleppo. It was here at Ugarit that precious documents from the fourteenth century B.C., written in cuneiform script, were found. The cosmopolitan character of Ugarit is reflected in the variety of languages represented in these documents: Akkadian, Hurrian, Hittite, and Ugaritic. Documents written in the latter language have, among other things, furnished us with a vast literature that shed welcome light on Canaanite religious beliefs and practices, some of which are referred to in the Old Testament.

Close to the north end of the coastal plain, Mount Cassius (5,771 ft. [1760 m.]) forms a prominent landmark along the shore of the Mediterranean. Just north of this, the plain of Antioch/Alalakh provides a swampy but adequate connecting route from the Mediterranean to Aleppo on the east. The steep scarp of the Amanus Mountains (ca. 6,000 to 7,000 ft. [1830 to 2130 m.]) rises to the north of the plain, and through these mountains a pass leads to the Cilician Plain and on to Anatolia.

East of the coast, behind Arvad and Ugarit, rise the Nuseiriyeh Mountains (4,000 to 5,380 ft. [1220 to 1640 m.]) along a north-south axis. Both the gentle western and steep eastern slopes were forested in antiquity, forming an impassible barrier for east-west traffic.

To the east of the Nuseiriyeh Mountains is the low-lying, marshy Ghab Valley. The Orontes River meanders through this swampy area, flowing from south to north before swinging around north of Mount Cassius and exiting into the sea via the Antioch Valley.

To the east of the Ghab rises Jebel Zawiyeh (3,080 ft. [940 m.]) with gentle eastern slopes that eventually blend into the steppe land that runs to the Euphrates. In the north, this plateau was dominated by the city of Halab (Aleppo), while the southern portion of the plateau was often controlled by Hamath on the Orontes, a city/country located just north of the traditional boundaries of the land of Canaan (see map p. 92). About half-way between these two centers lies Tell Mardikh, ancient Ebla. The startling discoveries of artifacts and documents at Ebla have begun to shed welcome light on the history of the third millennium B.C. in this entire steppe area.

The Geography of Mesopotamia

Life at the eastern end of the Fertile Crescent is dominated by the Tigris and Euphrates rivers. This large, amorphous region is bounded on the east by the Zagros Mountains, which run from southeast to northwest, separating Mesopotamia from Iran. The Zagros and Malatya mountains enclose the region on the north, while the northern reaches of the Syro-Arabian Desert help define the habitable area on the west and south. Most of this area, which in historical studies is often called "Mesopotamia," lies in what today is Iraq, while the rest is located in Syria, Turkey, and Iran. The name Mesopotamia is derived from the Greek and means "land between the rivers." Originally it may have referred to the land between the Euphrates and the Habur rivers, for it is used in the Septuagint (the Greek translation of the Old Testament) to refer to Aram Naharaim (NIV; lit., "Aram of the two rivers"), which was located near Nahor (Gen 24:10). "Mesopotamia" was used by Polybius (second century B.C.) and Strabo (first century A.D.) to refer to the area between the Euphrates and the Tigris. Today it is used by extension to refer to the land between and beside these two great rivers.

The Euphrates and Tigris both have their origins in the mountains of Armenia and are fed by the melting snows and local rains of this rugged northern area, which receives 20 to 40 inches (500 to 1000 mm.) of precipitation annually. Although the source of the Tigris is within a few miles of where the Euphrates passes, the two rivers diverge and follow different paths. The Euphrates, also known as "the River" in the Bible, is over 1,780 miles (2865 km.) long. It begins near Erzurum in Turkey and, after flowing through the mountains of Armenia in a southwesterly direction, heads due south as it leaves the mountains. When it crosses the North Syrian Plain (see map p. 62) near Carchemish, it is only some 100 miles (160 km.) inland from the Mediterranean Sea. It then turns southeast and continues its gradual descent to the Persian Gulf.

After the Euphrates passes through the Syrian plain, limestone escarpments hem it in on both sides from Abu Kamal to Hit, leaving only a narrow alluvial valley for farming. Since this area between Abu Kamal and Hit receives only 4 to 8 inches (100 to 200 mm.) of rain each year, agriculture is primarily confined to the narrow river

MESOPOTAMIA

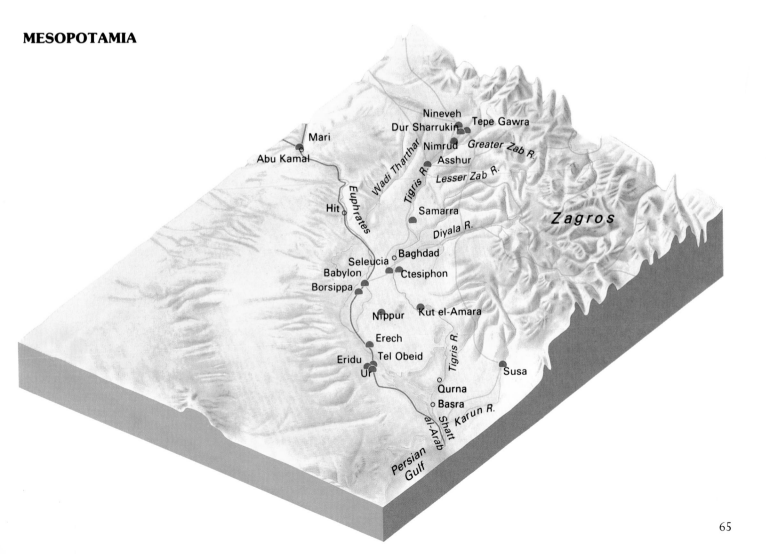

valley, although some grain crops are grown on the steppes where flocks of sheep and goats feed on the winter grass cover.

The Tigris, which begins in Lake Hazar southeast of Elazig, only 2 or 3 miles (4 km.) from the Euphrates, is 1,150 miles (1850 km.) long. After leaving the mountains of Armenia, the Tigris flows south and is fed from the east first by the Greater and then by the Lesser Zab rivers. These two rivers in fact double the amount of water flowing in the Tigris. This area is the old heartland of Assyria, and great cities (including Nineveh and Asshur) were once located along the banks of the Tigris. Today this highland region is largely deforested and heavily eroded, but during the winter months grain crops are grown. Winter rains—10 to 20 inches (250 to 500 mm.) annually—are the primary source of moisture for the crops. In some periods, irrigation canals have been used as well, although this involved somewhat advanced technology and large amounts of capital, for the Tigris is lower than the surrounding tableland. From the Greater Zab south to near Samarra there are few canals, scant rainfall (ca. 8 inches [200 mm.] annually), and little habitation.

Near Samarra, however, the landscape changes. Canals begin to branch off the Tigris to the east and to the southwest, and the "delta" or plain region of the Tigris and Euphrates begins. This plain is triangular in shape and is marked on the north by a line drawn from Samarra southwest to Hit, on the southwest by a line from Hit to Basra, and on the east by a line from Basra to Samarra. Near Baghdad the Tigris and Euphrates are only 18 miles (29 km.) apart, although they diverge again before actually joining at Qurna, northwest of Basra. The low-lying landscape between the two rivers is flat, expansive, and treeless. The silt, deposited over the millennia, is 15 to 25 feet (4.6 to 7.6 m.) deep.

Since this area receives only 4 to 8 inches (100 to 200 mm.) of rain each year, agriculture is dependent on irrigation techniques. Although the courses of the Tigris and Euphrates have in this region changed from time to time, the channels of both rivers are basically above the surface of the surrounding plain. If the rivers overflow their embankments in the spring, vast stretches of the plain are inundated. These inundations are somewhat problematic, for the amount of water brought down each year is very erratic. This irregularity can mean devastating floods in some years and disastrous droughts in others. Even when the flooding is neither too much nor too little, it comes too late for the winter crops and too early for the summer ones. Thus the residents of the area from time immemorial have tried to harness the rivers by diverting flood waters to low-lying areas upstream (e.g., into the Tharthar depression) to avoid flooding downstream.

Because in this area the Tigris and Euphrates are higher than the surrounding countryside, canals and channels crisscross the plain, bringing irrigation water to the crops during the fall, winter, and spring months. Since the water is slow-moving and the plain is very flat, these canals and channels often silted full, and it was necessary to organize labor gangs to clean them out. To coerce residents to show up and actually do the work, a rather strong local government was needed, and many city-states sprang up. At various times one of these city-states would gain supremacy over the others, and during that period a region was often named after its ruling city. Thus the geographical, political, and chronological terminology has often been derived from the names of cities (e.g., Sumer, Akkad, Ur, and Babylon).

After repeated cleanings, the banks of the canals and channels became so high that it was difficult to clean out the waterways. New waterways, parallel to the old ones, were dug. Eventually, low-lying fields lacking proper drainage were enclosed by the canals and channels. Water that entered these fields for the most part evaporated, leaving behind various minerals. In addition, since the water table in the plain was high, water and salts percolated out of the ground to the surface of the fields and added to the problem of salinization of the soil. As early as the third and second millennia B.C., and even into modern times, good agricultural land was lost because of this. First wheat could no longer be grown in the salty soil; then barley, which can tolerate more salt, could no longer be grown; and eventually, even date palms stopped producing fruit. When the land could no longer support barley or date palms, the people would move on to more fertile fields to raise their crops, leaving behind the useless land. Thus, the plain between the Tigris and Euphrates, rather than being a uniformly lush region, is an area where fertile irrigated fields alternate with infertile wastelands.

The southern part of the plain, where the Tigris and the Euphrates come close together, turns into marshland and eventually into swamp. In ancient times the Tigris and Euphrates entered the Persian Gulf separately; today they join at Qurna and form the Shatt al-Arab, which flows into the gulf. The area is hot, humid, and mosquito-infested. The Ma'dan, the swamp Arabs, inhabit the area today, living in reed huts constructed on high ground or on floating bogs. Their reed huts, along with their reed canoes, are reminiscent of the life of ancient inhabitants of this area. The area is certainly not prime agricultural land, and the natives subsisted by hunting wild fowl and wild boars, by fishing, and by tending date palms. Today rice is also grown. Archaeological remains are scanty in this region.

Internally, Mesopotamia produced enough foodstuffs to feed its population, although at times grain had to be shipped from the southern plain to Assyria. Land transport was mainly by foot or donkey, although the camel was probably introduced by the second millennium B.C. Land transport in the southern plain was impeded by the need to cross the Tigris and Euphrates rivers, as well as by the numerous canals and channels. In addition, the plain was often covered by mud and/or inundated by flood water during the winter and spring.

The main thoroughfares for travelers going from north to south were the rivers and canals. Bulk goods (such as timber and stone) were transported down the Tigris and Euphrates on rafts. These rafts were basically wooden platforms placed over inflated animal skins and could carry up to 35 tons (39 metric tons) of cargo. After the trip down the river was completed and the cargo had been delivered, the wooden frames were sold and the skins packed onto donkeys for the return trek northward. This type of vessel was used on both the Euphrates and the Tigris, although the Euphrates was a bit easier to navigate. Since in antiquity bridges were almost unknown, people often made use of these rafts (today called

The Euphrates at Dura Europus.

kalaks) to cross the rivers and canals. Guffahs—large circular baskets covered with bitumen, that could carry up to twenty people—were also used for this purpose.

Because Mesopotamia lacked many raw materials, it was necessary to import them from near and far. Although the sources varied from period to period, tin was imported from Iran, Afghanistan, and the Caucasus regions, silver from the Taurus Mountains, common timber from the Zagros Mountains, prized cedar wood from the Lebanon and Amanus mountains, and copper from many areas to the northeast, northwest, and even from sources reached via the Persian Gulf. In addition, luxury items were imported from India (spices and cloth) and south Arabia (frankincense and myrrh), both by overland transport and by sea.

One of the main routes of international as well as local significance that passed through Mesopotamia began at Nineveh in the north and ran westward via Shubat-Enlil (= Chagar Bazar?), Guzana, and Haran to Carchemish (see also map p. 62). From Carchemish, roads led northwest into Anatolia, westward to the Mediterranean, and southward toward Damascus, Israel, and Egypt. At Nineveh, connecting routes led northwest, via Diyarbakir, directly into Anatolia; eastward through difficult passes in the Zagros into Persia; and of course southward, via the Tigris, to the delta region.

In addition, an important route led northwest along the Euphrates, from Sippar in the delta toward Mari. From Mari it continued along the Euphrates to Carchemish, while another branch headed westward across the steppe/desert to Tadmor. From the delta, routes led east and southeast through the Zagros to the Persian plateau and other points eastward. In the first millennium B.C., routes also led southwest through the Arabian desert toward sources of frankincense and myrrh in southern Arabia. During peaceful times, caravans would ply these and other routes, while in less stable eras the great armies of Assyria, Babylonia, Persia, etc., set out on campaigns of conquest and devastation along these same paths.

Although remains of human occupation in Mesopotamia date back at least to the Neolithic period (ca. 8000 to 4000 B.C.), Mesopotamia, like Egypt, entered the light of history at the beginning of the Early Bronze Age (ca. 3150 B.C.). Scholars have grouped the cultural and historical eras in Mesopotamia into the following general periods:

DATES	PERIODS
8000–5000	Neolithic
5200–5000	Hassuna
5000–4500	Samarra, Halaf, Eridu
4500–3800	Tell el-'Obeid
3800–3200	Erech
3200–3000	Jemdet Nasr
3000–2500	Early Dynastic
2500–2000	Sumer and Akkad
2000–1600	Old Babylonian (and Isin & Larsa)
1600–911	Kassite and Early Assyrian
911–612	Assyrian
625–539	Neo-Babylonian
539–331	Persian
312–248	Seleucid
248–A.D. 226	Parthian
226–636	Sassanid

It should be noted that only rarely did one of these cultures pervade the whole of Mesopotamia; more often than not, they influenced larger and smaller areas surrounding their respective city-states/villages. The civilizations that sprang up along the two great rivers were constantly pressured by tribes located in the mountains to the north, in the Zagros to the east, and in Elam to the southeast, as well as by Bedouin marauders coming from the Syro-Arabian Desert. However, in many periods the Mesopotamian rulers were eager and able to hold these enemies at bay, sometimes even gaining territory at their expense. Of particular note for biblical studies are the westward expansions of the Assyrians, Neo-Babylonians, and Persians during the first millennium B.C. These expansions and their significance will be discussed in the Historical Section.

Since life in Mesopotamia can be characterized as a "mud culture"—crops were grown in mud; houses, palaces, temples, ziggurats, etc., were built of mud—it was only natural that mud or clay should often be used as a medium for communication. By 3100 B.C. cuneiform (wedge-shaped) writing had developed in Mesopotamia. This script was used to write a number of different languages (including Sumerian, Akkadian, Assyrian, Hittite, Babylonian, Persian, Ugaritic, and Eblaite) in a way similar to the use of Latin characters in writing English, German, and French. Cuneiform, which at first was composed of pictographs, quickly developed into stylized wedges, impressed on clay tablets by reeds. Many of the languages that adopted the cuneiform script used syllabic rather than alphabetic characters, along with determinatives—signs placed before and after words to indicate the class in which the word belonged (e.g., wooden objects, cities, mountains, etc.). Eventually, over 500 signs were used.

Cuneiform was deciphered in the nineteenth century, and since that time thousands upon thousands of cuneiform documents have been discovered in Mesopotamia, Armenia, Anatolia, Syria, Israel, and even in Egypt. This script was eventually discontinued in the first century A.D., after having been in use for over three thousand years. From these millennia a rich and varied literature has been preserved: myths and epics, legal texts, ritual texts, hymns and prayers, laments, omens, letters, and historical documents. The historical documents, especially those of the kings of Assyria and Babylonia of the first millennium B.C., are of great significance for biblical studies. These, as well as other relevant texts, will be mentioned at the appropriate places in the Historical Section.

ANNUAL CYCLE IN SOUTHERN MESOPOTAMIA

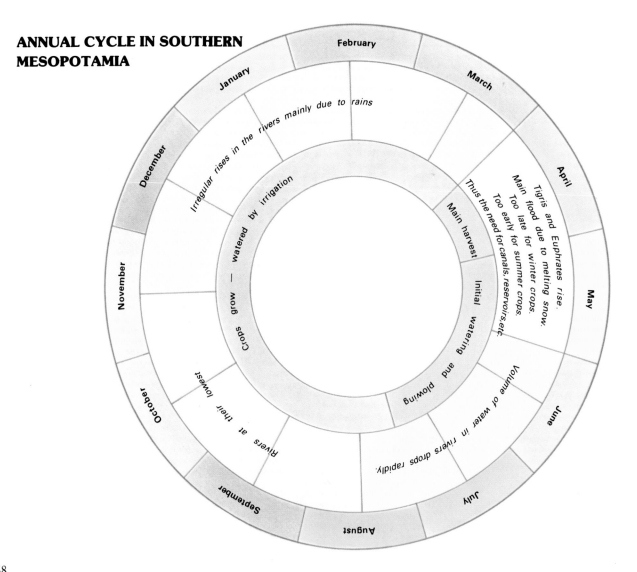

Historical Section

Arch of Titus in Rome which commemorated his conquest of Judea in A.D. 70

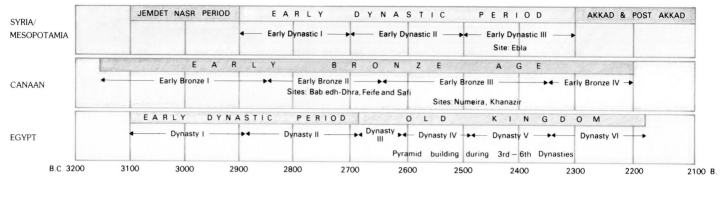

The Pre-Patriarchal Period

Garden of Eden (Genesis 1–3)

The Book of Genesis recounts in very terse yet picturesque language the history of the universe and the world from the time of creation until the call of Abram/Abraham. The second section of the creation account focuses on the creation of the first humans. The Bible places these sinless people in a perfect environment called the Garden of Eden.

The name Eden, if derived from Hebrew, means "delight" and is rendered "paradise" in the Septuagint (the Greek translation of the Old Testament). However, some scholars have suggested that Eden is related to the Sumerian/Akkadian word *edin(u)*, meaning "plain," and that this is a description of the location of Eden. It is of course possible that the author might have had both of these ideas in mind when using the term. In any case, it seems that Eden was the name of a locality and that the special garden mentioned was planted in the eastern portion of it (Gen 2:8). It is described as containing trees and an abundance of water. We can infer that it was in a warm climate—note the mention of fig trees and the lack of clothes (3:7). The major river that watered Eden is said to have separated into four headwaters called Pishon, Gihon, Tigris, and Euphrates (2:10–14). The latter two rivers are well known, but the identity of the first two is not, and their identification usually depends on where one places the garden.

The first of two major views places Eden in eastern Turkey, in Armenia, near the headwaters of the Tigris and the Euphrates. If this is correct, then the Pishon and the Gihon might be identified with other rivers in the area, such as the Araxes and the Murat, or they may now be nonexistent. This view has the advantages of locating Eden at a high altitude, from which the river(s) flowed down, and of uniting the symbolism of Eden, the place of the beginning of history, with the Ararat region, the place where the second beginning, with Noah and his descendants, took place. However, this region does not match the warm conditions implied in the biblical account.

The second view places Eden in southern Mesopotamia (modern Iraq). This view has the advantage of locating the garden in a warmer climate along the two identifiable rivers, the Tigris and the Euphrates. The Pishon and the Gihon

could then have been tributaries of the Tigris and/or Euphrates, though the text seems to indicate that one river was divided into four branches—reminiscent of a delta region—rather than four tributaries coming together to form

Section of a mid 16th century map by H. Weisel entitled *Lands of the Dispersion from Babel.*

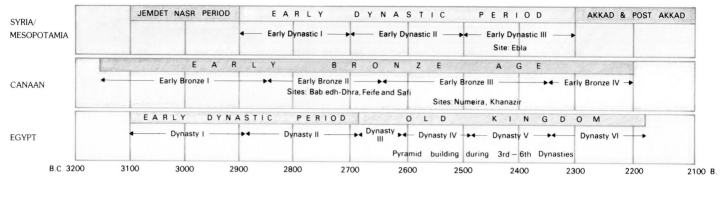

70

one river. Alternatively, the Pishon and Gihon could have been canals that branched off the Tigris and the Euphrates, but their paths through Havilah and Cush seem to imply considerable length.

The identification of Havilah and Cush is also difficult. Havilah (Gen 2:11–12) may be a country/region located in Sinai and/or Arabia (Gen 25:18), a locality where there were supplies of gold, aromatic resins (RSV "bdellium"; Heb. *b*e*dolah*), and onyx. If this was the case, it is interesting to note that the Israelites wandered in this barren area for forty years, observing firsthand the disastrous effects of the curse and receiving manna from heaven—which looked like resin (Heb. *b*e*dolah*; Num 11:7). The "land of Cush" usually refers to the land south of Egypt but north of Ethiopia, but it might possibly also refer to a portion of Arabia or, according to some, a territory in the mountains east of the Tigris River. Thus, although the exact location of Eden continues to elude modern interpreters, its theological and spiritual significance has certainly been appreciated by both ancients and moderns alike.

The Table of Nations   *Genesis 10*

The biblical text describes the progress of sin in the world after the fall of the first humans into sin and their expulsion from the Garden. The sinfulness of humankind was judged climactically in the Flood (Gen 6–9), after which a new beginning for humanity was initiated through the line of righteous Noah. Genesis 10 describes how the nations of the then-known world were derived from Noah's three sons—Japheth, Ham, and Shem. Their seventy descendants mentioned in this list are considered to have been the ancestral heads (= eponyms) of the clans and nations that bore their names (v. 32). The list is divided into three major sections, beginning with those peoples farthest removed from Israel's horizon and moving toward her near neighbors.

First, the fourteen descendants of Japheth are listed (vv. 2–5); special attention is given to the "sons" of Javan, with

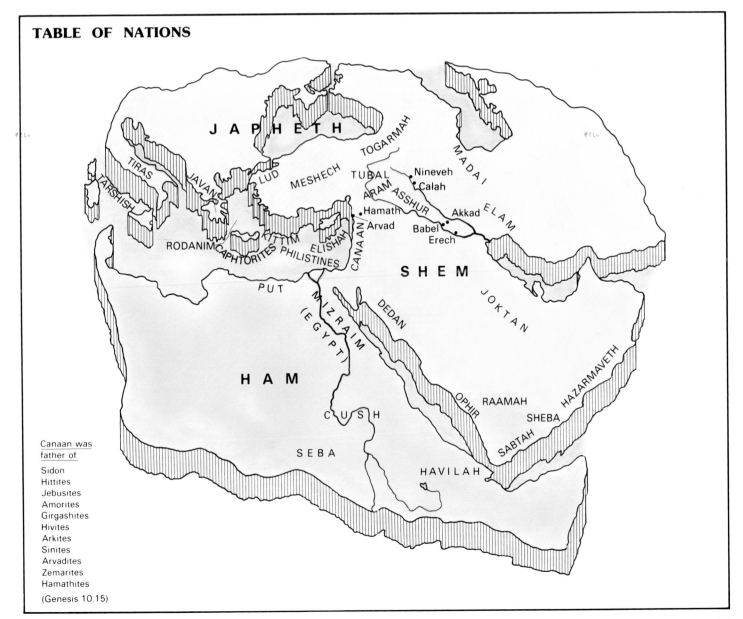

TABLE OF NATIONS

Canaan was father of:

Sidon
Hittites
Jebusites
Amorites
Girgashites
Hivites
Arkites
Sinites
Arvadites
Zemarites
Hamathites

(Genesis 10:15)

whom the Israelites came most often into contact. Although not all of the peoples/nations can be certainly identified, commonly accepted identifications include Gomer = Cimmerians, Madai = Medes, Javan = Ionians, Ashkenaz = Scythians, Elishah = Alashiya/Cyprus, and Rodanim = Rhodes. The general area where these peoples lived was to the west and north of the land of Israel.

The second portion of Genesis 10 (vv. 6–20) lists the thirty-one descendants of Ham. Generally accepted identifications for the descendants of Ham include Cush = Ethiopia/Nubia, Mizraim = Egypt, Put = Libya, Canaan = Canaan, Sheba = Saba (in southern Arabia), Dedad = Dedan (the el-Ula oasis in Arabia), Caphtorites = Cretans, Arkites = Arqad (in Lebanon), Arvadites = Arvad, Ham-athites = city of Hamath, in addition to peoples well known from the Old Testament: Philistines, Sidonites, Hittites, Jebusites, Amorites, Girgashites, Hivites, and others. In the main, the descendants of Ham settled in and around the land of Israel but also to the southeast and in Africa. The list gives special attention to the descendants of Canaan (vv. 15–19), with whom the Israelites came into very close contact, and to the cities associated with the warrior Nimrod (vv. 8–12). The first four of the cities mentioned in connection with him were important political/cultural centers in Shinar, in southern Mesopotamia, while the latter four (v. 11) were located along the upper Tigris River and are mentioned in connection with Nimrod's northern migration.

The third and final section of the list contains the twenty-

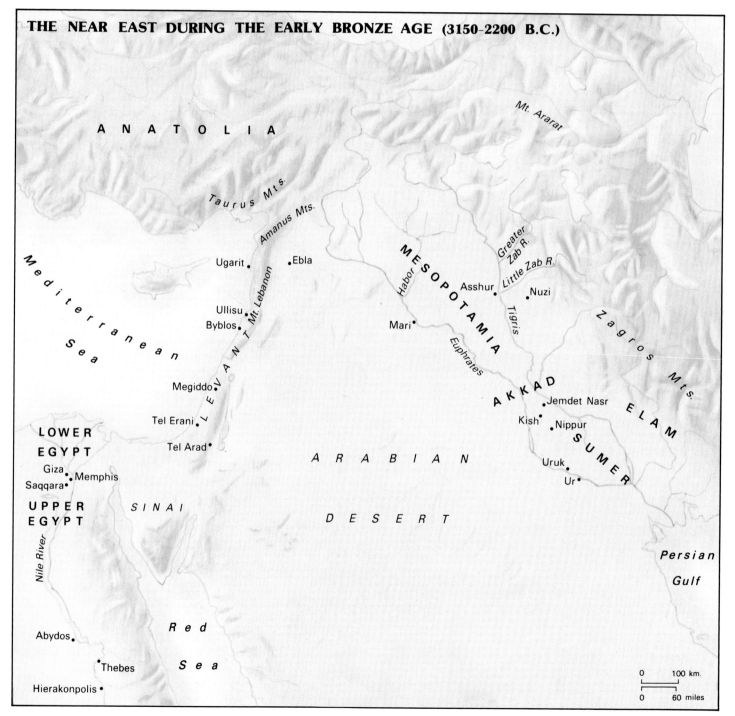

THE NEAR EAST DURING THE EARLY BRONZE AGE (3150-2200 B.C.)

six descendants of Shem (vv. 22–31). As is typical in Genesis, this, the most important line, is dealt with last—Abram/Abraham being a descendant of Shem. The people mentioned in this list mainly settled to the northeast and southeast of Israel. Commonly accepted identifications include Elam = Elam, Asshur = Asshur/Assyria, Arphaxad = Chaldeans/Kasdim(?), and Aram = Arameans. The list gives special attention to the descendants of Joktan, people who evidently were the eponymous heads of various Arabian tribes.

Although modern linguists sometimes speak of Hamitic and Semitic languages—making a seemingly vague reference to this text—these language-classification schemes are modern in origin, and it is not necessary to try to explain the list in Genesis 10 in terms of related languages. Because some of the peoples mentioned in the list appear for the first time in extrabiblical documents of the first millennium B.C., some scholars have concluded that the list must date from that period. However, it is quite possible that these "late-appearing" peoples were known as tribes that existed in the second half of the second millennium B.C. but happened not to be noted in extrabiblical documents until later periods. Simply put, the purpose of the list in Genesis 10 was to describe how the descendants of Noah were fruitful and filled the earth (9:1; cf. 1:22, 28).

Mesopotamia—Early Bronze Age

It was during the Early Bronze Age (ca. 3150–2200 B.C.)[1] that some of the countries of the Near East entered into the light of history. In Mesopotamia, the beginning of this era, called the Jemdet Nasr Period (3100–2900 B.C.), forms the transition from the Protoliterate to the Early Dynastic Period. During this period in Mesopotamia writing began, and large cities, containing examples of monumental architecture (such as temples, palaces, and fortifications), were first built on the plains near the Tigris and Euphrates rivers. This urban revolution was hastened by the use of newly developed copper tools and weapons, while the interaction of the people of the cities with those of the surrounding countrysides led to an increase in the population. This was the era, according to the Sumerian King List, during which the long-lived members of the pre-Flood dynasties ruled.

The urban revolution continued during the Early Dynastic Period (2900–2300 B.C.). The leadership of the country passed between great cities such as Kish, Uruk, and Ur. It seems that there was no strong central government controlling the whole area; rather, individual city-states ruled over limited territories, with first one and then another gaining dominance. These city-states seem to have had a unified culture, religion, and language, known today as Sumerian. The religious center of this civilization was the city of Nippur, but it is difficult to determine whether kings or priests were the dominating elements within the various city-states. It is to this period that much of the Akkadian epic literature owes its origin, although the now extant copies of this literature come from later times.

The Early Dynastic Period came to an end when a Semite—Sargon of Akkad, from the area north of Sumer—took control of the old city-states. Sargon had already conquered territory to the northeast and the west; according to the texts, he eventually pushed into Anatolia to Purushkhanda. He also led conquests into Elam to the east and to Tilmun in the south. Thus it was Sargon who established the first empire in the Mesopotamian region. His grandson, Naram-Sin, seems to have been especially active in the west, campaigning as far as the Amanus, Taurus, and Lebanon mountains, even reaching the Mediterranean coast near Ullisu. During this period of great prosperity the arts flourished, literature developed, and many foreign contacts were made. The Sargonic Empire (2300–2100 B.C.) came to an end because of internal and external pressures (the latter from the Guti, a mountain tribe), but the idea of a large, unified empire became a recurring concept that continued to express itself at various periods in Mesopotamian history.

Egypt During the Early Bronze Age

At the end of the fourth millennium B.C., Egypt, too, was moving out of the prehistoric period into the full light of history. During the Early Bronze Age there were two major eras in Egyptian history: the Early Dynastic Period and the Old Kingdom. Just prior to, or at the beginning of, the Early Dynastic Period (1st and 2nd Dynasties; 3100–2686 B.C.), Lower Egypt (the delta region) and Upper Egypt (the Nile Valley south of Cairo) were united into a single state. This union was symbolized by the king's crown, which combined elements of both the white crown of Upper Egypt and the red crown of Lower Egypt. The geographical origin of the 1st Dynasty may have been in Hierakonpolis, south of Thebes, but the cemeteries of the kings and officials were located at Abydos, Saqqara, and elsewhere. It seems that during this period Memphis was established as the capital, and it remained the capital throughout the Old Kingdom period (2686–2160 B.C.).

The first king of the 1st Dynasty (3100–2890 B.C.) was Narmer, who has been identified by some with Menes, a somewhat legendary figure known from classical sources. The pallet of Narmer shows him wearing the crowns of both Upper and Lower Egypt, indicating his authority over both regions. It seems likely that Egypt had some contacts with Palestine during his reign, for pottery inscribed with Narmer's name has been found at Tel Erani and Tel Arad. It also seems that Egypt had contacts with Mesopotamia, since cylinder seals of the Protoliterate period have been found in Egyptian cemeteries and Mesopotamian-style niched facades were used on Egyptian tombs. Artistic motifs (such as the intertwined necks of animals) and the early use of the pictographic writing system also seem to indicate Mesopotamian influence upon Egypt.

The 3rd Dynasty through the 8th Dynasty are collectively known as the Old Kingdom (2686–2160 B.C.). It was during this period that many aspects of Egyptian life reached their classical form: the traditional southern boundary at the first cataract was established, the symbols of hieroglyphic writing were stabilized, traditional administrative structures were put into place, and artistic compositions assumed their stylized forms. By the end of the period, the traditional twenty-two nomes (districts) of Upper Egypt were well established, although the twenty-nome structure of the Delta was not finalized until later.

The Old Kingdom is known as the age of the pyramid builders, the first of whom was Djoser. This king from the 3rd Dynasty (2686–2613 B.C.) is known not only for centralizing the government in Memphis but especially for his stepped pyramid, which he constructed at Saqqara, 2 miles (3 km.) west of Memphis. Thirty-four pyramids, out of a total of forty-seven, were built during the Old Kingdom period.[2] The pyramids are thought to symbolize the power of the king as well as to emphasize his association with the sun god Re. During this period the kings themselves were considered to be gods, and the pyramids served not only as burial places but also as religious centers where the cult of the deceased god-king was practiced. Typically, a pyramid consisted not merely of the monument itself but was rather a large complex of structures that included the pyramid, a temple for the king-cult (on the east), an enclosure wall, sometimes a small pyramid (for the Ka-spirit [?]), mastaba tombs (rectangular in shape with sloping sides and a flat roof) for officials who had served the king, small pyramids for the queens, and a processional avenue that led from the main complex eastward to the river bank where it joined a temple that had been built at the river landing. In addition, houses for the priests

and caretakers of the complex were located nearby. The 4th, 5th, and 6th dynasties are considered to have been the high point of the Old Kingdom, and the pyramids of three of the kings of the 4th Dynasty (2613–2494 B.C.)—those of Cheops, Chephren, and Mycerinus, located at Giza—are the most famous of the pyramids of Egypt.

Although the Old Kingdom is well known because of the pyramids, not many documents from which a history of the period can be reconstructed have been preserved. It is known that there were extensive contacts with Nubia to the south, from which luxury items such as gold, ivory, and ebony were obtained. To the north, Egyptian gold work has been found in Turkey, while stone vases of Chephren and Pepi I have been found at Tell Mardikh (Ebla), and additional Egyptian artifacts at Byblos. These data, along with the tomb inscription of Uni (see below), indicate important Egyptian contacts with the Levant.

The stability of the country began to crumble during the rule of the fifteen kings of the 7th and 8th dynasties (2181–2160 B.C.). During this time, and even at the end of the 6th Dynasty, the power of the nomarchs and other officials was growing at the expense of the king. The collapse of the Old Kingdom was probably due to internal factors, such as the economic burdens brought about by the high maintenance costs of the pyramid cults, by weak kings, and possibly by a series of below-normal inundations of the Nile that led to famine. These factors, along with the incursions of Asiatic peoples into the delta region, seem to have led the country into the turbulent days of the First Intermediate Period.

Early Bronze Age city wall with semi-circular tower at Arad.

Palestine in the Early Bronze Age

Although human settlement in Palestine has had a long history,[3] it was not until the country passed from the Chalcolithic period (fourth millennium B.C.) to the Early Bronze Age (3150–2200 B.C.) that the transition from small, scattered settlements to large urban centers took place. Although it is probable that this was a local development, some have suggested that the building of new urban centers reflects the fact that a new population element had entered the country. Broshi and Gophna, in their report of Early Bronze sites in modern Israel (those located north of an imaginary line running from Beersheba to Arad), note a total of 260 sites, of which 47 are over 10 acres (4 ha.) in size.[4] They have estimated that the average urban population during the period could have been in the neighborhood of 150,000.[5] Not until three thousand years later, during the Roman and Byzantine periods (37 B.C.–A.D. 640), would the number of large settlements in Israel again approach the magnitude of those found in this early period. Evidently the population group was Semitic, for in later written documents the names of many of the towns that they founded are clearly Semitic (e.g., Megiddo, Beth-yerah, Jericho, Aphek, etc. For the preservation of place names through the ages, see pp. 201–8).

Most of the large urban centers were protected by strong city walls, often massive in size; those at Megiddo and Beth-

74

yerah were close to 25 feet (7.5 m.) thick. Some were built of mud brick laid on stone foundations (e.g., Megiddo, Beth-yerah, Arad), while others were massive stone constructions (e.g., Tel Yarmuth, et-Tell). Some of the walls had protruding semicircular towers built into them to aid in the defense of the city (e.g., Arad, et-Tell). At Arad it is estimated that forty such towers were placed at intervals along the 3,840-foot (1170-m.) wall.

Although apsidal buildings are known from the period, typical houses were rectangular in shape with the entry placed close to the center of one of the long walls—hence the name "broad house." From street level, one would usually descend a few steps into a house. Archaeologists have discovered that the door socket, on which the door swung, was normally placed on the left side of the entry. Low benches lined the walls of the houses, and often small mortars used for the grinding of grain were found in or on the floors. On occasion one or more stone slabs, located along the long central axis of the house, have been found; these were evidently used to support pillars, which in turn supported the roof of the building. The clay model of an Early Bronze house, found at Arad, indicates that the buildings were flat-roofed and windowless.

At Megiddo, et-Tell, Bab edh-Dhra, and Arad, large public buildings, all in the shape of "broad houses," have been found, which appear to have served as temples. At Megiddo four such buildings were discovered in the sacred area. Three of them, similar in plan and measurements, were built in close proximity to the large (25 feet [7.5 m.] in diameter) circular altar.

Alongside the large urban centers one would normally expect correspondingly large cemeteries, but this is not usually the case. However, large burial grounds have been found at Bab edh-Dhra and Feifa, Early Bronze cities located at the southeastern end of the Dead Sea.[6] At Bab edh-Dhra, it is estimated that some 20,000 tombs contain the remains of 500,000 people—and the cemetery at Feifa is almost as large! Since the number of burials seems to be larger than the number of people that could have lived in these cities, and since some of these are secondary burials (the bones were brought from elsewhere and reburied here), it appears that these cemeteries may have been used as common burial sites for many other Early Bronze urban centers.

In addition to the numerous shaft tombs, in which a shaft 3 feet (1 m.) in diameter was sunk 6 feet (2 m.) deep and from which one to five burial chambers branch out, there are both round and rectangular charnel houses (bone houses). The rectangular ones, 10 to 25 feet (3 to 7.5 m.) in length, are built on the "broad house" pattern. In one charnel house the remains of close to 300 bodies were found, and an initial study of bones from the cemetery indicates that some of the populace were as tall as 6 feet 4 inches (193 cm.)!

In contrast to Egypt, Ebla, and Mesopotamia, no archives dating to the Early Bronze Age have yet been found in Palestine. As far as the written record goes, we are thus limited to such historical references as are found in the literature of the neighboring countries. At Abydos in Egypt, the tomb inscription of Uni describes how he led five campaigns to the "land of the Sand-Dwellers" during the reign of Pepi I (2289–2255 B.C.; *ANET*, 227–28). Although the "land of the Sand-Dwellers" in other contexts could refer to Sinai, it seems probable in this case that Canaan, to the northeast of Sinai, is indicated, since [fortified] enclosures, fig trees, and vines are mentioned in connection with the land. Indeed, the reference in the text to a prominent mountain height situated close to the sea and called the "Antelope-Nose" could refer to the promontory of Mount Carmel that juts out into the Mediterranean.

Another source of historical data that could pertain to Canaan during this period is the Ebla archive, which was discovered in the late 1970s. Early reports indicated that Canaanite cities such as Hazor, Megiddo, Gaza, Urusalima, Salem, Lachish, Dor, Ashtaroth, and Joppa, as well as Sodom, Gomorrah, Admah, Zeboiim, and Bela were mentioned in the texts.[7] Since then, the claim that the last three names appear in the texts has been withdrawn, and the mention of some of the other geographical names has been called into question. However, if any Canaanite place names do in fact appear in the texts, their appearance will shed welcome light on the history of this otherwise relatively dim period.

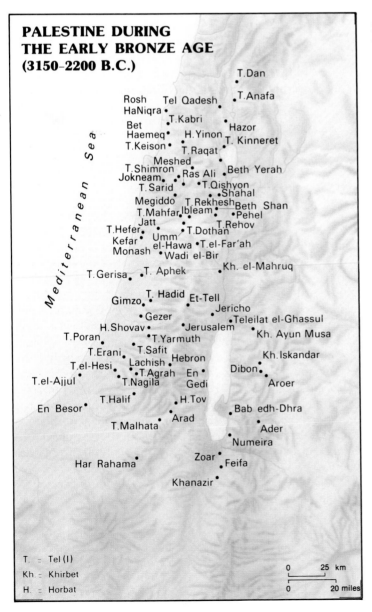

PALESTINE DURING THE EARLY BRONZE AGE (3150–2200 B.C.)

T. = Tel (l)
Kh. = Khirbet
H. = Horbat

0   25 km
0   20 miles

75

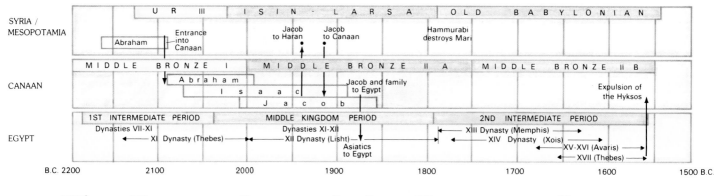

SYRIA / MESOPOTAMIA	U R I I I	I S I N · L A R S A	O L D B A B Y L O N I A N			

SYRIA / MESOPOTAMIA: U R III — I S I N · L A R S A — O L D B A B Y L O N I A N
Abraham — Entrance into Canaan — Jacob to Haran — Jacob to Canaan — Hammurabi destroys Mari

CANAAN: M I D D L E B R O N Z E I — M I D D L E B R O N Z E II A — M I D D L E B R O N Z E II B
Abraham — Isaac — Jacob — Jacob and family to Egypt — Expulsion of the Hyksos

EGYPT: 1ST INTERMEDIATE PERIOD — MIDDLE KINGDOM PERIOD — 2ND INTERMEDIATE PERIOD
Dynasties VII–XI — Dynasties XI–XII — XIII Dynasty (Memphis) — XIV Dynasty (Xois) — XV–XVI (Avaris) — XVII (Thebes)
XI Dynasty (Thebes) — XII Dynasty (Lisht) — Asiatics to Egypt

B.C. 2200   2100   2000   1900   1800   1700   1600   1500 B.C.

The Patriarchs and the Egyptian Sojourn

The end of the third millennium B.C. (ca. 2200–2000 B.C.) marks the beginning of the era of the biblical patriarchs: Abraham, Isaac, Jacob, and Joseph. Genesis 12–50 records Abram's emigration from Ur of the Chaldeans, in southern Mesopotamia,[1] to Canaan (ca. 2091 B.C.) and the events surrounding the lives of Abraham, Isaac, and Jacob in and around the land of Canaan. This section of Scripture concludes by describing the circumstances surrounding the migration of Jacob and his family to Egypt about 1876 B.C., 215 years after Abram had entered Canaan, which marks the beginning of the period of the sojourn of the Israelites in Egypt.

Although the dating of the patriarchs is somewhat problematic, the Bible presents some rather straightforward "relative dates" (e.g., Abram was 75 when he departed from Haran, Gen 12:4) from which some "absolute dates" (specific years, such as 2091 B.C.) can be derived.[2] The keystone in the attempt to convert "relative" to "absolute" dates is the passage found in 1 Kings 6:1:

In the four hundred and eightieth year after the Israelites had come out of Egypt, in the fourth year of Solomon's reign over Israel, in the month of Ziv, the second month, he began to build the temple of the Lord.

It is generally agreed that Solomon began his reign in 970 B.C. (an "absolute date"),[3] which means that his fourth year (a "relative date") would have been 966 B.C. Since this, according to the text, was 480 years after the Exodus, the Exodus must have taken place ca. 1446 B.C.[4] The biblical text indicates that the Exodus took place 430 years after Jacob and his family entered Egypt (Exod 12:40), which implies that this descent occurred about 1876 B.C. From data given in Genesis (12:14; 21:5; 23:1; 25:7, 26; 35:28–29; 47:9) one can work back to the date of the birth of Abraham (2166 B.C.) and determine that the probable date of his entrance into Canaan was 2091 B.C.[5] These and other "absolute dates" derived from the internal biblical chronology will be used in this atlas, and the dates so generated will—where possible—be correlated with extrabiblical data in an attempt to help define the geographical, archaeological, and cultural environment in which biblical events occurred.

As stated, the above data and the internal chronology found in Exodus and Genesis indicate that Abram was born in 2166 B.C. Abram's time was an era of relative peace and prosperity in southern Mesopotamia, during which his home

city of Ur controlled most of the other city-states in the region. This era, known as the Ur III period (ca. 2130–2022 B.C.), is well-known from the thousands of cuneiform documents that have been found in Ur, Lagash, Umma, Drehem, Nippur, and other cities. During this period many of the old Sumerian epics and myths, which had originated in the Early Dynastic Period (see above), were put into their final form. These documents show that a resurgent Sumerian culture was again flourishing in the region, albeit for the final time. Thousands of economic, legal, and judicial texts witness to the complex and pervasive roles of the palace and the temple in the everyday life of the people. The rich archaeological finds from Ur indicate that it was a thriving commercial center during this entire period. It was from such a culturally advanced city that Abram began his earthly pilgrimage of faith (Gen 11:31; Acts 7:4).

When Abram was about seventy years old (ca. 2096 B.C.) he, along with his wife, Sarah; his nephew Lot; his father, Terah; and a group of household retainers, left Ur of the Chaldees[6] for the "land of Canaan" (Gen 11:31). There were two major routes that Abram might have taken on his journey from Ur to Haran. One headed north, through what would later become Assyria, before it turned westward through the Jezirah to Haran (a total distance of ca. 670 mi. [1080 km.]; see p. 67). The other route proceeded northwest, alongside the Euphrates River, to the city of Mari, and from there continued to Haran via the Euphrates and Balik rivers (a total distance of ca. 630 mi. [1010 km.]). It is estimated that the trip would have taken at least thirty-one actual days of travel at the pace of twenty miles per day, and this figure does not include needed days of rest.

Haran ("roadway"), also known from extrabiblical texts, was an important caravan city around 2000 B.C. It is not known how long Abram stayed in Haran, but it appears that he settled there for at least a year, for his father Terah died there. The roots of Abraham in the Haran/Aram area were such that the Israelites would later refer to their ancestor as a "wandering Aramean" (Deut 26:5).

At the age of seventy-five (ca. 2091 B.C.; Gen 12:4), Abram departed from Haran, setting out for "the land of Canaan" (12:5). Later, during the fifteenth and fourteenth centuries B.C., "the land of Canaan" was a definite geopolitical entity, known both to the Egyptians and to the Israelites, with specific boundaries (see p. 91 and map p. 93). Yet the

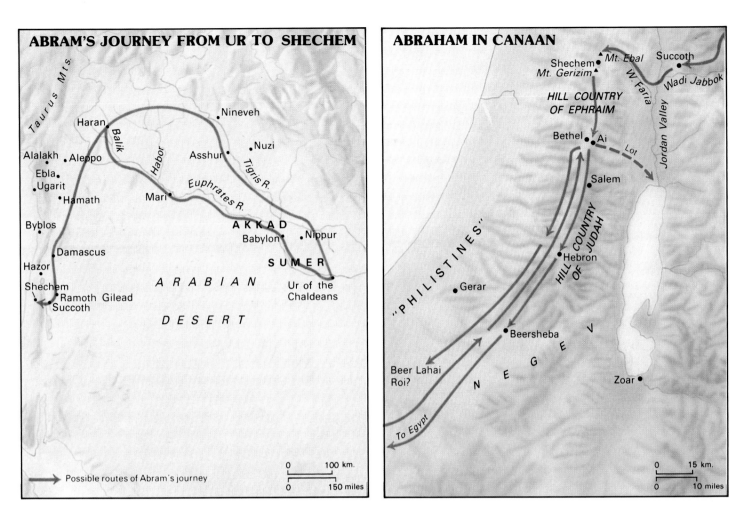

ABRAM'S JOURNEY FROM UR TO SHECHEM

Taurus Mts.
Haran
Balik
Nineveh
Alalakh
Aleppo
Habor
Nuzi
Ebla
Asshur
Ugarit
Tigris R.
Hamath
Mari
Euphrates R.
Byblos
AKKAD
Damascus
Babylon
Nippur
Hazor
SUMER
Shechem
ARABIAN
Ur of the Chaldeans
Ramoth Gilead
Succoth
DESERT

0   100 km.
0   150 miles

→ Possible routes of Abram's journey

ABRAHAM IN CANAAN

Shechem   Mt. Ebal   Succoth
Mt. Gerizim   W. Faria   Wadi Jabbok
HILL COUNTRY OF EPHRAIM
Bethel   Ai   Lot
Jordan Valley
Salem
"PHILISTINES"   HILL COUNTRY OF JUDAH
Hebron
Gerar
Beersheba
N E G E V
Beer Lahai Roi?
Zoar
To Egypt

0   15 km.
0   10 miles

antiquity of the term has been disputed. Was it actually in existence as early as the patriarchal age (2091 B.C.), or was it a term that came into use during the second half of the second millennium B.C.? Until recently, the latter was assumed to be the case, for biblical and extrabiblical references to Canaan had been found in ancient documents dating from 1450 to 450 B.C. but not earlier. Now, however, an early usage of Canaan as a geopolitical term is attested in the Mari documents that date to about 1800 B.C.,[7] and the reference to "Dagan [a deity] of Canaan" in the Ebla tablets (ca. 2400 B.C.) indicates the name's great antiquity.[8] Thus its use in the Patriarchal narratives need not be anachronistic.

Abram's route from Haran to Canaan probably took him south through Damascus into Transjordan, to the area of Ramoth Gilead. From there he would have descended into the Jordan Valley, possibly via the Wadi Jabbok to Succoth, where he would have crossed the Jordan River into Canaan. He probably entered the Hill Country of Manasseh via the relatively broad and gentle Wadi Faria, which took him up into the mountains just a few miles north of Shechem. All totaled, this trip covered about 400 mi. (640 km.) and took at least twenty actual days of travel. This basic route to and from Haran is of some importance, for it probably was later used by Abram's servant as he went to secure a bride for Isaac (Gen 24), by Jacob as he fled from his brother Esau to his uncle Laban who lived in Paddan Aram (Gen 27–29), and again by Jacob on his return to Canaan (see esp. Gen 31:19–33:20).

Shechem, Abram's first stop in the land of Canaan, has been identified with Tell Balatah. It is located near the watershed between the twin mountains of Ebal and Gerizim. Roads from all directions feed into this high, plateau-like valley, and from early times Shechem served as the major urban center in the Hill Country of Ephraim and Manasseh. Although Shechem has been excavated, it is not necessary to try to find any particular archaeological remains from this period (ca. 2091 B.C.), for the biblical evidence does not demand that an actual city was located there in Abram's day. It was at Shechem, at the site of the "great tree of Moreh," that the Lord appeared to Abram and promised, "To your offspring I will give this land." In response to this promise Abram built an altar and worshiped God there (Gen 12:7).

From Shechem Abram traveled south, through the Hill Country of Ephraim, to a mountain situated east of Bethel and west of Ai. There he pitched his tent and constructed another altar (Gen 12:8). The topographic details given in this passage fit very well with the usual identification of Bethel with modern Beitin and Ai with et-Tell.[9] At the time of Abram's arrival, the large Early Bronze Age city of Ai, which covered 27 acres, had been in ruins for hundreds of years, while the archaeological evidence regarding habitation at Bethel is ambiguous; there may have been a small Middle Bronze I (MB I) settlement there during Abram's time.[10] Abram continued his journey southward through the Hill Country of Judah to the Negev (Gen 12:9). The route he traveled from Shechem to Bethel/Ai, to Hebron, and on to

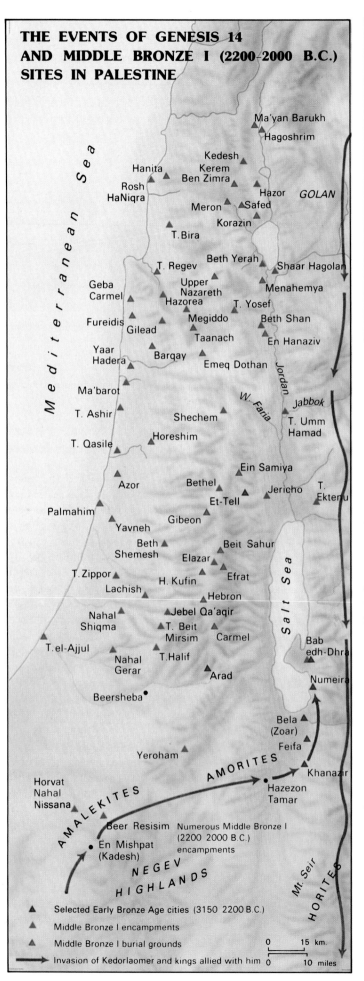

THE EVENTS OF GENESIS 14 AND MIDDLE BRONZE I (2200–2000 B.C.) SITES IN PALESTINE

Ma'yan Barukh
Hagoshrim
Kedesh
Hanita
Kerem
Ben Zimra
Rosh HaNiqra
Hazor
GOLAN
Meron
Safed
Korazin
T. Bira
Beth Yerah
T. Regev
Shaar Hagolan
Geba Carmel
Upper Nazareth
Menahemya
Hazorea
T. Yosef
Fureidis
Megiddo
Beth Shan
Gilead
Taanach
Yaar Hadera
Barqay
En Hanaziv
Ma'barot
Emeq Dothan
W. Faria
T. Ashir
Shechem
Jabbok
Horeshim
T. Umm Hamad
T. Qasile
Ein Samiya
Azor
Bethel
Jericho
T. Ekteru
Palmahim
Et-Tell
Gibeon
Yavneh
Beth Shemesh
Beit Sahur
T. Zippor
Elazar
Efrat
Lachish
H. Kufin
Hebron
Nahal Shiqma
Jebel Qa'aqir
T. Beit Mirsim
Carmel
T.el-Ajjul
T.Halif
Bab edh-Dhra
Nahal Gerar
Arad
Numeira
Beersheba
Bela (Zoar)
Yeroham
Feifa
Horvat Nahal Nissana
AMORITES
Khanazir
AMALEKITES
Hazezon Tamar
Beer Resisim
En Mishpat (Kadesh)
Numerous Middle Bronze I (2200 2000 B.C.) encampments
NEGEV HIGHLANDS
Mt. Seir
HORITES

▲ Selected Early Bronze Age cities (3150 2200 B.C.)
▲ Middle Bronze I encampments
▲ Middle Bronze I burial grounds
➤ Invasion of Kedorlaomer and kings allied with him

0   15 km.
0   10 miles

78

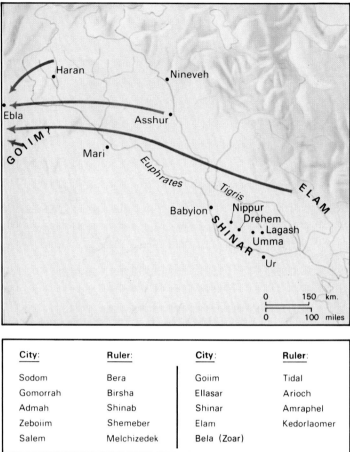

Haran   Nineveh
Ebla   Asshur
GOIIM?
Mari   Euphrates   Tigris   ELAM
Babylon   Nippur
Drehem
SHINAR   Lagash
Umma
Ur

0   150 km.
0   100 miles

City:	Ruler:	City:	Ruler:
Sodom	Bera	Goiim	Tidal
Gomorrah	Birsha	Ellasar	Arioch
Admah	Shinab	Shinar	Amraphel
Zeboiim	Shemeber	Elam	Kedorlaomer
Salem	Melchizedek	Bela (Zoar)	

Beersheba/Negev, was subsequently used very frequently throughout sacred history. This route is often called the "Ridge Route" (see p. 28) but could also be called the "Route of the Patriarchs" during this period.

The country in which Abram now lived was no longer characterized by the large Early Bronze urban centers, for these had collapsed by 2200 B.C., if not earlier. The reason for this collapse is not completely clear, but possibilities include Egyptian invasions (Pepi I?), internal conflicts, attacks by the MB I peoples, or a combination of the above. In any case, the characteristics of the MB I period (2200–2000 B.C.), during which Abraham lived, are well known.

Instead of living in large fortified cities, people of the MB I period lived in tents (tents are mentioned twenty-two times in the patriarchal narratives) and huts. In the Negev, where numerous settlements have been found and excavated, the typical settlement consisted of a cluster of small, flimsy, circular or rectangular installations grouped around a central courtyard.[11] Only a few "large" settlements have been found (Horvat Nahal Nissana, Har Yeruham, Be'er Resisim), and these are less than three acres in size and unwalled. In addition, numerous intermediate and single-unit settlements have been found scattered over the Negev Highlands, the Uvdah Valley, and southern Transjordan.

Although remnants of this civilization have been found at tells in the northern parts of the country (e.g., Bethel, Tell Beit Mirsim, Jericho, Megiddo), no fortifications and no public buildings have been discovered in Palestine, perhaps indicating that these settlements were poor and temporary. Evidently the Hill Country of Judah was not heavily settled during the MB I period, probably because it was still covered with relatively dense forests.

The burial customs of the MB I people were quite unique. Their tombs were usually shaft tombs, oftentimes hewn into the hard limestone hills of Palestine. A vertical shaft led to one or more chambers, but in contrast to the Early Bronze Age practice, one burial per chamber was the rule. Tens, or even hundreds, of these tombs are often found together (e.g., near what are called today Ein Samiya, Elazar, Efrat, Jebel Qa'aqir).[12] In the Golan region, Transjordan, and elsewhere, fields containing hundreds of dolmens have been found. These low, table-like structures were built out of three or four large rocks and were sometimes used to mark shallow grave sites. In other instances, especially in the Negev, piles of stones called *tumuli* mark the burial sites.

The identity of these MB I people in Palestine has not been firmly established.[13] Kenyon called them Amorites and proposed that they came from the east and northeast, from the deserts; Lapp, Kochavi, and Aharoni believed that they were Kurgan peoples who migrated south from the Caucasus Mountains. Dever, on the other hand, suggested that the MB I culture developed out of the Early Bronze (EB) civilization, while Cohen has recently suggested that the peoples came from the south, out of Sinai. In addition to the question of the geographical and ethnic origin of the MB I peoples, there is also considerable discussion concerning the relationship between them and the peoples of the preceding and succeeding eras (EB and MB II).[14] The current status of the question suggests that between 2200 and 2000 B.C. a seminomadic/pastoral population was moving about in Palestine and that for some reason they generally preferred to live on the fringes of the desert (e.g., in southern Transjordan and in the Negev Highlands) rather than in the more arable central and northern regions of the country.[15]

Soon after Abram entered Canaan, the land experienced one of its occasional droughts, which led to insufficient supplies of food and fodder. Abram, probably knowing that Egypt normally had sufficient supplies of food, crossed the northern Sinai peninsula, possibly following the way of Shur, to Egypt, where he found sustenance for his family (Gen 12:10–20).

The Egypt that Abram entered had been experiencing political and social upheavals for the last one hundred years. This turbulent era, known as the First Intermediate Period (2160–2040 B.C.), followed the collapse of the stable Old Kingdom (Pyramid Age; see above, pp. 73–74). Politically, Egypt was divided into at least two units. Kings of the 9th and 10th dynasties ruled the Nile Valley north of Abydos; their capital was the city of Herakleopolis, rather than Memphis. Simultaneously, the 11th Dynasty was established at Thebes in the south and ruled over the Nile Valley from Abydos in the north to Elephantine (near the first cataract) in the south. According to the description of this period found in the "Admonitions of Ipuwer" (*ANET*, 441–44), it was a time of great social unrest—the wealthy were consigned to perform menial tasks while the poor became their masters, the tombs of the kings were plundered, droughts (low inundations of the Nile) occurred, and death and destruction were everywhere.[16]

Although monumental remains are few, literary works such as the "Instruction for King Meri-ka-Re" (*ANET*, 414–

Dolmen in the Golan Heights

18) aid in understanding this era, as do the small-scale wooden models of scenes from daily life (boats, workshops, houses, etc.) that were found in the tomb of Meket-Re near Thebes (*ANEP*, 110 and 154). This First Intermediate Period came to an end around 2040 B.C. when Mentuhotpe II of the 11th Dynasty defeated the Heraklopolitan rulers and reunited the north with the south, ushering in the Middle Kingdom (2040–1786 B.C.).

Abram's return to Canaan from Egypt marked the beginning of nearly two hundred years of patriarchal residence in the land. From the biblical account it appears that most of this time was spent in the region of the Negev, with occasional trips to the Hill Country of Judah and Ephraim. The patriarchs were occupied with raising sheep and goats and growing grain crops (see, e.g., Gen 13:2, 5–7; 24:35; 26:12). This meant that from season to season they moved from one pastureland to another, but in all probability they returned to previous camps each succeeding year. Wells, probably dug in and near the junctions of wadis, provided water for their families and flocks. The digging of these wells was difficult, and thus the control of these sources of life-giving water was often disputed. Both Abraham and Isaac had conflicts with the king of Gerar[17] over the control of wells located between Gerar and Beersheba (Gen 21:25; 26:12–33).[18]

The attempt of Abram and his clan to live in the Bethel/Ai region in the Hill Country of Ephraim (Gen 13) seems to have been somewhat difficult. This may have been due to the fact that there was not enough grazing land in the area for his large herds because of extensive forests, or possibly because the Canaanites and Perizzites were hostile to him (13:7). In any case, Lot, Abram's nephew, chose to live in one of the cities located in the Jordan Valley while Abram remained in the hill country and Negev regions. The text indicates that the Jordan Valley was intensively cultivated at that time, in all probability being irrigated by ditches that conducted water from the powerful springs to the fields in the area. Although for a time Abram remained in the hill country, it does not seem that he or the other patriarchs spent a great deal of time in the region. Places like Shechem and Bethel/Ai were visited, altars built, Yahweh worshiped, and divine revelations received, and on one of the mountains in the "region of Moriah"—probably one of the mountains in the Jerusalem area[19]—Isaac was to have been sacrificed. Yet it appears that the major patriarchal encampment was in the (western) Negev.

The exception to this state of affairs was the patriarchal settlement close to Hebron in the hill country. This association with Hebron was to be expected, however, for throughout the ages Hebron was the contact point between the peoples of the Negev and the peoples of the hill country—the place where goods and services were bought and sold. At Hebron, Abraham purchased the cave of Machpelah (Gen 23), where ultimately Abraham and Sarah, Isaac and Rebecca, and Jacob and Leah were buried. Today, in the center of modern Hebron, the traditional burial sites of the patriarchs

are marked by a mosque and synagogue that are located in an old Crusader church that in turn was built within an enclosure wall that dates to the Herodian era (ca. 37–4 B.C.). Genesis 23:10 suggests that an actual city existed in Hebron during the days of Abraham, for it was in the city gate that he negotiated the purchase of the cave of Machpelah. To date, the city of Abraham's time has not been located, but the archaeological exploration of Hebron is only just beginning.[20]

Although Lot's choice of living in the well-watered Jordan Valley seemed logical from a human standpoint, he, in fact, faced a number of difficulties and twice had to be saved from death through the intervention of his uncle Abraham. For example, Genesis 14 relates how four kings from the north invaded the area and made war on the five kings of the plain who had revolted against their rule. The kings of the north

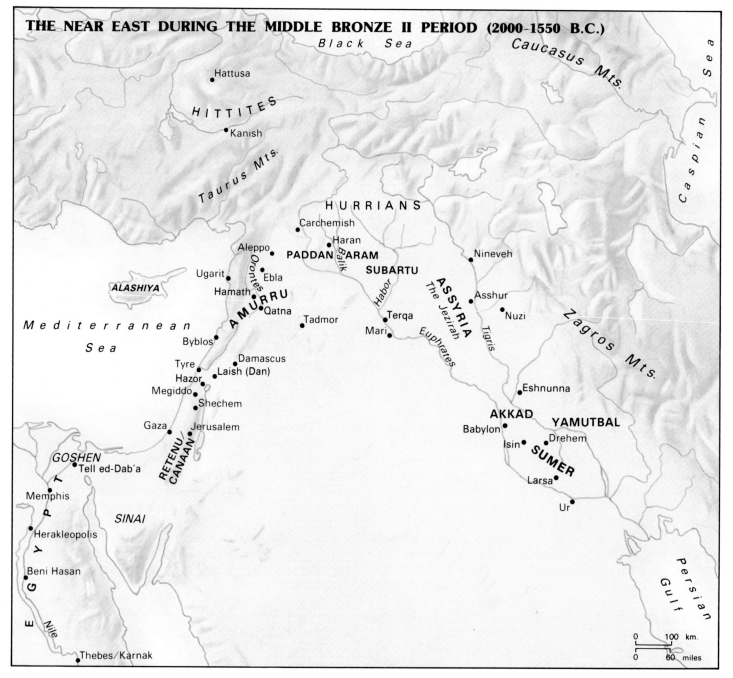

THE NEAR EAST DURING THE MIDDLE BRONZE II PERIOD (2000–1550 B.C.)

came from Shinar,[21] Ellasar,[22] Elam,[23] and Goiim.[24] Evidently their major objective was the conquest of the cities of Sodom, Gomorrah, Admah, Zeboiim, and Bela (i.e., Zoar).[25]

The four invading kings headed south along the Transjordanian Highway, defeating the Rephaite and Zuzite tribes in Gilead, the Emites in Moab, and the Horites in Mount Seir (Gen 14:5–6). The kings evidently continued south to El Paran before swinging northwestward into the Negev Highlands to En Mishpat, where they defeated the Amalekites (vv. 6–7).[26] Turning eastward, the four kings attacked and defeated the Amorites of Hazezon Tamar before initiating their major encounter with the five kings of the plain in the Valley of Siddim. This battle may have taken place in the salt badlands south of the Dead Sea or possibly in the area now covered by the southern third of the Dead Sea.[27] The defeated kings of the plain were taken captive and, along

with the booty, were carried off northwards as the invading kings returned to their homelands. Abram, together with his allies, pursued them as far as Dan and Hobah, rescuing Lot and the kings with whom he had been captured.[28] Upon Abram's return he met first with the king of Sodom in the "Valley of Shaveh (that is, the King's Valley)"[29] and then with "Melchizedek king of Salem" (v. 18).[30]

The second time Lot was delivered is recorded in Genesis 18–19, in the account of the destruction of Sodom and Gomorrah. These two cities, along with Zoar (the place to which Lot and his family fled to escape the destruction), had already been mentioned in Genesis 14. According to the internal biblical chronology followed here, the destruction of Sodom and Gomorrah took place about 2067 B.C. (i.e., toward the end of MB I [2200–2000 B.C.]). To date, no MB I sites with which any of the five cities could be identified have been discovered near the south end of the Dead Sea. Some have proposed that the cities are now buried under the south end of the Dead Sea; while this is possible, the recently receding waters of the sea have not revealed evidence of any ancient cities having been located there.

However, recent surveys and excavations along the Transjordanian foothills east and southeast of the Dead Sea have located five sites that date to the EB period (3150–2200 B.C.): Bab edh-Dhra, Numeira, Zoar, Feifa, and Khanazir (see p. 75). Some have wondered if these five sites could be the remains of the five cities mentioned in Genesis 14:2.[31] Given the current absolute dates attached to the various archaeological periods, this identification is difficult to maintain, for the only period during which these sites were all settled was the EB III period (ca. 2650–2350 B.C.), at least three hundred years prior to the date of the events mentioned in the Bible.[32] At this time, no sure identification of the five cities has been made.

Approximately one hundred years of Abraham's life were spent in the land of Canaan. At the time of his death (ca. 1991 B.C.) the country was moving from the "nomadic" MB I period into another "urban" age. The culture that was

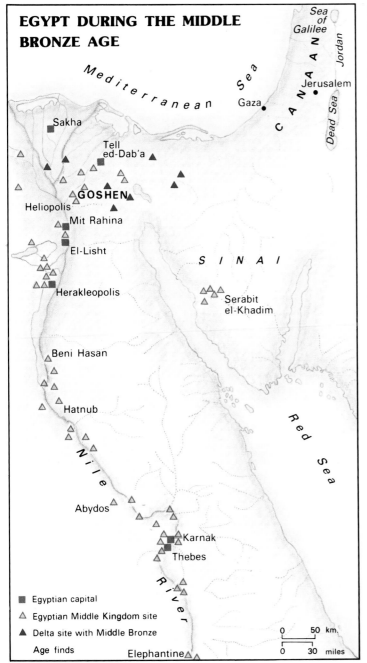

EGYPT DURING THE MIDDLE BRONZE AGE

■ Egyptian capital
△ Egyptian Middle Kingdom site
▲ Delta site with Middle Bronze
   Age finds

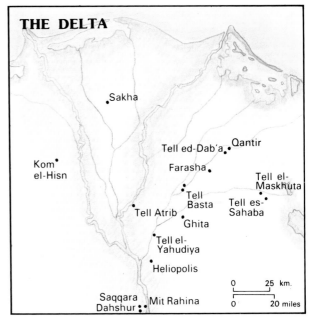

THE DELTA

established at the beginning of the MB II period (2000–1550 B.C.) actually continued well into the Late Bronze Age (1550–1200 B.C.). During the first part of the MB II period (MB IIA, 2000–1750 B.C.), Isaac and Jacob were active in the land, until 1876 B.C., when Jacob went down to Egypt. During the MB IIA period, new urban centers were built upon the ruins of earlier EB cities or over the temporary encampments of the peoples of the MB I period. Cities were now constructed with monumental city walls, gates, palaces, and temples.[33] Bronze replaced copper as the choice metal for making agricultural implements and weapons. New pottery forms were introduced, and evidence shows that contacts with Egypt now began to increase. Statues, scarabs, and other artifacts of Egyptian origin from the days of the 12th Dynasty are found at major sites in the Levant.

In Egypt, the period of the 12th Dynasty is known as the Middle Kingdom (2040–1786 B.C.). It was a time of great prosperity in a reunified Egypt. Pyramids were again being built (possibly as many as nine of them), administrative and bureaucratic structures were in place and functioning, and the arts and letters flourished; indeed, the Middle Kingdom is considered to be the "classical" period of Egyptian literature. Egypt, like Palestine, was turning from the inward confusion of the First Intermediate Period to a time of stability and even outward expansion. In Upper Egypt fortresses were built south of the second cataract to control the movement of the Nubians. Luxury goods, either originating in or transiting through Nubia, were shipped north. Commercial contacts with the Levant, especially with Byblos, were common, although the archaeological and literary evidence is not strong enough to indicate that Egypt "controlled" Canaan.

Egyptian contact with the Levant during this period is further reflected in the "Story of Sinuhe" (*ANET*, 18–23), a tale of an Egyptian who, upon the death of Amenemhet I (ca. 1962 B.C.), fled from Egypt to the Levant. He first journeyed

The stela of Hammurabi inscribed with laws.

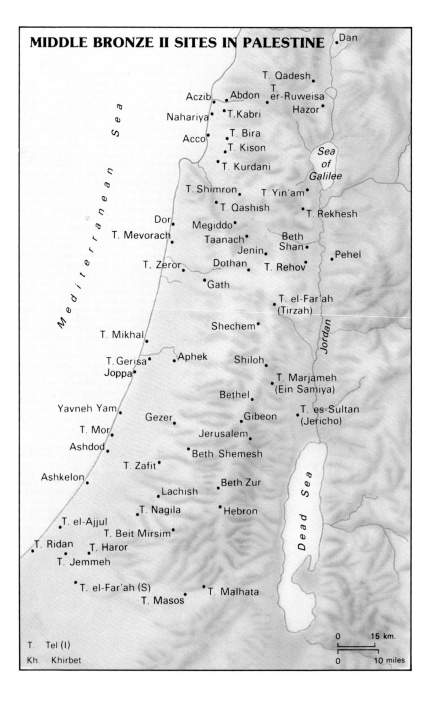

MIDDLE BRONZE II SITES IN PALESTINE

T.   Tel (l)
Kh. Khirbet

to the city of Byblos, on the coast of the Mediterranean Sea, but then turned inland toward Qedem, apparently located near the border of the eastern desert. He settled in the land of Araru (possibly in the region of Gilead or Bashan), where he was given land by a ruler of Upper Retenu,[34] and there he lived until he returned home to Egypt to die. The story describes how Sinuhe entertained and supported Egyptian messengers who passed through his country, and how he protected the frontier of his overlord's territory. It even gives a detailed description of the produce of the land of Retenu—figs, grapes, wine, honey, olives, fruit, barley, emmer-wheat, and cattle—a list that is strikingly similar to that found in Deuteronomy 8:8 with reference to the land of Canaan. In addition, Sinuhe's daily fare included bread, wine, cooked meat, roasted fowl, and milk. Although Sinuhe may have lived in a more "urban" context than his contemporaries Isaac and Jacob, it can be assumed that the patriarchs also enjoyed foodstuffs similar to those described in the story of Sinuhe.

In addition to the story of Sinuhe, a group of texts called the Execration Texts shed welcome light on life in the Levant during the MB IIA period (2000–1750 B.C.). These texts, discovered in Egypt, are divided into two groups. The earliest, written on bowls, consist of curses mentioning the names and locations of the persons execrated (cursed). Composed in the late twentieth or early nineteenth century B.C., the texts date to a time just prior to Jacob's descent into Egypt. About twenty towns and regions in the Levant are mentioned, including Jerusalem, Ashkelon, Beth Shan, Rehob, and Byblos. Since oftentimes several rulers are connected with one city or region, it seems that the common form of government at that time was the oligarchy.[35] The later Execration Texts, written on figurines that evidently represented captives, date to the late nineteenth century B.C. and thus to a time shortly after Jacob's descent into Egypt. These later texts mention some sixty-four geographical names from the Levant, and usually only one ruler is associated with each geographical name. The personal names from both groups of texts that can be analyzed are Amorite (West Semitic). Thus it seems that during the MB IIA period (2000–1750 B.C.) the ruling class in the Levant was of Semitic stock, as were probably the masses.

Two additional Egyptian inscriptions also illuminate MB IIA life in the Levant. The first is the Beni Hasan inscription (*ANET*, 229; *ANEP*, 3), which was found on the wall of the tomb of Khum-hotep III and dates to the sixth year of the king Sesostris II (ca. 1891 B.C.)[36]—only fifteen years before Jacob's descent into Egypt. The painting represents thirty-seven Asiatics bringing stibium, a substance used in the production of eye paint, to Egypt. The colorful dress of both the men and the women is well represented, as are their weapons, tools, and instruments. On the backs of the donkeys are bellows, or possibly copper ox-hide ingots, indicating that the company may also have included a group of traveling smiths. (It should be noted that at approximately this same time Joseph was sold to a caravan of Ishmaelites/Midianites who were transporting spices, balm, and myrrh from Gilead to Egypt [Gen 37:25, 36].) The picture is also a reminder that there were always Asiatics attempting to enter Egypt via her northeastern frontier for commercial purposes (as here), to avoid famine (as did Abram), or to find water

and pasturage for their flocks. To keep these Asiatics out, Amenemhet I (1991–1962 B.C.) dug a canal and built a corresponding "wall," not only to protect this northeastern frontier,[37] but also to provide water for the flocks of these peoples so that they would not have to enter Egypt to secure water.

The other relevant Egyptian text is a stele that dates to the reign of Sesostris III (1878–1843 B.C.). Titled "The Inscription of Khu-Sebek, Called Djaa," it briefly mentions an Egyptian military campaign to the foreign country of "Sek-mem" (= Shechem?), which, along with Retenu, fell to the Egyptians (*ANET*, 230). This brief portion of the inscription is suggestive of Egyptian activities in the Levant, but since the kings of Egypt from the Middle Kingdom have left no direct record of those activities, this inscription does not provide enough evidence to conclude any more than that this particular campaign was a limited, punative raid into Retenu.

According to the biblical data, Jacob and his family moved to Egypt in 1876 B.C., which would place this event early in the reign of Sesostris III (1878–1843 B.C.). Unfortunately, there are no Egyptian documents that make direct reference to the 430-year Israelite sojourn in Egypt, but the general features of Israel's life in Egypt can nevertheless still be outlined. According to Genesis 47:4, Jacob's family settled in the eastern delta of the Nile, in the agriculturally rich land of Goshen, where they evidently remained during their long stay in Egypt (cf. Exod 8:22 and 9:26). Although political stability was maintained in Egypt during the 12th Dynasty, conditions began to deteriorate during the 13th Dynasty (1786–1633 B.C.). There were more than fifty different "rulers" during the 154 years of the 13th Dynasty, and by the end of the period Nubia, to the south, was becoming more independent. In the western delta a rival 14th Dynasty (1786–1603 B.C.) was established, which boasted some seventy-six "kings" in 184 years.

During the 13th Dynasty, more and more Asiatics infiltrated the eastern delta until they became powerful enough to establish what are now known as the 15th and 16th dynasties (1674–1558 B.C.). This was the era of the "Hyksos" domination of the eastern delta; during this time their control occasionally even extended upstream along the Nile. These Asiatic rulers of Egypt were called "rulers of foreign countries" by the native Egyptians.[38] The Hyksos kings were evidently Amorites (West Semites) who had moved into the eastern delta from Asia. They had come from the Levant, where numerous city-states had been established by their compatriots.

During the second part of the Middle Bronze period (MB IIB, 1750–1550 B.C.) in Canaan, old cities were rebuilt and a number of new urban centers were established.[39] These city-states were defended by glacis (sloping ramps built of packed earth, stone, and plaster) and dry moats. Temple and palace architecture is well-known from the excavations at Hazor, Megiddo, Shechem, and other sites, indicating a high cultural level. The small finds of gold, silver, ivory, alabaster, etc. also indicate a great measure of prosperity in Canaan at this time. Militarily, the most important development was the introduction of the horse-drawn battle chariot. The charioteers, called *maryannu*, comprised a new social class that had to be reckoned with. These charioteers probably formed the power base on which the various city-states maintained

Wall painting from a tomb at Beni Hasan, c.1891 B.C., depicting a caravan of Asiatics.

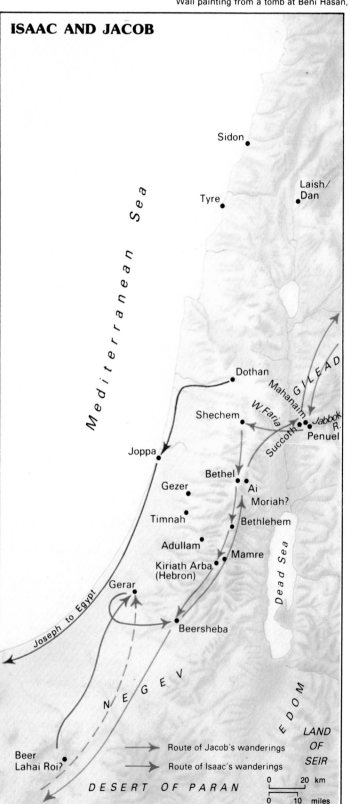

ISAAC AND JACOB

Route of Jacob's wanderings
Route of Isaac's wanderings

0   20 km
0   10 miles

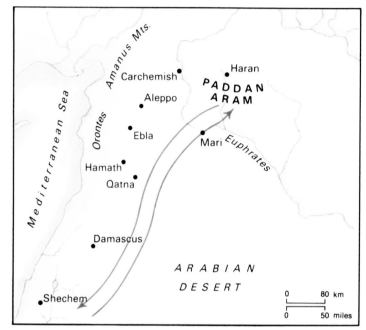

their existence. Besides typical cities built on tells, large enclosures were built in Canaan, Syria, and the eastern Nile delta. The purpose of these enclosures is disputed and may have changed over time, but initially some may have provided protected storage areas for chariots, horses, and related gear. The wide geographical distribution of similar architectural remains, pottery, defensive works, and large enclosures indicates continuing contacts between the regions of the Levant and Egypt.

During the MB II period there were also extensive contacts between Canaan and northern and southern Mesopotamia. The northern Mesopotamian connections are well-documented by information contained in the cuneiform tablets that were discovered at the city of Mari on the bank of the Euphrates River. These 20,000 tablets, dating to the late nineteenth and early eighteenth centuries B.C., shed welcome light on many aspects of life in the Ancient Near East during this period.[40] In particular, conditions in the Euphrates-Balik-Habur River region are described in detail—the very region where Jacob lived with his uncle Laban for some twenty years (= Paddan Aram). One Mari tablet actually refers to the "men of *Ki-na-aḫ-um*"—which is one of the earliest usages of "Canaan" as a geographical term.[41]

In addition, Canaanite cities (including Hazor and Laish [Dan]) are mentioned in the Mari texts. Of these, pride of place goes to Hazor, which to date has been found in seven Mari documents.[42] It is evident that Hazor was a very important city, for its ambassadors were found in royal courts all over the Near East. In addition, large quantities of tin were shipped to Hazor, which indicates that it was a major producer of bronze (one part tin, ten parts copper). The prominence of Hazor during this period is also seen in its sheer size—175 acres (71 ha.)—and from the rich finds discovered at the site.[43] Malamat is probably correct in noting that the statement "Hazor had been the head of all these kingdoms" (Josh 11:10) refers back to this period.[44]

The other major Palestinian city mentioned in the Mari texts is Laish (= biblical Leshem = Dan; Josh 19:47; Judges 18:29). It is mentioned along with Hazor as a recipient of deliveries of tin.[45] It should be noted that Wari-taldu, the ruler of Laish (Dan), bears a Hurrian, not an Amorite, name—one of several indications of the growing importance of a Hurrian element in the Levant. In fact, many of the rulers of city-states in the late MB II and Late Bronze (LB) ages, as well as some of the later kings of the Hyksos dynasties in Egypt, bore Hurrian names. The Hurrian element in the Levant became so important that at times Egyptians referred to the country as "Hurru Land."[46] Thus it seems that the Hurrian element in the population, which was growing during the MB II period, became quite prominent during the LB Age.

A good portion of Israel's stay in Egypt took place during the turbulent Second Intermediate Period (1786–1558 B.C.) and it may very well be that the "new king, who did not know about Joseph" (Exod 1:8) was a Hyksos. This would mean that the oppression of the Israelites began during the Hyksos reign. Additional support for this thesis is found in the statement that "the Israelites have become much too numerous for us" (1:9), which would fit much better in the mouth of a Hyksos king—limited in number as the Asiatics were—than in the mouth of a native Egyptian ruler.

The end of the MB II period (1550 B.C.) is not marked by any great cultural break in the Levant but rather by a historical event—the expulsion of the Hyksos from Egypt. The weak native 17th Dynasty (1650–1558 B.C.), which had ruled a portion of Upper Egypt from Thebes, was replaced by the 18th Dynasty, whose first king, Ahmose, drove the Hyksos from the country. Egyptian texts describe battles in the eastern Nile delta, the siege of the Hyksos capital of Avaris (= Tell el-Dab'a?), and the driving of the Hyksos rulers out of Egypt and back into Canaan (*ANET*, 230–34; 553–55). Ahmose besieged the Palestinian city of Sharuhen[47] for three years and, after conquering it, established an Egyptian base there at the southwest entrance to the land of Canaan. This was the area from which later Egyptian kings of the powerful New Kingdom (1558–1085 B.C.) launched their conquests of Canaan, increasingly bringing the land into the Egyptian sphere of influence.

At the end of the MB II period, Israel found herself in bondage in Egypt. She had increased in number, yet she did not possess the land promised to Abraham. She had been in Egypt for over three hundred years, but she was anything but a nation, and God, who had promised to be with her, seemed remote. In view of Israel's plight, the glowing promises given to Abraham, Isaac, and Jacob at the beginning of this era may have seemed to many to be incapable of fulfillment; yet it would be during the next phase of Near Eastern history, in the face of the most powerful nation on earth, that God would act decisively for his people.

Middle Bronze Age (c.1950 B.C.) city gate at Dan; mud brick arch with entrance way filled with dirt.

85

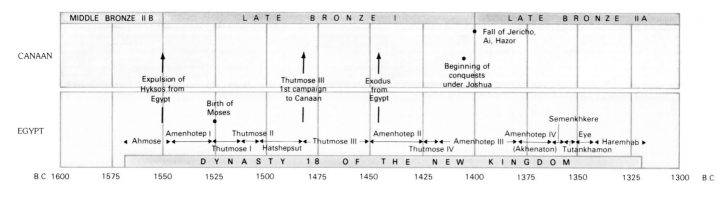

Exodus and Conquest

The Exodus from Egypt

One of the most important configurations of events in the Old Testament centers around the exodus from Egypt, the revelation of God's law at Sinai, and the establishment of Israel in the Promised Land. The reader of the record of God's acting in history and his revelation to his people cannot fail to be impressed with the wealth of historical and geographical data found in the biblical text. Since the Exodus, the wilderness wanderings, and the initial conquest of Canaan (Exod–Josh 11) form a continuous narrative covering approximately forty-five years, these events will be treated together in this chapter, while the settlement of the Israelites in the land (Josh 12–Judges) will be discussed in the next chapter.

According to the chronology adhered to in this atlas, the Exodus and conquest occurred at the end of the archaeological period known as the Late Bronze I Age (= LB I; 1550–1400 B.C.). In Egypt, the Israelites were suffering from

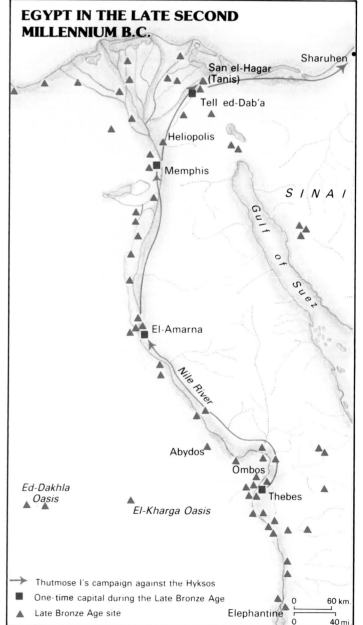

EGYPT IN THE LATE SECOND MILLENNIUM B.C.

→ Thutmose I's campaign against the Hyksos
■ One-time capital during the Late Bronze Age
▲ Late Bronze Age site

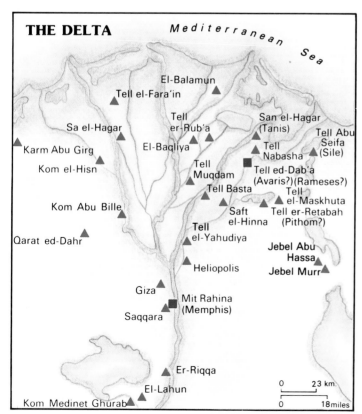

THE DELTA

oppression at the beginning of the New Kingdom, an Egyptian era that included the 18th, 19th, and 20th dynasties (1567–1085 B.C.). In particular, the first half of the 18th Dynasty coincided with the biblical events under consideration.

The first king of the 18th Dynasty, Ahmose (1570–1546 B.C.), not only unified Egypt but also expelled the Hyksos from the eastern delta. In addition, he pushed Egypt's northeastern frontier eastward across Sinai to Sharuhen and its southern boundary southward, up the Nile to the second cataract. Although not much is known about his immediate successor, Amenhotep I, the next king, Thutmose I (1525–1512 B.C.), is said to have conducted a military campaign through Canaan into Syria, even reaching the Euphrates River (*ANET*, 234, 239–40)! This was actually as far north as Egypt would expand during this period, for later kings would fight in Canaan and Syria, but not beyond the Euphrates. The purpose of the campaign of Thutmose I is not explicitly stated, but given the archaeologically attested destruction of many MB II sites in southwestern Canaan, in the hill country,[1] and elsewhere,[2] it seems as if he was trying to break the power base of the hated Hyksos and their allies. At about this same time a new political power was emerging in northern Mesopotamia—the kingdom of Mitanni. For the next one hundred years, Egypt and Mitanni would vie for control of the northern Levant. By the end of the reign of Thutmose I, Egypt had conquered territory stretching from Syria in the northeast to the fourth cataract of the Nile in the south. Egypt's territory had never before been so extensive, and it would never be again. From Nubia in the south, gold and luxury goods flowed northward, while Egypt imported cedar and other important forest and agricultural products from Canaan and Lebanon to the northeast.

During the reigns of Thutmose II and Queen Hatshepsut (1512–1482 B.C.), Egypt seems to have lost ground in Asia, for in 1482 B.C., at the beginning of Thutmose III's reign (1504–1450 B.C. [he was co-regent with Hatshepsut from 1504–1482 B.C., when at her death he became sole ruler]), he departed on the first of some seventeen campaigns into the Levant. His first expedition in 1482 B.C. was by far his most important, and in it he was able to secure control of much of the southern Levant.[3]

The first phase of his campaign took him from Sile (near the present-day Suez Canal) across northern Sinai to Gaza—covering a distance of 130 miles (210 km.) in nine or ten days. Although in his annals Gaza is called "That-Which-the-Ruler-Seized" (*ANET*, 235), in all probability it was already in Egyptian hands, for the day after his arrival he immediately, without laying siege to it, headed northward to Yaham. This distance of 75 miles (120 km.) was covered in eleven or twelve days, a bit slower than his trek across northern Sinai, yet fast enough to indicate that he met with little resistance along the way. Since the enemy was headquartered at Megiddo, it was necessary to cross the formidable barrier of Mount Carmel (650 to 1,790 ft. [200 to 545 m.]). At Yaham, Thutmose held a war council to consider which of the three passes he would take across the mountain: the Zephath-Jokneam, the Aruna-Megiddo, or the Taanach pass. In spite of advice to the contrary, he, in his wisdom, chose the narrower, more difficult, and more direct route from Aruna to Megiddo. Fortunately for the invading

Egyptians, the Canaanites had split their chariot forces, stationing them northwest and southeast of Megiddo. Thus the Egyptians were able to emerge from the pass and set up camp near Megiddo unmolested. The next day the Egyptians engaged the Canaanites in battle. The Canaanites were thoroughly routed, and the survivors fled to Megiddo, where they were pulled up on ropes over the city wall into the fortress. After a siege of seven months the city was conquered, and considerable booty, including 924 chariots, was taken. The leader of the Canaanite coalition seems to have been the king of Kedesh (i.e., Kedesh on the Orontes), who had been joined by city-state rulers of Canaan, as well as by forces from Naharin, Mitanni, Hurru, and Kode. By capturing Megiddo, Thutmose III was able to defeat and capture the leaders of the revolt and was, in effect, able to take control of most of the southern Levant without having to lay siege to each individual city. No wonder a scribe wrote that "the capturing of Megiddo is the capturing of a thousand towns" (*ANET*, 237). This is not to say that no other cities were attacked and possibly destroyed, but the basic victory had been won at Megiddo. Mopping-up operations continued into the reign of Thutmose III, and it was not until his sixth campaign that Kedesh on the Orontes was actually taken (*ANET*, 239).

Three copies of the topographical text that commemorates Thutmose's victory have been discovered (*ANET*, 242–43). Two of these texts, probably composed soon after his first campaign, list 119 towns and regions that were now under his control, while the third lists 231! These rosters are the largest listings of geographical names from the Levant, of which approximately half have been identified with some certainty.[4] From the lists it is apparent that Gaza, Kumidi, and Sumur served as Egyptian administrative centers, and the areas of Egyptian involvement included the coastal plain, the Jezreel Valley, Lower Galilee, the Beqa Valley, and, in Transjordan, the Damascus and Bashan regions. It appears that Egypt was primarily interested in controlling the International Coastal Highway and the Transjordanian Highway, as well as the latter's connecting routes to the Mediterranean via the Jezreel Valley and/or Galilee. Conspicuous by their absence are cities in the Hill Country of Judah, Ephraim, and Manasseh—evidently indicating that these regions were sparsely settled at this time and that the centers that did exist did not pose any immediate threat to Egyptian interests in the area.

The other sixteen campaigns of Thutmose III are not nearly as well-documented as the first. The more important of them were the fifth, sixth, seventh, and eighth, while the remaining campaigns were evidently punitive raids and/or shows of force in the region.

Thutmose III's successor (and for a short period co-regent), Amenhotep II (1450–1425 B.C.), conducted three campaigns into the Levant. The descriptions of these campaigns (*ANET*, 245–48) seem to indicate that, although early in his reign the battles were fought in the northern Levant, by his ninth year he was fighting battles in the region of the Sea of Galilee—a clear indication that he had been losing ground in the area. Indeed, after his ninth year, Egyptian military activity in the Levant was very limited until the days of Seti I (1318–1304 B.C.). However, internally Egypt was very prosperous and stable during the latter part of Amenhotep II's reign and during the reigns of Thutmose IV and Amenhotep III (1425–1379 B.C.). It seems that Egypt had come to terms with its northern enemy, Mitanni, for both Thutmose IV and Amenhotep III married Mitannian princesses—evidencing good relations between the two nations. This new alliance may have been forged to meet the threat common to both, namely, the growing power of the Hittites in Anatolia and in Syria.

The oppression of the Israelites that had begun during the days of the Hyksos dynasties (1674–1558 B.C.) continued and probably intensified during the early rule of the 18th Dynasty (Exod 1:13–22). Although not all aspects of Israel's oppression are known in detail, the text indicates that "they built Pithom and Rameses as store cities for Pharaoh" (v. 11). Rameses was evidently in or near the land of Goshen, for at the time of the Exodus it was the starting point of the Israelite departure from Egypt (Exod 12:37; Num 33:3, 5). The exact location of Rameses is problematic. The older identification with Tanis now has to be abandoned because of the lack of early archaeological remains. The best candidate seems to be Tell el-Dab'a, located near modern Qantir. This huge mound has extensive Hyksos remains and may have been the Hyksos capital of Avaris. The use of the name Rameses is not attested this early for the site, so its appearance in the Bible may be due to the work of a copyist who "updated" the text for his readers.[5] The other city mentioned in the Bible, Pithom, can be identified either with Tell er-Retabah or Tell el-Maskhuta.[6]

Although a considerable amount of geographical data is presented in connection with the Exodus and the trek to the land of Canaan, the exact identification of many places and regions mentioned remains unknown. The major reason for this is the lack of continuity among the populace of the desert-wilderness regions of the Sinai peninsula, the Negev, and parts of southern Transjordan. Without this continuity of population, the preservation of ancient place names is almost impossible. The other difficulty is that archaeologists have not discovered any artifactual remains that can be attributed to the Israelites in those regions through which they traveled.[7] This, however, is somewhat expected, for a nomadic people, living in tents and using animal skins instead of pottery for containers, would leave few permanent remains behind. Thus scholars are divided in their opinions as to the location even of major landmarks such as the Red Sea and Mount Sinai.[8] Har-El noted that there were nine different proposals for the location of the Red Sea or Reed Sea—including three lakes near the Mediterranean Sea, four lakes along the line of the present-day Suez Canal, as well as the Gulf of Suez and the Gulf of Elath.[9] He also counted twelve different candidates for Mount Sinai: five in the southern part of the peninsula, four in the north, one in the center, one in Midian (Saudi Arabia), and another in Edom (southern Transjordan).

In spite of these uncertainties, a few suggestions can be made regarding the Exodus and wanderings. After leaving Rameses (Tell el-Dab'a), the Israelites journeyed to Succoth (possibly Tell el-Maskhuta in the Wadi Tumilat). It is well to note that for fear of their becoming discouraged because of war, "God did not lead them by the way of the land of the Philistines" (Exod 13:17 NASB). This well-known route across northern Sinai from Sile to Gaza was the one

Life along the Nile River.

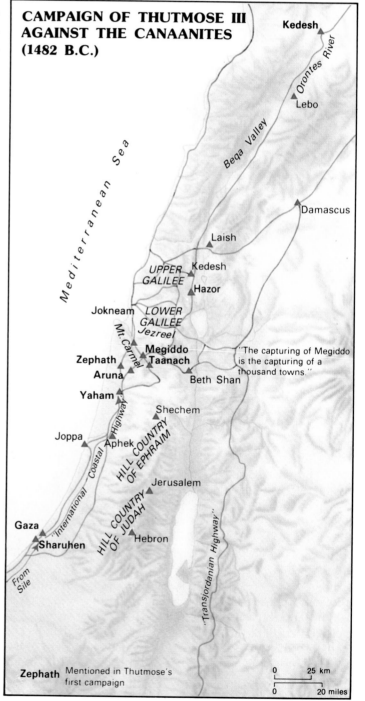

CAMPAIGN OF THUTMOSE III AGAINST THE CANAANITES (1482 B.C.)

Kedesh
Orontes River
Beqa Valley
Lebo
Damascus
Mediterranean Sea
Laish
UPPER GALILEE
Kedesh
Hazor
Jokneam
LOWER GALILEE
Jezreel
Mt. Carmel
Megiddo
Zephath
Taanach
"The capturing of Megiddo is the capturing of a thousand towns."
Aruna
Beth Shan
Yaham
Shechem
International Coastal Highway
Joppa
Aphek
HILL COUNTRY OF EPHRAIM
Jerusalem
Gaza
HILL COUNTRY OF JUDAH
Hebron
"Transjordanian Highway"
Sharuhen
From Sile

Zephath Mentioned in Thutmose's first campaign

0   25 km
0   20 miles

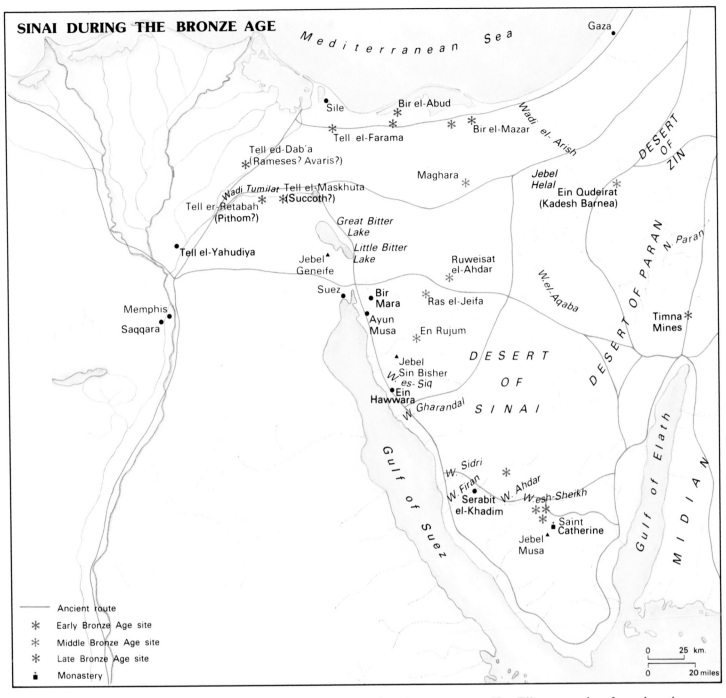

SINAI DURING THE BRONZE AGE

Mediterranean Sea

Gaza

Sile

Bir el-Abud

Tell el-Farama

Bir el-Mazar

Wadi el-Arish

DESERT OF ZIN

Tell ed-Dab'a (Rameses? Avaris?)

Maghara

Jebel Helal

Ein Qudeirat (Kadesh Barnea)

Wadi Tumilat Tell el-Maskhuta (Succoth?)

Tell er-Retabah (Pithom?)

Great Bitter Lake

Little Bitter Lake

Tell el-Yahudiya

Jebel Geneife

Ruweisat el-Ahdar

DESERT OF PARAN

N. Paran

Suez

Bir Mara

Ras el-Jeifa

W. el-Aqaba

Memphis

Saqqara

Ayun Musa

En Rujum

DESERT OF SINAI

DESERT OF PARAN

Timna Mines

Jebel Sin Bisher

W. es-Siq

Ein Hawwara

W. Gharandal

Gulf of Suez

Gulf of Elath

W. Sidri

W. Firan

W. Ahdar

W. esh-Sheikh

MIDIAN

Serabit el-Khadim

Saint Catherine

Jebel Musa

— Ancient route

* Early Bronze Age site

* Middle Bronze Age site

* Late Bronze Age site

▪ Monastery

0   25 km.

0   20 miles

Thutmose III and Amenhotep II had used so effectively on their frequent campaigns to Canaan, and it must have been well fortified by Egyptian troops.[10] Thus a northern route for the Exodus seems excluded. Since the Israelites were led by the "way of the wilderness to the Red Sea" (v. 18), it appears that they were heading southeast toward modern Suez.[11] The location of Etham ("fort" in Egyptian), Migdol ("fort" in Semitic), Baal Zephon, and Pi Hahiroth are problematic. Har-El's suggestion that Hahiroth refers to the low ground between Jebel Geneife and the Bitter Lakes is plausible but not certain. Etham and Migdol could be any one of a number of Egyptian forts located near the present-day Suez Canal.[12]

On the next stage of their journey the Israelites crossed the Red Sea. Since the Hebrew text literally means the "Reed Sea," many scholars look for a location in the lake/marsh areas that used to exist in the region through which the Suez Canal now passes. Har-El's suggestion for a location near the junction of the Great and Little Bitter Lakes is as plausible as any.[13] According to nineteenth-century travelers, the water at that spot was not very deep, and they even mention that at times the depth of the water decreased when the wind shifted. It is interesting to note that according to the text the "Lord drove the sea back with a strong east wind" (Exod 14:21). The location of Marah, where the water was bitter (15:23), and Elim, where there were twelve springs and seventy palm trees (v. 27), depends on where one locates Mount Sinai. If Har-El's suggestion of Jebel Sin Bisher is accepted, then the identifications of Marah and Elim with Bir Mara ("bitter well" in Arabic) and Ayun Musa ("the spring of Moses") are plausible. If the more traditional site of Sinai at Jebel Musa is maintained, then identifications of Marah and Elim with Ein Hawwara and Gharandal are also possible.

Mountains near Jebel Musa (Mount Sinai?).

Wadi Firan near Firan Oasis in southern Sinai

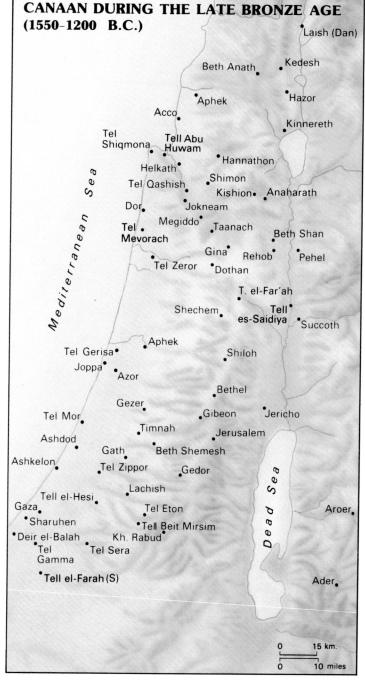

CANAAN DURING THE LATE BRONZE AGE (1550–1200 B.C.)

Laish (Dan)

Beth Anath

Kedesh

Aphek

Hazor

Acco

Kinnereth

Tel Shiqmona

Tell Abu Huwam

Hannathon

Helkath

Shimon

Tel Qashish

Kishion

Anaharath

Dor

Jokneam

Megiddo

Taanach

Beth Shan

Tel Mevorach

Gina

Rehob

Pehel

Tel Zeror

Dothan

T. el-Far'ah

Shechem

Tell es-Saidiya

Succoth

Aphek

Tel Gerisa

Shiloh

Joppa

Azor

Bethel

Gezer

Tel Mor

Gibeon

Jericho

Ashdod

Timnah

Jerusalem

Gath

Beth Shemesh

Ashkelon

Tel Zippor

Gedor

Lachish

Gaza

Tell el-Hesi

Tel Eton

Aroer

Sharuhen

Tell Beit Mirsim

Deir el-Balah

Kh. Rabud

Tel Gamma

Tel Sera

Tell el-Farah (S)

Ader

Mediterranean Sea

Dead Sea

0   15 km.

0   10 miles

The identification of Mount Sinai (Horeb) with Jebel Musa ("Mount Moses") is based on Christian tradition dating back to the fourth century A.D., about 1,750 years after the event. There, during the Byzantine period (A.D. 324–640), the desert monastery of St. Catherine was established. Although the Greek Orthodox monks today point out the very site of the giving of the Law, the place where the golden calf was erected, the plain where the Israelites camped, the site of the burning bush, etc., Har-El's suggested identification of Mount Sinai with Jebel Sin Bisher deserves careful attention.[14] Indeed, its location agrees with some of the biblical data. For example, it is located approximately three days' journey from Egypt (Exod 3:18; 5:3; 8:27) at a desert junction where there are fair supplies of water; possibly the Amalekites fought with Israel for control of this junction and the water sources (Exod 17). It is close to Egypt on the road that led directly from Midian to Egypt (the modern Darb el-Hagg, p. 61), and thus it would make a plausible location for the burning bush incident. Moses could have been bringing Jethro's sheep along this road in order to use the water and pasturage found on the eastern edge of the Nile delta (see above, p. 83, for the canal) when the Lord appeared to him in the burning bush. This is said to have taken place near the mountain where he would later worship him (3:1). Since it is reasonable to assume that Moses used the way of the wilderness on his return to Egypt, the meeting of Moses and Aaron at the "mountain of God" could well have been at this spot (Exod 4:27).

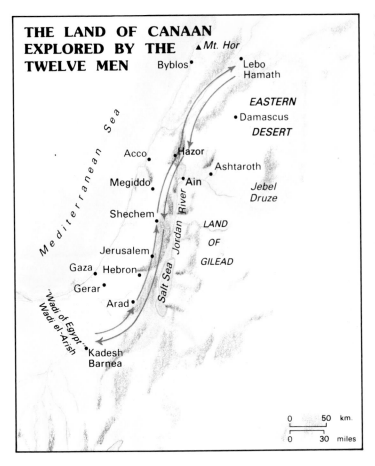

THE LAND OF CANAAN EXPLORED BY THE TWELVE MEN

After camping at Mount Sinai for about a year, the Israelites set out for the Kadesh Barnea region. This trek normally took eleven days (Deut 1:2), which fits the identification of Mount Sinai with Jebel Sin Bisher better than the identification with Jebel Musa. On their way they passed from the Desert of Sinai through the Desert of Paran to the Desert of Zin near Kadesh (Num 10:12; 33:36). These "deserts," or better, "wildernesses,"[15] are difficult to locate with accuracy, although the Desert of Paran[16] seems to have been large, covering most of the southern and central sections of the Sinai peninsula, while the Desert of Zin was evidently located to the north of this.[17] Along the way to Kadesh, several judgments of God befell the Israelites—at Taberah (Num 11:1–3), Kibroth Hattaavah (vv. 4–35), and Hazeroth (11:35–12:16). None of these places has been identified with certainty, for the place names have not been preserved in the area, although historical geographers—in the absence of better candidates—sometimes attach these names to the larger oases along the route.[18]

From the Kadesh region twelve men were sent to "explore the land of Canaan" (Num 13:2). They went up through the Negev[19] into the hill country, traveling as far north as Rehob and Lebo Hamath (13:21). It is clear that the "land of Canaan" is presented as a geopolitical entity with definable boundaries. These boundaries, which are described in Numbers 34:1–12 and Ezekiel 47:13–20, can be traced with some degree of accuracy. The southern boundary[20] stretched from the southeastern corner of the Salt Sea westward, ran south of Kadesh Barnea to the "Wadi of Egypt" (= W. el-Arish), and ended "at the [Mediterranean] Sea" (Num 34:3–5; Josh 15:2–4; Ezek 47:19). The Mediterranean Sea formed

the western boundary, but the northern one is a bit more difficult to define accurately (Num 34:6–9; Ezek 47:15–17, 20). The key point necessary to determine its proper line is "Lebo Hamath" (= "the entrance to Hamath [a country in Syria]"). This frequently mentioned northern point (twelve times; see the Gazetteer) has been well-identified with Lebweh, located in the Beqa Valley.[21] Geographical references that occur in the texts both before and after Lebo Hamath are surmised to be found near a general east-west line that runs through Lebweh. The boundary is described as running out into the eastern desert, where it swings to the south to include the Jebel Druze region, before turning westward to the hills at the southeast corner of the Sea of Kinnereth (Num 34:11). From there, the border followed the Jordan River south to the Salt Sea,[22] back to its starting point.

Since the account of the exploration of Canaan gives prominence to the Hebron region and the nearby Valley of Eshcol (Num 13:22–23), it is probable that the "spies" traveled the old patriarchal road, the "Ridge Route." Although other cities are not mentioned by name, they are described as being "fortified and very large" (v. 28). The land itself is described as being very fruitful, as evidenced by the large cluster of grapes, the pomegranates, and the figs that the spies brought back to camp with them (vv. 23–24). In addition, the land was described as flowing "with milk and honey" (v. 27), symbols of bounty and abundance.

Because of the people's disobedience (failing to enter the land at Yahweh's command), they were consigned to forty years of "wandering" in the "desert." After an abortive attempt was made to enter the land of Canaan (Num 14:39–45), the Israelites began their bleak wilderness experience. It seems that they spent much of their time in the desolate region between Kadesh and Ezion Geber (near/on the Red Sea [33:36]), in all probability camping near Kadesh, in the western Negev Highlands as well as in eastern Sinai.

At the end of this period the Israelites again found themselves in the Kadesh Barnea area. It was there that Miriam, Moses' sister, died (Num 20:1). It was there that Moses was disobedient to God's command, striking the rock twice when he should have spoken to it (vv. 2–13), and it was from Kadesh that Moses requested the king of Edom to allow the Israelites to pass through his land along the "King's Highway" (v. 17; in this passage possibly to be identified with today's Darb es-Sultan; see p. 51). Since this request was made from Kadesh, it is evident that the Edomites had extended their control from the Transjordanian Mountains westward, across the Arabah Valley into the Negev Highlands. In spite of Israel's promise to stay on the highway and to purchase water (vv. 17–19), their request was refused. Setting out from Kadesh, the Israelites arrived at Mount Hor, where Aaron died and Eleazar was appointed in his place (vv. 22–29). Although Mount Hor cannot be identified with certainty, Aharoni's suggestion of Imaret el-Khureisheh,[23] near Kadesh on the border of Edom, is much more plausible than the traditional spot, Jebel Nebi Harun, located in Transjordan.

After these events the Israelites attempted to enter Canaan from the south (Num 21:1–3). At first they were defeated by the king of Arad, who lived in the Negev, but then, after praying to God, the Israelites were victorious in their second encounter. In spite of this victory they decided not to enter Canaan from this direction; instead, they followed a circuitous path to the south and east. Their major route seems to have taken them south along the "way of the Red Sea" (= Darb el-Gaza) to Elath and Ezion Geber, then northward around (i.e., east of) the lands of Edom and Moab (Judges 11:18), traveling on what was called the "King's Highway" (Num 21:22; here the eastern branch of the Transjordanian Highway). From the "Desert of Kedemoth" (Deut 2:26) messengers were sent to Sihon, the king of the Amorites (who lived in Heshbon), requesting permission to pass, from east to west, through his territory to the Jordan River (v. 29). Sihon, who refused this request, marched to Jahaz, where he fought against and was defeated by the Israelites (Num 21:23–24). Having subdued Sihon, the children of Israel took possession of the land that he had controlled, from the Arnon River in the south to the Jabbok in the north (Num 21:24–25: Deut 2:36; Judges 11:22).

Some commentators believe that another "wave" of Israelites took a more westerly route, actually passing through Edomite and Moabite territory. The validity of accepting the use of such a route depends upon the certainty of the identification of certain towns—including Zalmonah, Punon, Oboth, and Iye Abarim (Num 21:1, 11; 33:41–44). But since none of these has been identified with complete certainty (even Punon's location can be challenged), it seems best to hold to a single, more easterly route rather than supposing a second route directly through Edom and Moab, for the text does not give any indication of direct conflict with them as the result of an invasion.[24]

Ever since Nelson Glueck's exploration of southern Transjordan (1932 to 1947), many have believed that an "occupation gap" in the area lasted from the nineteenth to the thirteenth centuries B.C.[25] If this were true, then the Israelites could not have encountered a sedentary population in the area (as the biblical account seems to imply). However, recent excavations and surface surveys have shown that this "occupation gap" really did not exist, for some MB II (2000–1550 B.C.) and LB (1550–1200 B.C.) sites have been located.[26] To be sure, the number and size of MB II and LB remains are not as extensive as those during some of the previous and later periods, but the "occupation gap" has been filled in recent years, and it is no longer necessary to doubt Israel's encounters with the kings of Edom and Moab and with Sihon, the king of the Amorites.

After securing Sihon's former territory, the Israelites marched north on the "way to Bashan." Og, the king of Bashan, who lived in Ashtaroth (Deut 1:4), came out and battled Israel at Edrei. The forces of this "giant" (3:11) were defeated, and his territory from the Jabbok River to Mount Hermon—including sixty cities as well as Gilead and Bashan—came under Israelite control (Num 21:33–35; Deut 3:4–11).

Additional events and speeches that occurred during Israel's encampment in the Plains of Moab, located between Beth Jeshimoth and Abel Shittim (Num 22:1; 33:49), are recorded in Numbers 21 through Deuteronomy 34. There the Israelites were blessed, rather than cursed by the prophet Balaam (Num 22–25), and it was there that the illustrious career of Moses drew to a close as he preached his last sermons before ascending Mount Nebo to die (Deut 34).

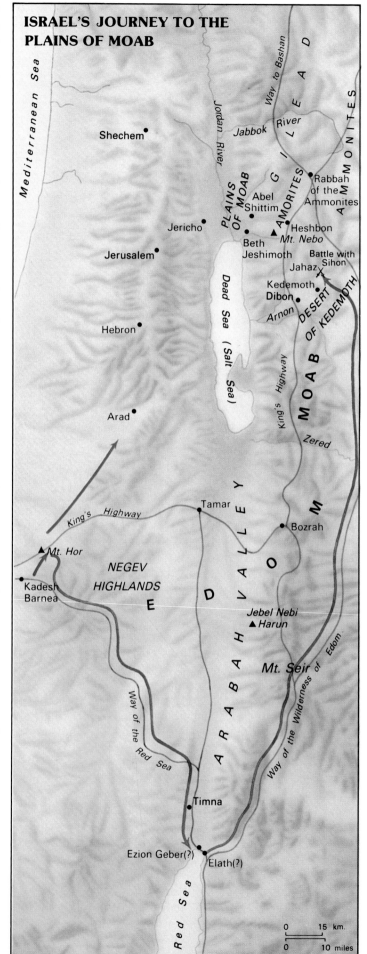

ISRAEL'S JOURNEY TO THE PLAINS OF MOAB

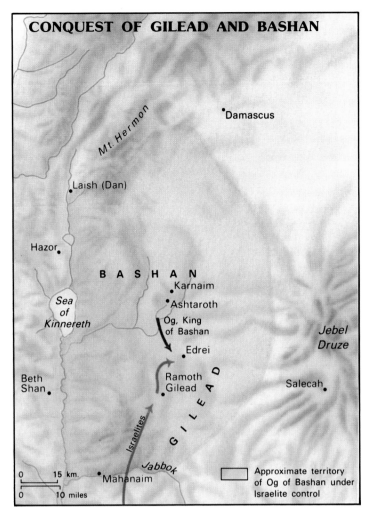

CONQUEST OF GILEAD AND BASHAN

Damascus

Mt. Hermon

Laish (Dan)

Hazor

B A S H A N

Karnaim

Ashtaroth

Og, King
of Bashan

Sea
of
Kinnereth

Edrei

Jebel
Druze

Beth
Shan

Ramoth
Gilead

G I L E A D

Salecah

Israelites

Jabbok

Mahanaim

0   15 km.

0   10 miles

Approximate territory
of Og of Bashan under
Israelite control

The Conquest of Canaan

After the death of Moses, Joshua led the Israelites into Canaan and directed the initial conquests in the land (Josh 1–12). Although the account is rather detailed, it should be remembered that in all probability, not every military event that took place under Joshua's leadership was recorded; rather, a number of key events were selected.[27] The initial phase of the conquest could have begun as early as 1406 B.C., forty years after the exit from Egypt. This initial phase probably did not take longer than seven years, although Joshua apparently lived until 1375 B.C.

Under Joshua's leadership Israel crossed the Jordan River at one of the fords located east of Jericho. The text indicates that this event took place in the spring of the year, for the Jordan was overflowing its banks after the winter rains and the (barley?) harvest was taking place (Josh 3:15); also, the Passover (March–April) was celebrated soon afterward at "Gilgal on the plains of Jericho" (5:10). Whereas the waters of the Red Sea had been "divided," the waters of the Jordan "piled up in a heap a great distance away, at a town called Adam in the vicinity of Zarethan, while the water flowing down to the Sea of the Arabah (the Salt Sea) was completely

cut off" (Josh 3:16; see p. 54). The Israelites set up camp at Gilgal,[28] where they circumcised the new generation and celebrated the Passover, and where, after the people tasted the produce of the land, the manna ceased. Gilgal evidently became an early tribal headquarters, and even a religious center, for it is mentioned in these and other capacities almost forty times in the Old Testament.

The first city to be captured by the Israelites was Jericho (Josh 6). This city has been well-identified with Tell es-Sultan, a 10-acre (4 ha.) mound situated beside a powerful spring in an otherwise arid region (6 in. [150 mm.] of rain annually). If an ancient city contained 150 to 200 people per acre, then at most 2,000 people lived at Jericho.[29] Although the name Jericho has been preserved in the name of the village er-Riha, and the geographical location of Tell es-Sultan matches that of Jericho as described in the Bible, the archaeological profile of the site does not completely correspond to the history of Jericho as found in the sources. If one holds to a late date for the conquest (i.e., ca. 1250–1230 B.C.), then according to the archaeological record no one was living at Jericho at the time when it was supposedly conquered by Joshua. However, if one holds to an early date for the conquest (i.e., ca. 1406 B.C.), then the archaeological profile fits much better. To be sure, archaeological remains from LB I (1550–1400 B.C.) are not plentiful on the tell, but pottery from nearby tombs indicates that people were living there at the time of the conquest.[30] In addition, it is interesting to note that scarabs of the early kings of the 18th Egyptian Dynasty up through the rule of Amenhotep III have been found at Jericho. Since the scarabs of later Egyptian kings are not found at Jericho, it is not unreasonable to conclude that this is because Jericho ceased to be a viable city during the reign of Amenhotep III (1417–1379 B.C.)— possibly due to the Israelite conquest around 1406 B.C. The much-sought-after walls that collapsed in the attack (Josh 6:20) can be considered to be the walls of the MB II city, found by Kenyon, which were used by people living at Jericho during LB I.[31]

The conquest of Ai (Josh 7 and 8) presents the historical geographer with serious problems. Biblical Ai is normally identified with the site named et-Tell. This identification is based on several factors, including Ai's geographical relationship to Bethel, which is said to lie to the west of it (Gen 12:8; Josh 8:9, 12). Thus the usual identification of Bethel with modern Beitin lends strong support to the identification of Ai with et-Tell. In addition, other geographical data in Joshua 7–8 concerning Ai—a place for the ambush party to the west of the city (8:13), a valley to the north (8:13), and a "place overlooking the Arabah" to the east (8:14)—all fit well with the et-Tell identification.[32] However, the archaeological picture of et-Tell does not agree at all with the historical data found in the Bible. According to the excavators, the large Early Bronze city was destroyed ca. 2400 B.C., and the site was not inhabited until ca. 1200 B.C.[33] Thus, no matter which date of the conquest is espoused, whether 1406 or 1250 B.C., the site was apparently unoccupied at the time it was supposed to have been conquered.

The search for an alternate site in the et-Tell region that could be identified with biblical Ai has not been successful. Although a number of solutions to the historical-archaeological problem have been proposed, all do violence to the biblical texts in some way.[34] Another approach has been suggested by David Livingston, who denies the Bethel = Beitin equation and has instead suggested that modern el-Bira[35] is Bethel and that Ai should therefore be sought to the east of it, specifically at Khirbet Nisya.[36] Livingston's proposal of disassociating Bethel from Beitin has been severely criticized by Anson Rainey on toponymic, historical, geographical, and archaeological grounds.[37] Thus, at the time of this writing, the solution to the "Ai problem" awaits further clarification.[38]

After the conquest of Ai, the Israelites moved northward to the Shechem area. Nearby, on Mount Ebal, Joshua built an altar to Yahweh, sacrificed, and wrote on stones (monumental, standing stones?) a copy of the Mosaic Law (Josh 8:30–35). Recently Adam Zertal has discovered and excavated what he calls a large religious complex near the summit of Mount Ebal; he identifies it with the altar mentioned in Joshua 8.[39] There on Mount Ebal and Mount Gerizim the Israelites read the curses and blessings of the law (Josh 8:33–34; Deut 27:11–14) as the covenant between the people and Yahweh was renewed.

Although the Israelites had made inroads into the hill country during the central campaign by conquering Jericho and Ai, it seems that a permanent foothold was still lacking,

for the next incident recorded in the Book of Joshua finds them back at their camp at Gilgal on the plains of Jericho.

When the people of the land of Canaan heard of the Israelite victories at Jericho and Ai, they banded together for mutual defense (Josh 9:1–2). However, a group of Hivites[40] living in the cities of Gibeon, Kephirah, Beeroth, and Kiriath Jearim (vv. 7, 17) chose to make a treaty with Israel. At the time when they made the treaty, the Israelites thought that the Hivites were "from a distant country" (v. 6). But Israel soon discovered that the Gibeonites lived in the heart of the land. However, Israel still observed the terms of the treaty and did not destroy the Gibeonites, although they consigned them to "serve as woodcutters and water carriers" (v. 23). When the king of Jerusalem heard of the Gibeonite-Israelite treaty, he was alarmed: a major neighboring city (10:2), Gibeon, had gone over to the side of the invading Israelites, and it, as well as its three allied cities, sat astride the two major roads that led from Jerusalem to the coast.[41] Thus Jerusalem's lifelines to the coast and to her Egyptian ally[42] were cut off, and she could become easy prey to the Israelites.

Jerusalem countered by assembling a coalition consisting of the kings of Hebron, Jarmuth, Lachish, and Eglon (Josh 10:5). As these rulers moved against the city of Gibeon,

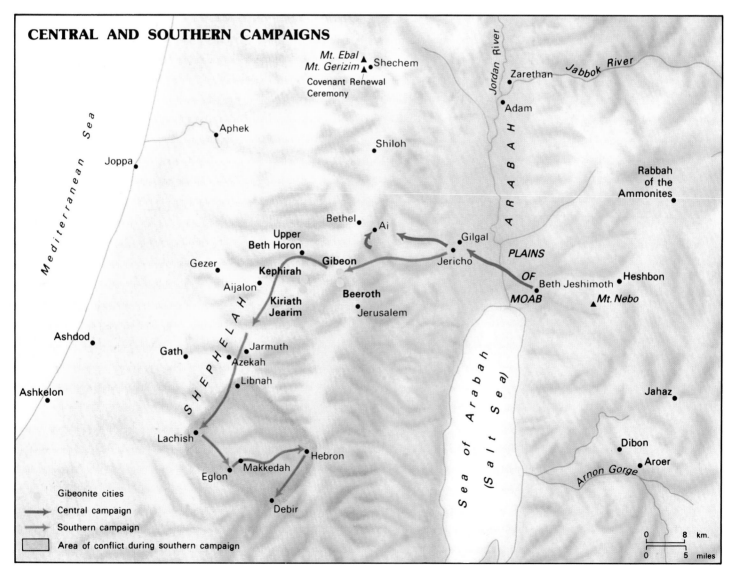

CENTRAL AND SOUTHERN CAMPAIGNS

Gibeonite cities
→ Central campaign
→ Southern campaign
▢ Area of conflict during southern campaign

probably to reopen the road to the coast, the Gibeonites appealed to Joshua for assistance on the basis of their treaty. Joshua responded by marching all night from Gilgal up into the hill country to relieve the siege of Gibeon. The coalition was defeated, and the kings and their armies fled westward, down the descent of Beth Horon, heading for the safety of their cities located in the Shephelah—to Yarmuth, Lachish, and Eglon (Josh 10). Their line of retreat led them through the Valley of Aijalon, past Azekah, to Makkedah.[43] The Israelites, with divine assistance—hailstones and a "prolonged day"—defeated these armies, and eventually the kings themselves were executed at Makkedah (vv. 22–27). Cities captured as a result of this campaign included Libnah, Lachish, Eglon, and Makkedah in the Shephelah, as well as Hebron and Debir, both located in the southern portion of the hill country.[44] Thus, what began as a rescue mission ended with the conquest of southern Canaan—the second major campaign led by Joshua.

The final phase of the Conquest—the northern campaign—occurred when Jabin, the king of Hazor, put together a coalition that included (among others) the kings of Madon,[45] Shimron, and Achshaph (Josh 11:1–3). These kings and their armies, horses, and chariots encamped at the "Waters of Merom" (vv. 4–5).[46] Although details are not given, the Israelite attack was successful, and as the defeated kings retreated, the Israelites pursued them to the Sidon region, to Misrephoth Maim, identified with the Litani River, and to the "Valley of Mizpah on the east" (v. 8), probably a portion of the Rift Valley north of modern Metulla. Jabin's city, Hazor, which "had been the head of these kingdoms," was burned (vv. 10, 13).[47] The Israelites, who evidently had no immediate use for them, hamstrung the horses and burned the chariots (v. 9). However, it is evident that the Israelites did not follow up their victory by establishing a settlement at Hazor, for archaeology shows that Canaanites reoccupied the city and lived there until its conquest by Deborah and Barak (Judges 4–5).

Thus, by the end of the fifteenth century B.C. the initial stages of the conquest of the land of Canaan had been completed. Yet the biblical writers were well aware that within Canaan there were still large portions of country that were controlled by non-Israelites (e.g., Josh 13:1–7). The apportionment of the land, the settlement of the Israelites in it, and the attempt to deal with the non-Israelite population groups would preoccupy the Israelites for the next four hundred years.

Old Testament Jericho, with modern oasis in the background.

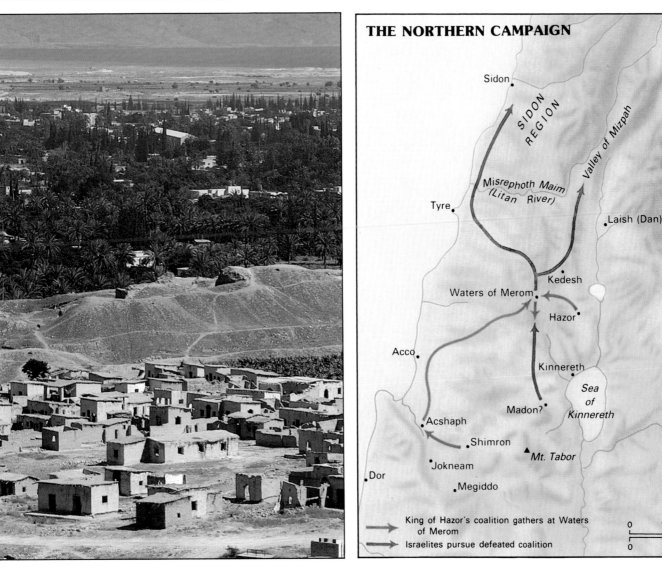

THE NORTHERN CAMPAIGN

Sidon

SIDON REGION

Valley of Mizpah

Misrephoth Maim (Litan River)

Tyre

Laish (Dan)

Kedesh

Waters of Merom

Hazor

Acco

Kinnereth

Sea of Kinnereth

Madon?

Acshaph

Shimron

Mt. Tabor

Jokneam

Dor

Megiddo

→ King of Hazor's coalition gathers at Waters of Merom

→ Israelites pursue defeated coalition

0   10 km.

0   6 miles

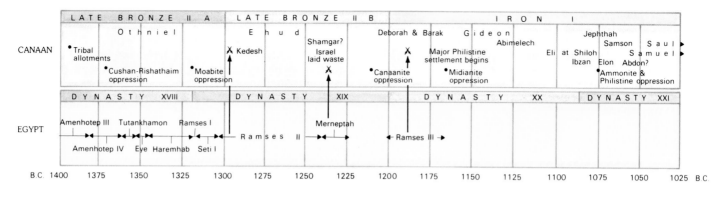

Settlement in the Land of Canaan

Allotment of the Land

Soon after the initial conquest of the land of Canaan had been completed, the Israelites began to grant territory to the various tribes. The basic record of these allotments is found in Joshua 13–21. Although the actual apportionment took place during the days of Joshua and Eleazar the son of Aaron (early fourteenth century B.C.; Josh 14:1; 19:51), it would seem that later copyists and editors of the Book of Joshua may have "updated" the lists of cities mentioned as belonging to the various tribes.

The tribal territories are described in two basic ways. In some instances the boundary of a given tribe is described as a line running from point A to point B to point C, etc., in a "dot-to-dot-to-dot" fashion (e.g., Judah's boundary in Josh 15:1–12). In some of these cases the descriptions are very detailed (e.g., Judah's and Benjamin's common boundary in the vicinity of Jerusalem; 15:7–9; 18:15–17), while in others the information supplied is very brief and sometimes vague (e.g., Naphtali's western boundary in 19:34). The second method of describing a territory is to simply list cities belonging to a given tribe, as in the cases of Judah (15:21–63) and Benjamin (18:21–28).

Judah   *Joshua 15; Judges 1:8–18*

The first tribe to be allocated territory in the land of Canaan was the tribe of Judah. The author of Joshua was particularly interested in this tribe, for all of chapter 15 (sixty-three verses) describes its allotment. The first twelve verses give a "dot-to-dot-to-dot" description of Judah's boundary. Its southern border (15:1–4) was identical with that of the land of Canaan (Num 34:3–5), while its northern border coincided first with the southern boundary of the tribe of Benjamin (Josh 15:5–10; 18:14–19) and then, following the path of the Nahal Sorek westward to the Mediterranean Sea (15:10–11), with the southern boundary of the tribe of Dan.

A description of the granting of Hebron and Debir to Caleb and Othniel is followed by a long list of cities. This list of 132 cities is divided into four major geographical areas: the Negev (Josh 15:20–32), the Shephelah (vv. 33–47), the Hill Country (vv. 48–60), and the Eastern Wilderness (vv. 61–62). These in turn are broken down into even smaller districts (notice the district totals in vv. 32, 36, 41, et al.) for a total of eleven districts within the tribe.[1] Most historical geographers believe that originally the city list functioned as an administrative document (for the collection of taxes, etc.) and propose adding an additional district to make a total of twelve, one for each month of the year.[2] The date of the city list is difficult to determine, but it has been suggested that it is not from Joshua's time (ca. 1400 B.C.), since archaeological surveys and excavations have turned up little evidence that many of the cities in the list existed then.[3] Late dates proposed for the list range from the days of Solomon (970–931 B.C.) to the period of the Babylonian exile (after 586 B.C.), with perhaps the most probable of these dates being in the reign of King Josiah (640–609 B.C.).[4]

This city list describes the essential heartland of Judah. Throughout much of its history, Judah was confined to the heights of the mountains, but during periods of strength, expansion westward into the Shephelah and southward into the Negev occurred. Only on rare occasions did Judah in fact control the Philistine Plain.[5] The rugged mountainous terrain was quite useful in providing Judah with a measure of defense against the hostile powers that were usually located on the coastal plain to the west.

Ephraim   *Joshua 16; Judges 1:29*

The second distribution was made to the tribe of Ephraim, the first son of Joseph. Only incomplete portions of its boundary description are given. Its southern boundary matched the northern one of Benjamin (Josh 16:1–5; 18:12–13), while on the west it theoretically was blocked from the sea by the tribe of Dan (19:40–48). Its northwestern boundary along the Kanah Ravine was well defined (16:8;

17:7–10), while on the northeast and east fewer border points are provided. For most of its history, Ephraim was confined to the rugged mountainous area. Deep V-shaped valleys provided it with security and inaccessible areas (see p. 40). Since no city list for the tribe of Ephraim is provided, relatively little is known about its population centers. In addition, some Ephraimites settled in the territory of Manasseh located to the north (16:9).

Manasseh   *Joshua 17; Judges 1:27–28*

The third lot fell to the second son of Joseph, Manasseh. While a portion of the tribe settled in the land of Gilead (see below), the other part settled in Canaan. Since, as in the case with Ephraim, no list of settlements is provided for Manasseh, there is somewhat of a "blank" spot on the map in comparison to tribes bordering it on the north and south. In addition, only the southwestern boundary is described in some detail (Josh 17:7–11), and thus its remaining borders are difficult to define with precision. Manasseh stretched from the sea to the Jordan River; the southern boundary was conterminous with Ephraim, while on the north, from west to east, Manasseh bordered on Asher, Zebulun, and Issachar. The boundary with these northern tribes evidently passed through the Jezreel and Harod valleys, which were divided among them. Cities such as Beth Shan, Ibleam, Dor, Endor, Tanaach, and Megiddo, while assigned to Manasseh (v. 11),[6] were difficult to capture due to the strength of the Canaanites in the plain, who possessed iron chariots (v. 16)—a fact well-known from the annals of Thutmose III (p. 87). It probably was not until the reigns of David and Solomon four hundred years later (i.e., 1010–931 B.C.) that the Israelites were able to take control of these powerful cities. Since the choice land on the plains was controlled by the Canaanites, the sons of Joseph (Ephraim and Manasseh) settled in the heavily forested hill country, cutting down trees to secure needed farmland (vv. 15–18).

Bottom of V-shaped valley with steep cliffs and rugged terrain in wadi bed.

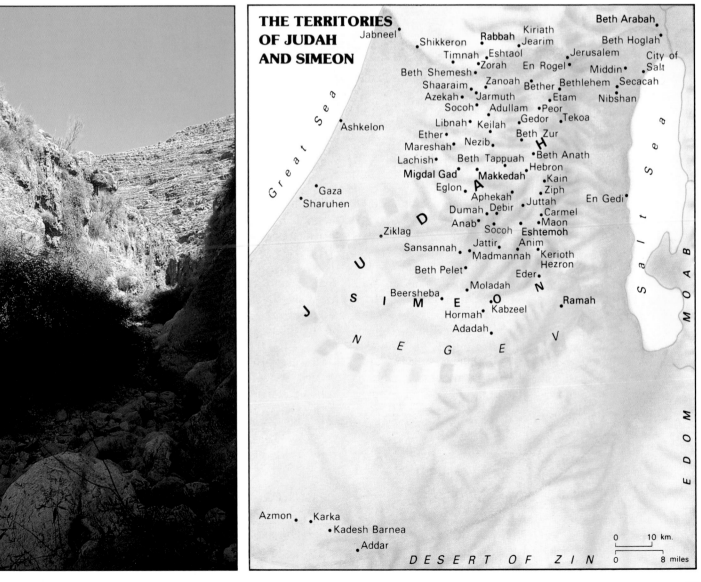

THE TERRITORIES OF JUDAH AND SIMEON

After the assignments to Judah, Ephraim, and Manasseh had been completed, the focus of activity shifted from Gilgal to Shiloh. At Shiloh, in the Hill Country of Ephraim, the tabernacle was set up. From there, Joshua sent out three men from each of the remaining tribes to prepare a written survey of the remaining portions of Canaan (Josh 18:4, 9).[7] Based on this survey, the remaining allotments were made.

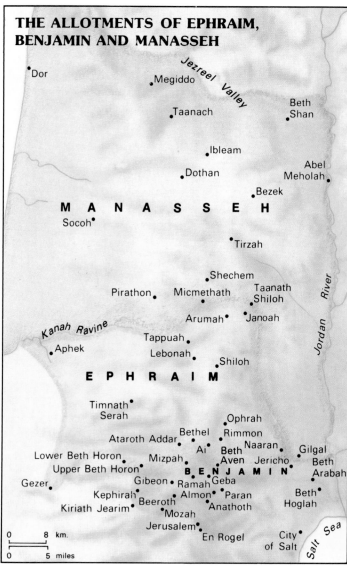

THE ALLOTMENTS OF EPHRAIM, BENJAMIN AND MANASSEH

Benjamin
Joshua 18:11–18; Judges 1:21

Benjamin's territory fell between the two powerful tribes of Ephraim and Judah. Its allotment is described in two ways: first by a boundary list and then by a list of cities in Benjamin's territory. Its northern boundary coincided with that of Ephraim and its southern with that of Judah. On the east it was bounded by the Jordan River, and on the west its boundary, instead of extending into the Aijalon Valley, confined Benjamin to the hills overlooking the valley. Of particular interest—as evidenced by the minute details—are the notations of the southern boundary in the Jerusalem area (Josh 18:16–17), where it is explicitly noted that Jerusalem was located in Benjamin, not in Judah, despite the fact that later a Judahite (David) would capture the city and make it his personal possession.

Benjamin's city list consists of two sections of twelve and fourteen cities respectively. The reason for its twofold character is debated; Aharoni, for example, argues that the list dates to the time of the divided monarchy (930–721 B.C.) and that the first section contains cities of Benjamin located in the Northern Kingdom, while the second section is composed of cities attached to Judah to the south.[8] While this is possible, it seems that the lists divide more into eastern and western groupings of cities, approximately along the line of the watershed in the mountains.

The strategic importance of Benjamin cannot be overemphasized. One of the main approach roads from the coastal plain into the hill country ran through its western portion (see p. 41). On the east, several roads led down into the Rift Valley and joined at the oasis of Jericho and from there proceeded eastward across the fords of the Jordan into Transjordan. Thus, throughout history, Benjamin was one of the "busiest" tribal areas, for invading international powers often entered the hills via the roads from the east or the west, and the northern and southern Israelite tribes occasionally met in battle in the territory of the Benjamites as they sought to expand their influence.

Simeon
Joshua 19:1–9; 1 Chronicles 4:24–43

The tribe of Simeon received territory inside the allotment of Judah. Of the seventeen cities mentioned as being assigned to Simeon (Josh 19:2–7), fifteen were previously mentioned in the city list of Judah—most in the Negev district but a few from the Shephelah district (e.g., Ether, Ashan [see 15:26–32, 42]). Simeon's primary location was in the western Negev, between Beersheba and the Mediterranean Sea. It should be noted that Simeon did not lose its tribal identity by being absorbed into the tribe of Judah (as is often thought), for it was still a distinct and growing tribe during the days of the Judean king Hezekiah (728–696 B.C.; 1 Chron 4:41). Indeed, the chronicler describes its expansion northwestward toward Gedor (LXX, Gerar) and eastward toward the Hill Country of Seir (1 Chron 4:42). Since Simeon's territory received only 10 inches (250 mm.) of rain each year, evidently the tribe specialized in keeping flocks, although in most years some grain crops could be grown.

Zebulun
Joshua 19:10–16; Judges 1:30

A correct understanding of the boundaries of the tribe of Zebulun is a key in attempting to understand the other tribal

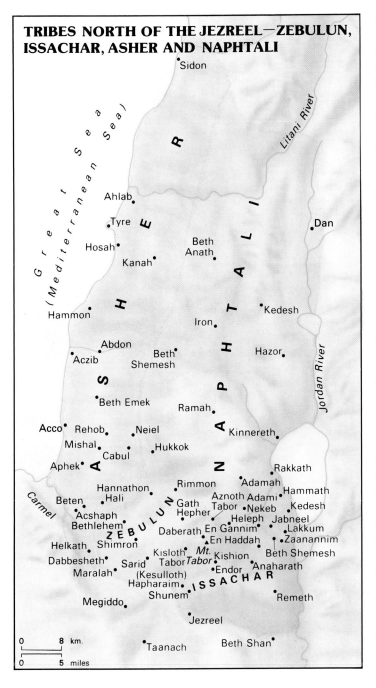

TRIBES NORTH OF THE JEZREEL—ZEBULUN, ISSACHAR, ASHER AND NAPHTALI

southwest it seems that cities such as Dabbesheth and Maralah were actually located in the valley itself, and that, on occasion, Zebulunite territory stretched across the valley to include a city such as Jokneam (cf. Josh 21:34). However, the tribe of Zebulun was not able to drive out the Canaanites who lived in Kitron and Nahalol (the Nahalal of Josh 19:15; see Judges 1:30).

Zebulun was situated near several major trade routes that ran through the Jezreel Valley, the east-west route that ran through Hannathon to Acco, and the route that connected Megiddo with Acco via Shimron and Hannathon. Because of its proximity to these routes, the Zebulunites were open to considerable outside influences and probably maintained commercial relations with Mediterranean port cities (Deut 33:18–19).

Issachar Joshua 19:17–23

The towns given to Issachar were located in the valleys and on the basalt heights of eastern Lower Galilee as well as in the eastern portion of the Jezreel Valley. Because of the basalt rocks and the lack of water sources, the heights were never densely settled; the major settlements were located in the valleys.[12] The description of the allotment of Issachar is composed of a city list, along with very brief boundary descriptions (Josh 19:22). Its northern line seems to have run from the hills overlooking the Jabneel Valley westward past Mount Tabor to Kesulloth. On the west, its boundary ran from Kesulloth to the city of Jezreel, indicating that only the eastern portion of the Jezreel Valley was within its territory. On the south, its boundary headed southeast from Jezreel, following the Harod Valley to the Jordan, its eastern limit.

Issachar's location was such that the major international highways ran close to its southern and western borders, and because of the relatively gentle terrain it would have been easy for armies on the march to invade. Indeed, major cities such as Beth Shan and Anaharath probably remained under non-Israelite control until the period of David and Solomon.

Asher Joshua 19:24–31; Judges 1:31

The tribe of Asher was apportioned territory in the northwestern corner of Israel. It was bounded on the south and east by Manasseh, Zebulun, and Naphtali and on the north by Phoenicia. The textual description of its territory seems to be an abbreviated boundary description that was combined with a city list.[13] Its territory stretched from Mount Carmel in the south to the Litani River on the north and theoretically included the coastal plain and the western hills of Upper and Lower Galilee. However, according to Judges 1:31, Asher was not able to take control of seven important cities located on the coastal plain: Acco, Sidon, Ahlab, Aczib, Helbah, Aphek, and Rehob. Thus the Asher-

allotments in Galilee, for Issachar, Naphtali, and Asher bordered it on the southeast, northeast, and northwest. First the southern boundary of Zebulun is given. Sarid, a city near the center of the southern border is the starting point, and the boundary is first traced westward from Sarid to Dabbesheth and then eastward from Sarid to Daberath, Japhia,[9] and Gath Hepher.[10] The boundary passed through Gath Hepher on the east side and circled around so that its northern portion touched Rimmon and passed through the modern Bet Netofa Valley to Hannathon. From there it headed southwest and south, following the Valley of Iphtah El (Wadi el-Malik) for a short distance and then the Wadi Musrarah to the Kishon. Fourteen cities are mentioned as being included in Zebulun;[11] most of them were in the south-central section of Lower Galilee (pp. 33–35). The greater part of Zebulun's allotment was confined to the high ground overlooking the Jezreel Valley to the south, yet in the ites were said to have "lived among the Canaanite inhabitants of the land." It probably was not until the days of David and Solomon that the plain came under Israelite control (1 Kings 4:16) and then only for a brief time, for it was soon traded to Hiram, king of Tyre, in exchange for financial benefits (9:10–14).

Strategically and economically, Asher's territory was very important. The one natural harbor of the whole country, Acco, was located there. The international north-south route along the coast ran through Asher, as did east-west routes that connected the port of Acco with Transjordan and even Damascus. During the Old Testament period, the maritime powers of Tyre and Sidon took great interest in controlling the area, to the economic detriment of Israel.

Naphtali

Joshua 19:32–39; Judges 1:33

The tribe of Naphtali was bounded on the south by Issachar and on the west by Zebulun and Asher. Its northern boundary is not recorded, but it probably extended as far as the Israelites settled—that is, south of an east-west line that coincided with the east-west portion of the Litani River. Its eastern boundary seems to have been the Jordan River and the Sea of Galilee, but the reference to "Judah" in Joshua 19:34 (see NIV footnote) is problematic.[14]

The outline of Naphtali's territory is first sketched by a boundary description, which is then supplemented by a city list. In the former, the report of its southern boundary with Issachar is most detailed. The starting point in the description is Heleph, from which the boundary proceeded to the "large tree in Zaanannim" (Josh 19:33); then points along the boundary are mentioned. It is clear that Naphtali controlled the Jabneel Valley, while Issachar was situated on the heights to the south of it. Then the border proceeded westward from Heleph to the Mount Tabor area and then northward along its common line with Asher. It is interesting to note how the prominent hill of Mount Tabor served as the meeting point for the boundaries of three tribes—Issachar, Naphtali, and Zebulun. Details of Naphtali's boundaries with Zebulun and Asher are not given, for they had already been described (vv. 10–16, 24–31).[15]

Since the city list contains only sixteen towns and the total is given as nineteen, it seems possible that the author omitted three cities that had already been mentioned in the boundary description—perhaps Heleph, Adami Nekeb, and Jabneel (Josh 19:33). In the city list the order proceeds geographically from south to north. The cities mentioned prior to Ramah were located in Lower Galilee, while those after it were in Upper Galilee (see p. 32).[16] Since a fair portion of Galilee was unoccupied prior to the Israelites' arrival, Naphtali was probably able to settle in the hills relatively early in the period of the Judges. However, it was unable, save for relatively brief periods of time, to take control of the larger Canaanite centers, such as Beth Shemesh and Beth Anath (Judges 1:33), which sat astride an important east-west road in Upper Galilee.

Dan

Joshua 19:40–48; Judges 1:34–35; Judges 17–18

The tribe of Dan was allotted territory to the west of Benjamin, and Dan's eastern boundary, on the western slopes of the mountains overlooking the coastal plain, coincided with the western boundary of Benjamin. Its southern boundary was identical to Judah's northern one and followed the Sorek Valley out to the Mediterranean Sea (Josh 15:10–11). Dan's northern boundary is not outlined, but from the cities mentioned and from comparison with the cities allotted to Ephraim (e.g., Gezer [16:3, 10]), its irregular shape can be surmised, and it appears to have stretched to "Me Jarkon" (i.e., to the Waters of the Jarkon [River] 19:46). Concerning several of the cities mentioned there is some uncertainty as to whether they belonged to Judah or Dan (e.g., Zorah [15:33; 19:41], Eshtaol [15:33; 19:41], Ir Shemesh [probably = Beth Shemesh; 15:10; 19:41], and Ekron [15:45; 19:43]).[17]

Dan's territory sat astride the Aijalon Valley, through which the major approach road into the Hill Country of Ephraim and Judah ran. In addition, the main international north-south route ran through Dan's western extension. Thus the great powers of antiquity were interested in controlling this territory, as were the powerful local Canaanite/Amorite chiefs, with the result that the Danites were not able to expand westward but were rather confined to the western slopes of the mountains in the Beth Shemesh, Zorah, Eshtaol, and Kiriath Jearim region (see Judges 1:34–35; 13–16). Not until the days of David and Solomon did Israel take control of Danite territory, and then only for a brief period of time (see 1 Kings 4:9; 2 Chron 2:16).[18]

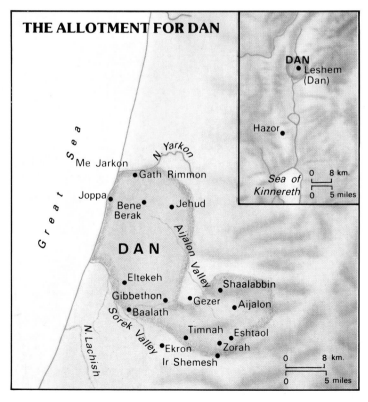

THE ALLOTMENT FOR DAN

Due to Amorite pressures, some of the tribe of Dan moved northward to Laish/Leshem, which they captured and renamed "Dan" (Judges 17–18). They thought that they had moved from an area of insecurity to one of security and prosperity (Judges 18:7, 27–28); yet later in biblical history this was the very area that invaders from the north (the Arameans, Assyrians, and others) attacked first.

Reuben, Gad, and Manasseh

Joshua 13:8–33;
Numbers 32

After the conquest of the kingdoms of Sihon and Og, but before crossing the Jordan River into Canaan, the tribes of Reuben, Gad, and part of Manasseh asked Moses to apportion to them the territory east of the Jordan, because of its suitability for raising their large herds and flocks (Num 32:1). After securing a pledge from them that the adult males would cross into Canaan and participate in the wars of conquest, Moses apportioned them territory according to their wish. Two descriptions of these allotments are given in the Bible: Numbers 32:33–42 and Joshua 13:8–33. The longer list in Joshua begins by mentioning cities at the extremities of the tribes (not dot-to-dot boundary descriptions) and then enumerates the cities belonging to each.

The tribe of Reuben (Josh 13:15–23; Num 32:37–38) received most of the territory stretching from the Arnon Gorge in the south to the city of Heshbon in the north (the Moabite tableland, or Mishor [see p. 55]), although at some point in time it seems that Gadites settled in some of their cities.[19] The territory allotted to Gad stretched from Hesh-

Terracing and destroyed "watch tower" in the hill country.

bon in the south to Mahanaim on the Jabbok River in the north and from just west of Rabbah (i.e., Rabbah of the Ammonites) to the Jordan River on the west. In addition it seems that Gad received the whole of the Jordan Valley east of the river, all the way up to the Sea of Kinnereth (Josh 13:27). Finally, certain clans from the tribe of Manasseh settled the territory north of the Jabbok (i.e., northern Gilead and the Bashan [see pp. 29–30, 52], probably north to Mount Hermon [Num 32:39–42; Josh 13:29–31]).

These tribes, although settled in the land of Gilead (in general the same as Transjordan), attempted to maintain relations with the other Israelite tribes in the land of Canaan (Josh 22). Throughout the remaining portion of Old Testament history, these tribes felt continuous pressure from a number of sources: from the Moabites south of the Arnon Gorge, who laid claim to Reubenite and Gadite territory north of the Arnon; from the Ammonites on the east, who made similar claims; from desert tribes, such as Midianites and Ishmaelites; from the Arameans of Damascus, who

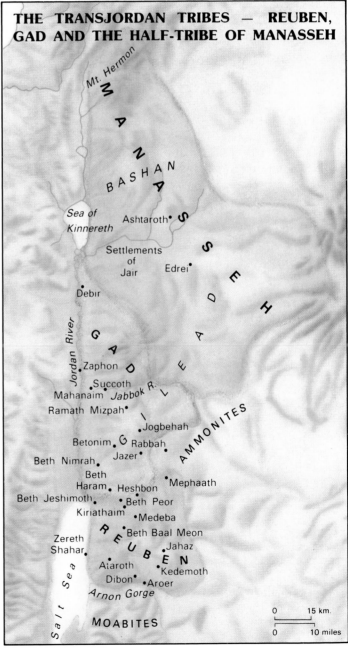

THE TRANSJORDAN TRIBES — REUBEN, GAD AND THE HALF-TRIBE OF MANASSEH

Mt. Hermon

M
A
N
A
S
S
E
H

BASHAN

Sea of Kinnereth

Ashtaroth

Settlements of Jair

Edrei

Debir

Jordan River

G
A
D

Zaphon

Succoth

Mahanaim *Jabbok R.*

Ramath Mizpah

G
I
L
E
A
D

Jogbehah

Betonim

Rabbah

AMMONITES

Jazer

Beth Nimrah

Beth Haram

Heshbon

Mephaath

Beth Jeshimoth

Beth Peor

Kiriathaim

Medeba

Zereth Shahar

R
E
U
B
E
N

Beth Baal Meon

Jahaz

Ataroth

Kedemoth

Dibon

Aroer

Arnon Gorge

Salt Sea

MOABITES

0   15 km.
0   10 miles

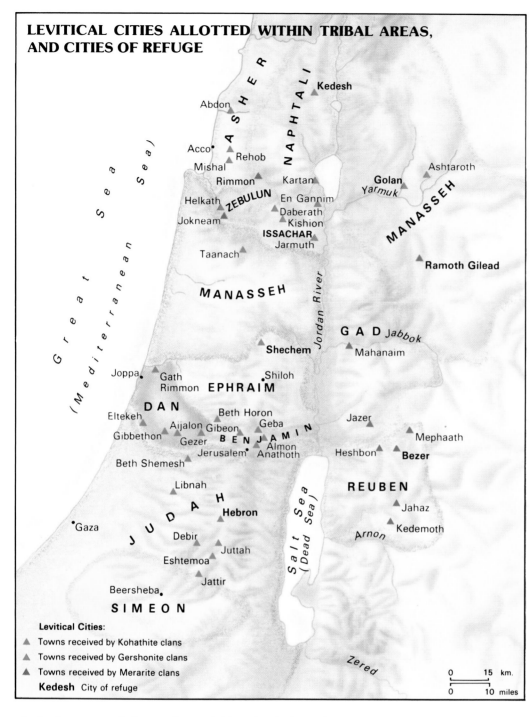

LEVITICAL CITIES ALLOTTED WITHIN TRIBAL AREAS, AND CITIES OF REFUGE

Kedesh
Abdon
Acco
Rehob
Mishal
Rimmon
Kartan
Ashtaroth
Helkath
En Gannim
Golan
ZEBULUN
Daberath
Yarmuk
Joknam
Kishion
ISSACHAR
Jarmuth
MANASSEH
Taanach

MANASSEH

Jordan River

GAD Jabbok
Shechem
Mahanaim

Joppa
Gath
Shiloh
Rimmon
EPHRAIM
DAN
Beth Horon
Eltekeh
Geba
Jazer
Aijalon Gibeon
Mephaath
Gibbethon
Gezer BENJAMIN
Almon
Heshbon Bezer
Jerusalem Anathoth
Beth Shemesh

REUBEN
Libnah

Gaza
JUDAH
Hebron
Jahaz
Debir
Kedemoth
Juttah
Eshtemoa
Arnon
Jattir

Beersheba

SIMEON

Salt Sea (Dead Sea)

Great Sea (Mediterranean Sea)

Levitical Cities:
▲ Towns received by Kohathite clans
▲ Towns received by Gershonite clans
▲ Towns received by Merarite clans
Kedesh City of refuge

Zered

0 ____ 15 km.
0 ____ 10 miles

Jordan River with ford

desired to control the north-south Transjordanian Highway that led to Arabia; and also from the Assyrians, who pressed similar claims. Despite these and other pressures, an Israelite/Jewish presence was maintained in Transjordan through the end of the biblical period and beyond.

Levitical Cities

Joshua 21;
1 Chronicles 6:54–81

As part of the process of settling in the land of Canaan, Joshua and Eleazar the priest assigned towns and their pasturelands to the Levites.[20] Not settled exclusively by Levites, forty-eight cities were assigned to the three Levitical clans, and approximately four such cities were designated from each of the tribes.[21] A good number of the cities were old Canaanite centers, some of which did not come under Israelite control until the days of David and Solomon, and it seems that Levitical settlement in those cities was probably delayed until that time. By the time of David, the Levites were involved not only with matters pertaining to God but also with "the affairs of the king" (1 Chron 26:29–32). Thus in their towns, scattered throughout Israel, they probably were spreading a godly influence through their teaching activities, but they also seem to have been promoting loyalty to the Davidic dynasty. It is possible, as Aharoni has suggested, that the Levitical cities not only served as religious but also as administrative centers.[22] Because of their attachment to the temple in Jerusalem and its chief patron, the Davidic king, it is no wonder that many Levites

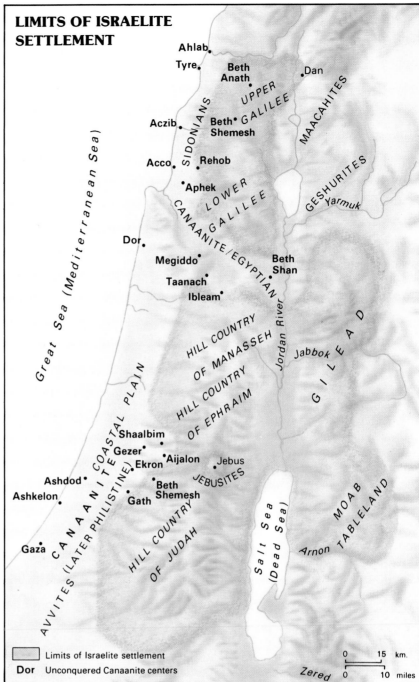

LIMITS OF ISRAELITE SETTLEMENT

Ahlab
Tyre
Beth Anath
Dan
UPPER GALILEE
SIDONIANS
Aczib
Beth Shemesh
MAACAHITES
Acco
Rehob
LOWER GALILEE
GESHURITES
Aphek
Yarmuk
CANAANITE/EGYPTIAN
Great Sea (Mediterranean Sea)
Dor
Megiddo
Beth Shan
Taanach
Ibleam
Jordan River
HILL COUNTRY OF MANASSEH
HILL COUNTRY OF EPHRAIM
Jabbok
GILEAD
Shaalbim
Gezer
Ekron Aijalon
Jebus
JEBUSITES
Ashdod
Beth Shemesh
CANAANITE COASTAL PLAIN
AVVITES (LATER PHILISTINE)
Ashkelon
Gath
MOAB TABLELAND
Salt Sea (Dead Sea)
Gaza
HILL COUNTRY OF JUDAH
Arnon

Limits of Israelite settlement

Dor   Unconquered Canaanite centers

Zered

0   15   km.
0   10   miles

moved south to Judah and Jerusalem at the time of the revolt of the north in the days of Jeroboam I (931–913 B.C.; 2 Chron 11:13–17).

Cities of Refuge

*Joshua 20;
Deuteronomy 4:41–43*

As part of the allotment process, six cities were set aside as places to which a person who committed manslaughter could flee. There the case would be tried (Josh 20:4, 6), and if it was indeed judged as manslaughter rather than murder, the slayer was required to remain in that city until the death of the high priest (Josh 20:6; Num 35:9–34; Deut 4:41–43; 19:1–14). Three of the cities were located to the west of the

Jordan River (Kedesh, Shechem, and Hebron) and three to the east (Golan, Ramoth, and Bezer). All of these cities were Levitical cities, where presumably the law of God was well-known due to the teaching activity of the Levites. Both sides of the Jordan had northern cities (Kedesh and Golan), central cities (Shechem and Ramoth in Gilead), and southern cities (Hebron and Bezer), so that the accused could readily find refuge from the hand of the "avenger of blood" (Josh 20:3).

Thus, in theory at least, by the end of the period of initial conquest, the land that God had promised to Abraham, Isaac, and Jacob had been assigned to their descendants, and religious and political institutions were in the process of being established. Yet, as the period of the Judges will show, complete possession of the land had not yet been attained. That remained for future generations to accomplish.

The Period of the Judges

At the end of the initial stage of the conquest of Canaan, which had been led by Joshua (ca. 1390 B.C.), the Israelites were well aware that not all of the land had been conquered, despite the fact that, theoretically at least, the land had been allotted to the various tribes. The southwestern portion of the land, which was then counted as Canaanite and which would later become Philistine, was not yet under Israelite control (Josh 13:2–3; Judges 3:3; and the Septuagint [Greek] translation of Judges 1:18—see NIV footnote). In fact, the whole of the coastal plain and its vicinity—including the cities of Gezer (Judges 1:29), Shaalbim, Aijalon (v. 35), and Dor (v. 27)—remained Canaanite. The Jezreel Valley and its southeastern extension to Beth Shan remained in Canaanite and/or Egyptian hands (vv. 27–28), while the Mediterranean coastline north of Mount Carmel was under Sidonian control (Josh 13:4; Judges 1:31–32; 3:3). Indeed, the whole of the land of Canaan north of an east-west line that ran through the east-west portion of the Litani River and Mount Hermon, up to Lebo Hamath, remained unconquered (Josh 13:4–5; Judges 3:3). In addition, there were foreign enclaves that remained independent, such as the city of Jebus (Jerusalem; Josh 15:63; Judges 1:21; 19:11) and the regions of the Geshurites (east of the Sea of Kinnereth) and Maacahites (in the Huleh Valley region; Josh 13:13). Most of these areas had come under Israelite control by the days of David and Solomon (e.g., see 1 Kings 4:7–19), although it is not possible to ascertain exactly when this happened in each case.

It is thus evident by process of elimination that the initial areas of Israelite settlement included (1) the hill countries of Judah, Ephraim, and Manasseh; (2) portions of Upper and Lower Galilee; and (3) Gilead and the tableland of Moab. The Israelites were in effect moving into areas that had not previously been densely populated, save for a few scattered urban centers such as Hebron and Shechem. The process of Israelite settlement must have proceeded in a somewhat peaceful fashion over the next 340 years, as farmsteads were established, scrub forests cleared, terraces built, and crops (especially grapes, olives, figs, and wheat) planted. In addition, the then recent invention of rock-hewn, plaster-lined cisterns allowed the people to settle in areas distant from springs, thus opening up new territorial vistas for the Israelites. It appears that throughout the period of the Judges (ca. 1370–1050 B.C.) Israel was able to remain in the mountains, somewhat aloof and removed from the threats of Egyptian kings (e.g., Seti I and Ramses II), who in the main were concerned with controlling the international routes through the country.

Israel was, however, threatened by lesser peoples, both near and far. In the process of settling down, some Israelites began to worship pagan deities, including Baal (who was thought to be responsible for the fertility of the land) and his consort Ashtoreth (goddess of war and fertility), as well as Asherah. As punishment for these sins, Yahweh sent foreigners who oppressed the Israelites. Eventually Israel cried out in repentance, and God sent "judges" who delivered Israel from her oppressors and ushered in periods of "rest." This cycle of lapse into sin, divine punishment, repentance, deliverance, and rest (Judges 2:10–19) is illustrated in the accounts of the six major judges (those whose exploits are recounted at length) and of the six minor judges (who receive only passing mention in the biblical text). Since the judges operated in various parts of the country, it is not necessary to assume that their periods of leadership were successive; in some cases their activities may have been concurrent. For example, the Ammonite oppression in Transjordan and the Philistine oppression from the west may have occurred at the same time, so that the judgeships of Samson and Jephthah may have coincided, with Jephthah active in the east and Samson in the west.

Although the literary presentation of the judges seems to be roughly in chronological order, in all probability the events recorded in Judges 17–21 took place early in the period (i.e., mid-fourteenth century B.C.). The Danite move from the region of the valleys of Aijalon and Sorek (Josh 19:47; Judges 17–18; and see 1:34–35) has already been mentioned (see p. 101), but it is well to note that the move was not attributed to Philistine pressure (that would come later), and that not all Danites moved from their tribal allotment. Later Samson, a Danite, would deal with the Philistines.

The final episode in the Book of Judges—that of the Levite and his concubine (chs. 19–21)—is set in the days of Phinehas, son of Eleazar (20:28), early in the fourteenth century B.C. It illustrates the moral corruption of the inhabitants of Gibeah and, evidently, of many in Benjamin as well, for the latter came to the defense of the former. All the Israelites from "Dan to Beersheba and from the land of Gilead [still distinguished from Canaan proper]" (20:1) assembled for battle against the Benjamites. The result of the various military encounters left only six hundred Benjamite men alive; from them the tribe eventually regained its numerical strength.

The account contains a number of interesting geographical features. For example, Benjamite connections with Jabesh Gilead (Judges 21:12) were established through intermarriage. The Ridge Route from Bethlehem to Ramah is described (19:10–15); note the south-north sequence of Bethlehem, Jebus (Jerusalem), Gibeah, and Ramah, as well as the fact that one needed to turn off the north-south Ridge Route and go east in order to get to Jerusalem (vv. 11–12). In addition, the description of the location of Shiloh—"to the north of Bethel, and east of the road that goes from Bethel to Shechem, and to the south of Lebonah" (21:19)—is the most detailed description of the location of any city mentioned in the Bible. Finally, the account of the Danites and that of the Levite together suggest something of a tribal vacuum in the Dan-Benjamin corridor, which separated Judah in the south from the northern tribes. Could the writer be preparing the reader for the Davidic move into Jerusalem (technically in Benjamin)? Or for the conflict over this territory between the northern and southern kingdoms during the divided monarchy (see below, pp. 124–27)? Whatever the case, both of the tribes in this corridor experienced serious difficulties early in the period of the Judges.

Throughout the period of the Judges, Egyptian sources shed welcome flashes of historical light on conditions in Canaan. In the late nineteenth century, Egyptian peasants discovered a large number of cuneiform tablets at el-Amarna, a site now known to have been the capital of the "heretic" king Akhenaton.[23] These tablets, of which almost four hundred have survived, date to the reigns of the Egyptian kings Amenhotep III (1417–1379 B.C.) and Akhenaton (1379–1362 B.C.). These clay tablets (some measure 2 by 2 in. [5 by 5 cm.], others are as large as 8 by 5 in. [20 by 13 cm.]) were written in Akkadian, the diplomatic language of the day. Although the content of these texts is varied, from the historical and geographical point of view the letters are of extreme interest. Correspondence between the king of Egypt and his contemporaries in Babylonia, Assyria, Mitanni, Alashia, and Hatti shed light on the international scene. In one of the letters, for example, the king of Babylonia complains that his caravan has been attacked at Hannathon in the land of Canaan and that since the land of Canaan is under Egyptian control, the king of Egypt is responsible for its fate (el-Amarna tablet number 8). However, most of the letters are records of the correspondence between the numerous city-state rulers in the Levant and the king of Egypt. This correspondence demonstrates that the Egyptians were treating Canaan with benign neglect yet still maintained nominal control over the area. Not that Canaan was in total chaos, but its numerous rulers were constantly forming alliances—first with one neighbor and then with another—in an effort to gain the upper hand in the country.

One of the most prominent of these manipulators was Labayu of Shechem. From his base in the hill country, he was reaching out in all directions like an octopus, attempting to take control of the trade routes that ran through the Sharon Plain, the Jezreel Valley, and the region of Pehel in Transjordan. Kings such as Biridiya of Megiddo complained of his antics, requesting the intervention of the Egyptians, while Labayu consistently swore his (feigned?) allegiance to the Egyptians. Eventually Labayu was murdered by his enemies in Canaan, but soon his sons were following in his footsteps.

Jerusalem, the other prominent hill country center, south of Shechem, is also represented in the correspondence. The ruler of Jerusalem, Abdi-hebda, was attempting to keep the Habiru at bay and was constantly interacting with the rulers of cities in the Shephelah (e.g., Gezer, Gath, Keilah, and Lachish). The web of intrigue there was similar in scope to that noted in the north.

When these letters were first discovered, some scholars thought that they were firsthand accounts of the Israelite (Hebrew) conquest of Canaan. However, the names of the kings of Jerusalem (Adoni-Zedek), Lachish (Japhia), and Gezer (Horam), mentioned in the Bible (Josh 10:3, 33), do not correspond to the names of the kings mentioned in the el-Amarna letters, namely Abdi-hebda (Jerusalem), Zimredda and others (Lachish), and Milkilu and Yapai (Gezer). According to the chronology adopted here, the events chronicled in these letters occurred soon after the initial conquests under Joshua (ca. 1406–1400 B.C.).

One of the most interesting groups mentioned in the el-Amarna letters are the Habiru, who were usually involved in

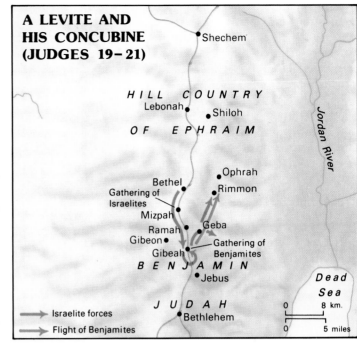

A LEVITE AND HIS CONCUBINE (JUDGES 19–21)

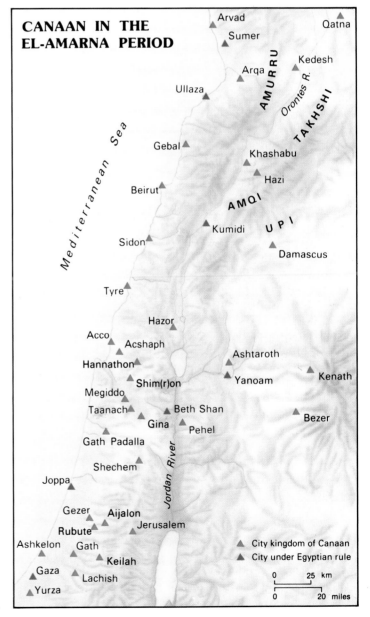

CANAAN IN THE EL-AMARNA PERIOD

anti-Egyptian activities and who threatened the stability of many of the city-states. It is possible that *Habiru* is related to *Hebrew*, and it may be that in some instances the activities of the Israelites (Hebrews), as they continued their conflict with the Canaanites and as they began to settle the hill country, are alluded to in the Amarna letters as activities of the Habiru. However, it does not appear that all Habiru were Hebrews, for the Habiru were active not only in the south but also in the northern Levant, where the Israelites were not active; nor were all Hebrews Habiru. Thus it does not seem possible to maintain a one-to-one correspondence between the Habiru and the Hebrews. In any case, it is interesting to note that cities such as Jericho, Bethel, Gibeon, and Hebron—cities in the Rift Valley and hill country that were conquered early by the Israelites—are not mentioned in the el-Amarna correspondence. Thus, although the letters do not seem to offer any one-to-one correspondence with known biblical events or personages, they do bear witness to the chaotic political conditions in Canaan and to Egyptian and Canaanite priorities along the coastal plain and in the valleys during the early fourteenth century B.C.—the very time when Israel was beginning to settle in the Hill Country of Judah and Ephraim.

The first of the six major judges was Othniel, son of Kenaz, who was Caleb's younger brother (Judges 3:7–11). The oppressor of Israel was Cushan-Rishathaim (= "Cushan, the doubly wicked"?), king of Aram Naharaim. The latter is usually identified with northwestern Mesopotamia, but this seems quite distant from Judah, where the oppression probably took place.[24] Kline has suggested that, in reality, Cushan-Rishathaim headed a band of Habiru who were oppressing the Israelites.[25] While chronologically the judgeship of Othniel and the events in the el-Amarna letters seem to coincide, Kline's thesis is difficult to prove. Others have suggested that "Aram" is corrupt for an original "Edom," for the Hebrew writing of the two names is almost identical except for two letters that could easily be confused due to similar appearance (ארם = Aram, אדם = Edom). This view would make the nearby Edomites the oppressors, a more logical enemy than distant Mesopotamia. Yet the appearance of "Naharaim" is still a problem.[26]

The second of the major Judges was Ehud, son of Gera, who was one of the surviving members of the tribe of Benjamin (Judges 3:15; and see above, p. 104). Eglon, the king of Moab, along with his Transjordanian neighbors, the Ammonites, and also the Amalekites,[27] oppressed Israel from their headquarters in the "City of Palms" (Jericho according to 2 Chron 28:15). Ehud, after delivering tribute to Eglon, killed him and escaped to Seirah (the forest) in the Hill Country of Ephraim (Judges 3:26–27). There he mustered the Israelite forces from the tribes of Benjamin and Ephraim and led them down into the Rift Valley to the fords of the Jordan River, where they were able to decimate the retreating Moabites and their allies. At least a portion of the land then enjoyed "peace" for eighty years (vv. 28–30).

Although the Bible does not mention it, the Egyptians were active in the land of Canaan at the end of the fourteenth and in the thirteenth centuries B.C. Egyptian reliefs, as well as stelas and portions of stelas found in Canaan tell of the activities of Seti I (1318–1304 B.C.) in the area. For example, it is known that he suppressed a revolt in the Beth Shan area

that had been led by the kings of the cities of Hammath and Pehel. Besides reasserting Egyptian control in the Beth Shan region, he subdued the Habiru in Mount Yarmuta (i.e., in territory that had been assigned to the tribe of Issachar). He also subdued Yenoam[28] in the Bashan and moved northward, conquering Hazor (lower city Level II) before moving further northward along the Phoenician coast.

His successor, Ramses II (1304–1237 B.C.), battled the Hittites at Kedesh on the Orontes in his fifth year (1298 B.C.), indicating that Canaan to the south was firmly under Egyptian control. Indeed, later the Hittites and Ramses II made a treaty that fixed their common boundary just to the south of Kedesh (ca. 1283 B.C.). In addition, "A Satirical Letter" (*ANET*, 476–78), dating to the thirteenth century B.C., also gives clear evidence of Egyptian control of the coastal plains and valleys of Canaan, noting that Egyptian chariots and messengers moved freely through the country.

Although Merneptah (1236–1223 B.C.), the successor of Ramses II, was not as powerful as his forerunner, his stele, among other items, mentions his victory over Israel:

> Desolation is for Tehenu (Libyans); Hatti is pacified;
> Plundered is the Canaan with every evil;
> Carried off is Ashkelon; seized upon is Gezer;
> Yenoam is made as that which does not exist;
> Israel is laid waste, his seed is not;
> Hurru is become a widow for Egypt!
> All lands together, they are pacified;
> Everyone who was restless, he has been bound
> by the king . . . Mer-ne-Ptah . . . .   (*ANET*, 378)

This is the first extrabiblical reference to "Israel," and it attests to Israelite presence in Canaan by at least 1231 B.C.

The question as to how all of this Egyptian activity could be going on in Canaan without being mentioned in the Bible is a relevant one. The most plausible solution to this problem is probably that the Egyptians and Israelites had different priorities in the land. The Egyptians were interested in the plains and open valleys, the places where the international routes ran, while the Israelites were striving to secure a foothold in the more rugged mountainous areas. Thus the encounters between the two peoples seem to have been minimal.

The first of the minor judges, Shamgar, son of Anath, is mentioned in Judges 3:31 and 5:6. The time of his activity is not certain, but it must be placed before the judgeship of Deborah and Barak (5:6). Thus a date in the late thirteenth century B.C. is possible. Since he was active against an early group of the Philistines, it seems reasonable to locate his activities in or near the Philistine Plain. Of his tribal affiliation nothing is known, although his name appears to be foreign (Hurrian?). Since he is called the "son of Anath" (a Canaanite goddess), it has been suggested that he came from the city of Beth Anath in Naphtali (Josh 19:38; Judges 1:33), but this would place his home far from the scene of his activity. On the other hand, he might have been from Beth Anoth, a city of Judah (Josh 15:59), which would place his home much closer to the assumed site of his exploits.[29]

During the first half of the twelfth century B.C., the Canaanites were again asserting themselves in northern Israel. Led by Jabin, the king of Hazor, and his commander Sisera, they oppressed northern Israel for some twenty years. During that time, village life was threatened and travel

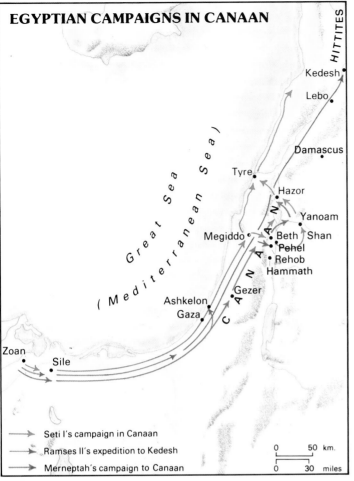

EGYPTIAN CAMPAIGNS IN CANAAN

→ Seti I's campaign in Canaan
→ Ramses II's expedition to Kedesh
→ Merneptah's campaign to Canaan

0   50 km.
0   30 miles

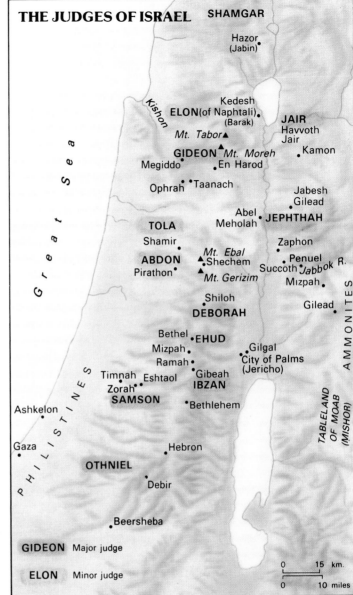

THE JUDGES OF ISRAEL

GIDEON Major judge

ELON Minor judge

0   15 km.
0   10 miles

on the roads was dangerous (Judges 5:6–7), due in part to the fact that military weapons were scarce in Israel (v. 8). Under the leadership of Barak of Kedesh Naphtali, and of the prophetess Deborah, whose headquarters were at the palm tree of Deborah between Ramah and Bethel in the Hill Country of Ephraim (4:4–6), the Israelite forces were mustered on the slopes of Mount Tabor at the northeastern end of the Jezreel Valley. Here on the wooded slopes of Tabor the Israelites were relatively safe from the operations of the nine hundred chariots controlled by Sisera (vv. 3–13). Initially Zebulun and Naphtali sent forces (v. 10), which were evidently joined by reinforcements from Ephraim, Benjamin, Makir (Manasseh), and Issachar (5:14–15). At the appropriate moment, Barak led his forces down the mountain to battle the Canaanites in the plain below. Due to a sudden downpour and the flooding of the Kishon River, the Canaanite chariots were rendered ineffective, and Israel scored a decisive victory (4:14–16; 5:20–21). Sisera, possibly fleeing back toward Hazor, was killed by the wily Jael, who drove a tent peg through his head while he slept. Instead of the Canaanites dividing the silver and plunder of the Israelites near Taanach, by the waters of Megiddo (5:19; possibly their major military camp),[30] it was Israel that was victorious, and the northern portion of the land experienced relative peace for forty years (v. 31).[31]

The exploits of Gideon, the judge who led Israel during the second half of the twelfth century B.C. against the Midianites, their allies the Amalekites, and other eastern peoples, are recorded in Judges 6–8. Each year these peoples invaded

Israel in the late spring/early summer, confiscating the newly harvested crops and grazing their livestock and camels in the fields. After seven successive years of this, Israel was becoming impoverished, and she cried to the Lord for help. Gideon, the Abiezrite from the tribe of Manasseh and the village of Ophrah, which overlooked the Jezreel Valley from the south, responded to God's call.[32] Mustering the tribes of Manasseh, Asher, Zebulun, and Naphtali at the spring of Harod, Gideon prepared for battle by culling his troops down to a select three hundred. Dividing this corps into three units, he surprised the Midianites—whose main camp was evidently on the northern slope of Mount Moreh at Endor (Ps 83:10)—with a night attack. The frightened Midianites fled in a southeasterly direction toward the Jordan River, Beth Shittah, Zererah, Abel Meholah, and Tabbath. At the request of Gideon, the Ephraimites joined the battle by seizing control of the fords of the Jordan and capturing the Midianite leaders Oreb and Zeeb. Gideon and his troops continued in pursuit of the fleeing Midianites eastward, passing Succoth and Peniel and heading up the Jabbok River into Gilead. Following the "route of the nomads east of

Nobah and Jogbehah" (Judges 8:11), he overtook the unsuspecting army of the eastern peoples at Karkor, a desert oasis in the Wadi Sirhan. After all but annihilating the opposing forces, Gideon and his men captured considerable booty. Subsequently, the land had peace for forty years.

Although Gideon's response to the request to rule over Israel was "no" ("The Lord will rule over you" [Judges 8:23]), one of his sons, Abimelech, whose mother was from Shechem, had different ambitions. By slaughtering seventy of his brothers at Gideon's home in Ophrah, Abimelech was able to set himself up as king in Shechem (Judges 9). Only Jotham, the youngest son of Gideon, survived the slaughter, and in a fable Jotham predicted how the people of Shechem and Abimelech would eventually destroy each other (vv. 7–20). This, in fact, occurred after only three years of Abimelech's rule. Gaal, Abimelech's adversary who had replaced him as the leader in Shechem, and his forces were killed, and when his allies, the citizens of Shechem, took refuge in the temple of El/Baal-Berith (v. 46),[33] Abimelech and his troops took wood from Mount Zalmon (Jebel el-Kabir[?] to the northeast of Shechem) and burned the tower down. Shortly thereafter, as Abimelech was laying siege to Thebez,[34] he approached too closely to a tower on the wall, and a woman dropped an upper millstone on his head, cracking his skull (vv. 52–55; 2 Sam 11:21).[35] It seems likely that Abimelech had been attempting to assert his kingship partly on the basis of Shechem's traditional role as the dominating city in the region. Shechem's dominance is well illustrated in the el-Amarna letters, which describe Labayu's antics in the region (see above, p. 105).

The date and extent of the activities of the two minor judges Tola (Judges 10:1–2) and Jair (vv. 3–5) are not known with certainty, but they were probably active in the late twelfth or early eleventh centuries B.C. Although Tola was from the tribe of Issachar, he lived and was evidently active in Shamir[36] in the Hill Country of Ephraim. Jair, on the other hand, was from the tribe of Manasseh and lived in Transjordan, in Gilead. There, in northern Gilead, he and his thirty sons judged Israel for twenty-two years. The towns they controlled were called Havvoth Jair ("Settlements of Jair")[37] and were located in the area of the boundary between the Bashan and Gilead, probably in the Yarmuk River region. Jair was buried in Kamon.

At the beginning of the eleventh century B.C., the Israelites were pressed on the east by the Ammonites and on the west by the Philistines. As was to be expected, Ammonite pressure was greatest in Gilead, but it was also exerted on Judah, Benjamin, and Ephraim (Judges 10:9). The major dispute was over the control of the tableland of Moab, the Mishor, as well as southern Gilead. This land was claimed at various times by the Moabites and Amorites (Num 21:26) and in this case by the Israelites and Ammonites. The elders of Gilead chose the previously outcast Jephthah to head their forces. Jephthah's argument that Yahweh had given the land to Israel, that Israel had taken it from the Amorites, and that Israel had lived there for three hundred years, was not accepted by the Ammonites (Judges 11:14–27). The ensuing battle with the Ammonites most likely took place south of Mizpah of Gilead (11:29–33), and the Ammonites were soundly defeated. Twenty of their towns were devastated, and the territory from Aroer[38] to the vicinity of Minnith[39]

and as far as Abel Keramim was secured (vv. 32–33).

In the aftermath of the Gileadite victory, the Ephraimites, who had been offended because they had not been invited to participate in the battle, crossed the Jordan River to Zaphon (possibly now the home and headquarters of Jephthah[?]; Judges 12:1) to fight with the Gileadites. In the battle that followed, the Ephraimites were routed, and fleeing survivors were executed as they attempted to cross the Jordan westward back to Ephraim—the famous "Shibboleth" incident (vv. 4–7). Jephthah's rule was short, only six years, and he was buried in a town in Gilead (v. 7). The story of Jephthah, like that of Gideon, illustrates how the tribes of Israel experienced pressure from their neighbors who lived in or on the fringes of the eastern desert.

Not much is known about the three minor judges that are mentioned next. Ibzan (Judges 12:8–10) led Israel for seven years from Bethlehem, which may have been either in Zebulun (Josh 19:15) or in Judah (cf. Josephus, *Antiq* 5.7.13 [271]). Elon (Judges 12:11–12) the Zebulunite led Israel for ten years from Aijalon, a city of Zebulun, and Abdon the son of Hillel (vv. 13–15) led the country for eight years. His home, Pirathon, was located in Ephraim in the Hill Country of the Amalekites (see above, p. 40). Evidently all of these judges led Israel during the first half of the eleventh century B.C.

Close to the beginning of the twelfth century B.C. a new political force began to make itself felt in the land of Canaan. These relative newcomers were peoples from the Aegean area that had been moving eastward and southward and had been migrating in small groups into the Levant and Egypt in the fourteenth and thirteenth centuries B.C. Called in Egyptian sources the Sea Peoples, these newcomers consisted of various tribal groupings, including the Tjekker, Danuna, Sherden, Tursha, Lukka, and Peleset (Philistines). Their migration in the thirteenth century B.C. brought to an end the Minoan civilization in Crete and the strong Hittite state in Anatolia, and they attacked northern Syria, including places such as Alalakh and Ugarit.

Moving southward into Canaan, the Sea Peoples were met by the Egyptian king Ramses III (1198–1166 B.C.), who in the eighth year of his reign (ca. 1190 B.C.) was able to defeat these invaders both on land and at sea.[40] The various tribes of the Sea Peoples began to settle along the coast of Canaan, primarily in seaport towns.[41] From the biblical standpoint, the most interesting of these peoples were the Philistines, who settled in their famous pentapolis of Gaza, Ashkelon, Ashdod, Gath, and Ekron. Although they brought with them elements of their Aegean cultural heritage—distinctive language, dress, pottery, weapons, etc.—they seem to have quickly assimilated major features of Canaanite culture, including its religion (note Canaanite deities such as Dagon, Ashtoreth, and Baal-zebub), pottery (their distinctive pottery disappeared by 1000 B.C.), and probably a Semitic language. They may have brought with them the technology for smelting and forging metal products, including those made of iron, and this seems to have given them a technological and military edge over the other peoples of Canaan (see, e.g., 1 Sam 13:19–22).[42] Their military capability was formidable from the start and included not only foot soldiers but also chariotry and horsemen (see the Medinet Habu Inscription of Ramses III [see above, note 40] and 1 Sam 13:5).

During the first half of the eleventh century B.C. the Philistines began to exert serious pressure on the Israelites. The natural place for this conflict between the people of the coast and the people of the hill country was in the buffer zone between them, the Shephelah. There, in its northern region, in the Valley of Sorek, the Nazirite judge Samson rose to meet the threat. The son of Danite parents from Zorah (evidently some Danites had not moved to northern Israel; see above, p. 104), Samson's base of operation was in Mahaneh (the camp) of Dan, which was located in the vicinity of Zorah and Eshtaol (Judges 13:25).

His earliest encounter with the Philistines was when he married a Philistine woman who lived in Timnah, which was located in the Sorek Valley west of Beth Shemesh. Later, as an offended husband, he burned the fields of grain, the vineyards, and the olive groves the Philistines maintained in the Sorek.[43] In response the Philistines pursued him into the Hill Country of Judah to the rock of Etam, where the fearful Judahites ("the Philistines are rulers over us," Judges 15:11) handed him over to the Philistines. However, he quickly gained the upper hand and was able to annihilate a number of them at (Ramath) Lehi (vv. 9–19), using a "donkey's jawbone."[44] Although his exploits had taken him to Ashkelon (13:19) and would eventually lead him to Gaza and Hebron (16:1–3), it was an affair with "a woman in the Valley of Sorek whose name was Delilah" that led to Samson's heroic but tragic death at Gaza (vv. 4–31).[45]

With the death of Samson, the last of the heroes of the Book of Judges passed from the scene. For 350 years (ca. 1400–1050 B.C.) the Israelites had been settling the land; yet even at the end of this long period, large pockets of non-Israelite populations still existed in the country. King Saul would provide protection from some of these enemies, especially the Ammonites and Philistines (whom Jephthah and Samson had not silenced completely), but it would be King David who would eventually bring them to submission.

The great battle of Ramses III against the Sea Peoples (Philistines) as depicted on a relief from temple of Ramses III at Medinet Habu, Thebes, c. 1198–1166 B.C.

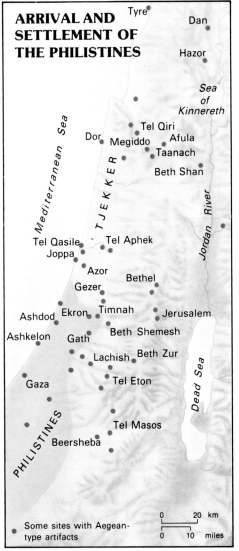

ARRIVAL AND SETTLEMENT OF THE PHILISTINES

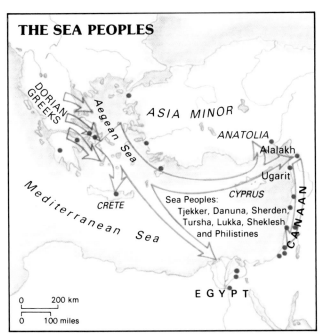

THE SEA PEOPLES

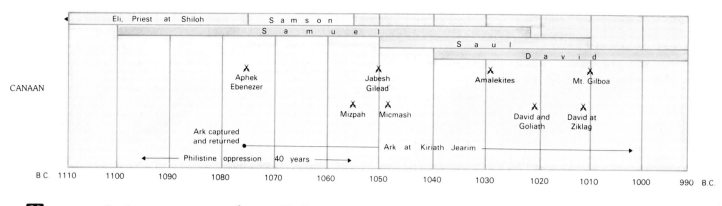

CANAAN

B.C. 1110   1100   1090   1080   1070   1060   1050   1040   1030   1020   1010   1000   990 B.C.

Transition to the Monarchy: Samuel and Saul

During the whole of the eleventh century B.C., Israel was in the process of shifting from the rule of judges to that of a monarch. Also, the Philistines were growing in strength and prowess, and it was almost inevitable that they would come into conflict with Israel.

At the beginning of the century (ca. 1100 B.C.), Samuel was born to parents who lived in the region of the Zuphites, in Ramathaim (1 Sam 1:1), very likely the same place as the Ramah where Samuel later made his home as an adult. During his childhood years he served the high priest Eli at the tabernacle at Shiloh (1 Sam 3). Probably one reason the tabernacle was located there was that the rugged terrain of the Hill Country of Ephraim that surrounded Shiloh provided natural topographical defenses, making it difficult for Israel's enemies to reach it.

When Samuel was approximately twenty-five (ca. 1075 B.C., about the same time Samson became active against the Philistines in the Sorek Valley), the Philistines mustered their forces at the city of Aphek, located by the headwaters of the Yarkon River, to prepare for an invasion into the hill country (1 Sam 4:1). To meet this threat, the Israelites set up camp near Ebenezer, now identified with Khirbet Izbet Sarta.[1] After an initial defeat, the Israelites believed that if the visual symbol of the presence of God would go with them into battle they would be victorious. Thus they brought the ark of the covenant from Shiloh to Ebenezer, much to the consternation of the Philistines. Yet when the time came for the battle, the Philistines soundly defeated the Israelites, and they even captured the sacred ark! Upon hearing news of this disaster, particularly of the loss of the ark, Eli the high priest collapsed and died (vv. 12–18). Although the Bible does not mention it, from the archaeological evidence it seems that Shiloh was destroyed at this time, in all probability by the Philistines.[2]

The ark of the covenant remained in Philistine hands for approximately seven months (1 Sam 6:1). At first it was taken to Ashdod and placed in the temple of Dagon. But the image of Dagon repeatedly fell over in obeisance to the ark, and a plague broke out in the city, so the ark was sent to Gath (5:1–8). There a similar plague broke out, and the troublesome ark was transferred to Ekron. For a third time a plague broke out in the city where the ark resided.

The rulers of the Philistines decided that a test should be made to determine if the ark really was the cause of the plagues: the ark, as well as offerings of gold tumors and gold rats, were placed on a cart, which was to be drawn by two cows that had young calves and that had never been yoked. If the cart headed toward the nearby Israelite city of Beth Shemesh, then the Philistines would know that Yahweh had brought this disaster (1 Sam 6:1–9). And indeed, as the five rulers of the Philistines watched from the ridge that overlooks the Sorek Valley to the northeast of Ekron, the cows pulling the cart headed eastward up the valley toward Beth Shemesh. The people of Beth Shemesh, who were harvesting wheat in the valley (which means that it must have been sometime around May),[3] rejoiced to see the ark and offered sacrifices in celebration of its safe return (vv. 10–18). But some of the people of Beth Shemesh looked into the ark—which only the high priest was allowed to do, and then only once a year, on the Day of Atonement—and God struck them down for their sin.[4] Because of this the ark was transferred to Kiriath Jearim, one of the four Gibeonite cities, where it remained for twenty years, until it was again taken into battle (14:18). It was not until David's reign, after the capture of Jerusalem (ca. 1003 B.C.), that the ark was moved to Jerusalem (2 Sam 6).

During his adult life, Samuel made his home in Ramah,[5] which was strategically located at the important junction of the west-east connecting route (Gezer–Beth Horon–Ramah–Jericho) and the north-south Ridge Route. There he built an altar to worship Yahweh (1 Sam 7:17). His annual duties, which were probably judicial and priestly, took him on a circuit that led from Ramah to Bethel, to Gilgal, and to Mizpah (7:16). It is interesting to note that all of these villages were situated on or east of the central watershed, away from areas to the west that were under Philistine control.

Even after the return of the ark, Philistine pressure on Israel continued. About 1055 B.C. Samuel gathered the Israelite tribes at Mizpah to pray for them and to offer sacrifices (1 Sam 7:5).[6] This assembly may have convened soon after Samson's death at Gaza, and it may have been called to deal with anticipated Philistine retaliation. The ensuing encounter between Israel and the Philistines probably occurred somewhere on the western side of the Benjamin Plateau. God intervened on Israel's behalf, sending a violent thunderstorm that panicked the Philistines. Israel, seizing the opportunity, pursued them westward toward the coastal plain, as far as Beth Car (identification unknown). In order to commemorate God's gracious assis-

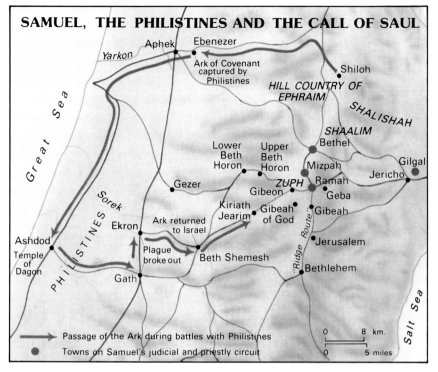

SAMUEL, THE PHILISTINES AND THE CALL OF SAUL

Passage of the Ark during battles with Philistines

Towns on Samuel's judicial and priestly circuit

Wadi Suweinit: possible site of Jonathan's manoeuvers against the Philistines.

tance in Israel's victory over the Philistines, Samuel set up a memorial stone called Ebenezer ("stone of help") between Mizpah and Shen (vv. 11–12).[7] As a result of this victory, Israel regained territory in the Ekron and Gath areas (vv. 13–14), but the lull in the Philistine threat would last only a few years.

While Samuel was ministering in the Benjamin region, two of his sons were serving as judges at the southern extremity of Israel, in Beersheba (1 Sam 8:1–3). Because of the corruption of these sons, and possibly because of new Philistine inroads into western Benjamin, the elders of Israel approached Samuel at his residence in Ramah, requesting that he appoint a king over them (vv. 4–5). At this point in the narrative (1 Sam 9), Saul of Benjamin is introduced. Looking for lost donkeys in the Hill Country of Ephraim, in the area of Shalisha and in the districts of Shaalim and Zuph, he finally approached Samuel in Ramah for guidance. After Saul was informed that the lost donkeys had been found, Samuel privately anointed him king (10:1). To help confirm in Saul's mind that he was God's choice, Samuel predicted certain events that would occur near Rachel's tomb at Zelzah on the border of Benjamin, at the great tree of Tabor, and at Gibeah of God (vv. 2–8).

These events indeed occurred, and at Gibeah of God (Nebi Samwil) Saul met "a procession of prophets [and] the Spirit of God came upon him in power" (1 Sam 10:10). Since Saul's family was from nearby Gibeon (1 Chron 9:35–40),[8] it is not surprising that as Saul descended from Gibeah of God, his uncle approached him with questions regarding what Samuel had said to him (1 Sam 10:15; Gibeah of God and Gibeon are only 1.5 mi. [2.5 km.] apart). Soon after, Israel was gathered at the central Benjamin site of Mizpah, and there Saul was chosen by lot to be king (vv. 17–27). After the selection process Saul returned to his (newly constructed?) residence in Gibeah (Tell el-Ful). Although this site had lain abandoned since its destruction after the affair of the Levite and his

concubine (Judges 20:33–45), Saul evidently built a fortress at this centrally located site and renamed it Gibeah or Gibeah of Saul (to avoid the ban on rebuilding a wicked city that had been destroyed? Deut 13:13–18); the earlier name Geba/Gibeah of Benjamin had been transferred to the nearby site of Jaba.[9] Here at Tell el-Ful (Gibeah of Saul), archaeologists have uncovered the remains of a fortress dating to the time of Saul. At this early stage in the monarchy, Saul's court must have been very small, for the feasts mentioned do not seem ostentatious (1 Sam 20:5–34) and the reference to Saul and his retainers under the tamarisk tree at Gibeah (22:6) bespeaks a very informal organizational structure.

Saul soon had the opportunity to exhibit his leadership qualities by mustering Israelite and Judean forces for the purpose of delivering the people of Jabesh Gilead from their Ammonite oppressors (1 Sam 11:1–13). Saul may have been eager to do this, for many Benjamites of Saul's day were probably descendants of women whose ancestral homes were in Jabesh Gilead (Judges 21:6–12). Leaving Gibeah of Saul, he proceeded northward to Bezek, where he prepared the forces of Israel and Judah for battle (1 Sam 11:6–8). After crossing the Jordan River, he was able to end the siege of Jabesh and defeat the Ammonites. Convinced of his prowess, Israel confirmed Saul as king at the old cultic center of Gilgal (vv. 14–15), and from that point on his kingship was not doubted by the populace at large.

Soon after this confirmation ceremony (possibly ca. 1048 B.C.)[10] Saul and his son Jonathan mustered small numbers of Israelite forces in Micmash, in the Hill Country of Bethel, and in Gibeah of Benjamin (1 Sam 13:2). These localities of Israelite control were again in central and eastern Benjamin, for it is probable that the Philistines controlled western Benjamin by means of garrisons at Gibeah of God (10:5) and Geba (probably = el-Jib [Gibeon] in this instance; Gibeon; 13:3).[11] With these garrisons, the Philistines' line of communication to the coastal plain, via the Beth Horon road, was secure. They were also in a position to make further inroads into the plateau area of Benjamin and to sever Israelite-Judean connections along the north-south Ridge Route. Militarily, the Israelites were at a distinct disadvantage, for they were dependent upon the Philistines for the manufacture and repair of their copper (and iron?)[12] agricultural and military implements (vv. 19–22).

Saul's son Jonathan met the Philistine threat head-on by assaulting and taking their garrison at Geba (Gibeon; 1 Sam 13:3). Since by this defeat the Philistines had lost their toehold in the hill country, and since the Israelites now controlled the Beth Horon approach, the Philistines evidently regrouped, possibly in the Aphek area, and then reentered the hill country via the more northerly route that led through Timnath Serah. This brought them into the northwestern and northeastern sections of the Benjamin plateau. Bringing with them chariots, horsemen, and foot soldiers, the Philistines set up camp at Micmash (v. 5). From there they sent out raiding parties to the north (Ophrah), west (Beth Horon), and east ("the border-land overlooking the Valley of Zeboim," vv. 17–18).

After assembling troops at Gilgal in the Jordan Valley near Jericho (prudently well away from the Philistine menace!), Saul and Jonathan moved into the hill country, establishing bases south of the Philistines at Gibeah/Geba of Benjamin (1 Sam 13:15–16) and at "Gibeah [of Saul]" (14:2). Then Jonathan and his armorbearer headed north from Geba to Micmash, crossing the wadi between the two villages (the modern Wadi Suweinit), in the process climbing down and up the cliffs (Seneh and Bozez) that lined the chasm (v. 4). At Micmash, Jonathan and his armorbearer subdued the guards of the Philistine camp (v. 14), and as the earth quaked, the Philistines panicked and ran (v. 15). Saul's watchmen, who had been observing from Gibeah of Benjamin (v. 16), informed him of the panic, and Saul led the remaining Israelite forces into the fray. Israelites who had been hiding in fear in the Hill Country of Ephraim to the north (v. 22) also joined the battle in the Beth Aven area, and they helped to drive the Philistines from the hill country back to the Aijalon region (v. 31).

Later in his reign (ca. 1025 B.C.), Saul had to deal with the Amalekites, who were apparently making an incursion into southern Israel. Saul mustered his troops at Telaim, possibly the same place as Telem of Judah (Josh 15:24, but identification unknown). Upon approaching the city of Amalek (recently identified with Tel Masos),[13] Saul instructed the Kenites—descendants/relatives of Moses' father-in-law, who at times dwelt in Judean territory (Judges 1:16; 1 Sam 27:10), but some of whom were now associated with the Amalekites—to separate themselves from the enemy (1 Sam 15:5–6). This accomplished, Saul attacked the Amalekites and slaughtered them from "Havilah to Shur, to the east of Egypt" (v. 7). To commemorate this victory, Saul set up a monument in "Carmel [of Judah]" (v. 12), which was

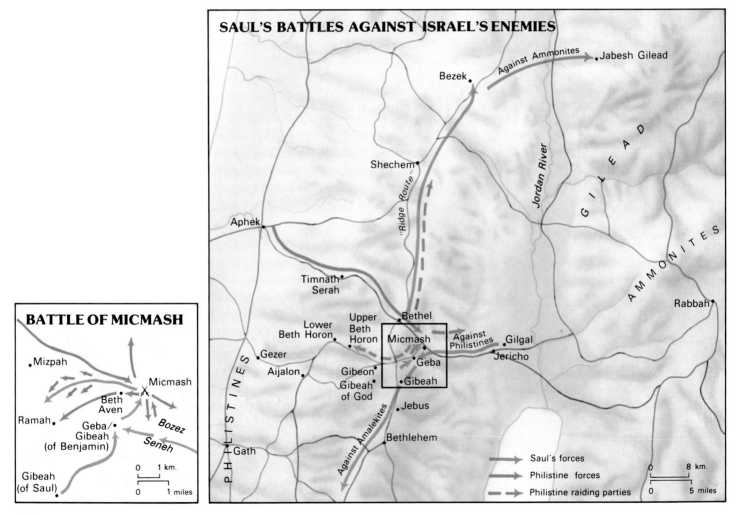

probably one of the southern Judean cities that had been harassed by the Amalekites. The subsequent victory celebration at Gilgal, however, was marred by the fact that Saul had not destroyed all that Yahweh had commanded him to destroy. Samuel informed him that because of this disobedience the kingship would be taken from him and given to his neighbor (vv. 24–35).

Besides noting Saul's victories over the Philistines and Amalekites, the biblical text mentions his victories over Moab, Edom, and the Ammonites to the east, and over the kings of Zobah to the north (1 Sam 14:47). Although these enemies were evidently kept at bay, it was not until the reign of David that Israel took control of these kingdoms, and then for only a brief period of time.

It was soon after the battle with the Amalekites that Samuel anointed David (1 Sam 16) and that David began to serve at Saul's court as a musician. The Philistines and Israelites were still vying for power, but now—probably to the relief of the Israelites—their battles were being fought in the Shephelah, the buffer zone between the Philistines on the west and the Israelite settlements in the mountains on the east. It is in this context that the battle of David and Goliath (1 Sam 17) in the valley of Elah should be placed. The Philistines, moving eastward from Ekron and Gath, camped at Ephes Dammim between Socoh and Azekah (17:1). The Israelites, defending the approaches to the hill country, camped on the north side of the valley (vv. 2–3), probably east of the Philistine camp. The encounter between David and Goliath took place in the broad valley itself, from which David took five smooth stones for his sling. Emboldened by David's example, Saul's troops successfully attacked the Philistines. The latter at first fled northward, on the Shaaraim road in the valley east of Azekah, and then, north of Azekah, they turned west and followed the valley to the security of their cities of Gath and Ekron (v. 52). This battle was probably one of a number that occurred between the Israelites and the Philistines in the Shephelah. For example,

in the Shephelah David defended the inhabitants of Keilah against the Philistines (23:1–13). Thus the account of David and Goliath not only provides numerous geographical details concerning the Valley of Elah region but also illustrates the fact that the Shephelah served as a military buffer zone between the inhabitants of the coastal plain and those of the mountains to the east.[14]

Following his stunning victory, chapters 18 through 21 of 1 Samuel describe David's growing popularity among the people and Saul's growing jealousy. These chapters are punctuated with descriptions of David's narrow escapes from Saul, most of the action occurring in the Benjamin area. For example, after Michal (David's wife) helped him escape from Saul (1 Sam 19:11–17), David fled to nearby Naioth, the Bedouin encampment that was close to Ramah.[15] Saul was overcome with a prophetic spirit as he approached Naioth, thus setting the stage for David's escape (vv. 18–24).

After a number of close encounters, David decided that it was necessary to leave the Benjamin Plateau in order to avoid Saul's wrath. With this decision, David began his year- or year-and-a-half-long flight from Saul. After receiving meager provisions of the sacred bread as well as the sword of Goliath from the priest who served at the tabernacle at Nob (1 Sam 21:1–7), David fled into the hands of his archenemy, Achish, the king of Gath (vv. 8–15)—possibly believing that Achish would welcome any enemy of Saul. However, Achish viewed David's arrival as an opportunity to rid himself of David, who had to flee for his life. At the cave of Adullam (Josh 15:35 clearly places it in the Shephelah) David gathered a fighting force of four hundred men. Throughout his career this group would give him unwavering military support, providing him with a power base from which to operate.

After he sent his parents to Moab—Davidic connections with Moab via Boaz and his Moabite wife, Ruth, are well attested (Ruth 4:9–22; 1 Chron 2:12–15)—David's movements are described in detail in 1 Samuel 22–27 (see map

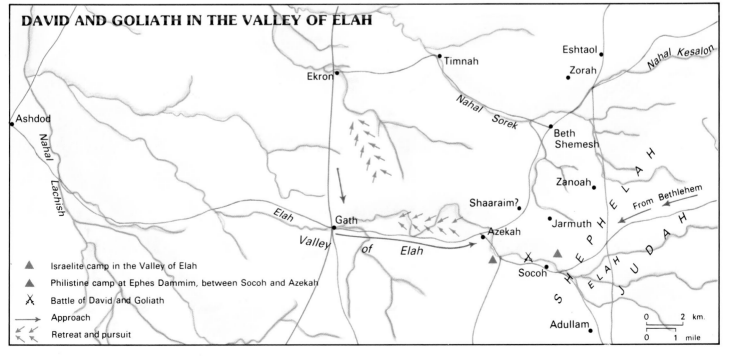

DAVID AND GOLIATH IN THE VALLEY OF ELAH

▲ Israelite camp in the Valley of Elah
▲ Philistine camp at Ephes Dammim, between Socoh and Azekah
✗ Battle of David and Goliath
→ Approach
↙↙ Retreat and pursuit

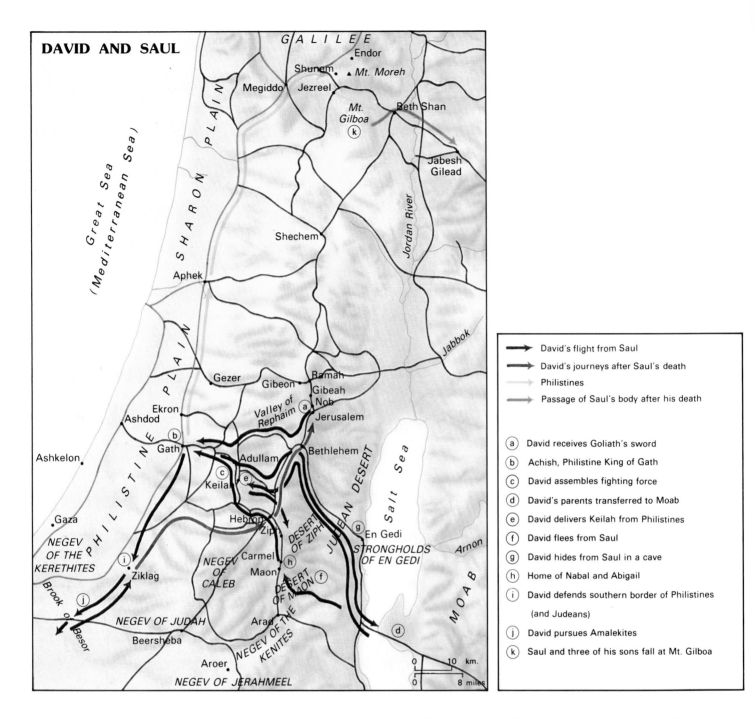

DAVID AND SAUL

Map legend:

→ David's flight from Saul
→ David's journeys after Saul's death
→ Philistines
→ Passage of Saul's body after his death

(a) David receives Goliath's sword
(b) Achish, Philistine King of Gath
(c) David assembles fighting force
(d) David's parents transferred to Moab
(e) David delivers Keilah from Philistines
(f) David flees from Saul
(g) David hides from Saul in a cave
(h) Home of Nabal and Abigail
(i) David defends southern border of Philistines
  (and Judeans)
(j) David pursues Amalekites
(k) Saul and three of his sons fall at Mt. Gilboa

p. 114). He was sometimes west of the Judean mountain ridge in the forest of Hereth (22:5), sometimes delivering Keilah from the Philistines (23:1–13). But most of the time he was east of the watershed, either in or on the fringes of the Judean desert. In this connection the tri-cities of Ziph, Carmel, and Maon are mentioned, as are the deserts of Ziph, Maon, Paran, and En Gedi as well as the Arabah and Jeshimon to the east and south.

Saul pursued David out into these deserts but was continually foiled in his attempts to capture him. It is probable that most of the local inhabitants in some way supported David—a fellow member of the tribe of Judah—and that David in turn "protected" the Judeans from their enemies. Exceptions to this supposed support included the inhabitants of Ziph, who at times attempted to deliver David into Saul's hands (1 Sam 23:19–29; 26:1–2), as did the insolent Nabal (a resident of Maon and Carmel), whose

beautiful wife Abigail married David after Nabal's untimely death (1 Sam 25). Since it would be difficult to support a band of six hundred men and their families in the Judean Desert, David's flight to En Gedi and the nearby Crags of the Wild Goats (23:29–24:2) was to be expected, for the freshwater spring at En Gedi is the largest on the western shore of the Salt Sea. Even though Saul's pursuit of David actually led him to the very cave where he was hiding, David still was able to escape (24:3–21).

Eventually David must have realized that he would either have to kill Saul in self-defense or else be killed by him. To avoid this, David, along with his troops, again sought asylum with Achish, the king of Gath. A year or so had passed since their previous encounter (1 Sam 2:10–15), and by this time Achish was well aware that David was indeed a true enemy of the Israelite king. Achish, planning to make use of David's troops and military prowess, stationed him at Ziklag.[16]

Tel Azeka, Valley of Elah and the Shephelah, looking southwest, near the spot of battle between David and Goliath.

There, on his southern border, David was to protect Achish against raiders from the south.

David, in fact, conducted raids on the Geshurites, the Girzites, and the Amalekites, all of whom evidently dwelt in northern Sinai between Ziklag and Shur (1 Sam 27:8). Leaving no survivors, David was free to perpetrate a lie by telling Achish, who lived in Gath (24 mi. [39 km.] to the north), that he had made raids on the Negev of Judah, the Negev of Jerahmeel, and the Negev of the Kenites (27:10), all of which are subdistricts of the biblical Negev.[17] In this way David was leading Achish to believe that Judean hostility toward David was growing, when in fact Judean appreciation for David was increasing because he was defending them from these desert bands!

After David had served sixteen months at Ziklag (1 Sam 27:7), the final confrontation between Saul and the Philistines began to unfold. It is difficult to pinpoint the exact cause of the battle. Possibly Israel, by camping at the spring by Jezreel in the north (29:1), was attempting to cut the line of communication between the Philistines and their allies garrisoned at Beth Shan. The Philistines responded to this threat by assembling their forces at Aphek, the point where the Philistine and Sharon plains meet, and from there they marched north and eastward, setting up camp opposite Israel on the southern slope of Mount Moreh at Shunem. By establishing their camp at Shunem they effectively cut the north-south lines of communication between Israelite settlements in Galilee and Manasseh.

As the Philistine and Israelite forces faced each other across the Harod Valley, David, whom the Philistines did not allow to take part in the battle (1 Sam 29), returned to Ziklag, only to find that the Amalekites had made a raid on the Negev of the Kerethites, the Negev of Caleb, Judean territory, and Ziklag, and that they had taken captive the women and children that had remained behind. David and his six hundred men pursued the retreating Amalekites southwest to the brook Besor,[18] and after crossing the brook with a small force he overtook the Amalekites, slaughtering them and rescuing the captive women and children. The spoil captured from the Amalekites was not kept by David and his men but was sent to the elders of Judah and distributed among cities located in the southern Hill Country of Judah and in the Negev (30:26–31).

Meanwhile, back in the Jezreel–Shunem region, the Israelites were engaged in a life-and-death struggle with the Philistines. Some of the fleeing Israelites went up Mount Gilboa, on the south side of the valley, possibly thinking that the mountain would offer protection from the pursuing Philistines, whose chariotry could not operate effectively in the rocky and forested mountainous terrain. It was there on Mount Gilboa that Saul and Jonathan died as a result of the battle. As part of the Philistine victory celebration the weapons of Saul and Jonathan were placed in the temple of the Ashtoreths and their headless bodies were fastened to the wall of Beth Shan in public display. The men of Jabesh Gilead, the town that Saul had delivered from the Ammonites and with which he may have had family ties (see above, p. 104), crossed the Jordan River, removed the bodies from the wall, and buried the first king of Israel, along with his son Jonathan, under a tamarisk tree at Jabesh.[19] With the burial of Saul and Jonathan the transition period between the period of the Judges and that of the monarchy had come to an end. Within a few years the idea of a dynastic monarchy would be firmly established, at least in the minds of the Judeans.

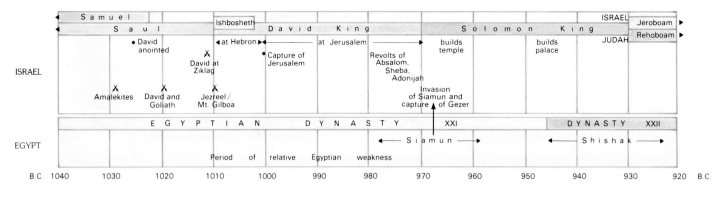

(Chart at top)

Samuel

Saul — Ishbosheth — David King — Solomon King — ISRAEL / Jeroboam — JUDAH / Rehoboam

ISRAEL

- David anointed
- at Hebron — at Jerusalem
- David at Ziklag
- Capture of Jerusalem
- Revolts of Absalom, Sheba, Adonijah
- builds temple
- builds palace
- Invasion of Siamun and capture of Gezer
- Amalekites
- David and Goliath
- Jezreel / Mt. Gilboa

EGYPTIAN DYNASTY XXI — DYNASTY XXII

EGYPT

← Siamun → ← Shishak →

Period of relative Egyptian weakness

B.C. 1040 1030 1020 1010 1000 990 980 970 960 950 940 930 920 B.C.

The United Monarchy: David and Solomon

After the death of Saul it was probably somewhat unclear in the minds of the common people whether a king should rule over them or not. One of the surviving sons of Saul, Ish-Bosheth, was established as "king over Gilead, Ashuri [= Asher?], and Jezreel, and also over Ephraim, Benjamin and all Israel" (2 Sam 2:9). The real power behind the throne, however, was Abner the son of Ner, the former commander of Saul's army, who had escaped with his life from the battle of Mount Gilboa. Ish-Bosheth ruled from the Transjordanian city of Mahanaim (a town discreetly removed from the clutches of the recently victorious Philistines).

In the south, after inquiring of the Lord, David moved from Ziklag to the city of Hebron, where he was anointed king of Judah (2 Sam 2:1–7, 11). It should be remembered that David had already helped the Judeans by protecting their southern flank from the Amalekites, Geshurites, and Girzites (1 Sam 27:8), and had ingratiated himself to them by sending gifts to eleven of their cities and to two local tribes (30:26–31). Thus it is no wonder that they accepted one of their own as king rather than the weak Benjamite Ish-Bosheth.

For a period of time there was war between the house of Saul and that of David, as exemplified by the battle of selected men from both armies at the pool of Gibeon (2 Sam 2:12–32). Abner, realizing the weak position of Ish-Bosheth, proposed to David that he would deliver "all Israel" to him in order to make him king of the entire country. In return, David promised to make Abner commander of his army. But before the arrangements could be completed, Joab intervened and killed Abner in cold blood (3:22–29).

Ish-Bosheth, now in a very weakened position, was murdered by two men from Beeroth, one of the old Gibeonite cities, possibly in revenge for Saul's extermination of many of their kinsmen (2 Sam 4:1–12; compare 21:1–14). At that point the elders of Israel came to David at Hebron, made a covenant with him, and anointed him king over Israel (5:1–3; 1 Chron 11:1–3).

The Philistines, who up to that time may have considered David a client king, realized that a united Israel posed a serious threat to their military and political control of the country. They responded by twice trying to divide the country into two parts by establishing themselves in the hill country in the Valley of Rephaim, southwest of Jerusalem. Twice they were defeated, and the last time David drove

them out of the hill country, via the Geba/Gibeon–Beth Horon road, back to Gezer and the coastal plain (2 Sam 5:17–25; 1 Chron 14:8–17).

After ruling in Hebron for seven years and six months (ca. 1010–1002 B.C.), David captured Jebus (Jerusalem) and made it his capital (2 Sam 5:6–10; 1 Chron 11:4–9; see pp. 188–99 for a detailed description of the city). Evidently Joab led in the capture of the city (1 Chron 11:6), probably gaining entrance to the fortress via the Gihon Spring and the Jebusite "watershaft" (2 Sam 5:8). The move of the capital from Hebron to Jerusalem was strategically very important. David's conquest of the non-Israelite city made it the personal possession of him and his descendants, so that neither Judah nor Israel could lay claim to it. Neither group would be offended by being governed from it, since it was situated on the boundary between the northern and southern tribes and was thus in a neutral location. By bringing the ark of the covenant to Jerusalem (2 Sam 6; 1 Chron 13) David made it the religious as well as the political center of a united Israel. From a defensive standpoint its mountainous location, removed from the coastal plain, meant that any enemies who wished to attack Jerusalem had to make the difficult ascent into the mountains with their chariots, siege machinery, etc., before they could even begin the attack on the city. In addition, its local topography (see p. 189) made it easily defensible on the west, south, and east.

It is to be assumed that David, after establishing his capital in Jerusalem, consolidated his kingdom internally before beginning his wars of expansion. This means that he must have taken control of the old Canaanite centers that were located in the Jezreel and Harod valleys—Megiddo, Taanach, Ibleam, and Beth Shan—along with the Canaanite centers located on the Plain of Acco and in Galilee (Judges 1:21–35). It appears that to the southwest David was able to subdue the Philistines, capturing the important city of Gath (1 Chron 18:1, although the parallel passage, 2 Sam 8:1, is difficult to interpret).

The exact sequence of David's wars of expansion, as described in 2 Samuel 8–12, is difficult to determine with precision, since the textual arrangement of the events is not necessarily their chronological order.[1] David's first war in the Transjordanian region was with the Ammonites. Their king, Nahash, who had been a friend of David, died, and his son Hanun became king in his place. David sent emissaries

116

The waterfall at En Gedi.

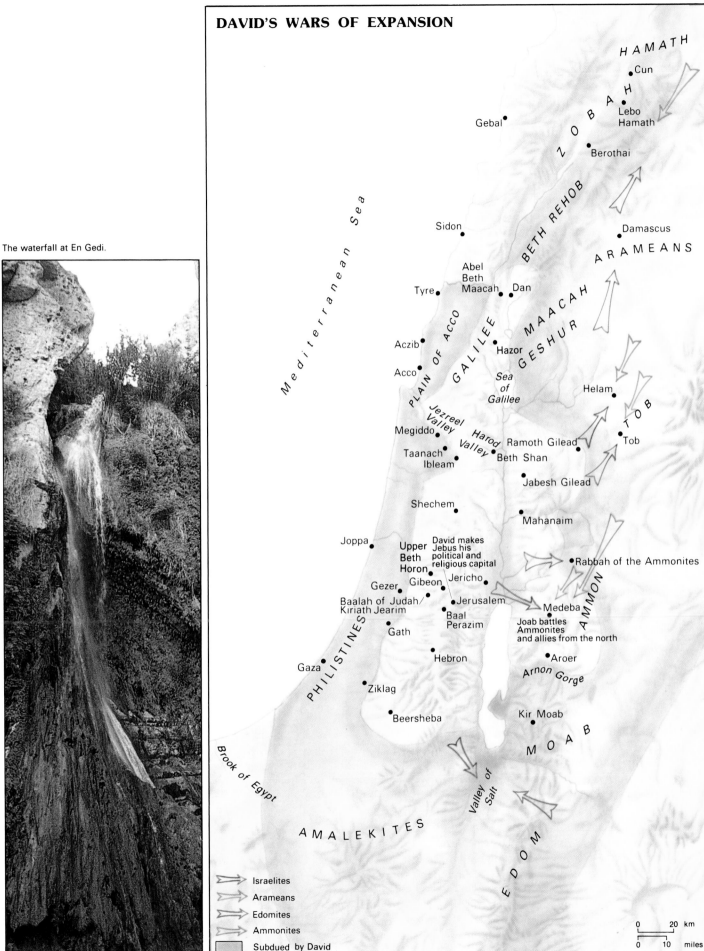

DAVID'S WARS OF EXPANSION

HAMATH

Cun

Z O B A H

Gebal

Lebo
Hamath

Berothai

Mediterranean Sea

Sidon

Damascus

BETH REHOB

ARAMEANS

Abel
Beth
Maacah

Dan

Tyre

MAACAH

GESHUR

Aczib

Hazor

Acco

PLAIN OF ACCO

GALILEE

Sea
of
Galilee

Helam

T O B

Jezreel
Valley

Megiddo

Harod
Valley

Ramoth Gilead

Tob

Taanach
Ibleam

Beth Shan

Jabesh Gilead

Shechem

Mahanaim

Joppa

Upper
Beth
Horon

David makes
Jebus his
political and
religious capital

Rabbah of the Ammonites

Gezer

Gibeon

Jericho

AMMON

Baalah of Judah
Kiriath Jearim

Jerusalem

Baal
Perazim

Medeba

Gath

Joab battles
Ammonites
and allies from the north

Hebron

Aroer

Gaza

Arnon Gorge

Ziklag

Kir Moab

Beersheba

M O A B

Brook of Egypt

Valley of Salt

AMALEKITES

E D O M

Israelites
Arameans
Edomites
Ammonites
Subdued by David

0   20 km
0   10   miles

117

to Hanun to congratulate him on his rise to the kingship, but instead of receiving the messengers graciously, Hanun mistreated them, thinking that they had come on a spy mission (2 Sam 10:1–5 and 1 Chron 19:1–5 have a somewhat comic description of their mistreatment). The Ammonites, realizing that their insult to David would lead to war, began to prepare for it by hiring mercenary troops from their neighbors to the north. Twenty thousand Aramean foot soldiers were supplied by the federated countries of Beth Rehob and Zobah, along with a thousand from the king of Maacah, a country located in the northeastern part of the Huleh Valley, while twelve thousand were supplied from the area of Tob (2 Sam 10:6). In addition, numerous chariots and charioteers were hired from Aram Naharaim (1 Chron 19:6–7).

These forces, combined with the Ammonite army, assembled at Medeba to fight the Israelite forces led by Joab. Joab found himself trapped between the Ammonites, stationed in and near the city of Medeba, and the Arameans, operating in the open countryside. By splitting their forces, Joab and his brother Abishai were able to drive off the Aramean and Ammonite forces (2 Sam 10:6–14; 1 Chron 19:6–15). It is likely that Israel continued to press its advantage in the area by conquering the territory of Moab (2 Sam 8:2; 1 Chron 18:2). It may have been at this time that Benaiah the son of Jehoiada, one of David's mighty men, distinguished himself by killing two sons of Ariel of Moab (2 Sam 23:20; 1 Chron 11:22). It is not clear why some Moabites were so harshly treated, especially since previously there had been good relations between Moab and David (David had sent his family to the king of Moab for safekeeping while fleeing from Saul, 1 Sam 22:3–4).

The Arameans, whose forces were still relatively intact following the battle of Medeba, regrouped at Helam, 35 miles (56 km.) east of the Sea of Galilee. Hadadezer, the king of Zobah and Rehob, supplemented his forces by bringing in additional Arameans from "beyond the River" (= Euphrates). In the ensuing battle, David and his troops emerged victorious, killing thousands of foot soldiers and hundreds of charioteers (2 Sam 10:15–19, but compare 1 Chron 19:16–19). It is probable, as Malamat has suggested,[2] that nearby Tob and Maacah passed into Davidic control at that time.

After the battle of Helam the Israelite forces may have returned to Rabbah to deal decisively with the Ammonites. While the army under the leadership of Joab was laying siege to the city, David was back in Jerusalem having his sinful affair with Bathsheba (2 Sam 11). David then had Bathsheba's husband, Uriah the Hittite, stationed close to the city wall during the siege of Rabbah, so that Uriah was "killed in the battle." After David repented of his sins (12:1–24), the royal citadel and water supply of Rabbah were captured. When the city itself was taken, David took the crown of the Ammonite king and placed it on his head (vv. 26–31; 1 Chron 20:1–3). Some of the Ammonites were executed for their participation in the revolt, and from that time on, David, probably via an appointed governor, ruled over the Ammonites.

The decisive blow against the Arameans came at a time when Hadadezer had gone north to quell the revolt of some of his previously loyal vassals who were now exploiting his weakened condition (2 Sam 8:3).[3] In this northern battle David defeated the Arameans of Damascus who had come to the aid of Hadadezer (vv. 5–6; 1 Chron 18:5–6). The spoils of war taken by David included chariots, chariot horses, gold shields, and a great quantity of bronze, which would later be used in the construction of the "Bronze Sea" in Solomon's temple (1 Chron 18:8). Eventually, the Aramean states of Beth Rehob and Zobah, along with their cities of Tebah, Berothai, and Cun, submitted to David's control (2 Sam 8:3–4, 7–8; 1 Chron 18:3–4, 7–8).

Finally, the army of David defeated the Edomites in the Valley of Salt, probably located to the south of the Dead Sea (2 Sam 8:13–14; 1 Chron 18:12–13). Although many Edomites were killed, Hadad, who was of royal Edomite descent, fled to Egypt via Midian and Paran and later returned to lead his people in revolt against Solomon (1 Kings 11:14–22).

By the end of the period of expansion David had gained control of many of the neighboring states. To the far north, Tou (or Toi), the king of Hamath, acknowledged David's supremacy by sending his son Joram (Hadoram) along with "gifts" of silver, gold, and bronze to Jerusalem. Certainly the Aramean states of Zobah, Beth Rehob, and Maacah now came under Israelite control. A garrison was placed in Damascus and tribute extracted from the populace (2 Sam 8:5–6; 1 Chron 18:5–6). It is probable that the state of Geshur, located just east of the Sea of Galilee, remained semi-independent; its king, Talmai, formed an alliance with David. This alliance was probably sealed by the marriage of Talmai's daughter to David; the offspring of their union was Absalom (2 Sam 3:3). It is thus no wonder that Absalom, after killing his half-brother Amnon (who had raped Absalom's sister Tamar), fled for refuge to Geshur, the homeland of his mother (13:37–39).

East of the Jordan the Israelites solidified their control of the land of Tob (in Gilead) and the portion of Moab north of the Arnon Gorge, so that the territory that had been assigned to the tribes of Reuben, Gad, and Manasseh was now firmly in Israelite hands. David assumed royal prerogatives over the Ammonites (2 Sam 12:30). He placed garrisons in Edomite territory, and the Moabites sent him tribute (2 Sam 8:2, 14; 1 Chron 18:13). To the south and the southwest the Amalekites and Philistines were subdued (2 Sam 8:12; 1 Chron 18:11). Thus all the countries surrounding Israel were now firmly under Davidic control.

Although the exact boundaries of the Davidic empire are not given, the chronicler, describing the bringing up of the ark from Kiriath Jearim to Jerusalem, notes that "David assembled all the Israelites, from the Shihor River of Egypt to Lebo Hamath" for the event (1 Chron 13:5). Since the Shihor is normally considered one of the eastern branches or canals of the Nile, located in the vicinity of the present-day Suez Canal, this implies that David controlled northern Sinai all the way to the eastern Nile delta. Never before and never again would Israelite control extend this far. The northernmost point, Lebo Hamath, was the northern boundary of the land of Canaan. Thus, while David and Solomon reigned, the Israelites did, in fact, rule over most of the land that had been promised them as an inheritance four hundred years earlier (Num 34).

As far as the core of David's kingdom (Israel proper) is concerned, east of the Dead Sea it stretched from Aroer in the south to Dan in the north; west of the Jordan Valley it

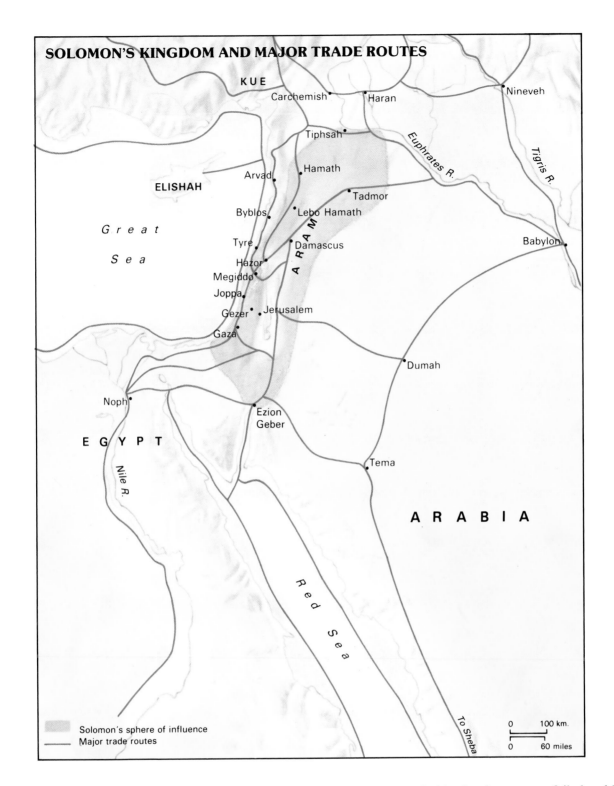

SOLOMON'S KINGDOM AND MAJOR TRADE ROUTES

Solomon's sphere of influence
Major trade routes

ports and some much needed agricultural hinterland. Solomon, in turn, could have received some unnamed cities, possibly located to the north and/or northeast of Phoenicia, in which he settled Israelites in order to control the territory near Hamath Zobah, thereby securing the trade routes through the area and providing bases for his merchants (1 Chron 8:1–4).

Toward the end of his reign, Solomon faced a number of serious problems. Internally, he had to face the dissatisfaction of some of the leaders of the northern tribes, who objected to his building projects and probably also to his taxation and conscription policies (1 Kings 11:27). This dissatisfaction can be seen in Jeroboam's rebellion against Solomon, although this abortive attempt failed and Jeroboam had to flee to Egypt, where he remained until Solomon's death (vv. 26–40). Externally, Hadad the Edomite became Solomon's adversary to the southeast (vv. 14–22), while to the northeast Rezon of Damascus became a leader of rebels who took control of and settled in Damascus (vv. 23–25). In addition, Solomon began to worship some of the foreign deities he had introduced into Jerusalem in deference to his foreign wives (vv. 1–8). It is thus evident that both internal and external factors were weakening the empire, and it is no wonder that it collapsed almost immediately upon the death of Solomon.

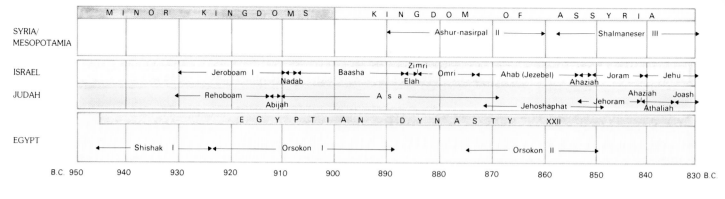

SYRIA/ MESOPOTAMIA	MINOR KINGDOMS	KINGDOM OF ASSYRIA Ashur-nasirpal II — Shalmaneser III		
ISRAEL	Jeroboam I — Nadab — Baasha	Zimri — Elah — Omri — Ahab (Jezebel) — Ahaziah — Joram — Jehu		
JUDAH	Rehoboam — Abijah — A s a	Jehoshaphat — Jehoram — Ahaziah — Athaliah — Joash		
EGYPT	EGYPTIAN DYNASTY XXII Shishak I — Orsokon I	Orsokon II		

B.C. 950 940 930 920 910 900 890 880 870 860 850 840 830 B.C.

The Divided Kingdom

Although Israel and Judah had been joined together for some seventy-three years under the leadership of David and Solomon, the continuation of the union was by no means assured. After the death of Solomon (930 B.C.), his son and successor, Rehoboam (930–913 B.C.), traveled north to the tribal center at Shechem in order to secure the continued allegiance of the northern tribes (1 Kings 12:1–19; 2 Chron 10:1–19). However, when the latter demanded relief from the oppressive tax burden Solomon had placed upon them, Rehoboam's response was that he would increase this burden. At this point the northern tribes rejected the supremacy of the Davidic dynasty and appointed Jeroboam (930–910 B.C.) as their first king. Rehoboam fled for his life back to Jerusalem and, at the behest of the prophet Shemaiah, refrained from invading the north (1 Kings 12:21–24; 2 Chron 11:1–4). Thus began the period of the divided kingdom (930–722 B.C.).

In the north, Jeroboam must have taken a number of economic and political steps to strengthen his grip on the country, but he is most famous for his religious maneuver of establishing worship centers at Dan and Bethel (1 Kings 12:26–33). By building sanctuaries at these two cities, which were located at the extremities of his country, he, in a sense, defined the limits of the territory under his control. In addition, by placing a sanctuary at Bethel, which was located on the Ridge Route only eleven miles (17.5 km.) north of Jerusalem, he in effect attempted to "detour" any worshipers who might be heading to the temple in Jerusalem. Since Jeroboam appointed non-Levitical priests to serve at his shrines and since the loyalty of most of the Levites was to the sanctuary in Jerusalem and to the Davidic dynasty, many of the Levites left their allotted cities in northern Israel (see map p. 102) and moved south, to the more hospitable territory of Judah (2 Chron 11:13–14).

The Egyptian pharaoh Shishak (945–924 B.C.), seeing the weakness of the divided kingdom, made plans for the invasion of both Judah and Israel. In response, Rehoboam constructed fifteen fortresses in Judah (2 Chron 11:5–12; see map p. 125) to ward off the attack. It is important to note that these forts were located in the Shephelah, the southern hill country, and along the edge of the Judean Desert; thus it is clear that by 925 B.C., within five years of the death of the powerful Solomon, the "empire" of his son was basically confined to the Hill Country of Judah! It is not known why Rehoboam did not fortify his northern border, but possibly

he was still hopeful of a reunion with the northern tribes.

Shishak's invasion of Judah is briefly described in the Bible (1 Kings 14:21, 25–31; 2 Chron 12:1–11), but his own inscription, located on the walls of the temple of Amun in Karnak, Egypt, documents it much more fully.[1] The invasion, which took place in Rehoboam's fifth year (925 B.C.), proceeded from the coastal plain into the Hill Country of Benjamin via the important approach road situated on the Beth Horon ridge as well as along one of the ridges to the south. Although Jerusalem was threatened, it avoided capture because Rehoboam paid large sums of tribute to Shishak (1 Kings 14:25–28; 2 Chron 12:9–11). Shishak's account of his campaign contains many details, including his invasion of Israel to the north, but it is difficult to determine his exact line of march. Apparently he moved northward toward Shechem, pursuing Jeroboam (who previously had found refuge with Shishak in Egypt [1 Kings 11:40]) to Tirzah, down the Wadi Faria into the Jordan Valley, and further into the hills of Gilead. Indeed, Jeroboam may have temporarily moved his capital to Penuel (12:25; Heb., but NIV Peniel), a city discreetly located in Transjordan away from the major thrust of Shishak's attack. In addition, the northern portion of Shishak's campaign included an attack on cities in the Jezreel Valley and the Sharon Plain. The second section of Shishak's inscription describes his conquest of some eighty-five settlements in the southern part of Judah in the Negev. This text and recent archaeological investigations[2] suggest that the fortresses that Solomon had built were destroyed by the Egyptian king, implying that the conveyers of luxury goods from southern Arabia now had to follow alternate routes (through Shishak's Egypt?) to Mediterranean ports. Thus effective control of the major trade routes through Israel slipped from Israelite and Judean hands, to the benefit of the Egyptians.

Israel and Judah, although both humbled by their experiences with Shishak, still took about twenty years to resolve the dispute over their common border. The first of several incursions was made by Rehoboam's son Abijah (913–910 B.C.), who invaded Israel and captured Bethel, Jeshanah, and Ephron, as well as the surrounding villages (2 Chron 13:2–20). This northern movement of the Judean border, which brought Jeroboam's cult center at Bethel under Judean control, lasted for approximately twenty years. It was the northern king Baasha (908–886 B.C.) who responded by pushing the border south to Ramah, only six miles (10 km.)

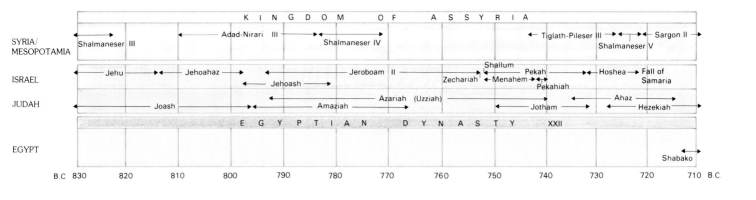

	B.C. 830	820	810	800	790	780	770	760	750	740	730	720	710 B.C.
SYRIA/MESOPOTAMIA	KINGDOM OF ASSYRIA												
	Shalmaneser III	Adad-Nirari III		Shalmaneser IV					Tiglath-Pileser III	Shalmaneser V	Sargon II		
ISRAEL	Jehu	Jehoahaz	Jehoash	Jeroboam II					Zechariah / Shallum / Menahem / Pekahiah / Pekah		Hoshea	Fall of Samaria	
JUDAH	Joash		Amaziah	Azariah (Uzziah)					Jotham	Ahaz	Hezekiah		
EGYPT	EGYPTIAN DYNASTY XXII											Shabako	

Podium (for throne of a king?) on the right side of the city gate at Dan.

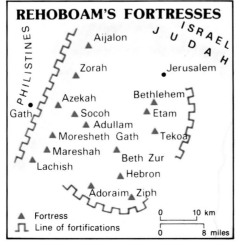

REHOBOAM'S FORTRESSES

PHILISTINES

JUDAH

ISRAEL

Aijalon

Zorah

Jerusalem

Azekah

Bethlehem

Gath

Socoh

Etam

Adullam

Moresheth Gath

Tekoa

Mareshah

Beth Zur

Lachish

Hebron

Adoraim Ziph

▲ Fortress

⊓ Line of fortifications

0   10 km

0   8 miles

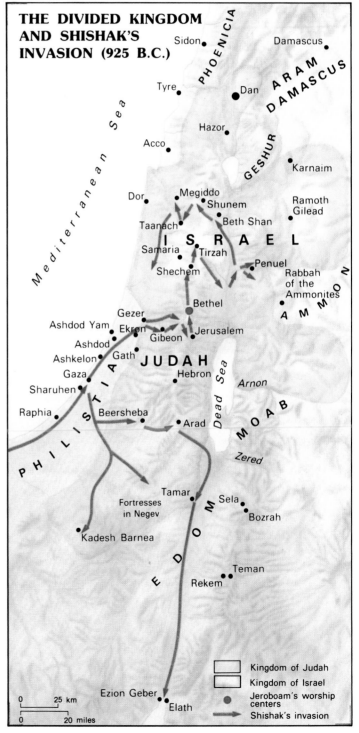

THE DIVIDED KINGDOM AND SHISHAK'S INVASION (925 B.C.)

PHOENICIA

Sidon

Damascus

Tyre

Dan

ARAM DAMASCUS

Hazor

GESHUR

Acco

Karnaim

Mediterranean Sea

Dor

Megiddo

Shunem

Ramoth Gilead

Taanach

Beth Shan

ISRAEL

Samaria

Tirzah

Shechem

Penuel

Rabbah of the Ammonites

AMMON

Bethel

Gezer

Ashdod Yam

Ekron

Jerusalem

Ashdod

Gibeon

Ashkelon

Gath

JUDAH

Gaza

Hebron

Dead Sea

Arnon

Sharuhen

Raphia

Beersheba

Arad

MOAB

Zered

Tamar

Fortresses in Negev

Sela

Bozrah

EDOM

Kadesh Barnea

Teman

Rekem

Ezion Geber

Elath

☐ Kingdom of Judah

☐ Kingdom of Israel

● Jeroboam's worship centers

→ Shishak's invasion

0   25 km

0   20 miles

125

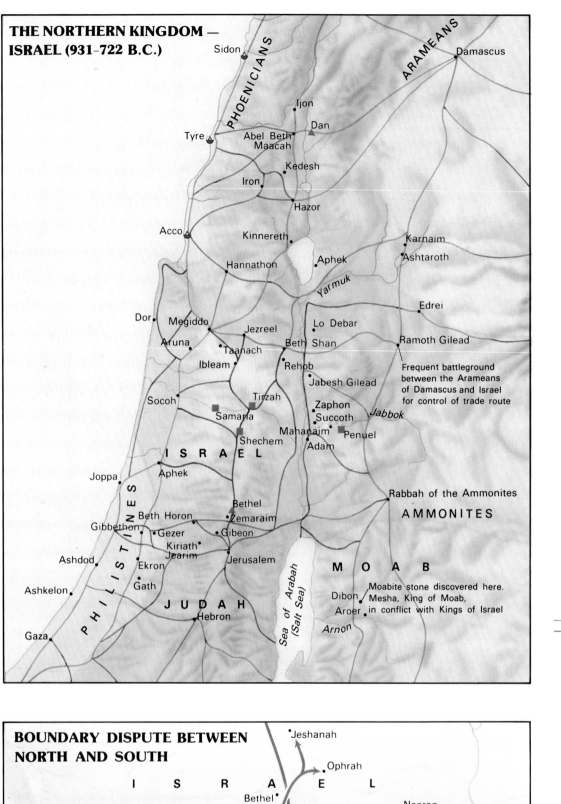

THE NORTHERN KINGDOM —
ISRAEL (931–722 B.C.)

Sidon

Damascus

PHOENICIANS

ARAMEANS

Ijon

Dan

Tyre

Abel Beth
Maacah

Kedesh

Iron

Hazor

Acco

Kinnereth

Karnaim
Ashtaroth

Hannathon

Aphek

Yarmuk

Edrei

Dor

Megiddo

Jezreel

Lo Debar

Ramoth Gilead

Aruna

Beth Shan

Taanach

Ibleam

Rehob

Socoh

Tirzah

Jabesh Gilead

Samaria

Zaphon
Succoth

Jabbok

Shechem

Mahanaim

Penuel

Adam

I S R A E L

Joppa

Aphek

Rabbah of the Ammonites

Bethel

AMMONITES

PHILISTINES

Beth Horon
Zemaraim

Gibbethon

Gezer

Gibeon

Kiriath
Jearim

Ashdod

Ekron

Jerusalem

M O A B

Ashkelon

Gath

J U D A H

Sea of Arabah
(Salt Sea)

Moabite stone discovered here.
Mesha, King of Moab,
in conflict with Kings of Israel

Dibon

Aroer

Gaza

Hebron

Arnon

Frequent battleground
between the Arameans
of Damascus and Israel
for control of trade route

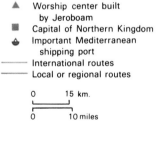

▲ Worship center built
by Jeroboam

■ Capital of Northern Kingdom

⚓ Important Mediterranean
shipping port

— International routes

— Local or regional routes

0   15 km.

0   10 miles

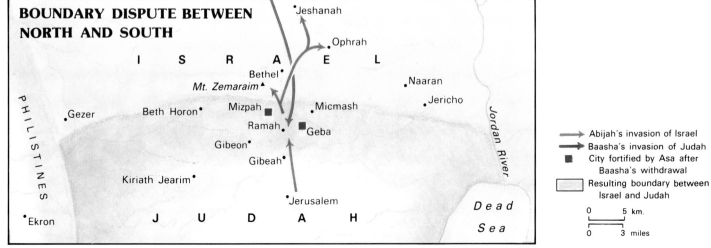

BOUNDARY DISPUTE BETWEEN
NORTH AND SOUTH

Jeshanah

Ophrah

I S R A E L

Bethel

Mt. Zemaraim ▲

Naaran

PHILISTINES

Gezer

Beth Horon

Mizpah

Micmash

Jericho

Ramah

Geba

Jordan River

Gibeon

Gibeah

Kiriath Jearim

Jerusalem

Dead

J U D A H

Sea

Ekron

→ Abijah's invasion of Israel

➡ Baasha's invasion of Judah

■ City fortified by Asa after
Baasha's withdrawal

▢ Resulting boundary between
Israel and Judah

0   5 km.

0   3 miles

126

north of Jerusalem. The Judean king Asa (910–869 B.C.) felt he needed assistance in meeting this Israelite threat and appealed to Ben-Hadad, king of Aram Damascus. Ben-Hadad, in turn, opened a northern front against Israel, invading and capturing Ijon, Dan, Abel Beth Maacah, Kinnereth, and other cities, all of which were located in the Rift Valley north of the Sea of Galilee (1 Kings 15:16–22; 2 Chron 16:1–6). Because of Ben-Hadad's attack, Baasha had to abandon his southward expansion plans, and Asa was able to push their common border northward. The resulting boundary, which left Bethel in Israel to the north and Mizpah and Geba in Judah to the south, formed the traditional boundary between the northern and southern kingdoms until the fall of the north in 722 B.C.

Throughout its 209-year history (930–722 B.C.), the Northern Kingdom was characterized by instability. Its nineteen kings came from nine different families, and eight of its kings were either assassinated or committed suicide. This instability was also illustrated by the fact that Israel had four capitals in succession: Shechem, Penuel, Tirzah, and Samaria. Shechem was initially selected because of its long history as a tribal and religious center. Penuel probably only served as a temporary refuge for Jeroboam as he fled from Shishak. Tirzah, situated east of the watershed at the head of the Wadi Faria, next served as a secure capital on the remote (east) side of the central mountains for approximately forty years. It was at the mid-point of Omri's reign (885–874 B.C.) that he purchased the hill of Shemer, built a new capital there, and named it Samaria (1 Kings 16:23–24). Since Samaria, on the western side of the mountain watershed, was situated close to an easy approach from the Sharon Plain via the Nahal Shechem, it was much more open to foreign influences than was Tirza or even Shechem. Indeed, Israel's treaty with the king of the Sidonians indicates its outward-looking orientation. The marriage of Ahab and Jezebel, the daughter of Ethbaal, king of the Sidonians, not only cemented this alliance, but Ahab's building of a temple and altar in Samaria for Jezebel's god Baal indicates that external influences on the Northern Kingdom were not merely economic, social, and political, but religious as well (vv. 31–33).

Although Israel was able to establish friendly relations with Judah to the south and Tyre and Sidon to the northwest, its relations with the Arameans of Damascus deteriorated. There were probably several causes for this conflict. For example, a strong Israel, occupying cities such as Dan, Ijon, Abel Beth Maacah, and Hazor, in effect controlled Damascus' east-west caravan route to the Mediterranean coast (see p. 32). Also, a powerful Israel meant that it, not Damascus, controlled the lucrative north-south incense route along the King's Highway in Transjordan. If Israel could control this route up to Ramoth Gilead, then spice and incense caravans could pass westward through Israelite territory to ports such as Acco, Tyre, and Sidon. From there, luxury goods could be loaded onto the ships of Phoenicia, Israel's new ally, and transported anywhere in the Mediterranean world. Thus, caravan transit revenues would benefit Israel rather than Damascus. It is no wonder that at least thirteen battles were fought between Israel and the Arameans and that several of them occurred at or near the strategic city of Ramoth Gilead.

On a number of occasions the Arameans pressed their advantage to the gates of Samaria—for example, during the days of Ahab (874–853 B.C.; 1 Kings 20:1–21) and J(eh)oram (852–841 B.C.; 2 Kings 6:24–7:8)—but in each instance they were driven off to lands east of the Jordan River. Despite the numerous conflicts between Aram and Israel, it was necessary for these two rivals to join together along with other nations of the Levant in order to meet the growing Assyrian threat when the Assyrian king Shalmaneser III (858–824 B.C.) began pushing westward and southward. A coalition of eleven or twelve Levantine kings met him in battle at Qarqar on the Orontes in 853 B.C. The only record of the battle comes from Shalmaneser's accounts, and, although he portrays himself as victorious, it is evident that the coalition temporarily blunted the Assyrian threat. Significant is the fact that Hadad-ezer of Damascus (= biblical Ben-Hadad I) supplied the most infantry (20,000 troops), while Ahab the Israelite provided the most chariots (2,000). Although the record of the number of chariots involved seems to have been inflated by Shalmaneser's scribes,[3] it is interesting to note that both Hadad-ezer and Ahab were considered to be the strongest of all the allied kings and that these two countries, which recently had been fighting each other and would do so again soon after the battle, appear as allies at Qarqar! In addition, it is well to note the appearance of Gindibu the Arab, who supplied 1,000 camels to the war effort—underlining the growing importance of the camel as a beast of burden, as well as Arabia's interest in affairs much to its north (i.e., its interest in protecting its northern spice and incense markets and terminals).

Soon after the battle of Qarqar, still in 853 B.C., Ben-Hadad and Ahab were again fighting each other at Ramoth Gilead. Ahab was killed in the battle (1 Kings 22:29–37; 2 Chron 18:28–34). With the death of the powerful Ahab, Moab, Israel's vassal, revolted (2 Kings 3:4–27 and Mesha Stela in *ANET*, 320–21), gaining its independence and capturing the tableland north of the Arnon Gorge as far as Medeba, Nebo, and Bezer, at the expense of the Israelite tribes of Gad and Reuben. In the north, Ahab's son Joram (852–841 B.C.) bore the brunt of Aram's continuing attack, and at one point the siege of Samaria was particularly severe, although ultimately the city was spared by divine intervention (6:24–7:8). Late in Joram's reign, Israel was again at war with the Arameans. Joram himself was wounded while fighting Hazael at Ramoth Gilead. While Joram was recuperating from his wounds at his winter palace in Jezreel, Jehu, the commander of Joram's army at Ramoth Gilead (who had been anointed by the prophet's representative), staged a coup, executing not only the king but also Jezebel and eventually all the remaining descendants of the line of Omri/Ahab (841 B.C.; 2 Kings 9 and 10).

In contrast to the Northern Kingdom, Judah exhibited much more stability during its 345-year history—from the time of Solomon's death (930 B.C.) until the sack of Jerusalem by the Babylonians (586 B.C.). Judah had nineteen kings, all of whom were from the Davidic dynasty.[4] In addition, at the time of Solomon's death Jerusalem had been firmly established as the religious and political capital of the south. Indeed, the Levites who lived in the north moved to Judah when Israel revolted, in order to maintain their connection with the temple worship.

As noted previously, the location of Rehoboam's fortresses and the route of Shishak's invasion (925 B.C.) clearly indicate that the southern kingdom was basically confined to the Hill Country of Judah and the Shephelah. During Rehoboam's rule (930–913 B.C.) Judah was no longer able to control the trade routes that ran through the coastal plain, the Negev, and Transjordan.

The chronicler's account of the reigns of successive Judean kings illustrates the theological principle that their expressions of fidelity and trust toward Yahweh led to blessing, prosperity, and strength, while their disobedience usually led to disaster, destruction, defeat, and eventually deportation. For example, during the early part of Asa's reign (910–869 B.C.), expressions of his trust in Yahweh were followed by his victory over the invading hordes of Zerah the Ethiopian at Zephathah near Mareshah (2 Chron 14). But later, Asa's lack of trust in the power of God to deal with Baasha's aggressive move southward (p. 127) and his reliance on an alliance with the pagan Ben-Hadad of Damascus eventually led to his ignominious death (16:7–14).

Jehoshaphat (872–848 B.C.), Asa's successor, instituted a series of religious and legal reforms. In addition, garrison cities, forts, and store cities were constructed and manned (2 Chron 17), and internal administrative districts and governorships were established (17:2). Jehoshaphat's power was such that the Philistines to the west and the Arabians to the south and east brought him tribute (vv. 10–11), possibly because he was again exercising Judean control over portions of the international trade routes.

Later in the reign of Jehoshaphat, the Moabites, Ammonites, and inhabitants of Mount Seir invaded Judah from the east (2 Chron 20). They evidently crossed the Salt Sea via a ford that led from the Lisan area westward, setting up camp at Hazazon Tamar (= En Gedi). From there they proceeded up the Pass of Ziz, evidently attempting to move up the road on the ridge just north of the Nahal Arugot. Jehoshaphat, after inquiring of the Lord, went out to meet them in battle. But before his arrival, the invading forces fought among themselves and slaughtered each other, so that the Judean army merely had to collect the booty left behind. Indeed, God had gone before the faithful Judeans.

In spite of his faithfulness to Yahweh, Jehoshaphat was also noted for establishing close relations with Israel to the north. In fact, his son Jehoram married Athaliah, a daughter of Ahab and Jezebel (2 Kings 8:18; 2 Chron 21:6), and Jehoshaphat even fought alongside Ahab in the battle of Ramoth Gilead (853 B.C.; see p. 127). When Ahab's son Joram experienced defeat in his encounter with Mesha, the king of Moab, in the northern Mishor area, Jehoshaphat permitted Joram to pass through Judah so that he could attack Moab from the southwest. Jehoshaphat and the Edomites even joined him in this unsuccessful endeavor (2 Kings 3:6–27).

Further evidence of Jehoshaphat's alliance with the north was his attempt to revive Israelite/Judean shipping on the Red Sea. Unfortunately, the Tarshish ships that Jehoshaphat and Ahaziah (853–852 B.C.) had constructed to go to Ophir barely left port before being wrecked at Ezion Geber (1 Kings 22:47–49; 2 Chron 20:35–37). Indeed, every recorded joint venture between Jehoshaphat and Israel was unsuccessful (the battle at Ramoth Gilead, the invasion of Moab, shipping on the Red Sea); yet when Jehoshaphat

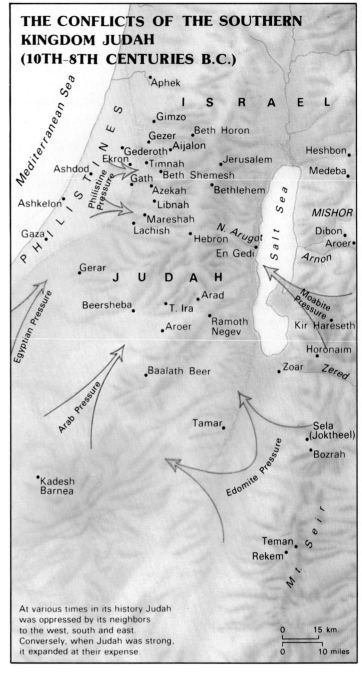

THE CONFLICTS OF THE SOUTHERN KINGDOM JUDAH (10TH-8TH CENTURIES B.C.)

At various times in its history Judah was oppressed by its neighbors to the west, south and east. Conversely, when Judah was strong, it expanded at their expense.

0   15 km.
0   10 miles

trusted in Yahweh, he was successful (the defeat of Moabites, Ammonites, and inhabitants of Mount Seir).

Jehoram, Jehoshaphat's son, who was co-regent with him from 853 to 848 B.C. and who had married Ahab's daughter Athaliah, was very wicked. During his reign (853–841 B.C.) Judah experienced a number of serious reversals. To the southeast, Edom revolted, as did Libnah in the Shephelah on the west (2 Kings 8:20–22; 2 Chron 21:8–10). The Philistines and Arabians, who had formerly brought tribute to Jehoshaphat, invaded Judah and even carried off members of the royal family (2 Chron 21:16–17).

At Jehoram's death, his son Ahaziah continued the alliance with Israel, fighting alongside Joram at Ramoth Gilead (2 Kings 8:28; 2 Chron 22:5). However, this close alliance led to Ahaziah's death: when he was visiting the wounded Joram in Jezreel, Jehu staged a coup and killed him along with Joram, Jezebel, and the last of Ahab's descen-

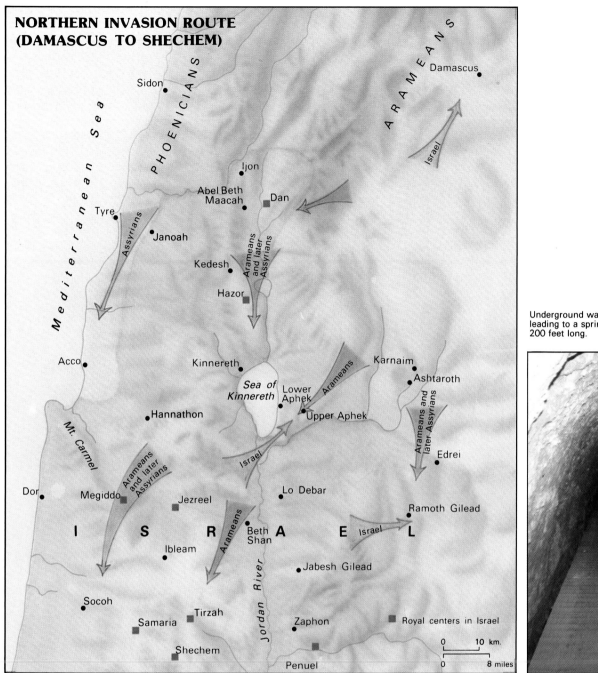

NORTHERN INVASION ROUTE (DAMASCUS TO SHECHEM)

Underground water system at Megiddo leading to a spring outside of city wall; over 200 feet long.

dents (2 Kings 9:27–28; 2 Chron 22:9).

Soon afterward, the royal Davidic line was almost annihilated by the wicked queen Athaliah (841–835 B.C.; 2 Kings 11). However, a priestly family rescued one child from the Davidic line (Joash) and secretly raised him for a number of years. At the age of seven Joash was crowned king, and the wicked Athaliah was executed (2 Kings 11:1–16; 2 Chron 23:1–15). During the early years of Joash's rule (835–796 B.C.), he and his mentor, Jehoiada the high priest, initiated religious reforms (2 Kings 12:1–12; 2 Chron 24:1–16). However, late in Joash's rule, after Jehoiada died at age 130, Joash forsook Yahweh for the worship of the Asherim and idols, and he even murdered the son of his godly advisor (2 Chron 24:17–20). Typically, disobedience led to disaster, and soon Joash felt the pressure of the Aramean king Hazael, who first attacked Gath in the Philistine Plain and then moved eastward into the hill country toward Jerusalem

(2 Kings 12:17–18). However, when Joash paid tribute to Hazael, the latter abandoned the attack on Jerusalem.

Disgruntled elements assassinated Joash (2 Kings 12:19–21; 2 Chron 24:25–27), and his son Amaziah ruled in his place (796–767 B.C.). Amaziah began his reign by subduing Edom and capturing Sela, renaming it Joktheel (2 Kings 14:7; 2 Chron 25:1–15). Soon Amaziah was worshiping captured Edomite gods, however, and his challenge to meet the Israelites in battle was answered by the Israelite king Jehoash, who defeated him in the battle of Beth Shemesh (2 Kings 14:8–14; 2 Chron 25:17–24). The Israelites continued on to Jerusalem, plundered the city, and destroyed portions of its walls. Amaziah's political support was at a low point, and as he fled Jerusalem he was assassinated by conspirators at the Judean city of Lachish (2 Kings 14:18–20; 2 Chron 25:26–28).

Amaziah was succeeded by his son Azariah (also called

Uzziah; 792–740 B.C.). Although Azariah reigned for a total of fifty-two years, because of co-regencies with Amaziah and Jotham, he was sole ruler for only seventeen years. He was judged by the ancient historians to have been a "good" king, and during his reign Judean influence spread considerably. On the west he captured Gath, Jabneh, and Ashdod (2 Chron 26:6–8). To the south and southwest the Arabs in Gur Baal and the Meunim paid tribute to him, as did the Ammonites on the east. In the south he constructed forts in the wilderness, subdued the Edomites, and rebuilt Elath on the Red Sea (2 Kings 14:22; 2 Chron 26:2). He thus reinstituted Judean control over the north-south trade routes that ran through the coastal plain and through Transjordan, as well as over the important east-west route that led from Edom/Arabia to the Mediterranean ports at Gaza and Ashdod. Because of this, it can be assumed that considerable revenues accrued to the Judeans, just as they had when Solomon had controlled these routes. In addition, Azariah fortified Jerusalem and built the Corner and Valley Gates. He was also famous for his agricultural pursuits, which made him known as one who "loved the soil" (2 Chron 26:9–15).

Despite all the blessings that Azariah and the Judeans enjoyed, he was reprimanded by the priests and struck with leprosy as divine punishment when he attempted to burn

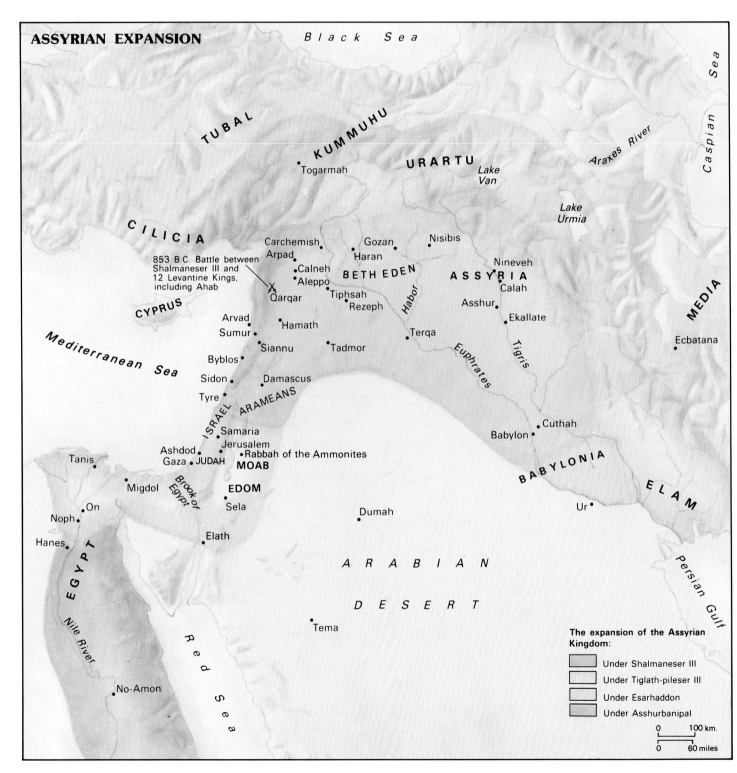

ASSYRIAN EXPANSION

853 B.C. Battle between Shalmaneser III and 12 Levantine Kings, including Ahab

The expansion of the Assyrian Kingdom:

Under Shalmaneser III

Under Tiglath-pileser III

Under Esarhaddon

Under Asshurbanipal

0   100 km.

0   60 miles

incense in the Holy Place of the temple (2 Chron 26:16–21). Evidently at that point (750 B.C.) his son Jotham succeeded him to the throne (750–732 B.C.). Although Jotham's kingship is only briefly described (2 Kings 15:32–38; 2 Chron 27:1–9), he was known for continuing in the ways of his father; the historian notes his building projects in Jerusalem as well as his construction of cities, forts, and towers in the Judean Hills. However, toward the end of his reign, when Ahaz was co-regent with him (apparently 735–732 B.C.), Pekah of Israel, Rezin of Aram Damascus, and probably the son of Tabeel of Transjordan attacked Judah. They were evidently attempting to replace the Davidic king with one of their own choosing, namely the son of Tabeel, who would join them in their anti-Assyrian alliance (2 Kings 16:5–6; 2 Chron 28:5–8; Isa 7:1–17). The Judeans, however, appealed to the Assyrian monarch Tiglath-Pileser III (744–727 B.C.) for assistance, and he willingly responded by attacking Israel in the north (2 Kings 16:7–10; 15:29; 2 Chron 28:16, 20–21; and see below, p. 133). Although the Judeans were relieved of immediate Israelite/Aramean pressures, they would later suffer at the hands of their Assyrian ally.

During Ahaz's reign (735–715 B.C.), religious and political conditions in Judah deteriorated. Children were made to pass through the fire, Baals were made and worshiped, and pagan rites at the high places were revived (2 Kings 16:2–4; 2 Chron 28:1–4). These religious setbacks were paralleled by political and geographical reversals: 120,000 Judeans were killed during the Israelite/Aramean invasion (2 Chron 28:6); Edom revolted and even invaded Judah (2 Kings 16:5–6); the Philistines invaded the Shephelah and the Negev, capturing Beth Shemesh, Aijalon, Gederoth, Soco, Timnah, Gimzo, and nearby villages (2 Chron 28:17–19). Indeed, at the time of Ahaz's death (715 B.C.), a low point in Judean history had been reached.

Meanwhile, in the Northern Kingdom, Jehu, after assassinating Jehoram (841 B.C.), continued his purge by wiping out the living male descendants from the family of Omri and by destroying the priests and worshipers of Baal as well as the temple of Baal at Samaria (2 Kings 10). Although not mentioned in Scripture, it is known from Assyrian records (*ANET*, 280–81) that Jehu paid tribute to Shalmaneser III (858–824 B.C.). The latter had invaded Aramean territory, captured cities in Gilead, and received tribute from Jehu and the kings of Tyre and Sidon at Baal-rosh (= Mount Carmel) in 841 B.C., evidently the first year of Jehu's reign. Although Israel survived under the leadership of Jehu and his successors, it did experience some defeats. For example, near the end of Jehu's reign, probably in the 820s, Hazael the Aramean invaded Israel, capturing Transjordanian lands belonging to the tribes of Manasseh, Reuben, and Gad, all the way south to the Arnon Gorge (2 Kings 10:32–33). To the southwest Hazael attacked Gath in the Philistine Plain as well as Judah and Jerusalem (12:17–18; 2 Chron 24:23–24), indicating that he must have been able to move freely through prime Israelite territory, including the Jezreel Valley and the Sharon Plain, in order to reach these targets.

Jehu's successor, Jehoahaz (814–798 B.C.), was also oppressed by the Arameans, both by Hazael and by his successor, Ben-Hadad. He too paid tribute to the Assyrians, namely to Adad-nirari (810–783 B.C.; *ANET*, 281). Militarily, Israel was reduced to 50 horsemen, 10 chariots, and 10,000 foot soldiers (2 Kings 13:7)—a very modest force compared with the reputed 2,000 chariots Ahab had mustered for the battle of Qarqar in 853 B.C.

From roughly 800 B.C. until 740 B.C. the Assyrians were preoccupied elsewhere in the Near East, and the Israelite kingdom was able to flourish. The final Israelite renaissance began during the days of Jehoash (798–782 B.C.), who inflicted several defeats on the Aramean Ben-Hadad and even overpowered arrogant Amaziah, the Judean king (see above, p. 129). The peak of Israelite expansion and prosperity was reached during the long rule of Jeroboam II (793–753 B.C.). The area of his influence stretched from Lebo Hamath

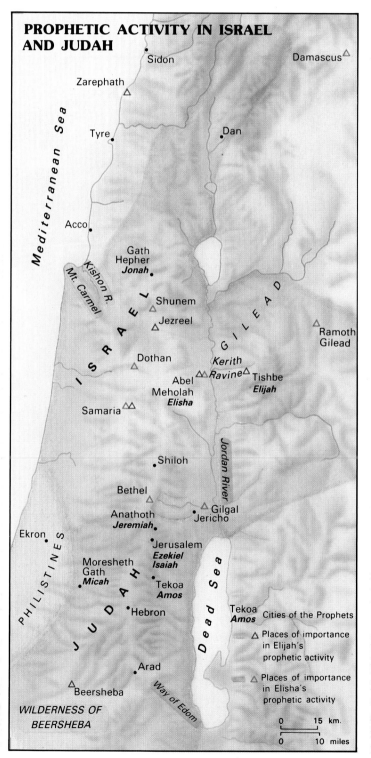

PROPHETIC ACTIVITY IN ISRAEL AND JUDAH

Mediterranean Sea

Sidon
Damascus △
Zarephath △
Tyre △
Dan △
Mt. Carmel
Kishon R.
Acco △
Gath Hepher
Jonah △
Shunem △
Jezreel △
G I L E A D
Ramoth Gilead △
Dothan △
Kerith Ravine △
Abel Meholah
Elisha
Tishbe
Elijah
Samaria △△
I S R A E L
Jordan River
Shiloh △
Bethel △
Gilgal △
Anathoth
Jeremiah △
Jericho △
Ekron
P H I L I S T I N E S
Jerusalem △
Ezekiel Isaiah
Moresheth Gath
Micah △
J U D A H
Tekoa
Amos △
Dead Sea
Hebron △
Tekoa
Amos △
Arad △
Beersheba △
Way of Edom
WILDERNESS OF BEERSHEBA

Cities of the Prophets
△ Places of importance in Elijah's prophetic activity
△ Places of importance in Elisha's prophetic activity

0   15 km.
0   10 miles

131

in the north to Judah and the Sea of the Arabah (= Salt Sea) in the south and included control over Damascus (2 Kings 14:25–29). Indeed, when the territories controlled by the Judean king Azariah (see above, p. 130) and those controlled by Jeroboam II are considered together, their combined area almost reached Solomonic proportions. Although the Bible is silent about the internal administrative structure of Israel during this era of great prosperity, sixty-three ostraca (broken pieces of pottery with writing on them) found in the excavation of the citadel at Samaria shed welcome light on this period. These ostraca record the receipt of wine and oil by persons living in Samaria from estates located in the surrounding villages. Many of the villages mentioned can be identified, and from the ostraca it is possible even to note on a map where various clans from the tribe of Manasseh were

located.[5] For the historical geographer this is a great bonanza, since the tribal description of Manasseh (Josh 16–17) is very brief and lacks a list of cities. Thus our knowledge of the heartland of Manasseh is greatly augmented by the Samaria ostraca.

Jeroboam's two successors ruled for a combined total of seven months, and both were assassinated. It was during the reign of Menahem (752–742 B.C.) that the presence of the Assyrian menace was again felt. Menahem assessed a 50-shekel levy against every wealthy man in order to pay 1,000 talents (ca. 37 tons) of silver to Tiglath-Pileser III (2 Kings 15:19–20 and *ANET*, 283).

It was Menahem's successor, Pekah (752–732 B.C.), who bore the brunt of the initial Assyrian onslaught. In order to meet the Assyrian threat, Pekah made an alliance with Rezin

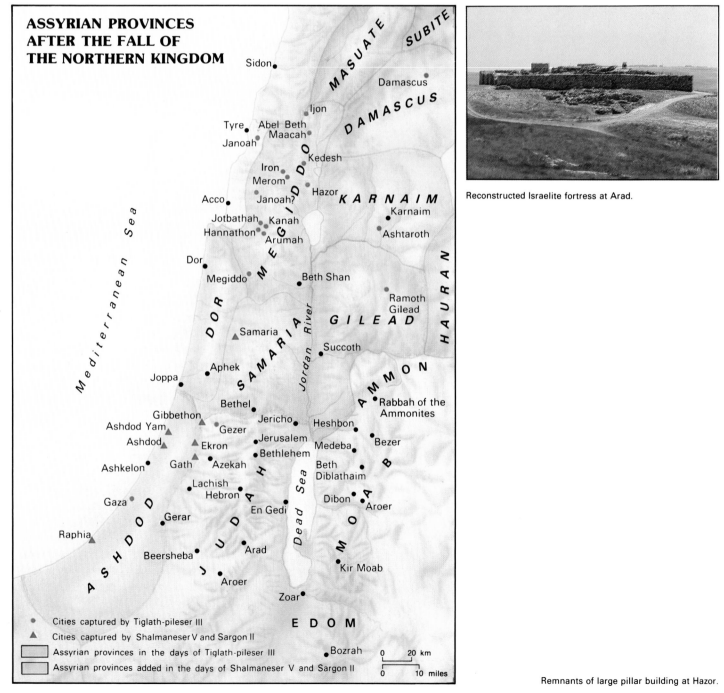

ASSYRIAN PROVINCES AFTER THE FALL OF THE NORTHERN KINGDOM

- • Cities captured by Tiglath-pileser III
- ▲ Cities captured by Shalmaneser V and Sargon II
- ▭ Assyrian provinces in the days of Tiglath-pileser III
- ▭ Assyrian provinces added in the days of Shalmaneser V and Sargon II

Reconstructed Israelite fortress at Arad.

Remnants of large pillar building at Hazor.

of Aram Damascus and with the influential son of Tabeel of Transjordan (Isa 7:5–6). These allies attempted to force the Judean king Ahaz into joining their coalition but, though able to devastate Judah and threaten Jerusalem, they were not successful (see above, p. 131). Biblical and especially Assyrian records describe Tiglath-Pileser III's invasions (2 Kings 15:29–30; *ANET*, 282–84). In 734 B.C. he marched down the Mediterranean coast, capturing cities all the way to Gaza and the Brook of Egypt. In 733 B.C. his army again returned, capturing northern Israelite cities such as Ijon, Abel Beth Maacah, Janoah, Kedesh, and Hazor (15:29), as well as cities in Naphtali (Galilee) and in Gilead. Finally in 732 B.C., after having cut off the routes for possible Egyptian and Israelite support, he attacked and captured Damascus. Rezin was deposed and Pekah assassinated, and in the latter's stead, Tiglath-Pileser III put Hoshea (732–723 B.C.) on the Israelite throne as a puppet king.

It was soon after the death of Tiglath-Pileser III (727 B.C.) that Hoshea, the last of the Israelite kings, revolted against the Assyrians, who responded by laying siege to Samaria. After a siege of three years, close to the end of the reign of Shalmaneser V (726–722 B.C.), Samaria fell to the Assyrians (2 Kings 17:4–6; 18:9–11; *ANET*, 284–85). The biblical writer, commenting on the tragedy that befell the Northern Kingdom in 722 B.C., states that it was due to the fact that as a nation the north had not heeded the warnings of their prophets—Elijah, Elisha, Jonah, Amos, Hosea—but had actively been involved in gross sins, including idolatry, sorcery, divination, and child sacrifice (17:7–23).

Although the Bible does not go into detail, the fall of Samaria was a very traumatic experience for the Israelites because the Assyrians were known for their savage treatment of rebels: not only looting, rape, and bondage, but also decapitation, impalement, and skinning people alive. However, not everyone was treated in this way, for Sargon II (721–705 B.C.) began a series of deportations whereby Israelites were consigned to Halah, to Gozan on the Habor River, and to towns in Media (2 Kings 17:6; 18:10–11). In their place, Sargon II and later Assyrian rulers settled foreign peoples from Babylon, Cuthah, Avva, Hamath, and Sepharvaim (17:24). These newcomers brought with them their worship of pagan deities, yet they also attempted to worship the "god of the land" (i.e., Yahweh; vv. 25–41). Evidently these newcomers, with their syncretistic blend of religions, were the forerunners of the religious/ethnic group later known as the Samaritans.

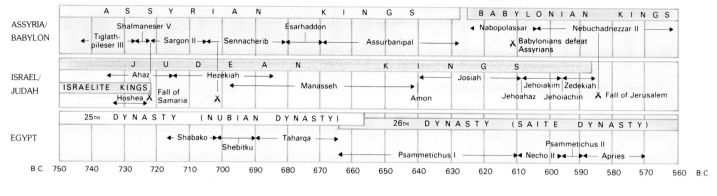

Judah Alone

The conquest of Damascus and the Northern Kingdom of Israel by the Assyrians brought the Judean kingdom temporary relief from military pressures between 735 B.C. and 722

B.C., but Ahaz's importation and promotion of pagan religious practices almost ensured that the south would also fall under God's judgment. And indeed, during the days of Ahaz

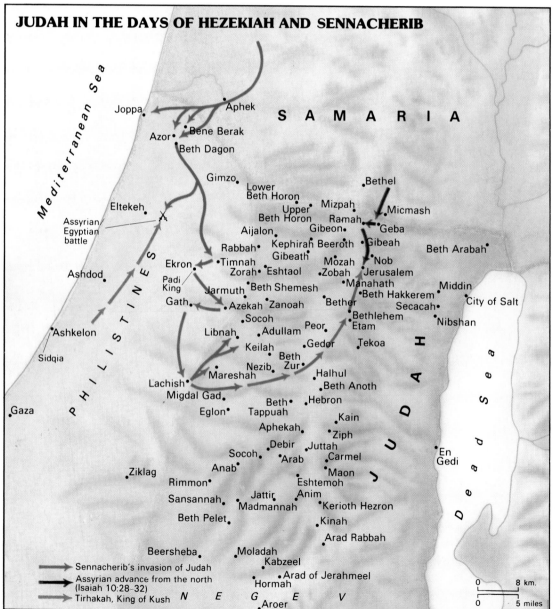

JUDAH IN THE DAYS OF HEZEKIAH AND SENNACHERIB

Mediterranean Sea

SAMARIA

Joppa
Aphek
Azor
Bene Berak
Beth Dagon
Gimzo
Lower Beth Horon
Upper Beth Horon
Bethel
Micmash
Mizpah
Ramah
Geba
Eltekeh
Aijalon
Gibeon
Gibeah
Assyrian/ Egyptian battle
Rabbah
Kephirah
Beeroth
Nob
Beth Arabah
Ekron
Timnah
Mozah
Jerusalem
Ashdod
Zorah
Eshtaol
Zobah
Middin
Padi King
Jarmuth
Beth Shemesh
Manahath
Beth Hakkerem
City of Salt
Gath
Azekah
Zanoah
Bether
Secacah
Nibshan
Socoh
Bethlehem
Etam
Ashkelon
Libnah
Adullam
Peor
Tekoa
Keilah
Gedor
Sidqia
Nezib
Beth Zur
Lachish
Mareshah
Halhul
Migdal Gad
Beth Anoth
Gaza
Eglon
Beth Tappuah
Hebron
Aphekah
Kain
Ziph
Debir
Juttah
Socoh
Arab
Carmel
Ziklag
Anab
Maon
En Gedi
Rimmon
Eshtemoh
Sansannah
Jattir
Anim
Madmannah
Kerioth Hezron
Beth Pelet
Kinah
Arad Rabbah
Beersheba
Moladah
Kabzeel
Arad of Jerahmeel
Hormah
N E G E V
Aroer

Dead Sea

PHILISTINES

J U D A H

→ Sennacherib's invasion of Judah
→ Assyrian advance from the north (Isaiah 10:28–32)
→ Tirhakah, King of Kush

0 ____ 8 km.
0 ____ 5 miles

City List of Judah (Joshua 15, 21–63)

Kabzeel, Eder, Jagur, **Kinah**, Dimonah, Adadah, Kedesh, Hazor, Ithnan, **Ziph**, Telem, Bealoth, Hazor Hadattah, **Kerioth Hezron** (Hazor), Amam, Shema, **Moladah**, Hazar Gaddah, Heshmon, **Beth Pelet**, Hazar Shual, **Beersheba**, Biziothiah, Baalah, Iim, Ezem, Eltolad, Kesil, **Hormah, Ziklag, Madmannah, Sansannah**, Lebaoth, Shilhim, Ain, Rimmon, **Eshtaol, Zorah**, Ashnah, **Zanoah**, En Gannim, Tappuah, Enam, **Jarmuth, Adullam, Socoh, Azekah**, Shaaraim, Adithaim, Gederah (Gederothaim), Zenan, Hadashah, Migdal Gad, Dilean, **Mizpah**, Joktheel, **Lachish**, Bozkath, Eglon, Cabbon, Lahmas, Kitlish, Gederoth, Beth Dagon, Naamah, Makkedah, Libnah, Ether, **Ashan**, Iphtah, Ashnah, **Nezib, Keilah, Aczib**, and Mareshah, **Ekron, Ashdod, Gaza**, Shamir, **Jattir, Socoh**, Dannah, Kiriath Sannah (**Debir**), **Anab, Eshtemoh, Anim**, Goshen, Holon, Giloh, **Arab**, Dumah, Eshan, Janim, **Beth Tappuah**, Aphekah, Humtah, Kiriath Arba (**Hebron**), Zior, **Maon, Carmel, Ziph, Juttah**, Jezreel, Jokdeam, Zanoah, Kain, Gibeah, Timnah, Halhul, Beth Zur, Gedor, Maarath, Beth Anoth, Eltekon, Kiriath Baal (Kiriath Jearim), **Rabbah, Beth Arabah, Middin, Secacah, Nibshan, City of Salt, En Gedi,**

Kabzeel   Cities which appear on the map

134

(735–715 B.C.) the Edomites successfully invaded Judah and took captives (2 Chron 28:17), while on the west the Philistines captured the cities of Beth Shemesh, Aijalon, Gederoth, Soco, Timnah, and Gimzo, all located in or near the Shephelah (vv. 18–19). Judeans living in these border areas probably fled into the Hill Country of Judah—at least temporarily—in order to save their lives. It must also be assumed that many Israelites from the Northern Kingdom moved south to Judah and Jerusalem to avoid the Assyrian onslaught of Tiglath-Pileser III, Shalmaneser V, and Sargon II. The growth of Jerusalem from a city of 37 acres (15 ha.) to 150 acres (61 ha.)[1] and the increase in the number of settlements in the Hill Country of Judah[2] during the reigns of Ahaz and Hezekiah (735–686 B.C.) are clear indicators of this influx of population.

With the death of wicked Ahaz in 715 B.C., Hezekiah's sole rule began.[3] During the early portion of his reign, Hezekiah initiated a series of religious reforms both inside and outside of Jerusalem. High places were torn down, sacred stones smashed, Asherah poles destroyed, and even the bronze snake (Nehushtan), which Moses had set up in the wilderness (Num 21:5–9), was broken into pieces (2 Kings 18:3–7; 2 Chron 29:2–19). In addition, the temple was reconsecrated, and a great Passover was celebrated in Jerusalem (2 Chron 29:20–30:27). Not only were the citizens of the Southern Kingdom included in the feast, but messengers were even sent to northern Israel, to what were now Assyrian provinces, with the result that some men of Manasseh, Zebulun, and Asher came to Jerusalem to participate.

The death of the Assyrian monarch Sargon II in 705 B.C. was the signal for many countries in the Near East to attempt to assert their independence. Hezekiah (728/715–686 B.C.), for example, was able to defeat the Philistines and regain territory as far as Gaza (2 Kings 18:8). In the process he evidently deposed petty kings who were still loyal to Assyria and replaced them with rulers more to his liking (e.g., Padi, the pro-Assyrian king of Ekron, was deposed and taken prisoner to Jerusalem).

Merodach-Baladan II (721–710 and 703 B.C.), the Babylonian king, was interested in encouraging anti-Assyrian activities on Assyria's southwestern flank and sent a delegation to Jerusalem, probably in 703 B.C., to encourage Hezekiah in his activities. Hezekiah's proud display of his wealth to this group led to Isaiah's frightening prophecy that in the future the Babylonians would carry off his riches and his descendants (2 Kings 20:14–18; Isa 39:3–7).

Hezekiah must have anticipated that sooner or later the new Assyrian monarch, Sennacherib (704–681 B.C.), would respond to his rebellious activities. In all probability Hezekiah stationed garrisons in strategic cities throughout the Hill Country of Judah and in the Shephelah. These garrisons were provided with officers, weapons, shields, and food supplies. In the excavation of numerous Judean cities from this period a large number of stamped jar handles have been found. These bear impressions of four-winged scarabs or two-winged sun disks and are also inscribed in Hebrew with the word "belonging to the king" followed by the name of one of four cities: Hebron, Soco, Ziph, and an unknown city, *mmšt*. These towns were evidently the centers of the royal vineyards from which produce was shipped to garrisons stationed in various cities.[4]

Hezekiah's preparations in and around Jerusalem were especially noteworthy. Springs in the vicinity of the city were stopped up, and a 1,750-foot-long (533 m.) water tunnel was dug through the solid rock in order to direct water from the Gihon Spring, located outside Jerusalem on the east, to a pool located within the city walls. This pool was also closer to the inhabitants of the newly settled western hill (see below, p. 194). In addition, Hezekiah repaired sections of Jerusalem's wall, constructed defensive towers, and reinforced the terraces upon which some of the city was built (2 Chron 32:2–8). It was at this time that a new wall was constructed in order to include the whole of the western hill within the fortified portion of Jerusalem. Indeed, Isaiah's speaking of "counting the buildings and tearing down houses to strengthen the wall" (Isa 22:10) has received archaeological confirmation by N. Avigad's discovery of a massive wall, 23 feet (7 m.) thick, located in the present-day Jewish quarter on the western hill.[5]

Hezekiah's internal preparations were augmented by the fact that Luli, king of Sidon, and Sidqia, king of Ashkelon, participated in the revolt. With the death of the pro-Assyrian Egyptian king Shabako in 702 B.C. and the accession of Shebitku (702–690 B.C.), there was probably a shift in Egyptian foreign policy to an anti-Assyrian—or at least a neutral—stance. With much of the southwestern portion of the Fertile Crescent in revolt, it was mandatory for Sennacherib to reassert his sovereignty there.

Sennacherib's response in 701 B.C. is one of the best-documented events in the ancient world. Scripture describes his invasion from the Judean standpoint (2 Kings 18–20; 2 Chron 32:1–23; Isa 36–39; very probably Mic 1:8–16; possibly Isa 10:28–32). From the Assyrian standpoint the "Prism of Sennacherib" (*ANET*, 287–88) describes his invasion in great detail, and this source can be supplemented by Sennacherib's recently discovered "Letter to God."[6] In addition, stone reliefs that lined the throne room of his palace in Nineveh depict various facets of his Judean campaign, including the graphic representation of his siege of the Judean city of Lachish.[7]

After marching westward from Assyria to the Mediterranean Sea, Sennacherib proceeded south along the Phoenician coast. Luli, the rebellious king of Sidon, fled, and the submissive Ethbaal was installed as king in his place. Other coastal cities—including Sidon, Mahalab, Uzu, Aczib, and Acco—submitted, and Sennacherib records how eight kings of Amurru brought him tribute. Continuing southward, Sennacherib captured Sidqia, the king of Ashkelon, and deported him, along with his dependents and gods, to Assyria. Cities in northern Philistia—including Beth Dagon, Joppa, Bene Berak, and Azuru—were captured. The Egyptians and Ethiopians, who had responded to Hezekiah's call for help, were defeated in the Plain of Eltekeh. It appears that Sennacherib then moved eastward, up the Sorek Valley. He captured the city of Timnah, thus cutting off the supply line between Ekron and her Judean ally, Hezekiah. This accomplished, the city of Ekron was conquered and its former king, Padi, who had been seized by Hezekiah, was reinstated. Moving south to the Elah Valley, Sennacherib captured first Azekah and then Gath.[8]

Sennacherib proceeded further south and assaulted the

Judean stronghold of Lachish. The siege and conquest of Lachish must have been one of the high points of Sennacherib's reign, for the throne room of his palace at Nineveh was decorated with reliefs depicting this conquest. The recent archaeological excavations at Lachish led by David Ussishkin of Tel Aviv University have proven conclusively that level three of that city was the one destroyed by Sennacherib. Indeed, in some areas 6 to 10 feet (2 to 3 m.) of ash and debris from the destruction have been found.[9]

From his camp at Lachish, and later from Libnah, Sennacherib sent his supreme commander, chief officer, and field commander with an army to demand the submission of Jerusalem (2 Kings 18:17). Although he was able to shut Hezekiah up as "a prisoner in Jerusalem, his royal residence, like a bird in a cage," Jerusalem never yielded to the Assyrian army. Throughout all of those difficult days, Hezekiah remained faithful in his trust in Yahweh.

In the end it was not Tirhakah, who later became the Cushite king of Egypt (2 Kings 19:9)[10], who rescued the Judeans. Instead, their deliverance came when the true and living God sent his angel to destroy 185,000 Assyrians (19:35–36; 2 Chron 32:21–22). Obviously, Sennacherib did not mention this disastrous loss of troops in his inscriptions; instead, he emphasized how he besieged and conquered forty-six strong cities and countless villages, how he confined Hezekiah to Jerusalem, and how many of the kings of the area, Hezekiah included, sent him tribute.

Not much is known about the later portion of Hezekiah's reign (715–686 B.C.) in the aftermath of Sennacherib's invasion. Evidently, his son Manasseh (697–642 B.C.) was co-regent with him for a few years. In spite of Sennacherib's losses on his Judean campaign, Assyria remained powerful. During the first part of Manasseh's long reign of fifty-five years the Assyrians were preoccupied with subduing revolts in the Babylonian and Elamite areas. In 689 B.C. Babylon was destroyed by Sennacherib, and it was not rebuilt until the days of his successor, Esarhaddon.

By the 670s the Assyrians had again become active along the Mediterranean coastline and in Egypt. However, Tirhakah (690–664 B.C.) was a very powerful and ambitious Egyptian monarch, eager to expand Egypt's influence northeastward, across Sinai into Israel. There he came into conflict with the Assyrians under Esarhaddon (681–669 B.C.) and Ashurbanipal (669–627 B.C.). In 674 B.C., the invading Esarhaddon was defeated by Tirhakah at el-Arish, but in 671 B.C., Esarhaddon won at Ashkelon and marched into Egypt proper, capturing Memphis. After a series of Egyptian revolts led by Tirhakah, Ashurbanipal pressed the Assyrian advantage south into Upper Egypt, where Thebes (NIV; Heb. No[-Amon]) was captured and sacked in 667 B.C., and Tirhakah fled for his life.

The books of Kings and Chronicles are silent about all of the above activities, and it must be assumed that for the most part Judah remained submissive to the Assyrians. In the biblical text Manasseh is primarily noted for the pagan religious rites that he reinstituted in Judah—including high places, altars for Baals, making an Asherah pole, worshiping the hosts of heaven, making children pass through the fire, and placing idols in the temple (2 Kings 21:2–9, 16; 2 Chron 33:1–20). At least at one point, however, Manasseh revolted and was taken captive by the Assyrians to Babylon for a short period of time (2 Chron 33:11–13). Possibly this occurred during the reign of Ashurbanipal, in 663 B.C., when Tyre (and Judah?) revolted. The Bible briefly describes how, when Manasseh repented of his sins, he was allowed to return to Jerusalem and rebuild the wall of the city, as well as to station "military commanders in all the fortified cities of Judah" (vv. 12–14). These projects may reflect the fact that the Assyrians considered him a loyal vassal, who, being situated close to Egypt, would aid them in their campaigns against the pharaohs.

Amon, the wicked son of Manasseh, ruled for only two years (642–640 B.C.) and was assassinated. He was followed by his eight-year-old son Josiah, who ruled for thirty-one years (640–609 B.C.). This young ruler certainly came under priestly and prophetic influence, for his reign was noted for a religious renaissance. In the eighth year of his reign (632 B.C.) Josiah sought God, and in his twelfth year (628 B.C.) he began to purge Judah and Jerusalem of their high places, Asherahs, and images. This purging also extended into what had been the Northern Kingdom, for towns in "Manasseh, Ephraim, and Simeon as far as Naphtali . . . throughout Israel" are mentioned (2 Chron 34:3–7).[11] Although the extent and nature of Josiah's influence/control in the north is not clear, the fact is that, at the time of the repair of the temple in his eighteenth year (622 B.C.), contributions were received not only from Judah, Benjamin, and Jerusalem, but also from Manasseh, Ephraim, and the remnant of Israel (vv. 8–13). All of this seems to indicate that he exerted some influence over some of the Israelites who remained in what used to be the Northern Kingdom. Nevertheless, the heartland of the major area under his control was probably confined to the Hill Country of Benjamin and Judah, stretching from Geba in the north to Beersheba in the south (2 Kings 23:8). Although a Hebrew ostracon has been found at the coastal site of Ashdod-yam (see ANET, 588, for the text), indicating the presence of Hebrew-speaking residents in the area, much of the Philistine Plain had probably been under Egyptian control ever since the campaign of the powerful Psammetichus I (664–610 B.C.) to Ashdod in 635 B.C. and his repulsion of the Scythians who had passed through Philistia in 627 B.C.

As mentioned above, during the final years of Manasseh's reign (697–642 B.C.) the Assyrians were increasingly preoccupied in southern Mesopotamia, attempting to control Babylon and the Aramean tribes, as well as in Elam. Ashurbanipal (669–627 B.C.) was followed by a series of weak Assyrian kings. In 626 B.C. the rebel Chaldean Nabopolassar (626–605 B.C.) captured Babylon from the Assyrians and initiated the process that would lead to the downfall of Assyria. By 620 B.C. Nabopolassar had established his control of southern Mesopotamia and was ready to move against Assyria itself.

However, to the northeast the powerful Medes, who had defeated the Scythians in 624 B.C., were also pressuring the Assyrians. A combined Egyptian-Assyrian army under Psammetichus I of Egypt and Sin-shar-ishkun of Assyria was able to deter Nabopolassar's expansion plans in 616 B.C., but in 614 B.C. the Medes actually captured and destroyed the Assyrian city of Asshur. The Medes and Babylonians then combined forces and in 612 B.C. conquered Nineveh. The last Assyrian ruler, Ashur-uballit II (612–609 B.C.), retreated

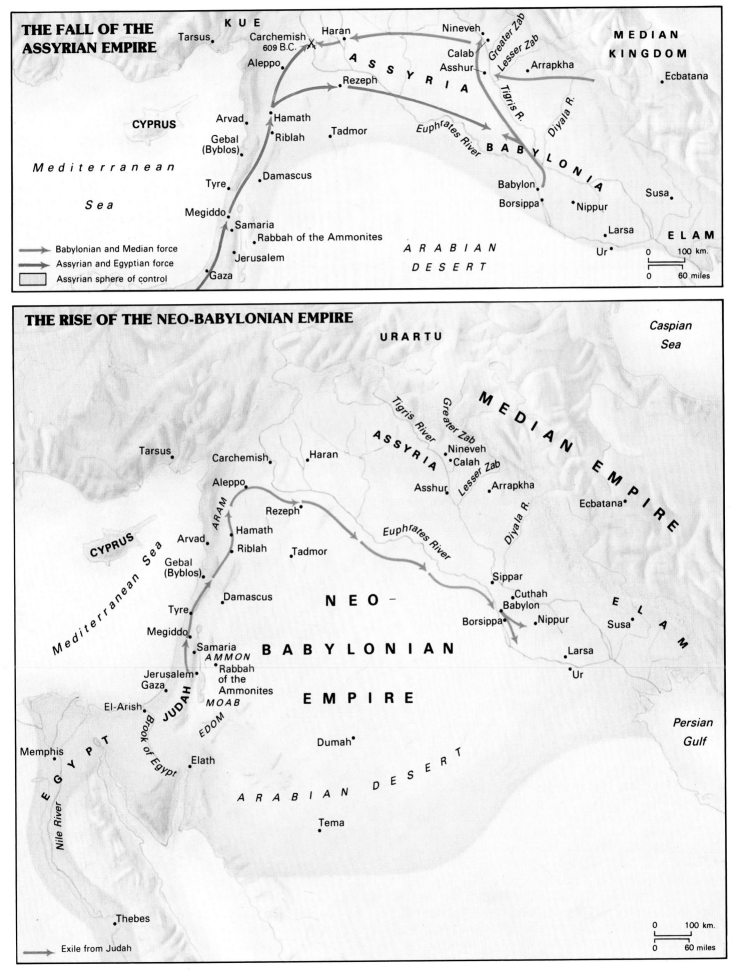

THE FALL OF THE ASSYRIAN EMPIRE

KUE
Tarsus
Carchemish
609 B.C.
Haran
Nineveh
Greater Zab
Lesser Zab
Calah
Asshur
Arrapkha
MEDIAN KINGDOM
Ecbatana
Aleppo
Rezeph
A S S Y R I A
Tigris R.
Diyala R.
CYPRUS
Arvad
Hamath
Riblah
Tadmor
Euphrates River
B A B Y L O N I A
Gebal (Byblos)
Mediterranean Sea
Tyre
Damascus
Babylon
Borsippa
Nippur
Susa
Megiddo
Samaria
Rabbah of the Ammonites
A R A B I A N   D E S E R T
Larsa
E L A M
Jerusalem
Ur
Gaza

→ Babylonian and Median force
→ Assyrian and Egyptian force
▭ Assyrian sphere of control

0   100 km.
0   60 miles

THE RISE OF THE NEO-BABYLONIAN EMPIRE

URARTU
Caspian Sea
Tarsus
Carchemish
Haran
A S S Y R I A
Tigris River
Greater Zab
Nineveh
Calah
Lesser Zab
M E D I A N   E M P I R E
Aleppo
Rezeph
Asshur
Arrapkha
Ecbatana
ARAM
Hamath
Riblah
Tadmor
Euphrates River
Diyala R.
Arvad
N E O -
Sippar
Cuthah
Babylon
E L A M
Gebal (Byblos)
Mediterranean Sea
Damascus
B A B Y L O N I A N
Borsippa
Nippur
Susa
CYPRUS
Tyre
Megiddo
Samaria
AMMON
Rabbah of the Ammonites
E M P I R E
Larsa
Ur
Jerusalem
Gaza
JUDAH
MOAB
Brook of Egypt
El-Arish
EDOM
Dumah
Memphis
E G Y P T
Elath
A R A B I A N   D E S E R T
Persian Gulf
Nile River
Tema
Thebes

→ Exile from Judah

0   100 km.
0   60 miles

westward and established a stronghold at Haran. There he and his Egyptian ally, Neco II (610–595 B.C.), attempted an unsuccessful defense of the city against the combined Median and Babylonian forces (610 B.C.). Retreating even further west, Ashur-uballit II attempted a counterattack in 609 B.C. As the Egyptian pharaoh Neco was heading north to assist his Assyrian ally, the Judean king, Josiah, evidently siding with the Babylonians, attempted to impede Neco's northward march at Megiddo, just north of the Mount Carmel pass. There the godly Judean was killed in battle in 609 B.C. (2 Kings 23:29–30; 2 Chron 35:20–27).

The Egyptian-Assyrian coalition was defeated by a Medo-Babylonian one at Carchemish in 609 B.C. This defeat was the blow that was fatal for the Assyrians, but the Egyptians merely retreated south, moving their staging area from Carchemish to Riblah. The people of Judah placed Josiah's son Jehoahaz on the throne in 609 B.C., but after a reign of only three months he was deposed by Neco and taken captive to Egypt, where he died (2 Kings 23:30–34; 2 Chron 36:1–4). Pharaoh Neco placed Eliakim on the throne in Jerusalem, changing his name to Jehoiakim (2 Kings 23:34–36; 2 Chron 36:4–5; Jer 22:11–12).

Jehoiakim's rule of eleven years (609–598 B.C.) was anything but godly. Although specific religious sins are not mentioned, he was a constant foe of Jeremiah the prophet (see Jeremiah, passim). He also imposed heavy taxes on the people in order to send tribute to Neco (2 Kings 23:35), and he evidently squandered money to build himself a new palace. Between 608 B.C. and 605 B.C. a series of battles between Egyptian and Babylonian forces took place near the Euphrates River. In 605 B.C., at Carchemish, Neco's forces were defeated by soon-to-be-king Nebuchadnezzar (605–562 B.C.), who pursued the Egyptians south to the Brook of Egypt, capturing Ashkelon along the way (604 B.C.). Judah was forced to change allegiance and become a Babylonian rather than an Egyptian vassal. At this time (605 B.C.) Nebuchadnezzar deported some of the talented upper-class Judeans, taking them captive to Babylon—recorded in Scripture as the first of four deportations of Judeans (Dan 1:1; Jer 46:2; compare 52:28–30). With the defeat of the Egyptians at Carchemish in 605 B.C., the Babylonians became heirs to territory that would eventually surpass the Assyrian Empire in extent. This new "world empire" is called the Neo-Babylonian Empire (605–539 B.C.).

In addition to the Babylonian oppression, the Judeans also suffered at the hands of Arameans, Moabites, and Ammonites during the reign of Jehoiakim (609–598 B.C.; 2 Kings 24:2–4). Toward the end of his reign, possibly after 601 B.C. (when Nebuchadnezzar had been repulsed at the border of Egypt by the Egyptians), Jehoiakim revolted against Babylonian overlordship.

Nebuchadnezzar was quick to respond and invaded Judah in 597 B.C. Just before Nebuchadnezzar's capture of the "city of Judah" (= Jerusalem)[12] on March 16, 597 B.C., Jehoiakim died. Jehoiachin, the third son of Josiah, ruled for only three months (598–597 B.C.) and presided over the fall of the city. In this second deportation (2 Kings 24:13–16), he and more than 10,000 Judeans—including officers, fighting men, craftsmen, and artisans—along with treasure from the temple and palace, were taken captive to Babylon. Jehoiachin remained a captive in Babylon[13] until his release

on March 22, 561 B.C. (25:27–30).

Nebuchadnezzar placed Mattaniah on the throne and changed his name to Zedekiah. Zedekiah ruled for eleven years (597–586 B.C.), at first as a loyal Babylonian vassal. Then, possibly around 588 B.C., when the Egyptian king Hophra/Apries (589–570 B.C.) led a military expedition to Tyre and Sidon, Zedekiah joined Edom, Moab, Ammon, Tyre, and Sidon (Jer 27:1–11; and evidently Egypt) in a revolt against Babylon. Nebuchadnezzar again responded quickly, and although the details of Nebuchadnezzar's line of march into Judah are not known, we do know from both the Bible (34:6–7) and from one of the Hebrew ostraca discovered at Lachish (number IV; *ANET*, 332) that he attacked the strategically important Shephelah cities of Lachish and

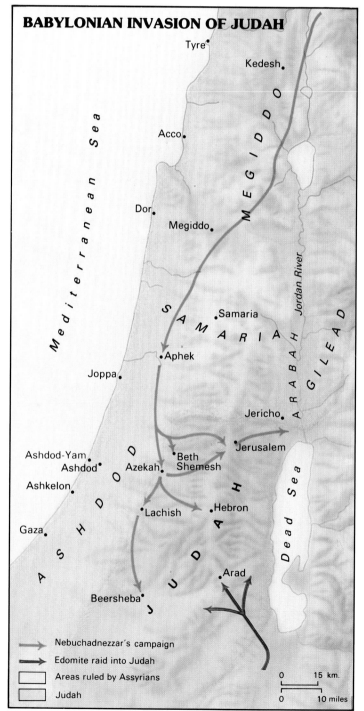

BABYLONIAN INVASION OF JUDAH

Tyre
Kedesh
Mediterranean Sea
Acco
MEGIDDO
Dor
Megiddo
Jordan River
SAMARIA
Samaria
ARABAH
GILEAD
Aphek
Joppa
Jericho
Jerusalem
Ashdod-Yam
Beth Shemesh
Ashdod
Azekah
ASHDOD
Ashkelon
Dead Sea
JUDAH
Lachish
Hebron
Gaza
Arad
Beersheba

→ Nebuchadnezzar's campaign
→ Edomite raid into Judah
▭ Areas ruled by Assyrians
▭ Judah

0   15 km.
0   10 miles

Azekah just as Sennacherib, the Assyrian, had a century earlier. On January 15, 588 B.C., Nebuchadnezzar began the siege of Jerusalem. The siege was lifted momentarily when rumors of Egyptian intervention circulated, but it was quickly reinstated. In July 586 B.C. Jerusalem was captured, and between August 14 and 17 the city was razed and the temple burned by Nebuzaradan, commander of the imperial guard. Zedekiah, who had fled toward the Arabah, was captured in the plain of Jericho and taken to Nebuchadnezzar's headquarters at Riblah. There his sons were executed, his eyes were put out, and he was deported to Babylon (2 Kings 25:1–7).

With the fall of Jerusalem in 586 B.C. the independent Israelite/Judean state, which had existed for more than four hundred years, had come to an end. The effect on the people of God must have been devastating: the holy city, where God had chosen to place his name, was in ruins, the temple of the true and living God had been destroyed, sacrifices had ceased, and the pathetic heirs of the once-great Davidic dynasty were now prisoners in exile. Had God abandoned his people? What had happened to the glorious promises that had been made to Israel's ancestors? The answers to these and many other questions would slowly come to the people of God during their period of exile. It would take a "second exodus," this time from Babylon rather than from Egypt, for God to deliver his people from the catastrophe that had befallen them.

The ruins of Babylon, with a view of the Ishtar Gate in the foreground.

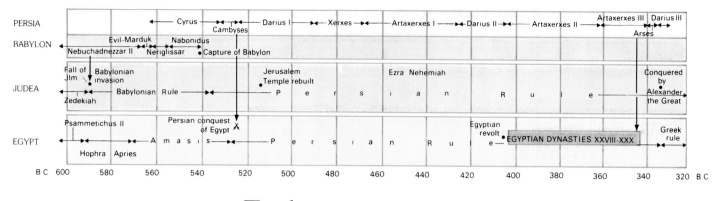

Exile and Return

With the capture of Jerusalem in 586 B.C. by the Babylonians, the Judean populace became quite scattered. Some Judeans were taken captive to southern Mesopotamia, some were allowed to remain in the land of Judah, while others fled to neighboring countries—including Ammon, Moab, and Egypt. As the main Babylonian force withdrew from Judah, Nebuzaradan, commander of the guard, appointed Gedaliah to be governor of those Judeans who remained in the land (Jer 40:1–41:15). Gedaliah established headquarters at Mizpah, 7.5 miles (12 km.) north of Jerusalem. The length of Gedaliah's rule is not known, but his authority was contested when Judeans returned from Ammon and Moab. Ishmael, who was employed by Baalis (king of the Ammonites, Jer 40:14), murdered Gedaliah, and also killed men of Shechem, Shiloh, and Samaria who had stopped at Mizpah while on their way to worship at the temple ruins in Jerusalem. Although some of the conspirators were caught and executed, Ishmael escaped to the Ammonite territory east of the Jordan River.

Since the Babylonians were still active in the area, (note the thirteen-year siege of Tyre that began in 585 B.C.), the Judeans, now under the leadership of Johanan, son of Kareah, were fearful of Babylonian reprisals (Jer 41:16–17). In spite of Jeremiah's instructions to remain and settle in the land, portions of the Judean community fled to Egypt, taking Jeremiah with them (42:1–44:30). Upon their arrival at Tahpanhes in the eastern delta of the Nile, Jeremiah prophesied that Nebuchadnezzar would set up his throne there and that the fleeing Judeans would be either killed or sent into exile (43:8–13). Jeremiah is not heard from again, and he evidently died in exile in Egypt. In 582 B.C. the Babylonians were again in the area of Judah, and at that time several thousand additional Judeans were taken into exile (52:30). It is not certain whether this fourth and final deportation was in response to the murder of Gedaliah, but Babylonian records tell of the subduing of the peoples of Ammon—to which the murderer Ishmael had fled—and Moab in that same year.

Specific details regarding life in Judea between the fall of Jerusalem in 586 B.C. and the first return from Babylon in 538 B.C. are lacking. Since the Babylonians did not import foreigners to settle areas recently vacated by exiled Judeans, there probably was a decrease in the density of population in some areas. It is commonly thought that the Edomites, who during the Old Testament period lived south and east of the Dead Sea in southern Transjordan, moved, under pressure from Arabs, into the southern portion of the Hill Country of Judah, to the region between Beth Zur and Beersheba. This population group later came to be known as the Idumeans (see below, p. 150).

At the eastern end of the Fertile Crescent, tribute, taxes, and income from trade flowed into the treasury at Babylon, and with this revenue Nebuchadnezzar aggrandized Babylon and other southern Mesopotamian cities. Weakness in Egypt led to its conquest by Nebuchadnezzar in 568 B.C., thus fulfilling the prophecy of Jeremiah (43:8–13). A former general, Amasis (568–526 B.C.), was placed on the Egyptian throne. However, Babylonian influence in Egypt was not permanent, for Amasis was able to pursue a rather independent political course. He initiated building projects at home and activities first against and then with Greek colonists in North Africa.

The Babylonian monarch Nebuchadnezzar was succeeded by Evil-Merodach (562–560 B.C.). It was during his reign that the Judean king Jehoiachin, who had been taken into exile in 597 B.C., was released on March 22, 561 B.C. (2 Kings 25:27–30; Jer 52:31–34). During Evil-Merodach's reign and during those of his successors—Neriglissar (559–556 B.C.) and Labasi-Marduk (556 B.C.)—new kingdoms were beginning to exert their authority. These included Lydia, in western Asia Minor (modern Turkey), and the Medes, located north and east of the Fertile Crescent. The latter were expanding westward into Urartian territory and even into northern Mesopotamia. The Medes and Persians fought each other at Ecbatana in 550 B.C. But soon after the battle the kingdoms were united under the leadership of the Persian ruler Cyrus (559–530 B.C.).

The final ruler of the Babylonian empire was Nabonidus (556–539 B.C.). During his early years he campaigned in Cilicia, Syria, Edom, and northern Arabia. By capturing Arabian cities—including Tema, Dedan, and Yathrib—he in effect took control of the trade routes that led through Arabia to the north and west. It was at Tema, an oasis in the Arabian Desert, that he took up residence for ten years, abandoning Marduk and worshiping Sin, the moon god. He left his son Belshazzar as chief administrator in Babylon (*ANET*, 315–16). During his absence from Babylon, the festival of the chief god Marduk was not celebrated, much to the distaste of the local populace and the priests. Indeed, the fall of Babylon to the Persians in 539 B.C. was attributed by

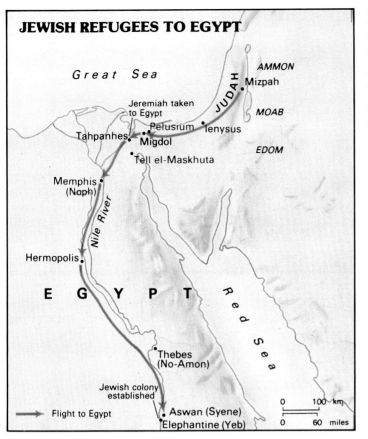

JEWISH REFUGEES TO EGYPT

Great Sea

AMMON

Mizpah

JUDAH

Jeremiah taken
to Egypt

MOAB

Pelusium

Ienysus

Tahpanhes

Migdol

EDOM

Tell el-Maskhuta

Memphis
(Noph)

Nile River

Hermopolis

E G Y P T

Red Sea

Thebes
(No-Amon)

Jewish colony
established

Flight to Egypt

Aswan (Syene)
Elephantine (Yeb)

0   100 km
0   60 miles

the Babylonians as divine judgment upon Nabonidus for allowing the festival to lapse.

Life in Babylon for the exiled Jewish populace must have been somewhat depressing, for their religious beliefs (which were based upon the promises of God) were intimately tied up with the land of Israel, from which they were exiled, and with Jerusalem, which was in ruins. In addition, the Davidic dynasty no longer ruled and its continued existence was in question, and the temple of Yahweh was in ruins (see Ps 137). The question that loomed large in the minds of the exiles was, Why? Yet in spite of this dismal state of affairs, at least portions of the Jewish community seem to have flourished. For example, Daniel became an advisor to kings and royalty (Nebuchadnezzar, Belshazzar, and Darius the Mede); Ezekiel was free to move about and minister to the needs of his people; the exiled Judean king Jehoiachin and his entourage received rations from the Babylonians (*ANET*, 308); and it seems that, economically, portions of the community prospered (fifth-century B.C. cuneiform tablets from Nippur relate some of the activities of the Jewish trading family of Murashu).

The collapse of the Babylonian empire, like that of the Assyrian one before it, was rather swift. After defeating the Medes in 550 B.C. at Ecbatana, Cyrus the Persian (559–530 B.C.) defeated a combined Babylonian, Egyptian, and Lydian army. Moving northwest into Asia Minor, Cyrus defeated Croesus, the powerful leader of the kingdom of Lydia, at Sardis (by 546 B.C.), with the result that Cyrus's territory stretched from Persia westward through Asia Minor to the coast of the Aegean Sea.

After defeating the Babylonians at Opis on the Tigris River, the capture of Babylon itself was relatively easy.

Cyrus entered the city in 539 B.C. He was hailed as a liberator and treated the populace with leniency. His popularity was further enhanced by the restoration of the god Marduk to its preeminence after the neglect it had suffered under the last Babylonian king, Nabonidus. The Persians, like the Babylonians, treated most of their subjects with informed enlightenment. The barrel inscription of Cyrus (*ANET*, 315–16) recounts how, under Persian rule, some peoples who had been exiled by the Babylonians were allowed to return to their homelands and how destroyed sanctuaries were rebuilt and divine images returned to their proper places.

It is within this general framework that Cyrus's decree regarding the Jews is to be placed (2 Chron 36:22–23; Ezra 1:1–4; 6:3–5). This decree permitted any Jew who wanted to do so to return to Judea. It also allowed for the temple to be rebuilt—with some royal financial support—and it commanded that the temple vessels were to be returned to Jerusalem. A total of 49,697 individuals returned to Judea with Sheshbazzar (Ezra 2:64–65). This was the largest of the three returns but even at that the number of returnees does not appear to be very great. Evidently a large number of Jews elected to remain in southern Mesopotamia, and there they formed the nucleus of what would become a rather large and powerful Jewish community. Many of the returnees listed in Ezra 2 are identified by family clans and occupations; however, within that chapter some are listed according to their towns of origin (vv. 21–35). Although it is not explicitly stated, most commentators assume that these people returned to their places of origin. If this is so, then a fair portion of returnees settled in twenty-one villages located primarily in the old tribal territories of Benjamin and Dan to the northeast, north, and northwest of Jerusalem. During this first phase of the first return, around 537 B.C., the sacrificial altar was reconstructed and sacrifices begun, the foundations for the temple were laid, and the Feast of Tabernacles was celebrated (Ezra 1–3). But because of the hostility of the Samaritans (4:1–4) work on the temple ceased until the second year of the rule of Darius (ca. 520 B.C.).

In the interim, Cyrus expanded his empire to the east, annexing territory that stretched all the way to the Indus and Oxus Rivers. He was fatally wounded while campaigning in the northeastern region of his empire, and upon his death Cambyses (530–522 B.C.), his son, assumed the throne. After executing his rivals and securing his position as king, Cambyses began making preparations for the invasion of Egypt. Mustering his army, possibly at Acco, Cambyses marched south along the Palestinian coast toward Egypt. An Arabian king (of Kedar?) supplied him with water and camels and in return was granted tax-free status for a territory in northern Sinai that stretched from Gaza to Ienysus (Herodotus 3.4–5), although the Arabian king did present a yearly "gift" of a thousand talents of frankincense to the Persian ruler (Herodotus 3.97). After initial victories at Pelusium and Memphis, Cambyses was eventually successful in capturing the whole of Egypt, which in turn became a Persian satrapy. While returning home, Cambyses, for some unknown reason, committed suicide near Mount Carmel in 522 B.C.

Within two years Darius I (522–486 B.C.), previously an

officer in the army, was able to secure the throne for himself by executing his rival, Gautama. He also put down revolts that had sprung up all over the empire: in Media, Parthia, Hyrcania, Armenia, and Babylonia. In 519–518 B.C. he reconquered Egypt, and the Persian Empire entered a relatively peaceful and prosperous era.

The second phase of the first Jewish return received impetus from the urgings of the prophets Haggai and Zechariah. During this second phase, the Judeans asked for and received permission to rebuild the temple. Under the leadership of Zerubbabel, work on the temple began in 520 B.C., and it was completed by 516 B.C. (Ezra 4:24–6:22), at which time a joyous Passover was celebrated in Jerusalem. Certainly the providence of God was involved in the timing of the rebuilding, but it is also interesting to note that permission to rebuild was granted in 520 B.C., just prior to Darius's Egyptian campaign mentioned above. Possibly Darius was trying to secure the loyalty of the Judeans by granting them their request.

Although the internal division of the Persian Empire changed from time to time, it was traditionally divided into large administrative units called satrapies; according to the Greek historian Herodotus (ca. 450 B.C.; 3.89–95) there were twenty such satrapies. But occasionally satrapies were combined and/or divided so that both their number and their extent varied. At the time of the first return from exile Judah was evidently in a large satrapy called "Babylon and Beyond the River [Euphrates]." From cuneiform documents it is known that Ushtannu was its governor (ca. 520 B.C.). It seems that by 520 B.C. the satrapy had been divided into at least two subunits, one of which was called "Beyond the River" (NIV = "Trans-Euphrates"; mentioned seventeen times in Ezra and Nehemiah). This administrative unit, which later became a separate satrapy (number five according to Herodotus 3.90), stretched from the Upper Euphrates–Orontes River region, southward through Lebanon, Syria, and Palestine into northern Sinai; not included were desert territory to the east and southeast and the Sinai coast from Gaza to Ienysus, which were under the control of the Arabs (Herodotus 3.5, 91). From both the biblical record (Ezra 5:3, 6; 6:6, 13) and cuneiform documents, it is known that Tattenai, a subordinate of Ushtannu, was the governor of Trans-Euphrates, and it was with him that Zerubbabel and Joshua had to deal in attempting to secure permission to

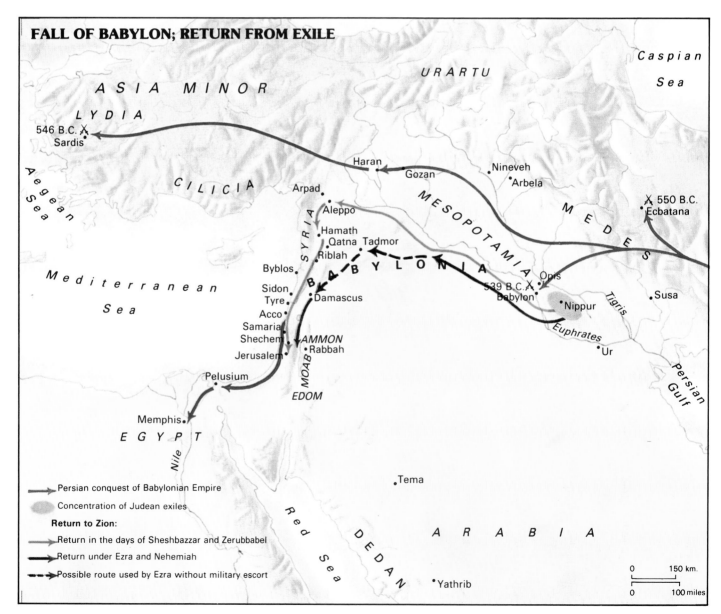

FALL OF BABYLON; RETURN FROM EXILE

Persian conquest of Babylonian Empire

Concentration of Judean exiles

Return to Zion:

Return in the days of Sheshbazzar and Zerubbabel

Return under Ezra and Nehemiah

Possible route used by Ezra without military escort

rebuild the temple (Ezra 5, 6).

During the reign of Darius I (522–486 B.C.), the Persian empire reached its greatest extent, stretching from the Indus River in the east all the way to Thrace and Macedonia in the west, and included Egypt and Libya in north Africa (satrapy six). During Darius's reign the minting of coins (the gold daric and the silver shekel) became common, the legal system of courts and judges that helped settle grievances was established, a postal system and roads (including the famous "Royal Road" that led from Sardis in Lydia to Babylon, Susa, and Persepolis) were in full operation, and even a major canal, connecting the Gulf of Suez and the Nile, was completed.

Toward the mid-point of Darius's long reign, ca. 500 B.C., trouble began brewing in the Aegean area with the Ionian revolt. The revolt was suppressed by the Persians, and the city of Miletus was captured and destroyed. But in 490 B.C. an invading Persian army suffered a serious defeat on the Greek mainland at Marathon. Persian retaliation was not immediate, for Darius died soon after the defeat, and the first few years of his son Xerxes' reign (486–464 B.C.) were spent quelling rebellions closer to home. However, in 480 B.C. Xerxes tried to subdue the Greek rebels. At Thermopylae he was successful, and he went on to capture and burn Athens; but his navy was routed at Salamis, and Xerxes was forced to retreat to Asia Minor. It seems that after this ill-fated expedition Xerxes became more interested in the internal affairs of his empire, embarking on a series of building projects at home. It was soon after these events that Esther was appointed as his queen (Esth 2:16–17; December 479 B.C. or January 478 B.C.), and the major events recorded in the Book of Esther have their setting in 473 B.C.

After Xerxes was assassinated, Artaxerxes I (464–424 B.C.) took the throne. Early in his reign, Egypt, with the help of Greece, revolted. This revolt (460–455 B.C.) was put down by the powerful general Megabyzus, who became the governor of the satrapy "Beyond the River." It was probably in the context of Persia's desire to secure the entrance into Egypt that additional concessions were granted to the Jews in 458 B.C. (Ezra 7:7–9). According to the royal decree (vv. 12–26), Ezra and an unlimited number of Jews were allowed to return to Judea. Concessions granted to the Jews included financial support from the royal treasury, the right of the Judeans to govern their own affairs on the basis

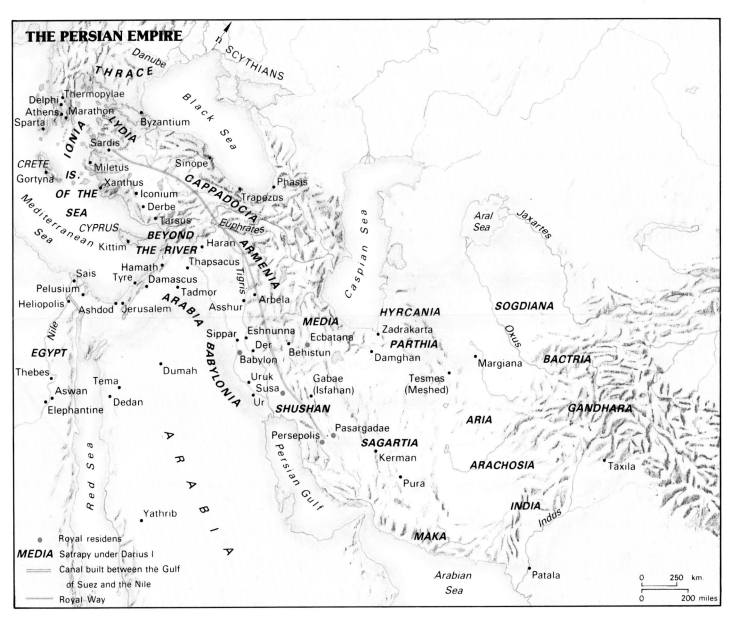

THE PERSIAN EMPIRE

• Royal residens
MEDIA Satrapy under Darius I
—— Canal built between the Gulf of Suez and the Nile
—— Royal Way

0   250 km.
0   200 miles

143

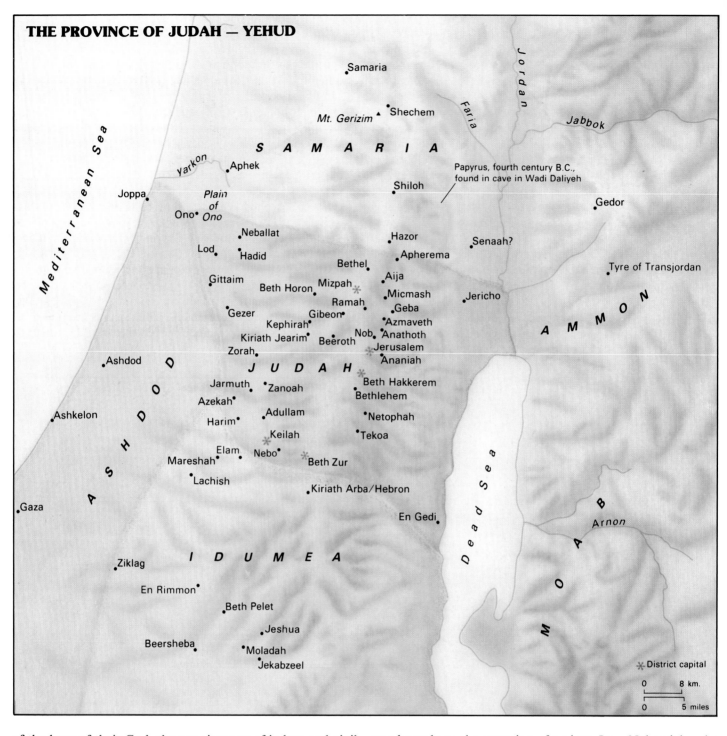

THE PROVINCE OF JUDAH — YEHUD

Samaria

Mt. Gerizim ▲ Shechem

S A M A R I A

Jordan

Faria

Jabbok

Yarkon

Aphek

Joppa

Plain
of
Ono • Ono

Shiloh

Papyrus, fourth century B.C.,
found in cave in Wadi Daliyeh

Gedor

Neballat

Hazor

Senaah?

Lod

Hadid

Apherema

Bethel

Tyre of Transjordan

Gittaim

Beth Horon Mizpah ✳

Aija

Micmash

Jericho

A M M O N

Ramah

Geba

Gezer

Gibeon

Azmaveth

Kephirah

Kiriath Jearim Beeroth Nob Anathoth

Zorah

Jerusalem ✳

Ashdod

Ananiah

J U D A H

Beth Hakkerem ✳

A S H D O D

Jarmuth • Zanoah

Bethlehem

Azekah

Adullam

Netophah

Ashkelon

Harim

Keilah ✳

Tekoa

Elam Nebo

Mareshah

Beth Zur ✳

Lachish

Kiriath Arba/Hebron

Gaza

En Gedi

Dead Sea

Arnon

I D U M E A

Ziklag

En Rimmon

M O A B

Beth Pelet

Jeshua

Beersheba

Moladah

Jekabzeel

✳ District capital

0   8 km.

0   5 miles

Mediterranean Sea

of the laws of their God, the appointment of judges and civil magistrates, and the granting of tax exemptions for temple personnel. Although the total number of Jews who returned with Ezra is not known, there were probably fewer than the 50,000 mentioned in connection with the first return, for only 1,758 adult males are mentioned in connection with the second one (8:1–20). The major accomplishment of the second return seems to have been a spiritual rebuilding of the Judeans—including the dissolution of intermarriages (ch. 9). During the period between the arrival of Ezra in 458 B.C. and that of Nehemiah in 445 B.C., an attempt was evidently made to rebuild the wall of Jerusalem (see the letter from this time in Ezra 4:7–23), but because of local opposition the rebuilding was not completed.

In 446 B.C. the dilapidated state of Jerusalem's defenses was brought to the attention of a pious Jew, Nehemiah, who was serving in the Persian court as cupbearer to King Artaxerxes. Artaxerxes responded favorably to Nehemiah's request to supervise the rebuilding of the wall of Jerusalem, possibly because he felt that a loyal Judean populace would help counteract those forces that had supported the satrap Megabyzus' revolt against the Persians. Nehemiah left for Judea in 445 B.C. armed with a letter from the king granting him permission to rebuild the wall, commanding other "governors of Trans-Euphrates" (Neh 2:7–9) to grant him safe passage, and ordering Asaph, the keeper of the king's forest, to provide him with timber. Upon arriving in Jerusalem, Nehemiah surveyed the condition of the defenses of the city (vv. 11–16). He then rallied the Judeans behind him and, despite opposition, rebuilt the walls in fifty-two

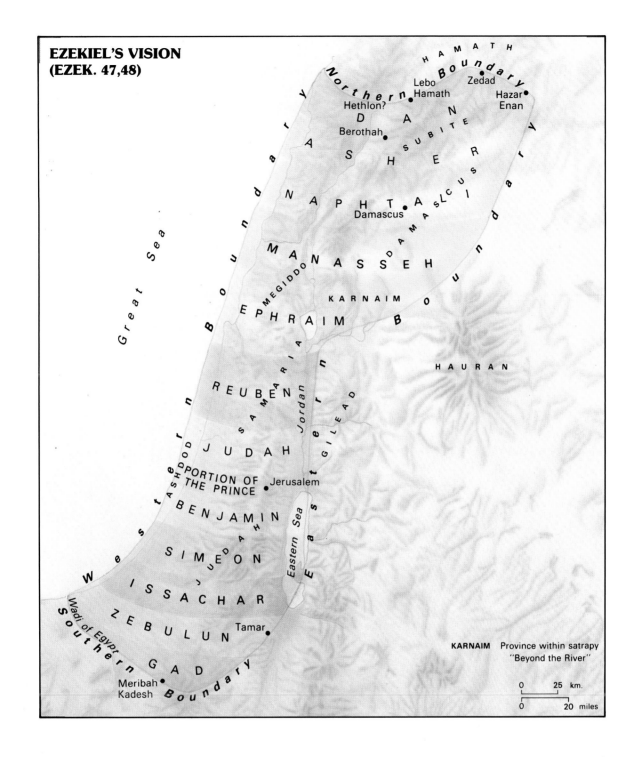

**EZEKIEL'S VISION
(EZEK. 47,48)**

Great Sea

Northern Boundary

HAMATH

Lebo Hamath
Hethlon?
Zedad
Hazar Enan

D A N

A S H E R

SUBITE

Berothah

N A P H T A L I

Damascus

DAMASCUS

Eastern Boundary

M A N A S S E H

Megiddo

E P H R A I M

KARNAIM

HAURAN

R E U B E N

Samaria

Jordan

Gilead

J U D A H

PORTION OF THE PRINCE

Jerusalem

Ashdod

Judah

B E N J A M I N

Eastern Sea

S I M E O N

I S S A C H A R

Western Boundary

Z E B U L U N

Wadi of Egypt

Tamar

G A D

Southern Boundary

Meribah
Kadesh

KARNAIM Province within satrapy "Beyond the River"

0   25 km.

0   20 miles

---

days (2:17–7:3).

With the walls completed, Ezra and Nehemiah led the people in a time of spiritual renewal that ultimately resulted in the signing of a covenant document whereby the people committed themselves to govern their lives in accordance with the Law of Moses. After serving for twelve years as governor (Neh 5:14; 13:6), Nehemiah returned to the Persian court in 433/432 B.C. He spent an undetermined period of time there and returned to Judea to serve again as governor, although his activities during his second term are not recorded.

From the biblical and extrabiblical data it is possible to gain a fair understanding of Judah's position in the Persian Empire. However, it is probable that during, or soon after, the days of Darius the large satrapy of "Babylon and Beyond

the River" was divided into at least two portions, so that "Beyond the River" became a satrapy in its own right, probably with Damascus as its capital.[1] By the time of Esther (ca. 473 B.C.) the Persian Empire was further divided into 127 provinces (Esth 1:1; 8:9), which, in turn, were combined in various ways to make up the satrapies. It is generally assumed that the provinces in the satrapy "Beyond the River" (e.g., Hamath, Subite, Damascus, Karnaim, Hauran, Gilead, Megiddo, Samaria, some of which were mentioned by the prophet Ezekiel [47:15–20]) which had been established by the Assyrians and maintained by the Babylonians, were also preserved by the Persians. Judah, too, was a province in the satrapy "Beyond the River."

To the north of Judah was the province of Samaria, whose governor, Sanballat the Horonite, came into direct conflict with Nehemiah (Neh 2, 4, and 6, passim). The extent of the Samaritan province is not known for certain, but it probably stretched from the Jezreel Valley in the north to Judah in the south and from the Jordan River in the east to the Sharon Plain in the west.[2] It is possible that the "plain of Ono," to which Sanballat tried to lure Nehemiah (6:2), was neutral territory, outside of both Judah and Samaria.

To the east of Judah and east of the Jordan River was the province of Transjordan, or Gilead. The governor there, at least during the days of Nehemiah, was Tobiah the Ammonite. This Tobiah was one of a series of rulers who came from a prominent Transjordanian family headquartered at Tyre of Transjordan (Iraq el-Emir) and who had close ties with Eliashib the priest in Jerusalem (Neh 13:4–7).[3] Not much can be said regarding the status of the area to the west, the Philistine Plain. Some of the coastal cities may have been granted to the cities of Tyre and Sidon, but this was a very fluid situation. This territory was possibly called "Ashdod," for the "men of Ashdod" are mentioned among Nehemiah's opponents (4:7).

Besides Sanballat and Tobiah, "Geshem the Arab" (Neh 6:1) joined in the hostilities against Nehemiah. He seems to have been the same person as the Geshem whose name was inscribed on a silver bowl found at Tell el-Maskhuta, located nine miles (14.5 km.) west of modern Ismailia in Egypt. His son Qaynu dedicated the bowl to the deity Han-Ilat (ANET, 657). In this inscription Geshem is called the king of Qedar (biblical Kedar). The extent of this kingdom is not known, but it probably included a portion of the northern desert of Sinai, which stretched along the Mediterranean coast from Gaza to Ienysus, and it probably extended south and eastward toward the Red Sea and Arabia. Geshem was likely involved in controlling the overland transport of luxury goods (e.g., gold, frankincense, myrrh, pearls, and spices) that passed through his territory on their way from Arabia to urban centers in the north and west.

As for Judah itself, it is evident that Jewish settlements were established in the old Benjamite territory north, east, and west of Jerusalem (Ezra 2:21–35; Neh 7:26–38; 11:31–36). On the west, in the Shephelah, Jews settled in En Rimmon, Zorah, Jarmuth, Zanoah, Adullam, Lachish, and Azekah (Neh 11:29–30). On the east, it is likely that Judean territory stretched to the bank of the Jordan River and to the shore of the Dead Sea. In the southern Hill Country of Judah the text mentions Jews residing in Kiriath Arba (= Hebron) and Dibon (identification unknown), and further south, in the region where the Hill Country of Judah meets the biblical Negev. The cities of Jekabzeel, Jeshua, Moladah, Beth Pelet, Hazar Shual, and Beersheba are mentioned, as are Ziklag and Meconah, both probably located in the western Negev (11:25–28).

In addition to the above data, hints regarding the internal structure of Judah can be gleaned from Nehemiah 3. This chapter describes how certain groups of men were engaged in rebuilding the walls of Jerusalem. In some instances the villages from which they came are mentioned. These villages include Keilah, Zanoah, Beth Zur, Tekoa, Beth Hakkerem, Jerusalem, Gibeon, Mizpah, and Jericho. Some terms (such as "district" and "half-district") that indicate the existence of administrative subdivisions within Judah are used in connection with Keilah, Beth Zur, Beth Hakkerem, Jerusa-

lem, and Mizpah. Although alternative schemes are possible, Aharoni's description of five districts—one located in the Shephelah (Keilah–Zanoah), three in the Hill Country of Judah (Beth Zur–Tekoa; Beth Hakkerem; and Jerusalem–Gibeah), and one in Benjamin (Mizpah–Jericho)—seems reasonable.[4]

Many, following Alt, have argued that from the time of the first return (538 B.C.) until the days of Nehemiah (445 B.C.) Judah was not an independent province but rather was a part of the province of Samaria. However, Avigad's studies have shown that, on the contrary, Judah was an independent province from the first.[5] His conclusion is based on a straightforward interpretation of the biblical (Ezra 5:14; Hag 1:1, 14; Neh 5:14–15; 12:26) and archaeological data (bulla, seals, jar-handle impressions, Elephantine papyri, and coins). Avigad was even able to reconstruct a tentative list of Judean governors, which includes Sheshbazzar, Zerubbabel, Elinathan, Yeho'ezer, Ahzai, Nehemiah, Bagohi, and Yehezqiyah—of which the first, second, and sixth are mentioned in the Bible.

At the end of the fifth century B.C. the biblical record becomes silent and we are dependent on a variety of sources to sketch out political and geographical developments. Upon the death of Artaxerxes I, Darius II (423–404 B.C.) became ruler of the Persian Empire. Glimpses into the life of the Jewish community in Judea are furnished by papyrus documents that were found at Elephantine, a site in southern Egypt (see ANET, 491–92). There a Jewish colony had established itself, possibly as early as the seventh or sixth century B.C., serving as a military garrison for the Egyptians. The papyrus documents show that the garrison had built a temple for worshiping Yahweh at Elephantine but that it had been destroyed around 410 B.C. It is also evident that the Jews of Elephantine on occasion looked to Jerusalem for guidance, for they corresponded with Bogoas/Bagohi, the governor of Judea.

Egypt, for its part, was able to gain a degree of independence from Persia during the 28th–30th dynasties (ca. 404–343 B.C.). During that time, Egypt maintained sporadic anti-Persian contacts with Greece (Sparta and Athens), Cyprus, Syria, and Palestine. Although a treaty between Greece and Persia was signed in 386 B.C., it was an uneasy peace between these two powers. On several occasions (373 and 351 B.C.) the Persians attempted to invade Egypt, and finally, on their third attempt, in 343 B.C., Artaxerxes III (359–338 B.C.) was successful. This victory inaugurated a ten-year period of harsh Persian rule in Egypt, which Alexander the Great's conquest in 332 B.C. brought to an end.

After the assassination of Artaxerxes III and the brief reign of Arses, Darius III Codomannus (336–330 B.C.) presided over the collapse of the Persian Empire as Alexander the Macedonian moved steadily eastward, conquering province after province. It was Alexander who captured the city of Persepolis, burning the magnificent palace that had been built by Xerxes, and in 330 B.C. the Persian Empire came to an end when Bessus, the satrap of Bactria, killed Darius III as the latter fled from the advancing Alexander. In the centuries following the arrival of Alexander (ca. 332 B.C.), the political, religious, linguistic, and cultural milieu of the Levant changed dramatically as Greco-Roman culture spread rapidly.

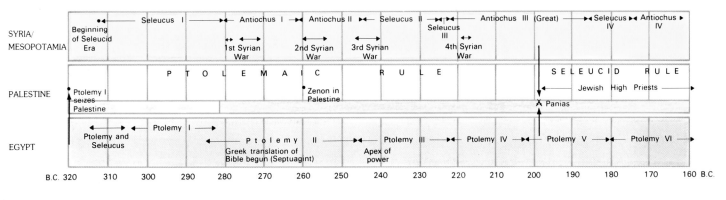

| | B.C. 320 | 310 | 300 | 290 | 280 | 270 | 260 | 250 | 240 | 230 | 220 | 210 | 200 | 190 | 180 | 170 | 160 B.C. |

SYRIA/MESOPOTAMIA: Beginning of Seleucid Era — Seleucus I — Antiochus I — Antiochus II — Seleucus II — Seleucus III — Antiochus III (Great) — Seleucus IV — Antiochus IV; 1st Syrian War, 2nd Syrian War, 3rd Syrian War, 4th Syrian War

PALESTINE: Ptolemy I seizes Palestine — PTOLEMAIC RULE — Zenon in Palestine — SELEUCID RULE; Panias; Jewish High Priests

EGYPT: Ptolemy and Seleucus — Ptolemy I — Ptolemy II (Greek translation of Bible begun [Septuagint]) — Ptolemy III (Apex of power) — Ptolemy IV — Ptolemy V — Ptolemy VI

The Arrival of the Greeks

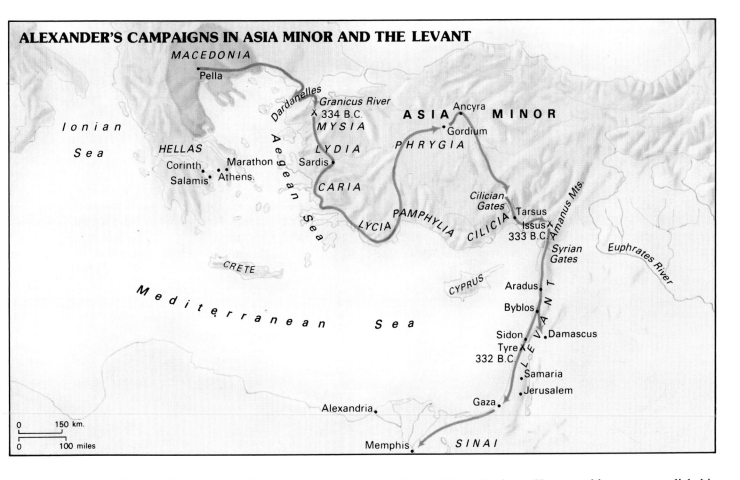

ALEXANDER'S CAMPAIGNS IN ASIA MINOR AND THE LEVANT

During the sixth, fifth, and fourth centuries B.C., the power of the various Greek city-states was growing to such an extent that they were beginning to challenge Persian supremacy in Asia Minor and elsewhere. The Persians, who had invaded Greece, were kept at bay by the Greek forces, which defeated them first at Marathon in 490 B.C. and then, ten years later, at Salamis. Through the remainder of the fifth century and during the first two-thirds of the fourth, the Greeks encouraged anti-Persian activities in Egypt, the Levant, and Asia Minor, but the extent of the territory under Persian rule in these areas remained virtually unchanged.

By the middle of the fourth century B.C. Philip II solidified his position as ruler of Macedonia in northern Greece. During his life he worked toward two great goals: the unification of the Greek city-states under his rule and the

overthrow of the Persians. He was able to accomplish his first goal by political as well as military means. In the process of unifying Greece he built his Macedonian army into a small but formidable fighting force. Unfortunately, Philip was assassinated in 336 B.C., after having completed plans for the invasion of Asia Minor.

At the time of his death, his son Alexander ("the Great"), born in 356 B.C., was well positioned to carry out his father's dreams. Although only twenty years old at the time, Alexander had been prepared for his new position as leader of Macedon: he had been educated by the Greek philosopher Aristotle and had led campaigns on behalf of his father during his teenage years. But before he could proceed with the invasion of Asia Minor, Alexander had to assert his dominon over neighboring countries and city-states as well as over Greece. This he was able to accomplish in a relatively short period of time, and then he was ready to proceed eastward to engage the Persians. Crossing the Dardanelles in 334 B.C., Alexander defeated the Persian satraps of Asia Minor at the Granicus River and then marched south through the provinces of Mysia, Lydia, Caria, Lycia, and Pamphylia in a counterclockwise direction. At Gordium, the ancient capital of Phrygia, he met Parmenio, his general, who had proceeded directly from Sardis to Gordium. The Greeks crushed resistance along both routes, captured cities, secured treasuries, and replaced Persian overlords.

Alexander proceeded from Gordium southeast to Tarsus, the capital of Cilicia, via Ancyra and the Cilician Gates. Continuing around the northeastern corner of the Mediterranean Sea, he passed through the Syrian Gates in the Amanus Mountains before realizing that behind him Darius, the Persian monarch, had assembled a large army at Issus. Retracing his steps, Alexander met and defeated Darius III at the battle of Issus in 333 B.C. In spite of considerable losses, however, Darius was able to flee eastward and began

to regroup his forces for a later battle with Alexander.

After his victory at Issus, Alexander marched south along the coast of the Levant, securing or seizing Aradus, Byblos, Sidon, Tyre (in 332 B.C., after the construction of a causeway to the island and a seven-month siege), Gaza (after a two-month siege), and other cities. In the meantime, contingents of Alexander's army secured the tribes in the Lebanon Mountains, and the strategic city of Damascus was captured by Alexander's general Parmenio. After Alexander had crossed northern Sinai, Egypt submitted to his rule, and he spent the winter of 332–331 B.C. there. At that time the city of Alexandria was founded on the western branch of the Nile near the Mediterranean Sea. This city became not only the capital of Egypt under the subsequent Egyptian Ptolemaic dynasty but also one of the leading commercial and intellectual centers of the Greco-Roman world.

After Alexander was declared the son of the Egyptian god Amon, which meant that he had been designated as the legitimate ruler of Egypt, he left Ptolemy in charge of administering the country and began to retrace his steps northward through the Levant. Although there is a tradition

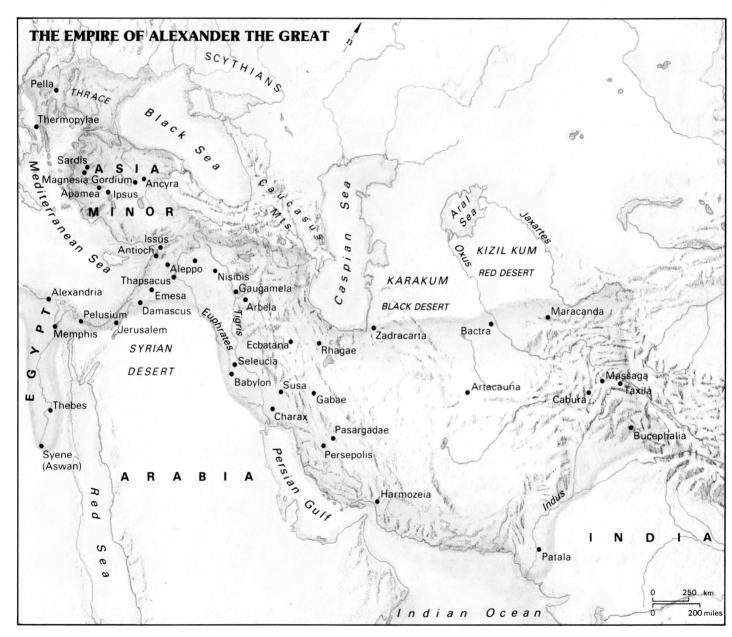

THE EMPIRE OF ALEXANDER THE GREAT

that Alexander visited Jerusalem, this is not certain, and his treatment of the Judeans is not known; it is probably to be assumed that the Jews did not interfere with his advance along the coast and that, in turn, they were not molested. The Samaritans to the north of Judea, however, murdered their governor (Andromachus), who had been appointed by Alexander; in retaliation, Alexander destroyed the city of Samaria and resettled it with Macedonian veterans. Thus a large foreign (Greek) element was added to the basically Samaritan/Semitic populace of the region.

Heading north and then east, Alexander passed through northern Mesopotamia, crossing both the Euphrates and the Tigris. To the east of the Tigris, on the plain between Gaugamela and Arbela, Darius was waiting with a large army. In the ensuing battle the Persians were soundly defeated, yet Darius himself was able to escape capture. He fled eastward, but just prior to being overtaken by Alexander, he was murdered by Bessus, the satrap of Bactria, a former ally. Thus nearly two hundred years of Persian rule in the Near East were brought to a close.[1]

Alexander continued his march eastward into the northeastern portions of the Persian Empire, to the Oxus and Jaxartes rivers (in the area of modern Afghanistan and Kashmir), and then headed south into the Indus Valley (in modern Pakistan). When his troops refused to continue east into India he embarked on a difficult march through the deserts and mountains of southern Persia (modern Iran) to Babylon.

Alexander may have intended to make Babylon the capital of his empire, although this is not certain; but before he was able to enjoy the fruits of a mature empire, he died in Babylon, in 323 B.C., at the age of thirty-two. It was years before the full impact of his conquests took effect, but it is worth noting here that the Near East was radically changed with the arrival of Greek language and culture.

Because Alexander died without leaving a designated successor, the period between 323 B.C. and 301 B.C. was one of controversy and war. At the outset, a number of his generals and regents (e.g., Perdiccas the regent, and later Antigonus Monophtalmus and his son Demetrius) quarreled over whether the kingdom should remain a united whole or whether it should be divided among the competing powers (e.g., Ptolemy I, ruler in Egypt, as well as Seleucus I, who laid claim to Syria and Mesopotamia). In 320 B.C. Ptolemy I annexed Palestine to Egypt, and a series of battles ensued that found him allied with Seleucus I and Lysimachus against Antigonus Monophtalmus and his son Demetrius. Following the battle of Ipsus in 301 B.C., in which Antigonus and his allies were defeated, there was a period of relative peace, during which time Antipater and Cassander were established in Macedonia and Greece; Lysimachus in Thrace and Asia Minor; Seleucus I in Syria, Mesopotamia, and Persia (all the way to the Indus River); and Ptolemy I in Egypt and Palestine.

Ptolemy was able to establish himself as the king of Egypt, and thus began the rule of his Greek dynasty, which lasted for almost three centuries, from 304 B.C. until 30 B.C. This dynasty consisted of at least sixteen different kings and queens who were called Ptolemy or Cleopatra. Not only was the king of Greek origin, but the ethnic background of much of the ruling administration was also Greek, and many of the native, non-Greek officials soon learned the Greek language

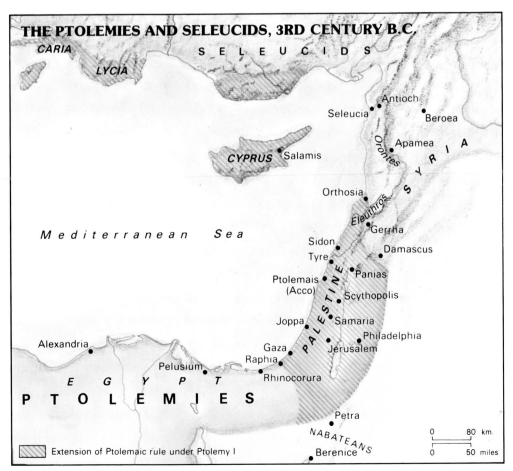

THE PTOLEMIES AND SELEUCIDS, 3RD CENTURY B.C.

CARIA
LYCIA
SELEUCIDS
Antioch
Seleucia
Beroea
Apamea
CYPRUS
Salamis
SYRIA
Orontes
Orthosia
Eleutheros
Gerrha
Sidon
Damascus
Tyre
Panias
Ptolemais
(Acco)
Scythopolis
PALESTINE
Joppa
Samaria
Alexandria
Philadelphia
Gaza
Jerusalem
Raphia
Pelusium
Rhinocorura
EGYPT
PTOLEMIES
Mediterranean Sea
Petra
NABATEANS
Berenice

Extension of Ptolemaic rule under Ptolemy I

0   80 km
0   50 miles

"Tomb of Zechariah" on east bank of Kidron Valley showing Hellenistic and Egyptian influences.

and adopted Greek customs. The capital of Egypt was moved to the recently established city of Alexandria. There Ptolemy I buried Alexander the Great, and he was able to establish the city as one of the leading commercial and intellectual centers of the world. During his reign the famous library of Alexandria was established, as was the scholarly center called the Museum. Since the early Greek rulers could neither speak Egyptian nor read hieroglyphics, it was necessary for them to rely on translators to communicate with the local populace and to understand the cultural history of Egypt. It was in this context, during the reign of Ptolemy I (304–282 B.C.), that Manetho, the Egyptian, wrote his famous history of Egypt in Greek, and it is from his lead that Egyptian history is normally divided into periods of thirty or thirty-one dynasties.

The political and military fortunes of Ptolemy I were varied, but at one time he was able to extend Ptolemaic rule not only to the island of Cyprus but also into southern Turkey, to Caria and Lycia, and even toward the Greek mainland, to Corinth. These territories (save that on the Greek mainland, which was held only briefly), would pass in and out of Ptolemaic hands during the third century B.C.

To the north of Palestine, Seleucus I (312–280 B.C.) was establishing a mighty kingdom. After defeating Lysimachus in 281 B.C., he even gained control of Asia Minor, so that his kingdom stretched from western Turkey, eastward through Syria, Mesopotamia, and Persia, to the Indus River. He established his capital at the city of Antioch, which was located on the Orontes River, near, but not on, the northeastern shore of the Mediterranean Sea. The influence of the Seleucid state was so pervasive that the calendrical system used in the Near East for hundreds of years was reckoned from the beginning of Seleucus I's reign in what is now known as 312 B.C. During the days of Seleucus I there was a period of relative peace between the Seleucid state in the north and Egypt in the south. This was probably due to the fact that Ptolemy I had saved Seleucus' life and had sheltered and supported him against their common foe, Antigonus.

Although the Ptolemies are usually considered to have been the rulers of Palestine during the third century B.C., the situation in fact was much more complex. During that century there was a series of four major wars pitting the Seleucids against the Ptolemies. These wars are called the Syrian Wars, and battles raged during the seventies, fifties, forties, and teens of the third century B.C. Although the Seleucids were at times able to invade and briefly control Palestine, the Ptolemies were, in the main, successful in defending and controlling their territory. In fact, during the Third Syrian War, in the late 240s, Ptolemy III (246–222 B.C.) even countered the Seleucids' aggression by invading their territory to the north and then marching eastward through Mesopotamia and Persia to the border of India. Even Seleucia, the port of Antioch, fell into Ptolemaic hands and remained under their control for over twenty years (ca. 240–219 B.C.). This extensive campaign came at a time when Ptolemaic rule was at the height of its power, but the conquest was not a lasting one.

During the third century B.C. Ptolemaic interest in Palestine was primarily twofold. First, Palestine was important as a buffer state, serving as Egypt's first line of defense against

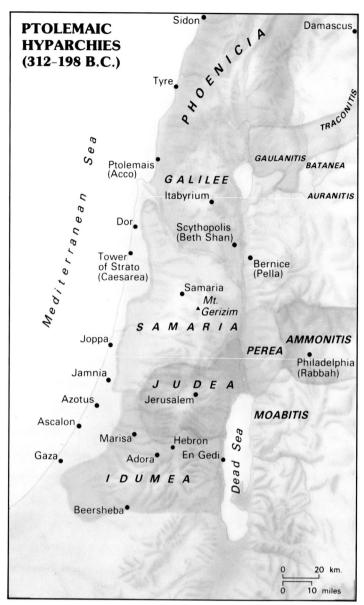

PTOLEMAIC HYPARCHIES (312–198 B.C.)

Sidon
Damascus
PHOENICIA
TRACONITIS
Tyre
Ptolemais (Acco)
GAULANITIS BATANEA
GALILEE
Itabyrium
AURANITIS
Dor
Scythopolis (Beth Shan)
Tower of Strato (Caesarea)
Bernice (Pella)
Samaria
Mt. Gerizim
Mediterranean Sea
SAMARIA
AMMONITIS
Joppa
PEREA
Philadelphia (Rabbah)
Jamnia
JUDEA
Azotus
Jerusalem
MOABITIS
Ascalon
Marisa
Hebron
En Gedi
Dead Sea
Gaza
Adora
IDUMEA
Beersheba

0   20 km.
0   10 miles

Seleucid aggression. In addition, Palestine served as an agricultural hinterland, from which Egypt could secure quality olive oil, wines, wood products, and, at times, slaves.[2]

The extent, depth, and precise nature of Ptolemaic rule in Palestine is difficult to determine with complete certainty, yet it is possible to describe its basic outline.[3] In general, Ptolemaic holdings stretched north along the Mediterranean Sea to the region of the Eleutherus River. However, inland, in Transjordan, they did not reach as far north as Damascus, which was usually under Seleucid control. The center of Ptolemaic administration was apparently located at Alexandria in Egypt, from which a governor and a director of revenues of Syria and Phoenicia controlled matters. Palestine[4] was divided into a number of administrative units called *hyparchies* in Greek. These were basically equivalent to Persian "provinces" (*medinah* in Aramaic). In general, each hyparchy had three major officials, all of whom were Greek: a governor, a financial officer, and a person in command of the army/police.

Not much is known about the hyparchy of Judea during the third century B.C. But since it had submitted to Alexander the Great, and since it was not deeply involved in the Syrian Wars, it is generally assumed that few changes

150

SELEUCID EPARCHIES (198–142 B.C.)

PHOENICIA

Panias
✗198 B.C.
Antiochia ●

Ladder
of
Tyre

Antiochenes
(Ptolemais) ●

Seleucia ● GAULANITIS
BATANEA

GALILEE

Philoteria ●

Seleucia
(Abila) ●

● Dora

Antiochia
Seleucia
(Gadara) ●

SAMARIA GALAADITIS

Samaria ●

Antiochia-on-●
Chrysorrhoas
(Gerasa)

S A M A R I A

AMMONITIS

PEREA

Philadelphia ●

Jamnia ●

Antiochia
(Jerusalem) ●

J U D E A

GALAADITIS

Azotus ●

Marisa ●

MOABITIS

Adora ●

Hebron ●
En Gedi ●

Gaza ● I D U M E A

Mediterranean Sea

P A R A L I A

Dead Sea

Beersheba ●

0   20 km.

0   10   miles

occurred in its size or internal administration, whose chief Jewish official was the high priest.

To the north of Judea, the hyparchy of Samaria underwent some change. The inhabitants of the city of Samaria had revolted against the governor whom Alexander had appointed, and they had burnt Andromachus alive. In retaliation, the city of Samaria was captured, its population executed or banished, and the city resettled with Macedonian veterans, thus establishing a viable Greek colony in and around the city. The remaining portion of the hyparchy of Samaria was probably dominated by the Samaritans, who maintained their religious and political institutions on and near Mount Gerizim.

To the north of Samaria were royal estates in the Jezreel Valley, and to the north of these was the hyparchy of Galilee, which is, in fact, mentioned in the Zenon papyri (see note 2). The precise identification of the administrative center of Galilee is not known with certainty, but it could have been at the fortress of Itabyrium, located on the top of Mount Tabor or, more probably, at Scythopolis (the "city of the Scythians" = OT Beth Shan).

To the north and west of Galilee, along the Phoenician coast, maritime cities such as Tyre and Sidon had a high degree of independence yet remained submissive to Ptolemaic rule, supplying ships and sailors for the formidable Ptolemaic navy as well as a merchant fleet. Indeed, during the third century B.C. the Ptolemies were the premier naval power in the eastern Mediterranean Sea. Further south along the Mediterranean coast the importance of Acco, the port of Galilee, was emphasized by the fact that it was one of the few cities to receive the dynastic name, Ptolemais. Further to the south, along the Sharon and Philistine plains, coastal cities—Dor, the Tower of Strato (later Caesarea), Joppa, Jamnia, Azotus (= OT Ashdod), Ascalon, and Gaza, among others—were influenced by Hellenistic civilization yet were able to retain varying degrees of independence within the context of maintaining at least nominal loyalty to the Ptolemaic dynasty.

To the east of the Philistine Plain was the hyparchy of Idumea. Its westward orientation, toward Greek influence, is emphasized by the fact that although its territory stretched east to the Dead Sea, its capital, Marisa, was located in its western region, in the Shephelah overlooking the coastal plain. In Transjordan, the large Assyrian/Babylonian/Persian districts were generally divided into smaller administrative units. It has been suggested that those districts whose names end in *-itis*, among others, were set up during the time of Ptolemaic rule; for example, the old Hauran district was divided into Traconitis and Auranitis. Besides the new district names, major cities were given Greek names, and a Hellenistic (or Hellenized) populace began to flourish in them: Rabbah of the Ammonites (NIV) was renamed Philadelphia, Pella/Pehel became Bernice, and in Cisjordan, as already noted, Acco became Ptolemais, Beth Shan became Scythopolis, etc. In these cities, it was the upper classes that were motivated to adopt Greek language and customs for economic as well as other reasons. However, it must be assumed that a rather large portion of the local population maintained their traditional Semitic languages (e.g., Hebrew, Aramaic) and customs, for later, after the veneer of Greco-Roman influence was removed, the Semitic influences still prevailed. For example, the name of the city of Scythopolis (Greek) eventually reverted to a form of the old name "Beth Shan" (Semitic), indicating that the local populace had continued using that name through centuries of Greco-Roman rule.

With the accession of Ptolemy IV (222–203 B.C.) to the Egyptian, and of Antiochus III (223–187 B.C.) to the Seleucid throne, the balance of power in the Levant began to shift in favor of the Seleucids. In the Fourth Syrian War (221–217 B.C.) Antiochus was able to recapture Seleucia, the port of the capital Antioch (219 B.C.), to push south into Galilee, the Jezreel Valley, and Transjordan (218 B.C.), and to advance all the way south to Gaza and Raphia (217 B.C.). However, the final Seleucid conquest of Palestine was thwarted for two more decades, as Antiochus was defeated at Raphia and the forces of Ptolemy IV were able to recapture Palestine and Phoenicia.

For the next decade Antiochus III was preoccupied with containing revolts in Asia Minor and the eastern regions of his kingdom. In 203 B.C. Ptolemy V (203–181 B.C.) acceded to the throne of Egypt at the age of seven—the first in a series of weak Ptolemaic kings who would be greatly influenced by wives, mothers, sisters, and generals. In 201

B.C. Antiochus III led a thrust into Palestine that would eventually culminate in the transfer of Palestine from Ptolemaic to Seleucid control. However, when Antiochus III turned his attention to the conquest of Pergamum in western Asia Minor, the Egyptian general Scopas reentered Palestine, reclaiming it for Egypt. Returning to confront this new threat, Antiochus III met Scopas in the decisive battle at Panias in 198 B.C.; the Egyptian army was routed, and Scopas was forced to flee to Sidon. In the aftermath of the battle Antiochus marched south through portions of Batanea in Transjordan and into Samaria and Judea. He evidently was well received by the Jewish population of Jerusalem, who aided him in the expulsion of the Ptolemaic garrison that had been stationed there. Thus began, as a result of the Battle of Panias, close to half a century of Seleucid control of Judea (198–142 B.C.).

During the rule of Antiochus III (223–187 B.C.) and the first portion of the reign of Seleucus IV (187–175 B.C.), the Judeans seem to have prospered under the leadership of the high priest Onias III (198–174 B.C.). Because the Jewish population of Jerusalem had so readily received Antiochus III, they were granted special privileges, including the restoration of Jerusalem, limited tax exemptions, subsidies for the temple, and permission to live according to their ancestral laws (Josephus, *Antiq* 12.3.3, 4 [138–46]).

However, the takeover of Palestine came at a time when Seleucid power was beginning to diminish. During the 190s, the Seleucids progressively lost control of their holdings in Asia Minor to an ascendent Rome, and in the Peace of Apamea (189 B.C.) they relinquished control of all their territory west of the Taurus Mountains. Seleucid control of the eastern portion of their empire was also being challenged, and, as will be described shortly, Palestine itself entered a period of turmoil and intrigue with the revolt of the Maccabees and the rise of the Hasmonean dynasty.

Given this state of flux within the Seleucid domains, and with only a limited number of historical sources to draw upon, it is possible to describe the geographical scene in Palestine in only the most general way, for it must be kept in mind that borders, spheres of influence, and whole populations of cities were constantly changing.[5] In general, it can be asserted that the Seleucids were much more interested in promoting the advancement of Greek language, culture, and customs than were the Ptolemies before them. They accomplished this not only by introducing all of these Greek elements in existing cities but also by establishing new cities on the model of the Greek *polis*, where the adult males who were eligible met together to govern the affairs of their city. The Seleucids also changed the Semitic names of cities to Greek ones, which indicates their pervasive influence in the countries that they controlled. For example, Jerusalem became Antiochia, Gerasa became Antiochia-on-Chrysorrhoas, Gadara became Antiochia Seleucia, Abila became Seleucia, and Ptolemais became Antiochenes. But these Seleucid names lasted for only a brief period of time, and then the names of cities often reverted back to their earlier designations. In addition, new cities, such as Antiochia (near Panias and Dan) and Seleucia in Gaulanitis, were also established.

It seems that the Seleucids preferred larger administrative units than those established under Ptolemaic rule, for they combined several Ptolemaic hyparchies to form a larger unit called an eparchy. Evidently there were four such eparchies in Palestine. One of the largest of these was the eparchy of Samaria, whose governor resided in the city of Samaria. Included in this eparchy were the districts of Judea, Samaria, Galilee, and Perea. The first three districts have been described above (pp. 150–51); Perea was located east of the Jordan River, just north of the Dead Sea. This small territory, which was bordered by Ammonitis on the east, probably consisted of old Tobiad domains that were now incorporated into Samaria.

To the south of the eparchy of Samaria was that of Idumea. Since Marisa, Azotus, Jamnia, and other cities were at times included in its territory, it evidently reached the Mediterranean Sea at least in a limited area. Along the coast of the Mediterranean Sea was Paralia, an elongated eparchy that stretched from the border of Egypt in the south to the Ladder of Tyre in the north, excluding the Idumean corridor to the sea in the Azotus-Jamnia region. On the east of Samaria, east of the Jordan River, was the large eparchy of Galaaditis, which included Batanea, Gaulanitis, Ammonitis, and Moabitis but excluded Perea. There in Transjordan, along the trade routes, Greek cities seem to have flourished. Eventually some of these cities united to form a league known as the Decapolis (see below, p. 160).

During the latter part of the rule of Antiochus III (223–187 B.C.) he experienced a series of defeats at the hands of the Romans, first at Thermopylae in 191 B.C. and then at Magnesia in 190 B.C. In 189 B.C. the Treaty of Apamea was signed, in which Antiochus relinquished control of much of Asia Minor and pledged to pay a heavy tribute to Rome. To insure payments, one of his sons, who would later rule as Antiochus IV, was taken as hostage to Rome. Antiochus III had great difficulty making the tribute payments, and he had to resort to the looting of temples to raise revenue for this purpose. In 187 B.C. he and some of his troops were killed by the Elymaeans while on such a looting expedition.

Antiochus III the Great was succeeded by his son Seleucus IV Philopater ("father-loving"), who ruled from 187 to 175 B.C. By adhering to the terms of the Peace of Apamea he was able to maintain good relations with Rome. He was also on good terms with the Egyptians, for Ptolemy V married his sister, who after the death of her husband in 181 B.C. governed Egypt until 176 B.C. as Cleopatra I. During the early part of Seleucus IV's reign he maintained good relations with the Judeans, even presenting gifts to the temple in Jerusalem (2 Macc 3:3). However, late in his reign a Jew named Simon, wanting to oust the pious Onias III from the office of high priest, tried to ingratiate himself with the Seleucid authorities by encouraging Apollonius, the governor of Coele-Syria and Phoenicia, to expropriate the Jerusalem temple treasury for the benefit of the king, Seleucus IV. Heliodorus, a high official of the king, was sent to Jerusalem to confiscate the treasure, but it is reported that due to divine intervention he was not able to carry out this plot (2 Macc 3). Near the end of his reign Seleucus IV sent his son Demetrius I to Rome to replace Antiochus IV as a hostage. Because of this exchange, Antiochus was able to usurp the throne upon the death of Seleucus IV in 175 B.C., and with the rise of Antiochus IV Judea entered a critical phase in its history, which will be taken up in the next chapter.

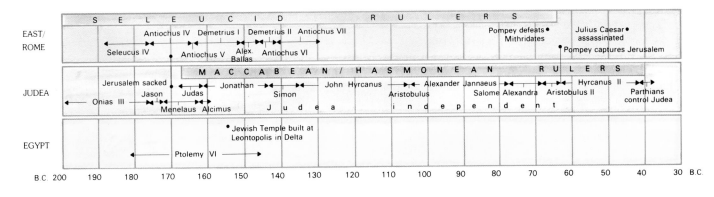

| | B.C. 200 | 190 | 180 | 170 | 160 | 150 | 140 | 130 | 120 | 110 | 100 | 90 | 80 | 70 | 60 | 50 | 40 | 30 B.C. |

EAST/ROME — SELEUCID RULERS — Seleucus IV, Antiochus IV, Demetrius I, Antiochus V, Demetrius II, Alex. Ballas, Antiochus VI, Antiochus VII; Pompey defeats Mithridates; Pompey captures Jerusalem; Julius Caesar assassinated

JUDEA — MACCABEAN / HASMONEAN RULERS — Onias III, Jerusalem sacked, Jason, Menelaus, Judas, Alcimus, Jonathan, Simon, Judea, John Hyrcanus, Aristobulus, independent, Alexander Jannaeus, Salome Alexandra, Aristobulus II, Hyrcanus II, Parthians control Judea

EGYPT — Ptolemy VI; Jewish Temple built at Leontopolis in Delta

The Maccabean Revolt and Hasmonean Dynasty

With the rise of Antiochus IV in 174 B.C. began a chain of events that culminated in the establishment of an independent Jewish state in 142 B.C., a state that lasted until the capture of Jerusalem by the Romans in 63 B.C. These events are of more than passing interest, for they had a direct influence on Jewish life and practice for the next two centuries and, in fact, have had a profound effect on Judaism to the present day.

Antiochus IV (174–163 B.C.) did not encounter much difficulty in seizing the Seleucid throne after the assassination of Seleucus III.[1] To counter the rising threat of a powerful Rome, Antiochus IV attempted to solidify his kingdom by uniting its diverse elements under the banner of Hellenism by encouraging his subjects to adopt Greek language, culture, religion, etc. In Judea certain elements of the population supported the Hellenizing process, and these gained more influence after Jason deposed the pious Onias III (2 Macc 4:7) and had himself appointed high priest by bribing Antiochus IV. Many Jews quickly adopted the new lifestyle (2 Macc 4), which meant breaking with their religious, cultural, and linguistic heritage. Soon afterward, around 171 B.C., Menelaus, another Hellenizer, had Jason removed and himself appointed to the high priesthood by offering Antiochus IV a larger bribe. He even had Onias III murdered. Thus official Judaism reached a low point as the office of high priest was sold to the highest bidder.

Antiochus IV successfully invaded Egypt in 169 B.C. but withdrew the same year, leaving a teenager (Ptolemy VI Philometer) as king of Egypt. In Judea it was rumored that Antiochus IV had died while in Egypt, and Jason, the former high priest, who thought that this would be an opportune moment to regain his lost position, attacked Jerusalem in an attempt to depose Menelaus. Antiochus responded by beating back the attack and recapturing Jerusalem. In the process, thousands of Jews were killed or sold into slavery, the temple treasury was plundered, and Antiochus, a Gentile, even entered the most sacred room of the temple, the Holy of Holies; access to this room was limited to the high priest, and then on only one day of the year, the Day of Atonement.

The following year (168 B.C.) Antiochus IV mounted a second attack on Egypt. As he advanced on the city of Alexandria he was met by the Roman legate C. Popilius Laenas, who presented him with Rome's ultimatum that he leave Egypt immediately. Antiochus IV tried to stall for time, but Laenas drew a circle around him in the sand and ordered him to make his decision before leaving the circle. In the face of Rome's threat, a humiliated Antiochus IV and his forces left immediately.

With Egypt denied him, Antiochus IV evidently decided to strengthen the southern approach to his kingdom by solidifying his position in Palestine. In 167 B.C. he dispatched troops to Jerusalem, where part of the population was slaughtered. In an attempt to Hellenize the population further, Jews were commanded to worship Zeus and other pagan deities, to burn their copies of the Torah, and to forsake the laws of their God (1 Macc 1:41–64). They were forbidden to observe the Sabbath, to celebrate their feasts, to sacrifice to God, and to circumcise their children. In addition, portions of the walls of Jerusalem were torn down and a pagan citadel, called the Acra, was constructed at a strategic location within the city. The temple in Jerusalem was turned into a temple of Olympian Zeus, and on December 16, 167 B.C., an unclean sacrifice was offered to him (2 Macc 6:1–11).

During the latter portion of his reign (167–164 B.C.), Antiochus IV undertook a series of campaigns to Parthia, Armenia, Persia, and Media, subduing the populace and plundering temple treasuries along the way. He eventually died in Persia in 164 B.C. While Antiochus was away on these campaigns, Lysias was left in charge of the territory west of the Euphrates River; thus it was he who had to deal with a serious rebellion in Judea. In 167 B.C. a delegate of Antiochus IV attempted to force Mattathias, a priest who lived in Modiin, to sacrifice to a pagan deity. Mattathias refused, but another Jew volunteered to perform the rite. Outraged, Mattathias killed both the Seleucid delegate and the errant Jew, and thus the Maccabean revolution began (1 Macc 2:1–48). The aged Mattathias soon died a natural death, leaving his five sons to carry the revolutionary torch (1 Macc 2:49–70).

The first and foremost leader of the revolution was Judas, the middle son, who was also called Maccabeus (probably "the hammerer"). Because of the prominence of Judas and the uniqueness of his nickname, this revolt is often called the Maccabean Revolt; however, the period of the revolt includes not only the days of his leadership but also those of his brother Jonathan (160–142 B.C.) and to some extent those of his brother Simon (142–135 B.C.) as well. Gaining the

153

support of the Hasidim, the "pious ones," who were true to ancient Jewish beliefs and practices, Judas and his followers went throughout the countryside, tearing down pagan altars and circumcising Jewish children.

The first attempt at suppressing the revolt was undertaken by Apollonius, the governor of the region and commander of the garrison at Samaria. As he marched south toward Judea, he was met by Judas and his troops and was defeated and killed (1 Macc 3:1–12). Soon afterward Seron, a Seleucid general, was sent to suppress the uprising. While attempting to enter the hill country from the coastal plain via the traditional Beth Horon road, Seron and his army were routed by Judas and his forces at the ascent of Beth Horon. Since this battle occurred in the same general area where Joshua had defeated the Amorite coalition through miraculous intervention (Josh 10), the writer of 1 Maccabees uses imagery from this earlier battle to describe the great achievement of Judas (1 Macc 3:13–26).

In 165 B.C. Lysias, the superior of Seron, assembled a large army under the combined leadership of Ptolemy, Dorimenes, Nicanor, and Gorgias. This army moved south along the coastal plain and set up camp at Emmaus, where the road to Jerusalem begins its ascent into the hill country. Judas mustered his warriors at the old tribal center of Mizpah in the Hill Country of Benjamin. While Gorgias and a portion of the Syrian army marched into the hills on a search-and-destroy mission, Judas and his men descended upon the portion of the Seleucid army that had remained at Emmaus in the Valley of Aijalon. The surprised Seleucids were defeated and retreated to the coast, as did Gorgias and his troops upon returning to their sacked camp at Emmaus (1 Macc 3:27–4:25).

After these three initial defeats, Lysias himself became personally involved in leading the Seleucid troops in a fourth campaign against the Maccabees (164 B.C.). Moving again south along the coastal plain, Lysias did not repeat the mistake of the two previous attacks—attempting to enter the hill country via the Aijalon Valley and Beth Horon road. Instead he continued south, probably to the friendly Hellenistic city of Marisa, and from there entered the Hill Country of Judah in the Adora/Hebron area, an Idumean region also friendly to the Seleucids. As Lysias marched north, Judas marched south along the watershed. The two armies met in battle at Beth Zur, a village located on the southern boundary of Judea. There, to the Judeans' great delight, the army of Lysias was routed; God was indeed favoring their righteous cause (1 Macc 4:26–35). Flushed with victory, Judas and his warriors marched to Jerusalem and recaptured the whole city, save the Acra, which remained in the hands of the Hellenizers. In the temple area, Judas commanded that the pagan altar be torn down and Yahweh's altar rebuilt. The temple was cleansed, and on Chislev 25 (December 14), 164 B.C., the temple was rededicated and proper Jewish sacrifices were resumed. This event has been commemorated by Jews through the ages as the Feast of Hanukkah, the Feast of Dedication (vv. 36–61).

After the death of Antiochus IV in 164 B.C., the power to rule was hotly contested between Lysias and a certain Philip, both of whom claimed to be the guardian of the boy Antiochus V (1 Macc 6:1–17; 2 Macc 9). While the Seleucid leaders were preoccupied with this internal matter, Judas

and his brothers were able to expand their influence in and around Judea. Jews who were being oppressed in Acrabeta, in the district of Samaria north of Jerusalem, and by the Beonites in Transjordan were delivered from their plight by Judas. To the northeast, Jews in the Gilead and Golan regions, in the villages of Bostra, Dathema, Alema, Caspein, Maked, Bosor, Charax, Raphon, and Carnaim, as well as those in Ephron and Scythopolis, also received relief from their oppressors because of Judas's successful military campaign in the area. While Judas was fighting in Transjordan, his brother Simon led an expedition to the Sharon Plain (Arbata), the Jezreel Valley, and western Galilee, relieving pressure on the Jews who lived in those areas. Finally, Judas himself led his men on raids to the south and southwest of Judea, harassing and/or capturing such cities as Hebron, Marisa, Azotus, and Joppa; yet in the end he was unable to hold these gains and was eventually forced to retreat to Odollam (= OT Adullam) in the Shephelah (1 Macc 5:1–68).

Despite these victories of Judas there was still a large influential portion of the populace who desired closer ties with the Seleucids and preferred the Hellenistic lifestyle. These Hellenizers appealed to Antiochus V for help, and Lysias was again sent to Judea with a large army. His line of march was similar to the one he had used previously: Coastal Plain–Marisa–Hebron–Beth Zur. Then, continuing north along the watershed of the Hill Country of Judah, he met Judas at the village of Beth Zechariah. In the battle Lysias

THE MACCABEAN REVOLT 167-152 B.C.

Acrabeta

S A M A R I A

Tephon
Lebonah

Jews killed by Bacchides on his return to Antioch.

Aramathea

Ber-zetha

Gophna
Apherema

Bethel
Jonathan permitted to settle at Micmash.

Lydda
Modiin
Lower Beth Horon
Eleasa
Beeroth
Mizpah
Micmash
Jericho

Gazara
Upper Beth Horon
Capharsalama
Adasa
Pharathon

Emmaus
Antiochus IV's attack on Jerusalem 167 B.C.
Temple rededicated 164 B.C. Feast of Hanukkah.
Jerusalem (Acra)

J U D E A
Bethlehem
Thamna
Beth Basi
Odollam
Beth Zechariah
Tekoa
Marisa
Beth Zur
Asphar

Dead Sea

I D U M E A

Judea at the beginning of the revolt

✗ Seleucid defeat at the hands of Judean rebels

✗ Judas' defeat

▪ Fortress set up by Bacchides

0   8 km.
0   5 miles

154

made use of war elephants, to the detriment of Judas's forces. In fact, one of Judas's brothers, Eleazar, was killed when one of the elephants fell on him—the first of the five brothers to die. Lysias was victorious at Beth Zechariah and proceeded to Jerusalem while Judas and his troops fled to the remote regions of the country (1 Macc 6:18–54). However, as Lysias was laying siege to the city he received word that his rival and archenemy, Philip, was marching from Persia to Syria to claim the Seleucid throne. Needing to return to Antioch, Lysias made peace with Judas, guaranteeing the Jews religious freedom (vv. 55–63), but demanding that the walls of Jerusalem be torn down. Thus, in spite of Judas's defeat, at least the religious gains of the revolt were preserved. However, Menelaus, the high priest, was accused by Lysias of being an instigator of the rebellion and was executed in Beroea and replaced by Alcimus, another Hellenizing high priest (2 Macc 13:3–8).

Upon returning to Syria, Lysias was able to defeat Philip. His achievement was short-lived, however, for Demetrius I, the son of Seleucus IV, who had been held hostage in Rome, had escaped and was heading for Syria. Demetrius I traveled to Syria via Lycia and landed at Tripolis, where the population rallied behind him as the legitimate heir to the throne. Lysias and his puppet ruler, Antiochus V, were deposed and executed (1 Macc 7:1–4).

Demetrius I confirmed Alcimus as high priest, but Alcimus still had to be established in Jerusalem. This was done by sending a military force to Jerusalem under the leadership of Bacchides, a powerful general in charge of all the territory west of the Euphrates River. The Hellenists of Jerusalem were, of course, willing to accept Demetrius I's appointment; but surprisingly, so were the Hasidim (the "pious ones"), because Alcimus was of legitimate, Aaronic, priestly descent. Thus Judas's allies temporarily abandoned the revolutionary movement. But Alcimus, after he had been installed as high priest, executed sixty Hasidim, and Bacchides killed even more Jews at Ber-zetha as he was returning to Antioch (1 Macc 7:5–25). With this turn of events the Hasidim returned to Judas, and the Maccabees began to pressure Alcimus and the Hellenizers.

Nicanor, the Syrian commander whom Bacchides had left in charge of the garrison at Jerusalem, tried to relieve the Maccabean pressure by venturing out of Jerusalem in an attempt to open the road that led from Jerusalem to the coastal plain. He was met and defeated by Judas at Capharsalama, six miles (10 km.) northwest of Jerusalem. Later, Nicanor again attempted to open the road, but this time he himself was killed in battle at Adasa. This victory is still celebrated as "Nicanor's Day," on the thirteenth day of the Jewish month of Adar (originally March 9, 161 B.C.; 1 Macc 7:26–50).

Judas knew that the powerful Bacchides would respond, and so he appealed to Rome for help, but this assistance would not arrive in time. In 160 B.C. Bacchides began his advance to Jerusalem. Passing south along the western shore of the Sea of Galilee he killed the Jews living in Arbela and proceeded through Samaria to Jerusalem. After arriving in Jerusalem, Bacchides, like Nicanor before him, marched northwest out of the city to secure the Beth Horon road to the coast. Judas and his troops met him near the village of Eleasa, and there the Maccabean forces were decimated.

Judas himself was killed, and the surviving members of his force fled to the Judean Wilderness, to the well of Asphar in the wilderness of Tekoa. There Judas's brother Jonathan attempted to rebuild the Maccabean fighting force. Bacchides, for his part, established a chain of fortresses in Judea at places such as Bethel, Jericho, Pharathon, Upper Beth Horon, Emmaus, Thamna, and Tekoa. Thus the revolt that had begun with Mattathias's deed at Modiin in 167 B.C. and had accomplished a number of significant goals (the temple area was regained, sacrifices had been reinstituted, military victories over superior forces had been won, and for a brief period of time minor territorial advances had been made) was in danger of collapse by 160 B.C. The charismatic leader Judas was dead, his forces dispersed, and the enemy securely in control of the countryside.

In 159 B.C. Alcimus, the high priest, died, and the Seleucids did not appoint a successor. Officially, Judea was under direct Syrian control; Bacchides remained in Jerusalem and from there governed a subdued populace. But in 157 B.C. Bacchides returned to Antioch, and Jonathan took advantage of his absence to resume hostilities. Jonathan and his troops seized the abandoned fortress of Beth Basi, 1.3 miles (2 km.) southeast of Bethlehem. Bacchides returned to Judea in 156 B.C. to deal with this new phase of the uprising and laid siege to Beth-basi. While Simon defended the fortress, Jonathan recruited additional forces from the Odomera and Phasiran tribes, who lived in the Judean Desert. Then both Simon and Jonathan attacked Bacchides' forces, and Simon was able to burn the latter's siege machinery. A weakened Bacchides sued for peace. The terms of the agreement gave Jonathan permission to settle in Micmash, seven miles (11 km.) north of Jerusalem, while the Hellenists remained in Jerusalem. When Bacchides again withdrew his forces from Judea, Jonathan was able to regain at least limited control of the countryside, although both Jerusalem and Beth Zur remained in the hands of the Hellenists.

This arrangement lasted for several years until Jewish-Seleucid relations entered a new phase in 152 B.C. At that time a certain Alexander Balas, who claimed to be the son of Antiochus IV, challenged the kingship of Demetrius I, who had become a very tyrannical ruler. In their rivalry both men attempted to win the loyalty of Jonathan. In what became a bidding war, Demetrius I released Jewish hostages and allowed Jonathan to move from Micmash to Jerusalem. Alexander Balas countered by appointing Jonathan as high priest and "Friend of the King," sending him the symbols of rulership—a purple robe and a diadem. Demetrius I increased his offer by promising Jonathan tax exemptions, the surrender of the Acra, the transfer of three toparchies from Samaria to Judea, subsidies for the army and the temple, and money for the rebuilding of the walls of Jerusalem. Jonathan eventually sided with Alexander Balas, and as a result of these intrigues he was able to better his position considerably. At the Feast of Tabernacles in 152 B.C. Jonathan wore the high priestly garments; thus the office was filled once again, this time by a Hasmonean. (The name Hasmonean was taken from a certain Hasman who was a priest from the family of Jehoiarib [1 Macc 2:1; 1 Chron 24:7] and who was the great-grandfather of Mattathias, the father of Jonathan and Simon and their brothers.)

Although Alexander Balas was able to defeat and kill Demetrius I, his struggle for the throne was not over, for Demetrius II returned from his refuge in Cnidus (close to Rhodes and Cos). Upon his arrival in the Levant in 147 B.C., the population joined him in opposition to Alexander Balas. Demetrius II appointed Apollonius as commander of Coele-Syria and sent him to attack Jonathan, who was supporting his rival. Jonathan had been able to attack and capture the port of Joppa, and it was between Joppa and Azotus that Jonathan and Apollonius met in battle. Apollonius was defeated and fled to Azotus, which was then also captured by Jonathan. Jonathan continued south to Ascalon and was well received there. Thus, twenty years after the beginning of the Maccabean revolt, the Judeans had proven themselves as a major military power. Recognizing this, Demetrius II gave Jonathan the district of Accaron as an estate and transferred the districts of Lydda, Aramathea, and Apherema to his control.

In 145 B.C. the internal Seleucid strife came to a head when the troops of Alexander Balas and Ptolemy VI met Demetrius II in battle near Antioch. Both Alexander Balas and Ptolemy VI died, and Demetrius II became the sole ruler of Syria. Although Jonathan and Demetrius II had been enemies, Jonathan sent him gifts, and Demetrius II, impressed with Jonathan's prowess and audacity, confirmed him as high priest and "Friend of the King" and granted him control of three districts of Samaria.

Demetrius II's sole rule and the new rapprochement with Jonathan were not to last long, for Tryphon, a general of Alexander Balas, claimed the Seleucid throne for Antiochus VI, a child of Alexander Balas who had been in safekeeping in Arabia. Initially Jonathan supported Demetrius II, but when the latter turned against him, Jonathan joined ranks with Tryphon and Antiochus VI. For this, Jonathan was made head of civil and religious affairs in Judea, while his brother Simon was placed in charge of the army. In 144 B.C. Demetrius II responded by invading Palestine and establishing a major base camp at Cadasa in Upper Galilee. Jonathan and his army moved north from Gennesaret on the north shore of the Sea of Galilee and met the forces of Demetrius II in battle near Hazor. Demetrius II's forces were defeated, and Jonathan captured the Syrian camp at Cadasa.

One year later, in 143 B.C., Jonathan again fought the army of Demetrius II, this time far to the north of Palestine on the Plain of Hamath, near the northern boundary of Coele-Syria. Again Demetrius II's army was defeated, and Jonathan was able to march through northern Coele-Syria, including Damascus, as a victor. Certainly Jonathan had become a military power to be reckoned with.

Demetrius II became preoccupied with the Parthians, which allowed Tryphon and Antiochus VI to strengthen their hold on Coele-Syria. Tryphon considered Jonathan to be too powerful and ambitious, and he marched south into Palestine in 143 B.C. Jonathan met him at Scythopolis with a strong army. Tryphon, fearful of direct combat, persuaded Jonathan to send all but 3,000 of his men home and then induced him to come to Ptolemais with only 1,000 men. After luring Jonathan into Ptolemais with only a token force, Tryphon turned on him and took him prisoner. With Jonathan as a hostage, Tryphon marched south along the coastal plain and from Philistia turned east into the Hill Country of Judea, via

the cities of Marisa, Hebron, and Beth Zur. His goal was to break the power of Jonathan's brother Simon and to regain Jerusalem. However, a severe snowstorm drove him into the warm Jordan Valley for relief, and from there Tryphon headed north for Antioch without having assaulted Jerusalem. En route to Antioch, at Bascama northeast of the Sea of Galilee, Jonathan was executed.

Upon his return to Antioch, Tryphon arranged the death of Antiochus VI and took the throne in his place. Naturally, Simon allied himself with Tryphon's opponent, Demetrius II. The latter, in recognition of Simon's loyalty, sent him a letter confirming Judea's complete independence. Thus 142 B.C. marked the official independence of the Judean state—the first time that it had been officially free from foreign domination since 586 B.C., when Jerusalem had fallen to the Babylonians.

The next year (141 B.C.) the siege of the Acra, begun under Jonathan, was completed. With the capture of the Acra, the whole of Jerusalem was in Hasmonean hands. Unfortunately Simon's ally, Demetrius II, was captured by the Parthians, and his brother Antiochus VII ruled in his stead. Simon allied himself with Antiochus VII against Tryphon, and in return Antiochus VII granted him permission to mint coins, a further indication of Judea's growing independence. In the meantime the Jews had conferred upon Simon the position of governor and of high priest "for ever, until a trustworthy prophet should arise" (1 Macc 14:25–43). Thus, it was during Simon's reign that the Hasmonean dynasty (142–63 B.C.), in a narrow sense, began to rule.

The power struggle between Tryphon and Antiochus VII continued for several years, until finally Antiochus VII captured Tryphon and forced him to commit suicide. Antiochus VII, fearing the growing power of Simon, sent Cendebeus into the Philistine Plain to recover territories that he felt Simon had unlawfully taken (e.g., Joppa and Gazara). Cendebeus established his headquarters at Jamnia and built the fortress of Kidron between Jamnia and Gazara. John Hyrcanus and Judas, sons of Simon, left their fortress at Gazara and attacked Cendebeus; the Syrians fled, and Hasmonean control of Philistia was reestablished.

However, even at this high point for the Hasmoneans, pro-Antiochus VII elements were evidently working in Judea, attempting to unseat Simon and to deliver Judea to the Seleucid king. Tragically, one of these attempts was successful. Ptolemy, son of Abubus, the son-in-law of Simon and governor of Jericho, invited Simon and his sons to a feast at the fortress of Docus and there assassinated all of them. Only John Hyrcanus, who was absent from the banquet, escaped the slaughter. Antiochus VII attempted to take advantage of the situation by invading Judea and laying siege to Jerusalem for more than a year. John Hyrcanus requested a truce for the Feast of Tabernacles, and surprisingly, Antiochus VII agreed, even sending gifts for the feast. With this signal that Antiochus was willing to negotiate, Jerusalem surrendered in 134 B.C. Although Antiochus VII's terms seemed harsh—the Jews had to pay five hundred talents in indemnity, hostages were taken, and the fortifications of Jerusalem were to be torn down—the terms were not as bad as they could have been; for the people were not slaughtered, and John Hyrcanus was allowed to maintain his position as governor and high priest.

PALESTINE OF THE MACCABEES AND THE HASMONEAN DYNASTY

Judea at the beginning of the revolt
Additions of Jonathan, 160–142 B.C.
Additions of Simon, 142–134 B.C.
Additions of Hyrcanus I, 134–104 B.C.
Additions of Aristobulus I, 104–103 B.C.
Additions of Alexander Janneus, 103–76 B.C.
Kingdom of Alexander Janneus

Damascus

Sidon

COELE-SYRIA

PHOENICIA

Panias

Tyre

Dan
(Antiochia)

Cadasa

Seleucia

Hazor

Bascama

Bethsaida   Gamala

Ptolemais

Gennesaret

Taricheae   *Sea
of
Galilee*   Dathema

Arbela   Hippus

GALILEE   Philoteria

Sepphoris

Dora

Mt. Carmel

Jezreel Valley

GALAADITIS

Strato's Tower

Scythopolis   Pella

SAMARIA

Gerasa

Samaria

Amathus

*Mt.
Gerizim* Shechem

Apollonia   Alexandrium

Acrabeta   Gadora

*P
E
R
E
A*

Philadelphia

Joppa

Aramathea

Apherema

Lydda

Docus   Jericho

Esbus

Jamnia

Gazara   *JUDEA*   Samaga

Azotus

Jerusalem

Accaron

Hyrcania   Medeba

Herodium

Ascalon

*P
H
I
L
I
S
T
I
A*

Beth Zur   Machaerus

Marisa

Anthedon

Adora   Hebron

Gaza

En Gedi

*D
e
a
d

S
e
a*

*M
O
A
B
I
T
I
S*

Gerar

Masada

Orda

IDUMEA

Raphia

Beersheba   Malatha

Rhinocorura

*N
A
B
A
T
E
A
N
S*

Wadi el-Arish

Mediterranean Sea

Petra

0	15 km.
0	10 miles

157

John Hyrcanus remained under the control of Antiochus VII until the latter was killed fighting against the Parthians in 129 B.C. With the death of Antiochus VII, strong Seleucid rule effectively ceased, and the Judeans could engage in expansionist activities. In 128 B.C. John Hyrcanus was able to seize Medeba and Samaga in Transjordan, which gave him at least partial control of the Transjordanian Highway. In the same year he attacked the Samaritans, who had been harassing the Jews, and destroyed their temple on Mount Gerizim. John Hyrcanus also established an alliance with Rome, and Rome confirmed his independence. In 125 B.C. he was able to move against Idumea, to the south of Judea, capturing the whole toparchy—including Hebron, Adora, and Marisa. The Idumeans were forced to convert to Judaism; thus the territory now controlled by John Hyrcanus stretched south all the way to Beersheba. Later in his reign, John Hyrcanus attacked the city of Samaria (ca. 108–107 B.C.) and, after a siege, drove out the Greeks who lived there. Despite this victory, only the district of Acrabeta, with its large Jewish population, was annexed to Judea. By the time of his death in 104 B.C., all of Samaria up to the Jezreel Valley was under Judean control.

After his rather long and successful reign, John Hyrcanus was replaced by his son Aristobulus I, who promptly eliminated other contenders for the positions of governor and high priest. He imprisoned all of his brothers save Antigonus, whom he eventually killed. Aristobulus I ruled for only a year (104–103 B.C.), but during that time he made a significant move north, conquering Galilee and forcing its non-Jewish inhabitants to convert to Judaism. Upon his death, his wife Salome Alexandra released his three brothers and appointed Alexander Jannaeus as king and high priest. She in turn married Alexander Jannaeus, in spite of the fact that the high priest was supposed to marry only a virgin.

Alexander Jannaeus's long reign (103–76 B.C.) could in some ways be considered the high point of Hasmonean power; yet it was marred by internal discord. On the positive side, Alexander Jannaeus was able to conquer and judaize the coastal plain from Gaza to Mount Carmel, except for Ascalon. He also conquered and controlled most of Transjordan from the southern tip of the Dead Sea north to Antiochia (= OT Dan)—excluding Philadelphia. Although his hold on this territory was challenged, the Hasmonean kingdom stretched at least briefly from Dan (Antiochia) in the north to Beersheba in the south, which meant that the traditional heartland of Israel was now under Jewish control.

However, with the assumption of this control came conflict with several successive Nabatean kings. The Naba-

The "seam" along the eastern wall of the temple enclosure; Herodian stones to the left of the seam, earlier stones to the right.

teans were an Arab people who had replaced the Edomites in Mount Seir and had made the rock-cut city of Petra their capital. They had since become the masters of the trade routes that led from southern Arabia north to Damascus and west to the Mediterranean Sea. Not only were products of Arabia (such as gold, frankincense, and myrrh) carried along these routes, but also spices from India and silk from China. The price of these goods at times doubled while in Nabatean hands. Since Alexander Jannaeus's kingdom sat astride the Transjordanian route to Damascus, he could control the northward movement of trade goods; he also controlled the Mediterranean coastline all the way to Rhinocorura, south of Gaza on the Wadi el-Arish. Thus the natural flow of goods from the southeast to the northwest, to the port of Gaza, was monitored by Alexander Jannaeus. As a result, several times during his governorship he met the Nabatean kings in battle, contesting supremacy over the trade routes.

On the negative side, during the reign of Alexander Jannaeus the internal conflict between the Sadducees and Pharisees came to a head. The governor/high priest sided with the Sadducees and, on occasion, went out of his way to offend the Pharisees. For example, during the celebration of the Feast of Tabernacles, instead of pouring the sacred water on the altar—as prescribed in Pharisaic tradition—he poured it on his feet. The worshipers at the temple responded by pelting him with lemons; Alexander, in turn, responded by massacring some six thousand Jews. Using foreign mercenaries, Alexander Jannaeus fought with his own countrymen over a six-year period, with the result that almost fifty thousand Jews were eventually killed in the conflict.

In 88 B.C. the Pharisees finally appealed to the Seleucid monarch Demetrius III for assistance. Ironically, the Pharisees, who were the spiritual descendants of the Hasidim (the "pious ones"), were driven to appeal to a ruler in the great line of Hellenizers (with whom they had been at war for almost a century). Demetrius III responded by invading Palestine and defeating Alexander Jannaeus at Shechem. However, some of the Jews who had at first summoned him belatedly decided that it would be better to live under Jewish rather than Seleucid rule, and they abandoned the cause of Demetrius III. With these desertions, Demetrius was forced to withdraw. Alexander Jannaeus, reinstated in Jerusalem, did not treat his opponents mercifully. Eight hundred Pharisees were crucified while their wives and children were put to death before their eyes and while Alexander openly engaged in an orgy with his concubines. This tragic incident illustrates the fact that the conflict between the Pharisees and Sadducees, evident even on the pages of the New Testament, was more than a theological dispute; its history was punctuated with literal life-and-death matters.

Alexander Jannaeus eventually died from an illness caused by his over-indulgent lifestyle. Before his death he realized that the Pharisees enjoyed popular support, and on his deathbed he instructed his wife Salome Alexandra to make peace with them. After his death, Salome Alexandra assumed civil rule (76–67 B.C.). Since she could not become high priest, she appointed Alexander Jannaeus's son Hyrcanus II to the position. Salome Alexandra made peace with the Pharisees as her husband had instructed her to do, and her rule as a whole was characterized by peace. However, there was constant agitation by Aristobulus II, the youngest son of Alexander Jannaeus, who wanted to have himself appointed high priest in place of his brother Hyrcanus II.

Within several months of the death of Salome Alexandra, Aristobulus II ousted Hyrcanus II from the high-priestly office and had himself appointed to that position, as well as to the governorship (67–63 B.C.). Hyrcanus II briefly retired to private life, but Antipater II, an Idumean who had been appointed governor of Idumea, maneuvered to use Hyrcanus II to help him gain control of Judea. Neither Antipater II nor his descendants could become high priest, for they were not of the Aaronic line; in fact, their very Jewishness was somewhat questionable, for the Idumeans had only become "Jewish" due to the exploits of John Hyrcanus I in 125 B.C. (see above, p. 158). Therefore, Antipater II formed a coalition with Hyrcanus II, who could qualify for the high priesthood, and induced Aretas, the Nabatean king, to attack Jerusalem in an attempt to overthrow Aristobulus II.

In the meantime, Rome had been advancing steadily eastward through Asia Minor; after Pompey defeated Mithridates of Pontius in 66 B.C., Rome's advance was swift. The Roman general Scarus was sent to Damascus (65 B.C.), and both Aristobulus II and Hyrcanus II appeared before him with gifts, hoping to be appointed high priest. Scarus confirmed Aristobulus II and forced Aretas to withdraw from Jerusalem. When Pompey himself arrived in Damascus (63 B.C.), Aristobulus II and Hyrcanus II appeared before him also, each hoping to be appointed high priest and ruler; this time, however, the Pharisees appeared also, requesting the abolition of Hasmonean rule.

Pompey seems to have delayed his decision as he undertook a campaign against the Nabateans. However, when Aristobulus II abandoned this campaign, Pompey turned on him and marched into Judea. Although the Roman general Gabinus was initially barred from Jerusalem, Pompey marched south through the Jordan Valley to Jericho and from there on up to Jerusalem. The backers of Hyrcanus II opened the gates of the upper city (the western hill) to Pompey, but the followers of Aristobulus II held out on the temple mount. After a three-month siege the Romans entered the temple area, and twelve thousand Jews were killed. In spite of the battle, the priests continued to offer sacrifices to the very end. After the capture of the temple, Pompey himself entered the Holy of Holies, but soon he ordered the temple to be cleansed and sacrifices to be reinstated. Aristobulus II and most of his family were taken as prisoners to Rome, and Hyrcanus II was installed as high priest for a second time (63–40 B.C.; he previously served from 76 to 67 B.C., see above), though with much more limited powers, for Judea and Jerusalem were now firmly under Roman control. Thus in 63 B.C. the Hasmonean state, independent since 142 B.C., officially ceased to exist. For the next century and a half, many Jews suffering under Roman rule would nostalgically look back on the Maccabean revolt and Hasmonean rule as the "golden days," when God had worked on behalf of his people. They remembered those years as a time when a "united" Jewish community drove off the Seleucids, a great world power. These selective memories would fuel the hearts of the Jews in A.D. 66 and A.D. 132, as the few and the weak, just as in the old days, would again attempt to throw off the yoke of their oppressors.

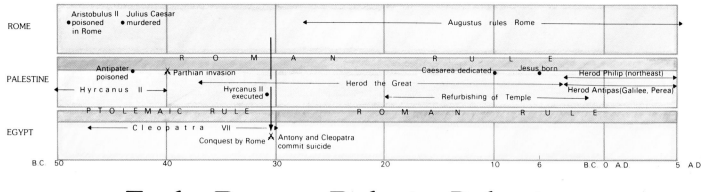

Early Roman Rule in Palestine

When Pompey withdrew from the Near East he left behind a proconsul to govern the province of Syria;[1] it is probable, but not certain, that Palestine also was under the control of this proconsul.[2] What is certain, however, is that the sphere of Jewish control was severely reduced. To the north of Judea, the Romans granted limited independence to the Samaritans, and the Valley of Esdraelon was detached from Galilee. Along the Mediterranean coast, cities from Raphia in the south to Dora in the north were granted autonomous status directly under the proconsul. In fact, the Jewish port of Joppa was detached from Judea. Cities to the east of the Jordan River—including Gadara, Hippus, Abila, Dium, Pella, and Gerasa—along with Scythopolis to the west of the Jordan, were also freed from Jewish control, and their gentile populations (which had been exiled by the Maccabees and Hasmoneans) were encouraged to return. Subsequently some of these Greek cities banded together into a league called the Decapolis ("ten cities"). The date of origin of this league of "ten" cities (the number varied from time to time) is disputed. The Romans may have encouraged the growth of these Greco-Roman cities in order to protect and control the Transjordanian Highway and its connection to the Mediterranean, to protect the settled areas from raiding desert tribes, and to counterbalance the strong Jewish population west of the Jordan River.[3] To the north and east of the Sea of Galilee, the Itureans were granted the Lake Semechonitis, Panias, and Gaulanitis areas but lost their outlets to the Mediterranean Sea. In the aftermath of these changes, Jewish territory was limited to Judea proper, to the mountains and desert south and east of Judea (= eastern Idumea), to Perea, and to a portion of Galilee.

The Romans appointed Hyrcanus II (63–40 B.C.), a son of the Hasmonean Alexander Jannaeus, as high priest and left him in charge of Jewish affairs. Early in the tenure of Hyrcanus II, however, his brother Aristobulus II and his two sons, Alexander and Antigonus, made several attempts to seize power in Palestine, but each time Gabinius, the proconsul of Syria (57–55 B.C.), was successful in subduing the rebels.

As proconsul, Gabinius oppressed those under him, and at one time he attempted to divide Jewish territory into five districts that had their headquarters at Sepphoris (Galilee), Amathus (Perea), Jericho, Jerusalem, and Adora (eastern Idumea). However, this arrangement was soon cancelled by decrees of Caesar. Gabinius' replacement, M. Licinius Crassus (54–53 B.C.), continued to oppress the Jews and confiscated two thousand talents of gold and eight thousand talents of precious objects from the temple in Jerusalem.

During the rule of Hyrcanus II (63–40 B.C.), the Roman Empire was racked by civil strife, which began when Caesar crossed the Rubicon in 49 B.C. and lasted until the death of Antony in 30 B.C. In 49 B.C. Caesar enlisted the help of the Hasmonean Aristobulus II to fight Pompey's followers in Palestine. But Aristobulus II was poisoned before he was able to leave Rome, and soon after that one of his sons, Alexander, was beheaded at Pompey's command. By 48 B.C. Caesar was gaining the upper hand against Pompey, pursuing him to Egypt. Caesar received welcome assistance when Hyrcanus II, the high priest in Jerusalem, instructed the Jews of Egypt to support Caesar. In addition, Antipater the Idumean, the power behind Hyrcanus, aided Caesar's ally, Mithridates of Pergamum, in the siege and capture of Pelusium in the eastern delta of the Nile. In return for their assistance, Caesar confirmed Hyrcanus II as high priest and ethnarch and appointed his colleague Antipater as procurator. Caesar also granted permission to rebuild the walls of Jerusalem, and it is possible that the port of Joppa and the Valley of Esdraelon were returned to Jewish control at this time (the summer of 42 B.C.).

Antipater secured his hold on the country by appointing his sons Phasael and Herod as governors in Jerusalem and Galilee. Herod demonstrated his ability to rule by vigorously subduing rebellious elements in Galilee. The Jewish authorities in Jerusalem attempted to curb Herod's growing power by accusing him of an illegal execution of one Ezekias, but the Roman governor, Sextus Caesar, intervened and ordered Herod's acquittal.

In 44 B.C. Julius Caesar was murdered, and civil war resumed in Rome. Cassius—who was one of the contenders in the civil war and who had become ruler of Syria—imposed a heavy tribute upon his subjects, including the Judeans, in order to finance his war efforts. Both Antipater and Herod were quite useful to him in raising taxes in Palestine, but Cassius' treatment of the Palestinian population was unduly harsh; for example, the residents of Lydda, Thamna, Gophna, and Emmaus were sold into slavery because of their failure to raise the revenue demanded by Cassius.

In 43 B.C. Antipater was poisoned while dining with Hyrcanus II. Herod, in turn, had Malichus, the murderer, assassinated, thereby avenging the death of his father. When Cassius left Syria in 42 B.C. conditions in the countryside became quite chaotic, and the ruler of the Phoenician city of Tyre seized portions of Galilee. However, during this period of instability Herod and Phasael were able to strengthen their control in both Judea and Jerusalem.

With the defeat of Cassius by Antony, a Roman general and rival of Octavian, the latter became master of Roman holdings in Asia. On two occasions Jewish leaders from Jerusalem requested Antony to dismiss Phasael and Herod, but Hyrcanus II was able to have them both confirmed in their positions. The concessions gained by Hyrcanus were short-lived, however, for in 40 B.C. the Parthians invaded Palestine. Having captured Damascus and Galilee, Pacorus,

the Parthian king, and Barzapharnes, his satrap, marched south to Jerusalem. Antigonus, the surviving son of Aristobulus II, hoped to reestablish Hasmonean sovereignty over the Jews and joined the Parthians as they marched on Jerusalem.

After the Parthians began the siege of Jerusalem, Phasael and Hyrcanus II were lured into a meeting with the Parthian king, at which time they were captured and put into chains. Phasael committed suicide while in captivity. The Parthians installed Antigonus II, the Hasmonean, as king and high priest in Jerusalem; Hyrcanus II's ears were mutilated, so that he was no longer fit to be high priest, and he was taken to Parthia as a prisoner.

As for Herod, he fled south from Jerusalem toward Tekoa and Orhesa, then eastward to the rock fortress of Masada. Leaving Joseph his brother there to defend his family, Herod continued on to Egypt when the Nabatean king Malchus II refused to help him. Braving fall storms on the Mediterra-

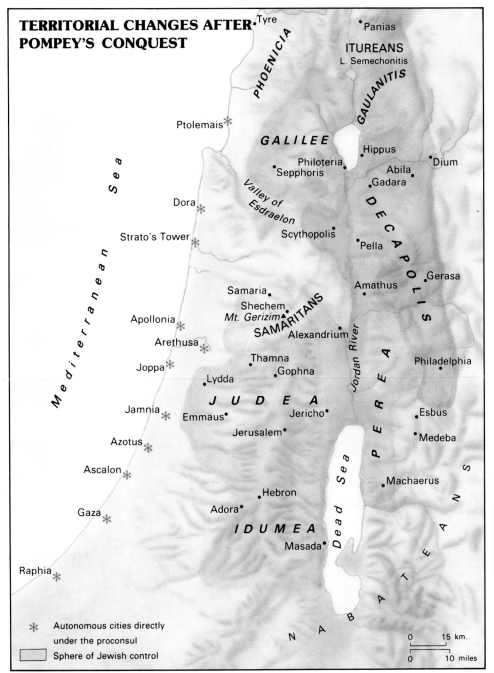

TERRITORIAL CHANGES AFTER POMPEY'S CONQUEST

Tyre
Panias
PHOENICIA
ITUREANS
L. Semechonitis
GAULANITIS
Ptolemais
GALILEE
Hippus
Philoteria
Sepphoris
Abila
Dium
Gadara
Valley of Esdraelon
DECAPOLIS
Dora
Scythopolis
Pella
Strato's Tower
Gerasa
Amathus
Samaria
Shechem
Mt. Gerizim
SAMARITANS
Apollonia
Alexandrium
Arethusa
P E R E A
Jordan River
Thamna
Philadelphia
Joppa
Gophna
Lydda
Jamnia
JUDEA
Jericho
Esbus
Emmaus
Jerusalem
Medeba
Azotus
Dead Sea
Ascalon
Machaerus
N A B A T E A N S
Hebron
Gaza
Adora
IDUMEA
Raphia
Masada

Mediterranean Sea

✳ Autonomous cities directly under the proconsul
☐ Sphere of Jewish control

0   15 km.
0   10 miles

Aqueduct bringing water to Caesarea.

nean, Herod made his way to Rome. There he was warmly received by Octavian and Antony, who were able to persuade the senate to appoint him king of Judea and to add Samaria and western Idumea to his realm.

The first portion of Herod's rule—from 40 B.C. until 37 B.C.—was a period of conquest during which Herod fought to gain control of the territory that the Romans had granted him. By the time he landed at Ptolemais in 39 B.C. the Parthians had already retreated from Palestine; however, much of the Jewish population was anti-Herodian, and Antigonus, the Hasmonean, ruled in Jerusalem.

Herod began his conquest of Palestine by moving south along the coastal plain, capturing the port city of Joppa, which had been in Jewish hands. He then proceeded inland to rescue his family from Masada, the fortress on the western shore of the Dead Sea where they had sought refuge while he was in Rome. This accomplished, he marched against Antigonus in Jerusalem, but his attempt to capture the city failed when Silo, the Roman commander who was assisting him, abandoned the siege and retreated to the warmer climate of the coastal plain, where he wintered his troops. Herod then left off the siege of Jerusalem and marched through Samaria to Galilee. After capturing the city of Sepphoris in a snow storm, he spent the winter of 39/38 B.C. there. During this period Galilee was subdued by Herod's forces, in spite of strong local opposition.

In 38 B.C. Herod visited his patron Antony in Samosata (a city in ancient Commagene, located in what is now southeastern Turkey) in order to secure support for his military activities. While he was away, the Roman commander Macherus moved eastward from the coast of Palestine and captured Emmaus, which guarded the roads that led up to Jerusalem from the west. At about the same time, Herod's younger brother, Pheroras, moved south down the Jordan Valley, and after refortifying the Alexandrium he set up his camp at Jericho to secure the eastern approaches to Jerusalem. Upon his return to Palestine, Herod led his troops from Jericho up into the mountains north of Jerusalem. There, at Isana, Antigonus's commander Pappus was defeated. With this victory the noose around Jerusalem was being tightened: Herod's people, the Idumeans, controlled the territory to the south of Judea and Jerusalem, while the Romans held Emmaus on the west, and Herod controlled the Benjamin Plateau to the north and Jericho on the east. The actual siege of Jerusalem began in the winter of 38/37 B.C., and the city fell into Herod's hands in the summer of 37 B.C. In the end, Antigonus was beheaded and Herod was established as ruler in Jerusalem.

Following this period of conquest there was a period of consolidation of Herod's kingdom, lasting from approximately 37 B.C. until 25 B.C. Internally, Herod faced considerable opposition from the Pharisees, from remnants of the Hasmonean family, and from portions of the populace and aristocracy. Throughout this period of consolidation, opponents were systematically eliminated or neutralized. For example, Herod executed forty-five members of the Sadducean aristocracy who had been supporters of Antigonus and confiscated their property to pay the demands of his overlord Antony.

Herod, of Idumean descent, was never accepted by the Jewish population at large as a true Jew. In fact, the "Jewishness" of all Idumeans was suspect, because they had been forcibly converted to Judaism during the reign of John Hyrcanus (134–104 B.C.). In an attempt to legitimize his claim to the kingship, Herod married Mariamne, a woman of Hasmonean descent, during the siege of Jerusalem in 38 B.C. Although Mariamne was never directly implicated in any intrigues against her husband, her Hasmonean relatives were. Indeed, her mother Alexandra was able to secure a Hasmonean foothold in the religious-political structure of the government by managing to have her seventeen-year-old son Aristobulus appointed as high priest. Aristobulus was very popular with the people, who saw him as a legitimate Jewish replacement for Herod, the Idumean. Enraged by this, Herod arranged for some of his friends to hold the young Aristobulus under water too long while they were swimming in one of the pools in Jericho. In spite of Herod's feigned grief over the "accidental" death of Aristobulus, it was well known that he, in fact, was the instigator of the deed.

During this period of consolidation additional members of the Hasmonean family were eliminated. Herod even had Mariamne, his beloved wife, executed in 29 B.C. out of intense jealousy, incited by rumors that were spread by his sister Salome and his mother, Cyprus. Within a year, Mariamne's mother, Alexandra, who had attempted to seize fortified positions in Jerusalem, was executed as well. The former high priest and friend of Herod, the aged Hyrcanus, had been executed previously (ca. 31 B.C.), and soon his male descendants were also eliminated, partially on the basis of rumors spread by Salome and Cyprus. Thus by the end of this period of consolidation (ca. 25 B.C.) most of the internal threats to his kingship had been removed.

In addition, Herod had to face a formidable external threat from Egypt in the person of Cleopatra, who had designs on reviving and expanding the Ptolemaic empire into Palestine and Arabia. Antony, her lover and the master of the east, submitted to her requests and granted her large portions of Herod's territory and of Arabia in 35 B.C. In this way she gained control of the coastlands of Phoenicia and Philistia, save for the cities of Tyre and Sidon. This severed Herod's direct connections to the Mediterranean Sea and thence to Rome. To the east of Herod's kingdom Antony gave Cleopatra the rich oasis of Jericho, where there were palm and balsam plantations and where perfumes were manufactured. Because she controlled both the Mediterranean coast and part of Arabia, Cleopatra was, in fact, able to control the lucrative spice and incense route that led from southern Arabia to the sea and from there to Rome.

Cleopatra seems to have had designs on taking total control of Herod's kingdom, and she might eventually have been successful had it not been for significant changes internationally. Civil strife within the Roman Empire led to Antony's defeat at the hand of Octavian in 31 B.C. at the naval battle near Actium (Greece), and in 30 B.C. she and Antony committed suicide rather than face the wrath of Rome. While Antony and Cleopatra were losing power, Herod skillfully changed his allegiance from Antony to Octavian so that when the latter emerged victorious, Herod was in a position to benefit. And benefit he did, for Octavian returned to him the territories that he had lost to Cleopatra, including such cities as Jericho, Gadara, and Hippus on the east, Samaria in the central portion of his realm, and Gaza,

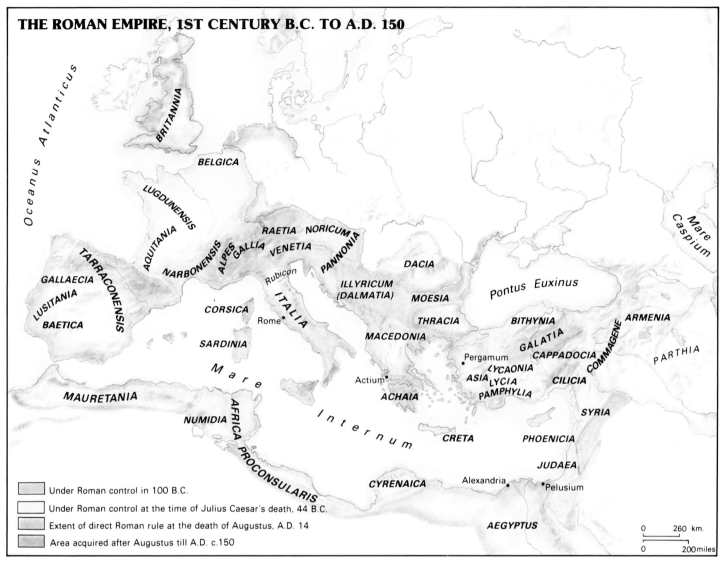

THE ROMAN EMPIRE, 1ST CENTURY B.C. TO A.D. 150

Oceanus Atlanticus

BRITANNIA

BELGICA

LUGDUNENSIS

AQUITANIA

RAETIA NORICUM

GALLIA VENETIA

ALPES

NARBONENSIS

Rubicon

PANNONIA

DACIA

ILLYRICUM
(DALMATIA)

MOESIA

Pontus Euxinus

Mare Caspium

TARRACONENSIS

GALLAECIA

LUSITANIA

BAETICA

CORSICA

Rome

ITALIA

SARDINIA

THRACIA

MACEDONIA

BITHYNIA

GALATIA

Pergamum

LYCAONIA

CAPPADOCIA

COMMAGENE

ARMENIA

PARTHIA

ASIA
LYCIA
PAMPHYLIA

CILICIA

MAURETANIA

NUMIDIA

AFRICA PROCONSULARIS

Mare   Internum

Actium

ACHAIA

CRETA

SYRIA

PHOENICIA

JUDAEA

CYRENAICA

Alexandria

Pelusium

AEGYPTUS

Under Roman control in 100 B.C.

Under Roman control at the time of Julius Caesar's death, 44 B.C.

Extent of direct Roman rule at the death of Augustus, A.D. 14

Area acquired after Augustus till A.D. c.150

0   260 km.

0   200miles

Anthedon, Joppa, and Strato's Tower along the Mediterranean coast.[4] Thus, although at the midpoint of this period of consolidation Herod was in danger of losing his whole kingdom to Cleopatra, he was able to emerge from the crisis in a very strong position, both politically and territorially.

The third period of Herod's reign (25–14 B.C.) can be characterized as a period of prosperity, construction, and additional territorial gains.[5] It is interesting to note that Herod did not add to his kingdom primarily through military conquest but rather through territorial grants from his Roman overlords. As noted above, in 30 B.C. Octavian returned to him cities that had been given to Cleopatra by Mark Antony. In 23 B.C. Herod was entrusted with the task of subduing a band of marauders in Batanea, Auranitis, and Traconitis; having accomplished this, these territories were added to his realm. Then in 20 B.C., Gaulanitis, Ulatha, and Panias, some of the holdings of Zenododrus, the last king of the Itureans, were transferred to Herod's rule.

At that point Herod's kingdom had reached its greatest extent. In the south, its common boundary with the Nabatean kingdom ran somewhere in the vicinity of the Wadi Beersheba near the fortress Malatha. Along the Mediterranean Sea his territory stretched from south of Gaza to slightly north of Caesarea, his holdings only interrupted by the free city of Ascalon. Although the tip of Mount Carmel

and the Plain of Acco were excluded from his kingdom, large portions of Lower and Upper Galilee were included. The northernmost limit of his kingdom was at Panias. To the northeast his kingdom included Gaulanitis, Batanea, Auranitis, and Traconitis. Herod did not hold the cities of the Decapolis nor the kingdom of the Nabateans, which lay east of the Jordan River and Dead Sea. However, Perea, a strip of land immediately east of the Jordan, stretching from approximately Amathus in the north to Machaerus in the south, was included in his kingdom.

The internal organization of Herod's realm can only be outlined, but it included large traditional administrative units—Idumea, Judea, Samaria, Galilee, and Perea. These larger units (meris in Greek) were further subdivided into twenty or so districts (toparchies), each of which was governed by a strategus appointed by Herod. In addition, newly acquired territories (including Gaulanitis, Batanea, Auranitis, and Traconitis) were administered directly by the king as military districts. In these largely uninhabited regions Herod was able to settle people who would be indebted and loyal to him. Finally, there were royal estates that were scattered throughout the country, the most important of which were situated in the fertile Jezreel Valley and in and around Jericho.

Because of his early fear of Cleopatra and his constant fear that his Jewish subjects might revolt, or even that his Nabatean neighbors might attack, Herod took a number of measures to secure his kingdom. He established at least two military colonies: one at Gaba, which guarded the northwest entrance to the Jezreel Valley, and one at Esbus (OT Heshbon), which protected his eastern frontier from Nabatean aggression. In addition, Herod built or rebuilt a string of fortresses in or near the wilderness that overlooked the Rift Valley from the west. These included the Alexandrium, Cypros, Hyrcania, Herodium, Masada, and Malatha, as well

as Machaerus east of the Dead Sea. These fortresses were normally furnished with royal amenities (such as palaces and baths), and troops were garrisoned in or near them. They not only could be used to control nearby territory but also could serve as places of retreat and security if Herod had to flee the country (e.g., Masada) or as prisons (e.g., Hyrcania), and one even served as a mausoleum (the Herodium).

Another technique Herod used to neutralize the potential threat from the Jewish population was to build and rebuild cities along Greco-Roman lines and settle Gentiles in them.

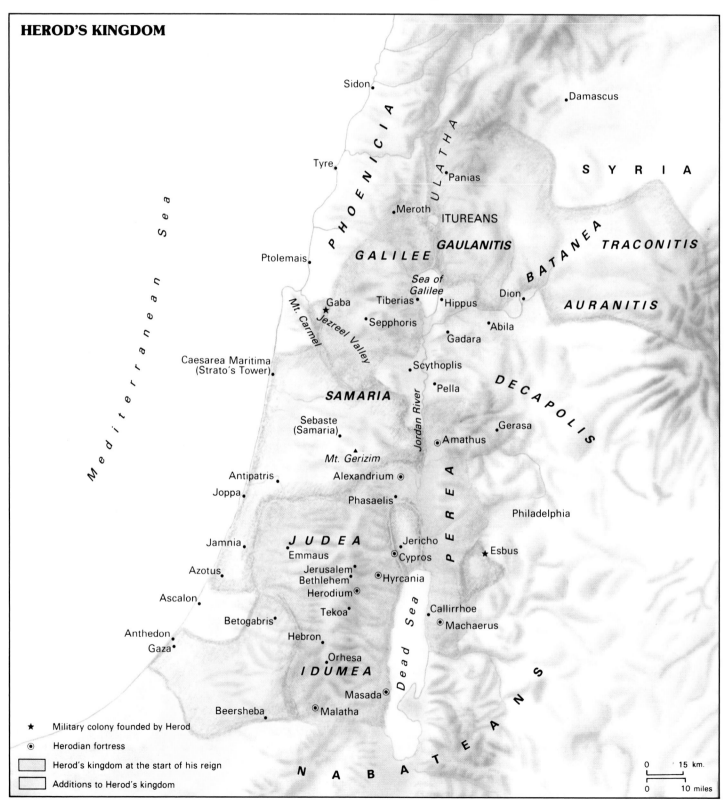

HEROD'S KINGDOM

★ Military colony founded by Herod

◉ Herodian fortress

Herod's kingdom at the start of his reign

Additions to Herod's kingdom

0   15 km.

0   10 miles

For example, Samaria was rebuilt, renamed Sebaste (the Greek name for Augustus, the emperor), and settled with Gentiles. There, as well as in other Greco-Roman cities, Herod built temples to Augustus and to pagan deities, as well as theaters, amphitheaters, and other structures. Thus he could retreat from the Jewish population with their restrictive scruples to places like Sebaste in order to indulge in a pagan lifestyle. It is easy to understand why Alexander and Aristobulus, the two sons of his Hasmonean wife, Mariamne, were executed at Samaria, rather than in a predominantly Jewish city such as Jerusalem.

With the return of most of the Mediterranean coastline, Herod moved to reestablish a secure port for himself from which he could maintain constant contact with Rome. He was also anxious to have a port in the northern part of his country from which he could export grain crops to Rome and elsewhere from his Gaulanitis, Batanea, Auranitis, and Traconitis territories and from his royal estates in the Jezreel Valley. There were several cities that could have served as ports for Herod, but of the two major candidates, Joppa was predominantly Jewish in character and too far south, and while Ptolemais was in the north, it was in Phoenician and Syrian hands. Thus he selected a small landing called Strato's Tower as the place where he constructed a new port to suit his purposes. Strato's Tower was well situated, for an easy pass through the Mount Carmel range connected it with the Jezreel Valley and the rich agricultural areas northeast of the Sea of Galilee. In addition, it had convenient connections with Sebaste and Antipatris to the east and south. Thus Herod built Caesarea Maritima at Strato's Tower, naming it after the emperor. To do this, swamp land was drained and fresh water was brought, via tunnels and aqueducts, from springs located at the foot of Mount Carmel, 12 miles (19 km.) to the northeast. A huge port, larger than Piraeus, the port of Athens, was built, including breakwaters, docks, and quays. Magnificent buildings were constructed in the city, such as a temple to Augustus, a theater, an amphitheater, and other public structures. It took more than twelve years to build the city, which was dedicated in 10 B.C. with special cultural activities, including athletic contests, theatrical performances, and gladiator fights, to mark the occasion. Over the ensuing years Caesarea continued to expand and grow in importance, so that it soon became the capital of the country, a position it would hold for almost six hundred years.

Herod also lavished a great deal of his attention and energy on Jerusalem. There, in 20 B.C., he initiated one of his great building projects—the refurbishing of the entire temple area. The temple platform was almost doubled in size, and great colonnades were built around its perimeter. Even the sacred temple itself, along with related buildings, was rebuilt and beautified. However, always wanting to remain in control of the populace, Herod also strengthened the Antonia fortress, which overlooked and controlled all of the temple precincts. For himself he built a magnificent palace on the western edge of the western hill and fortified the approach to it from the north by building three huge towers, which he named after Hippicus (a friend), Mariamne (his wife, whom he had executed), and Phasael (his brother). In addition, he either built or rebuilt the theater, amphitheater, and stadium, and he may have constructed a portion of the aqueduct that brought fresh water to Jerusalem from springs to the south.

During this prosperous period strong contacts were maintained with Rome, where two of his sons were being educated. Herod himself was busy either visiting or hosting close personal friends of the emperor, and the period seems to have reached its culmination with the visit of the emperor's very close associate, Agrippa, to Herod's kingdom in 15 B.C.

During the fourth period of Herod's rule (15 B.C.–4 B.C.) major building projects, such as the remodeling of the temple, continued, while others (e.g., the construction of Caesarea) were completed. Friendly relations were maintained with Rome, although on at least one occasion Herod was called to account by the emperor Augustus. The major concern of this era, however, was the question of which of Herod's sons would succeed their aging father as king.

The prime contenders for the throne were Antipater, the son of Doris, and Alexander and Aristobulus, two sons of Mariamne. During this time of intrigue, plots, slander, and duplicity, Herod drew up at least six wills, naming first one and then another of his sons as his successor. But in the end, Herod had Alexander and Aristobulus executed by strangulation at Samaria (7 B.C.), and ordered the death of Antipater only five days prior to his own death in 4 B.C.

Toward the end of this period Herod's health deteriorated rapidly. Even the hot baths of Callirrhoe, east of the Dead Sea, could not bring relief to the agony of his incurable disease, and Herod, in much pain, died in Jericho in the spring of 4 B.C. Even though the Jewish population rejoiced at his death, his family and soldiers gave him a lavish funeral, carrying his body with great pomp in a jewel-studded gold coffin from Jericho to his mausoleum, the Herodium.

At his death, Herod left behind a kingdom that was economically and materially prosperous. Many of the building projects that he had undertaken to aggrandize himself and to ingratiate himself with Rome were of such magnitude that remains of them have been preserved down through the centuries. Remnants of them are still visible to travelers today. Throughout his reign he attempted to maintain very good relations with the Romans; because of this there was a measure of peace and stability in his kingdom. However, this peace was maintained at a price, for those of his subjects who agitated against his or against Roman rule were dealt with harshly. Even among his own family he executed two of his ten wives, at least three of his sons, his brother-in-law, and his wife's grandfather. Thus, when Magi from the east appeared in Jerusalem in Herod's presence asking, "Where is the one who has been born king of the Jews?" it is no wonder that "when King Herod heard this he was disturbed, and all Jerusalem with him" (Matt 2:1–3). His slaughter of the baby boys of Bethlehem to remove a possible threat to his throne (vv. 16–18) was certainly in keeping with his character. Thus, from one standpoint, he could be called "Herod the Great," but from other standpoints he might be called "Herod the Despicable." And from an eternal standpoint, the lasting achievements of the one buried in the Herodium—a magnificent stone monument—can in no way be compared with those of the One born at Bethlehem, almost within the shadow of the Herodium.

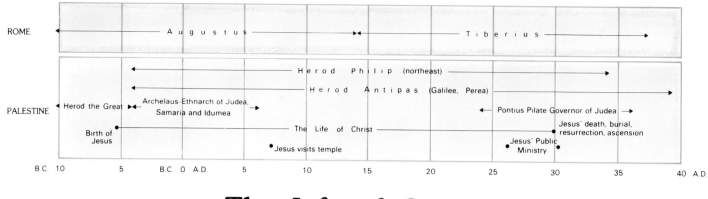

ROME										

A u g u s t u s ◄───────────────► ◄► T i b e r i u s

Herod Philip (northeast)

Herod Antipas (Galilee, Perea)

PALESTINE ◄─ Herod the Great ►◄ Archelaus-Ethnarch of Judea, Samaria and Idumea ─► Pontius Pilate Governor of Judea ─►

Jesus' death, burial, resurrection, ascension

The Life of Christ

Birth of Jesus

Jesus visits temple

Jesus' Public Ministry

B.C. 10   5   B.C. 0 A.D.   5   10   15   20   25   30   35   40 A.D.

The Life of Christ

At the time of the death of Herod the Great the question of who would succeed him had still not been resolved, although his sixth and final will designated Archelaus as king of Idumea, Judea, and Samaria; Antipas as ruler in Galilee and Perea; and Philip as governor of the lands northeast of the Sea of Galilee. But before Archelaus could assume the kingship, his appointment had to be confirmed, and to that end both he and Antipas traveled to Rome. In the meantime, anti-Herodian and anti-Roman elements of the population revolted, and it took the personal intervention of Varus, the legate of Syria, plus three legions, to suppress the rebellions.

In Rome, Archelaus, Antipas, and Philip, who had joined them, were confirmed as rulers over their designated territories. However, Archelaus was not given the title of king but rather the lesser title of "ethnarch," although the possibility was left open that in the future he could be promoted to king if his performance warranted it.[1] Archelaus's ten-year rule (4 B.C.–A.D. 6) was a brutal one, to the extent that he even slaughtered some of his Jewish and Samaritan subjects. In the Jordan Valley he built a village north of Jericho and had the audacity to name it after himself—Archelais. Close by he diverted life-giving waters from the village of Neara to his own palm groves. It was during his unjust rule that Mary, Joseph, and the baby Jesus returned to Galilee from Egypt. It is no wonder that they avoided returning to Judea, for they were "afraid to go there" when they heard that Archelaus was ruling in place of his father (Matt 2:19–23). Instead, they proceeded to Galilee, the territory of Antipas, and settled in the village of Nazareth.

Antipas, who eventually received the dynastic name Herod, ruled for more than forty years (4 B.C.–A.D. 39) over both Galilee and Perea.[2] Each of these two disjointed territories had a considerable Jewish population, which Herod Antipas was able to keep in check. Soon after taking control of Galilee and Perea he rebuilt the city of Sepphoris (3 B.C.–A.D. 10), which served as his capital; Varus, the Roman legate, had destroyed it in 4 B.C. when he entered the country to subdue rebellious elements in Galilee.

The Galilee ruled by Antipas stretched from the Esdraelon Valley in the south to the Baca/Gischala area in the north, and from Thella in the Rift Valley on the east to Chabulon overlooking the Plain of Acco on the west (Josephus, War 3.3.1–2 [35–43]). The area north of Bersabe and Kefar

Hananiya was higher in elevation and was called Upper Galilee by Josephus. This region of mountains and deep valleys was remote, and the outside contacts of its inhabitants may have been directed as much toward Tyre to the northwest as to Ptolemais directly to the west. To the south, Lower Galilee was much more open to outside influence, and its broad, spacious valleys provided good land for growing grain crops. Josephus, writing of both Upper and Lower Galilee, describes them as having soil so fertile that even the laziest of their inhabitants could make a good living.

Galilee must have been intensively cultivated and densely populated in Jesus' day, although Josephus' statistic of 15,000 people living in even the smallest villages (which would imply that Galilee had 3,000,000 inhabitants) must be grossly inflated (War 3.3.2 [41–44]). There may, in fact, have been a population of approximately 300,000 living in the two-hundred or so cities and villages that Josephus says were in existence. In Jesus' day the largest of the cities was probably Sepphoris, which may have had a population of 50,000. Antipas had furnished the city with Greco-Roman institutions (e.g., a theater), and its beauty was such that Josephus called it the "ornament of all Galilee" (Antiq 18.2.1 [27]); for a brief period it was called Autocratoris.[3] This city overlooked valuable farmland and was close to an important east-west route that connected the cities of the Decapolis and the Gaulanitis regions with the port of Ptolemais. Other large cities of Galilee included Tiberias, Taricheae, Gabara, Jotapata, and Japhia.

Jesus was raised in the small village of Nazareth, only 3.5 miles (5.6 km.) southeast of the capital Sepphoris and 1.5 miles (2.4 km.) east of Japhia. Although Nazareth itself was small and insignificant, its residents probably had numerous contacts with their more cosmopolitan neighbors. In all probability they came into contact with some of the caravans and Greek-speaking gentile traders who passed through Sepphoris on the north and/or the Esdraelon Valley (= OT Jezreel Valley) on the south.

When Jesus began to minister at about the age of thirty (ca. A.D. 26),[4] he seems to have spent much more time in Lower than in Upper Galilee. It is recorded that on several occasions he visited and taught in his hometown of Nazareth, where he was not welcome. He also ministered at Cana of Galilee, which has been identified as the antiquity site of

166

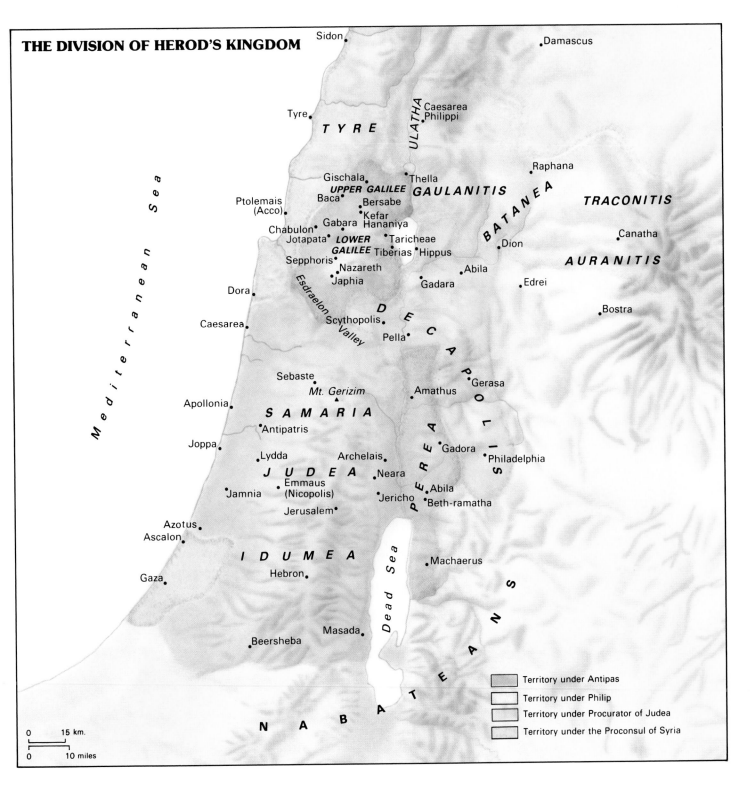

THE DIVISION OF HEROD'S KINGDOM

Sidon

Damascus

T Y R E

ULATHA

Caesarea
Philippi

Tyre

Raphana

Gischala
Thella
UPPER GALILEE
GAULANITIS

BATANEA

TRACONITIS

Baca
Bersabe

Ptolemais
(Acco)

Kefar
Hananiya
Gabara

Canatha

Chabulon
Jotapata
LOWER
GALILEE
Taricheae

Dion

AURANITIS

Sepphoris
Tiberias
Hippus

Nazareth
Abila

Japhia
Gadara

Edrei

Dora

Esdraelon

Bostra

Caesarea
Scythopolis
Valley
D
E
C
Pella
A

Sebaste
P
O
Amathus
Gerasa
L

Mt. Gerizim
I

Apollonia
S A M A R I A
S

Antipatris
P
E
Gadora
R

Joppa
E
Philadelphia
A

Lydda
Archelais
Neara

J U D E A
Abila

Jamnia
Emmaus
(Nicopolis)
Jericho
Beth-ramatha

Jerusalem

Azotus
Ascalon

I D U M E A
Machaerus

Gaza
Hebron
Dead Sea

N
Masada

Beersheba
A
B
A
T
A
E
A
N
S

Mediterranean Sea

	Territory under Antipas
	Territory under Philip
	Territory under Procurator of Judea
	Territory under the Proconsul of Syria

0   15 km.

0   10 miles

Khirbet Qana, located 8 miles (13 km.) north of Nazareth. It was in Cana that he performed his first miracle—turning water into wine at a wedding feast (John 2:1–11). On another occasion, also in Cana, he healed the son of a Roman official who had come to him from Capernaum (4:43–54), and it appears that Nathanael, one of his disciples, was originally from Cana (21:2).

It is about twelve miles (20 km.) from Cana to the Sea of Galilee, about a five- or six-hour walk. It was there, along the northern shore of the Sea of Galilee, that Jesus spent much of his time during his public ministry. In those days (ca. A.D. 26–30) the largest city on the sea was the newly

built city of Tiberias (Josephus, *Antiq* 18.2.3 [36–38]). Herod Antipas had constructed this city between A.D. 18 and 22 and had transferred his capital there from Sepphoris. He had adorned the city with a luxurious palace for himself, a stadium, a synagogue, and possibly a city wall. He had hoped to settle Jews in the city, but religious Jews were reluctant to live there because it was rumored to have been built over a cemetery; thus the city must have had a mixed Jewish and gentile population at best. To the south of the city were hot baths that were noted for their therapeutic properties. The Gospels never record that Jesus entered Tiberias, although the Sea of Galilee is called the "Sea of

167

Tiberias'' in John 6:1 and 21:1, and, on one occasion, boats from Tiberias are said to have arrived with passengers wanting to see Jesus (6:23).

Four miles (6.4 km.) to the northwest of Tiberias, along the western shore of the sea, is the probable site of the New Testament city of Magadan (Matt 15:39). This is the place visited by Jesus after the feeding of the four thousand on the other side of the lake. The parallel text in Mark (8:9) has ''Dalmanutha'' in place of ''Magadan,'' and it is not certain whether the two places were identical. Possibly Dalmanutha was the port of Magadan.[5] Compounding the uncertainty regarding the name and location of the site is the fact that the KJV, using late Greek manuscripts, reads ''Magdala'' in Matthew, and early Christian tradition held the site to be the home of Mary Magdalene. In addition, the same site seems to be called ''Taricheae'' (''the place of salted fish'') by Josephus, who refers to Taricheae as a large city on the

shore of the sea and the location of a bloody battle between Jews and Romans during the first Jewish revolt (ca. A.D. 66–70; Josephus, *War* 3.10.1–10 [462–542]).

Proceeding from Magadan six miles (9.6 km.) in a clockwise direction around the north shore of the Sea of Galilee, one comes to the village of Capernaum. Apart from Jerusalem, this is the most important of all the villages mentioned in the gospel accounts, for it was here that Jesus established his headquarters for the major portion of his public ministry. Three of his disciples were from Capernaum, and Peter and Andrew had evidently moved there from Bethsaida (Mark 1:29). According to archaeological investigations, the village spread out for a quarter of a mile (0.4 km.) along the seashore. It is probable that fishing was the major occupation of the inhabitants, although it is possible that basalt implements (e.g., olive presses and grain grinders) were produced there as well. The village sat astride

Fisherman on the Sea of Galilee.

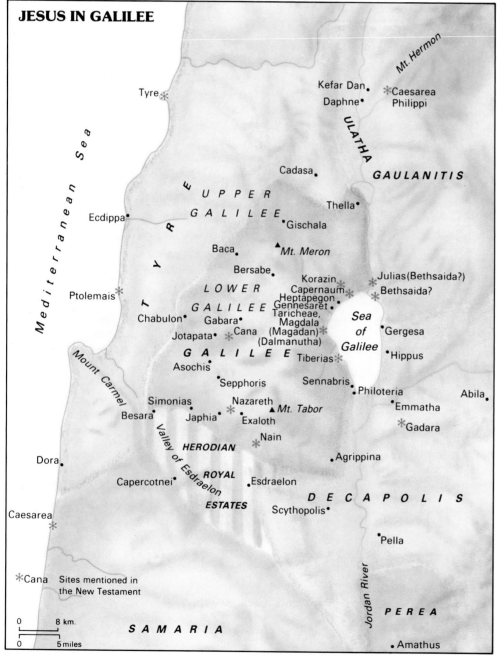

JESUS IN GALILEE

the International Route that ran from the Mediterranean Sea to Transjordan and Damascus, and it seems that a customs station was located there because of its proximity to the Jordan River and Philip's territory (Matt 9:9). Capernaum was large or important enough for a Roman centurion and his troops to be stationed there (8:5–9), as was an officer of the king (John 4:46). Jesus healed many there, including the servant of the centurion (Matt 8:5–13), the paralytic who was let down through the roof of a dwelling (Mark 2:1–12), and Peter's mother-in-law, who suffered from a fever (1:29–31). The Franciscans, who now own most of the site of Capernaum, have excavated a beautiful white limestone synagogue that dates from the fourth century A.D.; underneath it they have discovered the massive foundation walls of a black basalt synagogue that preceded it.[6] This earlier synagogue probably dates back to the days of Jesus and was the one in which he preached while at Capernaum. Early

Christian presence at the site is evidenced by the remains of several churches that were built over a house thought to have been the house of Peter (9:33).

Although it is difficult to pinpoint exactly the location of many of Jesus' activities in the neighboring countryside, by the fourth century Christian tradition had localized the site of the Sermon on the Mount (Matt 5–7), the feeding of the five thousand (14:13–21), and the appearance of the resurrected Lord to his disciples (John 21) near the place of seven springs—Heptapegon (Tabgha). This area, which is approximately 1.8 miles (3 km.) west of Capernaum, may indeed have been the site of these events, and ancient and modern churches have been built in the area to commemorate them. In addition, between Capernaum and Tabgha there is a small bay on the seashore in the shape of a natural theater that may have been the spot where Jesus "got into a boat and sat in it, while all the people stood on the shore. Then he told them many things in parables, saying . . ." (Matt 13:2–3).[7]

Two miles (3.2 km.) to the northwest of Capernaum are the remains of the city of Korazin. Although it is only mentioned as being cursed by Jesus because of its failure to repent, it is implied that Jesus had visited the place, for miracles had been performed there (Matt 11:20–24). The city is located in a basalt region, and all of the buildings were made out of the hard black rock. Excavations at Korazin have not yielded many finds from the time of Jesus, for many of the preserved remains were built in the second to the fourth centuries A.D. or later, including the black basalt synagogue.[8]

The third important village/city that Jesus visited is Bethsaida.[9] The probable location of this city is the mound called et-Tell, which is located east of the Jordan River about 1.5 miles (2.4 km.) before it enters the Sea of Galilee. This city was built by Philip, the son of Herod the Great, early in his reign (4 B.C.–A.D. 34), probably as a way station on the International Highway that led to the Mediterranean and as a port for himself on the Sea of Galilee (the ancient shoreline may have been further north than it is now). He named the city Julias, after Julia, the emperor's daughter. According to Josephus, Philip himself died there at the end of his peaceful rule (*Antiq* 18.4.6 [108]). Recently, additional support has been marshaled for the theory that there were in fact two Bethsaidas, one in Philip's territory (Bethsaida-Julias) and the other "in Galilee" (John 12:21). The latter has been tentatively identified with the small site of Araj, located very close to the shore of the Sea of Galilee. It is proposed that at the time of Jesus the Jordan followed a more easterly course than it does now, so that Araj at that time was west of the river, i.e., "in Galilee." Only Jerusalem and Capernaum are mentioned more frequently in the Gospels than Bethsaida, which was the birthplace of Peter and Andrew (1:44) and the home of the apostle Philip (12:21). In Bethsaida a blind man was healed (Mark 8:22–26), and in a deserted place nearby, probably along the northeast shore of the sea, the feeding of the four thousand took place. It too, along with Korazin and Capernaum, was "cursed" by Jesus because of the unbelief of its inhabitants.

To the northeast of Bethsaida lay Philip's territory, which included Gaulanitis, Batanea, Auranitis, Traconitis, and Ulatha.[10] During the days of Jesus, most of this territory was settled by Gentiles—except western Gaulanitis, which may

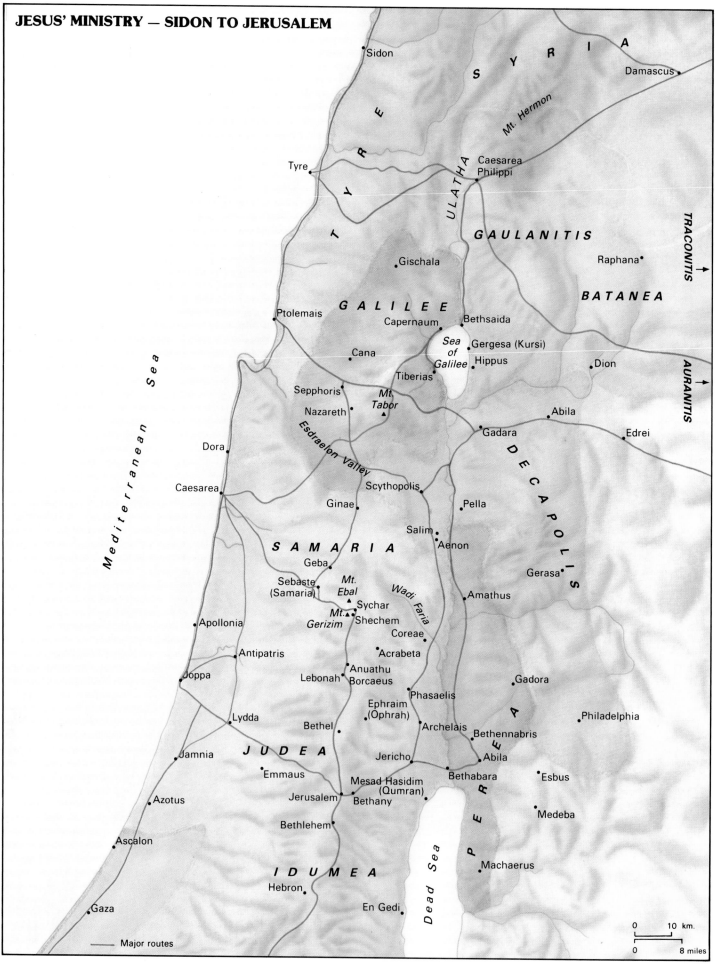

JESUS' MINISTRY — SIDON TO JERUSALEM

Sidon

Damascus

S Y R I A

Mt. Hermon

Tyre

T Y R E

U L A T H A

Caesarea Philippi

TRACONITIS

G A U L A N I T I S

Gischala

Raphana

B A T A N E A

Ptolemais

G A L I L E E

Capernaum

Bethsaida

Sea of Galilee

Gergesa (Kursi)

Cana

Hippus

Dion

Tiberias

AURANITIS

Sepphoris

Mt. Tabor

Nazareth

Abila

Gadara

Edrei

Mediterranean Sea

Esdraelon Valley

D E C A P O L I S

Dora

Scythopolis

Caesarea

Ginae

Pella

Salim

Aenon

S A M A R I A

Geba

Gerasa

Sebaste (Samaria)

Mt. Ebal

Sychar

Wadi Faria

Shechem

Amathus

Mt. Gerizim

Coreae

Apollonia

Acrabeta

Antipatris

Anuathu Borcaeus

Gadora

Lebonah

Phasaelis

Joppa

Ephraim (Ophrah)

Philadelphia

Lydda

Bethel

Archelais

Bethennabris

J U D E A

Jericho

Abila

Jamnia

Emmaus

Bethabara

Esbus

Azotus

Mesad Hasidim (Qumran)

P E R E A

Jerusalem

Bethany

Medeba

Bethlehem

Ascalon

Dead Sea

Machaerus

I D U M E A

Hebron

Gaza

En Gedi

0   10 km.

0   8 miles

—— Major routes

have been Jewish—but it is evident that Jesus did not spend much time there. However, on at least one occasion he traveled with his disciples to the vicinity of Caesarea Philippi, about twenty-five miles (40 km.) north of Bethsaida. There, at the headwaters of the Jordan and at the foot of Mount Hermon, Herod the Great had built a white marble temple in honor of the emperor; and there his successor, Philip, built a large city that he named after the emperor—adding his own name to the title to distinguish it from Caesarea Maritima. Philip made Caesarea Philippi the capital of his territory, and it must have been a thriving city, for it was situated along the highway that led from Damascus to Tyre and Sidon. It was in the vicinity of Caesarea Philippi that Peter made his "Great Confession," stating that he believed that Jesus was "the Christ, the Son of the living God" (Matt 16:13–20). Soon afterwards Jesus was transfigured in the presence of Peter, James, and John (Matt 17:1–8; Mark 9:2–8; Luke 9:28–36). Because of the close sequence of events in the gospel narratives, it is possible that the Transfiguration also occurred in this region, perhaps on Mount Hermon, or on one of the nearby peaks, such as the Hermonit. Other candidates for the place of transfiguration have been suggested by scholars, including Mount Meron (Jebel Jarmak) and Mount Tabor, but none of them commands as much textual or geographical support as the Mount Hermon vicinity.

To the south of Philip's territory was a region known as the Decapolis.[11] This was a group of cities that were either founded or rebuilt as Greco-Roman cities during the Hellenistic and Roman periods. Their populations were mainly gentile, although when they were controlled by the Jews for a short period of time—from the days of Alexander Jannaeus (103–76 B.C.) until the arrival of Pompey (63 B.C.)—they contained a large Jewish population. This group of cities was evidently originally ten in number—hence the name Decapolis ("ten cities")—but it often included more than ten cities in later years. It included, east of the Rift Valley from north to south, Damascus, Raphana, Canatha, Dion, Hippus, Abila, Gadara, Edrei, Bostra, Pella, Gerasa, and Philadelphia (modern Amman), as well as Scythopolis west of the Jordan.

The Decapolis was not an area frequently visited by Jesus, for he had said that his mission was primarily to the "lost sheep of Israel" (Matt 15:24), but on one occasion he healed a demon-possessed man, who, after having been healed, went into the Decapolis to tell of all that Jesus had done for him (Mark 5:20). This event is recorded in all three of the Synoptic Gospels, but Mark and Luke seem to mention only the most prominent of the two men who were healed (Mark 5:2; Luke 8:27; cf. Matt 8:28). Aside from the problem of the number of men healed, the various Greek manuscripts offer different readings as to the place where the healing(s) occurred: "the region of the Gerasenes [or Gadarenes or Gergesenes]" (Matt 8:28; cf. Mark 5:1; Luke 8:26). The identification of the site of the healing with the Decapolis city Gerasa (modern Jerash) is problematic, for Jerash is situated thirty-five miles (56 km.) south of the Sea of Galilee. Unless that city possessed some territory on the southeastern shore of the sea—a supposition that has not been proved—then the city is too far south for it to be the correct site. The placement of the event near the Decapolis city of Gadara

(modern Umm Qeis) is more plausible, since it is only six miles (10 km.) southeast of the sea and would be more likely to have possessed lakeshore territory than Gerasa; however, this is not certain either. Since the fifth century, Christian tradition has placed the event at Gergesa (modern Kursi), which is on the eastern shore of the Sea of Galilee directly opposite Taricheae and Tiberias. There a monastery was founded to commemorate the healing, and it is easy to imagine a herd of swine (an indication that this was gentile territory) hurtling down the nearby hills into the sea.

To the south and west of the Decapolis was the region called Perea. This is a shortened form of a Greek phrase that can be translated as "other side of the Jordan" or "regions across the Jordan." According to Josephus (*War* 3.3.3 [46]), it was bounded on the north by Pella and stretched to the south of Machaerus. On the west the Jordan River was its boundary, and on the east it approached, but did not include, the Decapolis city of Philadelphia. From the time of Jonathan's capture of the area (152 B.C.), the region was settled by Jews. Its capital was Gadora, and other prominent cities or forts included Amathus, Abila, Beth-ramatha (Livias/Julias), Callirrhoe, and Machaerus. Herod Antipas was granted this territory after the death of his father and controlled both it and Galilee. Perea, Galilee, and Judea are called "the three Jewish provinces" in the Mishnah.

It is evident that Jesus ministered in Perea, since Luke 9:51–18:34 places quite a few events there. In addition, John was baptizing "at Bethany on the other side of the Jordan" (John 1:28). This Bethany is difficult to locate precisely, but it may have been in the vicinity of Bethennabris or a spot closer to the Jordan, near the Wadi el-Kharrar. It was probably in this area that Jesus was baptized.

Later, the gospel writer notes that John was "baptizing at Aenon near Salim, because there was plenty of water" (John 3:23). This Aenon ("springs") is also difficult to identify with certainty. Some authorities suppose that John had not moved from his earlier spot and that Aenon should be located in the region of "Bethany beyond the Jordan." However, there is no Salim close by. Others, noting its literary context in John 3–4, locate the place in Samaria at the headwaters of the Wadi Faria, 5.5 miles (8.8 km.) north of the village of Salim, at or near the Old Testament site of Tirzah. But it seems best to follow the suggestion of the early church historian Eusebius (fourth century A.D.) that it was located in the Jordan Valley near Salim, seven miles (11 km.) south of Scythopolis, just west of the Jordan River. This would place John's activities in the territory of the Decapolis, just outside the reach of Herod Antipas (who had been annoyed by his preaching) and of Pilate (who might have considered him a revolutionary). In the end, John was beheaded by Herod Antipas because of his condemnation of Herod's divorce and remarriage. According to Josephus, the execution took place at the fortress of Machaerus, at the southern extremity of Perea (away from John's followers? *Antiq* 18.5.2 [116–19]).

Jews living in Perea probably had close contacts with Jerusalem, for it was an easy matter to cross the fords of the Jordan opposite Jericho, near where John had originally been baptizing, and then to pass through Jericho on the way up to Jerusalem. Since the days of Alexander the Great, Jericho had been something of a royal estate, generally owned and operated by the ruling monarch.[12] The Hasmonean rulers had built palaces there; Cleopatra had rented it to Herod for a few years; and Herod and his son Archelaus built and rebuilt aqueducts, plantations, fortresses, palaces, and pools in the area. Herod had his wife's brother (Aristobulus) murdered in Jericho, and Herod himself died there. In Jesus' day Jericho was controlled by the Romans, and its plantations were spread out over a large area. To the north of Jericho were the villages/plantations of Archelais, Phasaelis, and Coreae. It seems evident that there must have been a road running up the west side of the Jordan Valley connecting these communities and probably continuing all the way up to Scythopolis.

Jericho figures prominently in the Gospels. Jesus mentioned it in the parable of the Good Samaritan (Luke 10:25–37) and passed through it himself as he traveled from Perea to Bethany on his way to raise Lazarus from the dead (John 10:40–11:54). It was there that two blind men (Matt 20:29–34; Mark 10:46–52; Luke 18:35–43), including Bartimaeus (Mark 10:46), were healed, and it was there that Zacchaeus, the tax collector, was told to come down from a tree so that Jesus could dine with him in his house (Luke 19:1–10).

From Jericho a well-traveled road ran up to Jerusalem through the dry, chalky wilderness. Along this fifteen-mile (24-km.) stretch of road the parable of the Good Samaritan has its setting. After an uphill walk of six to eight hours from Jericho, one approached the back (east) side of the Mount of Olives. Slightly to the south of the old Roman road was the village of Bethany, the home of Mary, Martha, and Lazarus, today called el-Azariyeh (named after Lazarus). Jesus stayed in the house of these friends on many occasions, and events such as the teaching of Mary, the raising of Lazarus, and the anointing with precious oil took place there. It was in the Bethany/Bethphage area that Jesus mounted a colt and rode it into Jerusalem (on what is now commemorated as Palm Sunday), and later that same week he and the disciples made the same trip together for the last time, to the Upper Room in Jerusalem. During that final week of Jesus' life he spent several days teaching in Jerusalem, but it appears that he returned to Bethany every night.

The road from the east was of course not the only road leading into and out of Jerusalem. The Ridge Route led southwest out of Jerusalem toward Bethlehem, Hebron, and Beersheba. It passed through Judea to Idumea and then on into the Negev. From there one could proceed east to Transjordan and Arabia, southwest to Sinai, or west toward Egypt. Except in the birth narrative, the Gospels do not record any activity of Jesus south of Jerusalem.

To the north of Jerusalem the Ridge Route headed toward Shechem. In Jesus' day the territory of Judea stretched some thirty-five miles (56 km.) north of Jerusalem to the area of Anuathu Borcaeus and Acrabeta. It was probably early in his public ministry in this region that "Jesus and his disciples went out into the Judean countryside [north of Jerusalem], where he spent some time with them, and baptized . . . although in fact it was not Jesus who baptized, but his disciples" (John 3:22; 4:2). Late in his ministry, after raising Lazarus and after learning of a plot on his life, Jesus withdrew with his disciples to this same area, to a "village called Ephraim" (11:54). Although New Testament Ephraim has not been identified with absolute certainty, it is probably

to be equated with Old Testament Ophrah (modern et-Taiyiba). This village was located east of the watershed on the edge of the wilderness and could have provided a convenient place of retreat.

To the north of Anuathu Borcaeus was the district of Samaria, which reached to the southern edge of the Esdraelon Valley, to the village of Ginae (modern Jenin). This district, like Judea and Idumea to the south, was governed in Jesus' day by the Roman official Pontius Pilate. The district was named after the Old Testament city of Samaria, then called Sebaste, and the Samaritans dominated large portions of the area. An important route that ran through the district of Samaria was used by the Jewish inhabitants of Galilee on their pilgrimages to Jerusalem (Josephus, *Antiq* 20.6.1 [118]). According to Josephus, this journey took three days at a minimum (*Life* 52 [269]), which implies at least two overnight stays along the way. After crossing the Valley of Esdraelon, heading south, Jewish pilgrims entered Samaria at Ginae. It was probably in this area, "along the border between Samaria and Galilee" (Luke 17:11), that Jesus met and healed ten lepers, one of whom was a Samaritan (vv. 12–19). He may have been traveling "along the border" because he and his disciples had encountered Samaritan opposition as they attempted to enter Samaria; Josephus records that on at least one occasion Jews had met stiff resistance at Ginae (*Antiq* 20.6.1 [118]; *War* 2.12.3 [232]).[13]

Typically, Jewish pilgrims would have continued south from Ginae toward Shechem. It seems reasonable to assume that they would have had to spend the night in the area of Geba, about a day's walk from Galilee. Where Jewish pilgrims or travelers would find acceptable accommodations is difficult to imagine. It does not seem reasonable to expect that they would have stayed in Samaritan or gentile homes, so they may have had to camp out in the open. From the Geba region, the caravans would have continued south, passing Mount Ebal and Mount Gerizim on the next day's journey. Exiting the district of Samaria, they would have entered Judea before settling in for the night, possibly in the el-Lubban (= OT Lebonah) region. The third and final day of their journey would have taken them on into Jerusalem. It was probably near el-Lubban, at the overnight stop nearest Jerusalem, that Jesus' parents realized that he was missing from the caravan that was heading back to Galilee (Luke 2:41–50). Indeed, Jesus must have traveled this route quite frequently for "every year his parents went to Jerusalem for the Feast of the Passover" (v. 41).

On one memorable occasion early in his public ministry, Jesus stopped at Jacob's well near the town of Sychar (modern Askar) at midday (John 4:4–6); note that it is about a half-day's journey north from the el-Lubban overnight stop to Sychar. While his disciples went off to the village to purchase food, he met the Samaritan woman at the well. There, near the foot of the Samaritan holy mountain, Mount Gerizim, he pointed her to the real source of living water so that she, and others like her, could worship God in spirit and truth (vv. 4–42).

Although Jesus traveled the roads north and east of Jerusalem on a number of occasions, only one event is placed west of the city. This was his appearance to the two disciples on the road to Emmaus (Luke 24:13–35). According to the best Greek manuscripts, Emmaus was 60 stadia (ca. 7 mi. [11 km.]) from Jerusalem. From the Crusader period on (A.D. 1099–1291), the villages of Abu-Ghosh and el-Qubeibeh have both been suggested as the biblical Emmaus, since they are each about 7 miles (11 km.) from Jerusalem. However, both traditions are very late (Middle Ages). A third site that is considered a candidate for the biblical Emmaus is near modern Qaloniya/Motza. This site is 3.5 miles (5.6 km.) west of Jerusalem on the Roman road that led from Jerusalem to Joppa. One ancient source that refers to it as Emmaus says that Vespasian, the Roman emperor, ordered the settling of eight hundred retired veterans in a colony there (Josephus, *War* 7.6.6 [216–17])—hence the name Colonia/Qaloniya. If this is the biblical site, then the distance in Luke 24:13 (7 mi. [11 km.]) is the distance from Jerusalem to Emmaus and back, i.e., the distance of a round trip. However, this is a very questionable interpretation of the passage in Luke. A fourth possible site for biblical Emmaus is the city of Emmaus/Nicopolis, which was well-known in Roman times. The name of the ancient city was preserved in the now-destroyed Arab village of Imwas, which overlooked the strategically important Aijalon Valley. However, this site is about 19 miles (30 km.) from Jerusalem.

On the other hand, one important Greek manuscript reads "160 stadia" (= ca. 20 mi. [32 km.]) instead of "60 stadia" (= 7 mi. [11 km.]), which would place the biblical city at the same site as this well-known Roman city. It seems that the Imwas-Emmaus identification is the most probable, but it is not without difficulties.[14]

It was back in the Jerusalem area, on the Mount of Olives, that Jesus departed from his disciples, concluding his earthly ministry (for Jesus in Jerusalem, see pp. 199–200). It is quite amazing to reflect on the worldwide, and indeed cosmic, significance of the message and work of this first-century itinerant Jewish prophet, especially when one considers that he only ministered for three or four years, that he left behind only a small band of loyal followers, and that his ministry was primarily confined to a rather small province of the Roman Empire, located on its distant southeastern frontier. But the New Testament writers were anxious to establish that it was not through the might of Herod the Great nor through the power of the Roman emperors, but through him that all the nations of the earth would be blessed (Gen 12:3; Gal 3:6–15).

Natural theater on the north shore of the Sea of Galilee; possibly where Jesus addressed the crowd from a boat. (Matthew 13)

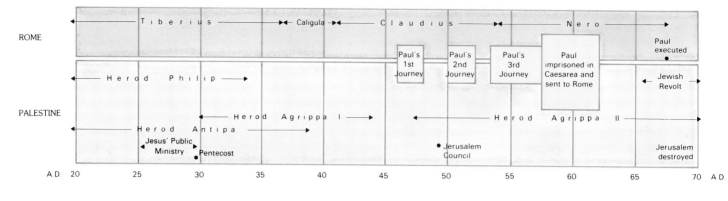

| | A.D. 20 | 25 | 30 | 35 | 40 | 45 | 50 | 55 | 60 | 65 | 70 A.D. |

The Expansion of the Church in Palestine

At the time Jesus' death, Pilate was governor of Idumea, Judea, and Samaria, while Antipas and Philip still held their respective positions in the north. Philip died in A.D. 34, and his territory (Gaulanitis, Batanea, Auranitis, and Traconitis) was transferred to the control of the province of Syria.[1] But in A.D. 37 the districts were detached from Syria when the Roman emperor Caligula appointed Herod Agrippa I (A.D. 30–44) as the ruler over Philip's old domain. When in A.D. 39 Antipas foolishly requested an improvement of his position, he was banished to Gaul, and Galilee and Perea were added to the realm of Herod Agrippa I. In A.D. 41 the emperor Claudius, grateful for Agrippa's assistance in helping him secure the throne, added Samaria, Judea, and Idumea to Agrippa's holdings. With these additions, Agrippa's kingdom was as extensive as that of his grandfather, Herod the Great. However, his large realm did not hold together for long, for at the peak of his power Agrippa was struck down with a terminal illness, and he died in Caesarea in A.D. 44 (Acts 12:19–23; Josephus, *Antiq* 19.8.2 [343–52]).

Scripture records a select number of events from the history of the early church between the resurrection of Jesus and the death of Agrippa I (A.D. 44; Acts 1–12). The sequence followed in the Book of Acts tells of the growth of Christianity from its beginning in Jerusalem, through the expansion into Judea and Samaria, to its spread throughout the Roman world (1:8). After Jesus' ascension the disciples gathered in Jerusalem to wait for the fulfillment of his promise that the Holy Spirit would be poured out upon them. Acts 2 records this special manifestation of the Spirit on the disciples at the feast of Pentecost, fifty days after Passover. At the time, Jerusalem was filled with Jewish pilgrims who had come from various parts of the Roman world, from the Parthian Empire on the east, and from Africa on the southwest. The pilgrims had come to celebrate the three great Jewish festivals: Passover/Unleavened Bread, the Feast of Weeks, and the Feast of Tabernacles, and were staying in Jerusalem for a period of several months. After hearing unlearned Galileans witness to them of the living Christ in their native languages, a number of them were converted to the new faith, and the initial core of disciples began to teach them about Jesus.

The early chapters of Acts describe the growth and persecution of the church in Jerusalem (chs. 2–7). Opposition to the early church grew as an increasing number of Greek-speaking Jews (Hellenists) joined the ranks of the followers of Jesus and as some of them joined others in making explicit the implications of their new-found faith in its relationship to Judaism. This persecution culminated with the stoning of Stephen. With that, a sizeable segment of the Jerusalem church scattered throughout Judea and Samaria (8:1), and as the believers dispersed they shared their faith with others. One of these enthusiastic preachers was Philip, who "went down to a city in Samaria" (v. 5; one always goes "up to" or "down from" Jerusalem). In this unnamed city—it probably was not Samaria/Sebaste, for that was predominantly gentile—inhabitants of the district of Samaria were converted and received the Holy Spirit. Indeed, even Peter and John (pillars in the Jerusalem church, Gal 2:9), who had come to pray for the new converts, willingly preached the gospel in Samaritan villages as they returned to Jerusalem (Acts 8:25).

Acts 8 also describes Philip's activities south and west of Jerusalem. There, Philip met the Ethiopian official who was reading from the prophecy of Isaiah as he returned to Africa. After Philip explained the meaning of the passage, the Ethiopian believed, was baptized, and "went on his way rejoicing" (vv. 26–39). The site of this event is difficult to locate precisely, but since the Ethiopian was riding in a chariot it seems that he must have been traveling on a developed road. It may very well have been that he was traveling on the road that led from Bethlehem to the Valley of Elah, the route that David had taken when he carried supplies to his brothers (1 Sam 17) and the one that the Romans eventually paved and marked with milestones. This road led south from the Valley of Elah through the low rolling hills of the Shephelah to Betogabris (near OT Mareshah = Hellenistic Marisa) and continued from there west to Gaza. From Gaza a road continued west across northern Sinai into Africa. It seems reasonable to assume that Philip continued preaching in the Shephelah before moving out into the Philistine Plain (Azotus; Acts 8:40) and then north, along the coast to Caesarea, where he eventually settled (Acts 21:8).

Others from Jerusalem were also active in the coastal plain area. Peter, for example, healed Aeneas at Lydda and then moved on to the Jewish port of Joppa, where he raised Tabitha from the dead (Acts 9:32–42). At Joppa Peter received his vision of the unclean animals and soon after-

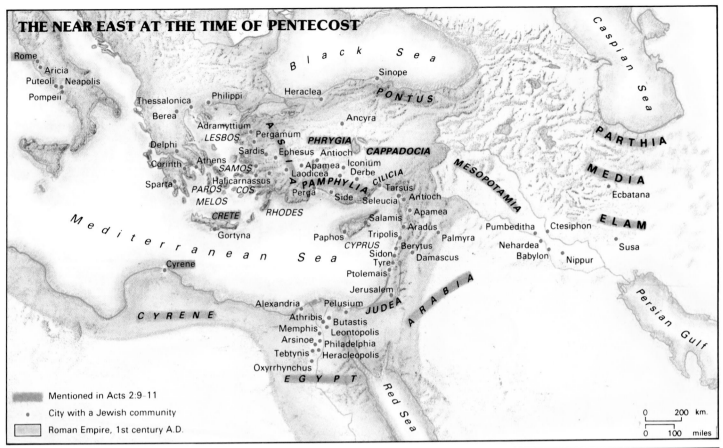

THE NEAR EAST AT THE TIME OF PENTECOST

Rome
Aricia
Puteoli Neapolis
Pompeii
Thessalonica   Philippi
Berea
Adramyttium
LESBOS   Pergamum
Delphi   Sardis Ephesus Antioch
Corinth   Apamea Iconium
Athens   SAMOS   Derbe
Sparta   Halicarnassus   PAMPHYLIA CILICIA
PAROS   COS   Perga   Side   Tarsus
MELOS   Seleucia   Antioch
CRETE   RHODES   Apamea
Gortyna   Salamis   Aradus
Paphos   Tripolis   Palmyra
Cyrene   CYPRUS   Sidon   Damascus
Tyre
Ptolemais
Jerusalem
Alexandria   Pelusium   JUDEA
Athribis
CYRENE   Memphis   Butastis
Arsinoe   Leontopolis
Tebtynis   Philadelphia
Oxyrrhynchus   Heracleopolis
EGYPT

Black Sea
Sinope
PONTUS
Heraclea
Ancyra
PHRYGIA   CAPPADOCIA
MESOPOTAMIA
Laodicea
Pumbeditha   Ctesiphon
Nehardea
Berytus   Babylon   Nippur
ARABIA
Red Sea

Caspian Sea
PARTHIA
MEDIA
ELAM
Ecbatana
Susa
Persian Gulf

Mediterranean Sea

▬ Mentioned in Acts 2:9–11
• City with a Jewish community
▢ Roman Empire, 1st century A.D.

0 ___ 200 km.
0 ___ 100 miles

ward he accepted an invitation to go to the house of Cornelius, a centurion living in Caesarea. As Peter shared the gospel, Cornelius and others believed, and the Holy Spirit was poured out on them. Thus it was at Caesarea, the huge port city that Herod had built, the city of the residence of the Roman governor (Pilate may still have been procurator), that the gospel began to make inroads into the gentile world on the shores of the Mediterranean Sea.

Meanwhile, the persecution of the church continued in Jerusalem and Judea. It was when Saul, a zealous Pharisee, armed with official sanction, was traveling to Damascus in order to persecute the believers there that the risen Lord appeared to him. The route he took cannot be determined, nor can the spot where the Lord appeared to him be located, although he was probably in northern Transjordan when the event occurred. After spending a short time in Damascus, Paul retired to Arabia (= the area of the Nabatean king Aretas IV), where he remained for three years (Gal 1:17). After briefly returning to Damascus, he traveled to Jerusalem for a two-week visit (Acts 9:26–29; Gal 1:18–19), and then he departed for Tarsus, his home city in Cilicia (southeastern Turkey).

In the Book of Acts, little attention is given to the events between the conversion of Saul (ca. A.D. 32/33) and the death of Agrippa I (A.D. 44), but during that time the church continued to grow and opposition to it increased. Agrippa I put to death James the brother of John, and when he saw that this pleased the Jews he attempted to execute Peter as well (Acts 12).

After the death of Agrippa I at Caesarea in A.D. 44, inept and offensive procurators ruled much of Palestine. Various Jewish groups attempted to revolt (e.g., Theudas, and the

KINGDOM OF AGRIPPA I — PALESTINE AFTER JESUS' DEATH

SYRIA
Abila
Sidon   Damascus
PHOENICIA
Caesarea
Philippi
Tyre
GAULANITIS   TRACONITIS
BATANEA
Ptolemais
GALILEE   AURANITIS
Sepphoris   Tiberias   Gadara
Scythopolis   DECAPOLIS
Caesarea
Sebaste
SAMARIA   Gadora
Joppa   Antipatris   Philadelphia
Jericho
Azotus   Jerusalem
JUDEA   PEREA
Gaza   Dead Sea
IDUMEA
NABATEANS

Mediterranean Sea

0 ___ 25 km.
0 ___ 20 miles

▢ Agrippas I's Kingdom, till A.D. 44

sons of Judas the Galilean), but none was successful. In the meantime, Herod Agrippa II was being granted more and more territory by the Romans, so that by the time of the Jewish revolt (A.D. 66–70) he was in control of Gaulanitis, Batanea, Auranitis, Traconitis, and portions of Galilee.

During this time (i.e., A.D. 44–66), Paul was traveling on his three great missionary journeys (see the next chapter), and he returned to Judea for visits after his second and third journeys. After his third journey he was imprisoned in Jerusalem, having been accused of bringing a Gentile into the temple area. Because of a plot on Paul's life he was transferred by night to Caesarea. The military escort that accompanied him traveled by horseback to Caesarea via Antipatris (= OT Aphek). The route from Jerusalem to Antipatris can only be surmised; possibly the detachment followed the old Beth Horon road, or they may have taken the road that ran further north through Gophna and Thamna. In any event, Paul spent over two years imprisoned at

Caesarea. During that time he appeared before two different procurators, Felix and Festus, as well as before the ascending Jewish king, Agrippa II. In the end, Paul appealed to Caesar and was escorted to Rome under guard (see next chapter).

During this period the Roman governors of Palestine continued to offend Jewish sensitivities and did little to restrain the Gentiles of Caesarea who were harassing the Jews. For example, Florus, building on the atrocities of his predecessors, even confiscated a portion of the sacred temple treasury. It was during his tenure (A.D. 64–66) that Jews all over Palestine revolted: in Caesarea, in Jerusalem, and in Galilee.[2] In Jerusalem the Temple Mount and the Antonia fortress were seized, and Roman forces were shut up in the three towers just north of Herod's palace on the western hill. By the end of the summer of A.D. 67 all of Jerusalem was under Jewish control. In response, the Roman legate of Syria marched south with the Twelfth Legion and

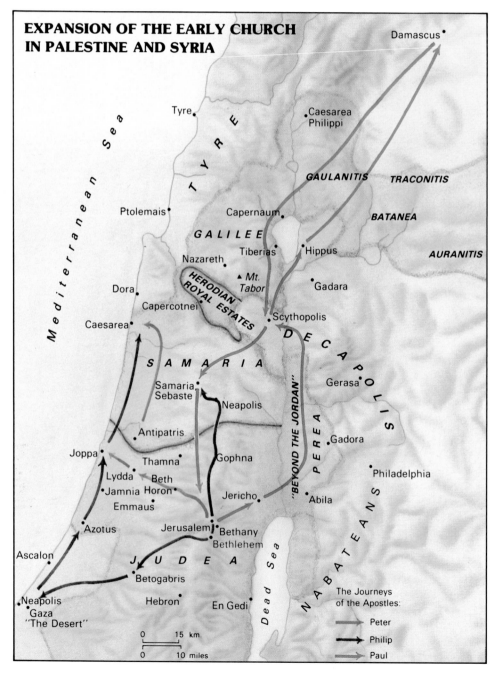

EXPANSION OF THE EARLY CHURCH IN PALESTINE AND SYRIA

The Journeys of the Apostles:

Peter

Philip

Paul

Jewish city of Gamala in the Golan; besieged by Romans in A.D. 67.

attempted to regain Jerusalem. But the attempt failed, and the legion was decimated while withdrawing down the Beth Horon road.

Although the Jewish rebel forces faced serious internal divisions throughout the revolt, a Jewish government was established, coins were struck, and military districts (commands) were set up. The most famous of those commanders was Josephus, the son of a priest, who was entrusted with the defense of Galilee. Later Josephus would become famous as a historian of this and earlier periods.

The emperor, Nero (A.D. 54–68), sent his general Vespasian to crush the revolt. Vespasian established his headquarters in Ptolemais and set out to deploy the three legions at his disposal: the Tenth, the Twelfth, and the Fifteenth. His first objective was to secure the northern part of the country, specifically Lower Galilee. After retaking Sepphoris, he laid siege to the fortress of Jotapata. Although most of the defending garrison died, their commander, Josephus, saved his life by surrendering to the Romans. Approaching the Sea of Galilee from the south, Vespasian proceeded through Tiberias to Taricheae. There he met stiff Jewish resistance but defeated the rebel forces after bloody land and sea battles. East of the Sea of Galilee, at Gamala, the Jewish forces also fought valiantly, but again the Romans prevailed, and most of the defenders were slaughtered. Places in Upper Galilee, such as Cadasa (= OT Kedesh) and Gischala, were

captured, so that by the end of A.D. 67, Galilee was under Roman control.

In the meantime, Roman troops marched south along the coast, capturing the Jewish port of Joppa and destroying the small Jewish navy. Further south, such cities as Jamnia and Azotus were captured, and to the east the Romans secured Samaritan territory in the Mount Ebal and Gerizim region.

In the spring of A.D. 68 fighting resumed, and it appears that Vespasian's goal was first to isolate and then to capture Jerusalem. To this end the Romans invaded Perea, the Jewish territory to the east of the Jordan River. In addition, the Fifth Legion moved south, along the coast, and captured the Shephelah, including the cities of Betogabris, Caphartobas, and Emmaus. The Fifth Legion was stationed at Emmaus to guard the western approaches to Jerusalem. The Romans also marched eastward through Samaria, down the Wadi Faria to Coreae, and from there south, down the west side of the Jordan Valley, to Jericho. After Jericho was captured, the Tenth Legion was stationed there to guard the eastern approach to Jerusalem. Raiding parties from Jericho were sent out into northern Judea against such cities as Acrabeta and Gerasa.

In June of A.D. 68 Nero, the emperor, committed suicide, and although the leadership in Rome was in turmoil (there were three rulers within a one-year period), Vespasian was able to keep up the pressure in Judea. By mid-summer of

AGRIPPA II'S KINGDOM TILL THE JEWISH REVOLT

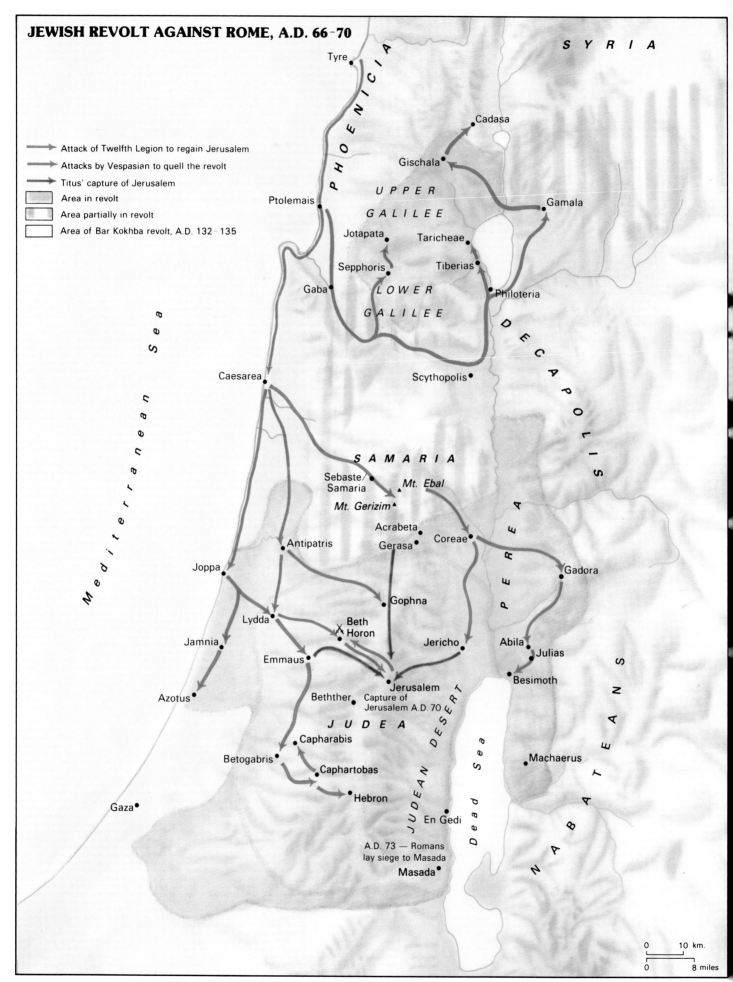

JEWISH REVOLT AGAINST ROME, A.D. 66-70

S Y R I A

→ Attack of Twelfth Legion to regain Jerusalem
→ Attacks by Vespasian to quell the revolt
→ Titus' capture of Jerusalem
Area in revolt
Area partially in revolt
Area of Bar Kokhba revolt, A.D. 132-135

Tyre

P H O E N I C I A

Cadasa

Gischala

U P P E R
G A L I L E E

Gamala

Ptolemais

Jotapata

Taricheae

Sepphoris

Tiberias

Gaba

L O W E R
G A L I L E E

Philoteria

D E C A P O L I S

Mediterranean Sea

Caesarea

Scythopolis

S A M A R I A

Sebaste/
Samaria

Mt. Ebal

Mt. Gerizim

Acrabeta

Coreae

P E R E A

Antipatris

Gerasa

Joppa

Gophna

Gadora

Lydda

Beth
Horon

Jericho

Jamnia

Abila

Emmaus

Julias

Jerusalem

Besimoth

Azotus

Bethther

Capture of
Jerusalem A.D. 70

J U D E A

J U D E A N   D E S E R T

N A B A T E A N S

Capharabis

Dead Sea

Betogabris

Machaerus

Caphartobas

Hebron

Gaza

En Gedi

A.D. 73 — Romans
lay siege to Masada

Masada

0   10 km.

0   8 miles

A.D. 69, Gophna and Acrabeta, both to the north of Jerusalem, and Hebron and Capharabis to the south, had been captured, leaving only Jerusalem, the Judean Desert, Masada, and Machaerus in Jewish hands.

In the summer of A.D. 69 Vespasian's troops declared him emperor. Vespasian returned to Rome to assume the throne, and in the summer of A.D. 70 it was his son, Titus, who captured Jerusalem. Titus approached Jerusalem from the north with the Twelfth and Fifteenth Legions. In addition, the Fifth Legion left its camp at Emmaus and ascended to Jerusalem from the west, while the Tenth Legion left Jericho and approached it from the east. Jerusalem was under siege from the end of May until the middle of August; Josephus describes the intense suffering of the inhabitants. Section after section of the city was methodically captured, and in August the Temple Mount was taken. On the ninth of Ab (ca. August 28) the Romans set fire to the temple. The upper (western) portion of Jerusalem held out for a few weeks longer but soon fell to the Romans. Although Jerusalem had been captured and destroyed, it was not abandoned, and the Romans stationed the Tenth Legion there in order to prevent further hostilities.

The capture of Jerusalem in A.D. 70 marks the end of the Jewish revolt, although the Romans had to engage in mopping-up operations, particularly in the Judean Desert. In A.D. 73 they had to lay siege to the massive rock fortress of Masada, located near the shore of the Dead Sea. There, 960 of the 967 Jewish defenders decided to commit suicide and to die as free individuals rather than to be captured by the Romans. Again, it is Josephus who describes that tragic moment in Jewish history.

The destruction of the temple and the cessation of sacrificial worship necessitated a dramatic change in Jewish life. The Sanhedrin, now dominated by the Pharisees, reconstituted itself at Jamnia and gave new direction to Jewish life and practice. Jewish life was now focused in the villages and cities outside of Jerusalem throughout Palestine.

In the early second century (A.D. 132–35) the Jewish people again attempted to throw off the Roman yoke. This second revolt, in contrast to the first, appears to have been carefully planned in advance. While the Romans were preoccupied in other parts of the empire, Simeon Bar Kokhba was declared the leader of the Jewish people by the highly respected Rabbi Akiba. The rebellion had its center in and around Jerusalem and Judea. An effective Jewish administration was set up, and even coins were struck. Initially the Jews enjoyed a number of military successes, evidently even wiping out a Roman legion. However, the Romans again responded in strength and sent several legions into the region to suppress the revolt. Bar Kokhba had to abandon Jerusalem and retreat to Bethther, 7 miles (11 km.) southwest of Jerusalem. The Romans laid siege to his fortress, and he and his garrison were wiped out. With the end of the second Jewish revolt, the emperor Hadrian ordered Jerusalem to be destroyed and rebuilt as a Roman colony named Aelia Capitolina, with Jews forbidden entrance into the city. In order to further eradicate the "Jewishness" of the land, its name was changed from Judea to Palestine.[3]

Inscription in Caesarea's aqueduct describing how the Tenth Legion dedicated its work to the Emperor Hadrian.

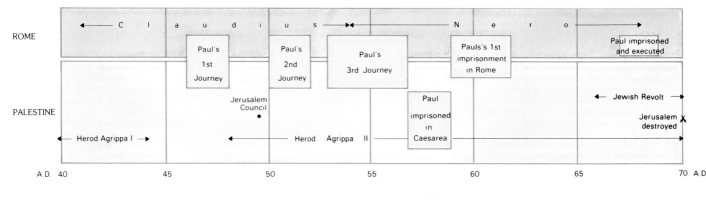

ROME — Claudius, Nero

Paul's 1st Journey | Paul's 2nd Journey | Paul's 3rd Journey | Pauls's 1st imprisonment in Rome | Paul imprisoned and executed

PALESTINE — Jerusalem Council • | Paul imprisoned in Caesarea | Jewish Revolt ← | Jerusalem destroyed X

Herod Agrippa I → | ← Herod Agrippa II

A.D. 40   45   50   55   60   65   70 A.D.

The Journeys of Paul

The Early Life of Saul

During the period between the ascension of Jesus and the fall of Jerusalem to the Romans (A.D. 30–70) the gospel message was preached not only in Jerusalem, Judea, and Samaria (Acts 1–12) but throughout the Roman world (Acts 13–28). The major figure involved in this enterprise was Paul. Born in the Greco-Roman city of Tarsus, on the southeastern coast of Asia Minor, Saul (later renamed Paul) was sent to Jerusalem to study under the famous teacher Rabbi Gamaliel (22:3; cf. 5:34). While in Jerusalem, Saul witnessed the stoning of Stephen (ca. A.D. 35), but soon afterward he was converted to Christianity on the road to Damascus (Acts 9). After spending three years in Arabia and making short visits to Damascus and Jerusalem, Saul returned to Tarsus, from which he apparently ministered in both Cilicia and northern Syria.

The major city of Syria was Antioch.[1] It was located to the southeast of Tarsus and was one of three chief cities in the eastern Mediterranean. Located in northern Syria on the Orontes River, about 16 miles (25 km.) from the sea, Antioch was founded by Seleucus I (Nicator; 312–280 B.C.). Over the years it had developed into a leading commercial center, since it was located at the western end of land routes leading from Mesopotamia to the Mediterranean and because it also served as the northwestern terminus for the spice and incense route from southern Arabia. For many years it had been the capital of the Seleucid kingdom, and it became the capital of the Roman province of Syria, serving as Rome's last major outpost vis-à-vis the kingdom of Parthia to the east. It was mainly gentile in character, but a considerable number of Jews lived there, for they had received property rights and citizenship because of the assistance they had rendered to various Seleucid causes.

It is probable that some Christians who fled Judea because of persecution sought refuge in Antioch and began to share their faith with its inhabitants. Because of the success of the new faith, the Jerusalem church sent Barnabas to investigate the situation (Acts 11:22). After spending some time in Antioch, Barnabas, who had assisted Saul previously, went to Tarsus to seek Saul's help in the ministry at Antioch. For a few years (ca. A.D. 43–45) Barnabas and Saul ministered together at Antioch, the place where believers were first called "Christians" (v. 26).

Paul's First Missionary Journey

After spending several years in Antioch, during which time Barnabas and Saul had made a trip to Jerusalem to deliver a gift for famine relief (Acts 11:28–30), Barnabas and Saul were set aside by the church in Antioch to be ministers to other parts of the Roman world. It was from Antioch's important harbor Seleucia that Saul set out on the first of his three missionary journeys (ca. A.D. 46–48). Barnabas and Saul set sail for the island of Cyprus (140 by 53 miles [225 by 85 km.]) some 80 miles (130 km.) to the west, landing at Salamis, which was located on the eastern edge of the island just below the "finger," which points toward Antioch. There at Salamis, the largest city on the island, they preached in the synagogue before moving overland to Cyprus' administrative capital, Paphos, on the southwestern edge of the island. At Paphos, the proconsul of Cyprus, Sergius Paulus, was converted after having heard the gospel and having seen the judgment that fell on the sorcerer Elymas.

From Paphos, Paul and Barnabas sailed 170 miles (270 km.) northwest to ancient Pamphylia, on the southern coast of modern Turkey. Bypassing the port of Attalia, they proceeded up the Kestros River to Perga, one of the largest cities of the province. At Perga, for unknown reasons—jealousy? sickness? home-sickness? fear?—John Mark left them and returned to Jerusalem (Acts 13:13). Paul and Barnabas evidently did not remain very long in Perga but headed north, up into the rugged Taurus Mountains. After climbing the steep, forested southern slopes, they entered the broad lofty plateau area called Pisidia. From there they continued north into Phrygia, an area that had been settled by peoples from Macedonia or Thrace. The districts of Pisidia and Phrygia were closely related, so that the city of Antioch, technically in Phrygia, was also associated with Pisidia and thus came to be known as "Pisidian Antioch"

180

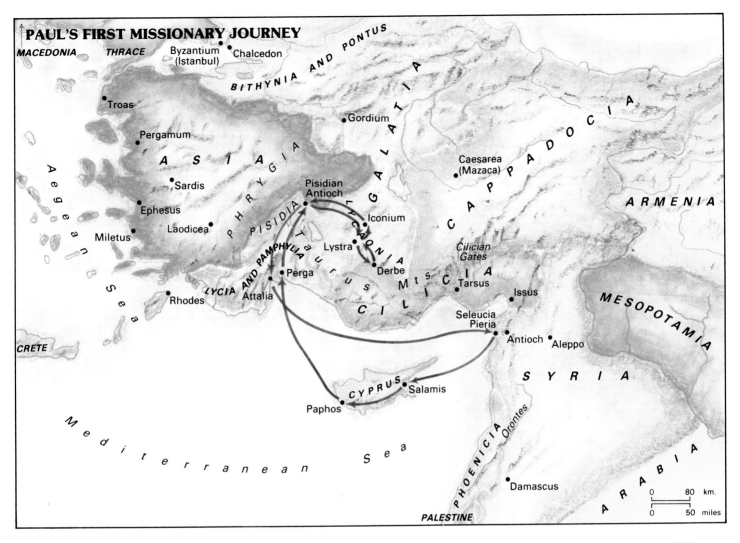

PAUL'S FIRST MISSIONARY JOURNEY

(v. 14). This city, situated at the base of a mountain range, sat astride the great road that led from Syria to the Ionian coast. Antioch also served as the administrative center of southern Galatia, the large Roman province of which Pisidia and Phrygia were a part. Paul and Barnabas preached in the synagogue in Pisidian Antioch for several Sabbaths. Although the Jews were not overly receptive to their message, the Gentiles were, and the gospel message spread "through the whole region" (v. 49). However, opposition soon developed, and Paul and Barnabas were expelled from the city.

Moving 80 miles (130 km.) to the southeast, they arrived at Iconium, another important commercial center on the road from Syria to Asia. There Paul and Barnabas again preached in the synagogue, and a large number of Jews and Gentiles believed. Once again, however, opposition and threats on their lives forced them to flee, this time to the Lycaonian cities of Lystra and Derbe.

Possibly Paul and Barnabas thought that Lystra would serve as a place of retreat from the antagonism they had been encountering, since it was not one of the larger cities of the region. But after Paul and Barnabas healed a man who had been crippled from birth, the Lycaonians, who believed that the gods had previously visited their ancestors, thought that the gods were visiting them again, and they identified Barnabas with Zeus and Paul with Hermes. Paul and Barnabas dissuaded the townspeople from worshiping them, but when Jews from Antioch and Iconium arrived they incited the populace to stone Paul, and they dragged him out of the city, thinking that he was dead. It is interesting to note that there probably was not a strong Jewish presence in Lystra, since no synagogue is mentioned, although apparently Timothy, whose mother was Jewish, was from the city. In addition, the lack of order and justice, evidenced in the treatment of Paul, seems to imply that the Roman presence was minimal, or at least that justice was greatly influenced by local prejudices; this was true in spite of the fact that Lystra had been made a Roman colony.

From Lystra Paul and Barnabas traveled east 60 miles (100 km.) to Derbe (to be identified with Kerti Huyuk or Devri Sehri, 2.5 mi. [4 km.] to the southeast of Kerti Huyuk) at the eastern edge of the province of Galatia. After preaching in the city Paul and Barnabas did not take the short route via the Cilician Gates and Tarsus back to Syrian Antioch; instead, they revisited and strengthened the churches they had just established in Lystra, Iconium, and Pisidian Antioch. Retracing their steps south through the Taurus Mountains, they crossed the narrow plain of Pamphylia to the beautiful port of Attalia and from there sailed back to Antioch. Thus on Paul's first journey, important churches were established on Cyprus and in southern Galatia, and from strategically placed cities such as Pisidian Antioch and Iconium the new converts could influence many who passed along the thoroughfares of Asia. On Paul's first trip some Jews, but many more Gentiles, were brought into the

PAUL'S SECOND MISSIONARY JOURNEY

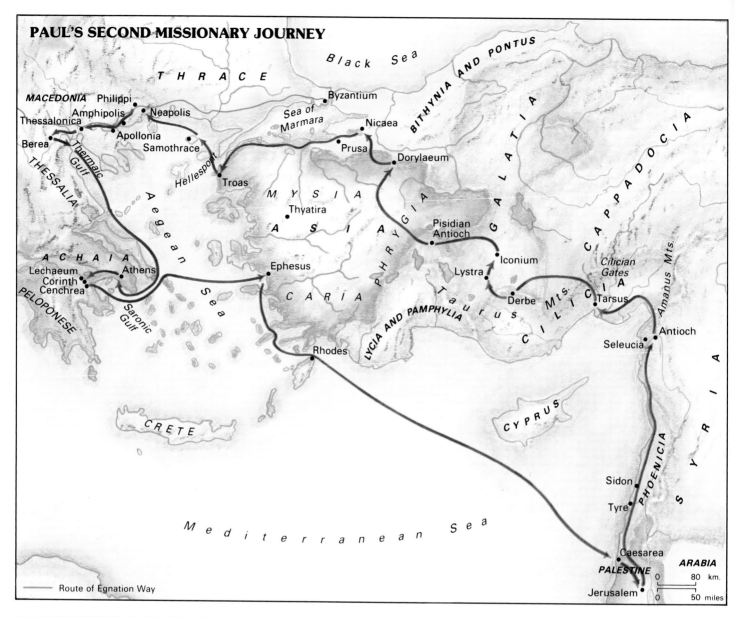

Black Sea

THRACE

MACEDONIA · Philippi
Amphipolis · Neapolis
Thessalonica · Apollonia
Berea · Samothrace
Thermaic Gulf
THESSALIA
Byzantium
Sea of Marmara
Nicaea
Prusa
Dorylaeum
BITHYNIA AND PONTUS

Hellespont
Troas

MYSIA
Thyatira

ASIA

PHRYGIA
GALATIA
CAPPADOCIA

Pisidian Antioch
Iconium
Lystra
Cilician Gates
Amanus Mts.

ACHAIA
Lechaeum
Corinth
Cenchrea
PELOPONESE
Athens
Saronic Gulf

Aegean Sea

Ephesus

CARIA

Taurus Mts.
Derbe
Tarsus
CILICIA
Antioch
Seleucia

LYCIA AND PAMPHYLIA

Rhodes

CRETE

CYPRUS

PHOENICIA

SYRIA

Mediterranean Sea

Sidon
Tyre

Caesarea
PALESTINE
ARABIA
Jerusalem

——— Route of Egnation Way

0   80 km.
0   50 miles

ATHENS IN ROMAN TIMES

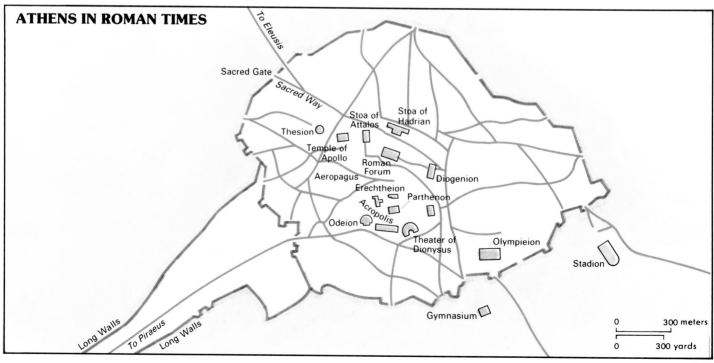

To Eleusis

Sacred Gate
Sacred Way

Stoa of Attalos
Stoa of Hadrian

Thesion
Temple of Apollo
Roman Forum
Aeropagus
Diogenion
Erechtheion
Parthenon
Acropolis
Odeion
Theater of Dionysus
Olympieion
Stadion

Gymnasium

Long Walls
To Piraeus
Long Walls

0   300 meters
0   300 yards

church.

Although Jewish proselytes had been joining the church since its earliest days, it was through the ministry of Paul and Barnabas that large numbers of Gentiles first began entering the church directly. This raised the question of the gentile converts' relationship to the Mosaic Law. To help answer the question, Paul and Barnabas traveled to Jerusalem to participate in the apostolic conference that had been called to discuss the issue (Acts 15; ca. A.D. 49/50). After major presentations by believing Pharisees, Peter, and Barnabas and Paul, James pronounced the decision that only minimal ritual demands would be requested of gentile converts so as to promote unity between believing Jews and Gentiles. Armed with this verdict, Paul and Barnabas returned to Antioch to minister there.

Paul's Second Missionary Journey

Both Paul and Barnabas were anxious to revisit the churches they had established on their first journey, but they disagreed on the question of the suitability of John Mark as a traveling companion. Because of this disagreement they decided to separate; Barnabas took John Mark and traveled to Cyprus (possibly they had family connections there), while Paul took Silas and headed toward Asia Minor. On this second journey (ca. A.D. 50–52) Paul and Silas traveled north from Antioch and walked through the Amanus Mountains to Cilicia. In all probability they stopped at Paul's home city of Tarsus and then headed northwest through the Cilician Gates, a pass in the Taurus Mountains, and after that continued west, sharing the decision of the Jerusalem council regarding the status of gentile converts with the churches at Derbe, Lystra, Iconium, and Pisidian Antioch. Along the way, at Lystra, Timothy joined Paul and Silas on their westward journey.

Soon after leaving Pisidian Antioch they had to choose whether to continue on the road that led west to the Ionian coast through districts such as Caria and Lycia of the province of Asia or to head north toward Dorylaeum. Choosing the latter route, they traveled north through Phrygia, preaching the gospel as they went. Passing southwest of Bithynia, they turned northwest to Nicea or Prusa and from there continued west along the northern border of Mysia, another district of the province of Asia, to the port city of Troas.

Situated near the Hellespont (the modern Straits of Dardanelles, which connects the Black Sea and the Sea of Marmara with the Aegean Sea), at the end of a caravan route from the east and close to Europe, Troas enjoyed great prosperity as a Roman colony. However, Troas was not to be the terminus of the Pauline journey, for here Paul evidently met Luke, a physician and the author of Luke-Acts, and, in response to a vision of a man from Macedonia, Paul and his party (now including Luke) sailed from Troas to Europe.

After anchoring for the night at the island of Samothrace,

the ship landed in Macedonia at Neapolis (modern Kavalla in Greece). From Neapolis the party continued 10 miles (6 km.) inland to the prominent city of Philippi. Founded in the Hellenistic period and named after Philip of Macedon, the father of Alexander the Great, Philippi was situated on the "Egnatian Way"—an important Roman road that led from Dyrrachium, on the western coast of modern Albania on the Adriatic Sea, to Byzantium 540 miles (870 km.) to the east. This strategic road was part of the system that connected Rome with its eastern provinces. As a Roman colony, Philippi seems to have been predominantly populated by Gentiles, for evidently the Jewish population was not large enough to warrant a synagogue. At the place of prayer by the River Gangites, west of the city, Paul met Lydia, the purple-cloth dealer from Thyatira. Paul ministered in the city while staying at her house. In Philippi Paul healed a slave girl who was demon-possessed, and as a result her owners had Paul and Silas thrown into prison. After the earthquake in the middle of the night and the subsequent conversion of the prison guard and his family, the leaders of Philippi begged Paul and Silas to leave the city, and the two men complied. Since the "we" section (Acts 16:10–17) that began at Troas ends here, it may be assumed that Luke remained behind to minister at Philippi. It seems that the ministry at Philippi was very successful, for in Paul's letter to the church there he expresses very warm feelings for the people and does not reprimand the members for doctrinal divergencies.

From Philippi Paul and Silas traveled 68 miles (110 km.) west along the Egnatian Way to Thessalonica via Amphipolis and Apollonia. Thessalonica was founded in 315 B.C. and was named by Cassander for his wife. Located at the northern edge of the Thermaic Gulf (Thessalonica's earlier name had been Therma—"Hot Spring"), it had become not only a district capital but also the chief port for all of Macedonia. Paul and Silas preached in the synagogue for three Sabbaths, and a number of Jews, God-fearing Greeks, and prominent women believed. But opposition developed once again. A mob stormed the house of Jason, where Paul was staying, so Paul and Silas departed that evening. It seems that even after that short, three-week stay Christianity took root in Thessalonica, as Paul's two letters to the church there indicate. Evidently the gospel rapidly spread from Thessalonica into the hinterland, for within the next eighteen months Paul wrote and commended the church that "The Lord's message rang out from you not only in Macedonia and Achaia–your faith in God has become known everywhere" (1 Thess 1:8).

Paul and Silas next moved 50 miles (80 km.) southwest to Berea (modern Verria) where they entered the synagogue and preached. The people of Berea were known for their desire to study the Scriptures, and a number of Jews as well as Greek men and women believed, but Jews from Thessalonica agitated the crowds of Berea, and Paul departed for the coast, leaving Silas and Timothy behind. Paul evidently traveled by ship to Athens, where he awaited the arrival of his companions.

The Athens that Paul visited was no longer the administrative capital of southern Greece, which was now the Roman province of Achaia—Corinth held that honor—but it was still renowned as a cultural and intellectual center. Since its Golden Age in the fifth century B.C., it had been filled with temples and altars to all kinds of gods. These temples and altars lined the road that ran from Piraeus, the port of Athens, to the city itself. The Agora (marketplace) and the Acropolis to the southeast were also filled with shrines. Paul preached in the marketplace as well as in the synagogue, and as a result was invited by a group of Epicurean and Stoic philosophers to address the philosophical assembly called the Areopagus (= "hill of Area"). By the time of Paul's appearance in Athens, the meeting place of this group had moved from the well-known rocky hill west of the Acropolis to the Royal Colonnade in the northwestern corner of the Agora. There Paul presented the gospel of Jesus to that learned group (Acts 17:22–31 contains a summary of that sermon). Although a number of Athenians were converted, there does not seem to have been a ready acceptance of the gospel, so Paul left for Corinth, the capital of Achaia, 40 miles (65 km.) to the west of Athens.

Corinth was a bustling administrative and commercial center at that time.[2] It had been sacked by the Romans in 146 B.C. but refounded as a Roman colony in 44 B.C. It owed its prosperity to its geographical location: it was just south of the narrow isthmus (4 mi. [6.5 km.] wide) that connected the Greek mainland with the Peloponnese, and all traffic between them had to pass through Corinth. In addition, the ancients preferred to portage passengers and cargo across the isthmus rather than taking the longer and more dangerous trip by sea around the southern tip of the Peloponnese. Corinth controlled the port of Cenchrea on the Saronic Gulf to the east, and its counterpart, Lechaeum on the Corinthian Gulf, to the northwest, so it certainly drew revenue from the trade that flowed through the isthmus.

In this boom town, famous for its immorality (Strabo states that there were one thousand prostitutes for the temple of Aphrodite alone) Paul ministered for over eighteen months. Here the gospel was eagerly received and the

church established. Paul probably penned both of his letters to the church at Thessalonica during this stay in Corinth. In time, Paul was accused by disgruntled Jews of violating their religious law, but Gallio, the proconsul of Achaia, would not accept their complaints.

After his extended stay, Paul, in the company of Priscilla and Aquila, with whom he had been living, left Corinth via the port of Cenchrea for the 250-mile (400-km.) journey to Ephesus. Stopping in Ephesus for a brief time, he left Priscilla and Aquila behind and set sail for Caesarea, some 600 miles (970 km.) distant. Upon arriving at Caesarea he went up to Jerusalem and reported to the church the results of his journey. Then he returned north to his starting point and home base, Syrian Antioch. On this second journey Paul had the opportunity to revisit the Galatian churches and to deal with their doctrinal problems (see Paul's letter to the Galatians) in light of the Jerusalem Council, and to preach the gospel in Europe—that is, in Macedonia and Achaia.

Paul's Third Missionary Journey

After spending some time in Syrian Antioch, Paul set out on his third journey (ca. A.D. 53–57). He probably began by retracing the route of his second journey through Galatia and Phrygia to Pisidian Antioch. But this time, instead of heading north, he continued west into the province of Asia, to Ephesus. This great city was one of the three major cities of the eastern Mediterranean (the other two were Syrian

Temple of Apollo at Corinth.

Antioch and Alexandria, Egypt). It had become an important commercial center, since caravan routes from the east converged there, while it was from there that shipping lanes to the west originated. Paul spent three years ministering in Ephesus "to the Jews first but also to the Greeks," and it is very probable that he or his converts carried the gospel message to additional cities in Asia. Certainly many of the Asian cities addressed by John in the first three chapters of Revelation—Ephesus, Smyrna, Pergamum, Thyatira, Sardis, Philadelphia, and Laodicea—were founded and/or nurtured by Paul.

Besides being an important transportation hub, Ephesus contained the temple of the fertility goddess Artemis (called Diana by the Romans), which was so large and so magnificent that it was considered one of the wonders of the ancient world. Because of the success of the gospel in Ephesus there was a serious decline in business associated with the worship of the goddess Artemis. Thus Demetrius the silversmith incited the Ephesians, who had assembled in the 24,000-seat theater, against Paul and other Christians, but the town clerk was able to dissuade the mob from carrying out any illegal acts.

Apparently soon afterward Paul set out for Macedonia, probably via Troas (2 Cor 2:12–13). In Macedonia he probably revisited the churches at Philippi, Thessalonica, and Berea, and it may well have been at this time that he continued westward along the Egnatian Way to, or into, Illyricum (Rom 15:19). Sometime during this period it appears that he wrote 2 Corinthians in preparation for his arrival at Corinth (the first letter had been written while he was living in Ephesus). After ministering in Macedonia, Paul continued south to Achaia and spent three months wintering in Corinth. It was probably at that time that he wrote his famous letter to the church at Rome, advising them of his intention to visit them as he proceeded to the western parts of the empire.

When spring came Paul planned to sail directly to Judea in order to reach Jerusalem by Pentecost, but because of a threat on his life he abandoned that plan and instead traveled overland to Philippi (Acts 20:3–6). After the Feast of Unleavened Bread he sailed for Troas (on a local cargo ship?), a trip that took five days. After spending seven days at Troas (where Eutychus was raised from the dead after falling out of a window), Paul walked the 20 miles (32 km.) overland to Assos while the remainder of his party traveled by ship. Sailing down the Ionian coast, they stopped at Mitylene (a port on the island of Lesbos), at the islands of Kios and Samos, and at Miletus. Miletus had formerly been

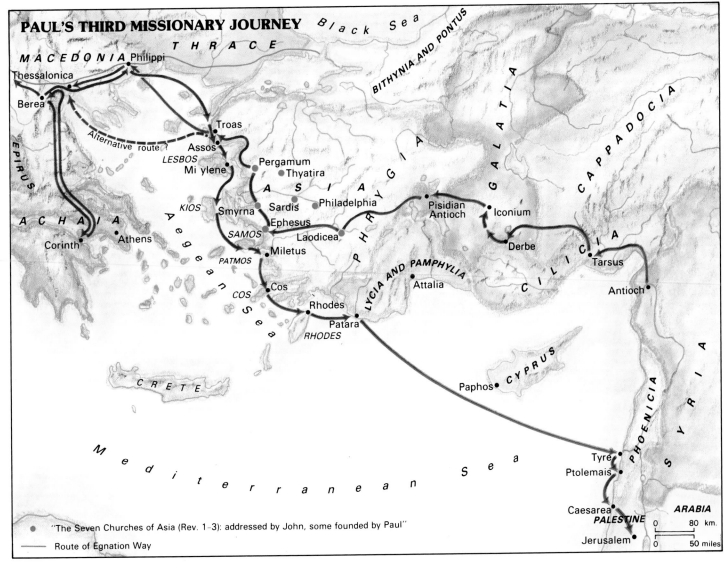

PAUL'S THIRD MISSIONARY JOURNEY

● "The Seven Churches of Asia (Rev. 1–3): addressed by John, some founded by Paul"

— Route of Egnation Way

one of the chief ports of Asia, but because of the silting of its harbor it was beginning to lose its importance to Ephesus. When Paul reached Miletus, he summoned the elders of the Ephesian church, who traveled 30 mi. [48 km.] to Miletus to spend a few days with their beloved teacher.

After a tearful good-bye, Paul and his party set sail from Miletus. After reaching the island of Cos, they continued to Rhodes and on to the southern shore of Asia Minor, to Patara, a seaport in the province of Lycia. Boarding a cargo vessel that was heading for Phoenicia, they sailed past Cyprus and landed at Tyre. While cargo was being unloaded Paul had a chance to spend seven days with the disciples there; then from Tyre they continued on to Caesarea, stopping briefly at Ptolemais along the way. Paul, against the advice of some Christians, continued on to Jerusalem, where he greeted the elders of the church and completed the purification rites associated with a vow that he had made. Although he may have intended to return to Antioch as usual, Jerusalem was, in fact, the terminal point of his third journey, as it was here that he was arrested (see above, p. 176). After being transported to Caesarea, he remained imprisoned there for a few years (ca. A.D. 57–59) before finally appealing to Caesar for justice.

Paul's Journey to Rome

For the trip to Rome, Paul was placed in the custody of a centurion named Julius. Along with a small party that included Aristarchus and probably Luke, Paul was placed on a ship from Adramyttium (the name of a harbor on the west coast of Asia Minor, east of Assos). The ship's route took it to Sidon and then on to the southern coast of Asia, to Myra, a major port of call for grain ships bound for Rome. There Paul and his party transferred onto a cargo ship that was to sail directly to Italy. Because of adverse winds, the ship was not able to reach Cnidus on the southwestern tip of Asia Minor (Turkey), and rather than attempting to cross the open sea to the southern tip of the Peloponnese, it sailed south, intending to pass on the lee (south) side of the island of Crete (140 by 35 mi. [225 by 55 km.]). Sailing along the southern coast of Crete, the ship passed up a winter anchorage at Fair Havens in an attempt to reach what the captain thought was a more desirable port at Phoenix, 50 miles (80 km.) further west. Since the fast (= Day of Atonement; Acts 27:9) was

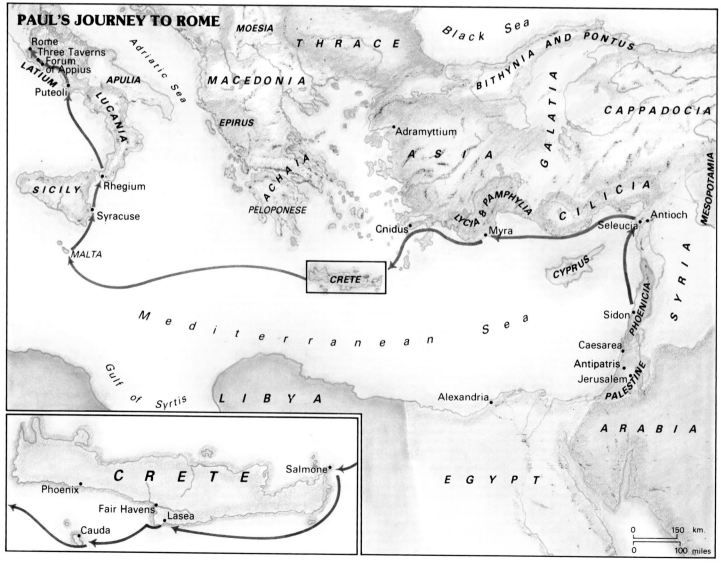

186

already over, it must have been late fall, and sailing on the Mediterranean in that season became precarious.

Indeed, a "northeaster" (Acts 27:14 NIV) wind sprang up, and the ship was driven off course. As it was passing on the lee side of the island of Cauda (ca. 23 mi. [37 km.] from Crete) the ship had to be lashed together, and as the storm continued there was considerable danger that the ship would run aground and be wrecked on the sandbars of Syrtis, off north Africa. Instead the ship eventually ran aground on the island of Malta, 60 miles (96 km.) south of Sicily. All 276 passengers were saved, but the ship and its cargo were lost.

After wintering three months on the island, they boarded another Alexandrian ship and sailed to Italy via Syracuse (on Sicily) and Rhegium. They landed at Puteoli (modern Puzzuoli) in spite of the fact that it was 140 miles (225 km.) south of Rome, as Puteoli was a favorite terminus for ships coming from the east. A good road connected it with Rome; along this road, at the Forum of Appius (43 mi. [69 km.] south of Rome) and at Three Taverns (33 mi. [53 km.] south) Paul was greeted by Christians from the capital.

The Rome of Paul's day was a huge city with a population of more than one million. It was situated on the banks of the Tiber River, 18 miles (29 km.) inland from the Adriatic Sea. It had spread beyond its traditional seven hills and even beyond its ancient fortifications. As the capital of the empire, it boasted the imperial palaces on the Palatine Hill and the temples of Jupiter and Juno on the Capitoline. Below these hills was the forum, with additional temples and public buildings. Theaters, amphitheaters, hippodromes, and other monuments graced the city, but its beauty was tempered by the fact that over half its population were slaves, and a large portion of the nonslaves lived in squalid conditions in high-rise apartment buildings of four and five stories and were dependent on the free distribution of food for their subsistence.

The Book of Acts concludes with Paul having resided in Rome for two years (ca. A.D. 59–61/62), under house arrest, without ever having had his case go to trial. From that point on we are dependent on early Christian tradition for our knowledge of the activities and fate of Paul. According to tradition, Paul was released from prison around A.D. 62 and traveled to various parts of the Mediterranean world—probably to Crete (Titus 1:5) and possibly to Spain. Also according to tradition, he was arrested and imprisoned again in A.D. 67/68, and it was during this time that he penned his final letter (2 Tim). Finally, tradition claims that during the time of the Neronian persecution (ca. A.D. 68) Paul was executed outside the walls of Rome, along the road to Ostia.

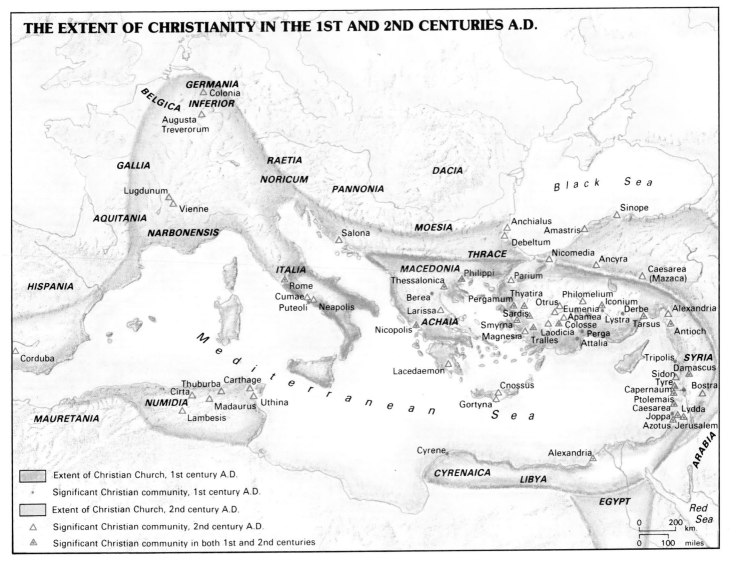

THE EXTENT OF CHRISTIANITY IN THE 1ST AND 2ND CENTURIES A.D.

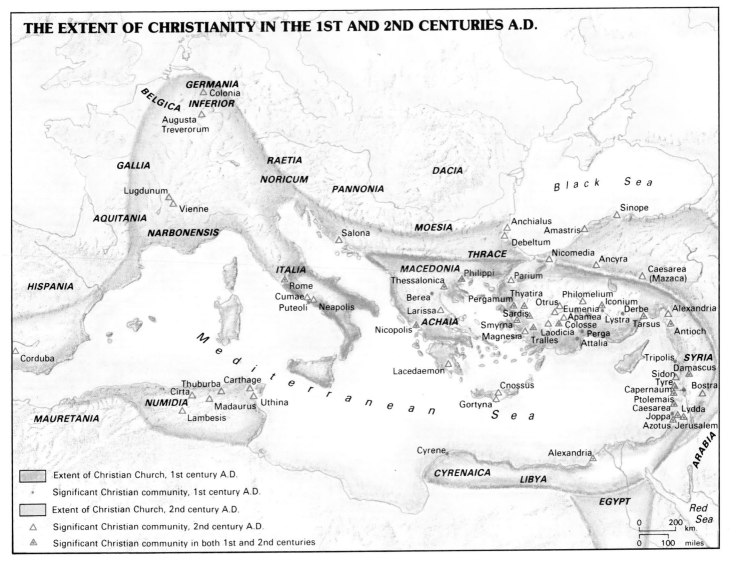Legend:
Extent of Christian Church, 1st century A.D.
Significant Christian community, 1st century A.D.
Extent of Christian Church, 2nd century A.D.
Significant Christian community, 2nd century A.D.
Significant Christian community in both 1st and 2nd centuries

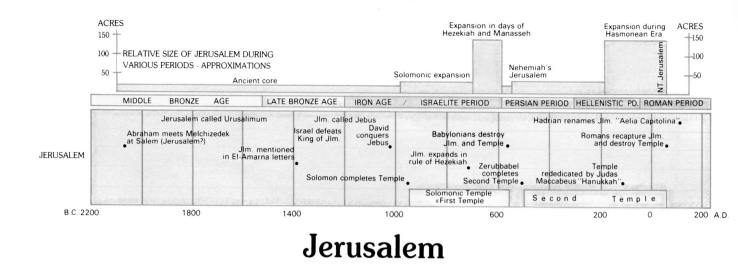

ACRES
150
100 — RELATIVE SIZE OF JERUSALEM DURING
50   VARIOUS PERIODS · APPROXIMATIONS

Expansion in days of Hezekiah and Manasseh

Expansion during Hasmonean Era

ACRES
150
100
50

Ancient core

Solomonic expansion

Nehemiah's Jerusalem

NT Jerusalem

| MIDDLE | BRONZE | AGE | LATE BRONZE AGE | IRON AGE / ISRAELITE PERIOD | PERSIAN PERIOD | HELLENISTIC PD. | ROMAN PERIOD |

JERUSALEM

Jerusalem called Urusalimum

Jlm. called Jebus

David conquers Jebus

Hadrian renames Jlm. "Aelia Capitolina"

Abraham meets Melchizedek at Salem (Jerusalem?)

Israel defeats King of Jlm.

Babylonians destroy Jlm. and Temple

Romans recapture Jlm. and destroy Temple

Jlm. mentioned in El-Amarna letters

Jlm. expands in rule of Hezekiah

Zerubbabel completes Second Temple

Temple rededicated by Judas Maccabeus "Hanukkah"

Solomon completes Temple

Solomonic Temple = First Temple

Second Temple

B.C. 2200   1800   1400   1000   600   200   0   200 A.D.

Jerusalem

Jerusalem holds a special place in the hearts and thoughts of Jews, Christians, and Moslems.[1] Of all the cities in the Bible, this is the most prominent one: it is mentioned 667 times in the Old Testament and 139 times in the New. Although today Jerusalem boasts a population of over 450,000 people, its origins were humble.

Jerusalem did not become an important city because of its proximity to any major international highway. In fact, it is quite removed from the coastal and the Transjordanian highways. The only route that passed by it was the north-south Ridge Route, and even that ran about a half mile west of the ancient core of the city. A west-east road that connected Gezer on the coastal plain and Jericho in the Jordan Valley via Beth Horon, Ramah, and Geba passed 5.5 miles (9 km.) north of Jerusalem. Although this route was the most natural approach into the hill country, whether from the east or the west, it was primarily of local significance.

Its location in the Hill Country of Judah, at an elevation of 2,500 feet (760 m.), gave Jerusalem the benefit of many natural defenses. The Dead Sea, the Rift Valley cliffs, and the wilderness provided protection on the south and east, while the latter two provided security on the northeast as well. It was also difficult to approach Jerusalem from the west because the hills of the Shephelah and the deep, V-shaped valleys carved into the hard limestone of the Judean hills formed a rugged and treacherous landscape. It was somewhat easier to approach Jerusalem from the north or south, along the Ridge Route, but access to the Ridge Route from either the coast or the Rift Valley was difficult. Thus, besides being removed from the main routes of commerce and military expeditions, Jerusalem enjoyed the security of its natural defenses.

If Jerusalem was not a natural center of commerce because of its location, neither was it situated in the heart of

View of Jerusalem as it was in 1917; from southeast looking northwest.

an extraordinarily rich agricultural region. In fact, Jerusalem was perched right on the boundary between the desert and the sown, and across the Mount of Olives, to the east, one runs immediately into the fringes of the Judean Desert. But Jerusalem itself receives ample supplies of winter rain (approximately 25 in. [640 mm.] per year), as do the hills to the west, so that they are able to produce a variety of crops. During early periods, however, agricultural activities must have been quite limited due to the extensive tree cover on the hills in and around the city. Beginning in the Bronze Age (ca. 3100 B.C.), and continuing into later periods, large trees were cut down to provide timber for buildings and ships, while both larger and smaller trees were used to fuel the fires in lime and pottery kilns and to heat houses in the winter months. Areas that had been cleared could be used for agricultural purposes, and on the more level terrain—e.g., in the Valley of Rephaim to the southwest of Jerusalem—grain crops were planted (Isa 17:5). To the north, south, and west of Jerusalem the natural hillside terraces were enhanced as small fields were cleared of boulders, fences and retaining walls were built, and crops were planted. By the time of the United Monarchy (ca. 1000 B.C.), all three crops in the famous triad of grain, olives, and grapes were being grown in the Jerusalem area, along with other crops. In spite of all this, Jerusalem never really became a large exporter of agricultural produce.

In addition to its unimpressive commercial and agricultural qualities, Jerusalem is not overwhelming from a topographical standpoint. Hills surround its ancient core so that standing on these hills one actually looks down on the city. Roughly speaking, the ancient city can be visualized as sitting on a rise in the bottom of a large bowl, where the rim of the bowl is higher than the rise within it.

Biblical Jerusalem was built on two parallel north-south ridges. The western ridge, which is the higher and broader of the two, is bounded on the west by the Hinnom Valley. This valley, which begins northwest of the city, turns due south and then due east, forming distinctive limits on the western and southern sides of the ridge. The narrower and lower eastern ridge is bounded on the east by the Kidron Valley, which in the Jerusalem area flows basically north to south. After being joined by the Hinnom, the Kidron turns to the southeast and proceeds through the barren Judean Desert to the Dead Sea. Both the Hinnom and the Kidron are mentioned in the Bible, but the valley between them, which separates the eastern and western ridges, is not. For lack of a better name, geographers often call it the Central Valley, or—following the lead of the Jewish historian Josephus—the Tyropoeon ("Cheesemakers") Valley (*War*. 5.4.1 [140]).

On the north, both ridges continue to rise as they veer to the northwest. The major valleys—the Hinnom Valley, the Central Valley, and a tributary of the Kidron—all veer off in that direction as well. The west-east Transversal Valley, which flows into the Central Valley, forms the natural northern boundary of the western ridge, yet in some periods of Jerusalem's history, the city expanded along that ridge to the northwest. The northern limit of the eastern ridge is not quite as noticeable as it continues rising to the northwest, interrupted only by some minor depressions that flow into the Bezetha Valley. Because of the easier approaches from the north and the northwest, invading armies have often assaulted Jerusalem from a northerly direction.

In many ways the western ridge is the more natural one to settle on, both because it has a relatively large surface area and thus can support more people, and because it is higher and seems to have better natural defenses (higher, steeper slopes) than the eastern ridge. In spite of these features, it was the lower, cigar-shaped, 15 acre (6 ha.), southern portion of the eastern ridge that was settled first. The reason why the ancient core of Jerusalem developed on this insignificant, down-in-a-basin hill was that the only good-sized spring in the whole area—the Gihon Spring—was located alongside the eastern ridge in the Kidron Valley.

The earliest settlement on the southern portion of the eastern ridge reaches back to the late Chalcolithic and Early Bronze ages, as evidenced by pottery discovered in recent excavations. To date, however, no city wall or buildings have been found that date unequivocally from these periods. From the Middle Bronze I (MB I) period (2200–2000 B.C.) there are very few remains, although MB I tombs have been discovered on the Mount of Olives, and some think that there may have been additional MB I tombs on the hill that eventually became the site of the Solomonic temple.[2] According to the chronology adopted in this atlas, it would have been during this period that Abram, returning from rescuing Lot, met Melchizedek, the king of Salem (Gen 14:18; this Salem is evidently to be identified with Zion [Jerusalem], for the two terms occur in synonymous parallelism in Ps 76:2). This meeting took place "in the Valley of Shaveh (that is, the King's Valley)," which in the Book of Samuel is said to have been close to Jerusalem (Gen 14:17; 2 Sam 18:18).

Later in his life Abraham took his son Isaac to one of the mountains in the "region of Moriah" to sacrifice him (Gen 22:2). The chronicler later identifies the mountain where

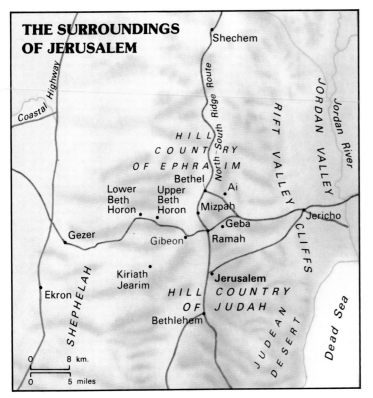

THE SURROUNDINGS OF JERUSALEM

Coastal Highway

Shechem

North-South Ridge Route

Jordan Ridge Route

JORDAN VALLEY

RIFT VALLEY

Jordan River

HILL COUNTRY OF EPHRAIM

Bethel

Ai

Lower Beth Horon

Upper Beth Horon

Mizpah

Geba

Jericho

Gezer

Gibeon

Ramah

CLIFFS

SHEPHELAH

Kiriath Jearim

Jerusalem

HILL COUNTRY OF JUDAH

Ekron

Bethlehem

JUDEAN DESERT

Dead Sea

0   8 km.

0   5 miles

Solomon erected the temple as "Mount Moriah" (2 Chron 3:1). Thus the biblical text places two events in the life of Abraham in close proximity to Jerusalem.

There is no mention in the Bible of Jerusalem during the Middle Bronze II period (2000–1550 B.C.)—unless Abraham should be placed in this period. However, Jerusalem is mentioned several times in the Execration Texts (see above p. 83). Among the cities, countries, and tribes mentioned, Urusalimum (= Jerusalem; meaning "foundation of the god Shalim" or "city of peace") is mentioned several times along with its various rulers. Archaeological excavations have confirmed the existence of Jerusalem during this period (ca. 2000 to 1750 B.C.), and although excavated building remains are few, 360 feet (110 m.) of a large wall, 20 feet (6 m.) thick, have been uncovered by Kenyon and Shiloh. This wall was apparently built about 1800 B.C. and it continued in use, with rebuilds, until the end of the Judean monarchy (586 B.C.).[3] The discovered portions lie about two-thirds of the way down the eastern slope of the eastern ridge. Evidently this site was high enough above the Kidron Valley and far enough away from the foot of the Mount of Olives to be defensible, yet it was far enough down the slope to provide maximum surface area for the city as well as easy access to the Gihon Spring. In spite of the large portions of the wall that have been uncovered, the exact location of the remaining sections on the south, west, and north is quite conjectural. Pottery finds, or the lack thereof, make it evident, however, that the walled city was confined to the southern

portion of the eastern ridge; it covered an area of approximately 15 acres (6 ha.) and housed 2,000–2,400 people.[4] Basically the city remained this size until it began to expand northward during the days of David and Solomon.

Around 1400 B.C. the Israelites began their conquest of the land of Canaan. After their initial thrust into the hill country and the capture and destruction of Ai, the Gibeonites made a nonaggression, mutual-defense treaty with Israel (see above p. 94). When the king of Jerusalem, Adoni Zedek, heard of this, he realized that his major line of communication with the coast, and hence to Egypt, was in jeopardy. To counter this threat he assembled a coalition of four other Amorite kings and attacked Gibeon (see map p. 94). In compliance with the treaty, Joshua and the Israelites came to the aid of the Gibeonites, and in the ensuing battle the king of Jerusalem was killed. The text does not indicate, however, that Jerusalem itself was captured at this time, although evidently shortly thereafter the tribe of Judah attacked and burned the city (Judges 1:8). But it does not seem that Judah settled in the city, for Jerusalem is mentioned in six of the el-Amarna letters (see above pp. 105–6), and the correspondence clearly indicates the non-Israelite character of the city during the reigns of the Egyptian pharaohs Amenhotep III and Akhenaton (ca. 1400–1350 B.C.). In fact, reference is made to the ruler of Jerusalem, Abdi-Heba, a name that does not correspond to the Adoni Zedek mentioned in the Bible.

At some point during the period of the Judges (ca. 1400–1050 B.C.), probably earlier rather than later, Jerusalem came

View of the City of David (bounded by roads on east and west) from south looking north; Temple Mount to the north.

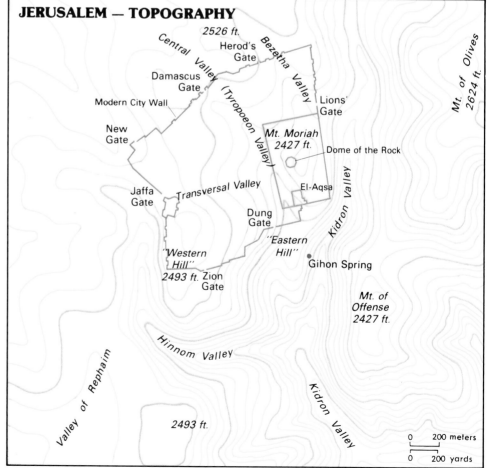

JERUSALEM — TOPOGRAPHY

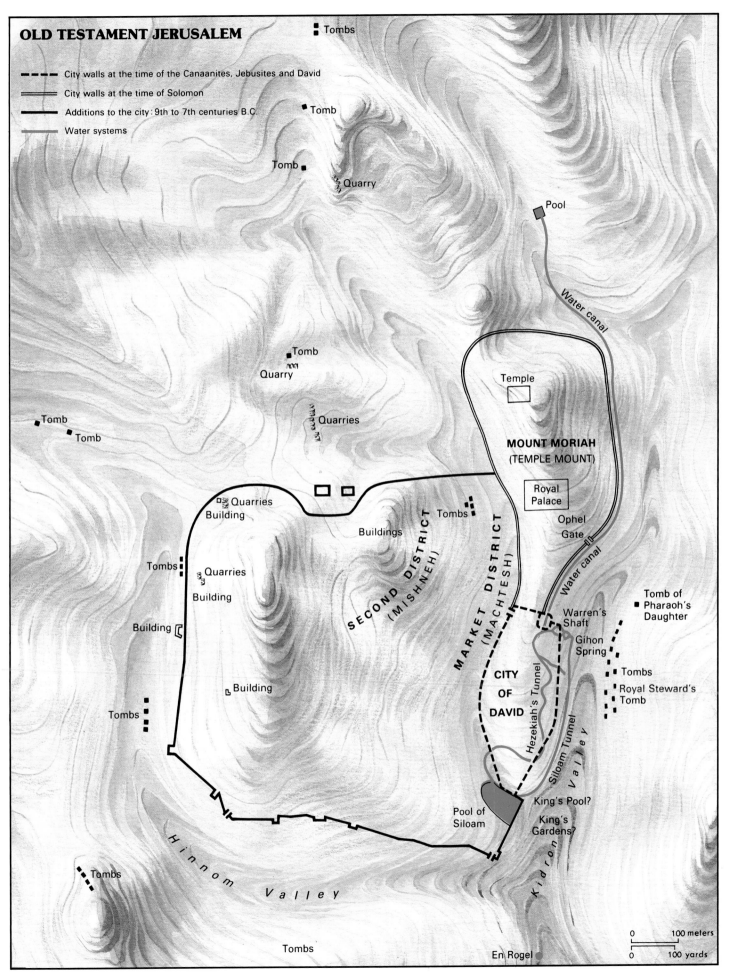

OLD TESTAMENT JERUSALEM

- ▪▪ **Tombs**
- - - - City walls at the time of the Canaanites, Jebusites and David
- ═══ City walls at the time of Solomon
- ▬▬▬ Additions to the city : 9th to 7th centuries B.C.
- ─── Water systems

Tomb

Tomb

Quarry

Pool

Water canal

Tomb

Quarry

Temple

Quarries

Tomb
Tomb

**MOUNT MORIAH
(TEMPLE MOUNT)**

Quarries
Building

Buildings

Tombs

Royal
Palace

Ophel
Gate

Water canal

Tombs

Quarries

Building

**SECOND DISTRICT
(MISHNEH)**

**MARKET DISTRICT
(MACHTESH)**

Warren's
Shaft

Gihon
Spring

Tomb of
Pharaoh's
Daughter

Building

**CITY
OF
DAVID**

Tombs

Royal Steward's
Tomb

Building

Tombs

King's Pool?

Pool of
Siloam

King's
Gardens?

H i n n o m

V a l l e y

K i d r o n   V a l l e y

Tombs

En Rogel

0   100 meters
0   100 yards

191

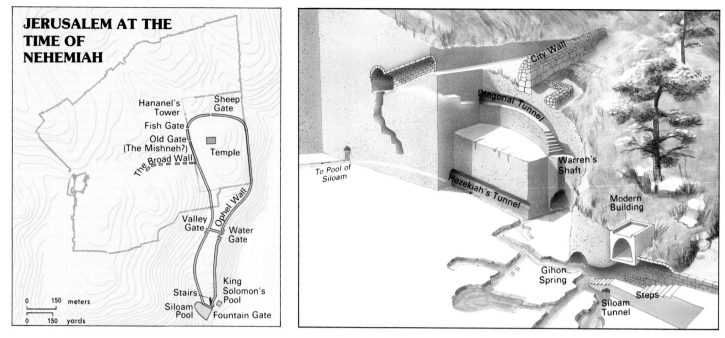

Ancient water systems of Jerusalem, near the Gihon Spring.

under the control of the people called Jebusites and was named Jebus. This status of Jerusalem is reflected in the story of the Levite and his concubine (Judges 19–21) where it is called "Jebus . . . this city of the Jebusites . . . an alien city" (19:11–12). In addition, in the description of the boundaries of the tribes of Judah and Benjamin, which date from this period, Jebus is mentioned as a point on the border, and it is specifically noted that it was located within the tribal allotment of Benjamin, not Judah (Josh 15:8; 18:16; but compare 15:63).

But it was the Judahite David who, after being installed as king over the northern tribes as well as over Judah, captured the city in his seventh year (ca. 1003 B.C.) and made it his capital. In the description of the conquest of the city it is noted that Joab was instrumental in its capture (1 Chron 11:6) and that in some way his use/capture/control of the *sinnor* (NIV "water shaft," 2 Sam 5:8) was a crucial aspect of the assault. Although a number of suggestions have been made regarding the nature of the *sinnor,* it seems best to associate it with the "Jebusite" water system discovered by Charles Warren in 1867 and cleared by Y. Shiloh in 1980.[5] The purpose of this system was to enable the residents of the city to have access to the waters of the Gihon Spring, which lay outside of the city wall, during times of siege. To do this, a diagonal tunnel, 128 feet (39 m.) long was cut in the rock. At the end of the tunnel a vertical shaft, 36 feet (11 m.) deep, was carved out. The foot of this shaft was connected to the Gihon Spring by a horizontal tunnel 66 feet (20 m.) long, so that water from the spring could flow to the foot of the shaft. Thus the inhabitants of the city could obtain water without ever having to go outside the city wall, by lowering their buckets down the vertical shaft. If the *sinnor* is a reference to the vertical shaft, then the biblical reference could imply that Joab and his men climbed up the shaft and in turn surprised the Jebusite garrison. If the *sinnor* refers to the horizontal tunnel, then possibly Joab was able to divert the waters of the Gihon so that the Jebusites were denied access

to their water supply and eventually had to capitulate to Joab's forces.[6]

With the capture of Jerusalem David accomplished several important goals. First, he removed a foreign enclave from a border area and thus removed a potentially divisive threat to the Israelite tribes. Second, because of Jerusalem's neutral location—not in the heartland of Judah, like Hebron, and not in the northern part of Israel—it was a capital acceptable to both David's own tribe of Judah as well as to the tribes of the north who had recently acknowledged him as king. By capturing Jerusalem himself, it became his and his descendants' personal property that could not be claimed by his own or any other tribe—it became the royal seat of the Davidic dynasty. In addition, David brought the ark of the covenant from Kiriath Jearim to Jerusalem, thus establishing it as the major worship center for all the Israelite tribes (2 Sam 6:1–23; 1 Chron 13:1–14).

The city that David captured was small—approximately 15 acres (6 ha.)—in size, with a population of 2,000–2,400. He evidently took up residence in the old Jebusite fortress called Zion, and from that point on, it, as well as the city as a whole, could be called the "City of David" (e.g., 2 Sam 5:7). Part of the foundation of this fortress may be the semicircular stepped structure, along with the Late Bronze Age terraces, which Shiloh has discovered on the upper portion of the eastern slope of the eastern ridge.[7] David also engaged in building projects in the city, including the construction of his own palace (2 Sam 5:11). Toward the end of his reign David purchased the threshing floor of Araunah the Jebusite, a site north of and higher than the ancient city core; this is the place where Solomon eventually built the temple (2 Sam 24:18–25; 1 Chron 21:18–26).

Soon after Solomon's accession to the throne, David died and was buried in the City of David (1 Kings 2:10). Evidently a royal cemetery was established where many of his descendants, up through Hezekiah (d. 686 B.C.), were buried. The search for the Tombs of the Kings of Judah

Tomb on the grounds of the Ecole Biblique in Jerusalem; from the 8th or 7th century B.C. Students peer into a burial repository below an empty burial bench.

within the City of David has been long and futile. The rock-hewn cavities excavated by R. Weill had been so quarried away that it is impossible to state with assurance that they were in fact tombs, let alone tombs that date to the time of David. The "tombs" discovered by B. Mazar are from a period later than David's, are not "in the City of David," and do not exhibit any of the fine decorative elements that one would expect in a royal tomb.[8] Some of the tombs surveyed east of the City of David, in the modern village of Silwan, give some evidence of having been the burial site for members of the upper classes of Jerusalem (e.g., a tomb of a "Royal Steward" was discovered), but they seem to date to the eighth century B.C.[9] North of Jerusalem, on the grounds of the Ecole Biblique, truly magnificent tombs of the Iron Age have been discovered, but they too are not "*in* the City of David."[10] Thus, to date, no sure claim for the tomb of David has come to light.

In the fourth year of his reign (966 B.C.) Solomon began building the temple, a task that took seven years. The building itself was composed of two rooms, a holy place in which the ten candelabra, the table for the bread of the Presence, and the incense altar were placed. The most sacred area was called the Holy of Holies, and in it the ark of the covenant was kept. The building faced east and was only 90 feet (31.2 m) long, 30 feet (10.4 m.) wide, and 45 feet (15.6 m.) high. The whole building was surrounded by courtyards in which were located the sacrificial altar, lavers, etc. The exact location of the temple is not known, although an old tradition places it in the immediate vicinity of the existing Moslem shrine called the Dome of the Rock. Given this location, it is debated whether the sacrificial altar or the Holy of Holies was located on top of the rock that is covered by the Moslem structure. However, others have suggested that the temple was located either south or north of the Dome area. In recent years, A. S. Kaufman has strongly argued that it was located to the north, that the Dome of the Spirits was the site of the Holy of Holies, and that some traces of rock carvings in the area are in fact remnants of the Solomonic temple.[11]

To the south of the temple, but north of the ancient core of Jerusalem, possibly in the vicinity of the present-day El Aqsa mosque, Solomon built his palace and the Palace of the Forest of Lebanon (1 Kings 7:1–12). Both of these structures have been compared by David Ussishkin to similar structures found in Anatolia and northern Syria.[12] The Palace of the Forest of Lebanon was probably a large basilica-type structure that may have served as a ceremonial armory. The palace itself was probably of the *bit-hilanni* style, and thus it would have included the ceremonial colonnaded portico, the throne hall or the Hall of Justice, and then, around the great courtyard, Solomon's quarters, a hall for pharaoh's daughter, and service areas.

In all probability, other administrative and military buildings were located nearby. It is possible that this royal acropolis, built at least in part on earth-and-stone fill north of the City of David but south of the temple complex, at the narrow neck of the ridge that connected the two areas, was in early times called the Millo (NIV "supporting terraces"; 1 Kings 9:15, 24; 11:27) but later came to be known as the Ophel (the acropolis).[13] Evidently Solomon strengthened the wall of Jerusalem and included the Millo/Ophel, as well as the temple area, within the confines of the wall. Thus the walled city must have expanded in size from 15 acres (6 ha.) to approximately 37 acres (15 ha.). Since the newly enclosed areas were not densely populated, Solomonic Jerusalem may have had a population of 4,500 to 5,000 people.

Among the increased population were at least some of the foreign wives whom Solomon married. It was for them that Solomon built a number of pagan shrines "on a hill east of Jerusalem" (1 Kings 11:7–8)—probably on the southern portion of the Mount of Olives. The location of these shrines was such that they towered over both the City of David and the temple of the true and living God.

With the secession of the north from the south after Solomon's death (930 B.C.), Solomon's successors ruled over a much smaller territory consisting of Judah and a portion of Benjamin. Jerusalem remained the seat of the government for the Davidic dynasty, and the Solomonic temple continued to be the focal point for Yahwistic worship.

During the period of the Divided Monarchy (930–722 B.C.), Jerusalem was attacked a number of times: once by the Egyptian pharaoh Shishak during the reign of Rehoboam (925 B.C.; 1 Kings 14:22–28; 2 Chron 12:2–4; see p. 124 and map p. 125) and once by Hazael of Aram Damascus, during the reign of Joash (ca. 813 B.C.; 2 Kings 12:17–18; 2 Chron 24:17–24). But in each instance, lavish gifts, taken from the temple treasury, bought off the aggressors. In the days of Amaziah of Judah, however, Joash of Israel attacked the city and "broke down the wall of Jerusalem from the Ephraim Gate to the Corner Gate—a section about six hundred feet long" (ca. 790 B.C.; 2 Chron 25:23). Although in this passage and in other places several gates of the city are mentioned, it is difficult to pinpoint their location in the city walls, save perhaps that the "Valley Gate" may be the massive gate discovered by Crowfoot and Fitzgerald (1927–28).[14]

Although the biblical text does not refer to any major expansion of Jerusalem during the period of the Divided Monarchy, some building activity is mentioned. We are told that Joash (835–798 B.C.) repaired the temple, probably in response to pagan Athaliah's alterations of the structure, but details are lacking (2 Kings 12:4–16; 2 Chron 24:4–14). We are also told that during the eighth century B.C. "Uzziah built towers in Jerusalem at the Corner Gate, at the Valley Gate and at the angle of the wall . . ." (2 Chron 26:9) as he strengthened the defenses of the city—possibly in response to the growing Assyrian threat in the person of Tiglath-Pileser III. It seems very probable that during Uzziah's reign (792–740 B.C.) and during the reign of his successors Jerusalem expanded westward so as to include the southern portion of the western ridge. The large increase in the size of Jerusalem at this time was probably due to the fact that settlers from the Northern Kingdom moved south so as to avoid the Assyrian onslaught; they may have thought that Jerusalem would never be taken by a foreign power because the temple of Yahweh was there, and that Yahweh would never allow such an indignity to be perpetrated.

Soon after the fall of the Northern Kingdom in 722 B.C., Hezekiah revolted against his Assyrian overlords (see above p. 135) and he needed to make defensive preparations for all Jerusalem. Evidently it was during his reign that the suburb that had developed on the southern portion of the western ridge was enclosed by a new wall. In his excavations in the modern Jewish Quarter of the Old City of Jerusalem, Professor N. Avigad discovered a 210-foot (65-m.) segment of this massive wall that was 23 feet (7 m.) thick, and in places is preserved to a height of 10 feet (3 m.).[15] Subsequently, additional fragments of this wall have been found in the citadel at the Joppa Gate. Although certainty is not possible, it seems that in Hezekiah's day the whole southern portion of the western ridge was included within the city wall so that the total area of the walled city had swelled to 150 acres (61 ha.) and boasted a population of about 25,000.[16]

Since the major water supply of the city, the Gihon Spring, was at some distance from the newly enclosed suburb and thus was exposed to enemy attack, Hezekiah devised a plan to divert the water to a spot inside the city walls, closer to the western hill. He did this by digging an underground tunnel that followed a serpentine path to a point in the Central Valley which, although was outside of the old city wall of the City of David, was inside the newly constructed city wall. This diversion of the spring water is mentioned not only in the Bible (2 Kings 20:20; 2 Chron 32:30), but also in a Hebrew inscription that was discovered at the southern end of the 1,750-foot (533-m.) tunnel.

In 701 B.C. Sennacherib the Assyrian attacked (see above pp. 135–36). Although he sent some of his army and commanders to Jerusalem to demand its surrender—Sennacherib boasted that he had shut Hezekiah up in Jerusalem like a bird in a cage—he had to retreat when, according to the biblical text, a large portion of his army was destroyed through divine intervention.

The eighth century witnessed unprecedented growth in Jerusalem. The city expanded in size from 37 acres to about 150 acres (from 15 to 61 ha.). Evidence that the city was so large comes not only from the portions of the city wall that have been discovered but also from noting the location of the cemeteries of the city, which were of course outside the city limits. Iron Age tombs from this period have been discovered on the lower slopes of the Mount of Olives to the east, on the bank of the Hinnom Valley to the south and west, and scattered to the north of Jerusalem. Jerusalem remained basically this size until its destruction in 586 B.C.

During the eighth and seventh centuries B.C. there were both good and bad rulers in Jerusalem. On the negative side were Ahaz and Manasseh, both of whom burned (sacrificed) children in the Valley of Ben Hinnom (2 Chron 28:3; 33:6; cf. 2 Kings 23:10). It was during Ahaz's reign that at least a portion of the temple area was remodeled and a new altar, based upon a pagan pattern from Damascus, was built to replace the old one (2 Kings 16:10–18). However, during this period there were also two godly kings, Hezekiah and Josiah, who worked to undo the abominations of their predecessors by taking steps to cleanse and refurbish the temple. It was during such a rebuilding, in the days of Josiah (ca. 622 B.C.), that the Book of the Law was discovered and in obedience to its commands additional reforms were instituted (2 Kings 22; 2 Chron 34).

But because of the continuing sins of the people and their leaders, God's judgment fell on Jerusalem in 605, in 597, and climactically in 586 B.C.—the year when the Babylonian king Nebuchadnezzar destroyed both the city and the temple. In excavations in the city of David, Shiloh has found considerable remains of the buildings that were destroyed in this conflagration. In one four-unit house an ostracon mentioning a certain Ahiel was found. In another, extensive burning was evident.[17] And in a third, partially excavated, building, fifty-one bullae (clay lumps used to seal the strings that bound folded papyrus documents) were found. Among the eighty-two legible Hebrew names is "Gemaryahu, the son of Shaphan," a scribe in the court of the Judean king Jehoiakim (cf. Jer 36:9–11). Unfortunately, the papyrus documents to which the bullae were attached have perished, but evidently some type of public archive was located here.[18]

Although the temple and major buildings of Jerusalem were destroyed by the Babylonian army, there are indications that some Jews remained in or near Jerusalem.[19] Almost fifty years after the destruction of the city, a large scale return to Jerusalem began in response to the decree issued by Cyrus in the first year of his reign (539 B.C.). Led by Sheshbazzar, 49,897 people returned to Jerusalem from Babylon and rebuilt the temple altar and reinstituted sacrificial worship. It was not until the days of the Persian monarch Darius, however, that Jews, under the leadership of Zerubbabel, were able to actually rebuild the temple (520–516 B.C.; Ezra 6). Although no certain remains of this temple have been found, the Bible indicates that it was a much more modest structure than its Solomonic predecessor (Ezra 3:12).[20]

The second return from Babylon was led by Ezra the scribe (458 B.C.) and was noted for its spiritual accomplishments. There may have been an attempt to rebuild the city wall at this time (Ezra 4:12), but the actual rebuilding of the walls had to wait another thirteen years until the days of Nehemiah (445 B.C.). In the Book of Nehemiah, portions of three chapters specifically relate to the character of Jerusalem at that time. Chapter 2 describes Nehemiah's night journey around the walls; chapter 3 describes the actual rebuilding of the walls, towers, and gates; and chapter 12 describes the dedication processions around the walls. It appears that Nehemiah's city was considerably smaller than

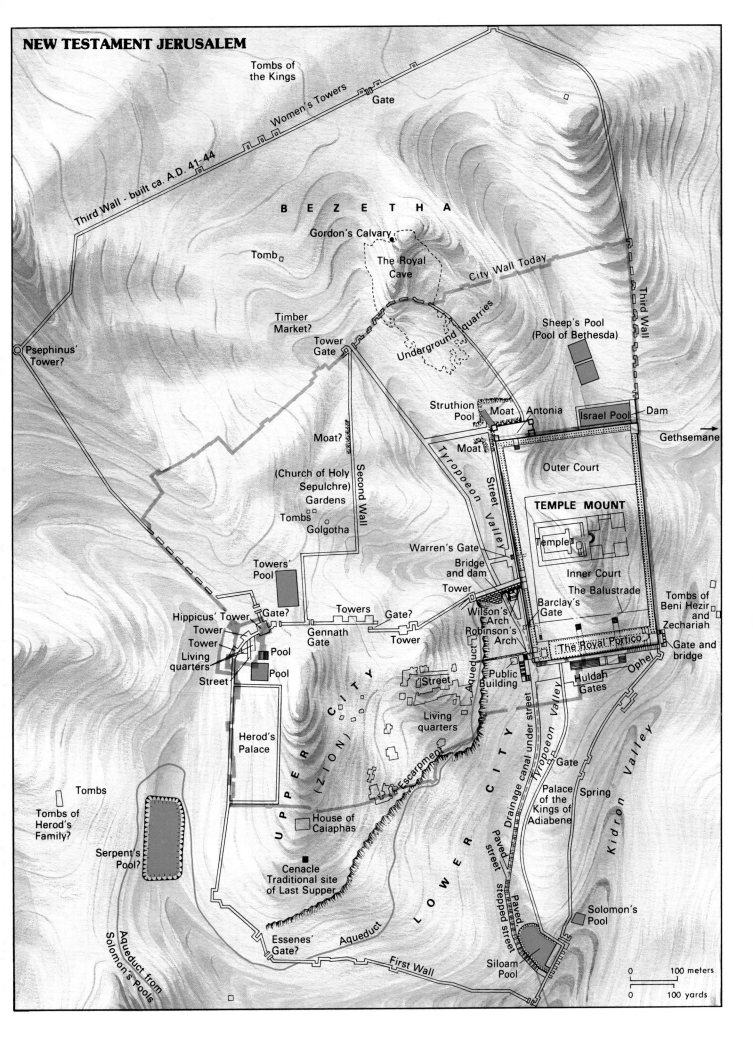

NEW TESTAMENT JERUSALEM

Tombs of
the Kings

Women's Towers   Gate

Third Wall – built ca. A.D. 41-44

B E Z E T H A

Gordon's Calvary

Tomb

The Royal
Cave

City Wall Today

Third Wall

Psephinus'
Tower?

Timber
Market?

Tower
Gate

Underground quarries

Sheep's Pool
(Pool of Bethesda)

Struthion
Pool   Moat   Antonia

Israel Pool   Dam

Moat?

Moat

Gethsemane

Tyropoeon

Outer Court

(Church of Holy
Sepulchre)
Gardens

Second Wall

Street

Valley

TEMPLE MOUNT

Tombs

Golgotha

Temple

Towers'
Pool

Warren's Gate

Bridge
and dam

Inner Court

The Balustrade

Tombs of
Beni Hezir
and
Zechariah

Tower

Hippicus' Tower

Tower

Tower

Living
quarters

Street

Gate?

Towers

Gennath
Gate

Gate?

Tower

Pool

Pool

Wilson's
Arch

Robinson's
Arch

Barclay's
Gate

The Royal Portico

Gate and
bridge

U
P
P
E
R

C
I
T
Y

Street

Aqueduct

Public
Building

Huldah
Gates

Ophel

Living
quarters

L
O
W
E
R

C
I
T
Y

Drainage canal under street

Tyropoeon

Valley

Gate

Tombs

Herod's
Palace

House of
Caiaphas

Escarpment

Palace
of the
Kings of
Adiabene

Spring

Kidron

Valley

Tombs of
Herod's
Family?

Serpent's
Pool?

Cenacle
Traditional site
of Last Supper

Paved

stepped street

Paved

street

Solomon's
Pool

Essenes'
Gate?

Aqueduct

First Wall

Siloam
Pool

Aqueduct from Solomon's Pools

0   100 meters

0   100 yards

the one that had been destroyed by the Babylonians. In fact, it was basically confined to the eastern ridge and was of Solomonic proportions. This is indicated by the fact that no structures or other artifacts from the Persian or early Hellenistic periods have been found in Avigad's extensive excavations on the western hill—a clear indication that it was not settled from 586 to ca. 200 B.C.[21] In addition, the fact that it took only fifty-two days to refortify the city also indicates that the long line of "Hezekiah's Wall" was not rebuilt at this time. Although the general location and/or geographical sequence of a good number of gates, towers, and buildings mentioned in the book of Nehemiah can be surmised, it is difficult to equate most of them with any known archaeological remains.

From the time of Nehemiah (445 B.C.) until the beginning of the second century B.C., not too much is known about Jerusalem. In 332 B.C. Alexander the Great conquered the Levant, but his so-called visit to Jerusalem is usually considered to be legendary. After his death in 323 B.C. the Ptolemies of Egypt gained control of Palestine and Judah, and it is generally assumed that under their benign rule a priestly aristocracy governed from Jerusalem. However, at the end of the third century B.C. there was considerable conflict in the area, and Jerusalem suffered at the hands of the Ptolemies. Early in the second century B.C. the Seleucid

king Antiochus III defeated the Ptolemies (198 B.C.), and the change in rule was welcomed by most of the Jewish population. With his support, repairs were made to the temple and a large pool—possibly the Pool of Bethesda—was constructed (Ecclus 50:1–3).

During the reign of Antiochus IV (175–164 B.C.), however, relations between the Jews and the Seleucids took a decided turn for the worse as Antiochus and his Jewish supporters pressed for a Hellenizing program among all of the Jews. The temple in Jerusalem was desecrated and a statute of Olympian Zeus was set up in its precincts (168 B.C.). In addition, other Greek structures were erected in Jerusalem including a gymnasium and a citadel. The citadel, called the Akra in Greek, was built on the eastern ridge just south of the temple area and was so tall that it towered over the temple area. Although Judas Maccabeus' forces were able to retake Jerusalem, to purify the temple (164 B.C.), and to reestablish sacrificial worship, the Seleucid garrison in the Akra remained a thorn in the side of the Jews until Judas's brother Simon (142–135 B.C.) captured and demolished it—even leveling the hill upon which it had stood (Josephus, *Antiq.* 13.6.7 [215]). To date, no remains of the Akra have been found, and because of its complete destruction and its probable location either under and/or near the southern portion of the present-day Moslem sacred area, it is not too

Artist's reconstruction of Herodian Temple complex, view from the southwest looking northeast.

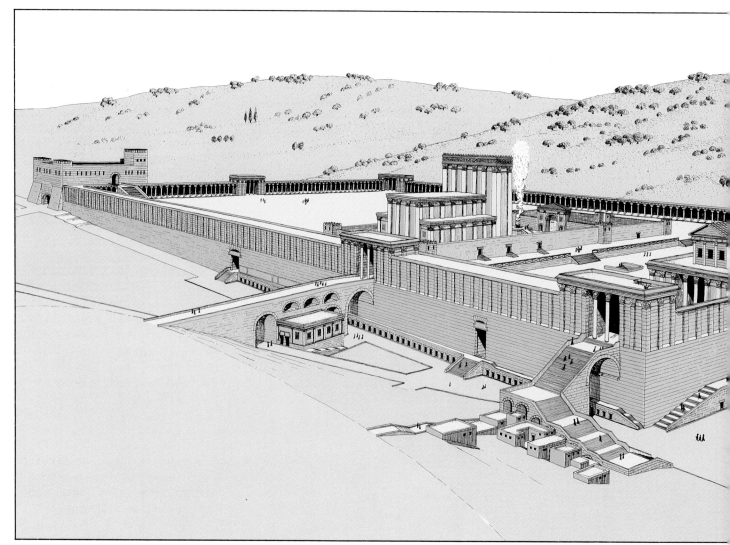

likely that any will be found in the future.[22]

Simon also completed the building of the walls of Jerusalem, a project that his brother Jonathan had begun earlier (1 Macc 10:10–11; 13:10). Although specific literary details regarding the exact line of the walls built by the Hasmoneans is not available, Josephus implies, and archaeological excavations confirm, that they were built along the line of Josephus' "First Wall" (see map p. 195). Indeed, not only has Avigad found significant remnants of the Hasmonean wall, which basically followed the east-west line of "Hezekiah's Wall"—thereby fortifying the northern boundary of the western ridge—but additional portions of the Hasmonean wall have been discovered in the present-day citadel, under the north-south wall to the south of the citadel, and also on the upper slope of the southern portion of the western ridge overlooking the Valley of Hinnom.[23] Thus the whole southern portion of the western ridge was once again inside the city after a gap of almost four hundred years. Avigad has also found pottery and some remains of modest buildings in his excavations in the Jewish quarter, thus confirming that renewed settlement on the western hill began during the Hasmonean period.[24]

From literary sources it is evident that the Hasmoneans built a palace on the eastern slope of the western ridge, overlooking the Temple Mount (Josephus, *Antiq.* 20.8.11

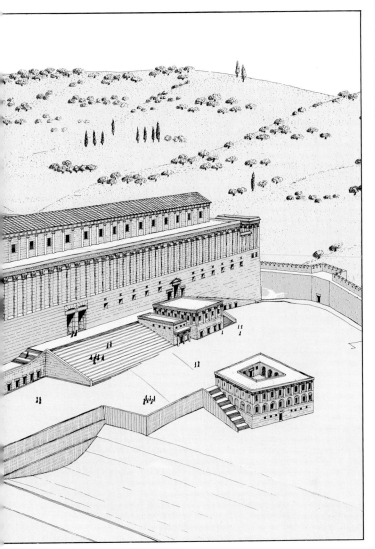

[189–90]), as well as a bridge that spanned the Central Valley and connected the palace with the temple precincts. This bridge was evidently a predecessor of what today is known as "Wilson's Arch." The only large-scale monuments from the Hellenistic period that are preserved in Jerusalem are several prominent mausoleums located in the Kidron Valley at the foot of the Mount of Olives: the Tombs of Beni Hazir and Zechariah. It is interesting to note that stylistically these tombs combine Hellenistic, Egyptian, and local characteristics, thus illustrating in monumental form the various cultural forces that influenced Jewish life during this period.

Jerusalem experienced additional growth and aggrandizement during the long and prosperous reign of Alexander Jannaeus (103–76 B.C.), but specifics are generally lacking in the historical sources. At the end of the Hellenistic age the Hasmonean brothers Aristobulus and Hyrcanus II vied with each other for the high priesthood and control of the country. In the end Pompey intervened and marched on Jerusalem (see above, p. 159). After setting up his camps to the southwest and northwest of the city, the upper city (the quarters on the western ridge) was handed over to him by the followers of Hyrcanus. However, the supporters of Aristobulus put up a defense on the eastern ridge. In response, Pompey erected a siege dike around the ridge and, after building assault ramps, attacked the temple area from the west, across the ruins of the bridge that had spanned the Central Valley, and also from the north, attacking the "Baris" fortress. Upon capturing the temple area he entered the Holy of Holies, but he soon allowed the resumption of sacrificial worship. The arrival of Pompey marked the beginning of the long period of control of Jerusalem by Rome and its Byzantine successor, which would last until the time of the Persian and Arab conquests (A.D. 614 and 639), save for brief periods during the first and second Jewish revolts.

At the beginning of the period of Roman rule Jerusalem experienced great expansion, construction, and beautification under the leadership of the Roman client king Herod the Great (37–4 B.C.). Pride of place must certainly go to Herod's refurbishing of the temple and the Temple Mount. Although he was limited in what he could do to the temple building itself—the divine word and tradition dictated its basic dimensions—he spent over a year and a half beautifying and refurbishing the structure. He did not face similar restrictions when it came to the courts that surrounded the temple, and so he expended great sums on expanding these. He is said to have doubled the size of the platform area so that it reached its present size of 40 acres (16.2 ha.). Although no remnants of Herod's temple have been found that can be identified as such with certainty,[25] the huge platform on which its courts were built has survived. The area is now occupied by Moslem structures and is called the Haram esh-Sharif—the Noble Sanctuary. In constructing this large platform, Herod made use of some existing walls, especially on the east, but he expanded the platform to the north, west, and south. Indeed, the western expansion was such that part of the Central Valley was filled in and covered over, and today some twenty-six courses of Herodian stones, founded upon bedrock, are still standing. These stones are cut so precisely that no mortar was used in the construction of the wall. A typical stone weighs 2 to 10 tons (1.8 to 9 metric tons), while the largest of the known stones measures 46 x 10 x 10 feet (14 x 3 x 3 m.) and weighs 415 tons (376 metric tons)! Almost all the stones, except the very low foundation courses that were covered by dirt, have a very flat and finely chiseled boss, and around the edges is a finely dressed narrow margin (see photo on p. 158).

Along the upper perimeter of the huge temple platform Herod built or refurbished a number of covered colonnades. The most famous of these was the southern one, the "Royal Colonnade." It was composed of 162 columns arranged in four rows, forming a long basilica-shaped building. The columns themselves were 27 feet (8 m.) high and 4.6 feet (1.4 m.) in diameter and were crowned with Corinthian capitals. Although nothing of the colonnade remains today, the appearance of its outer wall can be surmised from the pilaster-recessed design that is evident in the Herodian structure that encloses the Tomb of the Patriarchs in Hebron.

To the south of the Temple Mount, Benjamin Mazar has discovered large portions of the formal staircase that led up to the Huldah Gates.[26] The foundations of the gates are still visible in the southern wall of the Haram enclosure (the so-called double and triple gates). Although they are now closed, the underground passages that lead up to the top of the mount inside the wall are still preserved. In his excava-tions along the southern portion of the western enclosure wall, Mazar has found portions of the north-south street, a city drain, and most interestingly, the piers that supported a platform and staircase that led south, from a gate in the southern section of the western wall of the Temple Mount into the Central Valley.[27] Mazar also found a large dressed stone inscribed in Hebrew with the words "For the place of the trumpet blowing."[28] Evidently, this stone had fallen from its position on the southwest pinnacle of the Temple Mount where it had marked the spot where the priest stood to blow the trumpet to announce to the citizens of Jerusalem the beginning of the Sabbath, New Moon, New Year, etc.

It took Herod almost ten years to complete the major construction on the Temple Mount, but crews were still working on the project during Jesus' lifetime (John 2:20, ca. A.D. 28) and even during the rule of the procurator Albinus (A.D. 62–64; Josephus *Antiq.* 20.9.7 [219]) on the eve of the first Jewish Revolt, which began in A.D. 66. To the northwest of the temple Herod rebuilt the "Baris" fortress and named it the Antonia, after his friend Mark Antony. This fortress, situated on a rocky scarp, towered over the temple area and housed a garrison whose duty it was to monitor and control the crowds that gathered in the temple precincts.

On the western ridge Herod built a magnificent palace for

Part of the aqueduct system (the "syphon") that brought water to Jerusalem from the springs to the south; date uncertain.

himself on a site located in the present-day Armenian Quarter of the Old City. Only portions of its substructure have been preserved.[29] To the north of his palace he built a massive defensive complex consisting of three towers named Hippicus (after a friend), Phasael (after his brother), and Mariamne (after his beloved wife, whom he had executed). The massive base of one of these towers (probably Hippicus or Phasael) still remains in the present-day citadel complex just southeast of the Jaffa Gate. In addition, Herod built a second wall that began near these towers—by the Gennath Gate—and ran to the Antonia fortress, enclosing the northern "Second Quarter" of the city (Josephus, *War* 5.4.2 [146]). The exact line of this wall is not known, but it probably ran through the Muristan Quarter of the Old City to the area of the present-day Damascus Gate, and thus it enclosed a portion of the northern reaches of the Central Valley—called the Tyropoeon Valley by Josephus. Of the location of other Herodian structures such as the hippodrome, stadium, theater, and amphitheater little is known. However, Avigad's recent excavations in the Jewish quarter on the eastern slope of the western ridge have yielded significant evidence regarding life in this area during the Herodian period.[30] Large houses have been excavated that contained courtyards, ritual baths, fresco-covered walls, fine pottery, stoneware dishes, huge stone pots, carved stone tables, mosaic floors, etc. The nature of the archaeological finds—among them the discovery of a weight with the name of a priestly family, Kathros—and data from literary sources make it evident that priestly and other aristocratic families lived in this area.

The Jerusalem that Jesus knew during his ministry (ca. A.D. 26–30) was basically the same as Herodian Jerusalem described above.[31] On one of his visits to the city, he healed a thirty-eight-year-old paralyzed invalid at the Pool of Bethesda, north of the Temple Mount near the Sheep Gate (John 5:1–14). Portions of a double pool that could have been surrounded by "five covered colonnades"—one on each side and one in the middle separating the two pools—have been discovered just north of the Temple Mount. On another occasion Jesus healed a blind man whom he sent to the Pool of Siloam to wash (John 10).

Most of the information about Jesus in Jerusalem comes from the period of the last week of his earthly ministry. Jesus evidently spent the nights of this last week with his friends in Bethany, 1.5 miles (2.5 km.) from Jerusalem on the east side of the Mount of Olives, and he made his Triumphal Entry into Jerusalem on a donkey that he had mounted in the Bethphage area. After crossing the Mount of Olives he

View from the Mount of Olives looking west over Jerusalem.

descended into the Kidron Valley to shouts of "Hosanna." Although he may have entered the temple complex from the north or east, as has traditionally been supposed, it is more probable that he approached it from the south, via the monumental staircase that led up to the Huldah Gates. On Monday he again entered the temple area, and this time he drove out the money changers who were possibly operating in the Royal Colonnade along the southern perimeter of the Court of the Gentiles. On Tuesday Jesus once again entered the temple complex and evidently later in the day spent time teaching his disciples on the Mount of Olives.

After resting in Bethany on Wednesday, Jesus sent several of his followers into the city to secure a room and prepare a meal so that he could celebrate the Passover with his disciples. In spite of the fact that the structure on the traditional site of the Last Supper (the Cenacle) dates from the Crusader period (at least 1,100 years after the event), it is probable that the site itself, located on the southern portion of the western ridge in a well-to-do, possibly Essene, section of town, is close to the spot where the meal took place. After the meal, Jesus and his disciples went down to the Garden of Gethsemane, at the western foot of the Mount of Olives, near the Kidron Valley. There, after praying for a while, he was captured and taken prisoner. That night he appeared before Caiaphas the high priest, before Pilate the procurator, and before Herod Antipas, the ruler of Galilee, who was in Jerusalem for the festival. The exact site of each of these interrogations is not known, but it is probable that the residence of Caiaphas was somewhere on the southern portion of the western ridge, and it is possible that Herod Antipas was staying in the old Hasmonean palace on the eastern slope of the western ridge, overlooking the temple. Although Jesus may have appeared before Pilate at the Antonia Fortress, as has traditionally been maintained, it is more probable that as ruler of the country Pilate was residing in Herod's palace and that Jesus was interrogated, humiliated, and condemned there.

According to the gospel accounts, Jesus was led outside the city, crucified, and buried in a nearby tomb belonging to Joseph of Arimathea. In Jerusalem today there are two localities that lay claim to being the place of these events. The first of these is Gordon's Calvary, to the north of the present-day Damascus Gate, with the nearby Garden Tomb. Although this site lies outside the ancient as well as the present-day city wall and is quite amenable to certain types of piety, there is no compelling reason to think that this is either Calvary and/or the tomb—in fact, the tomb may date back to the Iron Age (1000–586 B.C.), and thus could not have been a tomb "in which no one had yet been laid" (Luke 23:53).[32]

More compelling, although still not certain, is the suggestion that the Church of the Holy Sepulchre marks the spot of these dramatic events. It is probable that this site was outside the walled city of Jesus' day and was in fact a burial ground. Very ancient Christian traditions, dating back to at least the days of Eusebius (fourth century A.D.), suggest that the church marks the more probable of the two sites. The New Testament records that after his resurrection Jesus appeared to his disciples for forty days and then, in the presence of his assembled disciples on the Mount of Olives, ascended into heaven.

During the early apostolic period (ca. A.D. 30–41) the church was centered in Jerusalem. A number of events are mentioned in connection with the activities of Peter, John, Stephen, and others as having taken place in Jerusalem, such as house meetings, appearances before the Sanhedrin, and imprisonments, but it is difficult if not impossible to pinpoint the exact location of these events. In the temple precincts a paralyzed man who was sitting at the "Beautiful Gate" (probably the gate that led into the court of women) was healed, and it is apparent that the early Christians often met in Solomon's Colonnade (Acts 3:11; 5:12)—probably the colonnade along the inner side of the eastern enclosure wall of the temple precinct.

Since the days of Herod the Great (37–4 B.C.) the city had been steadily expanding northward and finally, during the reign of Herod Agrippa I (A.D. 41–44), an attempt was made to enclose the northern quarter of the city (Bezetha). This wall ran northwest from the present-day Jaffa Gate to the Tower of Psephinus (probably in or near the present-day Russian Compound) and from there turned east to the Kidron Valley, at which point the wall turned south to join the northeastern corner of the Temple Mount (Josephus, War 5.4.2–3 [147–60]). However, Agrippa became fearful that the Romans might accuse him of rebellion, and he stopped work on the wall. Archaeologists have discovered long sections of the east-west portions of this wall north of the present-day Old City Wall.[33]

After the death of Agrippa I (A.D. 44) Roman procurators again ruled Jerusalem directly until the outbreak of the first Jewish revolt (A.D. 66–70). One of the immediate causes of the revolt was Emperor Caligula's attempt to have his statue erected in the temple in Jerusalem. The governor of Syria, Cestius Gallus, had some initial success in subduing the revolt in A.D. 66 but was not able to capture Jerusalem. The Jews were then able to gain control of the city and most of the remainder of the country. For the next three years the Romans, slowly but surely, subdued the rebels. In the spring of A.D. 70 the Fifth, Tenth, Twelfth, and Fourteenth legions, and their slave captives, about 80,000 men in all, advanced on Jerusalem. The Jews attempted to fortify the third, or northern, wall that Agrippa I had begun, but by the end of May the Romans had breached it. A few days later the second wall was also breached and a siege dike was set up around the remainder of the city. The suffering within the city was severe, and in late July the Antonia Fortress was attacked and captured. From there the Romans advanced into the temple precincts, and on the 9th of Ab (August 28) the temple was burned. By the end of September the lower city (the old City of David) and the upper city (on the southern portion of the western ridge) had been captured. Although Josephus' figures of 1,000,000 Jews dead and 97,000 captured are probably exaggerated, the figures do illustrate the magnitude of the defeat. Titus, the Roman general who later became emperor, ordered much of the city to be razed, save the three towers just north of the Herodian Palace. These he left standing as mute tribute to the greatness of the city that he had just captured.

The Disciplines of Historical Geography

Judeo-Christian beliefs are deeply rooted in space and time. Rather than elaborating an abstract system of theology, the Bible by and large presents history as a concrete form of theology: what God has done in history shows who he is and what he is like. Consequently, there has always been a keen interest in matters related to biblical history. Not only have people asked questions regarding what happened, why it happened, and who was involved, but they have also been interested in knowing where events took place and where and under what conditions people lived.

This interest in historical and geographical details is already evident in the biblical period. On occasion during that period, the transmitters of oral traditions, the authors and editors of texts, and the copyists of scrolls realized that some of their hearers or readers might not recognize the geographical references in a given historical account, and they therefore inserted the then-contemporary name of a place so that the historical setting of an event would be more intelligible to the hearers and readers. Thus the hearers and readers were informed that Bela (a name they were not familiar with) was the same as the city they knew as Zoar (Gen 14:2), that the Valley of Siddim was the same as the Salt Sea (14:3), En Mishpat as Kedesh (14:7), Kiriath Sepher as Debir (Josh 15:15), Kiriath Arba as Hebron (15:52), Kiriath Baal as Kiriath Jearim (15:60), Luz as Bethel (Judges 1:23), and so on.

Aramaic translation, 5th cent. B.C., of Behistun Inscription of Darius I, the Great, recounting his many city conquests.

Philology: Textual Studies

Although modern research on the subject of historical geography did not begin until the time of Napoleon's invasion of Egypt and part of the Levant in 1798–99, biblical geography has been a subject for study since at least the days of Eusebius (fourth century A.D.). Textual materials, both biblical and extrabiblical, have provided the main impetus as well as much of the raw data for the study of Bible geography. One of the main aims of biblical geographers has been to identify biblical place-names and other geographical references with existing cities, towns, villages, antiquity sites, regions, etc. With some of these identifications in hand, one can further attempt to define tribal and clan allotments, administrative districts, and boundaries between states. Furthermore, an understanding of the historical-geographical setting of an event can greatly aid in the overall understanding of the biblical narratives.

Two main sources of textual material are available to the biblical geographer. The first is, of course, the Bible itself, which, although it is by no means mainly a book about geography or history, does include much material of a historical-geographical nature. The second source of textual material is the ancient inscriptions that have been found in the Near East.

The Bible

In his comprehensive book *The Land of the Bible: A Historical Geography,* Yohanan Aharoni notes three classes of biblical documents of geographical interest: historical-geographical descriptions, territorial descriptions, and the records of military expeditions and conquests.[1] The first of these, the *historical-geographical descriptions,* appear to have been composed primarily for geographical purposes. Among them are the Table of Nations (Gen 10), the list of conquered Canaanite kings (Josh 12), and possibly the descriptions of "the land that remains" (Josh 13:1–6, Judges 3:1–4), as well as the wilderness itinerary of the Israelites (Num 33).

Of special interest to the historical geographer are the *territorial descriptions* scattered throughout the historical books of the Bible. These are of two types: boundary descriptions and town lists. In some instances the area belonging to a state or tribe is defined by means of a boundary description. Some of these boundary descriptions are very brief: only "terminal points" are given. Examples are the description of the land of Israel as stretching "from Dan [in the north] to Beersheba [in the south]" (e.g., 2 Sam 24:2) and the description of the Promised Land (Exod 23:31), which lists four "terminal points": "from the Red Sea [south(east)], to the Sea of the Philistines [= Mediterranean; northwest], and from the desert [southwest] to the River [= Euphrates: northeast]."

But in other cases the boundary descriptions are much more detailed, and a number of points along a border are mentioned sequentially—in a "dot-to-dot-to-dot" fashion. Examples of this technique include the description of the boundaries of the land of Canaan in Numbers 34:1–12 and several of the tribal boundary descriptions in Joshua, such as those of Judah (15:2–12), Benjamin (18:12–20), Ephraim (16:1–9), Manasseh (17:7–11), and Zebulun (19:10–16). To be sure, in some instances these descriptions appear to have been abbreviated, but others, such as the description of the border between Judah and Benjamin in the Jerusalem area (Josh 15:7–9; 18:15–17), remain quite detailed.

For the historical geographer, the "terminal point" descriptions are somewhat useful in determining the perceived boundaries of states and tribes, but they are quite general. The "sequential" boundary descriptions are often much more useful. They can be plotted on a map, and because the names usually follow a logical geographical sequence, the location of unknown places can be surmised. For example, the exact location of Ekron, a Philistine town, was disputed for many years, but its general location was known because the biblical text placed it on the western portion of the northern boundary of Judah—specifically, to the west of Beth Shemesh but to the east of Jabneel (Josh 15:10-11), two towns whose identifications were generally agreed upon.

In addition, territories were described by drawing up a list of the names of the towns assigned to a given tribe or district. Although the date and function of these town lists have been the subject of much dispute, we are certain that at least one of them, the list of twelve Solomonic districts in 1 Kings 4:7–19, was used for administrative purposes. Prominent among these rosters are the town lists of Judah (Josh 15:21–63; more than 100 towns are mentioned!), Simeon (Josh 19:2–8; 1 Chron 4:28–33; 17 towns), and Benjamin (Josh 18:21–28; 26 towns), as well as the lists of levitical towns (Josh 21; 1 Chron 6:54–80; about 48 towns), although there are many others.[2]

The town list of Judah is of special interest because it is so extensive and because it is divided into at least nine or ten districts (the Septuagint even includes an eleventh district, around Bethlehem, in Josh 15:59; see the NEB for a translation). Even though the date and original function of the town list of Judah in Joshua 15 has been the subject of debate, it has proved very useful in assisting to identify the location of disputed towns. For example, Debir, which some authorities located at Tell Beit Mirsim in the Shephelah, was really located in a southern hill country district (v. 49),[3] while Adullam, which some located in the Judean Hill Country, was actually located in the northern district of the "western foothills" (= Shephelah; v. 35). Thus a list like this can potentially help peg at least the general placement of biblical towns whose locations are in dispute.

The third type of biblical material, besides historical-geographical and territorial descriptions, are the *records of expeditions and conquests.* Thus the routes of military expeditions, such as those of Abijah (2 Chron 13:19), Ben-Hadad (1 Kings 15:20), and Tiglath-Pileser (2 Kings 15:29), among others, can be traced with some certainty. Given the reasonable assumptions that these expeditions followed a more or less sensible geographical progression and that the texts faithfully record these invasions, the identification of certain biblical towns can be confirmed, while in the case of unknown towns, at least their general location can be surmised. For example, although the exact location of Janoah is disputed, it is reasonable, on the basis of 2 Kings 15:29, to place it in the vicinity of Abel Beth Maacah, Kedesh, and Hazor.

Extrabiblical Texts

During the last one hundred years, numerous epigraphic finds have been made in Egypt, Mesopotamia, and Syria, and to a lesser extent in Palestine/Israel. By far the most substantial corpus of texts relevant to the historical geography of the Bible has come from Egypt. Major finds from the Middle Bronze II period (2000–1550 B.C.) include the Execration Texts (texts invoking a curse), with their listing of geographical, personal, and tribal names in the southern Levant, and the Story of Sinuhe, with its description of the land of Upper Retenu, which also includes incidental geographical and cultural references to the land of Canaan.[4]

From the Late Bronze Age (1550–1200 B.C.; the period of the Exodus, conquest, and settlement of the Israelites in Canaan) there is a wealth of information, including a description of the driving of the Hyksos from Egypt back into Canaan. From the 18th Egyptian dynasty, some of the campaigns of Thutmose III (1504–1450 B.C.), especially the first, are recorded in his annals and elsewhere in great detail. Copies of his great topographical list include at least 119 geographical names from the Levant. Also to be mentioned are the descriptions of the campaign of Amenhotep II (1540–1425 B.C.) into Canaan during the early years of his reign. In addition, from the reigns of Amenhotep III (1417–1379 B.C.) and Akhenaton (1379–1362 B.C.), there is the diplomatic archive, written in Akkadian, which was discovered at el-Amarna. It details Egyptian-Levantine relations as well as the internal struggles in the land of Canaan.

From the 19th Dynasty, the campaigns of Seti I (1318–1304 B.C.) and Ramses II (1304–1237 B.C.) are quite well known, and the stele of Merneptah (1236–1223 B.C.) even mentions "Israel" as being among other groups living in the southern Levant. These texts are supplemented by the Papyrus Anastasi I, which describes the geography of Canaan in some detail, as well as by the story of Wen-Amon and other texts. From later periods, only the account of Shishak's invasion of Israel (925 B.C.), with its listing of close to 150 settlements in Israel and the Negev, is of major importance.

Epigraphic finds from Mesopotamia make less of a contribution to the historical geography of the Bible than those from Egypt, although references to Hazor and Laish (= Dan) in the cuneiform tablets found at the Syrian site of Mari shed welcome light on the Middle Bronze II period. From the eighth, seventh, and sixth centuries B.C., the records of the expeditions of Assyrian and Babylonian kings (e.g., those of Tiglath-Pileser III, Sargon II, Sennacherib, Esarhaddon, Ashurbanipal, Nebuchadnezzar II) also supply a fair amount of relevant geographical detail regarding Israel and its neighbors. In addition, it is possible that the tablets discovered in northern Syria, at Tell Mardikh (ancient Ebla), will contribute to what until now has been an "epigraphic dark age" in our geographic understanding of Palestine, namely the third millennium B.C.

Epigraphic finds in Israel and Jordan have been scarce. A few cuneiform texts from the Late Bronze Age (1550–1200 B.C.) have been discovered at Tell el-Hesi, Beth Shemesh, Mount Tabor, Taanach, Hazor, and Aphek, but their contribution to the historical geography of the land has been minimal. From the Iron Age (1200–586 B.C.), the ostraca (pottery fragments with writing on them) discovered at Samaria shed welcome light on a portion of the tribal inheritance of Manasseh, an area the Bible does not treat in detail (Josh 17). The Moabite Stone provides information about the region east of the Dead Sea during the eighth century B.C. From Israel proper, the Arad ostraca contain a few geographical references, as do the ostraca discovered at Lachish. (Translations of many of these texts, as well as many of those from Egypt and Mesopotamia can be found in *Ancient Near Eastern Texts Relating to the Old Testament*.[5])

Finally, from the Hellenistic and early Roman periods, classical authors (e.g., Herodotus), papyri from Egypt (the Zenon papyri), the Septuagint, the books of the Apocrypha, the Dead Sea Scrolls, Josephus, as well as other epigraphic finds, all contribute to our historical geographical understanding of the intertestamental and New Testament periods (= Second Temple period).

One of the goals of textual studies in historical geography is to attempt to write as complete a history as possible of a given place or territory, based on all the available resources. The collection of all references to a given town or territory in the literary sources can be quite complex, for there may have been several towns that had the same name or a single town or territory may have had more than one name. But even if a similar name for a town is used in various languages, the researcher must deal with the problem of how a name was transcribed, since the phonetic and spelling systems of the various languages do not completely coincide. Thus a given place-name may occur in Hebrew, Egyptian, and Babylonian documents, but the name may not refer to the same place in all documents, while on occasion apparently different names may well refer to the same place.

A further complication is that some of the documents were written long after the date of the events they record. This means that a geographical name used in such a document or section of a document may be the name that was used at the time of the event or the name of the site that was used at the time of writing. For example, although Genesis records events said to have occurred in the days of Abraham, Isaac, and Jacob, certainly the book was written some time after the recorded events, and, as stated above, the writer in several instances took care to give the new name of a town along with the old one.

It is clear from the preceding that the body of primary textual material to be mastered by the serious student of historical geography of the Bible is considerable, and a working knowledge of Hebrew, Aramaic, Greek, Latin, Ugaritic, and of the various forms of Egyptian hieroglyphics, Assyrian, and Babylonian is desirable. This is obviously a daunting task, and cooperation between experts of the various languages and dialects is a necessity.

Toponymy: Study of Place Names

So far it has been noted that a study of the "primary" ancient sources, biblical and extrabiblical, alerts us to the fact that a certain settlement existed in ancient times, and that often these same sources give us clues as to the general geographical location of the site—in the north or south, in the hills or plains, proximity to other towns and villages, etc. One of the most successful ways of trying to attach the ancient name of a settlement to its correct site on the ground and in turn to its place on a modern map, is to see if its name has been preserved through the centuries down to the present time.

At first glance this line of investigation (formally known as the study of toponymy) may seem somewhat futile, given the thousands of years that separate us from the time of the Bible. But the well-watered areas of the land of Israel/Palestine have been inhabited by a rather continuous chain of indigenous peoples who could have, and in many cases in fact have, handed down the name of a given place, usually orally, from generation to generation.[6] Thus names like Jerusalem, Hebron, Acco, and Tiberias have been preserved for thousands of years. The preservation of ancient place-names has been helped by the fact that through the ages the languages of the indigenous population groups have all been Semitic. Thus, Canaanite was related to Hebrew, Hebrew in turn to Aramaic, and Aramaic to Arabic, recognizing of course that there were also many linguistic differences between these languages. However, in more remote areas, e.g., Sinai, there seem to have been significant gaps in the chain of indigenous inhabitants, and thus the ancient geographical names have not been well preserved through the centuries.

Since the preservation of place-names has been primarily an oral process, the modern investigator can either consult local, indigenous sources (usually Arabic-speaking)—who, by the way, are becoming fewer and fewer due to large-scale population movements in the Levant—or he/she can consult written works that have codified the oral traditions at certain points in time. These more recent written sources are "secondary" witnesses to places mentioned in the "primary" sources of the biblical era (but they are of course primary sources for their own eras). Major secondary sources include Josephus, rabbinic literature, the Onomasticon of Eusebius, which was translated and expanded upon by Jerome, the pilgrim itineraries from the Byzantine and Crusader periods, the works of Arab geographers, and the work of the Jewish scholar Eshtori ha-Parchi and others.

The modern study of toponymy began with the trip of Edward Robinson and Eli Smith to Palestine in 1838. Robinson was a great biblical scholar who had mastered all of the primary and most of the secondary materials available in his day. His expertise was supplemented by that of his former pupil, Smith, then a missionary in Beirut, who was fluent in many Arabic dialects and who accompanied him on that first trip. It was on that trip and on one made by Robinson alone in 1852 that the names of many biblical places were correctly identified as being preserved by "modern" local toponyms.

Although many individual contributions have subsequently supplemented their pioneering work, it was the great British survey of Palestine between 1871 and 1877 that added substantially to the available toponymic data. As a result of this survey, twenty-six large-scale maps, covering roughly the area from Dan to Beersheba, west of the Jordan and Dead Sea, were published, along with a number of volumes describing the topographical, cultural, linguistic, and archaeological findings of the survey. Of special interest is the volume of Arabic place names compiled and revised by E. Palmer. Although the work of Robinson and Smith and that of the British team are not free from error, and in spite of the fact that more recent mappings/surveys and archaeological excavations by governments, institutions, and individuals in the area have corrected and supplemented their work, those two sources remain great written repositories of local indigenous oral toponymic traditions that existed prior to the advent of the modern era.

Modern toponyms may preserve the name of an ancient settlement, but those names may not always be attached to the exact place where the biblical settlement was located. For example, the ancient site of biblical Jericho has been located at Tell es-Sultan, but the name was preserved at the nearby village of er-Rahia. While "er-Rahia" may not look like "Jericho" to a layperson, experts who are familiar with the sounds, scripts, and phonetic laws of Hebrew, Aramaic, and Arabic are able to confidently make such identifications. Thus identifications such as Micmash with the Arab village of Mukhmas, Upper Beth Horon with Beit Ur el-Foqa, and

Typical hill country village, with dirt-roofed dwellings, stone and brush fences and gardens.

many others, are fairly certain. Besides the ancient name being preserved at the ancient site itself or in the name of a nearby village, it may also be preserved in the name of a nearby tomb (the name Gezer was preserved in the name of the tomb of Sheikh Jezari on the top of the tell) or water source (biblical Beth Shemesh was preserved at the spring of Ain Shems located near the ancient site, and the name of Jabesh [Gilead] has been preserved in the name of the Wadi Yabis, along which it was located).

In addition to the complication that the name may not be preserved exactly at the ancient site, it might also be expected that an intrusive population group and/or language (such as Greek or, to a lesser extent, Latin, during the Hellenistic and Roman periods) might further complicate matters. However, this is not often the case. For example, even though the official name of Beth Shan was changed to Scythopolis during the Hellenistic period, the new name did not stick, for evidently the local population preserved the older Semitic name, and with the departure of Greco-Roman influence the use of a form of the more ancient name again came to the fore. Thus the name had been preserved up until very recent times as the name of the small Arab village of Beisan, which was located near the foot of the tell where the biblical town was located. On the other hand, forms of the Greek and Latin names of cities that were established during the Roman period have often been preserved by the local Semitic populace: Tiberias is preserved as Tabariyeh and Caesarea as Qeisarieh. However, in a few rare instances, old Semitic names have been replaced by a Greco-Roman counterpart: for example, biblical Shechem was renamed Neapolis during the Greco-Roman period, and it is that name which is preserved in the name of the modern city Nablus.

The above examples are but a few instances of the complicated process of name transmission and preservation through the ages. Of course, any suggested site identification is greatly enhanced if the ancient name can be traced through a number of the "secondary" sources mentioned above, especially if those sources come from different time periods and place the settlement consistently in the proper geographical area. If this is the case, then one can be reasonably certain that the name has been preserved by the local populace, and one can assert with a reasonable degree of assurance that the ancient site was situated at or near the locale of the "modern" toponym.

Archaeology

The process of matching a geographical name with a given antiquity site, usually a town, tell, or khirbet, involves the attempt to match the known history of a place (see above) with the archaeological remains found at the proposed site. For example, when places such as Bethel, Ai, Hebron, Gerar, and Shechem are mentioned in the narratives of the lives of Abraham, Isaac, and Jacob, does this mean that all of them or just some of them were cities at the time of the patriarchs? (A gate mentioned in connection with Hebron [Gen 23:18], and a building with a second story in connection with Gerar [26:8], at least imply that these were urban areas.) If one believes that the text faithfully records the events that took place during the patriarchal era, then one reasonably expects to find archaeological remains from that period at the antiquity sites that are candidates for Gerar, Hebron, etc. On the other hand, if one believes that the purpose of the text is other than historical, and that the stories are legendary, then one need not expect to find remains from the period of the recorded event at the site. Thus the writing of a "history" of an ancient site can be a rather complex task, and the resulting "history" depends to a large extent on the presuppositions that the researcher brings to the task.[7]

But once a "history" of a city has been written, the researcher attempts to determine which of perhaps several antiquity sites located in the general area that has been proposed as the probable location is in fact the actual location of the ancient city. Once a prime candidate has been chosen, often on the basis of initial surface surveys of several sites (see below), archaeological excavations can begin. It must be noted in passing that, although the emphasis in this essay is on the role that archaeology can play in site identification, usually other reasons are more prominent in selecting antiquity sites for archaeological excavation. These include such factors as the site's size, historical importance, and regional significance, and the need for emergency salvage operations in the wake of modern building activities, etc.

Today two major methods are used in excavating a tell. The first can be called the "trench method" (or Wheeler-Kenyon method): the archaeologists select an area of the mound, usually somewhere near its edge, where they sink a trench that resembles a thin slice taken from a layer cake.

Characteristically shaped tel, Tell el-Hammeh, in the Jordan Valley.

They hope that this trench will in fact intersect all the occupation levels (strata) represented within the mound and also that it will intersect any fortifications that might be preserved along its flank. This "trench" is actually a series of five-by-five-meter squares, set in a line and sometimes arranged in pairs, which have a one meter divider (baulk) separating them. As the excavation progresses, scrupulous records are kept, and drawings, photographs, and measurements are made. Thus the exact provenience of each artifact, be it a pot, a piece of jewelry, or something else, is recorded and it can later be studied in relation to the context in which it was found. In addition, the architectural remains (walls, buildings, floors, fortifications, etc.) are plotted in an effort to reconstruct the layout and defenses of the ancient settlement. As the excavators progress, they attempt to sort out the various "levels" or "strata" of occupation that are represented in the tell. Some tells, such as Megiddo or Hazor, may have more than twenty strata, while others, such as the lower city at Arad, may have four or even fewer. Once excavated, the finds from a given stratum (pottery, jewelry, etc.) are gathered together into an "assemblage" from which one can draw conclusions regarding the culture

Why Are There Tells?

The ancients did not set out to build tells. Rather, it often took centuries for tells to develop. The following are some of the more important factors that entered into the complex process of the formation of tells.

1. People preferred to live in regions with good agricultural land and/or pasturage.

2. Often people wanted to live close to major or even minor "roads," which may have led to the settlement of some sites. Other sites may have developed due to their religious significance, their proximity to special nature resources, etc.

3. People preferred to settle close to a source of fresh water - a spring, a well, or, more rarely, a flowing stream.

4. By settling on a hill or a rise near a water source, people could more easily monitor the surrounding landscape and defend themselves.

5. If stone walls, foundation walls, or even just stones from structures of previous inhabitants of a site were available, these could easily be reused in the building of a new settlement. In some areas of the country, the accumulation of mud from mud bricks also significantly contributed to the rise of a tell.

Since there was a limited number of water sources with a limited number of hills near them, and since on these sites building materials from previous settlers were often available, it was here that new settlements were built over old ones, a process that was often repeated many times over, so that in the end the distinctive mounds now known as tells were formed.

Aerial view of Tel Beersheba, showing excavated sections.

Restoring pottery in a local museum.

of the people who lived at that time. To assist in the sorting out of the strata, the sides of the five-meter squares are kept perfectly vertical, and thus the archaeologists are able to look back on these as reference points that help them gather additional data on the strata that they have been digging through. Indeed, photographs and/or drawings of these vertical surfaces become part of the permanent record of the excavation.

Once a "trench" has been excavated down to virgin soil or bedrock, there is a high degree of probability that it has intersected all the strata on the tell. Almost always the lower strata are from an earlier date than the upper ones, but how can this relative dating sequence be transformed into an absolute one? Inscriptional evidence mentioning a known and datable historical figure or event, found in a given stratum, can be very useful in setting boundaries for the dates of that stratum and of other strata. Unfortunately, not much inscriptional evidence from the biblical period is found in the tells of Israel/Palestine, with the exception of coins from the Hellenistic and Roman periods. In some cases modern technology can help, such as the use of the carbon-14 method for the dating of organic remains, but these techniques are not as precise as archaeologists desire—at least not for the historical periods in question.

Another important factor that enters into the dating process is the principle of "typology." Given that one stratum is older than another, one is able to compare the stylistic development of artifacts (oil lamps, cooking pots, gates, palaces, temple designs, etc.) from early to more recent periods. Over the past fifty years these typologies,

Sequence of oil lamps from different periods.

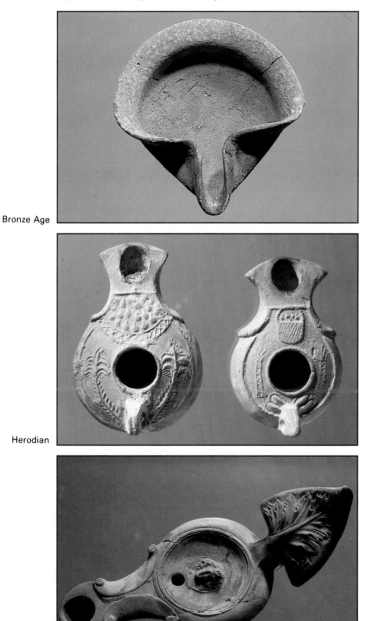

Bronze Age

Hellenistic

Herodian

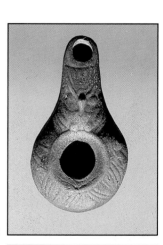

Samaritan

Roman

Byzantine

207

particularly pottery types with their various forms, decorations, and textures, have become well established, and various forms have been linked to strata which in turn can be correlated to Egyptian and/or Mesopotamian history where their absolute chronologies have been established with a fair degree of certainty. Thus today, in spite of the lack of epigraphic finds, a given stratum can usually be dated on the basis of the type of pottery it contains.[8]

This trench method of excavation is a valuable technique, for it allows the archaeologist to get an overview of the total history of the tell with relatively little outlay of time and money. In addition, this method leaves large areas of the tell untouched so that future generations of archaeologists, with better techniques and equipment, can return to re-excavate the site to check and improve upon earlier conclusions. However, since only a small area of the tell is opened up, usually only parts of buildings and of other interesting structures may be uncovered—indeed, it may be that a given stratum is represented elsewhere on the tell but is actually totally absent in the area where the probe trench was sunk, and thus incomplete and inaccurate conclusions may be drawn regarding the occupational history of the site.

A second method of excavation, often used in conjunction with the first, aims at opening up large areas of the tell so as to be able to appreciate over-all building designs, town planning, etc. These are worthy goals, but this method is quite time consuming and costly, and once a given stratum has been completely removed from the mound, it can never be re-excavated. In fact, some of the great controversies of modern archaeology have little chance of resolution because past excavators have completely removed the strata in question from a mound, and their published, or sometimes unpublished, results may lead to all kinds of ambiguity.

Excavation, no matter what method is used, is a costly undertaking. In modern times a technique called "surface survey" has led to some very productive results at a comparatively low cost. In this method, surface features (topography, wall outlines, installations, etc.) of a tell are drawn to scale, and pottery sherds (broken pieces) are collected from all over the top, sides, and bottom of the mound, on the assumption that some artifacts from the edge of each stratum will have worked their way to the surface. Often, in an attempt to refine the process, certain areas are selected in advance, and the sherds from each area are kept separate from those found in other areas. This at times is helpful in developing a more accurate history of the occupation of the site. In either case, an archaeologist, through pottery analysis, can come to some initial conclusions as to when the mound was occupied. It must be remembered, however, that the sherds from a given stratum may not have worked their way to the surface, sides, or foot of the tell, and thus the resulting occupational history may be incomplete. But by using this method, a large number of antiquity sites can be quickly surveyed and a general occupational history of each site can be developed.

Thus for the historical geographer, the excavation or survey of a proposed site can help either to confirm or cast doubt on the proposed identification of that site. If the archaeological data do not conform to the known history of a site, then alternate proposals may be made. For example, for a number of years it was thought that Tell esh-Sheikh Ahmad el-Areini fit the geographical description of the Philistine city of Gath, based on the interpretation of the historical sources that was then current, and it was identified as such on printed maps. However, when the site was excavated and no Philistine remains were found, the identification was dropped, maps were revised, and alternative suggestions were then made as to the true identification of Philistine Gath.

In other instances, the historical geographer, using written sources, may be almost certain regarding the geographical setting of an ancient settlement and the identification of a tell with that settlement, yet when the archaeological profile of the site in question does not fit with the known history of the site, the geographer may begin to question the thoroughness of the survey or excavation and/or his or her interpretation of the historical documents. Thus archaeology, which has many other roles and goals in reconstructing the ancient past, can help lend or limit support for a proposed identification of an ancient settlement and in some cases lead the investigators to a reevaluation of their historical sources. But usually at the conclusion of the process of site identification, the researcher is able to say that the proposed identification is either certain, probable, possible, or untenable—with the understanding that even "certain" identifications at times need to be revised in light of new evidence and/or fresh interpretations of old evidence.

Geography

Although the discipline of geography is a very broad one, certain aspects of it, such as the investigation of local topography, geology, soil types, water sources, and climatic conditions, among others, are useful in studying ancient settlement patterns, the location of routes of travel, and the economic base of a region. Since the early chapters of this book have dealt with how the ancients lived their lives in their immediate environment, these topics will not be treated here, and the reader is referred to the appropriate regional studies in the Geographical Section of this atlas (pp.11–68).

Conclusion

Although this essay has emphasized the fascinating process of site identification—how an ancient settlement can or cannot be identified with an actual antiquity site which in turn can be represented as a dot on a map in an atlas—the historical geographer is also interested in broader questions, such as historical reconstructions and how the ancients lived life in context. How did their immediate environment influence their lives and how, in turn, did they structure their environment? By following up on such geographical questions, as well as on ecological ones, and with the input from the disciplines of philology, toponymy, and archaeology, we can begin to draw a total regional picture. Along this line, detailed regional investigations have already begun in earnest, and they promise to occupy the attention of historical geographers in the years ahead.

Notes

Introduction to the Middle East as a Whole, pp. 12–15

[1] The portion of this route that ran from Gaza to Megiddo to Hazor, often near the coast, is labeled in many works as the "Way of the Sea" or the "Via Maris." This name is based on the Latin translation of Isaiah 9:1 [MT 8:23]. Recently, it has been shown that this portion of the route was not called by this name during the biblical period, and alternate suggestions for the biblical "Way of the Sea" have been proposed. See Z. Meshel, "Was There a 'Via Maris'?" *IEJ* 23 (1973): 162–66, and A. F. Rainey, "Toponymic Problems: The Way of the Sea," *Tel Aviv* 8 (1981): 146–49.

The Geography of Israel and Jordan, pp. 16–56

[1] Y. Karmon, *Israel: A Regional Geography* (New York: Wiley-Interscience, 1971), p. 178 but, compare D. Baly, *The Geography of the Bible*, new and revised edition (New York: Harper & Row, 1974), p. 154.

[2] M. Ben-Dov, "[נֶפָה] — A Geographical Term of Possible 'Sea People' Origin," *Tel Aviv*, 3:2 (1976): 70–73.

[3] "The Journey of Wen-Amon," *ANET*, 25–29.

[4] See "The Arival of the Greeks," p. 213, fn. 4 for a brief discussion of this term.

[5] I. Schattner, *The Lower Jordan Valley*, vol. 11 of *Scripta Hierosolymitana* (Jerusalem: Magnes), p. 23.

[6] Ibid., p. 35.

[7] Har-El, M. "The Pride of the Jordan–The Jungle of the Jordan," *BA* 41 (1978): 69.

[8] See the Moabite Stone, line 13 in *ANET*, 320–21.

The Geography of Egypt, pp. 57–61

[1] It has been estimated that more than twenty feet of silt has been deposited in the fields since 3000 B.C.

[2] The categories used here follow those outlined by Y. Aharoni, *The Land of the Bible*, rev. and enl. ed., trans. and ed. A. F. Rainey (Philadelphia: Westminster, 1979), 93–97.

The Geography of Syria and Lebanon, pp. 62–64

[1] D. Baly and A. D. Tushingham, *Atlas of the Biblical World* (New York: World, 1971), 13.

The Pre-Patriarchal Period, pp. 70–75

[1] See, for example, *EAEHL* 1:340.

[2] J. Baines and J. Malek, *Atlas of Ancient Egypt* (New York: Facts on File, 1980), 140–41.

[3] See, for example, Y. Aharoni, *The Archaeology of the Land of Israel*, ed. M. Aharoni, trans. A. F. Rainey (Philadelphia: Westminster, 1982), 9–47.

[4] M. Broshi and R. Gophna, "The Settlements and Population of Palestine During the Early Bronze Age II–III," *BASOR* 253 (1984): 41–53.

[5] Ibid., 45.

[6] For a convenient summary of the data, see H. Shanks, "Have Sodom and Gomorrah Been Found?" *BAR* 6:5 (September/October 1980): 26–36.

[7] See, for example, the early work of G. Pettinato, "The Royal Archives of Tell Mardikh-Ebla," *BA* 39:2 (May 1976): 46, and D. N. Freedman, "The Real Story of the Ebla Tablets, Ebla and the Cities of the Plain," *BA* 41 (1978): 143–64, but compare the negative comments of the Ebla "team" as reported by J. D. Muhly, "Ur and Jerusalem Not Mentioned In Ebla Tablets, Say Ebla Expedition Scholars," *BAR* 9:6 (November/December 1983): 74–75.

The Patriarchs and the Egyptian Sojourn, 76–85

[1] For an alternative view, which places Ur in northwestern Mesopotamia, see C. H. Gordon, "Where Is Abraham's Ur?" *BAR* 3:2 (June 1977): 20–21, 52.

[2] A "relative date" is a date that is given in relation to some other person, event, etc. (e.g., the "fourth year of Solomon"). An "absolute date" attempts to describe such a date in terms of our Gregorian calendar. If chronological studies can demonstrate that Solomon began to rule in 970 B.C., then the fourth year of his reign (a "relative date") would be 966 B.C. (an "absolute date," i.e., according to the Gregorian calendar). However, since the 970 B.C. starting point is based on historical probabilities, if that date were shown to be incorrect by additional historical studies, and that, say, 980 B.C. was the correct date for the beginning of Solomon's rule, then the "absolute date" for the fourth year of his reign would be changed to 976 B.C. Thus

"absolute dates" are not absolutely certain. In the second millennium B.C. there may be variations of twenty years or so in "absolute dates," depending on the chronology scheme one adopts, while in the early first millennium B.C. the variations are probably less than five years, and at the end of the first millennium B.C. possible variations are usually limited to a year or so. Thus the reader should note that the "absolute dates" used in this atlas are not "fixed in granite" but are used to provide convenient and reasonable pegs on which one can hang historical events.

[3] Thiele, after having discovered the keys from which an internally consistent pattern of relative dates for the kings of Judah and Israel could be derived, was able to establish absolute dates for this interlocking structure of kings by linking it to known, datable contacts of the kings of Judah and Israel with Assyrian monarchs—e.g., Ahab's involvement with Shalmaneser III at the Battle of Qarqar in 853 B.C. (E. R. Thiele, *The Mysterious Numbers of the Hebrew Kings*, rev. ed. [Grand Rapids: Zondervan, 1983], 43–60, 67–87). Thus, the total chronological scheme for the kings of Judah and Israel was put on a firm foundation, and the absolute dates for these kings, including Solomon, were established.

[4] The debate among evangelical scholars regarding this "early date" for the Exodus continues, yet the date preferred in this atlas, 1446 B.C., is supported by the plain reading of the text and fits reasonably well with the finds of extra-biblical Palestinian archaeology and Egyptian history. See, for example, J. J. Bimson, *Redating the Exodus and Conquest* (Sheffield: Almond Press, 1981); L. Wood, *A Survey of Israel's History*, rev. ed., ed. D. O'Brien (Grand Rapids: Zondervan, 1986), 65–86; and G. L. Archer, Jr., *A Survey of Old Testament Introduction*, rev. ed. (Chicago: Moody, 1986), 222–34; and J. J. Bimson and D. Livingstone, "Redating the Exodus," *BAR* 13:5 (September/October 1987): 40–68, but compare B. Halpern, "Radical Exodus Dating Fatally Flawed," *BAR* 13:6 (November/December 1987): 56–61.

[5] For a detailed description of the internal, relative, biblical chronology from Solomon's day back to the patriarchal era see, e.g., Wood, *Survey*, 19–25, 65–86.

[6] The term "Chaldees," or "Chaldean," usually refers to the people of southern Mesopotamia during the first millennium B.C. It has been suggested that the term was added to the Hebrew text of Genesis during that period to help explain where Ur—not remembered by the Israelites(?)—had been located.

[7] G. Dossin, "Une mention de Cananéens dans une lettre de Mari," *Syria* 50 (1973): 277–82.

[8] For example, see conveniently, L. Vigano, "Literary Sources for the History of Palestine and Syria: The Ebla Tablets," rev. and ed. D. Pardee, *BA* 47:1 (March 1984): 11.

[9] Z. Zevit, "The Problem of Ai," *BAR* 11:2 (March/April 1985): 61–62.

[10] *EAEHL*, 191–92; Bimson, *Redating*, 58, 69.

[11] For a popular description of the MB I period, see R. Cohen, "The Mysterious MB I People—Does the Exodus Tradition in the Bible Preserve the Memory of Their Entry into Canaan?" *BAR* 9:4 (July/August 1983): 16–29.

[12] R. Gonen, "Was the Site of the Jerusalem Temple Originally a Cemetery?" *BAR* 11:3 (May/June 1985): 54.

[13] For a survey of suggestions, see Cohen, "Mysterious MB I People."

[14] Indeed, in light of Cohen's Negev discoveries, that MB I (2200–2000 B.C.) settlements are found directly on top of EB II (2850–2650 B.C.) settlements, many are being led to a re-evaluation of the relative relationship between the two cultures. Could EB and MB I be partially contemporary? Did the MB I culture begin earlier than 2200 B.C., and/or did EB last longer than 2200 B.C. (see note 32)?

[15] This settlement pattern seems extremely illogical and probably should enter into the discussion of the questions mentioned above (see note 14).

[16] Most think this document was written during the Middle Kingdom and describes conditions of the First Intermediate Period; however, some (e.g. M. Lichtheim, *The Old and Middle Kingdoms*, vol. 1 in *Ancient Egyptian Literature: A Book of Readings* [Berkeley: University of California, 1973], 194–95) believe that it is a rather late literary document describing the general theme of "social chaos" instead of referring to actual historical conditions during a specific historical period.

[17] For the early use of the term "Philistine" in connection with the King of Gerar, see K. A. Kitchen, "The Philistines," in *Peoples of Old Testament Times*, ed. D. J. Wiseman (Oxford: Oxford University Press, 1973), 53–78.

[18] Note the meaning of Beersheba: Beer (= "well") sheba (= "of seven" or "swearing"); see Gen 21:32 and 26:33.

[19] The site of Solomon's temple is identified as Mount Moriah (2 Chron 3:1). This identification is also found on a tomb inscription from the seventh century B.C. discovered at Khirbet el-Qom (W. G. Dever, "Iron Age Epigraphic Material from the Area of Khirbet el-Kom," *Hebrew Union College Annual* 40–41 [1969–1970]: 139–204) and is supported in the writings of Josephus, first century A.D. (*Antiq* 7.13.4 [329–34]).

[20] The modern city has spread out in all directions, covering many of the valleys and hills where one would expect to find relevant archaeological remains, making excavation difficult and possibly destroying some archaeological evidence in the process. (See Bimson, *Redating*, 72–73), but for a preliminary report of recent excavations, see A. Ofer, "Tell Rumeideh - 1984," *Excavations and Surveys in Israel 1984*, vol. 3 (Jerusalem: The Israel Department of Antiquities and Museums, 1985),

94–95. For a report concerning an "exploration" of the "tombs of the patriarchs," see N. Miller, "Patriarchal Burial Site Explored for First Time in 700 Years," *BAR* 11:3 (May/June 1985): 26–43.

[21] Usually interpreted as an ancient name for the land of Babylon; but a more northern "Assyrian" location has also been proposed (*ZPEB*, 1:407).

[22] Location unknown; possibly a town in the Haran region (*NBD*, 323).

[23] Southwest Persia/Iran.

[24] Meaning "nations"; identification uncertain but possibly located in Syria (*ZPEB*, 2:771).

[25] Note that the Bible includes the explanation that ancient Bela was now called Zoar, indicating that in the days of the writer of Genesis (or, according to some scholars, alternately in the days of a later copyist) the location of Bela was no longer well known and so the writer/editor provided his readers with a "modern" clue as to its location. Notice the additional "updatings" also found in Genesis 14; "Valley of Siddim" updated by "Salt Sea" (14:3), "Ashteroth" by "Karnaim" (14:5), "Shaveh" by "Kiriathaim" (v. 5), "En Mishpat" by "Kadesh" (v. 7), possibly "Hazazon" by "Tamar" (v. 7), and the "Valley of Shaveh" by "King's Valley" (v. 17). Elsewhere in the patriarchal narratives note the following "updatings": "Ur" by "Chaldeans" (11:31; 15:7), "Kiriath Arba" by "Hebron" (23:2; 35:27), and "Luz" by "Bethel" (28:19; 35:6; passim).

[26] For the identification of these cities and regions, see the Gazetteer.

[27] The tarpits (Gen 14:10) add local color to the narrative, for Josephus states that in antiquity bitumen was gathered from the sea (*War* 4.8.4 [476–85]; and above, p. 45).

[28] The mentioning of "Dan" in the narrative is problematic, for its early name "Laish/Leshem" was not changed to "Dan" until the period of the Judges (ca. 1400–1050 B.C.; Josh 19:47; Judg 18:29). Possibly a later editor "updated" the text by substituting Dan for Laish, or, less probably, another, today unknown, more northern Dan is in view. The location of Hobah, north of Damascus, is not certain.

[29] Exact location unknown, but apparently close to Jerusalem, (see 2 Sam 18:18).

[30] Salem is evidently to be identified with Jerusalem (Ps 76:2).

[31] For a survey of the literature regarding the cities of the plain, see D. Howard, Jr., "Sodom and Gomorrah Revisited," *JETS* 27:4 (December 1984): 385–400.

[32] The internal biblical chronology seems secure; thus one is left to speculate regarding the nature of the archaeological periods and their dating. Is it possible that the EB II/III and MB I periods are chronologically much closer than normally granted (Cohen, "Mysterious MB I People," 26–28)? Could these periods even have overlapped? If so, this would explain why many MB I settlements are found in the arid regions of Palestine (the Negev and Transjordan); for if the fertile hill country and plains were densely settled by the powerful EB peoples, as evidenced by their numerous large cities, and in addition thick forests were still common in the mountain regions, then the intrusive MB I people(s) were forced to live in marginal areas (it is absurd to suppose that they chose to live in these areas if the more fertile plains and hills to the north were devoid of population and available for settlement as the current archaeological dating scheme proposes). If the EB II/III and MB I periods are concurrent, and if the dating of the end of this "reconstructed period" could be pushed down to about 2000 B.C. (this does not appear to be probable at this time), then the five EB III sites southeast of the Dead Sea could possibly be identified with the five cities of the plain. In addition, the alleged reference to Sodom and Gomorrah in the Ebla tablets (presently dated ca. 2400 B.C.) would be more relevant to the actual cities mentioned in the Bible. In truth, given the present archaeological data, no sure identification of Sodom, Gomorrah, Admah, Zeboiim, and Bela (Zoar) has been made; yet when two of the EB III sites (Numeria and Feifa) are described as being covered with ashy soil or a thick spongy charcoal substance, indicating a fiery destruction, one continues to wonder (H. Shanks, "Have Sodom & Gomorrah been Found?" *BAR* 6:5 (September/October 1980): 29–30).

[33] For a recent archaeological description of the MB II Period, see Y. Aharoni, *The Archaeology of the Land of Israel* , ed. M. Aharoni, trans. A. F. Rainey (Philadelphia: Westminster, 1982), 90–112.

[34] Retenu was one of the Egyptian names for Canaan at this time. The origin, meaning, and boundaries of Retenu are however, disputed; possibly "Upper Retenu" referred to the area north of the Jezreel Valley while "Lower Retenu" lay to the south of the valley (Y. Aharoni, *The Land of the Bible*, rev. and enl. ed., trans. and ed. A. F. Rainey [Philadelphia: Westminster, 1979], 66–67).

[35] For a detailed treatment of both the Story of Sinuhe and the Execration Texts, though not espousing the patriarchal connections mentioned here, see A. F. Rainey, "The World of Sinuhe," *Israel Oriental Studies* 2 (1972): 369–408.

[36] For a recent study of this inscription, see W. H. Shea, "Artistic Balance Among the Beni Hasan Asiatics," *BA* 44 (1981): 219–28.

[37] W. H. Shea, "A Date for the Recently Discovered Eastern Canal of Egypt," *BASOR* 226 (1977): 31–38.

[38] The translation of Hyksos as "shepherd kings" derives from Josephus' use of a mistranslation of the Egyptian term (hq3 ḫ3św t). In addition, Josephus' descriptions both of the Hyksos as an invading horde and of the length of their rule in Egypt at 511 years (*AqAp* 1.14 [75–92]), are not now generally accepted.

[39] For recent surveys of the archaeological finds of this period, see Aharoni, *Archaeology*, 90–112 and W. Dever, "The Middle Bronze Age: The Zenith of the Urban Canaanite Era," *BA* 50:3 (September 1987): 149–77.

[40] For a survey of Ancient Near Eastern and Biblical connections, see A. Malamat, "Mari," *BA* 34:1 (1971): 2–22.

[41] Dossin, "Une mention de Cananéens." The exact location of Canaan at this time is difficult to determine but it may have been to the north of Galilee.

[42] See A. Malamat, "Silver, Gold and Precious Stones from Hazor? Trade and Trouble in a New Mari Document," *Journal of Jewish Studies* 33:1–2 (1982): 70–79, for references to the Mari texts and to his numerous provided studies of this topic.

[43] See Y. Yadi, *Hazor: The Rediscovery of a Great Citadel of the Bible* (London: Weidenfeld and Nicolson, 1975).

[44] A. Malamat, "Hazor 'The Head of All Those Kingdoms,' " *JBL* 79 (1960): 12–19. It is doubtful however, that Hazor was the capital of Amurru, for the texts seem to indicate that Amurru was located to the north of Hazor.

[45] A. Malamat, "Syro-Palestinian Destinations in a Mari Tin Inventory," *IEJ* 21:1 (1971): 31–38.

[46] For Hurru Land see Aharoni, *Land of the Bible*, 67. But the currently meager textual evidence from Canaan itself (several personal names contained in a cuneiform tablet describing a lawsuit, found at Hazor) indicates an Amorite (West Semitic) population (W. W. Hallo and H. Tadmor, "A Lawsuit from Hazor," *IEJ* 27 [1977]: 10). Note that in the Mari texts, the name of the king of Hazor is Ammorite.

[47] A. Kempinski, "Tell el-Ajjul—Beth-Aglayim or Sharuhen?" *IEJ* 24 (1974): 145–52, has argued convincingly for the identification of Sharuhen with Tell el-Ajjul rather than Tell el-Fara (south).

Exodus and Conquest, pp. 86–95

[1] J. M. Weinstein, "The Egyptian Empire in Palestine: A Reassessment," *BASOR* 238 (1981): 43–46.

[2] R. Gonen, "Urban Canaan in the Late Bronze Period," *BASOR* 253 (1984): 61–73.

[3] Literary sources describing this campaign can be found in *ANET*, 234–43.

[4] See Y. Aharoni, *The Land of the Bible* , rev. and enl. ed., trans. and ed. A. F. Rainey (Philadelphia: Westminster, 1979), 152–66, for a basic discussion of this text with references, and now Z. Gal, "The Late Bronze Age in Galilee," *BASOR* 272 (1988): 79–84.

[5] See C. F. Aling, "The Biblical City of Ramses," *JETS* 25:2 (June 1982): 129–37. Later, during the XIX dynasty, a residence city for Rameside rulers was built in the area, possibly at Tell Abu el-Shafia, north of Qantir. In Egyptian sources this would have been called Pi-Ramesse. Those who hold to a late-date theory of the Exodus (ca. 1250 B.C.) argue that it was this city that the Israelites built—probably for Rameses II (1304–1237 B.C.)—the biblical city of Rameses being a shortened form of the Egyptian "the estate of Ramses." However, J. J. Bimson and D. Livingston argue that the name Rameses is used "retrospectively" in Exodus 1:11 to refer to building activities that took place in the Qantir region from the nineteenth to the seventeenth centuries B.C. ("Redating the Exodus," *BAR* 13:5 [September/October 1987]: 42–43).

[6] Pithom may be a form of Egyptian Per-Atum ("the estate-temple of Atum"), shortened to Pi-Tum. Remnants of a temple dedicated to Atum have been found at nearby Tell el-Maskhuta, and both Tell el-Maskhuta and nearby Tell er-Retabah contain the necessary archaeological remains (Bimson and Livingston, "Redating," 43).

[7] This is true unless one engages in a wholesale redating of archaeological periods. See, e.g., E. Anati, "Has Mt. Sinai Been Found?" *BAR* 11:4 (July/August 1985): 42–57, but compare W. H. Steibing, Jr., "Should the Exodus and the Israelite Settlement in Canaan Be Redated?" *BAR* 11:4 (July/August 1985): 58–69, and, from a different angle, R. Cohen, "The Mysterious MB I People—Does the Exodus Tradition in the Bible Preserve the Memory of Their Entry into Canaan?" *BAR* 9:4 (July/August 1983): 16–29.

[8] For a complete description of various viewpoints regarding the Exodus and wanderings from the geographical standpoint, see M. Har-El, *The Sinai Journeys: The Route of The Exodus* (San Diego: Ridgefield, 1983). His Hebrew name means "Mountain of God"!

[9] M. Har-El, "The Exodus Route in the Light of Historical-Geographical Research," in *Geography in Israel*, ed. D. H. K. Amiran and Y. Ben-Arieh (Jerusalem: Israel National Committee International Geographical Union, 1976): 374.

[10] Oren mentions a dozen New Kingdom archaeological sites between the Suez Canal and the Bardawil lagoon: E. D. Oren, "Migdol: A New Fortress on the Edge of the Eastern Nile Delta," *BASOR* (1984): 35.

[11] "The way of the wilderness" may have been the road running from Egypt, through Suez, across Sinai to Elath (see p. 60).

[12] Oren, "Migdol," 31, notes that a number of Migdols are mentioned in New Kingdom texts and points out that the Migdol of the Exodus cannot be Tell el-Her as maintained in some Bible atlases (e.g., *MBA*)—because of the lack of proper archaeological remains (34–35).

[13] Har-El, "Exodus Route," 377–80.

[14] Ibid., 383–91.

[15] Often times a *midbār* (NIV "desert") is a mountainous, rock-strewn, barren region.

[16] The name "Paran" seems to be preserved in the name of the largest oasis in southern Sinai, the Feiran Oasis.

[17] Possibly Kadesh was located on the border of the Desert of Paran and the Desert of Zin (Num 12:16; 33:36).

[18] If Jebel Sin Bisher is accepted as Mount Sinai, then the name of biblical "Rithmah" (Num 33:18) may be preserved in the "modern" "Ein [spring of] Rithmah" in the Wadi Suder; see Har-El, "Exodus Route," 392.

[19] Numbers 13:17, 22 implies that the "Negev" is not merely a directional word "south" but is actually a region located to the north of Kadesh.

[20] Although a number of places along the southern boundary cannot be identified with certainty (see the Gazetteer), the location of those mentioned above are reasonably certain. For a detailed study of the boundary of the land of Canaan see Aharoni, *Land of the Bible,* 67–77.

[21] Ibid., 72–73, 439.

[22] That the Jordan River formed a definite boundary between the "land of Canaan" to the west and the territory to the east—often called the "land of Gilead"—is well-illustrated in Scripture (e.g., Josh 22; and Judg 21:9–12).

[23] Aharoni, *Land of the Bible* , 202. Imaret el-Khureisheh is a low but prominent hill located at the junction of a number of roads; its summit is surrounded by a mysterious stone wall.

[24] See, for example, the comments of L. Wood, *A Survey of Israel's History*, rev. ed., ed. D. O'Brien (Grand Rapids: Zondervan, 1986), 131–32, but compare Aharoni, *Land of the Bible*, pp. 55–56.

[25] For a convenient evaluation of Glueck's views in light of recent work, see G. L. Mattingly, "The Exodus-Conquest and the Archaeology of Transjordan: New Light on an Old Problem," *Grace Theological Journal* 4 (1983): 245–62 and Bimson and Livingstone, "Redating," 43–44.

[26] The MB II and LB sites are listed and commented on by Mattingly, "Exodus-Conquest," 253–56. Sites listed include Amman, Tell Safut, Sahab, Na'ur, Madeba, Khirbet el-Mekhayyat, and Qla'et-Twal (among others recently surveyed).

[27] Compare the selectivity of the Gospel accounts as well as Acts.

[28] The exact location of Gilgal is unknown, but it was reasonably close to Jericho.

[29] Y. Shiloh, "The Population of Iron Age Palestine in the Light of a Sample Analysis of Urban Plans, Areas, and Population Density," *BASOR* 239 (1980): 30.

[30] For a summary of the compatibility of the evidence, see B. K. Waltke, "Palestinian Artifactual Evidence Supporting the Early Date of the Exodus," *Bibliotheca Sacra* 129 (January 1972): 33–47.

[31] Even Yigael Yadin publicly espoused this view shortly before his death: H. Shanks, "BAR Interviews Yigael Yadin," *BAR* 9:1 (January/February 1983): 17. It seems logical that the "lack" of fortified cities during the LB I age (see Gonen, "Urban Canaan in the Late Bronze Period") can be explained by the fact that walls of the MB II cities were in use at least a century later than archaeologists usually grant. See also Bimson and Livingston, "Redating," 45–46, 51–53.

[32] A. Zevit, "The Problem of Ai," *BAR* 11:2 (March/April 1985): 61–62.

[33] Ibid., 58.

[34] Ibid., 61–64, has a summary of proposals.

[35] Actually Ras et-Tahuna (grid ref. 170146) in el-Bira.

[36] D. Livingston, "Location of Bethel and Ai Reconsidered," *Westminster Theological Journal* 33 (1970): 20–44, and "Traditional Site of Bethel Questioned," *Westminster Theological Journal* 34:1 (1971): 39–50.

[37] A. F. Rainey, "Bethel Is Still Beitin," *Westminster Theological Journal* 33 (1971): 175–88. In addition, no walled city has been discovered at Khirbet Nisya (Bimson and Livingston, "Redating," 48–51).

[38] Zevit's proposal, that the biblical account is nothing more than a bard's tale, is difficult to accept for those who hold a high view of Scripture: Z. Zevit, "The Problem of Ai," 67–68.

[39] A. Zertal, "Has Joshua's Altar Been Found on Mt. Ebal?" *BAR* 11:1 (January/February 1985): 26–42; but compare the rejoinder of A. Kempinski, "Joshua's Altar—An Iron Age I Watchtower," *BAR* 12:1 (January/February 1986): 42–49.

[40] For this group of people, see conveniently *ZPEB* or more extensively T. Ishida, "The Structure and Historical Implications of the Lists of Pre-Israelite Nations," *Biblica* 60 (1970): 461–90, and B. Mazar, "The Early Israelite Settlement in the Hill Country," *BASOR* 241 (1981): 75–85.

[41] See p. 41 for a description of the Beth Horon road. The second road (and its branches) that the Gibeonites controlled led west from Gibeon along ridges that passed through Kephirah or Kiriath Jearim to the Valley of Aijalon.

[42] It is evident from the el-Amarna letters that the king of Jerusalem was at least partially dependent on Egyptian support for his defense (see el-Amarna letters numbers 287, 288, and 289 in *ANET*, 488–89).

[43] For the identification of Makkedah, D. Dorsey, "The Location of Biblical Makkedah," *Tel Aviv* 7 (1980): 185–93.

[44] Since the text does not explicity state that these cities were burned, it is not necessary to look for 1400 B.C. burn levels at each of these antiquity sites. Indeed, from the text, all that can be gathered is that their populations were slaughtered: see, e.g., E. H. Merrill, "Palestinian Archaeology and the Date of the Conquest: Do Tells Tell Tales?" *Grace Theological Journal* 3 (1982): 107–21. It is evident from archaeological finds—pagan temples, pagan cult objects, etc.—as well as from the el-Amarna correspondence, that non-Israelites returned to inhabit the "conquered" cities.

[45] The reading "Madon" (Josh 11:1; 12:19) is problematic. Possibly the city was close to Khirbet Madin, south of the Horns of Hattin, the Khirbet preserving the biblical name Madon. However, Aharoni suggested the reading "Merom" in place of "Madon," following the Greek translation of the Old Testament and the Merom of the phrase "Waters of Merom" mentioned in 11:5 and 11:7 (*Land of the Bible*, 117–18, 226)—the Hebrew letters represented by "r" and "d" are very similar in appearance and could be confused. However, it is difficult to see why a postulated Merom in 11:1 would be changed to Madon; for the former occurs twice in the context, and one would not expect a scribe to change the well-attested Merom to Madon. It is more probable that the Hebrew reading "Madon" is original.

[46] The location of Old Testament Merom is disputed, but Aharoni's suggested identification of Tell el-Khirbeh (*Land of the Bible*, 225–26; grid ref. 190275)—a Canaanite fort located at the junction of several roads in Upper Galilee—is plausible (see A. Rainey, "Merom, Waters of," *ZPEB*, 4: 192–93, for a detailed discussion). However, it is difficult to imagine how chariots (Josh 11:4) operated effectively in this rugged region. It would make more sense for these kings to make their defense either more to the south—in or near the Jezreel Valley—as a later Jabin, also king of Hazor, did in his battle with Deborah and Barak (Judg 4–5), or nearer to Hazor.

[47] The city that evidences destruction that can be attributed to Joshua is the pre-el-Amarna city of Level III (Lower City), which was destroyed about 1400 B.C. The Level II city would then have been destroyed by the Egyptian Seti I about 1300 B.C., while Level I was destroyed by Deborah and Barak (ca. 1200 B.C.). All the above fits well with the biblical data; however, if one maintains that Level I was destroyed by Joshua (ca. 1200 B.C.), then one is left with no destruction by Deborah and Barak or one must transpose the two accounts (e.g., Aharoni in *MBA*, 46–47); both solutions are contrary to the plain reading of the text. For a discussion of Hazor, see Waltke, "Palestinian Artifactual Evidence," 42–47.

Settlement in the Land of Canaan, pp. 96–109

[1] Ten are listed in the Hebrew text, while an additional eleventh district composed of the cities of "Tekoa, Ephrathah, that is Bethlehem, Peor, Etam, Culom, Tatam, Sores, Carem, Gallim, Baither, and Manach: eleven cities in all with their hamlets" (Josh 15:59b, NEB), is found in the Septuagint (Greek translation of the Old Testament).

[2] This is done, for example, by using one or both of the two Benjamin districts (Josh 18:21–27) and adding one or both of them to Judah; see Y. Aharoni, *The Land of the Bible*, rev. and enl. ed., trans. and ed. A. F. Rainey (Philadelphia: Westminster, 1979), 347–56; F. M. Cross and G. E. Wright, "The Boundary and Province Lists of the Kingdom of Judah," *JBL* 75 (1956): 221–24. On the other hand, it is possible that the cities of Simeon (Josh 19:1–9), listed as being in the Negev (15:21–32), formed a separate district to make a total of twelve.

[3] See, for example, M. Kochavi, "The Land of Judah," pp. 19–89 in *Judaea, Samaria, and the Golan: Archaeological Survey 1967–1968*, ed. M. Kochavi (Jerusalem: Carta, 1972) [Hebrew].

[4] Judah's recorded allotment would then be an example of an early boundary descriptior was later supplemented by the addition of the city list (vv. 21–63).

[5] For example, during the days of kings Uzziah (790–739 B.C.), Hezekiah (728/15–686 B.C.), and Josiah (640–609 B.C.). Possibly Josh 15:45–47 reflects this situation, but Judah evidently did not take this area during the period of the Judges (Judg 1:18, following the Septuagint "Not"; see NIV footnote).

[6] English translations usually indicate that these towns were "within" or "in" Issachar and Asher, but a better translation of ב (the Hebrew preposition) would be "beside."

[7] There is no reason to doubt that this was accomplished in Joshua's day, but it is not necessary to assume that the following tribal descriptions all date to his time. It is possible that the original material was updated from time to time, or even replaced by more "modern" lists. For a recent popular account of the excavations at Shiloh, see I. Finkelstein, "Shiloh Yields Some, But Not All, of Its Secrets," *BAR* 12:1 (January/February 1986): 22–41.

[8] Aharoni, *Land of the Bible*, 315, 355–56. It seems to some that the boundary description and the city list do not reflect the same historical time period, for the territory outlined in each does not appear to coincide. For example, the boundary description seems to indicate that Bethel was in Ephraim (18:12; cf. 16:2 and Judg 1:22–26), while the city list includes it as a city of Benjamin (Josh 18:22). In addition, Ophrah, if correctly identified, is located considerably north of the northern boundary.

[9] Not to be identified with modern Yafa to the west of Nazareth (Aharoni, *Land of the Bible*, 437), for the site should be found after Daberath, and, in addition, "modern" Yafa lacks proper archaeological remains to be identified as biblical Japhia.

[10] Later the home of Jonah the prophet (2 Kings 14:25).

[11] Of those listed, the following were probably in Zebulun: Sarid, Maralah, Japhia, Gath Hepher, Eth Kaziz, Rimmon, Hannathon, Kattath, Nahalah, Shimron, Idalah, and Bethlehem. The form of the description of Zebulun's allotment seems to be composite: the boundary description is followed by a short city list, from which those cities mentioned in the boundary list have been deleted.

[12] For a discussion of the territory, the date of the list, and recent site identifications, see Z. Gal, "The Settlement of Issachar: Some New Observations," *Tel Aviv* 9 (1982): 79–86.

[13] See Aharoni, *Land of the Bible*, 257–58, for a discussion.

[14] Could the reference to Judah reflect a time when the Davidic dynasty controlled territory in the Bashan (i.e., during the days of David and Solomon)? In this regard see especially the Hebrew text of 2 Kings 14:28, which is relegated to a footnote in the NIV.

[15] The relationship between Hukkok, on the border of Naphtali (Josh 19:34) and Hukok (1 Chron 6:75), a levitical city in Asher, is problematic. Probably the levitical city 'Hukok' (1 Chron 6:75) is a variant for "Helkath" (see Josh 21:30).

[16] It is evident that the ancients were aware of this distinction. Josephus, for example, puts the boundary point between the two Galilees at Beer-sheba, today H. Beer Sheva, at Grid Ref. 189259 (*War* 3.3.1 [35–40]).

[17] Possibly "Timnah, Ekron" (19:43) should be read "Timnah of Ekron" to distinguish it from other Timnahs (e.g., those mentioned in Josh 15:57; 19:50; Judg 2:9; see Y. Aharoni, "The Solomonic Districts," *Tel Aviv* 3 [1976]: 7–10).

[18] For a discussion of the Danite list, see Aharoni, "Solomonic Districts," 6–10.

[19] Note the Gadite cities of Dibon and Ataroth (Num 32:34), the former assigned to Reuben (Josh 13:17) and the latter in Reubenite territory (Josh 13:15–23). Compare also Mesha's reference to Gadites in this Moabite territory in the ninth century B.C. (*ANET*, 320–21).

[20] Many have suggested that the lists (Josh 21; 1 Chron 6:54–81) are to be dated to the reigns of David and Solomon (1010–931 B.C.) rather than to the days of Joshua (ca. 1400 B.C.). This suggestion is made on the assumption that the lists reflect a time when Israel actually controlled these cities. For example, those mentioned from the tribe of Asher were under Israelite control only during portions of David's and Solomon's reigns; thus, that portion of the list must date from that era (Aharoni, *Land of the Bible*, 301). However, it might be that the list was originally an "ideal" (or a "utopian") register and that some of the cities may not have been settled by Levites until long after the days of Joshua. In fact, it might be that a later editor or copyist "updated" the list for his contemporaries.

[21] For a reconstruction of the original list, based upon the Joshua and Chronicles passages, see Aharoni, *Land of the Bible*, 303–4.

[22] Ibid., 305.

[23] For a recent popular discussion of Akhenaton, see D. B. Redford, "The Monotheism of the Heretic Pharaoh," *BAR* 13:3 (May/June 1987): 16–32.

[24] Othniel had earlier captured Debir in Judah and evidently resided there (Josh 15:15–19; Judg 1:11–15).

[25] M. Kline, "The Ha-Bi-Ru—Kin or Foe of Israel?—II," *Westminster Theological Journal* 20 (1957): 54–61.

[26] "Naharaim" is possibly a later scribal gloss inserted into the text after Aram had replaced Edom.

[27] Although the Amalekites are usually associated with the Sinai or Negev deserts, these particular oppressors may have been a branch of Amalekites living in or near the Hill Country of Ephraim (see Judg 5:14; 12:15 for hints of this association).

[28] Yenôam is now to be identified with T. esh-Shihab—following N. Naaman, "Yenôam," *Tel Aviv* 4 (1974): 168–77.

[29] It is also possible that the term "son of Anath" may not be intended to carry any geographical information; it might even have been a title of some sort. Anath was a war goddess.

[30] For a study of the military camp between Megiddo and Taanach, see A. F. Rainey, "The Military Camp Ground at Taanach by the Waters of Megiddo," pp. 61*–66* in *Y. Aharoni Memorial Volume*, Eretz-Israel 15 (Jerusalem: Israel Exploration Society, 1981), and "Toponymic Problems: Harosheth-Hagoiim," *Tel Aviv* 20 (1983): 46–48.

[31] Possibly Hazor was captured and destroyed at this time (i.e., level I of the lower and level XIV of the upper city, which was destroyed ca. 1230 B.C.). It is not necessary to transpose the account of Joshua's conquest of Hazor with that of the battle of Deborah and Barak (as Aharoni has done in *MBA:* 46, 47 and in *The Land of the Bible*. The destruction by Joshua (ca. 1400 B.C.) could be represented in the lower city in level III, that of the Egyptian king Seti I (ca. 1318 B.C.) in level II, and that of Barak (ca. 1230 B.C.) in level I. See B. Waltke, "Palestinian Artifactual Evidence Supporting the Early Date of the Exodus," *Bibliotheca Sacra* 129 (January 1972): 42–47.

[32] See Z. Gal, "The Settlement of Issachar: Some New Observations," *Tel Aviv* 9 (1982): 83, for this new identification.

[33] It is very possible that Baal-Berith (Lord of the Covenant, v.4) and El-Berith (God of the Covenant, v. 46) are merely different names for the same temple that was built on an artificial platform called the Beth Millo (House of Filling, v. 6). The massive tower/temple discovered in the excavation at Shechem may indeed be the Baal/El-Berith mentioned in the text.

[34] The location of Thebez is not certain. Some suggest an equation with modern Tubas, northeast of Shechem (grid 185192), while Aharoni suggested that Thebez may be a textual corruption for Tirzah (182188; Aharoni, *Land of the Bible,* 265).

[35] Other places mentioned include Abimelech's residence at Arumah (southeast of Shechem), Beer (to which Jotham fled—identification unknown), and Mount Gerizim (to the south of Shechem).

[36] The identification of Shamir with Samaria is not certain (e.g., *MBA:* 183).

[37] The NIV translates the same Hebrew expression differently in various places: Havvoth Jair (Num 32:41; Deut 3:14; Judg 10:4; 1 Chron 2:23) and "settlements of Jair" (Josh 13:30 [in Bashan]; 1 Kings 4:13 [in Gilead]).

[38] Probably not the Aroer near the Arnon Ravine but rather the one on the Ammonite border (Josh 13:25). Identification unknown.

[39] Identification unknown.

[40] For the text describing this victory, see *ANET,* 262–63, and *ANEP,* 7, 9, 57, 341, 813.

[41] It is debatable as to whether the Philistines conquered territory this far south or whether Ramses III settled them on land that was under his control. For the mention of a Tjekker settlement at the seaport of Dor, see the story of "The Journey of Wen-Amon to Phoenicia" (*ANET,* 25–29).

[42] Traditionally, scholars have suggested that the Philistines brought with them the technological know-how regarding working with iron; see, for example, J. D. Muhly, "How Iron Technology Changed the Ancient World—And Gave the Philistines a Military Edge," *BAR* 8:6 (November/December 1982): 40–52. But recently the leading role ascribed to the Philistines has been called into question: see, for example, the ambiguous comments of T. Dothan, *The Philistines and Their Material Culture* (New Haven: Yale University, 1982), 20–21, and the negative comments of Y. Aharoni, who argues that iron was not commonly used for commercial/military purposes until closer to the time of the Israelite monarchy (*The Archaeology of the Land of Israel,* ed. M. Aharoni, trans. A. F. Rainey [Philadelphia: Westminster, 1979], 156–57). The biblical text seems to indicate that the Canaanites made use of iron for military purposes, e.g., "iron chariots" (Josh 17:16, 18; cf. Judg 1:19), at the time of the conquest of Canaan under Joshua, i.e., 1400 B.C., yet there are some references that indicate it was considered a "precious metal" at that time as well; note its association with silver, gold, and bronze as part of spoil captured by the Israelites (Num 31:22; Josh 6:24; 22:8).

[43] Sorek means "choice grape."

[44] Location unknown, probably in the Hill Country of Judah.

[45] A Philistine temple discovered by A. Mazar at Tel Qasile had twin columns that supported the roof and lends archaeological data to the account of Samson's "bringing the temple of Dagon down."

Transition to the Monarchy, pp. 110–15

[1] M. Kochavi and A. Demsky, "An Israelite Village from the Days of the Judges," *BAR* 4:3 (September/October 1978): 19–21.

[2] For a discussion of Shiloh as a cult center see I. Finkelstein, "Shiloh Yields Some, But Not All, of Its Secrets," *BAR* 12:1 (January/February 1986): 22–41.

[3] Since the ark was in Philistine hands seven months (1 Sam 6:1), the Aphek-Ebenezer battle must have occurred in October, just before the rainy season began. It is interesting to note that according to the internal biblical chronology, Samson was alive and active in the Beth Shemesh region at this very time.

[4] For the problem of the number killed—50,070 (a very large number for this rural village context) or 70—see the commentaries; J.W. Wenham, "Large Numbers in the Old Testament," *Tyndale Bulletin* 18 (1967): 22; or the note in the *NIV Study Bible.*

[5] Samuel's Ramah is usually identified with modern er-Ram, yet Albright's old suggestion of identifying it with modern Ramallah also deserves consideration. If Ramallah is indeed the place, then Samuel would have made his annual circuit from Ramah to Bethel to Gilgal to Mizpah to Ramah without having to double back. Ramah means "height" or "high place," and the name would actually fit either site. For a full discussion, see A. F. Rainey, "RAMAH, RAMA," in *ZPEB,* 5:29–33.

[6] This date is suggested by L. Wood, *A Survey of Israel's History,* rev. ed., ed. D. O'Brien (Grand Rapids: Zondervan, 1986), 194.

[7] This "Ebenezer" is not necessarily the same place mentioned in 1 Samuel 4:1 and 5:1, though it could be. The identification of Shen is unknown.

[8] For the genealogical association of Saul with Gibeon, see A. Demsky, "The Genealogy of Gibeon (1 Chronicles 9:35–44): Biblical and Epigraphic Considerations," *BASOR* 202 (1971): 16–23.

[9] There were a number of villages located on the hills that dot the Benjamin Plateau, which were named in view of their elevated positions: for example, Ramah/Ramathaim (from the Hebrew root meaning "to be high"), Mizpah ("watchtower"), and from the Hebrew root gb^{c} (meaning "hill") such names as Geba, Geba of Benjamin, Gibeath, Gibeah of Benjamin, Gibeah of God, Gibeah of Saul, and Gibeon. The interchange of the names within the latter group is somewhat complex (see, e.g., 2 Sam 5:25 [Heb. Geba, see NIV note] and compare 1 Chron 14:16 [Gibeon]). For an important discussion of this complex problem, see A. Demsky's study, the outlines of which are followed here, "Geba, Gibeah, and Gibeon—An Historico-Geographic Riddle," *BASOR* 212 (1973): 25–31.

[10] For the possibility of adopting this chronology from the difficult verse 1 Samuel 13:1, see Wood, *Survey of Israel's History, 203.*

[11] See Demsky, "Geba," 30, for this identification.

[12] The early introduction of iron by the Philistines is now doubted, and the weapons mentioned in 1 Samuel 13:19–20 were probably made of bronze. See above, "Settlement in the Land of Canaan," note 42.

[13] M. Kochavi, "Rescue in the Biblical Negev," *BAR* 6:1 (January/February 1980): 27.

[14] Also seen here is the proximity of Gath to the Valley of Elah, thus confirming the identification of Gath with Tell es-Safi; see A. Rainey, "The Identification of Philistine Gath—A Problem in Source Analysis for Historical Geography," in *Nelson Glueck Memorial Volume,* ed. B. Mazar, Eretz-Israel 12 (Jerusalem: Israel Exploration Society, 1975), 63*–76*.

[15] For the meaning of Hebrew *naweh* as "pastoral abode," see A. Malamat "Mari," *BA* 34:1 (1971): 16–17.

[16] Y. Aharoni, *The Land of the Bible,* rev. and en. ed., trans. and ed. A. F. Rainey (Philadelphia: Westminster, 1979), 291.

[17] Ibid, 261, and "The Negeb of Judah," *IEJ* 8 (1958): 26–38.

[18] The NIV's "Besor Ravine" is a bit misleading, for the wadi in this area is not terribly deep.

[19] Later David would have the remains of Saul and Jonathan moved to the family tomb at Zela in Benjamin (2 Sam 21:12–14).

The United Monarchy: David and Solomon, pp. 116–23

[1] For a reasonable arrangement of David's wars of expansion, see A. Malamat, "Aspects of the Foreign Policies of David and Solomon," *JNES* 22 (1963): 1–17. His basic sequence of events is followed in the discussion.

[2] Ibid., 3.

[3] Ibid.

[4] R. Cohen, "The Fortresses King Solomon Built to Protect His Southern Border," *BAR* 121 (May/June 1985): 56–70; Z. Herzog, "Enclosed Settlements in the Negev and the Wilderness of Beer-sheba," *BASOR* 250 (1983): 41–49; R. Cohen, "The Iron Age Fortresses in the Central Negev," *BASOR* 236 (1979): 61–79.

[5] For a discussion of this thesis, see C. Rasmussen, "The Economic Importance of Caravan Trade for the Solomonic Empire," *A Tribute to Gleason Archer: Essays on the Old Testament,* ed. W. Kaiser, Jr., and R. Youngblood (Chicago: Moody, 1986), 153–66.

[6] Y. Ikeda, "Solomon's Trade in Horses and Chariots in Its International Setting," *Studies in the Period of David and Solomon and Other Essays,* ed. T. Ishida (Winona Lake, Ind.: Eisenbrauns), 215–38; C. Hauer, Jr., "The Economics of National Security in Solomonic Israel," *JSOT* 18 (1980): 63–73.

[7] N. Glueck, "Ezion-geber," *BA* 28 (1965): 70–87; H. Shanks, "Nelson Glueck and King Solomon—A Romance That Ended," *BAR* (March 1975): 10–16; B. Rothenberg, *Timna* (London: Thames and Hudson, 1972), 63, 180.

[8] S. Ahituv, "Economic Factors in the Egyptian Conquest of Canaan," *IEJ* 28 (1978): 93–105.

[9] D. Ussishkin, "King Solomon's Palaces," *BA* 36:3 (September 1973): 78–105; Y. Aharoni, *The Archaeology of the Land of Israel,* ed. M. Aharoni and trans. A. F. Rainey (Philadelphia: Westminster, 1982), 220–21, 226–34.

[10] For contrasting views of the dating of the palaces, see Aharoni, *Archaeology,* 205–8 (Davidic), and Ussishkin, "Solomon's Palaces," 94–104 (Solomonic).

[11] Y. Kaufman, "Where the Ancient Temple of Jerusalem Stood," *BAR* 9:2 (1983): 56–58.

[12] For this reading in place of Aloth, see F. Cross in G. E. Wright, "The Provinces of Solomon: (1 Kings 4:7–19)," *E. L. Sukenik Memorial Volume,* eds. N. Avigad, M. Avi-Yonah, H. Z. Herschberg, and B. Mazar, Eretz-Israel 8 (Jerusalem: Israel Exploration Society, 1967), 59*.

[13] For the identification of Aruboth see A. Zertal "The Roman Siege System at Khirbet el-Ḥamman (Narbata) in Samaria," *Qadmoniot* 14:3–4 (1981): 114.

[14] See Y. Aharoni, "The Solomonic Districts," *Tel Aviv* 3 (1976): 5–15 for various possibilities.

[15] T. Mettinger, *Solomonic State Officials: A Study of the Civil Government Officials of the Israelite Monarchy,* Coniectanea Biblica, Old Testament Series 5 (Lund: CWK Gleerups, 1971), 126–27.

[16] Mettinger, *Solomonic State Officials,* 112 for additional arguments.

[17] K. A. Kitchen, *The Third Intermediate Period in Egypt (1100–650 B.C.)* (Warminster: Aris & Phillips, 1973), pars. 231, 235; A. Malamat, "Aspects of the Foreign Policies of David and Solomon," *JNES* 22 (1963): 9–10.

[18] F. C. Fensham, "The Treaty Between the Israelites and Tyrians," *Supplements to Vetus Testamentum* 17 (1969): 71–87.

The Divided Kingdom, pp. 124–33

[1] For a complete discussion of the text, see K. A. Kitchen, *The Third Intermediate Period in Egypt (1100–650 B.C.)* (Warminster: Aris and Phillips (1973), pars. 252–60, 398–415, and also Y. Aharoni, *The Land of the Bible,* rev. and enl. ed., trans. and ed. A. F. Rainey (Philadelphia: Westminster, 1979), 323–30.

[2] R. Cohen, "The Fortresses King Solomon Built to Protect His Southern Border," *BAR* 11:3 (May/June 1985): 69–70.

[3] N. Naaman, "Two Notes on the Monolith Inscription of Shalmaneser III from Kurkh," *Tel Aviv* 3 (1976): 97–102, reduces the number from 2,000 to a more reasonable 200 chariots.

[4] Athaliah (841–835 B.C.) was the only female and non-Davidic ruler.

[5] Aharoni, *The Land of the Bible,* 356–68.

Judah Alone, pp. 134–39

[1] M. Broshi, "The Expansion of Jerusalem in the Reigns of Hezekiah and Manasseh," *IEJ* 24 (1974): 21–26 and H. Shanks, "Yigal Shiloh," *BAR* 14:2 (March/April 1988): 20–21.

[2] M. Kochavi, "The Land of Judah," in *Judea, Samaria and the Golan: Archaeological Survey 1967–1968,* ed. M. Kochavi (Jerusalem: Carta, 1972), 19–89.

[3] For the difficult question regarding the dates of Hezekiah's reign, see E. R. Thiele, *The Mysterious Numbers of the Hebrew Kings,* rev. ed. (Grand Rapids: Zondervan, 1983), 129–38, 174–76.

[4] See, for example, A. F. Rainey, "Wine from the Royal Vineyards," *BASOR* 245 (1982): 57–62 and the references to previous literature cited there.

[5] N. Avigad, *Discovering Jerusalem* (Nashville: Thomas Nelson, 1983), 46–60.

[6] N. Naaman, "Sennacherib's 'Letter to God' on His Campaign to Judah," *BASOR* 214 (1974): 26–28.

[7] For ancient near eastern texts and pictures, see conveniently *ANET,* 287–88 and *ANEP,* figs. 371–74; and for the order of events, see K. A. Kitchen, *The Third Intermediate Period in Egypt (1100–650 B.C.)* (Warminster: Aris and Phillips, 1973),

pars. 126–37, 345–54, as well as Y. Aharoni, *Land of the Bible*, rev. and enl. ed., trans. and ed. A. F. Rainey (Philadelphia: Westminster, 1979), 367–400.

[8] See Naaman, "Sennacherib's 'Letter to God'," for the text describing this phase of the campaign.

[9] D. Ussishkin, "Answers at Lachish," *BAR* 5:6 (November/December 1979): 16–39.

[10] At the time of the Egyptian-Assyrian encounter, Sebitku (702–690 B.C.) was, in fact, the king of Egypt, but evidently it was his twenty-year-old brother, Tirhakah, who led the Egyptian forces on their campaign in Philistia. Since Tirhakah would become king (690–664 B.C.), it seems that the biblical writer uses the title "the Cushite king of Egypt" retrospectively. For this whole question, see Kitchen, *Third Intermediate Period*, pars. 128–29, and A. F. Rainey, "Taharqa and Syntax," *Tel Aviv* 3 (1976): 38–41.

[11] Possibly some Simeonites had moved northward from their tribal allotment in the Beersheba region (Josh 19:1–9; cf. 2 Chron 15:7).

[12] For the text from the Babylonian Chronicle, see *ANET*, 564.

[13] Note the tablet from the early sixth century B.C., found in Babylon, that mentions food rations given to Jehoiachin the king of Judah (*ANET*, 308).

Exile and Return, pp. 140–46

[1] For a detailed description of the history and geography of "Trans-Euphrates," see A. F. Rainey, "The Satrapy 'Beyond the River,'" *Australian Journal of Biblical Archaeology* 1:2 (1969): 51–78.

[2] For a detailed treatment of the province of Samaria in light of the fourth-century B.C. papyri from the Wadi Daliyeh, see F. M. Cross, "Papyri of the Fourth Century B.C. from Daliyeh: A Preliminary Report on Their Discovery and Significance," in *New Directions in Biblical Archaeology*, ed. D. N. Freedman and J. C. Greenfield (Garden City: Doubleday, 1969), 41–62, and F. M. Cross, "A Reconstruction of the Judean Restoration," *JBL* 94 (1975): 4–18.

[3] For an extensive treatment of this family, see B. Mazar, "The Tobiads," *IEJ* 7 (1957): 229–38.

[4] Y. Aharoni, *The Land of the Bible*, rev. and enl. ed., trans. and ed. A. F. Rainey (Philadelphia: Westminster, 1979), 418; but compare M. Avi-Yonah, *The Holy Land from the Persian to the Arab Conquest (536 B.C.–A.D. 640): A Historical Geography*, rev. ed. (Grand Rapids: Baker, 1977), 19–23.

[5] N. Avigad, *Bullae and Seals from a Post-Exilic Judean Archive*, Qedem 4 (Jerusalem: Hebrew University Press, 1976), 30–36.

The Arrival of the Greeks, pp. 147–52

[1] For predictions regarding the coming of Alexander the Great (goat with a prominent horn) and the defeat of the Persians (ram with two horns), see Daniel 8 and 11:1–3.

[2] The Zenon archive is a group of papyrus documents that were found at Philadelphia in the Fayum, west of the Nile. They shed much light on Egyptian-Palestinian commercial relations, among other things. These documents detail a trip that Zenon, an Egyptian official during the rule of Ptolemy II, took to Palestine in 259 and 258 B.C. Places that he visited include Pegae, Jerusalem, Abila, Tyrus, Lacasa, Naveh, Eeitha, Beth-anath, Cades, and Ptolemais, and his activities indicate that Palestine served as an important agricultural hinterland for Egypt.

[3] The following discussion is based on the detailed treatment of M. Avi-Yonah, *The Holy Land from the Persian to the Arab Conquests (536 B.C. to A.D. 640): A Historical Geography* (Grand Rapids: Baker, 1977), 32–41.

[4] For lack of a better name, the term "Palestine" is used in this and the following chapters in a rather ambiguous way. At times it will refer to the traditional territory that was included in the "Land of Israel." At other times it may include not only this but also Transjordanian territory (such as Gilead and/or Moab and Edom) and also the territorial holdings of the controlling government further north. This may be disconcerting, but the fact is that during the Hellenistic Period (332–63 B.C.) the boundaries of all the countries, provinces, districts, etc., were constantly changing. In addition, the term, like all the names for this area of the world, is problematic in that it carries with it indications of the political persuasion of the modern user. By using this term I am not attempting to make any modern political statement. I have decided to use this name during the Greco-Roman period as a general term of reference, for it was first used by the Greek historian Herodotus (ca. 450 B.C.; 1.105; 2.106; 2.104; 7.89; 3.5) at that time. Although the name is apparently derived from the word "Philistia" (= Greek Palestine), and it may have originally referred only to the limited area of Philistine settlement along the southern coast, it later came to be used in a broad way. It was also used by the Jewish historian Josephus in the late first century A.D. In any case, it is very difficult to define the exact boundaries of Herodotus' "Palestine," and that might give us some justification to use the term in a general way as well. Thus the writer—and reader—need not be constantly assaulted with a long list of provinces and/or districts when referring to the territory of the southern Levant.

[5] The following description makes use of the detailed discussion of M. Avi-Yonah, *Holy Land*, 42–52.

Macabean Revolt and Hasmonean Dynasty, pp. 153–59

[1] No attempt has been made to document each statement with regard to ancient or secondary sources. The interested reader can directly consult First and Second Maccabees as well as Josephus' works (*The Jewish War* and especially *Jewish Antiquities*). For a standard, detailed work that footnotes every reference and contains a detailed bibliography of ancient as well as modern works, see E. Schurer, *The History of the Jewish People in the Age of Jesus Christ*, ed. and rev. G. Vermes, F. Millar, and M. Black (Edinburgh: T. & T. Clark, 1979), 1:125–242. For a detailed technical discussion of the historical geography of this period, see M. Avi-Yonah, *The Holy Land from the Persian to the Arab Conquests (536 B.C. to A.D. 640): A Historical Geography* (Grand Rapids: Baker, 1977), 42–85.

Early Roman Rule in Palestine, pp. 160–65

[1] The historical account of most of the events referred to in this chapter can be found in the appropriate sections of Josephus' works (*The Jewish War* and *Jewish Antiquities*). For a standard, detailed work that footnotes every reference, see E. Schurer, *The History of the Jewish People in the Age of Jesus Christ*, ed. and rev. G. Vermes, F. Millar, and M. Black (Edinburgh: T. & T. Clark, 1979), 1:233–329. For a detailed technical discussion of the historical geography of this period, see M. Avi-Yonah, *The Holy Land from the Persian to the Arab Conquests (536 B.C. to A.D. 640): A Historial Geography* (Grand Rapids: Baker, 1977), 77–85.

[2] For the use of the term "Palestine," see "Arrival of the Greeks," note 4.

[3] For a recent discussion of the league, see S. T. Parker, "The Decapolis Reviewed," *JBL* 94 (1975): 437–41.

[4] For a detailed technical discussion of the historical geography of Herod's Kingdom, see Avi-Yonah, *The Holy Land*, 86–101.

[5] Reports of recent archaeological excavations and investigations of Herodian remains can be found in recent issues of the *Biblical Archaeology Review* and the *Biblical Archaeologist*.

Life of Christ, pp. 166–73

[1] For a detailed historical survey of the rule of Archelaus see, E. Schurer, *The History of the Jewish People in the Age of Jesus Christ*, ed. and rev. G. Vermes, F. Millar, and M. Black (Edinburgh: T. & T. Clark, 1979) 1:330–35, 353–57; and for a study of the geographical background of the period, see M. Avi-Yonah, *The Holy Land from the Persian to the Arab Conquests (536 B.C. to A.D. 640): A Historical Geography* (Grand Rapids: Baker, 1977), 102–7.

[2] For a detailed historical survey of the rule of Herod Antipas, see Schurer, *History of the Jewish People*, 340–53, and the bibliography cited there.

[3] For a recent popular survey of the history and archaeology of Sepphoris, see E. M. Meyers, E. Netzer, and C. L. Meyers, "Sepphoris 'Ornament of All Galilee'," *BA* 49:1 (March 1986): 4–19.

[4] There is some variety regarding the exact dates of Jesus' ministry. "Traditional" dates will be followed here—see T. W. House, *Chronological and Background Charts of the New Testament* (Grand Rapids: Zondervan, 1981), 102–3, but compare H. Hoehner, *Chronological Aspects of the Life of Christ* (Grand Rapids: Zondervan, 1977).

[5] Regarding the identification of Dalmanutha, see J. C. Laney, *Geographical Aspects of the Life of Christ*, second edition (doctoral dissertation presented to Dallas Theological Seminary, 1977), 150–55, but compare B. Pixner, "The Land of Galilee that Jesus Walked: A Historical Map," (Rosh Pina, Israel: Corazin, 1983).

[6] For a popular description of recent discoveries at Capernaum, see J. F. Strange and H. Shanks, "Synagogue Where Jesus Preached Found at Capernaum," *BAR* 9:6 (November/December 1983): 24–31.

[7] For the acoustical properties of a natural theater on the shore of the Sea of Galilee between Capernaum and Tabgha, see B. C. Crisler, "The Acoustics and Crowd Capacity of Natural Theaters in Palestine," *BA* 39:4 (December 1976): 134–38.

[8] Z. Yeivin, "Ancient Chorazin Comes Back to Life," *BAR* 12:5 (September/October 1987): 22–36, and "Korazim—1983/84," *Excavations and Surveys in Israel 1984* 3 (1984): 66–71.

[9] For a recent discussion of the location of Bethsaida, see B. Pixner, "Searching for the New Testament Site of Bethsaida," *BA* 48:4 (December 1985): 207–16.

[10] For a detailed history of Philip's rule, see Schurer, *History of the Jewish People*, 336–40 and the bibliography and ancient sources cited there; and for the geography, see Avi-Yonah, *The Holy Land*, 102–7.

[11] For a listing of the cities of the Decapolis (Matt 4:25; Mark 5:20; 7:31), see Pliny (A.D. 23–79) *Natural History* 5.16 [74]. For a recent discussion, see S. T. Parker, "The Decapolis Reviewed," *JBL* 94 (1975): 437–41.

[12] For an ancient description of Jericho and the surrounding region, see Josephus (*War* 4.8.2–3 [451–75]).

[13] Luke 17:11–19 appears to record the beginning of Jesus' final journey from Galilee to Jerusalem. Given the detour around Samaria, it can be surmised that Jesus and his disciples headed east from the Ginae area to the region of Scythopolis, and from there they could have headed south on either side of the Jordan River. The next locality that they passed through was Jericho at the south end of the Jordan Valley (Luke 19:1).

[14] Codex Sinaiticus and the Palestinian Syriac read 160 stadia, but it may have been that a copyist changed the distance from 60 to 160 in order to make it conform to the well-known Emmaus/Nicopolis. Another difficulty has to do with the problem of the two disciples covering the distance to and from Jerusalem in such a short period of time. For additional details see the appropriate articles in *ZPEB*, *ISBE*, or *IDB*.

Expansion of the Church in Palestine, pp. 174–79

[1] For the ancient extrabiblical texts pertaining to this period, see the relevant sections in Josephus (*The Jewish War* and *Jewish Antiquities*). For a standard, detailed work that footnotes every reference, see E. Schurer, *The History of the Jewish People in the Age of Jesus Christ*, ed. and rev. G. Vermes, F. Millar, and M. Black (Edinburgh: T. & T. Clark, 1979), 1:336–55; for the historical geography see M. Avi-Yonah, *The Holy Land from the Persian to the Arab Conquests (536 B.C. to A.D. 640): A Historical Geography* (Grand Rapids: Baker, 1977), 102–17.

[2] For a moving description of the revolt, see Josephus, *The Jewish War*, passim.

[3] For a discussion of this term, see "Arrival of the Greeks," note 4.

The Journeys of Paul, pp. 180–87

[1] For descriptions of the various cities that Paul visited on his journeys, see J. Finegan, *The Archeology of the New Testament: The Mediterranean World of the Early Christian Apostles* (Boulder, Colo.: Westview 1981), and E. Yamauchi, *The Archaeology of New Testament Cities in Western Asia Minor* (Grand Rapids: Baker, 1980) and the bibliographies cited there.

[2] For recent descriptions of Corinth, see J. Murphy-0'Connor, "The Corinth that Saint Paul Saw," *BA* 47:3 September 1984): 147–59, and his *St. Paul's Corinth, Texts and Archaeology* (Wilmington, Del.: Michael Glazier, 1983).

Jerusalem, pp. 188–200

[1] There are numerous studies on the history and archaeology of Jerusalem. The interested reader is invited to consult the works noted below or the recent survey of W. Harold Mare, *The Archaeology of the Jerusalem Area* (Grand Rapids: Baker, 1987), in which additional bibliographic references can be found.

[2] R. Gonen, "Was the Site of the Jerusalem Temple Originally a Cemetery?" *BAR* 11:3 (May/June): 44–55.

[3] Y. Shiloh, *Excavations at the City of David I: 1978–1982*, Qedem 19 (Jerusalem: The Institute of Archaeology of the Hebrew University, 1981), 28.

[4] The population estimates used in this chapter are based on M. Broshi's estimates: "Estimating the Population of Ancient Jerusalem," *BAR* 6:2 (June 1978): 12 and "The Expansion of Jerusalem in the Reigns of Hezekiah and Manasseh," *IEJ* 24 (1974): 20–26.

[5] The actual dating of the construction of this water system is in dispute, but there does not seem to be any compelling reason to abandon a pre-Davidic date for its construction. Y. Shiloh, "Jerusalem's Water Supply During Siege—The Rediscovery of Warren's Shaft," *BAR* 7:4 (July/August 1981): 24–39 for a recent description of the system.

[6] B. Mazar, *The Mountain of the Lord*, assisted by G. Cornfeld and D. N. Freedman (Garden City, NY: Doubleday, 1975), 168–69.

[7] Y. Shiloh, "The City of David: 1978–1983," in *Biblical Archaeology Today*, ed. J. Amitai (Jerusalem: Israel Exploration Society, 1985), 455–57.

[8] Mazar, *The Mountain*, pp. 186–87.

[9] D. Ussishkin, "The Necropolis from the Kingdom of Judah at Silwan, Jerusalem," *BA*, 33 (1970): 34–46.

[10] H. Shank's, "Have the Tombs of the Kings of Judah Been Found?" *BAR*, 13:4 (July/August 1987): 54–56. For a description of the tombs themselves see G. Barkay and A. Kloner, "Jerusalem Tombs From the Days of the First Temple," *BAR* 12:2 (March/April 1986): 22–39 and for the suggestion that they might be the tombs of later Judean kings see A. Kloner, "The 'Third Wall' in Jerusalem and the 'Cave of the Kings' (Josephus *War* V 147)," *Levant* 18 (1986): 121–29.

[11] A. S. Kaufman, "Where the Ancient Temple of Jerusalem Stood," *BAR* 9:2 (March/April 1983): 40–59.

[12] D. Ussishkin, "King Solomon's Palaces," *BA* 36 (1974): 78–105.

[13] It is difficult to pinpoint the exact location and function of the Millo and the Ophel. The former literally means "filling" and in contrast to the interpretation adopted above, it has been suggested that it refers to the supporting terraces that were built on the steep slopes and upon which buildings were constructed—thus the need to keep them in good repair. The term "Ophel" seems to be a reference to the royal acropolis, which was situated on the eastern ridge between the City of David to the south and the Temple Mount to the north. Indeed, Ophels, or acropolises, are mentioned in connection with the cities of Samaria (2 Kings 5:24) and Dibbon (*ANET*: 320 [lines 21–22]), royal centers of the northern kingdom and of Moab respectively. In the biblical text possibly the term Millo was used early in the period of the monarchy, but was later replaced by the term Ophel, or alternatively, the Millo might have been something more limited within the Ophel. For a report on the discovery of a gate and/or public building from the area where the Ophel was located see E. Mazar, "Ophel Excavations, Jerusalem," *IEJ* 37 (1987): 60–62, and "Royal Gateway to Ancient Jerusalem Uncovered," *BAR* 15:3 (May/June 1989): 38-51.

[14] J. W. Crowfoot and G. M. Fitzgerald, *Excavations in the Tyropoeon Valley, 1927*, Annual of the Palestine Exploration Fund 5 (London, 1929).

[15] N. Avigad, *Discovering Jerusalem* (Nashville: Thomas Nelson, n.d.), 46–60.

[16] M. Broshi, "Estimating," 12.

[17] Y. Shiloh, *Excavations*. pp. 28–29.

[18] Y. Shiloh, "The City of David: 1978–1983," pp. 460–62.

[19] For textual evidence see 2 Kgs 25:9 and in addition note that eighty men were going up to Jerusalem to the "house of the Lord," "bringing grain offerings and incense" (Jer 41:5) after the destruction of the temple, thus indicating that some type of worship was going on amid the ruins of the temple. In addition, tombs from this period have been found in the vicinity of Jerusalem, and the artifacts in them seem to indicate that some prosperous people were still living in the area—see G. Barkay, "St. Andrew's Church Jerusalem," *IEJ* 26 (1976): 57–58 and "News from the Field: The Divine Name Found in Jerusalem," *BAR* 9:2 (March/April 1983): 14–19. Further, it is evident that the Babylonians had left large portions of Jerusalem's wall intact, for Nehemiah 3 emphasizes the rebuilding of certain gates and towers, but not the entire perimeter of the wall. This supposition would also help account for the brevity of time needed to refortify the city—52 days. It is also possible that a significant beginning had been made in constructing the walls at an earlier time (Ezra 4:12). See H. G. M. Williamson, "Nehemiah's Walls Revisited," *PEQ* 116 (1984): 81–88.

[20] But compare A. S. Kaufman, "Where the Ancient Temple of Jerusalem Stood."

[21] Avigad, *Discovering Jerusalem*, 61–63.

[22] Y. Tsafrir, "The Location of the Seleucid Akra in Jerusalem," *Revue Biblique*, 82:4 (1975): 501–22 and B. Mazar, "The Temple Mount," in *Biblical Archaeology Today*, ed. J. Amitai (Jerusalem: Israel Exploration Society, 1985), 463–68.

[23] Avigad, *Discovering Jerusalem*, 65–75.

[24] Ibid., 74–79.

[25] But compare A. S. Kaufman, "Where the Ancient Temple of Jerusalem Stood."

[26] Mazar, *The Mountain*, 140–48.

[27] Ibid., 135ff.

[28] Ibid., 138ff.

[29] A. D. Tushingham, "Excavations in the Armenian Garden on the Western Wall," in *Excavations in Jerusalem 1961–1967: Volume I*, ed. A. D. Tushingham (Toronto: Royal Ontario Museum), 25–44.

[30] Avigad, *Discovering Jerusalem*, 81–204.

[31] G. Barkai, "The Garden Tomb: Was Jesus Buried Here?" *BAR* 12:2 (March/April): 40–57.

[32] For a convenient summary of all aspects of Jerusalem during the time of Jesus see J. Wilkinson, *Jerusalem as Jesus Knew It: Archaeology as Evidence* (London: Thames and Hudson, 1978).

[33] For a recent discussion of the dating and function of the "Third Wall," with references to earlier literature, see Kloner, "The Third Wall."

The Disciplines of Historical Geography, pp. 201–8

[1] This division into types is taken from Y. Aharoni, *The Land of the Bible: A Historical Geography*, rev. edition ed. by A. G. Rainey (Philadelphia: Westminster, 1979): 81–104. For a more complete treatment of topics mentioned here, as well as additional examples and bibliographhy, his work should be consulted.

[2] See Aharoni, pp. 87–91.

[3] M. Kochavi, "Khirbet Rabud = Debir," *Tel Aviv* vol. 1:2–33.

[4] For brief discussions of many of the texts mentioned here, see the appropriate chapters in the Historical Section of this atlas. For more detailed treatments see Aharoni, *The Land*, passim.

[5] *Ancient Near Eastern Texts Relating to the Old Testament*, 3rd edition, ed. F. B. Pritchard (Princeton: Princeton University, 1969).

[6] For in-depth overviews of toponymy see Aharoni, *The Land*, pp. 105–30 and the more recent survey of A. F. Rainey, "Toponymics of Eretz-Israel," "Bulletin of the American Schools of Oriental Research 232" (1978): 1–17. The examples that follow are drawn from their works.

[7] The historical reconstructions found in the historical section of this atlas indicate what great respect I have for the text as it stands, but many researchers have come to differing conclusions in this regard.

[8] Massive destruction levels that can be correlated with knwon historical events are very useful in anchoring the chronology of pottery types. For example, the destruction of Lachish III can be assigned to Sennacherib (701 B.C.), while that of level II is assigned to Nebuchadnezzar (587/6 B.C.). Thus the dating of the assemblages from those levels is fairly certain.

Bibliography

Abel, F.-M. *Géographie de la Palestine: Géographie physique et historique*, vol. 1. Third edition. Paris: J. Gabalda, 1933.

_____. *Géographie de la Palestine: Géographie politique. Les villes*, vol. 2. Third edition. Paris: J. Gabalda, 1938.

Aharoni, Y. *The Land of the Bible*. Revised and enlarged edition. Translated from Hebrew and edited by A. F. Rainey. Philadelphia: Westminster, 1979.

_____. *The Archaeology of the Land of Israel*. Edited by M. Aharoni, translated from Hebrew by A. F. Rainey. Philadelphia: Westminster, 1982.

Aharoni, Y., and Avi-Yonah, M. *The Macmillan Bible Atlas*. Revised edition. New York: Macmillan, 1977.

Amitai, J., ed. *Biblical Archaeology Today: Proceedings of the International Congress on Biblical Archaeology Jerusalem, April 1984, Jerusalem: Israel Exploration Society, 1985.*

Archer, G. L., Jr. *A Survey of Old Testament Introduction*. Revised edition. Chicago: Moody, 1975.

Atlas of Israel. Third English edition. New York: Macmillan, 1985.

Avi-Yonah, M. *The Holy Land from the Persian to Arab Conquests (536 B.C. to A.D. 640): A Historical Geography*. Revised edition. Grand Rapids: Baker, 1977.

_____. *Gazetteer of Roman Palestine*. Qedem 5. Jerusalem: The Institute of Archaeology, the Hebrew University, and Carta, 1976.

Avi-Yonah, M., and Stern, E., eds. *Encyclopedia of Archaeological Excavations in the Holy Land*, 4 vols. Jerusalem: Massada Press, 1975–1978.

Avigad, Nahman. *Discovering Jerusalem*. Nashville: Thomas Nelson, 1980.

Baines, J., and Malek, J. *Atlas of Ancient Egypt*. New York: Facts On File, 1982.

Baly, Denis, *The Geography of the Bible*. New and revised edition. New York: Harper & Row, 1974

Baly, D., and Tushingham, A. D. *Atlas of the Biblical World*. New York: World, 1971.

Beek, M. A. *Atlas of Mesopotamia*. Translated by D. R. Welsh and edited by H. H. Rowley. New York: Thomas Nelson, 1962.

Beitzel, Barry J. *The Moody Atlas of Bible Lands*. Chicago: Moody, 1985.

Bimson, J. J. *Redating the Exodus and Conquest*. Journal for the Study of the Old Testament Supplement, 5. Sheffield: Sheffield University Press, 1978.

Blaiklock, E. M., and Harrison, R. K., eds. *New International Dictionary of Biblical Archaeology*. Grand Rapids: Zondervan, 1983.

Bright, J. *A History of Israel*. Third edition. Philadelphia: Westminster, 1981.

Bromiley, G. W., ed. *The International Standard Bible Encyclopedia*. 4 vols. Revised edition. Grand Rapids: Eerdmans, 1979–1988.

Cornell, T., and Matthews, J. *Atlas of the Roman World*. New York: Facts On File, 1982.

Excavations and Surveys in Israel. Vol. 1—. Jerusalem: Israel Department of Antiquities and Museums, 1982—.

Grollenberg, L. H. *Atlas of the Bible*. London: Thomas Nelson, 1959.

Hallo, W. W., and Simpson, W. K. *The Ancient Near East: A History*. New York: Harcourt Brace Jovanovich, 1971.

Hayes, J. H., and Miller, J. M., eds. *Israelite and Judean History*. Philadelphia: Westminster, 1977.

Kallai, Zecharia. *Historical Geography of the Bible: The Tribal Territories of Israel*. Jerusalem: Magnes Press, Hebrew University, 1986.

Karmon, Y. *Israel: A Regional Geography*. New York: Wiley-Interscience, 1971.

Kitchen, K. A. *The Third Intermediate Period in Egypt (1100 – 650 B.C.)*. Warminster, England: Aris & Phillips, 1973.

Levi, P. *Atlas of the Greek World*. New York: Facts On File, 1980.

Mare, W. Harold. *The Archaeology of the Jerusalem Area*. Grand Rapids: Baker, 1987.

May, H. G., ed. *Oxford Bible Atlas*. Third edition revised by J. Day. New York: Oxford 1984.

Mazar, Benjamin. *The Mountain of the Lord*. Garden City, N.Y.: Doubleday, 1975.

Merrill, E. H. *Kingdom of Priests: A History of Old Testament Israel*. Grand Rapids: Baker, 1987.

Miller, J. M., and Hayes, J. H. *A History of Ancient Israel and Judah*. Philadelphia, Westminster, 1986.

Monson, J., ed. *Student Map Manual: Historical Geography of the Bible Lands*. Jerusalem: Pictorial Archive, n.d.

Naaman, N. *Borders and Districts in Biblical Historiography, Seven Studies in Biblical Geographical Lists*. Jerusalem: Simor, 1986.

O'Connor, Jerome Murphy. *The Holy Land: An Archaeological Guide from Earliest Times to 1700*. New edition. Oxford: University, 1986.

Orni, E., and Efrat, E. *Geography of Israel*. Third revised edition. Jerusalem: Israel Universities Press, 1971.

Pritchard, J. B., ed. *Ancient Near East in Pictures Relating to the Old Testament*. Second edition. Princeton: Princeton University Press, 1969.

_____. *Ancient Near Eastern Texts Relating to the Old Testament*. Third edition. Princeton: Princeton University Press, 1969.

_____. *The Harper Atlas of the Bible*. New York: Harper & Row, 1987.

Robinson, E. *Biblical Researches in Palestine and Adjacent Regions*. 3 vols. Reprint edition. Jerusalem: Universitas Booksellers, 1970.

Schoville, K. N. *Biblical Archaeology in Focus*. Grand Rapids: Baker, 1978.

Schurer, E. *The History of Jewish People in the Age of Jesus Christ*. Vol. 1 edited and revised by G. Vermes, F. Millar, and M. Black. Edinburgh: T. & T. Clark, 1973.

_____. *The History of the Jewish People in the Age of Jesus Christ*. Vol. 2 edited and revised by G. Vermes, F. Millar, and M. Black. Edinburgh: T. & T. Clark, 1979.

_____. *The History of the Jewish People in the Age of Jesus Christ*. Vol. 3.1 edited and revised by G. Vermes, F. Millar, and M. Black. Edinburgh: T. & T. Clark, 1986.

Shanks, H., ed. *Recent Archaeology in the Land of Israel*. Washington D.C.: Biblical Archaeology Society, 1984.

_____, ed. *Ancient Israel: A Short History from Abraham to the Roman Destruction of the Temple*, Washington, D.C.: Biblical Archaeology Society, 1988.

Simons, J. *The Geographical and Topographical Texts of the Old Testament*. Leiden: Brill, 1959.

Smith, G. A. *The Historical Geography of the Holy Land*. Fontana Library edition, 1973, using the twenty-fifth edition. London: Collins, 1931.

Tenney, M. C., ed., *Zondervan Pictorial Encyclopedia of the Bible*. 5 vols. Grand Rapids: Zondervan, 1975.

Thiele, E. R. *The Mysterious Numbers of the Hebrew Kings*. New revised edition. Grand Rapids: Zondervan, 1983.

Thompson, J. A. *Handbook of Life in Bible Times*. Downers Grove, Ill.: InterVarsity, 1986.

van der Woude, A. S., ed. *The World of the Bible*. Bible Handbook, vol. 1. Translated by S. Woudstra from Dutch. Grand Rapids: Eerdmans, 1986.

Vogel, E. K. "Bibliography of Holy Land Sites," *Hebrew Union College Annual*, vol. 42 (1971):1-96.

Vogel, E. K., and Holtzclaw, B. "Bibliography of Holy Land Sites, Part II," *Hebrew Union College Annual* 52 (1981): 1–92.

Wilkinson, John. *Jerusalem as Jesus Knew It: Archaeology as Evidence*. London: Thames and Hudson, 1978.

Wood, L. J. *A Survey of Israel's History*. Revised edition edited by D. O'Brien. Grand Rapids: Zondervan, 1986.

Wright, G. E., and Filson, F. V., eds. *The Westminster Historical Atlas to the Bible*. Revised edition. Philadelphia: Westminster, 1956.

Yamauchi, E. *The Archaeology of the New Testament Cities in Western Asia Minor*. Grand Rapids: Baker, 1980.

ATLAS CHAPTER	● Pre-Patriarchal Period pp. 70–75							
DATE 3200 B.C.	3100	3000	2900	2800	2700	2600	2500	2400
SYRIA/ MESO-POTAMIA		JEMDET NASR		EARLY DYNASTIC				
CANAAN		EARLY BRONZE						
EGYPT		EARLY DYNASTIC PERIOD DYNASTIES 1–2				PYRAMIDS DYNASTIES 3–6 OLD KINGDOM DYNASTIES 3–8		

ATLAS CHAPTER	● Settlement in Canaan and Judges pp. 96–109	● Samuel and Saul pp. 110–115 ● David and Solomon pp. 116–123	● Divided Kingdom pp. 124–133	● Judah Alone pp. 134–139

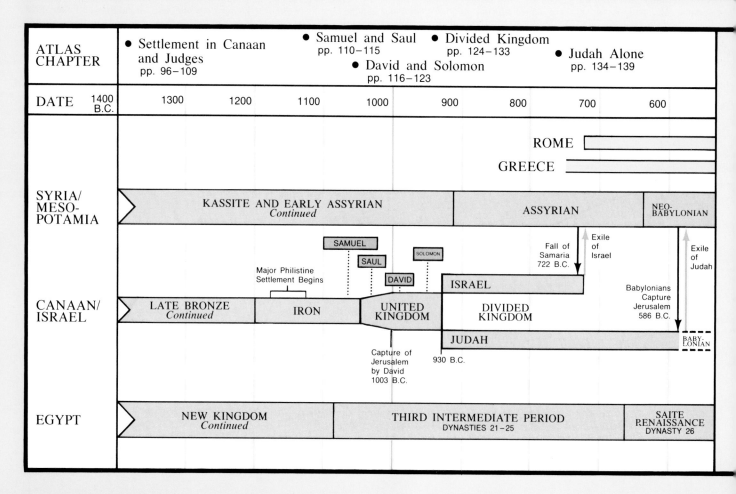

Biblical History

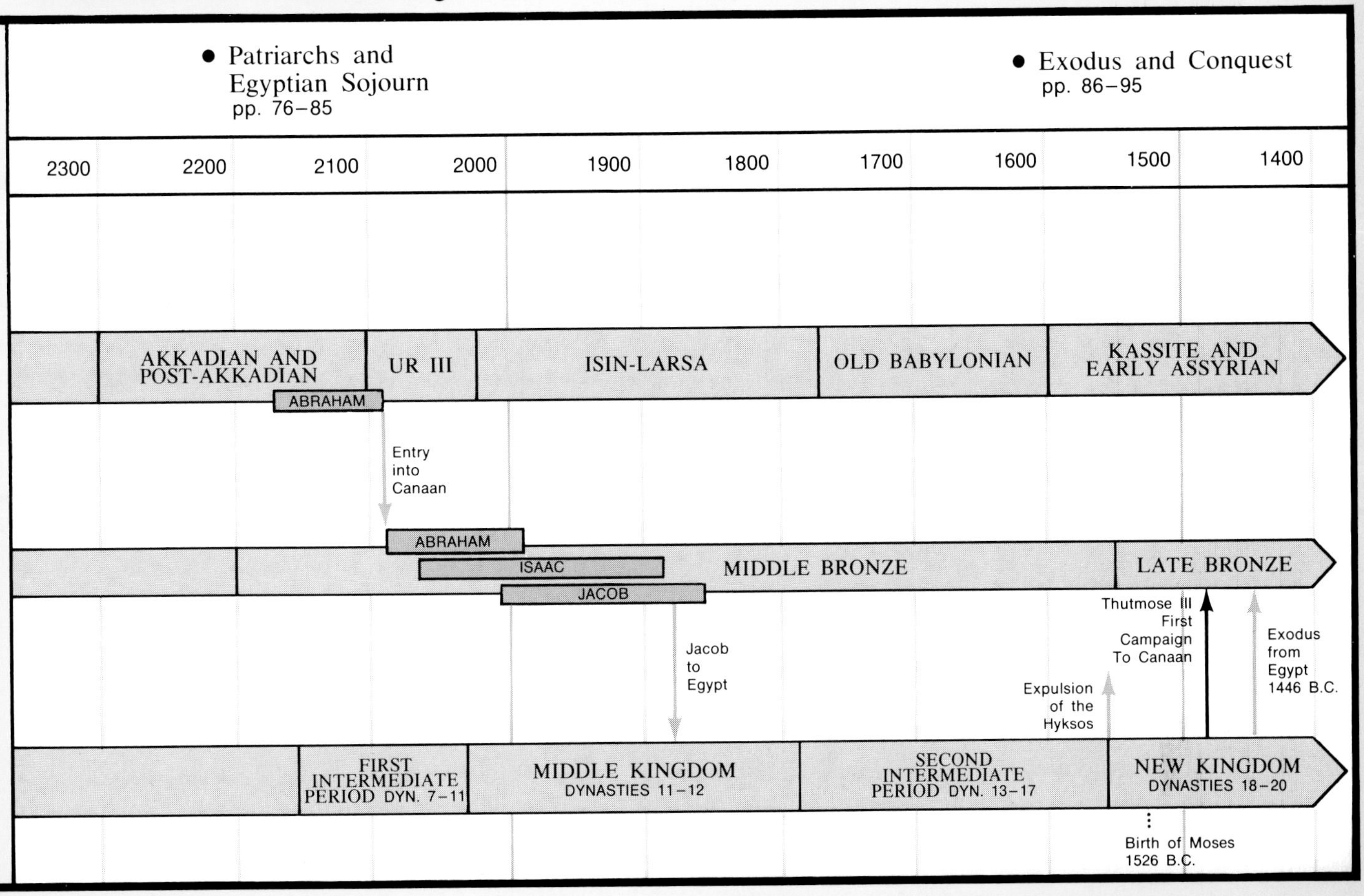

- Patriarchs and Egyptian Sojourn pp. 76–85
- Exodus and Conquest pp. 86–95

2300	2200	2100	2000	1900	1800	1700	1600	1500	1400

AKKADIAN AND POST-AKKADIAN	UR III	ISIN-LARSA	OLD BABYLONIAN	KASSITE AND EARLY ASSYRIAN

ABRAHAM

Entry into Canaan

ABRAHAM

ISAAC

JACOB

MIDDLE BRONZE   LATE BRONZE

Jacob to Egypt

Thutmose III First Campaign To Canaan

Exodus from Egypt 1446 B.C.

Expulsion of the Hyksos

FIRST INTERMEDIATE PERIOD DYN. 7–11	MIDDLE KINGDOM DYNASTIES 11–12	SECOND INTERMEDIATE PERIOD DYN. 13–17	NEW KINGDOM DYNASTIES 18–20

Birth of Moses 1526 B.C.

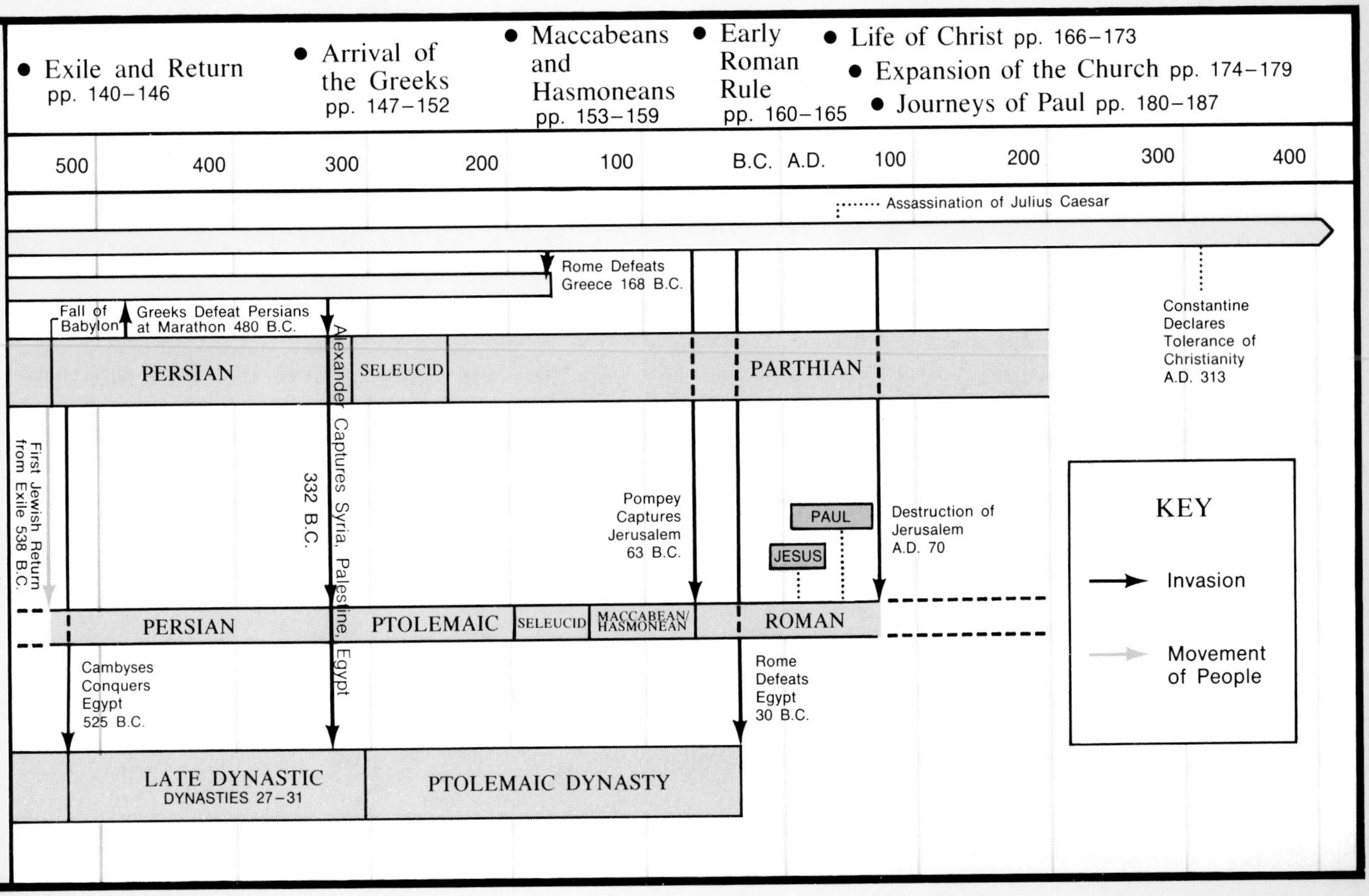

- Exile and Return pp. 140–146
- Arrival of the Greeks pp. 147–152
- Maccabeans and Hasmoneans pp. 153–159
- Early Roman Rule pp. 160–165
- Life of Christ pp. 166–173
- Expansion of the Church pp. 174–179
- Journeys of Paul pp. 180–187

500	400	300	200	100	B.C. A.D.	100	200	300	400

Assassination of Julius Caesar

Rome Defeats Greece 168 B.C.

Fall of Babylon

Greeks Defeat Persians at Marathon 480 B.C.

Constantine Declares Tolerance of Christianity A.D. 313

PERSIAN	SELEUCID		PARTHIAN

Alexander Captures Syria, Palestine, Egypt 332 B.C.

First Jewish Return from Exile 538 B.C.

Pompey Captures Jerusalem 63 B.C.

PAUL

JESUS

Destruction of Jerusalem A.D. 70

KEY

→ Invasion

→ Movement of People

PERSIAN	PTOLEMAIC	SELEUCID	MACCABEAN/HASMONEAN	ROMAN

Cambyses Conquers Egypt 525 B.C.

Rome Defeats Egypt 30 B.C.

LATE DYNASTIC DYNASTIES 27–31	PTOLEMAIC DYNASTY

Glossary of Terms

Aeolian	Soil deposited by the action of the wind
Alluvial	Soil/sediment deposited by flowing water
Beer	Well (Hebrew)
Beit	House (Arabic; Hebrew: Bet, Beth)
Beqa	Valley, basin (Arabic; Hebrew: Emeq)
Bet, Beth	House (Hebrew; Arabic: Beit)
Cisjordan	Area west of the Jordan Valley, or area west of the Rift Valley
Darb	Path, trail, road (Arabic)
Ein	Spring (Arabic; Hebrew: En)
Emeq	Valley, basin (Hebrew; Arabic: Beqa)
En	Spring (Hebrew; Arabic: Ein)
Har	Mountain (Hebrew; Arabic: Jebel)
Horbat	Ruin (Hebrew; Arabic: Khirbet)
Jebel	Mountain (Arabic; Hebrew: Har)
Khirbet	Ruin (Arabic; Hebrew: Horbat)
Kurkar	Fossilized dune sandstone
Levant	The land at the eastern end of the Mediterranean Sea
Makhtesh	Mortar- or cigar-shaped depression with steep cliff-like sides (Hebrew)
Mishor	Plain (Hebrew)
Nahal	River, stream, dry river bed (Hebrew; Arabic: Wadi)
Nahar	River (Hebrew; Arabic: Nahr)
Nahr	River (Arabic; Hebrew: Nahar)
Septuagint	The early Greek translation of the Old Testament
Tel	Antiquity mound (Hebrew; Arabic: Tell)
Tell	Antiquity mound (Arabic; Hebrew: Tel)
Transjordan	Area east of the Jordan Valley, or area east of the Rift Valley
Wadi	River, stream, dry river bed (Arabic; Hebrew: Nahal)

Index of Scripture References

Genesis

1–3	70–71
1:22, 28	73
2:8	70
2:10–14	70
2:11–12	71
3:7	70
6–9	71
9:1	73
10	71–73, 203
10:2–5	71
10:6–20	72
10:8–12	72
10:15–19	72
10:22–31	73
10:32	71
11:31	76
12–50	76
12:3	173
12:4	76
12:5	76
12:5–6	52
12:7	77
12:8	77, 93
12:9	77
12:10	25
12:10–20	79
12:14	76
13	79
13:2, 5–7	79
13:7	79
14	80, 81
14:2	81, 202
14:3	44, 45, 202
14:5–6	81
14:6–7	81
14:7	202
14:8	44
14:10	44, 45
14:17	189
14:18	81, 189
16:7	60
18–19	81
19:26	45
19:36–39	55
21:5	76
21:25	79
21:31	49
22:2	189
23	80
23:1	76
23:10	80
23:18	206
24	77
24:10	62, 65
24:35	79
25:7	76
25:18	71
25:26	76
25:30	55
26:8	206
26:12	25, 79
26:12–33	79
26:15–33	47
26:33	49
27–29	77
31:19–33:20	77
32:22–33:20	52
35:28–29	76
36:1–17	55

36:9	56
37:25	52, 83
37:36	83
46–50	59
47:4	83
47:9	76

Exodus

Exodus–Joshua 11	86
1:8	85
1:9	85
1:11	88
1:13–22	88
3:1	90
3:18	90
4:27	90
5:3	90
8:22	83
8:27	90
9:26	83
12:37	88
12:40	76
13:17	14, 27, 88
13:18	89
14:21	89
15:23	89
15:27	89
17	90
23:31	203

Numbers

10:12	91
11:1–3	91
11:4–35	91
11:7	71
11:35–12:16	91
13:2	91
13:7	49
13:21	91
13:22–23	91
13:22	49
13:23–24	91
13:27	91
13:28	91
14:39–45	91
20:1	91
20:2–13	91
20:14–20	55
20:16	51
20:17	23, 91
20:17–19	91
20:22–29	91
21–Deut 34	9
21:1–3	91
21:1	92
21:5–9	135
21:11	92
21:22	23, 92
21:23–24	92
21:24–25	92
21:26	108
21:33–35	92
22–25	92
22:1	92
32	55, 101–2
32:1	101
32:33–42	101
32:37–38	101

32:39–42	101
33	203
33:3	88
33:5	88
33:36	91
33:41–44	92
33:49	92
34	118
34:1–12	91, 203
34:3–5	91, 96
34:3	45, 51
34:6–9	91
34:7–11	16
34:11	91
34:12	16, 45

Deuteronomy

1:2	91
1:4	92
2:26	92
2:29	92
2:36	92
3:4–11	92
3:9	30
3:10	52, 55
3:11	92
3:13–14	30
3:17	22, 44, 45, 51
4:41–43	103
4:49	44
8:8	19, 83
11:8–17	26
11:14	25
13:13–18	111
26:5	76
27:11–14	94
33:18–19	99
34	92

Joshua

1–12	93
3–4	54
3:15	93
3:16	44, 45, 54, 93
4–5	95
5:10	93
6	93
7–8	43
7	93
8	93, 94
8–9	93
8:9	93
8:12	93
8:13	93
8:14	93
8:30–35	94
8:33–34	94
9:1–2	94
9:6	94
9:7	94
9:17	94
9:23	94
10	95, 154
10:1–15	47
10:2	94
10:3	105
10:5	94–95
10:22–27	95

10:31–33	48
10:33	105
11:1–3	95
11:2	22
11:4–5	95
11:8	95
11:9	95
11:10	85, 95
11:13	95
11:16	33
12–Judges	86
12	203
12:3	44, 45
12:4	30
13–21	96
13:1–7	95
13:1–6	203
13:2–3	104
13:4	104
13:4–5	16, 104
13:8–33	101–2
13:9	55
13:12	30
13:13	104
13:15–23	101
13:15–28	55
13:16	55
13:27	101
13:29–31	101
13:30	30
14:1	96
15	42, 96, 203
15:1–4	96
15:1–12	96
15:2–4	91
15:2–12	203
15:2	45
15:5–8	43
15:5–10	96
15:5	45
15:7–9	96, 203
15:8	192
15:10–11	96, 100, 203
15:10	100
15:15	12, 202
15:20–32	96
15:21–63	96, 203
15:24	112
15:26–32	98
15:32	96
15:33–47	96
15:33	100
15:35	113, 202
15:36	96
15:41	96
15:42	98
15:45	100
15:45–47	47
15:48–60	96
15:49	203
15:52	202
15:59	106, 203
15:60	202
15:61–62	96
15:63	104, 192
16–17	132
16	96–97
16:1–5	96
16:1–9	203
16:3	100
16:8	96

16:9	97
16:10	100
17	97–98, 204
17:7–10	97
17:7–11	97, 203
17:15–18	97
17:16	97
18:4	98
18:9	98
18:11–18	98
18:12–13	96
18:12–20	203
18:14–19	96
18:15–17	203
18:16	192
18:16–17	98
18:16–19	43
18:19	45
18:21–28	96, 203
19:1–9	98
19:2–7	98
19:2–8	203
19:10–16	98, 100, 203
19:15	99, 108
19:17–23	99
19:22	99
19:24–31	99–100
19:32–39	100
19:33	100
19:34	96, 100
19:35	35
19:38	106
19:40–48	96, 100–101
19:41	100
19:43	100
19:46	100
19:47	85, 104
19:51	96
20	103
20:3	103
21	102–3, 203
21:34	99
22	16, 52, 101

Judges

1:8	190
1:8–18	96
1:16	112
1:18	104
1:21	98, 104
1:21–35	116
1:23	202
1:27	104
1:27–28	36, 97–98, 104
1:29	96–97, 104
1:30	36, 98–99
1:31	99–100
1:31–32	33, 104
1:33	100, 106
1:34–35	100–101, 104
1:35	104
3:1–4	203
3:3	104
3:7–11	106
3:15	106
3:26–27	106
3:28–30	106
3:31	106
4	34

5 34
4:3–13 107
4:4–6 107
4:10 107
4:14–16 107
4:15 36
5:6 106
5:6–7 107
5:8 107
5:14–15 107
5:19 107
5:20–21 ....36, 107
5:31 107
6–8 107
7 34
8:11 108
8:23 108
9 108
9:7–20 108
9:46 108
9:52–55 108
10:1–2 108
10:3–5 108
10:9 108
11:14–27 108
11:18 92
11:22 92
11:29–33 108
11:32–33 108
12:1 108
12:4–7 108
12:8–10 108
12:11–12 108
12:13–15 108
13–16 ....47, 100
13:19 109
13:25 109
15:9–19 109
15:11 109
16:1–3 109
16:4–31 109
17–18 ....100–101, 104
17–21 104
18:7 101
18:27–28 101
18:29 85
19–21 ....104, 192
19:1 40
19:10–15 104
19:11 104
19:11–12 ....104, 192
20:1 104
20:21 16
20:28 104
20:33–45 111
21:6–12 111
21:12 104
21:19 104

Ruth

4:9–22 113

1 Samuel

1:1 110
2:10–15 114
3 110
3:10 16
4:1 110
4:12–18 110
5:1–7:2 48
5:1–8 110
5:2–5 46
6:1 110
6:1–9 110
6:10–18 110
7:5 110
7:11–12 111
7:13–14 111
7:16 110
7:17 110
8:1–3 111
8:4–5 111
9 111
10:1 111
10:2–8 111
10:5 111

10:10 111
10:15 111
10:17–27 111
11:1–13 111
11:6–8 111
11:14–15 111
13:2 111
13:3 ....111, 112
13:5 ....108, 112
13:15–16 112
13:17–18 112
13:19–21 47
13:19–22 ....108, 112
13:23–14:14 18
14:2 112
14:4 112
14:14 112
14:15 112
14:16 112
14:18 110
14:22 112
14:31 112
14:47 113
15:5–6 112
15:7 112
15:12 112
15:24–35 113
16 113
17 ....48, 113, 174
17:1 113
17:2–3 113
17:52 113
19:11–17 113
19:18–24 113
20:5–34 111
21:1–7 113
21:8–15 113
22–27 113
22:1–27:6 43
22:3–4 118
22:5 114
22:6 111
23:1–13 ....113, 114
23:19 43
23:19–29 114
23:24 51
23:29–24:2 114
24:3–21 114
25 114
26:1–2 114
26:1 43
26:3 43
27:7 114
27:8 ....115, 116
27:10 ....112, 115
28 34
29 115
29:1 115
30:26–31 ....115, 116

2 Samuel

1:12 40
2:1–7 116
2:11 116
2:12–32 116
2:9 116
2:29 22
3:3 118
3:22–29 116
4:1–12 116
4:17–25 116
5:1–3 116
5:6–10 116
5:7 192
5:8 ....116, 192
5:11 192
6 ....110, 116
6:1–23 192
8–12 116
8:1 116
8:2 118
8:3 118
8:3–4 118
8:5–6 118
8:7–8 118
8:12 118
8:13 44

8:13–14 118
8:14 118
10:1–5 118
10:6 118
10:6–14 118
10:15–19 118
11 118
11:1 27
11:21 108
12:1–24 118
12:26–31 118
12:30 118
13:37–39 118
14–19 119
17:24–29 119
18:6 119
18:18 189
20:1–2 119
20:1–22 ....119, 120
20:14 120
21:1–14 116
23:20 118
24:1–8 119
24:2 ....119, 203
24:7 16
24:18–25 192

1 Kings

1:5–10 120
1:5–27 120
1:11–48 120
2:10 192
2:13–35 120
3:1 121
4:7–19 ....104, 203
4:7 122
4:8 122
4:9 ....100, 122
4:10 122
4:11 122
4:12 122
4:13 30
4:15 122
4:16 ....100, 122
4:17 122
4:18 122
4:21–24 121
4:22–23 122
4:27–28 122
5:1–12 121
5:10 121
5:11 122
5:18 122
6:1 ....76, 122
7:1–12 193
7:13–14 122
9:10–14 100
9:11–14 122
9:15 ....36, 121, 122, 193
9:16 122
9:17–18 121
9:18 63
9:24 193
9:26 16
9:27–28 122
10:1–13 ....44, 121
10:14–27 122
10:26–29 121
10:28–29 121
11:1 121
11:7–8 193
11:14–22 ....118, 123
11:23–25 123
11:26–40 123
11:27 ....123, 193
11:40 124
12:1–19 124
12:21–24 124
12:25 ....52, 124
12:26–33 124
14:21 124
14:22–28 193
14:25–31 124
14:25–28 124
15 32
15:16–22 127
15:20 203

15:21 40
15:33 40
16 40
16:23–24 127
16:29–34 40
16:31–33 127
20:1–21 127
20:26 30
20:30 30
22:29–37 127
22:47–49 128

2 Kings

3:4 ....23, 55
3:4–27 127
3:6–27 128
4 34
6:24–7:8 127
8:18 128
8:20–22 128
8:28 128
9 127
9:27–28 129
10 ....127, 131
10:32–33 131
11 129
11:1–16 129
12:1–12 129
12:4–16 194
12:17–18 ....129, 131, 193
12:19–21 129
13:7 131
13:17 30
14:7 ....44, 129
14:8–14 129
14:18–20 129
14:22 ....16, 130
14:25 44
14:25–29 132
15 32
15:19–20 132
15:29 ....131, 203, 204
15:29–30 133
15:32–38 131
16:2–4 131
16:5–6 131
16:7–10 131
16:10–18 194
17:4–6 133
17:6 133
17:7–23 133
17:24 133
17:25–41 133
18–20 135
18:3–7 135
18:8 135
18:9–11 133
18:10–11 133
18:17 135
19:9 136
19:35–36 136
20:20 194
21:2–9 136
21:16 136
22 194
23:8 136
23:10 194
23:29–30 138
23:30–34 138
23:34–36 138
23:35 138
24:2–4 138
24:13–16 138
25:1–7 139
25:27–30 ....138, 140

1 Chronicles

2:12–15 113
2:23 30
4:24–43 98
4:28–33 203
4:41 98
4:42 98
5:16 ....38, 55
6:54–80 203

6:54–81 102–3
8:1–4 123
9:35–40 111
11:1–3 116
11:4–9 116
11:6 ....116, 192
11:22 118
13 116
13:1–14 192
13:5 118
14:8–17 116
18:1 116
18:2 118
18:3–4 118
18:5–6 118
18:7–8 118
18:8 118
18:11 118
18:12 44
18:12–13 118
18:13 118
19:1–5 118
19:6–7 118
19:6–15 118
19:16–19 118
20:1–3 118
21:18–26 192
24:71 155
26:29–32 102
27:25–31 119
27:29 38

2 Chronicles

1:14–17 121
1:15 122
1:16–17 121
2:3–16 121
2:10 121
2:15 121
2:16 ....47, 100
3:1 190
8:1–2 122
8:3 121
8:4 ....63, 121
8:5–6 121
9:13–24 122
9:14 121
9:26 121
10:1–19 124
11:1–4 124
11:5–12 124
11:13–14 124
11:13–17 103
12:1–11 124
12:2–4 193
12:9–11 124
13:2–20 124
13:19 203
14 128
16:1–6 127
16:7–14 128
17 128
17:2 128
17:10–11 128
18:28–34 127
20 128
20:1–30 44
20:16 44
20:35–37 128
21:6 128
21:8–10 128
21:16–17 128
22:5 128
22:9 129
23:1–15 129
24:1–16 129
24:4–14 194
24:17–20 129
24:17–24 193
24:23–24 131
24:25–27 129
25:1–15 129
25:11 44
25:17–24 129
25:23 193
25:26–28 129
26:2 ....16, 130

26:6–8 130	11:35 47	47:19 91	9:2–8 171	16:10–17 183
26:9 194	12 194	47:20 91	9:2–13 30	17:22–31 183
26:9–15 130	12:26 146		9:33 169	20:3–6 185
26:16–21 131	13:4–7 146	**Daniel**	9:42 35	21:7 33
27:1–9 131	13:6 145		10:46–52 172	21:8 174
28:1–4 131		1:1 138		22:3 180
28:3 194	**Esther**		**Luke**	27:9 ....26, 186
28:5–8 131		**Hosea**		27:14 187
28:6 131	1:1 145		2:41–50 172	
28:15 106	2:16–17 143	6:3 25	3:1 30	**Romans**
28:16 131	8:9 145		8:26 171	
28:17–19 131		**Joel**	8:27 171	15:19 185
28:17 135	**Job**		9:28–36 171	
28:18–19 135		2:20 44	9:51–18:34 171	**2 Corinthians**
28:20–21 131	24:5 51		10:25–37 172	
29:2–19 135		**Amos**	10:30 44	2:12–13 185
29:20–30:27 135	**Psalms**		17:11 172	
32:1–23 135		4:6–8 25	17:12–19 172	**Galatians**
32:2–8 135	76:2 189		18:35–43 172	
32:21–22 136	83:9 36	**Jonah**	19:1–10 172	1:17 175
32:30 194	83:10 107		23:53 200	1:18–19 175
33:1–20 136	137 140	1:3 47	24:13 173	2:9 174
33:6 194	147:14 19		24:13–35 172	3:6–15 173
33:11–13 136		**Micah**		
33:12–14 136	**Song of Songs**		**John**	**1 Thessalonians**
34 194		1:1 48		
34:3–7 136	7:5 36		1:28 171	1:8 183
34:8–13 136		**Habakkuk**	1:44 169	
35:20–27 138	**Isaiah**		2:1–11 ....34, 166	**2 Timothy** 187
35:22 37		3:17–19 19	3–4 171	
36:1–4 138	7:1–17 131		3:22 172	**Titus**
36:4–5 138	7:5–6 133	**Haggai**	3:23 171	
36:22–23 141	9:1 ....27, 32, 35		4:1–26 19	1:5 187
	10:28–32 135	1:1 146	4:2 172	
Ezra	17:5 189	1:14 146	4:4–6 172	**Revelation**
	22:10 135		4:4–42 172	
1–3 141	35:1 51	**Zechariah**	4:43–54 166	16:16 36
1:1–4 141	36–39 135		4:46 169	
2 141	39:3–7 135	14:8 44	5:1–14 199	**Ecclesiasticus**
2:21–35 ....141, 146	40:7–8 26		6:1 ....35, 168	
2:64–65 141		**Matthew**	6:23 168	50:1–3 196
3:12 194	**Jeremiah**		10 199	
4:1–4 141		2:1–3 165	10:40–11:54 172	**1 Maccabees**
4:7–23 144	2:12–13 19	2:16–18 165	11:54 172	
4:12 194	5:24 25	2:19–23 166	12:21 169	1:41–64 153
4:24–6:22 142	8:22 52	3:1–12 43	21 169	2:1 155
5 143	12:5 20	4:1–11 43	21:1 ....35, 168	2:1–48 153
5:3 142	22:6 52	5–7 169	21:2 166	2:49–70 153
5:6 142	22:11–12 138	8:5–9 169		3:1–12 154
5:14 146	27:1–11 138	8:5–13 169	**Acts**	3:13–26 154
6 ....143, 194	34:6–7 138	8:28 171		3:27–4:25 154
6:3–5 141	34:7 48	9:9 169	1–12 ....174, 180	4:26–35 154
6:6 142	36:9–11 194	11:20–24 169	1:8 174	4:36–61 154
6:13 142	40:1–41:15 140	13:2–3 169	2 174	5:1–68 154
7:7–9 143	40:14 140	14:13–21 169	2–7 174	6:1–17 154
7:12–26 143	41:16–17 140	15:24 171	3:11 200	6:18–54 155
8:1–20 144	42:1–44:30 140	15:39 168	5:12 200	6:55–63 155
9 144	43:8–13 140	16:13–20 ....30, 171	5:34 180	7:1–4 155
	46:2 138	17:1–8 171	7:4 76	7:5–25 155
Nehemiah	46:11 52	17:1–13 30	8 174	7:26–50 155
	49:19 ....20, 52	20:17–21:3 43	8:1 174	10:10–11 197
2 194	50:19 52	20:29–34 172	8:5 174	13:10 197
2 6 146	50:44 ....20, 52		8:25 174	14:25–43 156
2:7–9 144	51:43 51	**Mark**	8:26–39 174	
2:11–16 144	52:28–30 138		8:40 174	**2 Maccabees**
2:17–7:3 145	52:30 140	1:29 168	9 180	
3 ....146, 194	52:31–34 140	1:29–31 169	9:26–29 175	3 152
4 146		2:1–12 169	9:32–42 174	3:3 152
4:7 146	**Ezekiel**	5:1 171	9:43 47	4 153
5:14 145		5:2 171	11:22 180	4:7 153
5:14–15 146	27:6 30	5:20 171	11:26 180	6:1–11 153
6 146	39:18 30	8:9 168	11:28–30 180	9 154
6:1 146	47:13–20 91	8:22–26 169	12 175	13:3–8 155
6:2 ....47, 146	47:15–17 91	8:27–30 30	12:19–23 174	
7:26–38 146	47:15–20 145		13–28 180	
11:25–28 146	47:18 44		13:13 180	
11:29–30 146			13:49 181	
11:31–36 146			15 183	

Index of Persons

Abdi-hebda 105
Abdon 108
Abiathar 120
Abigail 114
Abijah 124
Abimelech 108
Abishai 118
Abner 116
Abraham (Abram) 14, 27, 28, 45, 47, 52, 70, 73, 76–81, 83, 85, 103, 189–90
Absalom 52, 118, 119
Abubus 156
Achish 113–15
Adad-nirari 131
Adoni-Zedek 105, 190
Adonijah 120
Aeneas 174
Agrippa 165; *see also* Herod Agrippa I, Herod Agrippa II.
Ahab 127, 128, 131
Ahaz 131, 133–35, 194
Ahaziah 128
Ahmose 85, 87
Ahzai 146
Akhenaton 105, 190
Albinus 198
Alcimus 155
Alexander Balas 155–56
Alexander Jannaeus 158–60, 171, 197
Alexander the Great 146–50, 171, 183, 196
Alexander (son of Herod the Great) 160, 165
Alexandra 158, 159, 162
Allenby 47, 52, 54
Amasa 119
Amasis 140
Amaziah 129, 130, 132, 193
Amenemhet I 82, 83
Amenhotep I 87
Amenhotep II 87–89
Amenhotep III 88, 93, 105, 190
Amnon 118
Amon 136, 148
Amos 25, 42, 133
Anath 32, 100, 106
Andrew 168, 169
Andromachus 149, 151
Antigonus 149, 150, 158, 160–62
Antiochus III 151, 152, 196
Antiochus IV 152–55, 196
Antiochus V 154, 155
Antiochus VI 156
Antiochus VII 156, 158
Antipater 149, 159–61, 165
Antipater II 159
Antony 160–63, 198
Apollonius 152, 154, 156

Apries 138
Aquila 184
Araunah 192
Archelaus 166, 172
Aretas 159, 175
Ariel 118
Aristobulus I 158
Aristobulus II 159–62
Aristotle 147
Arses 146
Artaxerxes I 143, 146
Artaxerxes III 146
Asa 127, 128
Asaph 144
Ashkenaz 72
Ashur-uballit II 136, 138
Ashurbanipal 136
Athaliah 128, 129, 194
Augustus 165
Azariah 130, 132

Baalis 140
Baasha 124, 127, 128
Bacchides 155
Bagohi 146
Barak 34, 36, 95, 106, 107
Barnabas 180–83
Bartimaeus 172
Barzapharnes 161
Barzillai 119
Bathsheba 118, 120
Belshazzar 140, 141
Ben-Hadad 127, 128, 131
Ben-Hadad I 127
Benaiah 118, 120
Bessus 146, 149
Biridiya 105
Boaz 113
Bogoas 146

C. Popilius Laenas 153
Caesar, Julius 160, 176, 186
Caiphas 200
Caleb 96, 106, 115
Caligula 174, 200
Cambyses 141
Cassander 149, 183
Cassius 64, 160, 161
Cendebeus 156
Cestius Gallus 200
Cheops 74
Chephren 74
Claudius 174
Cleopatra 43, 149, 152, 162, 163, 172
Cornelius 175
Crassus, M. Lucinius 160
Croesus 141
Cushan-Rishathaim 106
Cyrus 140, 141, 194

Darius I 141–43, 145, 146, 148, 149, 194
Darius II 146

Darius III 146, 148
David 16, 36, 40, 42, 43, 48, 52, 94, 97–100, 102, 104, 109, 110, 113–16, 118–20, 122, 124, 136, 174, 190, 192–94, 200
Deborah 34, 36, 95, 106, 107
Delilah 109
Demetrius (son of Antigonus) 149
Demetrius I 152, 155, 156
Demetrius II 156
Demetrius III 159
Demetrius (the silversmith) 185
Djaa 83
Djoser 74
Dorimenes 154
Doris 165

Eglon 106
Ehud 106
Eleazar (the priest) 92, 96, 102, 104
Eleazar (the Maccabean) 155
Eli 110
Eliakim 138
Eliashib 146
Elijah 37, 133
Elisha 34, 37, 133
Elnathan 146
Elon 108
Elymas 180
Esarhaddon 136
Esau 55, 56, 77
Esther 143, 145
Ethbaal 127, 135
Eusebius 171, 200
Evil-Merodach 140
Ezekias 160
Ezekiel 91, 141, 145
Ezra 141–44, 146, 194–96

Felix 176
Festus 176
Florus 176

Gaal 108
Gabinius 160
Gabinus 159
Gallio 184
Gedaliah 140
Gemaryahu 194
Gera 106
Geshem 146
Gideon 34, 107, 108
Goliath 48, 113
Gomer 72
Gorgias 154

Hadad 118, 123, 127, 128, 131
Hadad-ezer 127
Hadadezer 118
Hadoram 118
Hadrian 179

Haggai 142
Ham 71, 72
Hanun 116, 118
Hasman 155
Hatshepsut 87
Hazael 127, 129, 131, 193
Heliodorus 152
Herod Agrippa I 174–75, 200
Herod Agrippa II 176
Herod Antipas 32, 35, 166, 167, 171, 174, 200
Herod the Great 38, 43, 45, 160–67, 169, 171, 173–75, 197–200
Herodotus 57, 59, 141, 142
Hezekiah 98, 135, 136, 192, 194, 196–97
Hillel 108
Hippicus 165, 199
Hiram 100, 121–23
Hophra 138
Horam 105
Hosea 133
Hoshea 133
Hyrcanus II 159–61, 197

Ibzan 108
Isaac 28, 47, 76, 77, 79, 80, 82, 83, 85, 103, 189
Isaiah 135, 174
Ish-Bosheth 116
Ishmael 140

Jabin 95, 106
Jacob 28, 52, 60, 76, 77, 80, 82, 83, 85, 103, 172
Jael 107
Jair 30, 108
James (the disciple) 30, 171, 175
James (the Lord's brother) 183
Japheth 71
Jason (the high priest) 153
Jason (the Thessalonian) 183
Javan 71, 72
Jehoahaz 131, 138
Jehoash 129, 131
Jehoiachin 138, 140, 141
Jehoiada 118, 129
Jehoiakim 138, 194
Jehoram 127, 128, 131
Jehoshaphat 44, 128
Jehu 127, 128, 131
Jephthah 104, 108, 109
Jeremiah 42, 138, 140
Jeroboam I 52, 103, 123–24
Jeroboam II 132
Jeshua 142, 146
Jesus 30, 32–35, 43, 166–69, 171–74, 180, 184, 198–200
Jezebel 40, 127, 128
Joab 116, 118–20, 192
Joash 129, 193, 194

Johanan 140
John (the apostle) 30, 171, 174, 175, 185, 200
John (the Baptizer) 43
John Hyrcanus 156, 158–59, 162
John Mark 180, 183
Joktan 73
Jonah 47, 133
Jonathan (Maccabean leader) 153, 155–56, 171, 197
Jonathan (son of Saul) 11, 111–12, 115
Joram 118, 127, 128
Joseph of Arimathea 200
Joseph (the brother of Herod) 161
Joseph (the husband of Mary) 166
Joseph (the son of Jacob) 76, 83, 85, 96, 97, 161, 166, 200
Josephus 31, 35, 45, 166, 169, 171–72, 177, 179, 189, 197–200
Joshua 43, 47, 48, 54, 92–100, 101–5, 154, 190
Josiah 19, 37, 96, 136, 138, 194
Jotham 108, 130, 131
Judas Maccabeus 175, 196, 197
Julia 169
Julius Caesar 160, 176, 186

Kareah 140
Kenaz 106
Khu-Sebek 83
Khum-hotep III 83

Laban 77, 85
Labasi-Marduk 140
Labayu 105, 108
Laenus, C. Popilius 153
Lazarus 172
Leah 80
Lot 55, 76, 79–81, 97, 111, 189
Lot's wife 45
Luke 183, 186
Luli 135
Lydia 140, 141, 143, 148, 183
Lysias 153–55
Lysimachus 149, 150

M. Licinius Crassus 160
Maccabeus 153, 196
Madai 72
Malchus II 161
Malichus 161
Manasseh (the son of Hezekiah) 136, 194
Manetho 61, 150
Mariamne 162, 165, 199
Mark. See John Mark.
Mark Antony 163, 198
Martha 172

Mary (mother of Jesus) 166
Mary (of Bethany) 172
Mary Magdalene 168
Mattaniah 138
Mattathias 153, 155
Megabyzus 143, 144
Meket-Re 79
Melchizedek 81, 189
Menahem 132, 133
Menelaus 153, 155
Menes 73
Meri-ka-Re 79
Merneptah 106
Merodach-Baladan II 135
Michal 113
Milkilu 105
Miriam 92
Mithridates 159–60
Moses 89–90, 92, 101, 112, 135, 145
Mycerinus 74

Nabal 114
Nabonidus 140, 141
Nabopolassar 136
Nahash 116
Napoleon 47
Naram-Sin 73
Narmer 73
Nathan 120
Nebuchadnezzar 138–41, 194
Nebuzaradan 139, 140
Neco 37, 138
Neco II 138
Nehemiah 142, 144–46, 196
Ner 116
Neriglissar 140
Nero 177
Nicanor 154, 155
Noah 70, 71, 73

Octavian 161–63
Og 30, 92, 101
Omri 127, 131
Onias III 152, 153
Oreb 107
Othniel 96, 106

Pacorus 161
Padi 135
Pappus 162
Parmenio 148
Paul 33, 175, 176, 180, 181, 183–87
Pekah 131, 133
Pepi I 74, 75, 78
Perdiccas 149
Peter 30, 47, 168, 169, 171, 174–75, 183, 200
Phasael 160, 161, 165, 199
Pheroras 162
Philip (the evangelist) 174
Philip of Macedon 147, 183
Philip (the tetrarch) 30, 154–55, 166, 169, 171
Phinehas 104

Pilate 171, 172, 174, 175, 200
Pompey 159, 160, 171, 197
Priscilla 184
Psammetichus I 136
Ptolemy I 148–50
Ptolemy III 150
Ptolemy IV 151
Ptolemy V 151, 152
Ptolemy VI 153, 156

Qaynu 146

Rabbi Akiba 179
Rabbi Gamaliel 180
Ramses II 104, 106
Ramses III 108
Rebecca 80
Rehoboam 124, 127, 128, 193
Rezin 131, 133
Rezon 123
Ruth 113

Salome Alexandra 158, 159, 162
Samson 47, 104, 109, 110
Samuel 51, 110, 111, 113, 116, 189
Sanballat 145, 146
Sarah 76, 80
Sargon (of Akkad) 73, 133, 135
Sargon II 133, 135
Saul (king of Israel) 34, 40, 43, 47, 109–16, 118
Saul of Tarsus 175, 180; see also Paul.
Scarus 159
Scopas 152
Seleucus I 149, 150, 180
Seleucus III 153
Seleucus IV Philopater 152, 155
Sennacherib 48, 135, 136, 139, 194
Sergius Paulus 180
Seron 154
Sesostris II 83
Seti I 87, 104, 106
Sextus Caesar 160
Shabako 135
Shalmaneser III 127, 131
Shalmaneser V 133, 135
Shamgar 106
Sheba 22, 44, 72, 119–21
Shebitku 135
Shem 71, 73
Shemaiah 124
Sheshbazzar 141, 146, 194
Shishak 52, 61, 124, 127, 193
Shobi 119
Siamun 122
Sidqia 135
Sihon 92, 101
Silas 183
Silo 162
Simeon Bar Kokhba 179

Simon (brother of Jonathan) 197
Simon (a Maccabean Jew) 152–56
Simon the Tanner 47
Sin-shar-ishkun 136
Sinuhe 60, 61, 82, 83
Sisera 106, 107
Solomon 19, 36, 44, 47, 63, 76, 96, 97, 99, 100, 102, 104, 116, 118, 120–24, 127, 130, 190, 192, 193, 200
Stephen 174, 180, 200
Strabo 59, 65, 184

Tabeel 131, 133
Tabitha 174
Talmai 118
Tamar 118
Tattenai 142
Terah 76
Theudas 175
Thutmose I 87
Thutmose II 87
Thutmose III 36, 47, 61, 87, 88, 97
Thutmose IV 88
Tiglath Pileser III 131–33, 135, 194
Timothy 181, 183
Tirhakah 136
Titus 179, 187, 200
Tobiah 146
Toi 118
Tola 108
Tou 118
Tryphon 156

Uni 74, 75
Uriah 118
Ushtannu 142
Uzziah 19, 130, 194

Varus 166
Vespasian 173, 177, 179

Wari-taldu 85

Xerxes 143, 146

Yapai 105
Yehezqiyah 146
Yeho'ezer 146

Zacchaeus 172
Zadok 120
Zechariah (the prophet) 142, 197
Zedekiah 138, 139
Zeeb 107
Zenododrus 163
Zerah 128
Zerubbabel 142, 146, 194
Zimredda 105

Gazetteer and Index

The purpose of the Gazetteer and Index is to assist the reader of the Bible in locating places both in this atlas and on modern maps. The Gazetteer/Index lists all places found in the text and on the maps; page numbers in regular type refer to the text, those in bold type to the pages on which specific maps can be found.

Additional information is provided for biblical place names. First, a short description of the significance of a place is given, complete with biblical references. Note that not every reference is given for places mentioned numerous times in the Bible (e.g., Jerusalem, Babylon, Bethel); a concordance such as the *NIV Complete Concordance* lists all occurrences of place names. In addition, many places are treated in more detail in the text (e.g., Jerusalem, which is discussed in a separate chapter, and regions of the country such as the Bashan, Shephelah, Sea of Galiliee, Edom, Moab), and the reader should consult the appropriate portions of the text.

This description is followed, wherever possible, by an identification of the ancient site with a "modern" place; this material is in italic type. I have attempted to use the most up-to-date site identifications. Some identifications are disputed; in those cases I have cited the identification I think to be the most probable one. (For the process of site identification, see the chapter on "The Disciplines of Historical Geography.")

The modern designation of each site is given in English characters. A simplified system of transliteration from Arabic, Hebrew, Turkish, Greek, etc. into English has been used and is intended to be helpful to the general reader. In the case of sites located in Israel, the Arabic name is usually given first, followed by the Hebrew name. For places in the southern Levant (Israel, Jordan, and sometimes Lebanon and Syria), a six-digit grid reference is provided in parentheses to assist in precisely locating the place on standard 1:250,000, 1:100,000, and 1:50,000 maps available for those countries (the first three digits serve to locate the site on a north-south axis, while the last three digits locate it on an east-west axis). Also, for quick reference, the approximate distance ("as the crow flies") and direction of the site from a major known ancient place (such as Jerusalem, Joppa, Jericho, Nazareth, Acco, etc.) is given. Abbreviations are used for points of the compass (N = north(ern); NW = northwest(ern); NNW = north northwest(ern); etc.). For sites not in Israel, the country of their location is noted. Thus the reader will be able to quickly locate a place both in this Atlas and on a modern map.

For biblical places, NIV spellings have been used throughout. However, it will generally not be difficult to find placenames in this Gazetteer/Index no matter which version of the Bible one is using. In a few cases readers using other translations of the Bible may find it necessary to look in an NIV translation to check the spelling used there. For example, where the RSV has "Chinnereth" and "Negeb," the NIV uses "Kinnereth" and "Negev." But these instances are relatively few.

Because of the nature of an atlas, the descriptions and discussions of sites are brief. The interested reader should consult the standard dictionaries or encyclopedias such as *EAEHL, IDB, ISBE, NBD,* or *ZPEB,* or the standard works on historical geography such as those by Abel, Aharoni, Avi-Yonah, Kallai, etc., which are listed in the bibliography. Extrabiblical places mentioned in this atlas have not been annotated, but their locations can be found on the maps. The key to the abbreviations used in the Gazetteer/Index is found on p. 8. See also Glossary on p. 218.

Abana – River of Damascus mentioned by Naaman (2 Kings 5:12) – *Nahr Barada; begins in Anti-Lebanon mountains, flows SE through Damascus, ends in a marsh in the desert.*

Abarim – Mountain range in Transjordan, E of N end of Dead Sea; Mt. Nebo was part of the range (Num 27:12; 33:47–48; Deut 32:49; Jer 22:20).

Abdon – Levitical town in territory of Asher (Josh 19:28; 21:30; 1 Chron 6:74). – *Kh. Abdeh/T. Avdon (165272), 10 mi. NNE of Acco –* **99, 102**

Abel – See Abel Beth Maacah (2 Sam 20:18).

Abel Beth Maacah (Abel) – Town in N Israel. Joab pursued Sheba there (2 Sam 20:14–15). Captured by Ben-Hadad (1 Kings 15:20; called Abel Maim in 2 Chron 16:4) and later by Tiglath-Pileser III (2 Kings 15:29) – *Abil el-Qamh/T. Avel Bet Maakha (204296), N of Huleh Valley, 4 mi. W of Dan –* 28, 31, **31,** 32, **117, 119, 119,** 126, 127, **129,** 132, 133

Abel Keramim – Town in or on border of Ammonite territory, captured by Jephthah (Judges 11:33) – *Uncertain; possibly Naur (228142), 8 mi. SW of Amman in Jordan –* 108

Abel Maim – See Abel Beth Maacah.

Abel Meholah – Site along route of Gideon's pursuit of Midianites (Judges 7:22). Town in fifth Solomonic district (along with Beth Shan et al.; 1 Kings 4:12). Home of Elisha (19:16) – *T. Abu Sus (203197), 10 mi. S of Beth Shan in Jordan Valley –* 33, 98, 107, **107,** 122, 131

Abel Mizraim – Place where funeral procession of Jacob stopped for 7 days of mourning; also called "threshing floor of Atad" (Gen 50:11). Text says "near the Jordan," which does not fit route from Egypt to Hebron well – *Unknown.*

Abel Shittim (Shittim) – Near Jordan River in plains of Moab, NE of Dead Sea. Israel camped here (Josh 2:1; 3:1; Baalam incident, Num 25:1; 33:49; Mic 6:5) – *T. el-Hammam (214138), 8 mi. NE of NE end of Dead Sea –* 92, **92**

Abila (Beqa) – 175, 177

Abila (Decapolis) – 28, 30, 152, 160, **161, 164, 167, 168, 170,** 171

Abila (Perea) – 176–178

Abilene – Region/political unit NW of Damascus in Lebanese mountains and Beqa. Lysanias was tetrarch of Abilene at time of Jesus' birth (Luke 3:1).

Abronah – Stopping place during wilderness wanderings, between Jotbathah and Ezion Geber (Num 33:34–35) – *Uncertain; possibly Umm Rashrash/ Elath (145884) at N end of Red Sea.*

Abu-Ghosh – 173

Abu Kamal – 65, **65**

Abu Rudeis – 60

Abydos – 72, 73, 75, **78, 79, 81, 86**

Accaron – 156, 157

Acco – Chief Mediterranean port of Palestine in ancient times. In territory of Asher, who failed to occupy it (Judges 1:31). Probably under Israelite control during days of David, but ceded to Tyre by Solomon. Later called Ptolemais – *T. el-Fukhkhar/T. Akko (158258), 1 mi. E of Akko/Acre –* 16, **17,** 18, 25, 27, 28, 30, **31,** 32–34, 33, 36, 37, **82, 90, 91, 95, 99, 99,** 100, **102, 103, 105,** 117, 119, 120, 122, 125, **126,** 127, **129, 131, 132,** 135, **138,** 141, **142, 149, 150,** 151, **167, 204**

Acco, Plain of – 16, 17, **31,** 32, 33, **33,** 36, 37, 116, **117,** 122, 163, 166

Achaia – Province of Greece; main city: Corinth. Mentioned 9 times in NT. Achaia and Macedonia were the two major provinces of

Greece; on occasion Achaia could be used to refer to the whole of Greece – 163, 182, 183–85, **185–87**

Achor, Valley of – Place where Achan was executed (Josh 7:24, 26). On boundary between Judah and Benjamin (15:7); evidently a wilderness area (Isa 65:10; Hos 2:15) – *Possibly el-Buqeia, a large broad valley in the Judean Desert, 10 mi. ESE of Jerusalem.*

Acrabeta – 154, **154**, 157, 158, **170**, 172, 177, **178**, 179

Acshaph – Town assigned to Asher (Josh 19:25); its king participated in battle of Merom against Joshua (11:1; 12:20) – *Uncertain; possibly Kh. el-Harbaj/T. Regev (158240), 12 mi. S of Acco* – 95, **95**, 99, 105

Actium – 162, 163

Aczib (Asher) – Town assigned to tribe of Asher (Josh 19:29), which was not able to drive out inhabitants (Judges 1:31) – *Ez-Zib/T. Akhziv (159272), 10 mi. N of Acco.* – 18, **18**, 31, 32, **33**, 99, **99**, 103, 117, 134, 135

Aczib (Judah) – Assigned to tribe of Judah in Shephelah (Josh 15:44); mentioned in wordplay by Micah (1:14). Possibly Kezib (Gen 38:5) and Cozeba (1 Chron 4:21) are to be identified with Aczib – *Often identified with Kh. T. el-Beida/H. Lavnin (145116); but see Libnah.*

Adadah – Town in Negev district of Judah (Josh 15:22) – *Possibly same as Aroer (Negev; 148062); otherwise unknown* – **97**

Adam – Town along Jordan River where water heaped up at time of Israelite crossing (Josh 3:16) – *Tell ed-Damiyeh (201167) on E side of Jordan, ca. 16 mi. NNE of Jericho* – 28, 38, 40, **54**, 93, **94**, 126

Adamah – One of the fortified cities of Naphtali (Josh 19:36) – *Uncertain; possibly Qarn Hattin/H. Qarne Hittim (193245), 5 mi. W of Tiberias. But see Merom, Waters of* – 99

Adami Nekeb – Town on S boundary of Naphtali (Josh 19:33) – *Kh. et-Tell (ed-Damiyeh)/T. Adami (193239), 6 mi. SW of Tiberias* – **99**, 100

Adana – 62

Adasa – 154, 155

Addar – Town on S boundary of Judah (Josh 15:3) – *Possibly identical to Hazar Addar (Num 34:4)* – 97

Addon – Site in Babylon from which exiles returned (Ezra 2:59; Neh 7:61) – *Unknown.*

Ader – 75, 90

Adithaim – Town in Shephelah district of Judah (Josh 15:36) – *Unknown.*

Admah – Mentioned in connection with Sodom and Gomorrah (Gen 10:19; 14:2, 8; Deut 29:23). Symbol of God's judgment (Hos 11:8) – *Unknown; possibly SE of Dead Sea in Rift Valley* – 75, 81

Adora – See Adoraim – **150**, 151, 154, **154**, 157, 158, 160, **161**

Adoraim – Town fortified by Rehoboam (2 Chron 11:9). Called Adora, Dora, or Dor in documents from intertestamental period – *Dura (152101), ca. 5 mi. WSW of Hebron in Judean Hill Country* – 42, **43**, 46, 48, 125

Adramyttium – Port city on W coast of Asia Minor. In Caesarea, Paul boarded a ship from Adramyttium on first leg of his journey to Rome (Acts 27:2) – *Karatash near Edremid in W Turkey* – 175, 186, **186**

Adriatic Sea – Paul's ship was "driven across the Adriatic Sea" (Acts 27:27) – *Sea E of Italy, Sicily, and Malta, W of Albania, Greece, and Crete* – 183, **186**, 187

Adullam – Town in Shephelah conquered by Israelites (Josh 12:15) and allotted to Judah (15:35). Residents intermarried with tribe of

Judah (Gen 38:1). David fled to a cave there (1 Sam 22:1; 2 Sam 23:13; 1 Chron 11:15). Fortified by Rehoboam (2 Chron 11:7). Lamented over by Micah due to pending invasion of Assyrians (1:15). Inhabited after Babylonian Exile (Neh 11:30) – *Kh. esh-Sheikh Madhkur/H. Adullam (150117), 16.5 mi. WSW of Jerusalem in Shephelah* – **46**, **84**, **97**, 113, 113, 114, 125, 134, 144, 146, 154, 202

Adummim, Pass of – Site mentioned as being on N boundary of Judah (Josh 15:7) and S boundary of Benjamin (18:17) – *Eusebius places it halfway between Jericho and Jerusalem; possibly the "modern" Talaat ed-Damm ("ascent of blood"; 184136), 8 mi. ENE of Jerusalem.*

Aegean Sea – 108, **109**, 141, **142**, 143, **147**, 181, **182**, 183, **185**

Aelia Capitolina – Hadrianic name for Jerusalem (2nd cent. A.D.) – 179

Aenon – Near Salim; John baptized here (John 3:23) – *Much disputed: (1) NE of modern Nablus in Samaria, near sources of W Faria (182188); (2) E of Jordan River, opposite Jericho near W. Kharrar (203138); (3) 8 mi. SSE of Beth Shan at/near Umm el-Umdan (199199). Ancient sources seem to support (3)* – **170**, 171

Afghanistan – 67, 149

Africa – 14, 20, 22, 37, 47, 56, 57, 59, 61, 72, 140, 143, **163**, 174, 187

Afula – 109

Agrippina – **168**

Ahava (Canal) – In S Babylon (Ezra 8:15, 21, 31). Ahava may be name of town or district to/through which the canal flowed – *Unknown.*

Ahlab – Town in Asher where Canaanites lived (Judges 1:31) – *Problematic; possibly a variant of Mahalab (Josh 19:29 RSV; NIV "in the region of"); if so, then identical with Kh. el-Mahalib (172303), 5 mi. NNE of Tyre along Mediterranean coast* – 99, **103**

Ai – Abraham pitched his tent between Bethel and Ai (Gen 12:8; 13:3). Conquered by Joshua (Josh 7–12). After Babylonian exile Jews of Bethel and Ai returned to Judea (Ezra 2:28; Neh 7:32) – *Usually identified with et-Tell (174147), 10 mi. NNE of Jerusalem. Alternative sites have been proposed. Possibly there was a second Ai in Transjordan (Jer 49:3)* – 28, 43, **43**, 77, **77**, 79, 80, **84**, 93, 94, **94**, **98**, 189, 190, 205

Aiath – Town N of Jerusalem along enemy invasion route (Isa 10:28) – *Uncertain; possibly Kh. Haiyan (175145). According to some, alternate form of Ai.*

Aija – Town in which Benjamites settled after exile (Neh 11:31) – *Unknown; possibly identical to Ai or Aiath* – **144**

Aijalon (Dan) – Town assigned to tribe of Dan (Josh 19:42), who failed to take it (Judges 1:35). Levitical city (Josh 21:24) inhabited by Ephraimites (1 Chron 6:69) and Benjamites (8:13). Philistines fled toward Aijalon (1 Sam 14:31). Fortified by Rehoboam (2 Chron 11:10). Occupied by Philistines during reign of Ahaz (28:18) – *Yalo (152138), 13 mi. NW of Jerusalem in N Shephelah* – 41, **46**, 47, 48, **94**, 98, **102**, **103**, 104, **105**, 108, 112, **112**, **122**, 125, **125**, 131, **134**, 135

Aijalon (Zebulun) – Town in land of Zebulun (N Israel) where Elon the judge was buried (Judges 12:12) – *Unknown.*

Aijalon, Valley of – Valley where moon "stood still" as Joshua defeated the Amorite coalition (Josh 10:12) – *Wadi Selman/Emeq Ayyalon; valley named after nearby site of Aijalon* – 41, **43**, **46**, 47, 95, 98, 100, **100**, **128**, 154, **154**, 173

Ain (Bashan/Golan) – Town along E border of Canaan (Num 34:11) – *Uncertain; possibly Kh. Ayyun (212235), 3 mi. E of S end of Sea of Galilee* – **91**

Ain (Judah/Simeon) – Town assigned to both Judah and Simeon (Josh 15:32; 19:7). Levitical city (21:16; 1 Chron 4:32) – *Uncertain; probably in W Negev. Possibly Ain and Rimmon should be read together as a compound town name: Ain Rimmon.*

Ain Shems, spring of – 205

Akeldama – Field bought with Judas' "blood money," to be used for burials (Acts 1:19) – *Traditional identification: along S slope of Valley of Hinnom in Jerusalem.*

Akkad – City mentioned in Gen 10:10. Capital of Akkadia, ancient empire in Mesopotamia. Capital of dynasty of Sargon of Akkad at end of 3rd millennium B.C. Used in famous phrase "land of Akkad and Sumer" – *Unknown* – 13, 66, **71**, **72**, 73, **77**, 80

Alalakh – 64, 77, 108, **109**

Alashi(y)a – 105

Albania – 13, 183

Alema – 154

Alemeth – Levitical city (1 Chron 6:60; Josh 21:18, Almon) in territory of Benjamin – *Kh. Almit (176136), 4 mi. NE of Jerusalem.*

Aleppo – 13, 14, 28, **62**, 64, **77**, 80, 84, 130, **134**, **137**, **142**, 148, 181

Alexandria – City in Egypt on Mediterranean Sea. Established by Alexander (332/1 B.C.). Capital of Egypt, center of commerce and learning. Jews of Alexandria opposed Stephen in Jerusalem (Acts 6:9). Apollos was from here (18:24). Paul sailed on Alexandrian (grain) ship on part of voyage to Rome (27:6; 28:11) – 13, **58**, 147, 148, **148**, 149, 150, 153, **163**, **175**, 185, **186**, **187**

Alexandrium – **157**, 161, 162, 164, **164**

Allammelech – Town allotted to tribe of Asher (Josh 19:26) – *Unknown.*

Allenby Bridge – 52, **53**, 54

Allon Bacuth – Burial site of Deborah, Rebekah's nurse (Gen 35:8) – *Unknown; near Bethel.*

Almon – See Alemeth – **98**, 102

Almon Diblathaim – Stopping point of wandering Israelites (Num 33:46–47) between Dibon Gad and mountains of Abarim. See also Beth Diblathaim – *Uncertain; possibly Kh. Deleilat esh-Sherqiyeh (228116), E of Dead Sea, 21 mi. SE of Amman.*

Aloth – Solomonic district, described as "in Asher and in Aloth" (1 Kings 4:16) – *Uncertain; possibly should be read "Bealoth" or even "Zebulun"* – 122

Alush – Stopping point of wandering Israelites, between Dophkah and Rephidim (Num 33:13–14) – *Unknown.*

Amad – Town allotted to Asher (Josh 19:26) – *Unknown.*

Amalek, city of – Saul attacked it after mustering troops at Telaim. In Negev of Judah – *Uncertain; possibly T. Masos (146069), 8 mi. E of Beersheba* – 112

Amalekites, Hill Country of the – 108

Amam – Town in Negev district of Judah (Josh 15:26) – *Unknown.*

Amana, crest of – Mountain (SS 4:8), probably in Anti-Lebanon range.

Amanus Mountains – 12, **13**, 62, **62**, 64, 67, **72**, 73, **84**, **147**, 148, **182**, 183

Amastris – **187**

Amathus – **157**, 160, **161**, 163, **164**, 167, 168, **170**, 171

Amaw – Home of Balaam the prophet (Num 22:5 RSV; NIV "in his native land") – *Country W*

of Euphrates; main center: Emar, 50 mi. S of Carchemish.

Ammah, hill of – Hill where Joab ceased pursuing Abner (2 Sam 2:24) – *Uncertain; E of Gibeon on edge of wilderness.*

Amman – 13, 21, 23, 25, 52, 58, 171

Ammon – Country of the Ammonites, located E of the Jordan River. Capital: Rabbah (modern Amman) – 18, 117, 120, 121, 122, 125, 132, 137, 138, 140, 141, 142, 144

Ammonitis – 150, 151, 152

Amphipolis – Greco-Roman city, capital of first district of Macedonia in NE Greece. Paul passed through it on his way to Philippi on second journey (Acts 17:1) – *Neochori in NE Greece, 25 mi. SW of Philippi on Strymon (Struma) River* – 182, 183

Amurru – 62, 80, 135

Anab – Village in Hill Country of Judah (Josh 15:50) from which Joshua drove out the Anakim (11:21) – *Kh. Unnab es-Saghir (145091), 12 mi. SW of Hebron* – 97, 134

Anaharath – Town allotted to Issachar (Josh 19:19) – *Uncertain; possibly T. el-Mukharkhash/T. Rekhesh (194228), 8 mi. SW of S tip of Sea of Galilee* – 90, 99, 99, 105

Ananiah – Village to which Benjamites returned after exile – *El-Azariyeh (174131), 1.5 mi. E of Jerusalem (NT Bethany)* – 144

Anathoth – Levitical city in territory of Benjamin (Josh 21:18; 1 Chron 6:60). Two of David's warriors from there (2 Sam 23:27; 1 Chron 12:3). Abiathar banished there by Solomon (1 Kings 2:26). Along path of advancing Assyrian invaders (Isa 10:30). Birthplace of Jeremiah and site of his activity (Jer passim). Jews lived here after Babylonian exile (Ezra 2:23; Neh 7:27; 11:32) – *Ras el-Kharrubeh (174135), 2.5 mi. NE of Jerusalem; possibly nearby Der es-Sid is site of Jeremiah's Anathoth* – 42, 43, 98, 102, 120, 131, 144

Anatolia – 62–64, 67, 68, 73, 88, 108, 109, 193

Anchialus – 187

Ancyra – 13, 147, 148, 148, 175, 187

Anem – Levitical town in Issachar (1 Chron 6:73) – Possibly identical to En Gannim (Josh 21:29).

Aner – Levitical town in Manasseh (1 Chron 6:70). Josh 21:25 reads Taanach – *Unknown.*

Anim – Town in Hill Country of Judah (Josh 15:50) – *Kh. Ghuwein et-Tahta/H. Anim (156084), 11 mi. S of Hebron* – 97, 134

Ankara – See Ancyra.

Anthedon – 157, 163, 164

Anti-Lebanon Mountains – 62, 63, 64

Antioch (Pisidian) – Greco-Roman city in Phrygia, near Pisidia, visited by Paul on all his missionary journeys (Acts passim). Synagogue is setting for longest recorded Pauline sermon (13:14–41) – *In W-central Turkey, NE of Yalvac.*

Antioch (Syrian) – Greco-Roman city in SE Turkey, 15 mi. inland from Mediterranean Sea on Orontes River. Great metropolitan center of over 500,000 people. Christianity spread there after persecution of Stephen; Saul and Barnabas ministered here. "Home base" for Paul on his journeys. Mentioned 17 times in Acts – *Modern Antakya* – 62, 64, 148, 149, 150, 151, 155, 156, 175, 180, 181, 181, 182, 183, 184, 185, 186, 186, 187

Antioch, Plain/Valley of – 64

Antiochenes (See Ptolemais) – 151, 152

Antiochia (Jerusalem) – 151, 152, 158

Antiochia-on-Chrysorrhoas (Gerasa) – 151, 152

Antiochia Seleucia (Gadara) – 151, 152

Antiochus – 151

Antipatris – City to which Paul was taken by night under military escort from Jerusalem (Acts 23:31). Built by Herod the Great 9 B.C.; named after his father. Military relay station on border between Judea and Samaria – *Ras el-Ain/Afeq (143168), OT Aphek, ca. 11 mi. NE of Joppa* – 164, 165, 167, 170, 175, 176, 176–78, 186

Anuathu Borcaeus – 170, 172

Apamea (Syria) – 149, 175

Apamea (Turkey) – 148, 152, 175, 187

Aphek (Asher) – Town allotted to Asher (Josh 19:30), who were not able to drive out inhabitants (Judges 1:31) – *Tell Kurdaneh/T. Afeq (160250), 7 mi. SSE of Acco* – 99, 99, 103

Aphek (Phoenician) – Town on Sidonian-Amorite border (Josh 13:4) – *Afqa (231382), SE of Byblos in Lebanon.*

Aphek (Sharon) – City in SE corner of Sharon Plain at headwaters of Jarkon River. King killed by Joshua (Josh 12:18). Philistines mustered troops here for battle of Aphek (1 Sam 4:1) and again for battle of Gilboa (29:1). NT Antipatris – *Ras el-Ain/T. Afeq (143168), 11 mi. ENE of Joppa.* 16, 17, 18, 28, 38, 38, 46, 47, 74, 82, 88, 90, 94, 98, 110, 111, 112, 114, 115, 119, 126, 128, 132, 134, 138, 143, 176

Aphek (Upper and Lower) – Site of two Israelite/Aramean battles (1 Kings 20:26, 30; 2 Kings 13:17) – *Uncertain; possibly Kh. el-Asheq/En Gev (210143), close to E shore of Sea of Galilee* – Upper 29, 31, 129; Lower 30, 31, 129

Aphekah – Town in Hill Country of Judah (Josh 15:53) – *El-Habad (155098), 4 mi. SW of Hebron* – 97, 134

Apherema – 144, 154, 156, 157

Apollonia – City in Macedonia on Via Egnatia. Paul passed through here on second journey (Acts 17:1) on his way from Philippi to Thessalonica – *NE Greece but exact identity unknown* – 38, 39, 157, 161, 167, 170, 182, 183

Appius, Forum of – Paul met here by Roman Christians as he traveled to Rome (Acts 28:15) – *On Appian Way, about 40 mi. S of Rome.*

Apulia – 186

Aqaba – See Elath – 17, 18, 22, 23, 49, 51, 55, 56, 58, 60, 60, 61

Aqaba, Gulf of – See Elath, Gulf of – 22, 60

Aquitania – 163, 187

Ar (of Moab) – Town or region in Moab near Arnon River (6 times in OT) – *Uncertain; possibly el-Misna (224076), 15 mi. E of Dead Sea; possibly same as later Areopolis and Rabbath Moab.*

Arab – Town in the Hill Country of Judah (Josh 15:52) – *Possibly Kh. er-Rabiya (153093), 8 mi. SW of Hebron* – 134

Arabah – OT name for the Rift Valley between Sea of Galilee and Red Sea. In OT usually refers to Jordan Valley S of Sea of Galilee and N of Dead Sea – *Modern Ghor* – 17, 18, 22, 44, 49, 51, 52, 53, 54–56, 56, 60, 91, 92, 93, 94, 97, 114, 132, 138, 139

Arabah, Sea of the – Alternate name for Salt Sea (Deut 3:17; 4:49; Josh 3:16; 12:3; 2 Kings 14:25) – *Dead Sea* – 41, 51, 93, 94, 126, 132

Arabah Valley – See Arabah.

Arabia – Mentioned eight times in NIV; inhabitants ("Arabs") are mentioned as well. Can refer to the whole, or part, of the Arabian peninsula – *Large peninsula in SW Asia, predominantly occupied by Saudi Arabia* – 12, 22, 23, 28, 50, 51, 55–57, 58, 60, 60, 63, 67, 71, 72, 88, 102, 121, 123, 124, 127, 130, 140, 142, 143, 146, 148, 156, 159, 162, 172, 175, 175, 180, 181, 182, 185, 186

Arabian Desert – 12, 13, 16, 22, 28, 43, 52, 55, 65, 67, 68, 72, 77, 84, 130, 137, 140

Arabian Peninsula – 12, 13

Arabian Sea – 143

Arachosia – 143

Arad – City in Negev of Judah (Judges 1:16; some read Arad for Eder in Josh 15:21). Israelites fought with king of Arad on two occasions (Num 21:1; 33:40) – *T. Arad (162076), 17 mi. S of Hebron, but possibly "Canaanite Arad" was located at T. el-Milh/T. Malhata (152069), 11 mi. E of Beersheba* – 28, 42, 43, 44, 49, 49, 50, 60, 74, 75, 75, 78, 91, 91, 92, 114, 120, 125, 128, 130, 132, 138, 203, 206

Arad of Jerahmeel – 134

Arad Rabbah – 134

Aradus – 147, 148, 175

Arah – Town belonging to the Sidonians, NW of Israel (Josh 13:4) – *Unknown; RSV has "Mearah."*

Araj – See Bethsaida – 169

Aral Sea – 143, 148

Aram – Used 68 times in the NIV, usually to refer to the Aramean peoples (Semitic) and the land(s) in which they lived – *Indefinite geographically; NE of Israel, including area around Damascus, Syria, and upper Tigris-Euphrates Valleys. Used in compound names (e.g., Aram Damascus, Aram Maacah, Aram Zobah) to refer to small states* – 30, 62, 65, 71, 73, 76, 77, 85, 106, 118, 123, 127, 131, 133, 193

Aramathea – See Arimathea – 154, 156, 157

Aram Damascus – See Aram – 122, 125, 127, 131, 133, 193

Aramean kingdom of Damascus – Aramean population in and around Damascus who became subject to David (2 Sam 8:5, 6; 1 Chron 18:6).

Aram Maacah – Alternate name for Maacah (1 Chron 19:6).

Aram Naharaim – Abraham's servant searched for a wife for Isaac here (Gen 24:10). Balaam was from here (Deut 23:4). During period of judges, Cushan-Rishathaim was king (Judges 3:8). Ammonites hired horsemen and chariots from here to fight against David (1 Chron 19:6 and Ps 60, title) – *Region bounded by Upper Euphrates on W and Habur River on E* – 62, 65, 106, 118

Aram Zobah – Psalm 60 (title); see Aram and Zobah.

Ararat – Ark of Noah rested on "the mountains of Ararat" (Gen 8:4). Assassins of Sennacherib escaped to land of Ararat (2 Kings 19:37; Isa 37:38). Mentioned in Jer 51:27. Called Urartu in Assyrian inscriptions – *In modern Armenia; center in Lake Van region, where borders of Russia, Iran, and Turkey converge* – 12, 13, 70

Araru – 83

Arava – See Arabah – 17, 22

Araxes River – 70, 130

Arbata – 154

Arbela – 142, 143, 148, 149, 155, 157, 168

Arbel Pass – 28, 34, 34, 35

Archelais – 166, 167, 170, 172

Arethusa – 161

Argob – Name of Og's kingdom (Deut 3:4; 13, 14); mentioned as part of one of the Solomonic districts (1 Kings 4:13) – *In, or beside, the Bashan in N Transjordan* – 29, 30

Aria – 143

Aricia – 175

Ariel – Rare name for Jerusalem (Isa 29:1, 2, 7).

Arimathea – Home of Joseph who buried the body of Jesus in his tomb (Matt 27:57; Mark

15:43; Luke 23:51; John 19:38). See Arama-thea – *Rentis (151159), 16 mi. E of Joppa.*

Armageddon – Site of great eschatological battle (Rev 16:16) – *Usually identified with OT Megiddo (167221) on SW edge of Jezreel Valley, especially if the Greek name is derived from the Hebrew Har Megiddo = Mt. Megiddo. Alternative interpretations and identifications have been proposed (see commentaries)–* 36

Armenia – 65, 66, 68, 70, 142, **143**, 153, **163**, **181**

Arnon (Gorge/River) – Mentioned 25 times in NIV. Traditional N boundary of Moab and S boundary of the Amorites and later of Israelite tribe of Reuben – *Wadi Mujib in Transjordan, which flows from E to W into the Dead Sea opposite En Gedi –* 17, **18**, 22, 23, 28, **28**, 53, 55, **56**, 92, **92**, **94**, 101, **102**, 103, 114, 117, 118, **119**, **125**, **126**, 127, **128**, 131, **144**

Aroer – On boundary between Israelite and Ammonite territories (Josh 13:25) – *Unknown.*

Aroer (Negev) – Village with which David shared Amalekite spoils (1 Sam 30:28). Two of his mighty men came from here (1 Chron 11:44) – *Kh. Ararah/Aroer (148062), 12 mi. SE of Beersheba.*

Aroer (Reuben/Gad) – S limit of Sihon's kingdom, allotted to Reuben (Deut 3:12; 4:48; Josh 12:2; 13:9, 16; 1 Chron 5:8) but repaired/built by sons of Gad (Num 32:34). Located near Arnon Gorge (Deut 2:36; 3:12). Here Joab began census for David (2 Sam 24:5). Also mentioned in Judges 11:26; 2 Kings 10:33, and Jer 49:19 – *Arair (228097), ca. 14 mi. E of Dead Sea on N bank of Arnon –* 28, **28**, **56**, 75, **90**, **94**, 101, 108, 114, **114**, 117, 118, **119**, 120, 122, **126**, **128**, **132**, 134

Arpad – City/province in N Syria conquered by Assyrians. Always mentioned in connection with Hamath (2 Kings 18:34; 19:13; et al.) – *Tell Erfad, 25 mi. NNW of Aleppo –* 130, 142

Arqa – 105

Arqad – 72

Arrapkha – 137

Arsinoe – 175

Artacauna – 148

Arubboth – District headquarters of one of Solomon's administrators (1 Kings 4:10) – *Kh. el-Hammam (162201), 17 mi. NW of Shechem –* 122

Arumah – Abimelech, son of Gideon, fled here after being driven from Shechem (Judges 9:41) – *Kh. el-Ormah (180172), 5 mi. SE of Shechem –* **43**, 98, **132**

Aruna – 27, **28**, 33, 38, 87, **88**, 126

Arvad – Island/city, 2.5 mi. off Syrian coast. Famous for its powerful fleets (Ezek 27:8, 11) – *Er-Ruad (229473), ca. 30 mi. N of Tripoli –* 13, **62**, 64, **71**, 72, **105**, **123**, 130, **134**, 137

Ascalon – **150**, 151, 156, **157**, 158, 161, 163, **164**, 167, 170, 176

Ashan – Village in Shephelah district first allotted to Judah (but later given to Simeon (Josh 19:7; 1 Chron 4:32). Levitical city (1 Chron 6:59). David and his men roamed there (1 Sam 30:30) – *Uncertain; possibly Tell Beit Mirsim (141096), 12.5 mi. SW of Hebron. There may have been two Ashans: a Judahite in the Shephelah and a Simeonite in the Negev.*

Ashdod – Major Philistine city located in Philistine Plain, 22 mi. S of Joppa, 10 mi. N of Ashkelon. Mentioned 21 times in OT and in Acts 8:40 (Azotus). Usually under non-Israelite influence – *Esdud/T. Ashdod (117129), 3 mi. inland from the Mediterranean Sea –* 18, **18**, **28**, **46**, 47, **82**, 90, **94**, 103, 108, **109**, 110, **111**, **113**, 114, **125**, **126**, **128**, 130, **130**, **132**, **134**, 136, **138**, **143**, **144**, 146, 151

Ashdod-yam – **125**, **132**, **138**

Asher – Israelite tribe that settled in W Galilee and in and along the Plain of Acco – 32–34, 97, 99, **99**, 100, **102**, 107, 116, 122, 135

Ashkelon – Major Philistine city in Philistine Plain, 32 mi. S of Joppa, 12 mi. NNE of Gaza. Mentioned 13 times in OT. Usually under non-Israelite influence – *Asqalan/T. Ashqelon (107118), on the Mediterranean Sea –* 18, **18**, 47, **49**, **82**, 83, **90**, **94**, **97**, **103**, **105**, 106, **107**, 108, 109, **109**, 114, **125**, **126**, **128**, **132**, **134**, 135, 136, 138, **138**, **144**

Ashnah (Judah) – In first Shephelah district of Judah (Josh 15:33) – *Unknown.*

Ashnah (Judah) – In the third Shephelah district of Judah (Josh 15:43) – *Possibly Idna (147107), 8 mi. WNW of Hebron.*

Ashtaroth – Capital city of Og king of Bashan (Deut 1:4; Josh 9:10; et al.). Captured by Israelites and allotted to half-tribe of Manasseh (Josh 13:31). Levitical city (1 Chron 6:71; Josh 21:27, NIV "Be Eshtarah") – *T. Ashtarah (243240) in Transjordan, 22 mi. E of Sea of Galilee –* **18**, 23, 27, 28, **28**, **29**, 30, 52, **53**, 75, **91**, 92, **101**, **102**, **105**, **126**, **129**, 132

Ashteroth Karnaim – Early name, Ashteroth, is further identified by reference to Karnaim, which later replaced it as the chief city in the region (Gen 14:5).

Ashuri – 116

Asia – In NT times a Roman province covering W third of Turkey, from Aegean Sea to central highlands. Mentioned 19 times in NT. Paul established churches here. John wrote Revelation to seven of the churches here. Ephesus was evidently chief city – **163**, **175**, **181**, **182**, **185**

Asia Minor – **109**, 140, 141, **142**, 143, 147–50, **147**, 148–52, **148**, 159, 180, 183, 186

Askar – 172

Asochis – 168

Asphaltitis, Lake – 45

Asphar (Well of) – **154**, 155

As-Salt – 25

Asshur – Son of Shem (Gen 10:22; 1 Chron 1:17). Capital city of Assyria (Ezek 27:23; et al.) – *Qalaat Sherqat, 56 mi. S of Mosul/Nineveh on W bank of Tigris River in Iraq –* 13, **65**, 66, **71**, **72**, 73, **77**, **78**, 80, **130**, **134**, 136, **137**, 143

Assos – Port city in W Asia on hillside overlooking harbor. Paul passed through it on third journey (Acts 20:13–14) – *Behramkoy in Turkey –* 185, **185**, 186

Assyria – Country located along Upper Tigris River in modern Iraq. Great international power from ca. 900–600 B.C. Mentioned over 140 times in OT. took N Kingdom into captivity in 722 B.C. – 12, 16, 23, 62, 63, 66–68, 73, 76, **80**, 105, **130**, **134**, 135, 136, 137

Aswan – Town in Upper Egypt on border with Ethiopia (Ezek 29:10; 30:6; RSV: "Syene"). See also Sinim – *Aswan in S Egypt, 550 mi. S of Cairo at first cataract of Nile –* 57, **58**, 141, 143

Atad – Place of mourning for Jacob, near the Jordan (Gen 50:10–11) – *Unknown.*

Ataroth (Ephraim) – Town in NE Ephraim on border with Manasseh (Josh 16:2, 7) – *Unknown.*

Ataroth (Gad) – Transjordanian town allotted to Gad (Num 32:3, 34). Moabite Stone (10–14) states that Gad had always dwelt there – *Kh. Attarus, 9 mi. NW of Dibon (213109).*

Ataroth Addar – Village on border between Benjamin and Ephraim (Josh 16:5; 18:13) – *Uncertain; possibly Kh. Raddana (169146), 9.5 mi. NNW of Jerusalem –* 98

Athach – Town in S Judah to which David sent booty (1 Sam 30:30) – *Unknown; possibly a scribal error for Ether.*

Athara – 58

Atharim – Possibly a town in S Judah. Israelites traveled "along the road to Atharim" when attacked by king of Arad (Num 21:1) – *Unknown.*

Athens – City in Greece, visited by Paul on second and third journeys (Acts 17:15–16, 22; 18:1; 1 Thess 3:1). Major cultural and educational center at time of Paul – *5 mi. inland from the Aegean Sea –* **13**, 143, **143**, 146, **147**, 165, **175**, **182**, 183, 184, **185**

Athlit – 39

Athribis – 175

Atlantic Ocean – 163

Atroth Beth Joab – Possibly a village near Bethlehem (1 Chron 2:54) – *Unknown.*

Atroth Shophan – Village in Transjordan built by Gadites (Num 32:35) – *Uncertain; possibly Rujm Atarus, 1.5 mi. NE of Ataroth (Gad).*

Attalia – Port city in Pamphylia. From here route led into the interior; Paul and Barnabas set sail from here on their return to Antioch at end of first journey (Acts 14:25–26) – *Andaliya in S Turkey –* 180, 181, **181**, 185, **187**

Augusta Treverorum – 187

Auja – See Wadi Auja – 42, 43, 54

Auja (Spring) – 53

Auranitis – See Hauran – **150**, 151, 163, **164**, 165, **167**, 169, **170**, 174, **175**, 176, **177**

Autocratoris – 166

Avaris – 85, 88

Avedat – 28

Aven, Valley of – Valley in Lebanon, between Lebanon and Anti-Lebanon mountains. Part of Aramean kingdom of Damascus (Amos 1:5) – *Uncertain; possibly near modern Baalbek in Lebanon.*

Avith – Town in Edom. Home of Hadad son of Bedad, king of Edom (Gen 36:35; 1 Chron 1:46) – *Unknown.*

Avva – District/province from which Shalmaneser V took people and settled them in Israel (2 Kings 17:24) – *Unknown. See Ivvah –* 133

Avvim – Town allotted to Benjamin (Josh 18:23) – *Uncertain; probably in vicinity of Bethel.*

Ayun Musa – 60, 89, **89**

Ayyah – Town possessed by Ephraim (1 Chron 7:28) – *Unknown.*

Azekah – Shephelah town allotted to Judah (Josh 15:35), on border between Judah and coastal plain. Joshua pursued Amorite coalition towards it (10:10–11). David fought Goliath in its vicinity (1 Sam 17:1). Rehoboam fortified it (2 Chron 11:9); later Nebuchadnezzar attacked it (Jer 34:7; Lachish Letter 4). Reoccupied by Jews after the Exile (Neh 11:30) – *Kh. T. Zakariyeh/T. Azeqa (144123), 15 mi. NW of Hebron –* **43**, **46**, 48, **94**, 95, **97**, 113, **113**, **128**, **132**, **134**, 135, **138**, 139, **144**, 146

Azmaveth – Town where Jews lived after the exile (Ezra 2:24; Neh 12:29) – *Ras Dhukeir (174137) near Hizmeh, ca. 5 mi. NNE of Jerusalem –* 144

Azmon – Town on SW border of Canaan (Num 34:4) and Judah (Josh 15:4), E of the Wadi of Egypt (Wadi el-Arish) – *Uncertain; possibly Ein Muweilih (085010), 50 mi. SW of Beersheba –* 97

Aznoth Tabor – Landmark on SW border of Naphtali (Josh 19:34) – *Uncertain; possibly Kh. el-Jebeil/T. Aznot Tavor (186237), 3 mi. N of Mt. Tabor –* 99

Azor – 78, **90**, 109, **134**

Azotus – Greco-Roman name for Ashdod (Acts 8:40). See Ashdod – **150**, 151, **151**, 152, 154, 156, **157**, 161, **164**, 167, 170, 174, **175**, **176**, 177, **177**, **178**, **187**

Azuru – 135

Baalah (Negev) – Town in Negev district of Judah (Josh 15:29) – *Unknown; possibly identical to Baalath Beer.*

Baalah, Mount – Mountain on Judean-Benjamite border (Josh 15:11); probably near Baalath (Dan).

Baalah of Judah – Early name for Kiriath Jearim on border of Judah and Benjamin (Josh 15:9–10) from which David brought ark to Jerusalem (2 Sam 6:2; 1 Chron 13:6). Fortified by Solomon (2 Chron 8:6) – **117**

Baalath (Dan) – Danite town (Josh 19:44) – *Possibly el-Mughar (129138). May be referred to in 1 Chron 4:33 (N boundary of Simeonites in Shephelah) and in 2 Chron 8:6 and 1 Kings 9:18 (fortified by Solomon), although latter two references could be to Kiriath Jearim –* **100**, **120**, 121

Baalath Beer – Simeonite town in Negev (Josh 19:8), also called "Ramah in the Negev" – *Uncertain; see Ramah in the Negev –* **120**, **128**

Baalbek – 64

Baal Gad – Town in Valley of Lebanon (Josh 11:17; 12:7) at W foot of Mt. Hermon (13:5). N limit of Joshua's conquest – *Unknown.*

Baal Hamon – Solomon said to have had a vineyard there (SS 8:11). Possibly only a poetic expression – *Unknown.*

Baal Hazor – Place near border of Ephraim where Absalom executed Amnon (2 Sam 13:23) – *Jebel Asur/T. Asur (177153), 15 mi NNE of Jerusalem –* **18**, 40, **119**

Baal Hermon – Town on border of Manasseh in Transjordan (1 Chron 5:23). Hivites lived here (Judges 3:3) – *Unknown; probably near Mt. Hermon.*

Baal Meon – Town in Transjordan settled by Reubenites (Num 32:38; 1 Chron 5:8); at times under Moabite control (Ezek 25:9). Also called Beth Baal Meon (Josh 13:17), Beth Meon (Jer 48:23), and possibly Beon (Num 32:3) – *Main (219120), 23 mi. SW of Amman, 10 mi. E of Dead Sea.*

Baal Perazim – Place where David defeated Philistines soon after becoming king (2 Sam 5:20; 1 Chron 14:11): – *Uncertain; possibly ez-Zuhur (167127), 4 mi. SW of Jerusalem. –* **117**

Baal-rosh – **131**

Baal Shalishah – Place from which a supporter of Elisha came (2 Kings 4:42) – *Uncertain; possibly Kh. Marjame (181155), 16 mi NE of Jerusalem.*

Baal Tamar – Town or landmark between Bethel and Gibeah where Israelites lay in wait for pursuing Benjamites (Judges 20:33) – *Unknown.*

Baal Zephon – Site in/near Egypt mentioned in connection with Israelite camp at Pi Hahiroth/Migdol (Exod 14:2, 9; Num 33:7) – *Unknown; frequently identified with Tahpanhes/Tell Defenneh near N end of Suez Canal; more probably in area of Bitter Lakes* – 89

Bab edh-Dhra – **43**, 45, **56**, 75, **75**, **78**, 81

Babel – Place where tower reaching toward heaven was built (Gen 11:9) – *Unknown; probably in S Mesopotamia; possibly alternate name for Babylon* – 71

Babylon – Various forms of "Babylon" are mentioned 237 times in the OT and 11 times in the NT. Located in S Mesopotamia (Iraq) on Euphrates River, 50 mi. S of Baghdad. Capital of the Neo-Babylonian Empire (ca. 604–539 B.C.). Judeans were taken captive by the Babylonian king Nebuchadnezzar in 586 B.C. – 13, 14, **65**, 66, 77, **78**, 80, 123, 130, 133, 136, 137, 138–43, **142**, **143**, 145, 148, 149, 175, 194

Babylon and Beyond the River – 142, 145

Babylonia – Area in S Mesopotamia ruled from city of Babylon. See above – 12, 16, 18, 23, 62, 63, 67, 68, 105, **130**, **137**, 142, **142**, **143**

Baca – 166, **167**, **168**

Bactra – 148

Bactria – **143**, 146, 149

Baetica – 163

Baghdad – **13**, **65**, 66

Bahariya Oasis – 58

Bahurim – Site E of Mt. of Olives mentioned in connection with life of David (2 Sam 16:5; 17:18; 19:16; 1 Kings 2:8; 1 Chron 11:33) – *Uncertain; possibly Ras et-Tumeim (174133), 1.5 mi. NE of Jerusalem* – 119, **119**

Baither – Town allotted to Judah; mentioned only in Septuagint of Josh 15:59 (see NEB) – *Kh. el-Yahudi (162126), 7 mi. WSW of Jerusalem.*

Balah – Negev town allotted to Simeon (Josh 19:3) – *Unknown.*

Balik River – 62, **62**, 76, **77**, 80, 84

Bamoth – Stopping place for Israel in Transjordan, N of Arnon Gorge (Num 21:19–20) – *Unknown; possibly same as Bamoth Baal.*

Bamoth Baal – Site NE of Dead Sea to which Balak took Balaam to curse Israel (Num 22:41). Allotted to Reuben (Josh 13:17) but claimed by Moabites (Moabite Stone) – *Unknown.*

Barada River – 63, 64

Barqay – 78

Barsip – 62

Bascama – 156, **157**

Bashan – Mentioned some 60 times in OT. Area E and NE of the Sea of Galilee, bounded by the Rift Valley on the W, Mt. Hermon on the N, Mt. Bashan on the E, and Gilead on the S – **17**, **18**, 23, 29–31, **29**, 33–36, 52, **53**, 83, 87, 92, **93**, 101, **101**, 106, 108

Bashan, Mount/Mountains of – See Jebel Druze – 29, **29**, 30, **53**

Basra – **65**, 66

Batanea – **29**, 30, **150**, **151**, 152, 163, **164**, 165, **167**, 169, **170**, 174, **175**, 176, **176**, 177

Bealoth – Negev city allotted to Judah (Josh 15:24) – *Unknown; some suggest Kh. el-Mishash/T. Masos (146069), 8 mi. ESE of Beersheba. Possibly same as Baalath Beer, but cf. Hormah below.*

Beer (Hill Country of Ephraim) – Site near Mt. Gerizim to which Jotham fled from Abimelech (Judges 9:21) – *Unknown.*

Beer (Moab) – Site in Moab where Israelites secured well water (Num 21:16) – *Unknown.*

Beer Elim – Moabite town mentioned in oracle of Isaiah (15:8) – *Unknown.*

Beer Lahai Roi – "Well of the Living One that sees me." Place where angel of Yahweh appeared to Hagar (Gen 16:14). Frequented by Isaac (Gen 24:62; 25:11) – *Unknown; but Ein Muweileh (085010), 50 mi. SW of Beersheba (see Azmon) has been suggested –* 77, **84**

Beeroth – One of the four Gibeonite cities that made a treaty with Joshua (Josh 9:17). Allotted to Benjamin (Josh 18:25). Inhabitants fled to Gittaim (in Saul's day?) and two of them murdered Ishbosheth (2 Sam 4:2–3). One of David's elite troops came from here (2 Sam 23:37; 1 Chron 11:39). Settled after the exile by Jews (Ezra 2:25; Neh 7:29) – *Kh. el-Burj (167137), 4.5 mi. NW of Jerusalem –* 94, **94**, **98**, 116, 134, **144**, 154

Beer Resisim – 78, **78**

Beersheba – Capital of the Negev, mentioned 34 times in OT. Associated with Abraham, Isaac, and Jacob. Allotted to both Judah (Josh 15:28) and Simeon (19:2; 1 Chron 4:28). Mentioned as S boundary of Israel in phrase "from Dan to Beersheba." Mentioned in Joab's census (2 Sam 24:7) and story of Elijah's flight from Jezebel (1 Kings 19:3). Evidently a shrine/temple was here (Amos 5:5; 8:14), and Jews lived here in the postexilic period (Neh 11:27) – *Tell es-Seba/T. Beer Sheva (134072), 25 mi. SW of Hebron –* 16, **17**, **18**, 21, 25, 28, **28**, 39, 42, **43**, 46, 49, **49**, 50, **58**, 60, **60**, 74, 77, **78**, **78**, 79, **84**, **97**, 98, **102**, 104, **107**, **109**, 111, **114**, **117**, 119, **119**, **120**, 125, **128**, **131**, **132**, **134**, 136, **138**, 140, 144, **144**, 146, **151**, **157**, 158, 163, **164**, **167**, 172, 202, 204

Beersheba, Desert/Wilderness of – **131**

Be Eshtarah – See Ashtaroth.

Behistun – **143**

Beirut – **13**, **62**, 64, **105**

Beisan – See Beth Shan – 206

Beitin – 77, **93**, 94

Beit Sahur – 78

Beit Ur el-Foqa – See Beth Horon – 205

Bela – Former name of Zoar (Gen 14:2, 8) – *See Zoar –* 75, **78**, 81, 201

Belgica – See Belgium.

Belgium – 163, 187

Bene Berak – Town allotted to tribe of Dan (Josh 19:45) and attacked by Sennacherib of Assyria (Annals) – *Kheiriyeh/Bene-beraq (133160), 4.5 mi. NE of Joppa –* **100**, **134**, 135

Bene Jaakan – Place of Israelite encampment in Sinai/ Negev desert (Num 33:31–32; Deut 10:6 "wells of the Jaakanites") – *Unknown.*

Ben Hinnom, Valley of – See Hinnom, Valley of.

Beni Hasan – 80, 81

Benjamin – Youngest son of Jacob and name of tribe that descended from him. Tribal allotment to the NE, N, and NW of Jerusalem – 39, 41, 96, 98, **98**, 100, 104, 107, 108, 111–13, 116, 122, 136, 141, 146, 192, 193

Benjamin, Hill Country of – 41, 42, 47, 124, 136, 154, 202

Benjamin Plateau – 41, 42, 110, 112, 113, 162

Beon – Town in Transjordan (Num 32:3). See Baal Meon.

Beqa – See Lebanese Beqa – **18**, 20, 28, 31, 32, **62**, 64, 87, **88**, 91

Beracah, Valley of – Valley where Judeans collected booty during days of Jehoshaphat (2 Chron 20:26) – *Uncertain; in or near Judean Desert, possibly Wadi el-Arrub between Bethlehem and Hebron –* 42

Berea – Large Macedonian city visited by Paul on his second and possibly third journeys (Acts 17:10, 11, 13, 14; 20:4) – *In and around Verria in N Greece, 40 mi. W of Thessalonica –* 149, 155, **175**, 182, **183**, 185, **187**

Bered – Point mentioned in the story of the flight of Hagar from Sarai (Gen 16:14) – *Unknown; probably in S Israel or NE Sinai.*

Berenice – 149

Berenike – 58

Bernice – See Pella – **150**, 151

Berothah/Berothai – City on N boundary of Canaan (Ezek 47:16, Berothah). Controlled by Hadadezer, king of Hamath, but taken by David (2 Sam 8:8) – *Bereitan (257372), 30 mi. NW of Damascus –* **117**, 118, **145**

Bersabe – 166, **167**, 168

Berytus – 175

Ber-zetha – **154**, 155

Besara – 168

Besimoth – 178

Besor Ravine – Wadi in SW Israel that David crossed in pursuit of the Amalekites (1 Sam 30:9, 21) – *Wadi Ghazzeh/Nahal Besor* – **16, 17, 18, 28**, 46, 47, 49, 115

Betah – See Tebah.

Beten – Town allotted to Asher (Josh 19:25) – *Uncertain; possibly Kh. Ibtin/H. Ivtan (160241), in N coastal plain of Israel, 11 mi. SSE of Acco* – **99**

Bethabara – 170

Bet Haemeq – 175

Beth Anath – Town assigned to Naphtali (Josh 19:38); inhabitants became forced laborers of Naphtali (Judges 1:33) – *Uncertain; possibly Safed el-Battikh (Lebanon; 190289), 15 mi. SE of Tyre in Upper Galilee* – **31**, 32, **90, 97, 99, 100, 103, 106, 107**

Beth Anoth – Village allotted to Judah in a Hill Country district (Josh 15:59) – *Kh. Beit Anun (162107), 3 mi. NE of Hebron* – 106, **134**

Bethany (near Jerusalem) – Village on road to Jericho (Mark 11:1; Luke 19:29), less than 2 mi. from Jerusalem (John 11:18). Mary, Martha, and Lazarus lived here (John 11). It seems that Jesus spent evenings of week before Crucifixion here. Mentioned 11 times in NT – *El-Azariya (174131), 1.5 mi. E of Jerusalem, on E side of Mt. of Olives* – **172**, 199, 200

Bethany, on the other side of the Jordan – Place E of Jordan where John baptized Jesus (John 1:28); Jesus ministered near here (10:40–42) – *Uncertain; possibly near Wadi el-Kharar (203138), 6 mi. E of Jericho, E of Jordan, although several other sites have been proposed* – 171

Beth Arabah – Village on the boundary between Judah (Josh 15:6) and Benjamin (18:18). Assigned to both Judah (15:61) and Benjamin (18:22) – *Uncertain; possibly Ein el-Gharabah (197139), 4 mi. SE of Jericho* – 97, **98, 134**

Beth Arbel – Village devastated by Shalman (Hos 10:14) – *Irbid (229218), 20 mi. NW of Amman in Transjordan* – 54

Beth Ashbea – Town in Judah noted for linen workers (1 Chron 4:21) – *Unknown.*

Beth Aven – Town on N boundary of Benjamin, W of Jericho but E of Luz (Bethel; Josh 18:12) and near Ai (7:2). Philistines camped at Micmash, E of Beth Aven (1 Sam 13:5; 14:23). Noted for illicit worship (Hos 4:15; 5:8; 10:5) – *Uncertain; possibly T. Maryam (175141), 7 mi. NE of Jerusalem* – 98, 112, **112**

Beth Azmaveth – See Azmaveth.

Beth Baal Meon – Town allotted to Reuben (Josh 13:17). See Baal Meon – **101**

Beth Barah – Place in Jordan Valley near which Ephraimites were encouraged by Gideon to head off fleeing Midianites (Judges 7:24) – *Unknown; some emend the text to read "the fords of the Jordan."*

Beth Basi/Beth-basi – **154**, 155

Beth Biri – Town in Negev(?), inhabited by Simeonites (1 Chron 4:31). Parallel in Josh 19:6 has "Beth Lebaoth" – *Unknown.*

Beth Car – Israelites pursued Philistines from Mizpah W to a point below Beth Car (1 Sam 7:11) – *Unknown; probably in western Benjamin/Ephraim* – 110

Beth Dagon (Asher) – Boundary town of Asher in N Israel (Josh 19:27) – *Unknown.*

Beth Dagon (Judah) – Shephelah town allotted to Judah (Josh 15:41) – *Unknown* – **134**, 135

Beth Diblathaim – Town of Moab "cursed" by Jeremiah (48:22). See Almon Diblathaim – **132**

Beth Eden – Cursed by Amos along with Damascus and the people of Aram (1:5) – *Aramean principality near the upper Euphrates valley. Possibly equivalent to the "people of Eden" (2 Kings 19:12 = Isa 37:12) and "Eden" (Ezek 27:23). Called Bit-Adini in Assyrian sources* – 130

Beth Eked – Place where Jehu captured and slaughtered the relatives of Ahaziah of Judah (2 Kings 10:12, 14) – *Unknown; probably N of Shechem near Jezreel Valley.*

Bethel (Benjamin) – Town mentioned 71 times in the OT, second in number only to Jerusalem. Patriarchal center near which Abram pitched his tent (Gen 12:8; 13:3) and where Jacob dreamed of ladder ascending to heaven (28:19). Captured by Israelites (Josh 12:16), allotted to Benjamin (18:22). On Benjamin-Ephraim border (16:1–2; 18:13). Jeroboam built a worship center here containing a golden calf (1 Kings 12:29, 32–33). Thus Bethel became target of prophetic rebuke (e.g., Amos 4:4; 5:5–6). Resettled by Jews after the Babylonian exile (Ezra 2:28; Neh 7:32; 11:31). See also Luz – *Beitin (172148), 12 mi. N of Jerusalem* – 18, **18**, 28, 28, 40, 41, 43, **43**, 77–80, **77, 78, 82, 84, 90**, 93, 94, **94, 98**, 104, **105**, 106, 107, **107, 109**, 110, **111, 112**, 124, **125, 126**, 127, **131, 132, 134, 144**, 154, 155, **170, 189**, 201, 205

Bethel (Judah) – See Bethuel.

Bethel, Hill Country of – Hills in Bethel region through which the Ephraim-Benjamin border ran (Josh 16:2). Here Saul mustered his troops in preparation for battle with Philistines (1 Sam 13:2) – 111

Beth Emek – Town on boundary of Asher (Josh 19:27) – *T. Mimas/T. Bet Ha-Emeq (164263), 3.5 mi. NE of Acco* – 99

Bethennabris – **170**, 171

Bether – See Beththter – **97, 134, 178**

Beth Ezel – Town mentioned by Micah as in mourning due to attack (1:11), probably in days of Sennacherib (ca. 701 B.C.) – *Unknown; probably in Shephelah of Judah.*

Beth Gader – Haraph was its "father" (= ruler, sheikh; 1 Chron 2:51) – *Uncertain; possibly in territory of Judah, perhaps same as Geder.*

Beth Gamul – Town in Moab cursed by Jeremiah (48:23) – *Kh. el-Jumeil (235099), in Transjordan, E of Dead Sea, 33 mi. S of Amman.*

Beth Gilgal – Singers from Beth Gilgal participated in dedication of wall of Jerusalem (Neh 12:29) – *Unknown; probably in vicinity of Jerusalem.*

Beth Haggan – Ahaziah of Judah fled from Jehu "up the road to Beth Haggan" (2 Kings 9:27) and was wounded – *Jenin (178207), 11 mi. SE of Megiddo on S edge of Jezreel Valley* – **33**, 36, **38**

Beth Hakkerem – Hill country town allotted to Judah (Josh 15:59b; LXX). Here a signal (fire) could be raised for the Judeans fleeing from Jerusalem (Jer 6:1). In Nehemiah's day, capital of a district of Judah whose ruler participated in repair of Dung Gate of Jerusalem (Neh 3:14) – *Kh. Salih/Ramat Rahel (170127), 3 mi. SSW of Jerusalem, or less probably Ein Karim/En Kerem (165130), 5 mi. W of Jerusalem* – 41, **43, 134, 144**, 146

Beth Hakkerem Valley – **18, 19, 31**, 32, **33**

Beth Haram – Town in Transjordan allotted to Gad (Josh 13:7; cf. Num 32:36 "Beth Haran") – *Tell Iktanu (214136), 18 mi. WSW of Amman* – **101**

Beth Hoglah – Town SE of Jericho on border of Judah and Benjamin (Josh 15:6; 18:19); allotted to Benjamin (18:21) – *Uncertain; possibly Deir Hajlah (197136), 3.5 mi. SE of Jericho* – **97, 98**

Beth Horon (Upper and Lower) – Twin towns located 2 mi. apart on ridge guarding approach to hill country from coastal plain. In Ephraim near Ephraim-Benjamin border (Josh 21:22; 1 Chron 6:68); one, or both, a Levitical city (Josh 21:22; 1 Chron 6:68). Mentioned 14 times in OT. Joshua pursued fleeing Amorites past them (Josh 10:9–15). Solomon rebuilt them to protect one of the approaches to Jerusalem from the W (1 Kings 9:17; 2 Chron 8:5) – *Upper = Beit Ur el-Foqa (160143); Lower = Beit Ur et-Tahta (158144), 12 mi. NW of Jerusalem* – 28, 41, **43, 46**, 47, 48, 95, **94, 98, 102**, 110–12, 116, **117, 120**, 121, 124, **126, 128, 144**, 154, 155, **176, 176**, 177, **178, 188, 189**, 204

Beth Jeshimoth – Last camping place for Israel before crossing Jordan River into Canaan (on plains of Moab; Num 33:49). On extremity of Sihon the Amorite's territory (Josh 12:3). Allotted to Reuben (13:20) but later a town of Moab (Ezek 25:9) – *T. el-Azeimeh (208132), 22 mi. WSW of Amman* – 92, **92, 94, 101**

Beth Lebaoth – Town in Negev allotted to Simeon (Josh 19:6). Possibly same as Lebaoth (15:32) and Beth Biri (1 Chron 4:31) – *Unknown; in S Israel/Judah.*

Bethlehem (Judah) – Judean town mentioned 40 times in the OT, mostly in connection with David. Naomi and Ruth were from here, as was David. Fortified by King Rehoboam (2 Sam 23:24). Settled by Jews during postexilic period (Ezra 2:21; Neh 7:26). Mentioned 8 times in NT, chiefly in connection with birth of Jesus – *Beit Lahm (169123), 5 mi. SSW of Jerusalem* – 18, **18**, 28, 42, **43**, 44, **46**, 48, **84, 97, 99**, 104, **105, 107**, 108, **111, 112**, 114, **125, 128, 132, 134, 144**, 154, 155, **164**, 165, **170**, 172, 174, **176, 189**, 202

Bethlehem (Zebulun) – Town allotted to Zebulun (Josh 19:15). The judge Ibzan came from here (Judges 12:8, 10) – *Beit Lahm/Bet Lehem Hagelilit (168238), 7 mi. WNW of Nazareth* – 108

Beth Marcaboth – Village in Negev allotted to Simeon (Josh 19:5; 1 Chron 4:31) – *May be identical to Madmannah (which is preceded by Ziklag in the Negev list of Judah [Josh 15:31]); if not, then unknown; in S Judah.*

Beth Meon – See Baal Meon.

Beth Nimrah – Town allotted to Gad, near good grazing land (Num 32:36; Josh 13:27). Called Nimrah in Num 32:3 – *T. el-Bleibil (210146), in Transjordan, 18 mi. E of Amman* – **101**

Beth Ophrah – Town in/near Shephelah, mentioned in oracle of Micah (1:10) – *Uncertain; possibly et-Taiyibeh (153107), 5 mi. NW of Hebron.*

Beth Pazzez – Town allotted to Issachar (Josh 19:21) – *Uncertain; possibly Sheikh Mazghith (199221), 5.5 mi. N of Beth Shan.*

Beth Pelet – Town allotted to Judah, in Negev district (Josh 15:27). After exile, Jews settled here; evidently in Negev (Neh 11:26) – *Uncertain; possibly T. es-Saqti/T. Shoqet (141079), 6 mi. NNE of Beersheba* – **97, 134, 144**, 146

Beth Peor – Place in/near the plains of Moab where Israel camped. Setting for giving of laws of Deuteronomy (3:29; 4:46). Moses buried here (Deut 34:6). Allotted to Reuben (Josh 13:20) – *Uncertain; possibly Kh. esh-Sheikh Jayil (215133), 18 mi. WSW of Amman* – **101**

Bethphage – Village on Mt. of Olives, through which Jesus passed on way from Bethany to Jerusalem on day of Triumphal Entry (= Palm Sunday; Matt 21:11; Mark 11:1; Luke 19:29) – *Et-Tur (173131), 0.7 mi. E of Jerusalem* – **172**, 199

Beth-ramatha – **167**, 171

Beth Rehob – Aramean principality N of Israel. Laish/Dan was in/near it (Judges 18:28). Ammonites hired soldiers from here to fight David's troops (2 Sam 10:6). Called Rehob in

2 Sam 10:8 – *Probably located in Lebanese Beqa N of Israel* – **117**, 118

Bethsaida – City on N shore of Sea of Galilee. The disciples Philip, Andrew, and Peter were from here (John 1:44; 12:21). Jesus performed mighty works here (e.g., healed a blind man [Mark 8:22] and fed 5,000 in vicinity [Matt 14:13; Mark 6:30ff.]), yet it was cursed by him because of unbelief (Matt 11:21; Luke 10:13) – *Possibly there were two Bethsaidas, one W of ancient course of Jordan River, the other on E bank. The former would have been a small fishing village, "Bethsaida in Galilee" (John 12:21), located at el-Araj (208255), on shore of Sea of Galilee). In contrast, the latter was a large Gentile city, built by Herod Philip, tetrarch of Gaulanitis. Also called "Julias" and mentioned in extrabiblical literature – Et-Tell (209257), 1.5 mi. N of the lakeshore* – **31**, **34**, **35**, **157**, 168, **168**, 169, **170**, 171

Bethsaida-Julias – See Bethsaida and Julias – 169

Beth Shan – Major Canaanite city allotted to Manasseh, in or near Issachar (Josh 17:11; 1 Chron 7:29). They were not able to drive out inhabitants (Josh 17:16; Judges 1:27). Became a Philistine stronghold where bodies of Saul and Jonathan were hung on wall (1 Sam 31:10, 12; 2 Sam 21:12). In 5th Solomonic district (1 Kings 4:12). In Hellenistic period called Scythopolis and Nysa – *Tell el-Husn/T. Bet Shean (197212), 15 mi. SSW of Sea of Galilee* – 18, **20**, 25, **27**, **28**, 33, 36, **38**, 40, **53**, 54, **54**, 75, **78**, 82, 83, **88**, 90, **93**, 97, **98**, 99, **99**, 103, 104, **105**, 106, 107, **109**, 114, 115, 116, **117**, **119**, 120, **122**, 125, 126, **129**, 132, 151, 205

Beth Shemesh (Issachar) – Town in E Lower Galilee on boundary of Issachar – *Possibly Kh. Sheikh esh-Shamsawi/H. Shemesh (199232), but more probably T. el-Abeidiyeh (202232), 2 mi. S of Sea of Galilee near Jordan River* – **31**, 99

Beth Shemesh (Judah/Dan) – Town in N Shephelah on N boundary of Judah (Josh 15:10). Allotted to tribe of Dan (19:41), who was unable to occupy it (Judges 1:35). Levitical city (Josh 21:16; 1 Chron 6:59). Served as Judean outpost on border with Philistines. Ark of Covenant was returned here (1 Sam 6). In Solomon's second administrative district. Fortified by Rehoboam. Disputed by Israel (2 Kings 14:8–14; 2 Chron 25:21) and the Philistines (2 Chron 28:18) – *T. er-Rumeileh/T. Bet Shemesh (147128), 16 mi. W of Jerusalem* – 18, **28**, 43, **46**, 47, 48, **78**, 82, 90, **97**, 102, 103, 109, **109**, 110, 111, 113, 120, 122, 128, 129, 131, **134**, 135, **138**, 202, 203

Beth Shemesh (Naphtali) – Town in Upper Galilee allotted to Naphtali (Josh 19:38); Canaanites continued to live here but served as laborers to Naphtalites (Judges 1:33) – *Kh. T. er-Ruweisi/T. Rosh (181271), 17 mi. NE of Acco* – **31**, 32, **99**, 100, **103**

Beth Shittah – Site along route of Midianites fleeing before Gideon (Judges 7:22) – *Unknown; probably SE of Beth Shan in Jordan Valley* – 107

Beth Tappuah – Town allotted to Judah in hill country (Josh 15:53) – *Taffuh (154105), 3.5 mi. WNW of Hebron* – **97**, **134**

Bethther – OT Bether – **178**, 179

Beth Togarmah – N country noted for horses (Ezek 27:14); mentioned in prophecy against Gog (38:6) – *E Turkey, modern Armenia.*

Bethuel – Negev town allotted to Simeon (Josh 19:4 and 1 Chron 4:30, "Bethul". Probably same as the Bethel (1 Sam 30:27) to which David sent plunder. Parallel Judean list (Josh 15:30) has Kesil – *Unknown.*

Beth-yerah/Beth Yerah – 33, **34**, 54, 74, 75, **75**, 78

Beth Zechariah – 154, 155

Beth Zur – Town allotted to Judah in hill country (Josh 15:58). Populated by descendants of Caleb (1 Chron 2:45). Fortified by Rehoboam (2 Chron 11:7). Administrative center of a half-district in days of Nehemiah (3:16). Mentioned frequently in literature of intertestamental period – *Kh. et-Tubeiqeh (159110), 4.5 mi. N of Hebron* – 82, 97, **109**, 125, **134**, 140, **144**, 146, 154–56, **154**, **157**

Bet Netofa Valley – 99

Betogabris – 164, 174, **176**, **177**, **178**

Betonim – Town allotted to Gad (Josh 13:26) – *Kh. Batneh (217154), 16 mi. NE of Jericho in Transjordan* – **101**

Beyond the Jordan – 176

Beyond the River – See Trans-Euphrates – 62, 118, 142, 143, **143**, 145

Bezek – Town conquered by Simeonites and Judahites (Judges 1:4). Place where Saul mustered troops prior to battle with Ammonites at Jabesh Gilead (1 Sam 11:8) – *Latter at Kh. Ibziq (187197), 13 mi. NE of Shechem; former may be the same or a different, unknown, site* – **98**, 111, **112**

Bezer – One of the three cities of refuge E of the Jordan River (Deut 4:43; Josh 20:8). Also a Levitical city in Reubenite territory (Josh 21:36; 1 Chron 6:78) – *Uncertain; possibly Umm el-Amad (235132), 11 mi. S of Amman* – **53**, 102, 103, **105**, 127, **132**

Bezetha Valley – 189, 190

Bileam – See Ibleam.

Bilhah – Town allotted to Simeon (1 Chron 4:29). Probably same as Balah (Josh 19:3) and Baalah (15:29) – *Unknown; in S Judah.*

Bir el-Abud – 89

Bir el-Mazar – 89

Bir en-Nasb – 60

Bir Mara – 52, 60, 89, **89**

Bir Sidri – 60

Bithynia – Roman province in N Asia Minor (Turkey), along S coast of Black Sea. On second journey, Paul and Silas were forbidden to enter it (Acts 16:7); yet Peter later addressed the church here (1 Peter 1:1) – **163**, **181**, **182**, 183, **185**, **186**

Bitter Lakes – 60, 89, **89**

Biziothiah – Possibly town in Negev district allotted to Judah (Josh 15:28, NIV). More probably, following the LXX and Neh 11:27, the passage should be read "Beersheba and its settlements."

Black Sea – 13, 80, 130, 143, 148, 163, 175, 182, 183, **185–87**

Blue Nile – 57, 58

Bohan, Stone of – Marker on NE border of Judah (Josh 15:6) – SE Benjamin (18:17) – *Unknown; in Jericho region, but closer to Dead Sea.*

Bokim – "Weeping." Place where Israel wept in repentance (Judges 2:1, 5) – *Uncertain; possibly in hill country W of Jericho, near Bethel (cf. Gen 35:8: ". . . oak below Bethel. So it was named Allon Bacuth.").*

Bor Ashan – Place in S Judah where David and his men roamed and to which he sent plunder (1 Sam 30:30) – *Uncertain; possibly same as Ashan.*

Borsippa – 65, 137

Bosor – 154

Bostra – 154, 167, 171, **187**

Bozez – Cliff S of Micmash which Jonathan and his armor bearer climbed to attack Philistine garrison (1 Sam 14:4) – *Cliff on rim of Wadi Suweinit (ca. 176141), 7 mi. NNW of Jerusalem* – 112, **112**

Bozkath – Town in Shephelah district of Judah (Josh 15:39). Home of Jedidah, King Josiah's mother (2 Kings 22:1) – *Unknown.*

Bozrah (Edom) – City in N Edom located along caravan routes. Early king of Edom from here (Gen 36:33; 1 Chron 1:44). Focus of prophecies of judgment (Isa 34:6; 63:1; Jer 49:13, 22; Amos 1:12) – *Buseirah (208016), 25 mi. SE of S tip of Dead Sea in mountains of Edom* – 28, **28**, 55, **56**, 92, 125, **128**, 132

Bozrah (Moab) – Town in Moab mentioned in judgment prophecy of Jeremiah (48:24) – *Possibly same as Bezer.*

Bridge of Jacob's Daughters – 28

Britannia – 163

Brook of Besor – See Besor Ravine – 114

Brook of Egypt – See Egypt, Wadi of – 60, 117, 130, 133, **137**, 138

Bucephalia – 148

Buqeia – 42, **43**

Butastis – 175

Buz – Mentioned in an oracle of Jeremiah (25:23) – *Unknown; probably in the desert E of Palestine.*

Byblos – See Gebal – **13**, 18, **62**, 64, **72**, 74, **77**, 80, 82, 83, **91**, 123, 130, **137**, 142, 147, 148

Byzantium – 143, 181, 182, 183

Cabbon – Town allotted to Judah in a Shephelah district (Josh 15:40) – *Unknown.*

Cabul – Town near/in Plain of Acco allotted to Asher (Josh 19:27). Also name of district in same area ("Land of Cabul"); given by Solomon to Hiram of Tyre (1 Kings 9:13) – *Kh. Rosh Zayith (171253), 8 mi. ESE of Acco* – **99**, 120, 122

Cabura – 148

Cadasa – 156, **157**, 168, 177, 178

Caesarea/Caesarea Maritima – Built by Herod the Great (37–4 B.C.) in coastal plain. In NT times main port of Palestine. Mentioned 17 times in the NT, all in Acts. Visited by Philip (8:40) and Saul (9:30). Here Cornelius was converted to Christianity (Acts 10–11). Became Roman capital of Palestine. Herod Agrippa I died there (12:19). Paul passed through it at end of his second (18:22) and third (21:8, 16) journeys. Paul was prisoner here for several years before being shipped to Rome for trial – *Qaisariye (140212), 31 mi. N of Joppa* – **17**, 18, **18**, 33, 38, **38**, 39, 151, 163, **164**, 165, 167, 168, 170, 171, 174–76, **175–78**, 181, 182, 184, **185**, 186, **186**, 187, 205

Caesarea Philippi – At foot of Mt. Hermon, at the headwaters of the Jordan River. Formerly called Panias, renamed by Philip the tetrarch. In region of Caesarea Philippi Peter confessed that Jesus was the Christ (Matt 16:13–20; Mark 8:27–30). Also called "Neronias" for a brief period of time – *Banias (215295) on NE slope of Huleh Valley, ca. 50 mi. SW of Damascus* – 29, 30, **30**, **31**, 167, 168, 170, 171, **175–77**

Cairo – 13, 57, 58, 59, 61, 73

Calah – Important city of kingdom of Nimrod (Gen 10:11–12). Frequently mentioned in Assyrian texts. Residence of Assyrian kings from Ashurnasirpal II on – *Nimrud in N Iraq on E bank of Tigris River, N of where the Upper Zab joins it, about 22 mi. S of Nineveh* – **71**, 130, **137**

Caleb Ephrathah – If really a village, Hezron died here (1 Chron 2:24) – Unknown (but RSV, following the LXX, translates "after the death of Hezron, Caleb went in to Ephrathah, the wife of Hezron. . .").

Callirrhoe – 43, 44, 45, **164**, 165, 171

Calneh (S Mesopotamia) – City founded by Nimrod in Shinar (S Mesopotamia? Gen 10:10) – *Unknown (but possibly text is to be translated "all of them in the land of Shinar" [RSV]).*

Calneh (Syria) – The Calneh of Amos 6:2 is associated with a N Hamath and may be identical with Assyrian Kullani (Probably "Calno" [Isa 10:9] and "Canneh" [Ezek 27:23] are the same places as this N "Calneh" with slight spelling variations) – *Kullankoy, 8 mi. NW of Aleppo in Syria* – **130**

Calno – See Calneh.

Cana – **31**

Canaan – Geopolitical territory mentioned over 75 times in the OT (plus over 75 references to Canaanites). Mentioned in biblical and extra-biblical texts of second and first millennia B.C. Stretched from Desert of Zin and Kadesh Barnea in the S to Lebo Hamath in the N, and from the Mediterranean Sea to the Dead Sea, the Jordan River, and even E of Damascus (Num 34:1–12; Ezek 47:13–48:29. Especially prominent in patriarchal, Exodus, and conquest narratives – 14, 16, 27, 52, 59, 64, **71**, 72, 75–77, 79, **80**, 81–89, **81**, **90**, 91–98, **91**, 101, 102, 104–6, **105**, **107**, 108, **109**, 118, 190, 202, 203

Cana of Galilee – Village where Jesus performed his first and second miracles (John 2:1–11; 4:46–54). Home of Nathanael (21:2) – *Traditional site: Kefr Kana (182239), 4 mi. NE of Nazareth; more probable site: Kh. Qana (178247), 8 mi. N of Nazareth* – 33, **33**, 34, 166, 167, **168**, 170

Canatha – **167**, 171

Canneh – See Calneh.

Capercotnei – **168**, 176

Capernaum – Village mentioned 16 times in the NT in association with Jesus' ministry. His headquarters for much of his public ministry. Several of his disciples were from here, and many miracles were performed here. A fishing village with a toll booth and a synagogue, it was large enough to be the residence of a public official and a Roman centurion – *Tell Hum (204254), on N shore of Sea of Galilee, 2.5 mi. W of where Jordan enters the sea* – **31**, **34**, 35, 167–69, **168**, **170**, **176**

Capharabis – **178**, 179

Capharsalama – **154**, 155

Caphartobas – **177**, 178

Caphtor(ites) – Place from which the Caphtorites (Deut 2:23) and Philistines (Jer 47:4; Amos 9:7) came – *Probably Greek island of Crete* – **71**

Cappadocia – Roman province in E Asia Minor; served as a buffer on E frontier. Jews from Cappadocia were present in Jerusalem on Day of Pentecost (Acts 2:9). A church was established here (1 Peter 1:1) – *E Turkey* – **143**, **163**, 175, 181, 182, 185, 186

Carchemish – Major Hittite-Syrian town on the W bank of the Euphrates River, at important ford. Fought over by Assyrians, Egyptians, and Babylonians during the first millennium B.C. (Isa 10:9; Jer 46:2; 2 Chron 35:20) – *Jerablus, about 63 mi. NE of Aleppo* – 13, 62, 63, 65, 67, **80**, 84, 123, **130**, 137, 138

Carem – Village in hill country allotted to Judah. Mentioned in LXX text of Josh 15:59b (see NEB) – *Uncertain; possibly same as Beth Hakkerem.*

Caria – 147, 148, **149**, 150, **182**, 183

Carmel (Judah) – Village allotted to tribe of Judah (Josh 15:55). Mentioned in connection with Saul's defeat of the Amalekites (1 Sam 15:12). Prominent in story of David and Abigail, whose husband, Nabal, was from Carmel (1 Sam 25; 27:3; 30:5; 2 Sam 2:2; 3:3; 1 Chron 3:1). A Davidic warrior came from here (2 Sam 23:35; 1 Chron 11:37) – *Kh. el-Kirmil (162092), 7.5 mi. SE of Hebron on edge of Judean Desert* – **43**, **97**, 112, **114**, **134**

Carmel, Mount/Carmel Range – Prominent mountain that interrupts coastal plain in N

Israel. S border of Asher (Josh 19:26). Site of contest between Elijah and prophets of Baal (1 Kings 18). Later Elisha frequented the region (2 Kings 2:25; 4:25). Symbol of beauty and fruitfulness because of lush tree cover (SS 7:5; Isa 35:2; et al.); its withering became symbolic of destruction and desolation (Amos 1:2; 9:3; et al.) – 16, **17**, 27, **28**, 31, 32, 33, 36–39, 42, 44, 52, 75, **78**, 87, **88**, 99, **99**, 104, 112, 114, **129**, 131, **131**, 138, 141, **157**, 158, 163, **164**, 165, **168**

Carmel, Shephelah (foothill) of – **33**, 37, **43**

Carnaim – **154**

Carthage – **187**

Casiphia – Village in Babylonian territory from which Ezra summoned temple servants (Ezra 8:17) – *Unknown; probably in S Iraq.*

Caspein – **154**

Caspian Sea – 13, **80**, 130, 137, 142, 143, 148, 163, **175**

Cassius, Mount – **62**, 64

Caucasus (Mountains) – 67, 79, 80, **148**

Cauda – Small island in Mediterranean; ship Paul was traveling on passed it on lee side (Acts 27:16) – *Gaudhos/Gozzo, ca. 30 mi. S of W Crete* – **186**, 187

Cenchrea – One of two ports of Corinth; goods (and ships) were transported over the isthmus W to the port of Lechaeum. Here Paul had his hair cut in fulfillment of a vow before setting sail with Priscilla and Aquila for Syria on his second journey (Acts 18:18). Phoebe was later commended for her service to the church here (Rom 16:1) – *7 mi. SE of Corinth on Saronic Gulf* – **182**, 184

Central Mountain Range – 17

Central Valley – 189, 190, 194, 197–99

Chabulon – 166, **167**, **168**

Chagar Bazar – **62**, 63, 67

Chalcedon – 181

Chaldea – Region in S Mesopotamia (modern Iraq) at head of Persian Gulf. Chaldeans became powerful in seventh century B.C. and eventually established neo-Babylonian dynasty. Chaldea, Chaldean(s) mentioned 12 times in the NIV translation of the Bible. (In some places NIV translates the Hebrew for Chaldea/Chaldean[s] as Babylon/Babylonian[s]).

Chalsis – **177**

Charax – **148**, 154

Cilicia – Region/province in SE Asia Minor, part mountainous, part coastal plain. Tarsus was its leading city. Jews from here disputed with Stephen in Jerusalem (Acts 6:9). Paul's home was Tarsus (21:39; 22:3; 23:34), and he evangelized the area (15:23, 41; Gal 1:21). On his way to Rome, Paul's boat passed the coast of Cilicia (27:5) – *SE Turkey* – **130**, 140, **142**, 147, 148, **163**, 175, 175, 180, 181, 182, 183, **185**, 186

Cilician Gates – **147**, 148, 181, **181**, 182, 183

Cilician Plain – 64

Cirta – 187

Cisjordan – 20, 39, 51, 151

Cisjordan Range – 39

Cnidus – City on SW tip of Asia Minor; Paul's ship passed it on his way to Rome (Acts 27:7) – 156, 186, **186**

Cnossus – See Knossos – **187**

Coastal Plain – 16, **17**, 18, 19, 24, 38, 40–42, 46–48, 63, 64, 87, 96, 98–100, **103**, 104, 106, 110, 111, 113, 116, 122, 124, 128, 130, 151, 154–56, 158, 162, 174, 188

Coele-Syria – 152, 156, **157**

Colonia/Qaloniya – See Emmaus.

Colonia (Germania) – 187

Colosse – City in Roman province of Asia to which Paul wrote an epistle (Col 1:2). He probably had not visited it (2:1); by his day it had lost importance to Laodicea, 13 mi. to the NW – *In SW Turkey, in Lycus valley* – 187

Commagene – 162, 163

Corduba – 187

Coreae – 170, 172, 177

Corinth – Large Roman city strategically located just S of isthmus connecting mainland Greece with Peloponnese. Paul visited the city on his second (Acts 18:1–18) and third (probably 20:3) journeys; two of his letters to the church here are preserved. Commercial center, known for its wickedness – **147**, 150, 175, **182**, 183–85, **184**, **185**

Corinthian Gulf – 184

Corruption, Hill of – Hill where Solomon built altars for pagan deities Ashtoreth, Chemosh, and Molech; desecrated by Josiah (2 Kings 23:13) – *Probably S-most knoll on Mt. of Olives, 0.25 mi. E of Jerusalem.*

Corsica – 163

Cos – Small Greek island of SW coast of Turkey; Paul's ship passed it on third journey, going from Ephesus to Rhodes (Acts 21:1) – 156, **175**, 185, 186

Cozeba – Village settled by descendants of Judah (1 Chron 4:22). Possibly same as Aczib (Judah).

Craftsmen, Valley of the – Low-lying area in N Philistine Plain where descendants of Kenaz (1 Chron 4:14, see NIV note) and Benjamin (Neh 11:35) settled – *Roughly triangular area with Joppa, Lod, and Aphek at the points of the triangle and Ono near its center* – 47

Crags of the Wild Goats – 114

Crete – Greek Island in the Mediterranean Sea, 160 mi. long, located about 180 mi. S of Athens. Mentioned 7 times in the NT. People from Crete were in Jerusalem on the day of Pentecost (Acts 2:11). Paul's ship, on its voyage to Rome, passed S of Crete in a storm (27:7–16) – 13, 108, **109**, 143, 163, 175, 181, **182**, 185, 186, 186, 187

Crocodile River – See See Nahal Tanninim – 38

Crocodilon Polis – **38**, 39

Ctesiphon – **65**, 175

Cumae – 187

Cun – A town of Hadadezer, king of Zobah, from which David took large quantity of bronze (1 Chron 18:8) – *Uncertain; possibly Ras Baalbek (283406) in Lebanese Beqa, 55 mi. NE of Beirut* – **117**, 118

Cush – Country immediately S of Egypt but N of Ethiopia. Its heartland was between the second and third cataracts of the Nile; at times it expanded N to the first and S to the fourth cataract. On occasion, it seems to be associated with S Arabia (Gen 10:7) and possibly with Mesopotamia (2:13; 10:8?). Country and people mentioned ca. 50 times in OT – **58**, 59, 71, **71**, 72

Cushan – Only in Hab 3:7, in parallel with Midian. May be region in/near Midian. Cf. Moses' "Cushite wife" (Num 12:1).

Cuthah – City in S Mesopotamia. After fall of N Kingdom, Sargon II settled people from Cuthah in N Israel (2 Kings 17:24, 30) – *Possibly Tel Ibrahim, ca. 20 mi. NE of Babylon* – **130**, 133, 137

Cypros – 164, **164**

Cyprus – Third-largest island in Mediterranean, 45 mi. S of Turkey and 60 mi. W of Syria. Called Kittim (Gen 10:4; Num 24:24; et al.) in OT (in some cases translated "Cyprus" in NIV; Isa 23:1; et al.). Paul's traveling companion Barnabas was from Cyprus, which was also their first stop (Acts 4:36; 13:4). Barnabas and Mark revisited it (15:39). Paul passed it on several journeys (21:3; 27:4) – 13, 72, **109, 130, 137, 143,** 146, 147, 149, 150, **175,** 180, 181, **181, 182,** 183, **185,** 186, **186**

Cyrenaica – 163, 187

Cyrene – District capital of Roman province of Cyrenaica in N Africa. Simon, who bore Jesus' cross, was from Cyrene (Matt 27:32; Mark 15:21; Luke 23:26), Jews from here were in Jerusalem on Day of Pentecost (Acts 2:10), and Jews from Cyrene disputed with Stephen (6:9). Some of them were converted and preached the gospel (11:20; 13:1) – *Shakhat, in Libya, E of the Gulf of Sidra, about 100 mi. ENE of Benghazi, a few miles inland from the sea* – 13, **175,** 187

Dabbesheth – Village mentioned in description of S border of Zebulun, between Sarid and Jokneam (Josh 19:11) – *T. esh-Shammam/T.Shem (164230), 6 mi. NW of Megiddo* – 99, 99

Daberath – Town on border of Zebulun (Josh 19:12) but actually in Issachar (possibly same as Rabbith; Josh 19:20). Levitical city (Josh 21:28; 1 Chron 6:72) – *Daburiyeh (185233), 5 mi. E of Nazareth at the NW foot of Mt. Tabor* – 99, **99, 102**

Dacia – 163, 187

Dahshur – 81

Dalmanutha – Jesus went to the "region" of this village after feeding of 4,000 (Mark 8:10) – *Uncertain; may be identical to Magadan/Magdala (Matt 15:39; parallel text and variant). See Magadan* – 35, 168, **168**

Dalmatia – District in S part of Illyricum. Titus traveled there (2 Tim 4:10) – *W Yugoslavia on Adriatic Sea, around Dubrovnik region* – 163

Damascus – Major Syrian city. By extension name can refer to a geographical region or an Aramean kingdom. Used 43 times in OT and 15 in NT. Briefly controlled by David and Solomon, but Israel's foe throughout much of OT history. Antioch on the Orontes replaced it as capital of Syria in Hellenistic period. Paul had his famous vision on road to Damascus – *Esh-Sham/Dimasq (272324), oasis city at 2000 ft., E of the Anti-Lebanon mountains in Syria. Bordered on S, W, and N by mountains and fed by two rivers (biblical Barada and Pharpar)* – 13, 14, 16, **18, 20,** 21, 22, 23, 27, 28, **28, 29,** 30, 32, 36, 56, **58,** 62–64, **62,** 67, 77, **77, 80, 84,** 87, **88, 91,** 100, 101, 103, **105,** 107, 117, 118, **120,** 121, 123, **123, 125, 126,** 127, 128, **129, 130,** 131–34, **131, 132, 137, 142,** 145, 145, **147, 148, 148, 149,** 150, **150,** 156, 157, 159, 161, **164, 167,** 169, **170,** 171, 175, **175–77,** 180, **181,** 187, 193, 194, 200

Damascus Oasis – 30

Damghan – 143

Dan – Name of tribe of Dan was given to town of Laish/Leshem, which they conquered (Judges 18:7; Josh 19:47). Town name appears about 24 times in the OT (NIV). On N boundary of Israel. Used 7 times in familiar description of Israel's territory as stretching from "Dan to Beersheba" (2 times in reverse order). Usually first city to bear attack of invaders from the N. Here Jeroboam built sanctuary containing golden calf (1 Kings 12:29) – *T. el-Qadi/T. Dan (211294), 17 mi. NNE of Hazor at the NE edge of the Huleh Valley near the foot of Mt. Hermon* – 16, **17, 18,** 19, 20, **21,** 23, 25, **25,** 28, **28, 29,** 30–32, **31,** 50, **62,** 81, **82,** 84, 85, **95,** 96, **99,** 100, **100,** 101, **102,** 104, 109, **109, 117,** 118, 119, **119, 120,** 122, **122,** 124, **125, 126,** 127, **129, 131,** 141, **145,** 152, **157,** 158, 202–4

Dan Jaan – Place in N Israel mentioned in Joab's census itinerary (2 Sam 24:6). Could be village near town of Dan; possibly text should be read "to Dan and Ijon (Jaan)," two towns in the region also mentioned together in 2 Kings 15:29.

Dannah – Village in a hill-country district of Judah (Josh 15:49) – *Unknown.*

Danube – 143

Daphne – 168

Darb el-Gaza – 49, 60, 92

Darb el-Hagg – 49, 51, 60, **60,** 90

Darb es-Sultan – See King's Highway – 91

Dardanelles, Straits of – 147, 148, 183

Dathema – 154, 157

David, City of – Alternate name for Jerusalem. In Luke 2:11 used of Bethlehem, original home of David.

Dead Sea – See Salt Sea – 17, **18,20** 20, 22, 23, **28,** 42–45, **43,** 49, 51, 52, **53,** 54, 55, **56,** 75, 81, **81, 82,** 84, 90, 92, 102, 105, 109, 118, **119, 120, 125, 126, 131, 132, 138,** 140, **144,** 146, 150, 151, **151,** 152, **154, 157,** 158, **161,** 162–65, **164, 167, 170, 175,** 176, 178, 179, **188, 189, 189,** 203, 204

Debeltum – 187

Debir (Gad) – Gadite town in Gilead (Transjordan; Josh 13:26) – *If same as Lo Debar, then Umm ed-Dabar (207219) in Jordan Valley, 10 mi. S of Sea of Galilee* – **101**

Debir (Hill Country of Judah) – Canaanite city formerly known as "Kiriath Sepher" and "Kiriath Sannah" (Josh 15:15, 49). Conquered by Israelites (Josh 10; 11:21; 12:13) and later(?) by Othniel (15:15; Judges 1:11). Allotted to Judah (Josh 15:49). Levitical city (21:15; 1 Chron 6:58) – *Kh. Rabud (151093), 8.5 mi. SSW of Hebron* – 42, **43, 46, 82,** 94, 95, 96, **97,** 102, 107, 134, 201, 202

Debir (Judean boundary point) – Village (?) on N boundary of Judah near Valley of Achor (Josh 15:7) – *Unknown.*

Decapolis – Confederation of (usually) ten Greco-Roman (gentile) cities, primarily E of Sea of Galilee and Jordan Valley, including Pella, Dion, Philadelphia, Gadara, Gerasa, Hippos, Damascus, Scythopolis, Raphana, Kanatha, and others. People from region followed Jesus (Matt 4:25), who healed a demoniac here (Mark 5:20) and later visited region on his way to Galilee (7:31). Parts of region now in modern Syria, Jordan, and Israel – 35, 52, **53, 54,** 152, 160, **161,** 163, **164,** 166, **167, 168, 170, 171, 175–78**

Dedad – 72, 143

Dedan(ites) – Name of individual, a people, territory, and possibly settlement. Primarily in prophetic literature in connection with Arabian (Isa 21:13) places/peoples such as Tema, Buz (Jer 25:23), Edom (Ezek 49:8), Teman (25:13), and Sheba (38:13–14). Probably way station on incense route from S Arabia to Syria/Palestine – *El-Ula Oasis in W Arabia* – 71, 72, 140, 142

Deir Alla – 52, 53

Deir el-Balah – 90

Delphi – 13, 143, 175

Der – 143

Derbe – Lyconian city visited by Paul on his first (Acts 14:6, 20) and second (16:1) journeys. Paul's companion Gaius was from here (20:4) – *Kerti Huyuk in Turkey, 14 mi. NNE of Karaman, or Devri Sehri to SE of Kerti Huyuk* – 143, **175,** 181, **181,** 183, **187**

Destruction, City of – City in Egypt where the "language of Canaan" would be spoken and Yahweh would be worshiped (Isa 19:18) – *Unknown; some read "city of the sun" and identify it with Heliopolis or nearby T. el-Yehudiyah.*

Devri Sehri – 181

Dhahab – 60

Diblah – See Riblah.

Dibon (Judah) – Village in Negev settled by Jews after the Exile (Neh 11:25) – *Unknown; possibly same as Dimonah.*

Dibon (Moab) – One of the chief cities of Moab. Captured by Israel (Num 21:30), allotted to Reuben (32:3; Josh 13:17), built by Gad (Num 32:34; also called Dibon Gad [33:45–46]). Regained by Moab. Mentioned on Moabite Stone and in prophetic oracles (Isa 15 [probably same as "Dimon"]; Jer 48) – *Dhiban (224101), 13 mi. E of Dead Sea and 3.5 mi. N of Arnon Gorge* – 17, 18, 23, 53, 55, **56,** 75, 92, 94, 101, 126, 128, 132, 146, 171

Dibon Gad – See Dibon.

Dilean – Village in Judean Shephelah (Josh 15:38) – *Unknown.*

Dimnah – Zebulunite village named as a Levitical city – *Probably same as Rimmono (1 Chron 6:77) and Rimmon (Josh 19:13).*

Dimon – Variant of Dibon (Moab; Isa 15:9).

Dimonah – Negev town allotted to Judah (Josh 15:22) – *Unknown; possibly Dibon (Judah) is a variant of it.*

Dinhabah – Capital city of Bela, son of Beor, king of Edom (Gen 36:32; 1 Chron 1:43) – *Unknown.*

Dion/Dium – 160, **161,** 164, 167, 170, 171

Diyala River – 65, 137

Diyarbakir – 67

Dizahab – Place E of Jordan in Arabah, where Moses delivered (some?) of the messages in Deuteronomy (Deut 1:1) – *Unknown; the suggested Dhahab on the Red Sea (104769) does not seem to fit the biblical location.*

Docus – 156

Dophkah – Campsite in Sinai, somewhere between Egypt and Mt. Sinai (Num 33:12–13) – *Unknown.*

Dor – Port city whose king was defeated by Joshua (12:23). Allotted to Manasseh (17:11) but settled by Ephraim (1 Chron 7:29). Area around Dor was evidently called "Naphoth Dor" (Josh 11:2; 12:23; 17:11). Solomon placed special administrator here (1 Kings 4:11). Often under non-Israelite control. See also Naphoth Dor – *Kh. el-Burj/T. Dor (142224), 15 mi. S of Haifa, 8 mi. N of Caesarea* – 18, **18,** 33, 39, 75, **82,** 90, 95, 97, **98,** 103, 104, 109, 122, **122, 125, 126, 129, 132, 138,** 150, 151

Dor, Coast of – See Naphoth Dor – 16, **17,** 33, 39

Dora – OT Dor – 151, 157, 160, **161,** 167, 168, 170, 176

Dorylaeum – 82, 183

Dothan – Prominent town near which Joseph was sold by his brothers (Gen 37:17). Elisha was besieged here by the Syrians (2 Kings 6:13) – *T. Dothan (172202), 11 mi. NNW of Samaria and 5 mi. S of the Jezreel Valley* – 28, 33, 37, **38,** 39, 40, **82,** 84, 90, 98, 131

Dothan Valley – 33, 37, 39, 40

Drehem – 76, 78, 80

Dumah (Arabia, Edom?) – Son of Ishmael (Gen 25:14; 1 Chron 1:30) and founder of Arab tribe which may have had its center near Dumet ej-Jendel in Arabia, halfway between Persian Gulf and Gulf of Aqaba/Elath. Possibly same as Dumah mentioned by Isaiah (21:11), although it may have been in Edom – *Uncertain* – 13, 123, 130, 137, 143

Dumah (Judah) – Town allotted to Judah (Josh 15:52) – *Kh. ed-Deir Domeh (148093), 10 mi. SW of Hebron in the hill country* – 97

Dunqul Oasis – 58

Dura, plain of – Plain near Babylon where Nebuchadnezzar set up a colossal statue (Dan 3:1) – *Unknown; probably near Babylon.*

Dur Sharrukin – 65

Dyrrachium – 183

East, land of the – Sons of Abraham, save Isaac, were sent to this area (Gen 25:6) – *Uncertain; possibly SE of Israel in Midian/Arabia.*

Eastern Desert/Wilderness – 16, **17**, **18**, 23, 57, **58**, 83, 91, **91**, 96, 108

Eastern Sea – Dead Sea (Ezek 47:18; Joel 2:20; Zech 14:8) – 44, **145**

Ebal, Mount – Here Joshua built an altar and read the curses and blessings of the law (Josh 8:30, 33) as commanded (Deut 11:29; 27:4, 13). *Jebel Islamiyeh, 3,080-ft. peak just N of Shechem (176179)* – **18**, 38, 40, 77, **77**, 94, **94**, 107, 170, 172, 177, **178**

Ebenezer – Here the Israelites lost two battles to the Philistines (1 Sam 4:1; 5:1). Possibly same place where Samuel set up a stone to commemorate God's help in a later victory over the Philistines ("between Mizpah and Shen"; 1 Sam 7:12) – *Uncertain; possibly Isbat Sarta (146167), 13 mi. E of Joppa* – 38, 110, 111, **111**

Ebez – One of the towns allotted to Issachar (Josh 19:20) – *Uncertain; possibly unnamed site at grid 197227, 9 mi. N of Beth Shan.*

Ebla – 14, **62**, 64, **72**, 74, 75, 77, **77**, **78**, 80, 84, 203

Ecbatana – One of the capitals of Persian Empire. Here Darius found decree of Cyrus permitting temple in Jerusalem to be rebuilt (Ezra 6:2) – *Hamadan in Iran, 175 mi. SW of Tehran* – **13**, **130**, **137**, 140, 141, **142**, **143**, 148, 175

Ecdippa – 168

Ed-Dakhla Oasis – 58, 86

Eden – Locality in which there was the garden where the first humans were placed (Gen 2–4; cf. Ezek passim) – *Unknown; possibly in S Mesopotamia or Armenia* – 70, 71

Eden – Ezek 27:23 and 2 Kings 19:12. See Beth Eden.

Eder – Town allotted to Judah in the Negev district (Josh 15:21) – *Uncertain; possibly scribal error for Arad* – 97

Edom – Personal, tribal, and geographical name used (in various forms) 116 times in OT. Region S of Dead Sea, N of Red Sea, E of Rift Valley. On occasion expanded into Negev Desert W of Rift Valley. Usually hostile toward Judah – 22, 23, 43, **49**, 51, 55, 56, **56**, **60**, **84**, 88, 91, **92**, **97**, 106, 113, **117**, **120**, 121, **125**, 128–31, **130**, **132**, **137**, 138, 140, **141**, **142**

Edom, Mountains of – 53

Edom, Way of – 131

Edrei (Bashan) – Town in the Bashan. Residence of Og, king of Bashan, who was defeated by the Israelites (Num 21:33; Deut 1:4; 3:1, 10; Josh 12:4; 13:12). Allotted to Manasseh (Josh 13:31) – *Dera (253224), 60 mi. S of Damascus* – **29**, 30, **53**, 92, **93**, 101, **126**, **129**, 167, 170, 171

Edrei (Naphtali) – Town allotted to Naphtali (Josh 19:37) – *Unknown; probably in Upper Galilee.*

Efrat – 78, 79

Eglaim – Town, apparently on border of Moab (Isa 15:8) – *Uncertain; possibly Mazra (201078), on E shore of Dead Sea, on NE section of the Lisan.*

Eglath Shelishiyah – Town of Moab, mentioned in connection with Zoar (Isa 15:5) and Horonaim (Jer 48:34) – *Probably E, or SE, of S portion of the Dead Sea.*

Eglon – Village in Shephelah whose king joined king of Jerusalem against invading Israelites. Captured by Joshua (Josh 10:3, 5, 23, 34, 36, 37; 12:12). Allotted to Judah (15:39) – *Tell Aitun/T. Eton (143099), 11 mi. WSW of Hebron* – 94, 95, **94**, **97**, 106, **134**

Egnatian Way – 183, 185

Egypt – Major country in NE Africa – 12, **13**, 14, 16, 18, 20, 27, 28, 32, 51, 56, 57, **58**, 59–64, **60**, 67, 68, 71–76, **71**, 79, 80, **81**, 82–88, 86, 90, 91, 93, 105, 106, 108, **109**, 112, 118, 121–24, **123**, **130**, 133, 136, **137**, 138–43, **141–43**, 146–50, **148**, **149**, 151–53, 160–62, **163**, 166, 172, **175**, 185, **186**, **187**, 190, 196, 203

Egypt, River of – Alternate designation for Nile (Gen 15:18; Amos 8:8; 9:5).

Egypt, Wadi/Brook of – Prominent wadi that marked portion of S boundary of Canaan (Num 34:5; Ezek 48:28), of Judah (Josh 15:4, 47), and of Solomon's kingdom (1 Kings 8:65; 2 Chron 7:8). Mentioned elsewhere in the Bible as a prominent marker (2 Kings 24:7; Isa 27:12; Ezek 48:28) – *Wadi el-Arish, which drains N Sinai and flows into Mediterranean SW of Gaza; some identify it with more northerly Nahal Besor. To be distinguished from "River of Egypt" = the Nile* – 91, **91**, **145**

Ein (el-)Qudeirat – See Kadesh (Barnea) – 60, 89

Ein Faria – 24, 25, **25**

Ein Fashkha – See Ein Feshkha.

Ein Feshkha – 18, 22, 43, **43**

Ein Furtaga – 60

Ein Hawwara – 60, 89, **89**

Ein Khudra – 60

Ein Qudeirat – See Ein (el-)Qudeirat.

Ein Samiya – 78, 79, **82**

Ekallate – 130

Ekron – City in coastal plain on N border of Judah and S border of Dan (Josh 15:11, 46; 19:43). Important Philistine center (13:3); Judah had difficulty taking control of it (LXX of Judges 1:18). Mentioned 23 times in OT. Prominent in stories of capture of the ark (1 Sam 5–6) and of David and Goliath (17:52) – *Kh. el-Muqanna/T. Miqne (136131), 20 mi. SE of Joppa* – **18**, **43**, **46**, 47, 100, **100**, **103**, 108, **109**, 110, 111, **111**, 113, **113**, **114**, **125**, **126**, **128**, **131**, **132**, **134**, 135, **189**, 201

Elah, Valley of – Valley in which David killed Goliath (1 Sam 17:2, 19; 21:9) – *Wadi es-Sant, ca. 18 mi. WSW of Jerusalem* – **46**, 48, 113, **113**, 135, 174

Elam – Country NE of the Persian Gulf in modern Iran. In patriarchal narratives, its king, Kedorlaomer, invaded Canaan (Gen 14:1, 9). Later appears in the prophetic books and elsewhere. Became a satrapy in the Persian Empire; story of Esther is set in Susa, old capital of Elam. Elamites were present in Jerusalem on the Day of Pentecost (Acts 21:9) – 68, **71**, **72**, 73, **78**, 81, **130**, 136, **137**, **175**

Elam (Judea) – Town settled by Jews in postexilic period (Ezra 2:31; Neh 7:34) – *Uncertain; possibly Kh. Beit Alam/H. Bet Elem (145109), 10 mi. WNW of Hebron* – **144**

El-Amarna – 58, 61, 86, 105, 106, 108, 190, 203

El-Arish – See also Wadi el-Arish – **49**, 58, 60, **60**, 91, 136, **137**, 159

Elath – Place where Israel camped on trek to Canaan (Deut 2:8). From nearby Ezion Geber Solomon dispatched ships on Red Sea (1 Kings 9:26; 2 Chron 8:17). Uzziah recaptured and rebuilt it (2 Kings 14:22; 2 Chron 26:1–2); lost again in days of Ahaz (2 Kings 16:6) – *Possibly in/near Aqaba (150882), Jordanian city at N end of Gulf of Aqaba (= Gulf of Elath)* – **13**, 16, **17**, **18**, 19, 20, 22, 25, **25**, **28**, 49, **49**, 51, **52**, 56, **56**, **58**, 59, 60, **60**, **89**, 92, **92**, **125**, **130**, **137**

Elath, Gulf of – See Aqaba, Gulf of – 22, **49**, 50, 51, 55, 59, 61, 88

Elazar – 78, 79

El-Azariyeh – 172

Elazig – 66

El-Balamun – 86

El-Baqliya – 86

El Bethel – Alternate name for Bethel (Gen 35:6).

El-Bira – 94

Elealah – Village in Transjordan. Captured by Israelites (Num 32:3) and allotted to Reuben (v. 37). Recaptured by Moab and mentioned in prophetic oracles as among the cities of Moab (Isa 15:4; 16:9; Jer 48:34) – *el-Al (228136), 11 mi. SW of Amman.*

Eleasa – **154**, 155

Elephantine – 79, **81**, 86, **141**, 143, 146

Eleutherus – **149**, 150

Elim – Oasis with 12 springs and 70 palm trees where Israelites camped on their way to Mt. Sinai (Exod 15:27; 16:1; Num 33:9, 10) – *Possibly Ayun Musa, 9 mi. SE of Suez (if Jebel Sin Bisher is Mt. Sinai) or Wadi Gharandal, 55 mi. SE of Suez (if Jebel Musa)* – 89

Elishah – Place in/on Mediterranean from which blue and purple dyes were secured (Ezek 27:7) – *Probably (section of?) Cyprus, for other Ancient Near Eastern literature refers to Cyprus as Alashia* – **71**, **123**

El-Jib – 111

El-Kharga Oasis – 89

Elkosh – Home of Nahum the prophet (Nah 1:1) – *Unknown in spite of numerous suggestions.*

El-Lahun – 86

Ellasar – 81

El-Lisht – 81

El-Lubban – 172

Elon – Town allotted to Dan (Josh 19:43). In Solomon's second administrative district (1 Kings 4:9; = Elon Bethhanan) – *Unknown; in coastal plain, E of Joppa.*

Elon Bethhanan – Alternate name for Elon.

El Paran – Site near desert attacked by Kedorlaomer and allies (Gen 14:6) – *Possibly alternate name for Elath* – 81

El-Qantara – 59

El-Qubeibeh – 173

Eltekeh – Town allotted to Dan (Josh 19:44). Levitical city (21:23) – *Uncertain; possibly T. esh-Shallaf/T. Shalaf (128144), 11 mi. SSE of Joppa* – **100**, 102, **134**

Eltekeh, Plain of – 135

Eltekon – Town allotted to Judah, in hill country probably just N of Hebron (Josh 15:59).

Eltolad – Town allotted to Simeon (Josh 19:4; 1 Chron 4:29 = "Tolad") within allotment of Judah (Josh 15:30) – *Unknown; in Negev.*

El-Ula oasis – 72

Elusa – 28

El-Waarah – 29, 30

Emek Keziz – Town allotted to Benjamin, in E part of allotment (Josh 18:21) – *Unknown.*

Emesa – 148

Emmatha – 168

Emmaus – Town to which Cleopas and companion were going when Jesus appeared to them (Luke 24:13) – *Disputed. Best candidate is Emmaus/Nicopolis (Imwas; 149138, 19 mi. W of Jerusalem, thus matching the 160 stadia [= 20 mi.] of an important NT manuscript). Alternately, Emmaus/Colonia/Qaloniya is possible (Qalunya; 165133, 3.5 mi. W of Jerusalem, thus fitting the majority of NT manuscripts [60 stadia = 7 mi.] if NT indicates round-trip distance)* – 154, **154**, 155, 160, **161**, 162, **164**, 147, 170, 172, 173, **176**, 177, **178**, 179

Enaim – Town near which Tamar enticed Judah (Gen 38:14, 21) – *Probably variant of Enam.*

Enam – Town in N Shephelah district of Judah (Josh 15:34). Probably same as Enaim – *Uncertain; possibly Kh. Beith Ikka (151121), 5 mi. SE of Beth Shemesh.*

En Besor – 75

En Boqeq – 43, 44

Endor/En Dor – Town "within Issachar" assigned to Manasseh (Josh 17:11). Barak defeated Canaanites nearby (Ps 83:10). Saul consulted a medium here (1 Sam 28:7) – *Kh. Safsafeh/H. Zafzafot (187227), 2.5 mi. due S of Mt. Tabor* – 33, 34, 97, 99, 107, 114

En Eglaim – Town on shore of Dead Sea where according to Ezekiel fishermen will spread their nets when the waters of the sea become fresh (47:10) – *Unknown; probably S or SE of the Dead Sea as indicated by Bar Kokhba documents and Eusebius.*

En Gannim (Issachar) – Town allotted to Issachar. Levitical city (Josh 19:21; 21:29; 1 Chron 6:72 [= Anem]) – *Not Kh. Beith Jann (196235), which is too far SW for Issachar; rather Kh. ed-Dir (200229), 5 mi. SW of the Sea of Galilee* – 99, 102

En Gannim (Judah) – Town allotted to Judah, in N Shephelah (Josh 15:34) – *Unknown.*

En Gedi – Town allotted to Judah (Josh 15:62), on W shore of Dead Sea (Ezek 47:10) near edge of Judean Desert. David, fleeing from Saul, was drawn to its powerful spring (1 Sam 23:29; 24:1). Famous for its vineyards (SS 1:14). See Hazazon Tamar – *T. Jurn/T. Goren (187097), 25 mi. SE from Jerusalem* – 22, 28, 43–45, **43**, 49, 53, 75, 97, 114, 114, 128, **128**, **132**, **134**, **144**, 150, 151, 157, 170, 176, 178

En Haddah – Town allotted to Issachar (Josh 19:21) – *el-Hadatheh (195231), 6 mi. WSW of the Sea of Galilee* – 99

En Hakkore – Spring from which Samson drank (Judges 15:19) – *Unknown; probably in territory of Judah.*

En Hanaziv – 78

En Harod – 107

En Hazor – Town allotted to Naphtali, probably in Upper Galilee (Josh 19:37) – *Unknown.*

En Mishpat – Place (identified in text as "Kadesh") mentioned in connection with the campaign of four N kings against Sodom, etc. (Gen 14:7) – *Probably same as Kadesh Barnea* – 78, 81, 201

Enoch – City built by Cain in honor of son – *Unknown.*

En Rimmon – Place in Judea settled after exile (Neh 11:29) – *Unknown; possibly same as Rimmon in the N Negev* – **144**, 146

En Rogel – Spring just S of Jerusalem on boundary of Benjamin and Judah (Josh 15:7; 18:16). Here David's spies hid (2 Sam 17:17) and Adonijah's premature coronation took place (1 Kings 1:9) – *Bir Ayyub (172130), less than a mile S of Jerusalem in Kidron Valley* – 97, 98, 120, **191**

En Rujum – 89

En Shemesh – Spring on boundary between Benjamin and Judah, between Jericho and Jerusalem (Josh 15:7; 18:17) – *Ein Hod/"Spring of the Apostles" (175131), 2 mi. E of Jerusalem.*

En Tappuah – Spring near town of Tappuah, on boundary between Ephraim and Manasseh (Josh 17:7) – *See Tappuah (Ephraim).*

Ephes Dammim – Place were Philistines camped in preparation for battle with Saul's forces (1 Sam 17:1). Goliath was killed nearby (1 Chron 11:13). See Pas Dammim – *Not certain; probably on S side of Valley of Elah, ca. 1 mi. SE of Azekah (144123)* – 113

Ephesus – Most important city of Asia Minor, near shore of Aegean Sea. Port city at terminus of caravan route from E. Paul lived here for almost three years on his second journey and visited it on his third. Mentioned 18 times in NT; among the seven churches in Revelation (1:11; 2:1) – **175**, **181**, **182**, 184–86, **185**

Ephraim – Son of Joseph and name of tribe that descended from him. Name for tribal allotment, N of Benjamin, S of Manasseh, in rugged hill country. Territory included worship centers at Shiloh and Bethel – **17**, **18**, 19, 28, 38–40, **38**, 42, 47, 54, 96–98, **98**, **102**, 110–12, 116, 119, 122, 136, **145**, 172, 202

Ephraim (NT) – Town near desert where Jesus retreated after raising of Lazarus (John 11:45) – *Probably same as OT Ephron and Ophrah* – **170**, 172

Ephraim, forest of – Undefined region E of Jordan River, near Mahanaim and Jabbok River in central Gilead, where Absalom was killed (2 Sam 18:6) – 119, **119**

Ephraim, Hill Country/hills of – Rugged territory W of Jordan River where Ephraim settled. Thickly forested at time of conquest (Josh 17:15–18). Mentioned 32 times in OT – **38**, 40, 42, 77, **77**, 79, 80, 87, **88**, 98, 100, **103**, 104, **105**, 106–8, 110–12, **111**, 122, **170**, 189

Ephrath – Place near which Benjamin was born and Rachel died (Gen 35:16, 19; 48:7) – *Uncertain; seemingly in the territory of Benjamin, but some texts associate it with Bethlehem, S of Jerusalem (see Ephrathah).*

Ephrathah – Alternate name for Bethlehem (Mic 5:2; Josh 15:59a; LXX), also mentioned in the story of Ruth (4:11), although some have proposed that it is a district (Ps. 132:6) in which Bethlehem and other villages were located. There may also have been a Caleb Ephrathah (1 Chron 2:24) – *Either Bethlehem or its immediate vicinity, or a nearby place.*

Ephron – One of the villages N of Jerusalem which Abijah took from Jeroboam (2 Chron 13:19) – *Uncertain; possibly et-Taiyiba (178151), 13 mi. NNE of Jerusalem. Possibly the same as Ophrah (Josh 18:23) and Ephraim (NT)* – 124, 154

Ephron, Mount – Hill, or ridge, mentioned in the description of Judah's N boundary (Josh 15:9) – *Uncertain; W of Jerusalem and E of Beth Shemesh, probably in vicinity of Kiriath Jearim.*

Epirus – 185, 186

Erech – One of several cities founded by Nimrod (Gen 10:10). People from Erech were settled in the cities of Samaria by Ashurbanipal (Ezra 4:9) – *Warka, in Iraq, 160 mi. S of Baghdad, E of Euphrates River* – 65, 71

Eridu – 65

Er-Rahia – See Jericho – 204

Er-Riha – 93

Er-Riqqa – 86

Erzurum – 65

Esbus – OT Heshbon – 157, 161, 164, **164**, 170

Esdraelon, Valley of – OT Jezreel, Valley of – 36, 160, **161**, 166, 167, 168, **170**, 172

Esek – Well dug by Isaac (Gen 26:20) – *Unknown; between Beersheba and Gerar.*

Eshan – Judean town in hill country (Josh 15:52) – *Unknown.*

Eshcol, Valley of – Valley in Hebron area where spies cut a large cluster of grapes (Num 13:23, 24; 32:9; Deut 1:24) – *Uncertain* – 91

Eshnunna – 80, 143

Eshtaol – Village in N Shephelah, first allotted to Judah but then to Dan (Josh 15:33; 19:41). Some Danites moved N from the area (Judges 18:2, 8, 11). Samson's family was from the area (Judges 13:25; 16:31) – *Ishwa/Eshtaol*

(1511132), 14 mi. W of Jerusalem – **97**, **100**, **100**, **107**, **109**, **113**, **134**

Eshtemoa/Eshtemoh – Levitical city in Hill Country of Judah (Josh 15:50; 21:14; 1 Chron 6:57). David sent booty to its inhabitants (1 Sam 30:28) – *Es-Semu (156089), 9 mi. SSW of Hebron* – **97**, **102**, **134**

Es-Safa – 30

Etam (Judah) – Town allotted to Judah, in hill country near Bethlehem (Josh 15:59b; LXX). Fortified by Rehoboam of Judah (2 Chron 11:6) – *Kh. el-Khokh (166121), 2 mi. SW of Bethlehem* – **97**, **125**, **134**

Etam (Simeon) – Simeonite town in NW Negev or Shephelah (1 Chron 4:32) – *Unknown.*

Etam, rock of – Place where Samson stayed after battling Philistines (Judges 15:8, 11) – *Unknown; possibly near Etam of Judah* – 109

Etham – Place of Israel's encampment after leaving Succoth in Egypt (Exod 13:20; Num 3:6, 7, 8) – *Derived from Egyptian for "fort" and refers to one or more of the forts that guarded E frontier of Egypt in area of modern Suez Canal* – 89, **134**

Ether – Judean town in Shephelah (Josh 15:42). Later assigned to Simeon (Josh 19:7) – *Kh. el-Atr/T. Eter (138112), 4 mi. NE of Lachish* – **97**, 98

Ethiopia – See Cush – **58**, 59, 71, 72

Ethiopian Highlands – 57, 58

Eth Kazin – Town on NE boundary of Zebulun, between Gath Hepher and Rimmon (Josh 19:13) – *Uncertain; possibly Kefr Kenna (182239), 4 mi. NE of Nazareth.*

Et-Taiyiba – See Ophrah (Benjamin) – 172

Et-Tell – See Ai – 75, **75**, **78**, 77, 93, 169

Et-Tih Desert – 60

Et-Tur – 60

Eumenia – 187

Euphrates River – Major river (1,780 mi. long) that flows from Turkey through Syria and Iraq to the Persian Gulf. Mentioned 18 times in OT in connection with Garden of Eden and traditional boundaries of the Promised Land (Gen 15:8; Deut 1:7; 11:24; Josh 1:4); also in prophetic literature and in Rev 9:14 and 16:12. Also called "the great river" (e.g., Deut 1:7) and "the River" (e.g., Gen 31:21) – 12, **13**, 23, 27, 62–67, **62**, **65**, 70, 71, **72**, 73, 76, **77**, **78**, **80**, 84, 87, 118, 121, **123**, **130**, **137**, 138, 142, **142**, **143**, 144, **147**, **148**, 149, 153, 155, 202

Exaloth – 168

Ezel, stone – Place where David was to meet Jonathan (1 Sam 20:19) – *Unknown.*

Ezem – Town allotted to Judah in Negev district (Josh 15:29); later assigned to Simeon (Josh 19:3; 1 Chron 4:29) – *Unknown.*

Ezion Geber – Site at N end of Gulf of Elath/Aqaba where Israelites camped (Num 33:35–36); evidently in the Arabah (Deut 2:8). Here Solomon built ships to sail to Ophir (1 Kings 9:26; 2 Chron 8:17); Jehoshaphat's and Ahaziah's later maritime ventures were not as successful (1 Kings 22:48; 2 Chron 20:36) – *T. el-Kheleifeh (147884), at N end of Gulf of Elath/Aqaba although the archaeological profile does not completely agree with recorded biblical history and the island anchorage of Jezirat Faraun (135874), 9 mi. SW of Elath, has also been suggested* – 51, **56**, 91, **92**, **92**, **120**, **123**, **125**, 128

Fair Havens – Port on S-central coast of Crete where Paul was shipwrecked on journey to Rome (Acts 27:8) – *Bay near Lasea on S coast of Crete, E of Cape Littinos, 5 mi. E of Cape Matala* – 186, **186**

Fairan Oasis – 59

Faiyum Oasis – 58

Farafra Oasis – 58

Farasha – 81

Faria – See also Wadi Faria – **17, 18**, 20, 40, 52, 54, 77, 124, 127, **144**, 171, 177

Feifa – 45, 75, **56, 75, 78**, 81

Feiran Oasis – See Rephidim – 60, **60,**

Fertile Crescent – Modern term for the roughly crescent-shaped area that includes the fertile portions of Iraq, Syria, Lebanon, Israel, and Egypt; setting for most of the events of Ancient Near Eastern history – 12, **13**, 65, 135, 140

Foothills (western) – See Shephelah – 47

Forum of Appius – Stopping point on Appian Way, about 40 mi. S of Rome, where Paul was met by Christians from Rome (Acts 28:15) – **186**, 187

Fureidis – 78

Gaash – Mountainous region in/near Hill Country of Ephraim, N in which Joshua was buried at Timnath Serah (Josh 24:30; Judges 2:9). One of David's mighty men was from the ravines of Gaash (2 Sam 23:30; 1 Chron 11:32) – *Unknown; possibly rugged area ca. 15 mi. NW of Jerusalem.*

Gaba – 164, **164**, 178

Gabae – 143, 148

Gabara – 166, 167, 168

Gad – Son of Zilpah and Jacob and tribal name. Allotment NE of the Dead Sea along E side of Jordan Valley to Sea of Galilee – 53, 54, 101, **101, 102**, 118, **119**, 122, 127, 131

Gadara – City of the Decapolis. See also Gadarenes, region of the – *(Umm Qeis; 214229) located 6 mi. SE of the Sea of Galilee* – 29, 30, **54**, 152, 160, **161**, 162, 164, 167, 168, 170, 171, **175–78**

Gadarenes, region of the – Region E or SE of Sea of Galilee where Jesus healed the demoniacs (Matt 8:28). Parallel texts read "Gerasenes" (Mark 5:1; Luke 8:26, 37). Possibly the miracle took place in the region of Gerasa, but more probably near site of Kursi. See Gerasenes, region of the.

Gadora – 157, 167, 170, 171, **175–78**

Galaaditis – 151, 152, 157

Galatia – Region in central plateau of modern Turkey, which Paul visited on all three journeys (Acts 16:6; 18:23; third journey by implication). In Paul's day a Roman province that included portions of ancient kingdom of Galatia and others. Paul wrote epistle to the church here and referred to it (2 Tim 4:10), as did Peter (1 Peter 1:1). See also 1 Cor 16:1 – **163**, 181, **182**, 184, **185, 186**

Galeed – See Jegar Sahaduth.

Galilee – Region in northern Israel mentioned 6 times in OT and 64 in NT (60 in Gospels, 4 in Acts; 5 are to Sea of Galilee) – **17, 18**, 19, 30–36, **31, 33**, 51, 52, 54, 87, 99, 100, **114**, 115, 116, **117**, 122, 127, 133, **150**, 151, **151**, 152, 154–56, **157**, 158, 160–63, **161, 164**, 165–69, **168, 170**, 171, 172, 174, **175–77**, 176, 177, 200

Galilee, Lower – **17**, 30, **31**, 32–36, **34**, 88, **88**, 99, 100, **103**, 104, 163, 166, **167, 168**, 177, **178**

Galilee, Sea of – Harp-shaped lake in N Israel, 13.5 by 7.5 mi., 695 ft. below sea level. Mentioned 5 times in the Gospels. Also called "Sea of Tiberias," "the sea," "Sea of Kinnereth," and "Lake of Gennesaret." Much of Jesus' public ministry took place along its N shore – **18**, 20, 27, **28, 29**, 30–32, **31, 33**, 34–36, **34**, 51, 52, **53, 54, 54**, 81, 82, 87, 100, **117**, 118, 127, 155, 156, **157**, 160, **164**, 165–69, **168, 170**, 171, 177

Galilee, Upper – **17, 18**, 31–34, **31, 33**, 87, **88**, 99, 100, **103**, 104, 156, 163, 166, **167, 168**, 177, 178

Galilee of the Gentiles – 32

Gallaecia – 163

Gallia – 163, 187

Gallim (Benjamin) – Village in Benjamin, along the traditional military approach to Jerusalem from the N (Isa 10:30). Home of Palti, to whom Saul gave his daughter Michal (1 Sam 25:44) – *Uncertain; possibly in area of Gibeah and Anathoth (Isa 10:30), ca. 4 or 5 mi. N of Jerusalem.*

Gallim (Judah) – Town allotted to Judah (Josh 15:59b; LXX only, see NEB), in Bethlehem district S of Jerusalem – *Unknown.*

Gamala – 31, 157, 175, 177, **177**, 178

Gammad – Men of Gammad aided in defense of Tyre (Ezek 27:11) – *Unknown; probably in vicinity of Tyre; possibly same as Kumidi of el-Amarna letters.*

Gandhara – 143

Gangitis River – 183

Gareb, hill of – Hill in immediate vicinity of Jerusalem, possibly N or W of the city (Jer 31:39) – *Unknown.*

Gath – 28, 38, 47, 48, **82, 90, 95, 99, 103, 105, 105**, 108, **109**, 110, 111, **111**, 113–16, **113, 114, 117, 125, 126, 128**, 129–31, **132, 134**, 135

Gath (Padalla) – Possibly the Gath mentioned in 1 Chron 7:21 – *Jett (154200), in the Sharon Plain 12 mi. NW of Samaria, mentioned in extrabiblical sources as Gath Padalla* – 33, 38, **38, 82, 105**

Gath (Philistine) – One of the five cities of the Philistines (Josh 13:3; 1 Sam 6:17); possibly the chief city, for it had a "king" (1 Sam 21:10, 12) while the others had "lords." Home of Goliath (17:4). Mentioned approximately 34 times in OT – *T. es-Safi/T. Zafit (135123), 25 mi. SSE of Joppa* – 28, 43, 46, 47, 48, **82, 90, 94, 103, 105, 105**, 108, **109**, 110, 111, **111**, 113–16, **113, 114, 117, 125, 126, 128**, 129–31, **132, 134**, 135, 208

Gath Hepher – Village on E border of Zebulun in Lower Galilee (Josh 19:13). Home of Jonah the prophet (2 Kings 14:25) – *Kh. ez-Zurra/T. Gat Hefer (180238), 3 mi. NE of Nazareth* – 99, **99**, 131

Gath Rimmon (Dan) – Town allotted to Dan (Josh 19:45; 21:24); evidently later occupied by Ephraim (1 Chron 6:69) – *Uncertain, but usually identified with T. Jerisheh/T. Gerisa (132166), located in modern Tel Aviv, 4.5 mi. NE of Joppa, although the archaeological profile is problematic* – 100, 102

Gath Rimmon (Manasseh?) – Town in Manasseh allotted to Levitical clan of Kohathites (Josh 21:25); the parallel passage in 1 Chron 6:70 has "Bileam" (= Ibleam), which seems preferable. One Greek version of Josh 21:25 also has "Bileam."

Gaugamela – 148, 149

Gaul – 174

Gaulanitis – 24, 29, 30, **150, 151**, 152, 160, **161**, 163, **164**, 165, 166, 167, 168, 169, 170, 174, **175–77**, 176

Gaza – Town in SW Israel on border between the sown land of Canaan and Desert of N Sinai. Allotted to Judah (Josh 15:47), the Philistines settled there (13:3; Judges 1:18, LXX "Judah did not take," NIV fn.; 1 Sam 6:17; et al.). Usually, if not always, under non-Israelite control: Egyptians used it as base for expeditions N. Assyrians, Babylonians, et al. used it as base for invasions of Egypt. Mentioned 22 times in OT and once in NT (Acts 8:26) – *Ghazzeh/Azza (099101), 3.5 mi. inland from Mediterranean in SW Israel* – 13, 14, 16, **17**, 18, **18**, 22, 23, 25, 27, **28**, 46, 46, **47, 49**, 50, 51, 56, **58**, 59, **60**, 75, **80, 81**, 87, **88, 90**, 91, 92, **97**, 102, 103, 105, 107, 108–10, **109**, 114, 117, 119, 120, **123, 125, 126, 128**, 130, **130, 132,**

133, **134**, 135, **137, 138**, 141, 142, **144, 147**, 148, **149, 150**, 151, **151, 157**, 158, 159, **161**, 162, 163, **164, 167**, 170, 174, **175–78**, 189

Gazara – OT Gezer – 154, 156, 157

Geba (Benjamin) – A town allotted to the tribe of Benjamin (Josh 18:24) which served as a Levitical city (21:17; 1 Chron 6:60; 8:6). Located in an area disputed by Judah and Israel (1 Kings 15:22), it was near the N border of Judah after fall of N Kingdom (2 Kings 23:8; some suggest a more N Geba in this instance, but this proposal is not certain). Mentioned 15 times in the OT, it was located along the N approach to Jerusalem (Isa 10:29). After the Exile, Jews settled there (Ezra 2:26; Neh 7:30; 11:31; 12:29) – *Jeba (175140), 6 mi. NNE of Jerusalem* – 41, **43**, 98, 102, 105, 111, **111**, 112, **112, 126**, 127, **134**, 136, **144**, 188

Geba (Samaria) – 170, 172

Geba Carmel – 78

Gebal (Phoenicia) – City N of Israel on Phoenician coast not conquered by Israel, though part of Canaan (Josh 13:5). Solomon secured timber for temple from there (1 Kings 5:18), and men of Gebal served as "shipwrights" (Ezek 27:9). Also called Byblos – *Jebeil (210391), on Mediterannean coast, 18 mi. NNE of Beirut* – 64, **105, 117, 137**

Gebal (Transjordan) – Unidentified region, probably SE of Dead Sea (Ps 83:7).

Gebim – Site along traditional approach to Jerusalem from the N (Isa 10:31) – *Unknown; probably only a few mi. N of Jerusalem.*

Geder – Canaanite city conquered by Joshua (Josh 12:13) – *Unknown; possibly in N central Negev.*

Gederah – Town allotted to Judah in Shephelah (Josh 15:36; 1 Chron 4:23) – *Unknown.*

Gederoth – Town allotted to Judah in Shephelah (Josh 15:41). Conquered by Philistines in days of Ahaz (2 Chron 28:18) – *Unknown; in Shephelah, possibly in Valley of Elah area* – **128, 131**, 135

Gederothaim – According to NIV, alternate name for Gederah, rather than fifteenth town in a list said to contain fourteen (Josh 15:36). LXX reads "Gederah and her sheep pens," which may be preferable.

Gedor (Benjamin) – Two Benjamites from Gedor joined David at Ziklag (1 Chron 12:7) – *Unknown.*

Gedor (Judah) – Town allotted to Judah in hill country near Hebron (Josh 15:58). The Gedors mentioned in 1 Chron 4:4 and 4:8 are probably towns, but it is not certain if one or both of them are identical to this Gedor. (Some follow LXX and read "Gerar" for "Gedor" in 1 Chron 4:39) – *Kh. Jedur (158115), 7.5 mi. NNW of Hebron* – **90, 97**

Gedor (Simeon) – Possibly alternate form for Gerar (1 Chron 4:39, see LXX) – 98

Gedor (Transjordan) – 54, 144

Ge Harashim – Place on coastal plain where craftsmen settled (1 Chron 4:14). Probably same as "Valley of the Craftsmen" where Benjamites settled after the exile (Neh 11:35) – *On coastal plain, E of Tel Aviv/Joppa. Probably within Lod-Aphek-Joppa triangle.*

Geliloth (Benjamin/Judah) – Point on SE boundary of Benjamin near Pass of Adummim (Josh 18:17). Possibly same as Gilgal in Josh 15:7 – *Unknown.*

Geliloth (near Jordan River) – Unidentified site by Jordan River near which an altar was built (Josh 22:10–11; but RSV translates Geliloth as "the region about the Jordan").

Gennesaret – OT Kinnereth. Village on NW shore of Sea of Galilee at or near which Jesus and his disciples landed (Matt 14:34; Mark 6:53). The nearby plain (1 by 3 mi.) is named after it – *Kh. Ureime/T. Kinrot (200252), 6 mi. N of Tiberias* – **35**, 156, **157**

Gennesaret, Lake of – Alternate name for Sea of Galilee (Luke 5:1). See Gennesaret – 35

Gennesaret, Plain of – 34, 35

Gerar – Town near Gaza on SW border of Canaanite territory (Gen 10:19). Here Abraham, and later Isaac, encountered two "Philistine" kings, both named Abimelech (Gen 20:1–2; 26:1, 6). Herdsmen of Gerar quarreled with those of Isaac over water rights (26:20, 26). Asa of Judah pursued the Ethiopian Zerah in this area (2 Chron 14:13, 14) – *T. Abu Hureireh/T. Haror (112087), 17 mi. NW of Beer Sheba* – **28**, 46, **46**, 47, **49, 77, 79, 84, 91**, 98, **128, 157**, 205

Gerar, Valley of – Valley along which Gerar was located – *Probably Wadi esh-Sheriah/N. Gerar.*

Gerasa – 152, **157**, 160, **161**, 164, 167, 168, 170, 171, **176**, 177, **178**

Gerasenes, region of the – Place where Jesus healed the demoniac and where swine drowned in the sea (Mark 5:1; Luke 8:26, 37). – *Possibly near the site of Kursi (Chorsia/Gergesa; 211248) on E shore of Sea of Galilee where tradition placed it by the third century A.D.*

Gergesa – **34**, 35, **168**, 170, 171

Gerizim, Mount – Mountain just S of Mt. Ebal and city of Shechem from which the blessings were read at the covenant renewal ceremony (Deut 11:29; 27:12; Josh 8:33) and to which Jotham fled from Abimelech (Judges 9:7). Place of Samaritan worship, referred to as "this mountain" by the woman whom Jesus met at the well (John 4:20) – *Jebel et-Tur/Mt. Gerizim (176170), 30 mi. N of Jerusalem* – **18**, **38**, 40, 77, **77**, 94, **94**, 107, 151, 158, **161**, 164, 167, 170, 172, 177, **178**

Germania Inferior – 187

Gerrha – 149

Geruth Kimham – Place near Bethlehem where Johanan stopped before descending into Egypt (Jer 41:17) – *Unknown.*

Geshur – Small Aramean kingdom E and NE of Sea of Galilee that remained independent of Israel (Deut 3:14; Josh 12:5; 13:11, 13). David married daughter of Talmai king of Geshur and she bore Absalom (2 Sam 3:3), who fled to Geshur after executing Amnon (13:37, 38; 14:23, 32; 15:8). Later Geshur and Aram captured Israelite territory of Havvoth Jair (1 Chron 2:23) – 29, **29**, 30, **117**, 118, **119, 122, 125**

Geshur(ites) (south) – A people who lived S and SW of Philistia (Josh 13:2). David raided their territory when working for Achish king of Gath (1 Sam 27:8) – *Territory in NE Sinai* – 115, 116

Gethsemane – Garden (John 18:1) where Jesus went to pray with his disciples and where he was captured (Matt 26:36; Mark 14:32) – *E of Temple Mount in Jerusalem, on lower W slope of Mt. of Olives (Luke 22:39)* – 195

Gezer – City in N Shephelah whose king was defeated by Joshua (10:33; 12:12). Allotted to Ephraim (Josh 16:3), who failed to drive out Canaanites living there (Josh 16:10; Judges 1:29). Levitical city (Josh 21:21; 1 Chron 6:67). David drove Philistines from Gezer area to it (2 Sam 5:25; 1 Chron 14:16). Captured by Egyptian pharaoh and given as dowry to his daughter who married Solomon (1 Kings 9) – *T. Jezer (Abu Shusheh)/T. Gezer (142142), 17 mi. SE of Joppa* – **28**, 41, **43, 46**, 47, **75, 80, 82, 84, 90, 94, 98**, 100, **100, 102, 103**, 104–6, **105**, 107, 109, 110, **111, 112, 114**, 116, **117, 119**, 120, 121, 122, **123, 125, 126, 128**, 144, 188, **189**, 205

Ghab Valley – 64

Gharandal (Edom) – 55, 56, **56**

Gharandal (Sinai) – 89, **89**

Ghita – 81

Ghor – 20, 54

Giah – Site in Benjamin passed by Abner as he fled E from Gibeon pursued by Joab and Abishai (2 Sam 2:24) – *Unknown; in Benjamin, probably E of watershed near edge of wilderness.*

Gibbar – Ancestor of family that returned from exile (Ezra 2:20); parallel passage (Neh 7:25) has "Gibeon."

Gibbethon – Philistine village in N Philistia assigned to Dan (Josh 19:44). Levitical city (Josh 21:23). Here Baashah murdered Nadab (1 Kings 15:27) and Omri was proclaimed king of Israel (1 Kings 16:15) – *T. Melat/T. Malot (137140), 15 mi. SE of Joppa, 3 mi. W of Gezer* – **100**, 102, **126, 132**

Gibeah (Ephraim) – Place in Hill Country of Ephraim where Eleazar, son of Aaron, was buried (Josh 24:33). Abijah's mother was from here (2 Chron 13:2) – *Unknown.*

Gibeah (in/of Benjamin) – Town allotted to Benjamin (Josh 18:28). Its citizens abused Levite's concubine and city was destroyed as punishment (Judges 19–20); referred to in Hos 9:9; 10:9–10) – *T. el-Ful (172136), 3 mi. N of Jerusalem (site was later called "Gibeah [of Saul]")* – Two or three hundred years later Jonathan launched an attack on the Philistines from Gibeah in Benjamin (1 Sam 13:2, 15; 14:16) which was then located 3 mi. to the NE of the old site – *Jeba (175140).* Also mentioned in 2 Sam 23:29; 1 Chron 11:31; Isa 10:29; Hos 5:8 – **18**, 18, 28, 41, 104, **105**, 107, 111, **111**, 112, **112**

Gibeah (Judah) – Town allotted to Judah, in hill country SE of Hebron (Josh 15:57) – *Unknown.*

Gibeah (of Saul) – Several centuries after destruction of Gibeah (in/of Benjamin), Saul rebuilt it as his capital. Called Gibeah (of Saul) in narratives of 1 Sam (10:26; 11:4; 14:2; 15:34; 22:6; 23:19; 26:1; and 2 Sam 21:6). See also Gibeah in/of Benjamin – *T. el-Ful (172136)* – **112, 112**, 114, 126, 134, 146

Gibeah of God – Hill near Gibeon with Philistine outpost (1 Sam 10:5) where Saul met band of prophets (10:10). Once called Geba (1 Sam 13:3). See also Gibeon, high place at – *Nabi Samwil (167137), 5 mi. NW of Jerusalem* – 111, **111**, 112

Gibeath – 134

Gibeath Haaraloth – Site near Gilgal and Jericho where Israelites were circumcised after crossing Jordan (Josh 5:3) – *Unknown; vicinity of Jericho.*

Gibeon – Major hill country town that headed the Gibeonite (Hivite) league that tricked Joshua into making a treaty with them (Josh 9–11). Joshua saved the inhabitants from attacking Amorite coalition. Allotted to Benjamin (18:25). Levitical city (21:17). Probably Saul's hometown (1 Chron 9:35–39). Here Joab fought Abner (2 Sam 2–3) and David drove Philistines from vicinity (1 Chron 14:16, but called Geba in Heb. text of 2 Sam 5:25; see NIV fn.). Jeremiah cursed a prophet from Gibeon (28:1). Here Johanan fought with Ishmael (Jer 41:12, 16). Men from the town helped rebuild the walls of Jerusalem after the Exile (Neh 3:7; see also 7:25) – *El-Jib (167139), 6 mi. NW of Jerusalem* – 41, **43, 46**, 47, **78, 82, 90**, 94, 95, **94, 98**, 102, 105, 106, 111, **111**, 112, **112**, 114, 116, **117**, 119, 120, **125, 126, 134**, 144, 146, **189**, 190

Gibeon, high place at – Worship center near Gibeon where tabernacle was during reign of David and Solomon (1 Chron 16:39; 21:29; 2 Chron 1:3, 5, 13; probably also 1 Kings 3:4, 5; 9:2). See Gibeah of God.

Gibeon, Valley of – Valley in vicinity of Gibeon (el-Jib [167139]) where God fought for his people (Isa 28:21; possible reference to Joshua defeating the Amorites [Josh 10:10–12]) – *Unknown.*

Giddi Pass – 60

Gidom – Defeated Benjamites were pursued to Gidom where several thousand were killed (Judges 20:45) – *Unknown; probably in NE Benjamin.*

Gihon (river) – One of four rivers mentioned in connection with Garden of Eden (Gen 2:13) – *Unknown* – 70, 71

Gihon (spring) – The major water source for city of Jerusalem, just E of city in Kidron Valley. Here Solomon was crowned king (1 Kings 1:33, 38, 45). Hezekiah blocked its upper outlet (2 Chron 32:30) and repaired city wall above it (33:14) in anticipation of Assyrian advance on Jerusalem – *Ein Umm ed-Deraj/Ein Sitti Maryan* – 116, 120, 135, 189, 190, **191**, 192, 194

Gilboa, Mount – Mountain (range) where Saul and three of his sons died in battle against Philistines (1 Sam 28:4; 31:1, 8; 2 Sam 1:6, 21; 21:12; 1 Chron 10:1, 8) – *Jebel Fuquah/Mt. Gilboa, 17 mi. SW of Sea of Galilee, overlooking Jordan, Harod, and Jezreel Valleys* – **33**, 36, **38**, 39, 40, 42, **114**, 115, 116

Gilead (Land of) – Primarily geographical term for mountainous region S of Yarmuk, N of E-W line drawn at N end of Dead Sea, and stretching E of Jordan to edge of desert (occasionally used as a clan name and personal name). Used over 97 times in OT – 16, **17, 18**, 23, 27–30, **29**, 36, 52, **53**, 54, **54**, 55, 77, **78**, 81, 83, **84, 91**, 92, **92**, 97, 101, **101**, 103, 104, 107, 108, 111, **112**, 115, 116, 118, **119**, 120, 121, 124, 127, 128, 131, **131, 132**, 133, **138**, 145, 146, 154

Gilgal – Site W of Jordan River in vicinity of Jericho, where Israel camped when it entered Canaan (Joshua passim). Continued as worship center during days of Samuel and Saul (1 Sam passim) and later became symbol of wickedness (Hosea and Amos). Mentioned 35 times in OT – *Uncertain; possibly in the Kh. el-Mefjer area (193143), 1.3 mi. NE of OT Jericho* – 93–95, **94**, 98, **98**, 107, 110–13, **111**, **112, 131**

Gilgal (Ephraim) – Elisha and Elijah passed by it on way down to Bethel and Jericho (2 Kings 2:1). Later Elisha returned here (4:38) – *Unknown.*

Gilgal (Galilee?) – Among the list of kings defeated by Joshua is the "king of Goyim in Gilgal" (Josh 11:23; LXX: Galilee) – *Unknown; probably not same as other Gilgals.*

Gilgal (Judah) – Site on E portion of N boundary of Judah in vicinity of Pass of Adummim (184136; Josh 15:7), 8 mi. E of Jerusalem. Parallel passage in Josh 18:17 reads "Geliloth" – *Unknown.*

Giloh – Town allotted to Judah, in S hill country (Josh 15:51). Home of Ahithophel, counselor to David and Absalom (2 Sam 15:12; 23:34) – *Unknown.*

Gimzo – Town captured by Philistines in days of Ahaz (2 Chron 28:18) – *Jimzu/Gimzo (145148), 15 mi. ESE of Joppa* – 75, **128**, 131, **134, 135**

Gina – 90, 105

Ginae – **170**, 172

Gischala – 166, 167, 168, 170, 177, **178**

Gittaim – Village to which people of Beeroth fled (2 Sam 4:3). Jews lived here after the Exile (Neh 11:33) – *Ras Abu Humeid (140145), 14 mi. SE of Joppa* – 46, 47, **144**

Giza – **58, 72, 74, 86**

Gob – Place where David's men battled twice with Philistines (2 Sam 21:18–19). 1 Chron 20:4 implies that it is another name for Gezer.

Goiim – Tidal, king of Goiim, participated in attack on cities of the plain (Gen 14:1, 9). "Tidal" may be Hittite name – *Unknown* – **78**, 81

Golan – Transjordanian city of Manasseh, allotted to the Levites (Josh 20:8; 1 Chron 6:71). One of the six cities of refuge (Deut 4:43; Josh 21:27). In NT times there was a district known as Gaulanitis – *Sahm el-Jolan (238243), 18 mi. E of the Sea of Galilee* – 17, 18, 23, **78**, 79, **102**, 103, 154

Golan Heights – 28

Golgotha – Site (hill?) just outside NT Jerusalem where Jesus was crucified (Matt 27:33; Mark 15:22; John 19:17) – *Probably Church of Holy Sepulchre inside of present-day old city of Jerusalem.*

Gomorrah – One of the cities of the plain attacked by kings of the N (Gen 14). Destroyed because of its wickedness (Gen 18–19). It and Sodom became symbol of wickedness and judgment (23 times in Bible) – *Unknown; possibly one of Early Bronze III sites E and SE of the Dead Sea.* – 75, 81

Gophna – 74, **154**, 160, **161**, 176, **176**, **178**, 179

Gordium – 147, 148, **148**, 181

Gortnya – 143, 175, 187

Goshen (Egypt) – Region of Egypt where Jacob and his descendants settled (mentioned 15 times in OT). Possibly called "district of Rameses" later in history (Gen 47:11) – *Area of E Nile Delta, near and N of Wadi Tumilat* – 58, 59, **80**, **81**, 83, 88

Goshen (Judah) – Town allotted to Judah in S hill country (Josh 15:51). Also name of a region, possibly in same area (Josh 10:41; 11:16) – *Unknown.*

Gozan – City and region conquered by Assyrians (1 Kings 19:12; Isa 37:12) to which Israelites were deported (1 Kings 17:6; 18:11; 1 Chron 5:26) – *T. Halaf, 160 mi. NE of Aleppo (Syria) on a W tributary of Habor River* – **13**, **130**, 133, **142**

Granicus River – 147, 148

Great Sea – Alternate name for Mediterranean Sea (13 times in NIV).

Greece – Mentioned 7 times in NIV. Paul visited Greece on second and third journeys – *General area of modern Greece, depending upon time frame of text* – 12, **13**, 64, 143, 146–49, 162, 183

Gudgodah – Campsite of Israel during wilderness wanderings, between Moserah and Jotbatah (Deut 10:7; called "Hor Haggidgad" in Num 33:32, 33) – *Unknown.*

Gur – Spot near Ibleam (177205; S side of Jezreel Valley) where Ahaziah was mortally wounded by Jehu's servants (2 Kings 9:27) – *Unknown.*

Gur Baal – Uzziah of Judah defeated the Arabs who lived in Gur Baal (2 Chron 26:7) – *Uncertain; S or SE of Judah* – 130

Guvrin Valley – 46, 48

Guzana – See also Gozan – 67

Haarava – 51

Habor/Habur (River) – Deported Israelites were settled in Habor region by the Assyrians (2 Kings 17:6; 18:11; 1 Chron 5:26) – *Khabur River in NE Syria* – 62, **62**, 65, **72**, **77**, **80**, **84**, **130**, 133

Hadashah – Town in Judean Shephelah district (Josh 15:37) – *Unknown.*

Hadid – Town resettled by Jews after return from the Exile (Ezra 2:33; Neh 7:37; 11:34) – *El-Haditheh/T. Hadid (145152), 11 mi. ESE of Joppa on coastal plain* – **144**

Hadrach, land of – Subject of oracle of Zechariah (9:1). Called "Hatarikka" in Assyrian texts – *Tell Afis, 28 mi. SW of Aleppo, Syria.*

Haeleph – Town in Benjamin (Josh 18:28) – *Unknown; probably W of watershed.*

Hagoshrim – 78

Haifa – 25

Haifa Bay – 32

Hakilah, hill of – Hill in Judean Desert where Saul pursued David (1 Sam 23:18; 26:1) – *Unknown; probably near Ziph.*

Halab – See Aleppo – 64

Halah – Place in Gozan region near Habor River to which Israelites were exiled by Assyrians (2 Kings 17:6; 18:11; 1 Chron 5:26) – *Unknown* – 133

Halak, Mount – Point marking S limit of Joshua's conquests (Josh 11:17; 12:7) – *Uncertain; possibly Jebel Halaq, 28 mi. SE of Beersheba.*

Halhul – Town in hill country district of Judah (Josh 15:58) – *Halhul (160109), 4 mi. N of Hebron* – 134

Hali – Town allotted to Asher (Josh 19:25) – *Kh. Ras Ali/T. Hali (164241), 11 mi. SSE of Acco* – **99**

Halicarnassus – 175

Ham – Place in Transjordan where Zuzites lived (Gen 14:5) – *Ham (226213), 40 mi. NNW of Amman in Gilead.*

Ham, land of – Alternate name for Egypt (Pss 105:23, 27; 106:22) – **71**

Hamakhtesh Hagadol – 18

Hamath (Land of) – State just N of Canaan. Israelite territory reached to its S boundary during days of David, Solomon, and Jeroboam II. Mentioned 24 times in OT – *In NW Syria; capital city Hamath (= Hama; 312503), 120 mi. NNE of Damascus* – 13, 28, **62**, 64, **71**, **72**, **77**, **80**, **84**, 91, 104, **117**, 118, 121, 123, **123**, **130**, 132, 133, **137**, 142, 143, 145, **145**, 156

Hamath, Plain of – 156

Hamath Zobah – City in Aramean state of Zobah, captured by Solomon (2 Chron 8:3) – *Unknown; possibly in Beqa in Lebanon* – 121, 123

Hammath (Jordan Valley) – 38, 106, **107**

Hammath (Kenite) – Place of origin of some Kenites (1 Chron 2:55) – *Unknown.*

Hammath (Naphtali) – Town allotted to Naphtali (Josh 19:35) – *Hammam Tabariyeh/Hame Teveriya (201241), on W shore of Sea of Galilee* – 31, 33, **34**, 35, 99

Hammath Gader – 34, 35

Hammemat – 58

Hammon – Levitical city in Naphtali (1 Chron 6:76) – *Uncertain; possibly same as Hammoth Dor.*

Hammon (Asher) – Town allotted to Asher (Josh 19:28) – *Umm el-Awamid (164281), in Lebanon, 14.5 mi. NNE of Acco* – **99**

Hammoth Dor – Levitical town in territory of Naphtali (Josh 21:32). Perhaps identical to Hammath (Naphtali) of Josh 19:35 and Hammon of 1 Chron 6:76.

Hamonah – Symbolic name of town ("horde") in Valley of Hamon Gog (Ezek 39:16).

Hamon Gog, Valley of – Valley, possibly in Transjordan, where army of Gog will be slain and buried (Ezek 39:11, 15) – *Unknown.*

Hanes – Egyptian city mentioned in Isa 30:4 – *Unknown; possibly Heracleopolis Magna, 50 mi. S of Memphis or Heracleopolis Parva in E Delta* – 130

Hanita – 78

Hannathon – Town on NW boundary of Zebulun (Josh 19:14) – *T. el-Bedeiwiyeh/T. Hannaton (174243), 14 mi. SE of Acco* – 27, **28**, **31**, 33, 34, 36, **90**, 99, **99**, 105, **105**, **126**, **129**, **132**

Hapharaim – Town allotted to Issachar (Josh 19:19) – *Affuleh (177223), 6.5 mi. ENE of Megiddo* – **99**

Hara – Place to which Assyrians took exiled Israelites (1 Chron 5:26, but text is difficult; cf. 2 Kings 17:6; 18:11) – *Unknown.*

Haradah – Desert campsite of wandering Israelites (Num 33:24–25) – *Unknown.*

Haran – Site in N Mesopotamia on Balik River to which Abram migrated. Here Jacob lived with his uncle Laban. Later captured by the Assyrians; their last capital. Mentioned 11 times in OT, 2 times in NT – *Haran, 115 mi. NE of Aleppo in E Turkey, near Turkish-Syrian border* – 13, **62**, 63, 67, 76, 77, **77**, **78**, **80**, 84, **123**, 137, **138**, **142**, **143**

Harim – People of village participated in first return from Babylonian Exile (Ezra 2:32; Neh 7:35) – *Uncertain; possibly Kh. Hauran/Mezad Hakhlil (144117), 8 mi. NE of Lachish in Shephelah* – **144**

Harmon – If text is correct, a place to which Israelites were to be exiled (Amos 4:3) – *Unknown.*

Harmozeia – 148

Harod, spring of – Place where Gideon camped with his men in preparation for battle with Midianites (Judges 7:1) Two of David's mighty men were from a town of this name (2 Sam 23:25) – *Ein Jalud/En Harod (183217), 9 mi. WNW of Beth Shan* – 107

Harod, Valley of – 17, 18, 20, 25, 33, 34, 36, **38**, 40, 54, 97, 99, 115, 116, 122

Harosheth Haggoyim – Place where Sisera, commander of Jabin's army, resided or ruled over and to which his troops retreated in the face of Deborah and Barak's army (Judges 4:2, 13, 16) – *Uncertain; possibly reference to the forested region(s) of Galilee or, better, to gentile plantations in Jezreel Valley in vicinity of Taanach and Megiddo.*

Har Rahama – 75

Har Ramon – 51

Har Yeruham – See Yeruham – 78

Hashmonah – Campsite of Israelites during years of wanderings (Num 33:29–30) – *Unknown.*

Hatnub – 81

Hatti – 105, 106

Hattin, Horns of – See Alamah and Merom, Waters of – 34

Hattusa – 13, 80

Hauran – Assyrian district E of Sea of Galilee, mentioned in connection with boundaries of Promised Land (Ezek 47:16–17). Called Auranitis during the NT period. See Jebel Druze – *Territory just W of Jebel Druze* – 30, **132**, 145, **145**, 151

Hauran, Mount – 29, 30

Havilah – Land through which Pishon River ran (Gen 2:11) – *Various proposals, but unknown. Also known as region near which Amalekites settled (Gen 25:18; 1 Sam 15:7) – Probably NE Sinai or possibly E Negev* – 71, **71**, 112

Havvoth Jair – Settlements in N Gilead that had been part of the kingdom of Og. Settled by a descendant of Manasseh named Jair (Josh 13:30; Num 32:41; Deut 3:14). Possibly the judge Jair was from this region (Judges 10:4). Later part of a Solomonic district (1 Kings 4:13). At some time captured by Geshur and Aram (1 Chron 2:23). Also called "settlements of Jair" (Josh 13:30; 1 Kings 4:13) – *Probably the region of N Gilead near the Yarmuk River* – 29, 30, **107**, 108

Hazar, Lake – 66

Hazar Addar – Site on S boundary of Canaan (Num 34:4) – *Uncertain; possibly Ein Qedeis (100999) or the nearby fort (103000), ca. 51 mi. SW of Beersheba.*

Hazar Enan – Site on NE border of Canaan (Num 34:9, 10; Ezek 47:17; 48:1) – *Qaryatein (360402), 70 mi. NE of Damascus* – **62, 145**

Hazar Gaddah – Village in Negev district allotted to Judah (Josh 15:27) – *Unknown.*

Hazarmaveth – **71**

Hazar Shual – Village in Negev allotted to both Judah (Josh 15:28) and Simeon (19:3; 1 Chron 4:28). Jews settled here after the Exile (Neh 11:27) – *Unknown* – **146**

Hazar Susah – Negev village allotted to Simeon (Josh 19:5). Name means "corral of the mare." Probably identical to Hazar Susim, "corral of the horses" (1 Chron 4:31) – *Unknown; possibly stables or military stations.*

Hazar Susim – See Hazar Susah.

Hazazon/Hazazon Tamar – Place where kings of N defeated Amorites. *Uncertain, possibly Ein Husb/Hazeva (173024), 27 mi. SSW of Dead Sea. See Tamar* – **78, 81**

Hazazon Tamar (En Gedi) – Place where tribes from the E camped as they invaded Judah (2 Chron 20:2); identifid in text as "En Gedi" *Probably Ein Jidi/En Gedi (187097), at midpoint of W shore of Dead Sea* – **128**

Hazer Hatticon – On N border of Promised Land (Ezek 47:16). Because of position in the list, seems to be alternate form of, or scribal error for, Hazar Enan.

Hazeroth – Third campsite after Israelites left Mt. Sinai. Here Miriam and Aaron questioned Moses' marriage to a Cushite woman and his position as leader (Num 11:35; 12:16; 33:17–18; Deut 1:1) – *Uncertain; possibly Ein Khadra (096814), 40 mi. NE of Jebel Musa (Mt. Sinai?)* – **91**

Hazi – **105**

Hazor (Arabia?) – Probably settlements in Arabia attacked by Nebuchadnezzar (Jer 49:28–33) – *Unknown; probably in W or NW Arabia.*

Hazor (Benjamin) – Village where Benjamites settled after the Exile (Neh 11:33) – *Uncertain; in Benjamin Plateau N of Jerusalem.*

Hazor (Judah [1]) – Negev town allotted to Judah (Josh 15:23) – *Unknown; in S Judah.*

Hazor (Judah [2]) – Alternate name for Kerioth Hezron (Josh 15:25).

Hazor (Naphtali) – Large Canaanite city, head of kingdoms in area. Conquered by Joshua (11:1, 10, 11, 13; 12:19) and allotted to Naphtali (19:36). Its forces fought against Deborah and Barak (Judges 4:2, 17; 1 Sam 12:9). On major international route. Fortified by Solomon (1 Kings 9:15). Conquered by Tiglath-Pileser III of Assyria (2 Kings 15:29) – *T. el-Qedah/T. Hazor (203269), 9.5 mi. N of Sea of Galilee* – **13, 14, 28, 28, 29, 30, 31, 31, 33, 34, 35, 40, 75, 75, 77, 78, 80, 82, 83–85, 88, 90, 91, 95, 95, 99, 100, 105, 106, 107, 107, 109, 117, 119, 120, 121, 122, 123, 125, 126, 127, 128, 129, 132, 133, 144, 156, 157, 203, 206**

Hazorea – **78**

Hazor Hadattah – Negev town allotted to Judah (Josh 15:25) – *Unknown.*

Hebron – Town in Hill Country of Judah; earlier name Kiriath Arba (Gen 23:2). Here Abraham pitched his tent and built an altar (13:18), and purchased cave of Machpelah where patriarchs and their wives were buried (23:18; et al.). The Israelite spies passed Hebron (Num 13:22). Captured by Joshua and given to Caleb (Josh passim). Levitical city (21:11, 13) and city of refuge (20:7). David ruled from Hebron for 7½ years before moving his capital to Jerusalem (2 Sam passim). Here Absalom

began his revolt (2 Sam 15). (Re)fortified by Rehoboam (2 Chron 11:10). Mentioned 64 times in OT – *El-Khalil–Jebel er-Rumeideh (el-Khalil)//Hebron (160103), 20 mi. SSW of Jerusalem* – **17, 18, 18, 21, 25, 28, 28, 41–44, 43, 46, 48, 49, 50, 60, 75, 77, 77, 78, 80, 82, 84, 88, 91, 91, 92, 94–96, 94, 97, 102, 103, 104, 106, 107, 109, 114, 116, 117, 119, 119, 120, 125, 126, 128, 131, 132, 134, 135, 138, 144, 146, 150, 151, 154, 156, 157, 158, 161, 164, 170, 172, 176, 178, 179, 192, 198, 201, 204, 205**

Helam – Town to which Arameans retreated and where David defeated them (2 Sam 10:16–17) – *Uncertain; possibly Alma (267240), 35 mi. E of Sea of Galilee* – **117, 118**

Helbah – Town of Asher from which Canaanites were not driven out (Judges 1:31) – *Uncertain; may be alternate name for Ahlab* – **99**

Helbon – Damascus traded wine from Helbon with Tyre (Ezek 27:18) – *Uncertain; possibly Valley of Halbun, 12 mi. N of Damascus.*

Helech – Place from which Tyre hired mercenary soldiers (Ezek 27:11) – *Possibly Cilicia in SE Turkey.*

Heleph – Site at SW corner of boundary of Naphtali (Josh 19:33) – *Uncertain; possibly Kh. Irbadeh/H. Arpad (189236), 3 mi. NE of Mt. Tabor* – **99, 100**

Heliopolis – Major Egyptian religious center mentioned in Ezekiel's lament for Egypt (Ezek 30:17). Also called "On" in NIV (Gen 41:45, 50; 46:20), and possibly identified as the "temple of the sun" in Jer 43:13 – *Tell el-Hisn, near el-Matarieh, 10 mi. NNE of Cairo* – **81, 86, 143**

Helkath – Town on boundary of Asher (Josh 19:25). Levitical city (Josh 21:31; but parallel in 1 Chron 6:75 has "Hukok" – *Uncertain; possibly T. el-Qassis/T. Qashish (160232) at NW exit of Jezreel Valley, 17 mi. S of Acco* – **31, 33, 36, 90, 99, 102**

Helkath Hazzurim – Place where 12 men of Joab fought 12 men of Abner (2 Sam 2:16) – *Unknown; near Gibeon.*

Hellas (Greece) – **147**

Hellespont – **182, 183**

Hena – One of a number of cities captured by Sennacherib (2 Kings 18:34; 19:13; Isa 37:23) – *Uncertain; probably in N Syria.*

Hepher – King of Hepher defeated by Joshua (Josh 12:17). Incorporated into Solomon's third administrative district (1 Kings 4:10) – *possibly el-Ifshar/T. Hefer (141197), 25 mi. NNE of Joppa near coast of Mediterranean* – **122**

Hephzibah – Poetic name for Jerusalem (Isa 62:4).

Heptapegon – See also Tabgha – **34, 35, 168, 169**

Heraclea – **175**

Herakleopolis – **79, 80, 81, 175**

Heres, Mount – "Mountain of the sun." Place from which Danites were not able to drive out Amorites (Judges 1:35) – *Uncertain; possibly same as or near Ir Shemesh ("house/temple/city of the sun [god];" Josh 19:41), which apparently is same as Beth Shemesh ("city of the sun").*

Heres, Pass of – Place near which Gideon ceased pursuing defeated Midianites (Judges 8:13) – *Unknown; in Transjordan, probably in/near desert.*

Hereth, forest of – Place where David hid from Saul after leaving Moab (1 Sam 22:5) – *Uncertain; in Judah, possibly W or SW of Jerusalem* – **114**

Hermon, Mount – High mountain in NE Israel. N-most limit of Joshua's conquests (Josh 11:17; 12:1). Snow-covered most of the year, tributaries of the Jordan River originate at its base. Also called Senir, Sirion, and Baal

Hermon. Mentioned 14 times in OT – *Jebel esh-Sheikh or Jebel eth-Thalj, 27 mi. WSW of Damascus, 9,232 ft. high* – **16, 18, 20, 22, 23, 28–32, 28, 29, 31, 34, 62, 64, 92, 93, 101, 101, 104, 168, 170, 171**

Hermonit – **171**

Hermopolis – **141**

Herodian Royal Estates – **168, 176**

Herodium – **43, 43, 157, 164, 164, 165**

Heshbon – Capital city of Sihon, king of Amorites, conquered by Israel (Num 21:25–34; et al.). Allotted to Reuben but evidently became Gadite. Levitical city. Recovered by Moab and mentioned as Moabite in prophetic oracles (e.g., Isa 15:4; et al.). Mentioned 38 times in OT – *Hesban (226134), 12 mi. SW of Amman, may preserve the name, but OT site may have been at nearby Jalul where the archaeological profile fits the historical data better in some periods* – **17, 18, 23, 28, 28, 52, 53, 55, 92, 92, 94, 101, 101, 102, 120, 122, 128, 132, 164**

Heshmon – Negev town allotted to Judah (Josh 15:27) – *Unknown.*

Hethlon – Place on N portion of ideal boundary of Israel, between Mediterranean and Lebo Hamath (Ezek 47:15; 48:1) – *Unknown* – **145**

Hezron – Site along S boundary of Judah between Kadesh Barnea and Adar (Josh 15:3). Parallel passage in Num 34:4 has "Hazar Addar" – *Unknown.*

Hierakonpolis – **72, 73**

Hierapolis – Paul refers to church here (Col 4:13), which he may have established while in Ephesus – *In W Turkey, 6 mi. N of Laodicea and 12 mi. NNW of Colosse in Lycus valley.*

Hilen – Levitical city in Hill Country of Judah (1 Chron 6:58). Called Holon in Josh 15:51 and 21:15 – *Unknown.*

Hinnom, Valley of (Ben) – Valley to W and S of Jerusalem; part of border between Judah and Benjamin (Josh 15:8; 18:16). During later Judean monarchy a place of idolatrous worship (2 Kings 23:10; 2 Chron 28:3; 33:6; Jer 7:31; 32; 19:2, 6; 32:35). Mentioned as boundary limit in Neh 11:30 – *Wadi er-Rababi just W and then S of the Old City of Jerusalem. Joins the Kidron just S of the City of David* – **189, 190, 191, 194, 197**

Hippus – **29, 30, 34, 35, 157, 160, 161, 162, 164, 167, 168, 170, 171, 176**

Hispania – See Spain.

Hit – **65, 65, 66**

Hobah – Place N of Damascus to which Abram pursued Amraphel and other kings who had captured Lot (Gen 14:15) – *Unknown* – **81**

Holon (Judah) – Town allotted to Judah in S hill country (Josh 15:51). Levitical city (21:15); but parallel passage has Hilen (1 Chron 6:58) – *Unknown.*

Holon (Moab) – Town located on plateau of Moab (Jer 48:21) – *Unknown; E of Dead Sea, N of Arnon Gorge.*

Homs – **62–64**

Homs, Palmyra and Tadmor – **63, 64**

Hor, Mount (Lebanon) – Mountain on the N border of Canaan (Num 34:7–8) – *Uncertain; possibly Ras Shaqqa (213412), 30 mi. NNE of Beirut on Mediterranean.*

Hor, Mount (Negev) – Israelite campsite during wilderness wanderings where Aaron died (Num 20 passim; et al.). Mentioned 10 times in OT – *Uncertain; possibly Imaret el-Khureisheh (104017), 40 mi. SW of Beer Sheba* – **91, 91, 92**

Horbat Kufin – **78**

Horbat Shivta – **49**

Horbat Shovav – **75**

Horbat Toy – 75

Horbat Yinon – 75

Horeb – Alternate name for Sinai (17 times in OT). See Sinai – 90

Horem – Town allotted to Naphtali in Upper Galilee (Josh 19:38) – *Unknown.*

Horesh – Site in Desert of Ziph where David hid from Saul and met with Jonathan (1 Sam 23:15–16, 18–19) – *Uncertain; probably E of Ziph, 5 mi. SE of Hebron.*

Horeshim – 78

Hor Haggidgad – Israelite campsite in wilderness between Bene Jaakan and Jotbathah (Num 33:32–33). Called Gudgodah in Deut 10:7 – *Unknown.*

Hormah – Village in Negev allotted to Judah (Josh 15:30) and then to Simeon (19:4; 1 Chron 4:30). Here Israelites were first defeated by Canaanites (Num 14:45; Deut 1:44) but later captured and destroyed the town, which formerly had been called Zephath (Num 21:3; Josh 12:14; Judges 1:17). David sent booty to its inhabitants (1 Sam 30:30) – *Uncertain; possibly Kh. el-Meshash/T. Masos (146069), 8 mi. ESE of Beersheba, or T. Khuweilifeh/T. Halif (137087), 9.5 mi. NNE of Beersheba. But see Rimmon* – 97, 134

Horonaim (Moab) – A town of Moab mentioned in prophetic oracles (Isa 15:5; Jer 48:3, 5, 34) – *Uncertain; possibly el-Iraq (211055), 8.5 mi. E of S end of Dead Sea* – 56, 128

Horonaim (N of Jerusalem) – Place mentioned in story of Absalom's killing of Amnon (2 Sam 13:34) – *Unknown.*

Horvat Nahal Nissana – 78

Hosah – Village on N border of Asher (Josh 19:29) – *Uncertain; possibly T. Rashidiyeh (170293) in Lebanon, 3 mi. SSE of Tyre near Mediterranean* – 99

Hukkok – Town on W border of Naphtali (Josh 19:34) – *Uncertain; possibly Kh. el-Jemeijmeh/H. Gamon (175252), 12 mi. ESE of Acco* – 99

Hukok – See Helkath.

Huleh (Basin/Lake/Valley) – 17, 18, 20, 31, **31**, 32, **33**, 35, 104, 118

Humtah – Town in hill country allotted to Judah (Josh 15:44) – *Unknown.*

Hurru – 85, 87, 106

Hushah – Evidently a village of Judah (1 Chron 4:4) – *Uncertain; possibly Husan (162124), 4.5 mi. W of Bethlehem.*

Hyrcania – 43, **43**, 142, **143**, 157, 164, **164**

Ibleam – Town allotted to Manasseh beside Issachar (Josh 17:11); they were not able to drive out the Canaanites (Judges 1:27). Near it Jehu of Israel killed Ahaziah Judah (2 Kings 9:27). The Levitical town of Bileam (1 Chron 6:70) is probably identical with Ibleam – *Kh. Belameh (177205), 12 mi. SE of Megiddo* – **33**, 38, 75, 97, **98**, 103, 116, **126**, 129

Iconium – City visited by Paul and Barnabas on first journey (Acts 13:51; 14:1, 19, 21; 2 Tim 3:11) and mentioned in passing in Acts 16:2. In all probability Paul also visited it on his second and third journeys (16:6 and 18:23) – *Konya, in S central Turkey* – **143**, 175, 181, **181**, **182**, 183, **185**, 187

Idalah – One of the towns allotted to Zebulun (Josh 19:15) – *Uncertain; possibly Kh. el-Huwarah (167236), 6.5 mi. W of Nazareth.*

Idumea – District S of Judea in time of Jesus. People from here followed Jesus (Mark 3:8) – *Boundaries varied; Dead Sea on E, Beer Sheba on S, Beth Zur in N, near Marisa on W* – **144**, **150**, 151, **151**, 152, **154**, 157, 158–60, **161**, 162, 163, **164**, 166, **167**, 170, 172, 174, **175**, 177

Ienysus – 141, **141**, 142, 146

Iim – Negev settlement allotted to Judah (Josh 15:29) – *Unknown; in S Judah.*

Ijon – Village in N Israel, evidently in Naphtali, taken by Ben-Hadad (1 Kings 15:20; 2 Chron 16:4) and later Tiglath-Pileser III (2 Kings 15:29) as they invaded Israel from the N – *T. ed-Dibbin (205308), 9 mi. NNW of Dan in Lebanon* – **119**, **126**, 127, **129**, **132**, 133

Illyricum – Roman province in what is now W Yugoslavia and Albania. Paul evidently visited it on his second and/or third journeys (Rom 15:19). See also Dalmatia – **163**, 185

Imar – 62

Imaret el-Khureisheh – See Hor, Mount (Negev) – 91

Immer – Babylonian town from which exiles returned (Ezra 2:59; Neh 7:61) – *Unknown.*

Imwas – See Emmaus – 173

India – Country on E boundary of Persian Empire (Esth 1:1; 8:9) – *Area W of Indus River* – 22, 56, 57, 67, 142, **143**, 148, 149, 150, 159

Indian Ocean – 148

Indus (River/Valley) – 141, **143**, 148, 149

Ionia – 143

Ionian Sea – 147

Iphtah – Town allotted to Judah in a Shephelah district (Josh 15:43) – *Unknown.*

Iphtah El, Valley of – Valley on boundary between Zebulun (Josh 19:14) and Asher (19:27) – *Uncertain; possibly Wadi el-Malik* – 99

Ipsus – **148**, 149

Iran – 13, 65, 67, 149

Iraq – 12, **13**, 65, 70, 146

Iraq el-Emir – 146

Ir Nahash – Could be personal or geographical name (1 Chron 4:12) – *Uncertain; possibly Kh. en-Nahas (191010), 30 mi. S of Dead Sea in Jordan. Others suggest in Shephelah region of Judah.*

Iron – Town in Upper Galilee allotted to Naphtali (Josh 19:38) – *Yarun (189276), 22 mi. NE of Acco* – 31, **99**, **126**, 132

Irpeel – Town allotted to Benjamin (Josh 18:27) – *Unknown; in area N of Jerusalem.*

Ir Shemesh – Town allotted to Dan (Josh 19:41). Probably alternate form of Beth Shemesh – 100, **100**

Isana – 162

Isfahan – 143

Isin – 80

Island of the Sea – 143

Ismailia – 58, 60, **60**, 146

Israel – Name for Jacob and designation for his descendants and the territory in which they lived, basically from Dan to Beersheba. During Divided Monarchy (930–721 B.C.) it usually refers to the N Kingdom, although not exclusively. In postexilic times it can again designate the whole of God's people – 12, **13**, 14, 16, 18–20, 22–25, **23**, 27, 29–33, 36, 42, 44, 46, 47, 49, 50, 55, 63, 64, 67, 68, 71–74, 76, 83, 85, 86, 88, 90–92, 94, 99, 100, 102, 104, 106–13, **107**, 115, 116, 118, 119, **119**, **120**, 121, 122, 124, **125**, **126**, 127, 128, **128–31**, 131, 132, 134–36, **134**, 139, 141, **145**, 158, 171, 190, 192, 193, 202–4, 207

Issachar – Tribe of Israel mentioned 42 times in OT and once in NT. Settled in territory SW of Sea of Galilee – 34, 36, 99, **99**, 100, **102**, 106–8, 122

Issus – 147, 148, **148**, 181

Itabyrium – 150, 151

Italia – See Italy.

Italy – Peninsula, ca. 700 mi. long, that extends S from Europe, bounded on the E by the Adriatic and on the W by the Tyrrhenian Sea. Mentioned 4 times in NT (Acts 18:2; 27:1, 6; Heb 13:24) – 12, **163**, 186, 187, **187**

Ithlah – Town allotted to Dan (Josh 19:42) – *Unknown.*

Ithnan – Negev town allotted to Judah (Josh 15:23) – *Unknown.*

Iturea – During NT era, district N of Palestine ruled by Philip the tetrarch (Luke 3:1) – *Beqa area in Lebanon, just N of Israel, and mountain slopes on E and W of it* – 164

Ivvah – City/state in N Syria captured by the Assyrians (2 Kings 18:34; 19:13; Isa 37:13) from which people were brought to settle in Israel. Called Avva in 2 Kings 17:24 – *Unknown.*

Iye Abarim – Campsite of wandering Israelites, probably E of Rift Valley between Oboth and Zered Valley (Num 21:11; 33:44) – *Uncertain; possibly el-Medeiyineh (223041), 19 mi. ESE of Dead Sea on N slope of Zered Valley. Called Iyim in Num 33:45* – 92

Iyim – Alternate name of Iye Abarim (Num 33:45).

Jaakanites, wells of the – Campsite of Israelites during wilderness wanderings (Deut 10:6). Called "Bene Jaakan" in Num 33:32 – *Unknown.*

Jaar, fields of – Possibly a shorter form for Kiriath Jearim (Ps 132:6) where ark of covenant was during part of Saul's reign (1 Sam 7:2).

Jaba – 111

Jabbok (River) – River in Transjordan that flows N from near Amman and turns W to join the Jordan. Here Jacob wrestled with God (Gen 32:22). Traditional N boundary of the Amorites (Num 21:24; Deut 2:37; Josh 12:2). S boundary of Manasseh and N boundary of Reuben and Gad (Deut 3:16; Josh 12:2). Territory in vicinity was claimed by Ammonites (Judges 11:13, 22) – *Nahr ez-Zerka in Jordan* – **17**, 18, 20, 23, 28, **28**, 52, 53, 54, **54**, 77, **78**, **84**, 90, 91, 92, 93, 94, 101, **101–3**, 107, **107**, 114, **119**, **126**, 144

Jabesh – Short form of Jabesh Gilead.

Jabesh (Gilead) – Town in Gilead mentioned in various forms 19 times in OT. Here the surviving men of Benjamin took 400 women as wives (Judges 21). Saul (a Benjamite) rescued its inhabitants from an Ammonite attack (1 Sam 11). Men of Jabesh removed bodies of Saul and Jonathan from wall of Beth Shan (1 Sam 31; 1 Chron 10), and David took the bodies from Jabesh and buried them in Benjamin (2 Sam 2) – *T. el-Maqlub (214201) on the N bank of the Jabbok, 7 mi. E of the Jordan River and 13 mi. SE of Beth Shan* – **54**, 104, **107**, 111, **112**, 114, 115, **117**, **126**, 205

Jabez – Town where scribes lived (1 Chron 2:55), possibly in Bethlehem area – *Unknown.*

Jabneel Valley – See also Nahal Jabneel – 99, 100

Jabneel (Judah) – Town on W portion of Judah's N border (Josh 15:11) – *Yebna/Yavne (126141), 13 mi. S of Joppa. Same as Jabneh captured by Uzziah (2 Chron 26:6). Mentioned frequently in sources of intertestamental period and later as "Jamnia"* – 97, 202

Jabneel (Naphtali) – Town on S border of Naphtali (Josh 19:33) – *T. en-Naam/T. Yinam (198235), 3.5 mi. W of S end of Sea of Galilee* – 31, 33, 34, 99

Jabneh – 130

Jackal's Well – Well in vicinity of Jerusalem between Valley and Dung Gates (Neh 2:13) – *Unknown.*

Jacob's Well — Well near Sychar where Jesus met Samaritan woman (John 4:5–6) – *Bir Yaqub (177179), .5 mi. SE of Shechem.*

Jagur — Town in Negev district of Judah (Josh 15:21) – *Unknown.*

Jahaz — Transjordanian town captured from Sihon, king of Amorites (Num 21:23; Deut 2:32; Judges 11:20). Allotted to Reuben (Josh 13:18). Levitical city (Josh 21:36; called "Jahzah" in 1 Chron 6:78). Mentioned in prophetic oracles as Moabite town (Isa 15:4; Jer 48:34) – *Uncertain; possibly Kh. el-Medeiyineh (236110), E of Dead Sea, 11 mi. SE of Medeba* – **92, 92, 94, 101, 102**

Jahzah — Alternate form of Jahaz (1 Chron 6:78).

Jair, settlements of — Josh 13:30; 1 Kings 4:13. See Havvoth Jair – **101**

Jamnia — OT Jabneel (Judah) – **150, 151, 151, 152, 156, 157, 161, 164, 167. 170, 176, 177, 178, 179**

Janim — Judean town in hill-country district of Hebron (Josh 15:53) – *Unknown.*

Janoah (Ephraim) — Town on NE boundary of Ephraim (Josh 16:6–7) – *Kh. Yanun (184173), 6 mi. SE of Shechem* – **38, 98**

Janoah (Galilee) — Uncertain; possibly a town in Upper Galilee captured by Tiglath-Pileser III of Assyria (2 Kings 15:29) – *Yanuh (178296), ca. 6 mi. E of Tyre* – **28, 129, 132, 133, 203**

Japheth – **71**

Japhia — Town on S border of Zebulun (Josh 19:12) – *Usually identified with Yafa (176232), 1.5 mi. SW of Nazareth, but archaeological profile does not correspond with historical record* – **99, 166, 167, 168**

Japhletites, territory of the — Territory on SW border of Ephraim (Josh 16:3) – *Possibly NE of Beth Horon region.*

Jarkon/Yarkon River — See Nahal Yarkon and Me Jarkon – **27, 28, 38, 39, 46, 47, 100, 110, 111, 144**

Jarmuth (Issachar) — Levitical town in Issachar (Josh 21:29). Called "Ramoth" in 1 Chron 6:73 and "Remeth" in Josh 19:21 – *T. Remet (199221), 6 mi. NNE of Beth Shan* – **102**

Jarmuth (Judah) — Town in Shephelah whose king fought against Joshua (Josh 10:3, 5, 23; 12:11). Assigned to Judah (15:35). Jews settled here after return from the Exile (Neh 11:29) – *Usually identified with Kh. el-Yarmuk/T. Yarmut (147124), 17 mi. WSW of Jerusalem, but archaeological profile is problematic* – **94, 94, 97, 113, 134, 144, 146**

Jashubi Lehem — Judeans lived here (1 Chron 4:22) – *Unknown; text is difficult.*

Jatt – **75**

Jattir — Town in hill country allotted to Judah (Josh 15:48). Levitical city (21:14; 1 Chron 6:57). David sent spoils to its inhabitants (1 Sam 30:27) – *Kh. Attir/Yatir (151084), 13 mi. SW of Hebron* – **97, 102, 134**

Javan – **71**

Jaxartes (River) – **143, 148, 149**

Jazer — Transjordanian town of Sihon captured by Israelites (Num 21:32) and given to Gad (32:1, 3, 35; Josh 13:25). Levitical city (Josh 21:29; 1 Chron 6:81). David stationed soldiers here (1 Chron 26:31). Joab passed through area while taking a census (2 Sam 24:5). Later taken by Moabites (Isa 16:8, 9; Jer 48:32) – *Uncertain; possibly Kh. es-Sar (228150), 6.5 mi. W of Amman* – **101, 102, 119**

Jearim, Mount — Mountain (ridge?) on NW boundary of Judah (Josh 15:10) in vicinity of Kesalon – *Kesla; 154132, 11 mi. W of Jerusalem.*

Jebel as-Silsila – **58**

Jebel Barkal – **58**

Jebel Bishri – **62, 63**

Jebel Druze — See Nashan, Mount, and Harran, Mount – **17, 23, 29, 30, 91, 91**

Jebel ed-Dabab – **55, 56**

Jebel el-Aziz – **62, 62**

Jebel el-Kabir — See Zalmon, Mount – **108**

Jebel el-Maghara – **59**

Jebel el-Silsila – **57**

Jebel esh-Sharqia – **62, 63**

Jebel et-Tih – **60**

Jebel Geneife – **89, 89**

Jebel Helal – **49, 60, 89**

Jebel Jarmak – **171**

Jebel Karkom – **49, 60**

Jebel Murr – **86**

Jebel Musa — See Sinai (Desert of, Mount) – **60, 89–91, 89**

Jebel Nebi Harun – **91, 92**

Jebel Qaaqir – **78, 79**

Jebel Sin(n) Bisher — See Sinai (Desert of, Mount) – **60, 89–91, 89**

Jebel Sinjar – **62, 62, 63**

Jebel Sinn Bisher — See Jebel Sin(n) Bisher.

Jebel Sirbal – **60, 60**

Jebel Tih – **58, 60**

Jebel Umm ed-Daraj – **52, 53, 54**

Jebel Yalaq – **60**

Jebel Zawiyeh – **62, 64**

Jebus (Jebusite city) — Alternate name for Jerusalem, used from the time of Joshua up until the days of David. Mentioned in boundary descriptions of Judah and Benjamin (Josh 15:8; 18:16) and in city list of Benjamin (18:28); also in story of Levite and his concubine (Judges 19:10–11) and in story of David's conquest of Jebus (1 Chron 11:4). Jebusites mentioned frequently in Scripture – **103, 104, 105, 112, 116, 192**

Jegar Sahaduth — Stone marker set up in Transjordan (Gilead?) by Jacob and Laban (Gen 31:47). Called "Galeed" by Jacob – *Unknown.*

Jehoshaphat, Valley of — Valley near Jerusalem where nations are to be judged (Joel 3:2, 12) – *Traditionally identified with portion of Kidron Valley just E of Jerusalem.*

Jehud — Town allotted to Dan (Josh 19:45) – *El-Yehudiyeh/Yehud (139159), 8.5 mi. E of Joppa in coastal plain* – **100, 144**

Jekabzeel — Town in Negev settled by Jews after the Exile (Neh 11:25) – *Probably alternate form of Kabzeel* – **107, 144, 146**

Jemdet Nasr – **72**

Jenin – **18, 82, 105**

Jerahmeelites, towns of the — Settlements of Judahite clan in E Negev basin to which David sent booty (1 Sam 30:29) – *Probably area about 12 mi. E of Beersheba in E Negev.*

Jerash – **171**

Jericho (NT) — Jesus passed through Jericho on way to Jerusalem; healed the blind (Matt 20:29; Mark 10:46; Luke 18:35) and met Zacchaeus (Luke 19:1). Also mentioned in story of Good Samaritan (10:30) – *Spread out over a large oasis; Hasmonean and Herodian palaces located at Tulul Abu el-Alayiq (191139) along banks of Wadi Qilt, 9 mi. NNW of the Dead Sea* – **4, 154, 155, 156, 157, 159, 160, 161, 162, 163, 164, 165, 166, 167, 170, 171, 172, 175, 176, 177, 177, 178, 179, 188, 189**

Jericho (OT) — Town W of Jordan River. Mentioned 56 times in OT (once in NT; Heb 11:30), primarily to identify Israel's campsite in the Plains of Moab and esp. in connection with conquest of Canaan (Josh passim). Border city between Ephraim and Benjamin (Josh 16 and 18). Ehud killed Eglon here (called "City of Palms" in Judges 3:13). Also mentioned in the Elijah and Elisha narratives (2 Kings 2). Jews settled here after the Exile (Ezra 2:34; Neh 3:2; 7:36) – *T. es-Sultan (192142), 6 mi. W of Jordan River and 10 mi. NNW of Dead Sea, alongside a powerful spring* – **18, 20, 25, 28, 41–44, 43, 53, 54, 74, 75, 78, 78, 82, 90, 92, 93, 94, 94, 98, 106, 107, 110, 111, 112, 112, 117, 126, 131, 132, 138, 139, 144, 146, 204**

Jericho, Plain of – **92, 94, 138**

Jerusalem – *el-Quds/Jerusalem (172131)* – **13, 17, 18, 18, 21, 23, 24, 25, 28, 28, 33, 40–44, 43, 46, 47, 48, 53, 75, 80, 80, 82, 83, 88, 90, 91, 92, 94, 94, 96, 97, 98, 98, 102–5, 105, 109, 110, 111, 114, 116, 117, 118–24, 119, 120, 122, 123, 125, 126, 127, 128, 129–31, 130–32, 133, 134, 135, 136, 137, 138–42, 138, 142–45, 144, 146, 147–50, 149, 152–56, 154, 157, 159–62, 161, 164, 165, 167, 168, 169, 170, 171–77, 175–78, 179, 180, 182, 183–86, 185–87, 188–90, 189–92, 192–94, 195, 196–200, 204**

Jerusalem Plateau – **41, 42**

Jeshanah — Town in S Ephraim taken by Abijah of Judah from Jeroboam of Israel (2 Chron 13:19). A gate in Jerusalem was called Jeshanah Gate (Neh 3:6; 12:39); possibly road led from it to Jeshanah. Shen (1 Sam 7:12) is possibly a variant of Jeshanah (as LXX) – *Burj el-Isaneh (174156), 15.5 mi. N of Jerusalem* – **124, 126**

Jeshimon — Desert/wilderness area where David hid from Saul (1 Sam 23:19, 24; 26:1, 3) – *Dry, chalky wilderness, stretching from Ziph E and SE toward Dead Sea* – **43, 114**

Jeshua — Town in S Judah where Jews settled after the Exile (Neh 11:26) – *Uncertain; possibly T. es-Saweh/T. Jeshua (149076), 9 mi. ENE of Beersheba* – **144, 146**

Jezirah – **62, 62, 76, 80**

Jezreel (Issachar) — Town allotted to Issachar (Josh 19:18). Saul's troops camped near it in battle with Philistines (1 Sam 29:1–11). Later Ish-Bosheth ruled over area (2 Sam 2:9). It and the valley were included in fourth Solomonic district (1 Kings 4:12). Ahab had secondary palace there (18:45). Here Ahab took Naboth's vineyard (21:1). Site of Jehu's coup in which Joram and Jezebel were killed (2 Kings 9–10) – *Zerin/T. Yizreel (181218), 11 mi. WNW of Beth Shan and 8.5 mi. ESE of Megiddo* – **25, 33, 36, 38, 99, 99, 114, 115, 126, 127, 128, 129, 131**

Jezreel (Judah) — Town allotted to Judah (Josh 15:56). David's wife Ahinoam was from Jezreel (1 Sam 25:43; 27:3; 30:5; 2 Sam 2:2; 3:2) – *Unknown; probably about 8–10 mi. S of Hebron.*

Jezreel, Valley of — Large, triangular valley in N-central Israel. In Joshua's time (17:16) controlled by Canaanites. During days of Gideon, Midianites, Amalekites, and other eastern peoples raided and camped here (Judges 6:33). Mentioned in an oracle of Hosea (1:5) – *Valley that separates Hill Country of Manasseh from that of Galilee* – *Jezreel Valley 17, 18, 18, 27, 31, 32, 33, 33, 36, 37, 87, 88, 98, 99, 104, 105, 107, 117, 124, 131, 146, 151, 154, 157, 158, 163–66, 164*

Jogbehah — Town in Transjordan (Gilead) built up by Gad (Num 32:35). Gideon pursued Midianites in its direction (Judges 8:11) – *El-Jubeihat (231159), 7 mi. NW of Amman* – **101, 108**

Jokdeam — Town in hill country allotted to Judah (Josh 15:56). Possibly same as Jorkeam in 1 Chron 2:44 – *Unknown; probably in area 8–10 mi. S of Hebron.*

Jokmeam (east) – Town in fourth Solomonic district (1 Kings 4:12) – *Uncertain; possibly T. es-Samadi (196170) in Jordan Valley, 27 mi. S of Beth Shan* – **28, 38, 122**

Jokmeam (west) – Levitical city, evidently in vicinity of W Ephraim near Gezer and Beth Horon (1 Chron 6:68) – *Unknown.*

Jokneam – Canaanite town conquered by Israel (Josh 12:22). Border of Zebulun extended to ravine near it (19:11). Levitical city (21:34; in NIV translation of 1 Chron 6:77, even though it does not appear in Heb. text there) – *T. Qeimun/T. Yoqneam (160230), 7 mi. NW of Megiddo on S edge of Jezreel Valley at foot of Mt. Carmel* – **28, 31, 33, 36, 37, 75, 87, 88, 90, 95, 99, 102**

Joktan – **71**

Joktheel (Edom) – See Sela – **128, 129**

Joktheel (Judah) – Town in Shephelah allotted to Judah (Josh 15:38) – *Unknown.*

Joppa – Mediterranean port evidently allotted to Dan (Josh 19:46). Intermittently served as Judean port, for logs for first and second temples were shipped there from Lebanon (2 Chron 2:16; Ezra 3:7). Throughout much of OT period in non-Israelite hands. From here Jonah set sail (Jonah 1:3). Peter had his vision and received messengers from Cornelius here (Acts 9–11 passim). Mentioned frequently in extrabiblical literature – *Yafa/Yafo (126162), just S of modern Tel Aviv* – **17, 18, 18, 21, 25, 28, 46, 46, 47, 75, 84, 88, 90, 94, 100, 102, 105, 109, 117, 119, 120, 121, 122, 122, 123, 126, 132, 134, 135, 138, 143, 149, 150, 151, 154, 156, 157, 160, 161, 163, 164, 165, 170, 173, 174, 175, 176, 177, 177, 178, 187, 194**

Jordan (country) – **12, 13, 23**

Jordan (River) – The major river of Palestine. Flows from N to S, through Sea of Galilee to Dead Sea. Mentioned 181 times in OT, 15 times in NT – **16, 17, 18, 20, 23, 27, 28, 28, 29, 29, 30, 31, 31, 33, 34, 35, 36, 38, 43, 44, 52, 53, 54, 54, 77, 78, 79, 80, 81, 82, 91, 92, 93, 94, 97, 98, 98, 99, 99, 100, 101, 102, 103, 103, 105, 106–8, 109, 111, 112, 112, 114, 115, 118, 119, 119, 120, 122, 124, 126, 127, 129, 131, 138, 140, 144, 145, 146, 152, 156, 159, 160, 161, 162, 163, 166, 168, 169, 171, 172, 177, 188, 189, 204**

Jordan Valley – **23, 52, 53, 54, 77, 77, 79, 80, 101, 112, 122, 156, 159, 162, 166, 171, 172, 177, 189**

Jorkeam – If a place (1 Chron 2:44) and not a personal name, then possibly the same as Jokdeam of Josh 15:56 – *Unknown.*

Jotapata – **166, 167, 168, 177, 178**

Jotbah – Queen mother of Amon was from here (2 Kings 21:19) – *Kh. Jefat/H. Yodefat (176248), 9 mi. NNW of Nazareth.*

Jotbathah – Campsite of Israelites during wilderness wanderings (Num 33:33–34; Deut 10:7) – *Very uncertain; possibly Tabeh (139878), 5.5 mi. SW of Elath on W shore of Red Sea* – **132**

Judah – Son of Jacob whose descendants formed one of the 12 tribes. Bulk of Judah's territory was between Jerusalem and Beersheba. During Divided Monarchy, the S Kingdom was called Kingdom of Judah; later the territory became known as Judea – Judah **16, 17, 18, 19, 23, 27, 33, 39, 41–44, 43, 46, 47, 50, 52, 77, 79, 87, 96, 97, 98, 100, 102, 103, 104, 106, 108, 109, 111, 112, 113, 114–16, 119, 122, 122, 124, 125, 126, 127, 128, 128, 130–32, 131–36, 134, 137, 138, 138, 140, 141, 142, 144, 145, 146, 154, 188, 190, 192, 193, 196, 202**

Judah, Hill Country/Mountains of – **23, 27, 28, 42, 46, 47, 52, 77–79, 77, 87, 88, 96, 103, 100, 104, 106, 109, 113, 115, 121, 124, 128, 131, 135, 136, 140, 146, 154, 156, 188, 189**

Judea – Greco-Roman designation for territory/district/province that succeeded Davidic kingdom of Judah. Mentioned 43 times in the

NT, – **43, 140, 141, 143–46, 149, 150, 150, 151–56, 151, 154, 157, 158–63, 161, 163, 164, 166, 167, 170, 171, 172, 174–77, 175–78, 179, 180, 185**

Judean Desert/Wilderness of Judea – 41–44, **43, 47, 114, 114, 124, 155, 178, 179, 189, 189**

Julias – See Bethsaida – **168, 169, 171, 178**

Juttah – City in hill country allotted to Judah (Josh 15:55). Levitical city (21:16; NIV inserts "Juttah" into 1 Chron 6:59 [following some versions of the LXX], but the MT does not have the name) – *Yatta (158095), 5.5 mi. S of Hebron* – **97, 102, 134**

Kabir River – **63**

Kabzeel – Negev town allotted to Judah (Josh 15:21). One of David's warriors was from here (2 Sam 23:20; 1 Chron 11:22) – *Uncertain; formerly identified with Kh. Gharreh/T. Ira (148071), 8 mi. E of Beersheba. Also called Jekabzeel* – **97, 134**

Kadesh (Barnea) – Called Kadesh 14 times in OT and Kadesh Barnea 10 times. Mentioned in connection with Abraham (Gen 14:7; 16:14; 20:1). On S boundary of Canaan (Num 34:4; Josh 15:3). The spies returned to Israelite camp at Kadesh (Num 13:26). Moses' sister, Miriam, died here (20:1), as did Aaron at nearby Mt. Hor (v. 22). Israel camped here "many days" (Deut 1:46) – *Ein el-Qudeirat (096006), about 50 mi. SW of Beersheba* – **13, 16, 17, 18, 28, 49, 49, 60, 60, 78, 89, 91, 91, 92, 97, 102, 120, 125, 128, 201**

Kadesh, Desert of – Mentioned in Psalm 29:8. Since the setting of the Psalm seems to be N of Israel, the Kadesh referred to is probably Kedesh on the Orontes – *T. Nebi Mind (291444), about 75 mi. N of Damascus in Syria.*

Kafar Dan – **168**

Kain – Hill country town allotted to Judah (Josh 15:57) – *Kh. Bani Dar (164100), 3.5 mi. SE of Hebron* – **97, 134**

Kamon – Transjordanian town where the judge Jair was buried (Judges 10:5) – *Uncertain; possibly Qamm (218221), 11.5 mi. SE of the Sea of Galilee* – **107, 108**

Kanah (Asher) – Town allotted to Asher (Josh 19:28) – *Qana (178290), 7.5 mi. SE of Tyre in Lebanon* – **31, 32, 99, 132**

Kanah Ravine – Wadi draining W Ephraim and Manasseh and boundary between them (Josh 16:8; 17:9) – *Wadi Qana, which flows W out of Hill Country of Ephraim and Manasseh and joins the Nahal Shillo a few mi. W of Aphek* – **40, 96, 98**

Kanath – **53**

Kanish – **13, 80**

Karakum Desert – **148**

Karka – Settlement on SW boundary of Judah (Josh 15:3) – *Uncertain; possibly Ein el-Qeseimeh (089007), about 50 mi. SW of Beersheba in vicinity of Kadesh Barnea* – **97**

Karkor – Transjordanian site to which Zebah and Zalmunna fled from Gideon (Judges 8:10) – *Unknown* – **108**

Karm Abu Girg – **86**

Karnaim – Transjordanian city taken by Israel (Amos 6:13). Probably had replaced Ashtaroth (Karnaim) as regional center – *Sheikh Sa'd (247249), 23 mi. E of the Sea of Galilee* – **27, 28, 28, 29, 30, 93, 125, 126, 129, 132, 145, 145**

Karnak – **80, 81, 124**

Kartah – Levitical town in territory of Zebulun (Josh 21:34; MT of 1 Chron 6:77 does not have Kartah, see NIV note) – *Unknown.*

Kartan – Levitical town in territory of Naphtali (Josh 21:32) – *Uncertain; possibly the same*

as "Rakkath" of Josh 19:35 and Kiriathaim (Naphtali) 1 Chron 6:76 – **102**

Karun River – **65**

Kashmir – **149**

Kattath – Town allotted to Zebulun (Josh 19:15). Possibly same as Kitron (Judges 1:30) – *Unknown.*

Kavalla – See Neapolis (Greece) – **183**

Kebar River – Canal in ancient Babylon near which Nebuchadnezzar settled Jewish exiles (Ezek 1:3). Near it Ezekiel had some of his visions (1:1; 3:15, 23; 10:15, 20, 22; 43:3) – *Uncertain; possibly same as ancient "Naru Kabari" canal, which branched off from Euphrates NW of Babylon and rejoined it some 60 mi. S.*

Kedar – Arabian tribe S and SE of Israel, mentioned 10 times in OT – **141, 146**

Kedemoth – Transjordanian town assigned to Reuben (Josh 13:18). Levitical city (21:37; 1 Chron 6:79) – *Uncertain; possibly Aleiyan (233104), 20 mi. E of Dead Sea, N of Arnon River* – **92, 101, 102**

Kedemoth, Desert of – Wilderness region near Kedemoth from which Moses sent messengers to Sihon, king of Amorites (Deut 2:26) – **92, 92**

Kedesh (Issachar) – Levitical city in Issachar (1 Chron 6:72). See Kishion – *Unknown.*

Kedesh (Judah) – Town in Negev district of Judah (Josh 15:23) – *Unknown; some believe it to be identical to Kadesh Barnea, but not likely.*

Kedesh (Naphtali, Lower Galilee) – Home of Deborah's general, Barak (Judges 4:6, 9), who pursued Sisera toward it (4:11) – *Kh. Qedish/H. Qedesh (202237), 1 mi. W of S end of Sea of Galilee, overlooking sea* – **31, 34, 107, 107**

Kedesh (Naphtali, Upper Galilee) – Town conquered by Israel (Josh 12:22), allotted to Naphtali (19:37). Levitical city (21:32; 1 Chron 6:76) and city of refuge (Josh 20:7). Captured by Tiglath-Pileser III (2 Kings 15:29) – *T. Qades/T. Qedesh (199279), 17 mi. NNW of Sea of Galilee in Upper Galilee* – **32, 33, 77, 88, 90, 95, 99, 103, 107, 126, 129, 132, 133, 138, 177, 203**

Kedesh (on the Orontes) – **28, 62, 64, 87, 105, 106**

Kefar Hananiya – **166, 167**

Kefar Monash – **75**

Kehelathah – Israelite campsite during wilderness wanderings, between Rissah and Mt. Shepher (Num 33:22–23) – *Unknown.*

Keilah – Shephelah town allotted to Judah (Josh 15:44). David protected inhabitants from Philistines but had to flee when in danger of being handed to Saul (1 Sam 23). Jews settled here after the Exile (Neh 3:17–18) – *Kh. Qila (150113), 18 mi. SW of Jerusalem* – **46, 97, 105, 105, 113, 114, 114, 134, 144, 146**

Kenath – Transjordanian town captured by Nobah (Num 32:42), lost to Geshur and Aram (1 Chron 2:23) – *Qanawat (302241), 57 mi. E of the Sea of Galilee at the W foot of the Jebel Druze* – **29, 105**

Kephar Ammoni – Town allotted to Benjamin (Josh 18:24) – *Unknown; N of Jerusalem, possibly on E side of watershed.*

Kephirah – One of four "Gibeonite" (Hivite) cities that tricked Joshua into making covenant (Josh 9:17). Allotted to Benjamin (18:26). Resettled by Jews returning from exile (Ezra 2:25; Neh 7:29) – *Kh. el-Kefireh (160137), 8.5 mi. WNW of Jerusalem* – **94, 98, 134, 144**

Kerak – See Kir Hareseth – **25**

Kerem Ben Zimra – **78**

Kerioth (Moab) – Moabite town mentioned in prophetic oracles (Amos 2:2; Jer 48:24) – *El-Qereiyat (215105), 8 mi. E of Dead Sea.*

Kerioth Hezron – Negev town allotted to Judah (Josh 15:25); also called "Hazor" – *Uncertain; possibly Kh. el-Qaryatein/T.Qeriyot (161083), 12.5 mi. SSE of Hebron* – **97, 134**

Kerith Ravine – Elijah went here at time of prophesied drought (1 Kings 17:2–7) – *Unknown; probably a wadi E of Jordan River, some suggest the Wadi Jabesh* – **131**

Kerman – **143**

Kerti Huyuk – **181**

Kerub – Jews from here returned to Judah (Ezra 2:59; Neh 7:61) – *Unknown; in area of Babylonia.*

Kesalon – Town along W portion of Judah's N boundary (Josh 15:10) – *Kesla/Kesalon (154132), 11 mi. W of Jerusalem.*

Kesil – Town in Negev allotted to Judah (Josh 15:30). Probably same as Simeonite (19:4) Bethuel (1 Chron 4:30). See Bethuel.

Kestros River – **180**

Kesulloth – Town allotted to Issachar (Josh 19:18). Probably same as Kisloth Tabor in boundary description of Zebulun (v. 12) – *Iksal (180232), 2 mi. SE of Nazareth* – **99, 99**

Kezib – Town in Judean Shephelah where Shua gave birth to Shelah (Gen 38:5). See Aczib (Judah).

Khanazir – **45, 56, 75, 78, 81**

Khashabu – **105**

Khirbet Ayun Musa – See Nebo (Moab) – **75**

Khirbet el-Mahruq – **75**

Khirbet Ira – **42, 43**

Khirbet Iskander – **75**

Khirbet Izbet Sarta – See Ebenezer – **110**

Khirbet Nisya – **94**

Khirbet Qana – See Cana of Galilee – **34, 167**

Khirbet Rabud – See Debir – **90**

Khirbet Uza – See Ramoth Negev – **44**

Kibroth Hattaavah – "Graves of Desire." First Israelite camp after Mt. Sinai (Num 33:16–17). Here they craved food of Egypt and received quail; many died as punishment (11:34–35; Deut 9:22) – *Uncertain; probably in Sinai peninsula* – **91**

Kibzaim – Levitical city listed between Gezer and Beth Horon (Josh 21:22). Parallel list (1 Chron 6:68) has "Jokmeam," which may be same. See Jokmeam (W).

Kidon, threshing floor of – Site between Kiriath Jearim and Jerusalem where Uzzah died after touching the ark (1 Chron 13:9). Called "threshing floor of Nacon" in 2 Sam 6:6 – *Unknown.*

Kidron (fortress) – **156**

Kidron Valley – Valley immediately E of Jerusalem. David crossed it as he fled from Absalom (2 Sam 15:23). Solomon commanded Shimei not to cross it on pain of death (2 Kings 2:37). Site where illicit cult objects were destroyed during reforms of Asa, Hezekiah, and Josiah (1 Kings 15:13; 2 Kings 23:4, 6, 12; 2 Chron 15:16; 29:16; 30:14). Also mentioned by Jeremiah (31:40). Jesus and his disciples crossed it going from Upper Room to Garden of Gethsemane (John 18:1) – *N-S valley E of Jerusalem called (from N to S) Wadi ej-Joz, Wadi Sitti Maryam, Wadi Tantur Farun, Wadi Silwan, and eventually Wadi en-Nar, which flows SE through Judean Desert into Dead Sea* – **119, 120, 156, 189, 190, 190, 191, 195, 197, 200**

Kilmad – Mentioned after Asshur and other places as having traded with Tyre (Ezek 27:23) – *Unknown; probably not close to ancient Israel.*

Kinah – Negev town allotted to Judah (Josh 15:22) – *Uncertain; possibly Kh. Taiyib/H. Tov (163081), 19 mi. ENE of Beersheba* – **134**

King's Garden – Zedekiah and his troops fled Jerusalem via gate near it (2 Kings 25:2; Jer 39:4; 52:7). Nehemiah's workers repaired the wall of Jerusalem near it – *Uncertain; possibly S, E, or SE of Jerusalem in Kidron Valley. Possibly watered from overflow of Pool of Siloam at S tip of ancient Jerusalem.*

King's Highway – While in Kadesh (Barnea), Israel requested permission from king of Edom to use this route (Num 20:17). They made a similar request of Sihon, king of the Amorites, who ruled from Heshbon (21:22 and possibly Deut 2:27) – *First reference possibly to E-W route called Darb es-Sultan, which runs through Nahal Zin toward Edom. Second reference may be to portion of N-S Transjordanian route that connects Edom/Arabia with points N* – **23, 91, 92, 92, 127**

King's Valley – Valley of Shaveh, where Abram met king of Sodom after victory over invading kings is called "King's Valley" (Gen 14:17). Absalom erected pillar in "King's Valley" as a memorial (2 Sam 18:18) – *Uncertain; possibly in vicinity of Jerusalem if meeting with Melchizedek took place soon after above encounter and if Salem = Jerusalem (see Gen 14)* – **81, 189**

Kinnereth – Town allotted to Naphtali (Josh 19:35). Ben-Hadad conquered it (or the area; 1 Kings 15:20) – *Kh. Ureime/T. Kinrot (200252), on NW shore of Sea of Galilee. Called "Gennesaret" in NT* – **28, 31, 34, 35, 90, 91, 95, 99, 101, 126, 127, 129**

Kinnereth, Sea of – Common name for Sea of Galilee (Num 34:11; Josh 12:3; 13:27). Abbreviated form evidently used in Deut 3:17 and Josh 11:2, although these references could be to town. See Galilee, Sea of; Gennesaret, Lake of – **35, 91, 93, 95, 100, 101, 101, 104, 109, 129**

Kios – Paul's ship spent night off Kios (Acts 20:15) – *Greek island, 5 mi. W of central W shore of Asia Minor (Turkey)* – **185, 185**

Kir – Place to which Tiglath-Pileser III of Assyria carried captives from Damascus (2 Kings 16:9). The Arameans originated from Kir (Amos 9:7). Mentioned in Amos 1:4 and Isa 22:6 – *Usually thought to be in Mesopotamia but identity unknown.*

Kir Hareseth – Evidently chief city of Moab during period of Monarchy. Attacked by Israel, Judah, and Edom (2 Kings 3:25). Mentioned in prophetic oracles (Isa 16:7, 11; Jer 48:31, 36), often in parallel with Moab. Called "Kir in Moab" in Isa 15:1 – *El-Kerak (217066), 10 mi. E of Dead Sea* – **55, 56, 128**

Kiriath – See Kiriath Jearim.

Kiriathaim (Naphtali) – Levitical town in Naphtali (1 Chron 6:76) – *Uncertain; possibly same as Kartan in Josh 21:32.*

Kiriathaim (Reuben) – Transjordanian town assigned to Reuben (Num 32:37; Josh 13:19). Mentioned in prophetic oracles against Moab (Jer 48:1, 23; Ezek 25:9) – *Uncertain; possibly Qaryat el-Mekhaiyet (220128), 9 mi. E of Dead Sea* – **101**

Kiriath Arba – Older name (Judges 1:10) for Hebron (Gen 23:2; 35:27; Josh 14:15; 15:13, 54; 20:7; 21:11), also used after Babylonian exile (Neh 11:25). See Hebron – **84, 144, 146, 201**

Kiriath Baal – See Kiriath Jearim.

Kiriath Huzoth – Town in Moab to which Balak took Balaam (Num 22:39) – *Unknown, probably E of N end of Dead Sea.*

Kiriath Jearim – Town in old Hivite league with which Israel made treaty (Josh 9:17). Allotted to Judah (15:60) but on N border of Judah (v. 9) and SW border of Benjamin (18:14–15). Danites camped in the area (Judges 18:12). Later the ark was stored here (1 Sam 6:21, 7:1–2) until David brought it to Jerusalem (1 Chron 13:5–6; 2 Chron 1:4). Jeremiah (26:20) mentions a prophet from here. People from here returned to Judah after the Exile (Ezra 2:25; Neh 7:29). Also called "Kiriath Baal" (Josh 15:60; 18:14), "Baalah of Judah" (Josh 15:9, 10; 2 Sam 6:2; 1 Chron 13:6), and possibly "Kiriath" (Josh 18:28), "Jaar" (Ps 132:6), and as "Baalath" (2 Chron 8:6; 1 Kings 9:18) – *Deir el-Azar/T. Qiryat Yearim (159135); 8.5 mi. W of Jerusalem* – **18, 43, 48, 94, 94, 97, 98, 100, 110, 111, 117, 118, 121, 126, 144, 189, 192, 201**

Kiriath Sannah – See Debir (Hill Country of Judah).

Kiriath Sepher – See Debir (Hill Country of Judah).

Kir (in) Moab – Isa 15:1. See Kir Hareseth – **28, 28, 117, 120, 132**

Kish – **73**

Kishion – Town allotted to Issachar (Josh 19:20). Levitical city (21:28; the parallel in 1 Chron 6:72 has "Kedesh") – *El-Khirba/T. Qishyon (187229), 6.5 mi. SE of Nazareth near foot of S slope of Mt. Tabor* – **90, 99, 102**

Kishon River – River that drains Jezreel Valley from E to NW. Here Deborah and Barak fought Canaanites (Judges 4:7, 13; 5:21; Ps 83:9) and Elijah slaughtered prophets of Baal (1 Kings 18:40) – *Nahr el-Muqatta/Nahal Qishon* – **31, 32, 36, 99, 107, 107, 131**

Kisloth Tabor – See Kesulloth – **99**

Kitlish – Shephelah town allotted to Judah (Josh 15:40) – *Unknown.*

Kitron – Town in Zebulun from which Canaanites were not driven out (Judges 1:30). Possibly same as Kattath (Josh 19:15) – *Unknown* – **99**

Kittim – Descendant of Javan (Gen 10:4; 1 Chron 1:7) and ancient name for Cyprus (Num 24:24; Jer 2:4) and for city located on its SE coast. See Cyprus – **71, 143**

Kizil Kum Desert – **148**

Knossos – See Cnossus – **13**

Koa – Unknown people and/or country (Ezek 23:23), possibly NE of Babylonia.

Kode – **87**

Kom Abu Bille – **86**

Kom el-Hisn – **81, 86**

Korazin – Town visited by Jesus and cursed by him (Matt 11:21; Luke 10:13) – *Kh. Keraze (203257), 2 mi. N of Capernaum and Sea of Galilee* – **35, 34, 78, 168, 169**

Kue – Place from which Solomon purchased horses (1 Kings 10:28; 2 Chron 1:16) – *Roughly same area as Cilicia, in SE Turkey* – **121, 123, 137**

Kufrinia – **25**

Kumidi – **87, 105**

Kurkur Oasis – **58**

Kursi – See Gadarenes, region of – **34, 170, 171**

Laban (Sinai) – Israelite campsite (Deut 1:1). Possibly same as Libnah (Sinai) – *Unknown.*

Lacedaemon – **187**

Lachish – Town in Judean Shephelah (Josh 15:39) whose king was defeated by Joshua (Josh 10; 12:11). Fortified by Rehoboam (2 Chron 11:9). Amaziah of Judah fled here but was assassinated (2 Kings 14:19; 2 Chron 25:27). Captured by Sennacherib of Assyria (2 Kings

18:14, 17; 19:8; 2 Chron 32:9; Isa 36:2; 37:8; Mic 1:13) and by Nebuchadnezzar (Jer 34:7). Jews settled here after the Exile (Neh 11:30) – *T. ed-Duweir/T. Lachish (135108), 29 mi. WSW from Jerusalem* – **43, 46,** 48, 75, **75, 78, 82, 90, 94, 94,** 95, **97, 100,** 105, **105, 109, 125, 128,** 129, **132, 134,** 135, 136, 138, **138, 143,** 146, 203

Ladder of Tyre – See Rosh HaNiqra/Haniqra – **151,** 152

Lagash – 76, 78

Lahmas – Shephelah town allotted to Judah (Josh 15:40) – *Unknown.*

Laish – Older name for Dan (Judges 18:7, 14, 27, 29); also called Leshem (Josh 19:47). See Dan – **80,** 84, **84,** 85, **88, 90,** 93, **95,** 101, 203

Laishah – Town N or NNE of Jerusalem along traditional invasion route from the N (Isa 10:30) – *Unknown.*

Lakkum – Town on S boundary of Naphtali (Josh 19:33) – *Uncertain; possibly Kh. el-Mansurah/Kh. Kush (202233), 1.7 mi. SW of Sea of Galilee* – 99

Lambesis – 187

Laodicea – Greco-Roman city mentioned in letter to church at Colosse (2:1; 4:13, 15–16); one of the seven churches of Revelation (1:11; 3:14) – *Eski Hissar on S bank of Lycus River in SW Turkey, 8 mi. NW of Colosse* – **175, 181,** 185, **185, 187**

Larissa – 187

Larsa – 80, 137

Lasea – Paul's ship passed this port on way to Rome (Acts 27:8) – *Probably antiquity site 5 mi. E of Fair Havens on S-central coast of Crete* – 186

Lasha – Town mentioned in boundary description of Canaanite settlement (Gen 10:19) – *Uncertain; some seek it in vicinity of Sodom and Gomorrah (SE of Dead Sea) because of context; others suggest name may be corruption of Laish/Leshem/Dan (in N Israel).*

Lasharon – King of Lasharon was defeated by Joshua (12:18) – *Uncertain; possibly LXX reading "a king of Aphek of Sharon" is to be preferred? If an independent town, then unidentified.*

Lashon – See Lisan – 44

Latium – 186

Lebanese Beqa – See Beqa – 20, 28, 31, 32

Lebanon – Region N of Israel known for its high, often snow-covered, mountains and fertile valleys. Its cedar forests were famous. At times serves as symbol of stability, strength, and fertility. Mentioned 70 times in Bible – *Approximate area of modern country of Lebanon, excluding the narrow coastal plain (= Phoenicia), but possibly including portion of W Syria* – 12, **13,** 14, 52, 62–64, **62,** 67, 72, 73, 87, 121, 142, 148

Lebanon, Mount – 62, 72

Lebanon Mountains – 63, 64, 67, 73, 121, 140

Lebaoth – Town in Negev allotted to Judah (Josh 15:32). Possibly same as Beth Lebaoth (19:6) and Beth Biri (1 Chron 4:31) – *Unknown.*

Lebo Hamath – City on S edge of kingdom of Hamath, mentioned in Bible as being on N boundary of Canaan (Num 13:21; 34:8; Ezek 47:15, 20; 48:1). N-most point of "ideal" Israel (Josh 13:5; Judges 3:3; 1 Chron 13:5; 1 Kings 8:65; 2 Kings 14:25; 2 Chron 7:8; Amos 6:14) – *Lebweh (277397), in Lebanese Beqa (Valley), 45 mi. N of Damascus* – 28, **62, 88,** 91, **91,** 104, **107, 117,** 118, 121, **123,** 131, **145**

Lebonah – Town in Ephraim, S of Shechem but N of Bethel (Judges 21:19) – *El-Lubban (173164), 10 mi. SSW of Shechem* – **28, 38,** 98, 104, **105,** 154, 170, 172

Lebweh – 91

Lechaeum – **182,** 184

Lega, the – **29**

Lehi – Place where Samson killed 1,000 Philistines (Judges 15:9, 14, 19) – *Uncertain; possibly near Etam of Judah in Hill Country of Judah.*

Leja – 30

Leontopolis – 175

Lesbos – 175, **185, 185**

Leshem – Older name for Dan (Josh 19:47). Also called Laish. See Dan – 85, **100,** 101

Levant – 63, **72,** 74, 82–85, 87, 105, 106, 108, 127, 146–48, **147,** 151, 156, 196, 203, 204

Libnah (Judah) – Shephelah town conquered by Joshua (Josh 10; 12:15) and allotted to Judah (15:42). Levitical city (Josh 21:13; 1 Chron 6:57). Revolted against Judean rule during reign of Jehoram (2 Kings 8:22; 2 Chron 21:10). Sennacherib laid siege to it (2 Kings 19:8; Isa 37:8). Mother of last Judean king, Zedekiah, was from here (2 Kings 23:32; 24:18; Jer 52:1) – *Disputed, but possibly Kh. T. el-Beida/H. Lavnin (145116), 20 mi. SW of Jerusalem, 8 mi. NE of Lachish* – **46,** 94, 95, **97,** 102, 128, **128, 134,** 136

Libnah (Sinai or Negev) – Israelite campsite during wilderness wanderings (Num 33:20). Possibly identical with "Laban" (Deut 1:1) – *Unknown.*

Libya – Mentioned in prophetic oracles (Ezek 30:5; Nah 3:9). Jews from there were present in Jerusalem on Day of Pentecost (Acts 2:10) – *in N Africa, W of Egypt; Libya* – **13,** 57, 72, 143, **186, 187**

Lisan – See Lashon – **43,** 44, 51, 128

Lisht – **58,** 59

Litani/Litanni River – **29,** 30, **31,** 32, 62, **62,** 63, 64, 95, **95,** 99, **99,** 100, 104

Livias/Julias – 171

Lod – Town built by Benjamite (1 Chron 8:12) to which Jews returned after the Exile (Ezra 2:33; Neh 7:37; 11:35). Called Lydda in NT era – *El-Ludd/Lod (140151), 11 mi. SE of Joppa in coastal plain* – **46,** 144

Lo Debar – Home of Makir who housed Mephibosheth (2 Sam 9:4–5) and brought provisions to David when he fled from Absalom (17:27). Probably reconquered by Israel during days of Jeroboam II (Amos 6:13) – *Uncertain; possibly Umm ed-Dabar (207219), 10 mi. SSE of Sea of Galilee, E of Jordan River in Jordan Valley* – **54,** 119, **119, 126, 129**

Los Angeles – 23

Lower Egypt – Mentioned in prophetic oracles (Isa 11:11; Jer 44:1) – *Nile delta region, N of Cairo* – 57, **58,** 59, 61, **72,** 73

Lud – 71, 143

Lugdunenis – 163

Lugdunum – 187

Luhith – People from Moab are said to have fled in direction of this town (Isa 15:5; Jer 48:5) – *Uncertain; possibly Katrabba (209070), 6 mi. E of the Lisan of the Dead Sea or 6 mi. WNW of Kerak.*

Lusitania – 163

Luz – Canaanite town where Jacob met with God and renamed it Bethel (Gen 28:19; 35:6; 48:3). On boundary between Ephraim and Benjamin (Josh 16:2; 18:13). Bethel was captured by the house of Joseph (Judges 1:23). It is possible that Bethel (originally a worship center?) and Luz (the original town) were nearby each other but distinct (see NIV note to Josh 16:2). See Bethel (Benjamin).

Luz (Hittite) – Town founded by survivor of Canaanite Luz in "land of the Hittites"

(Judges 1:26) – *Unknown; probably somewhere in Lebanon/Syria.*

Lycaonia – 163, 181, **181**

Lycia – Roman province/region on W portion of S coast of Asia Minor. Paul changed ships at port of Myra in Lycia (Acts 27:5) on his voyage to Rome – *Remote, rugged inland and coastal region in SW Turkey; NE of Rhodes* – **147,** 148, **149,** 150, 155, **181, 182,** 183, **185,** 186, **186**

Lydda – Town where Peter healed Aeneas the paralytic (Acts 9:32, 35, 38). See Lod – **154,** 156, **157,** 160, **161,** 167, 170, 174, **176, 178, 187**

Lydia – Country in W Turkey, with Sardis as capital, whose most famous king was Croesus. Possibly also called "Lud" (Gen 10:13; 1 Chron 1:11). NIV has four references to Lydia and Lydians (Isa 66:19; Jer 46:9; Ezek 27:10; 30:5); however, these may really be to "Lud" (Heb.) and refer to an African people/nation – 140, 141, **142, 143,** 147, 148

Lystra – Lycaonian city visited by Paul and Barnabas (Acts 14:6, 8, 21) on first journey. Here they healed a crippled man, but the people turned on them and Paul was stoned and left for dead. Paul revisited Lystra on his second (16:1) and probably third (18:23) journeys. It seems that Timothy was from Lystra (16:1–5; 2 Tim 3:11) – *Mound N of Turkish village of Hatun Sarai in S central Turkey* – 181, **181, 182,** 183, **187**

Maacah – Small Aramean (Syrian) kingdom in N Israel whose territory was assigned to the half-tribe of Manasseh (Josh 12:5; 13:11), although its inhabitants were not driven out (13:13). Initially David's adversary (2 Sam 10:6, 8; 1 Chron 19:7) but became his vassal – *NE portion of Huleh Valley and NW slopes of Golan Heights* – 29, **29, 117,** 118, **119**

Maan – 56, **56**

Maarath – Hill country town allotted to Judah (Josh 15:59) – *Unknown; in region of Halhul and Beth Zur.*

Mabarot – 78

Macedonia – Roman province in N Greece, mentioned 23 times in the NT. Paul visited it on his second and third journeys. Paul refers to province and a number of Macedonian Christians in his letters (Rom, 1 and 2 Cor, Phil, 1 Thess, 1 Tim). Important cities included Philippi, Thessalonica, and Berea – *Mountainous region in N Greece, S Yugoslavia, and S Albania* – 143, **143,** 147, **147,** 149, **163,** 180, **181, 182,** 183–85, **185–87**

Machaerus – 157, **161,** 163, 164, **164,** 167, 170, 171, **178,** 179

Machbenah – Calebite settlement (1 Chron 2:49) – *Unknown; probably S of Hebron.*

Machpelah – Place near Hebron. Here a field, trees, and a cave were purchased by Abraham. Abraham, Isaac, and Jacob and their spouses (Sarah, Rebekah, and Leah) were buried there (Gen 23:9, 17, 19; 25:9; 49:30; 50:30) – *Haram el-Khalil in modern Hebron (160103)* – 80

Madai – 71

Madaurus – 187

Madmannah – Negev town allotted to Judah (Josh 15:31). Probably same as Beth Marcaboth in Josh 19:15 – *Kh. Tatrit (143084), 9 mi. NE of Beersheba* – **97, 134**

Madmen – Town mentioned in oracle against Moab (Jer 48:2) – *Uncertain; possibly Kh. Dimna (217077), 10 mi. E of Dead Sea in Jordan, 7.5 mi. N of Kerak.*

Madmenah – Town N of Jerusalem on line of traditional invasion route from the N (Isa 10:31) – *Unknown; probably S of Anathoth.*

Madon – Galilean town whose king, Jobab, assisted Jabin of Hazor in battle against

Joshua (Josh 11:1; 12:19) – *Uncertain; possibly same as Merom* – 95, **95**

Magadan – Jesus and disciples went to "vicinity of Magadan" after feeding of 4,000 (Matt 15:39). Parallel text (Mark 8:9) has "Dalmanutha" – *Uncertain; possibly Majdal (198247), 3 mi. NW of Tiberias on NW shore of Sea of Galilee* – 168, **168**

Magdala – Mary, one of Jesus' followers, was from here (John 19:25; 20:1, 18; and "Magdalene" 9 times in NT) – *Uncertain; possibly same as Magadan/Dalmanutha (NT) and Taricheae (Josephus)* – **34**, 35, 168, **168**

Maghara – 89

Magibsh – Town settled by Jews after return from exile (Ezra 2:30) – *Unknown.*

Magnesia – 148, 152, 187

Magog – Place or a people ruled by "Gog" (Ezek 39:3, 6) – *Uncertain; possibly Magog simply means "land of Gog," although some identify it with ancient kingdom of Lydia in W Turkey. In Revelation, Gog and Magog represent the heathen opponents of Messiah (20:8).*

Mahalab – 135

Mahanaim – Place where on return to Canaan Jacob met angels of God (Gen 32:2). On border between Gad and Manasseh (Josh 13:26, 30), but served as Levitical city in Gad (Josh 21:38; 1 Chron 6:80). Here Abner set up Ish-bosheth as king (2 Sam 2:8, 12, 29). David fled there when Absalom revolted (2 Sam 17:24, 27; 19:32; 1 Kings 2:8). One of Solomon's district centers (1 Kings 4:14) – *Uncertain; possibly edh-dhahab el-Gharbi (214177), 7 mi. E of Jordan River, N of Jabbok, or possibly T. er-Reheil (228177), 15.5 mi. E of Jordan River, N of Jabbok* – 52, **53**, **54**, **84**, **93**, 101, **101**, 102, 116, 117, 119, **119**, **122**, **126**

Mahaneh Dan – "Camp of Dan." Campsite at which 600 Danites camped before moving N (Judges 18:12). Probably W of Kiriath Jearim. In Samson's day evidently located between Zorah and Eshtaol (Judges 13:25) – *Uncertain; in N Shephelah in Zorah, Eshtaol, Kiriath Jearim area* – 109

Maka – 143

Makaz – One of several towns that formed second administrative distict of Solomon (1 Kings 4:9) – *Uncertain; probably in old Danite region in N Shephelah and/or N Philistia.*

Maked – 154

Makheloth – Israelite wilderness campsite between Haradah and Tahath (Num 33:25–26) – *Unknown.*

Makhtesh Ramon – 49

Makkedah – Five Amorite kings hid in cave of Makkedah and were captured by Joshua (Josh 10). This Shephelah town was captured (12:16) and allotted to Judah (15:41) – *Kh. el-Kum (146104), 8.5 mi. W of Hebron* – 95, **94**, **97**

Malatha – 157, 163, 164, **164**

Malatya Mountains – 62, 65

Malta – Island (18 x 9 mi.) where Paul was shipwrecked on way to Rome (Acts 28:1), called Melita by Greeks and Romans – *Malta, in Mediterranean, 58 mi. S of Sicily* – **186**, 187

Mampsis – 28

Mamre – Place near Hebron where Abraham and Isaac camped (Gen 13:18; 18:1; 35:27). The cave of Machpelah was "near" Mamre (23:17, 19; 25:9; 49:30; 50:13) – *Uncertain; possibly Ramat el-Khalil (160107), 2.5 mi. N of Hebron* – **84**

Manach – Hill country town allotted to Judah (Josh 15:59b; LXX) – *Possibly same as Manahath.*

Manahath – Town to which some Benjamites from Geba were carried captive (1 Chron 8:6; cf. 2:54). Maybe same as Manach – *El-Malhah/Manahat (167128), 4 mi. SW of Jerusalem* – **134**

Manasseh – Son of Joseph and Israelite tribe. Mentioned over 141 times in OT. Settled in hills S of Jezreel Valley and N of Ephraim, and in Gilead E of Jordan River – **17**, **18**, 19, 36–40, **38**, 42, 52, 54, 77, 87, 97–99, **98**, 101, **101**, **102**, 104, 107, 108, 115, 118, 122, 131, 132, 135, 136, 202, 203

Manasseh, Hill Country of – 38, **39**, 40, 77, 82, **103**, 104

Maon – Town in hill country allotted to Judah (Josh 15:55). Nabal, who was antagonistic toward David, was from Maon (1 Sam 25:2); David married his widow, Abigail – *Kh. Main (162090), 8 mi. SSE of Hebron* – 42, 43, 44, **97**, 114, **114**, **134**

Maon, Desert/Wilderness of – Wilderness area E and SE of Maon where David hid from Saul (1 Sam 23:24–25; 25:1) – **114**

Maracanda – 148

Marah – Oasis, about three-day journey from Egypt. Here Moses tossed piece of wood into the bitter ("Marah") water that became sweet (Exod 15:23; Num 33:8–9) – *Uncertain; possibly Bir Marah, 10 mi. E of Suez in W central Sinai; alternatively Ein Hawarah, 47 mi. SE of Suez* – 89

Maralah – Town on W border of Zebulun (Josh 19:11) – *Uncertain; possibly T. el-Ghaltah/T. Reala (166232), on NW edge of Jezreel Valley, 7 mi. NNW of Megiddo; or possibly T. Thorah/T. Shor (166228), 5 mi. NNW of Megiddo* – 99, **99**

Marathon – 143, **143**, 147, **147**

Mare Caspium – See Caspian Sea.

Mare Internum – See Mediterranean Sea.

Mareshah – Shephelah town allotted to Judah (Josh 15:44) and fortified by Rehoboam (2 Chron 11:8). Asa of Judah fought Zerah the Ethiopian in vicinity (14:9–10). In days of Jehoshaphat, Dodavahu of Mareshah prophesied (2 Chron 20:37). Mentioned in the prophecy of Micah (1:15). During Hellenistic and Roman periods it was an important center known as Marisa – *T. Sandahannah/T. Maresha (140111), 13 mi. NW of Hebron in Shephelah* – **43**, **46**, 48, **97** 125, 128, **128**, **134**, 144, 174

Margiana – 143

Mari – 13, 14, **62**, 63, **65**, 67, **72**, 76, 77, **77**, **78**, **80**, 84, **84**, 203

Marisa – See Mareshah – 48, **150**, 151, **151**, 152, 154, **154**, 156, **157**, 158, 174

Marmara, Sea of – **182**, 183

Maroth – Mentioned in prophecy of Micah (1:12) – *Uncertain; evidently in Judean Shephelah.*

Masada – 43, **43**, 45, **49**, 157, 161, **161**, 162, 164, **164**, 167, **178**, 179

Mashal – See Mishal.

Masrekah – Royal city of Edom associated with Samlah (Gen 36:36; 1 Chron 1:47) – *Unknown.*

Massaga – 148

Massah – Place near Horeb and Rephidim where Israelites complained about lack of water. Moses "struck" the rock and water came out (Exod 17:7; incident referred to in Deut 6:16; 9:22; 33:8 and Ps 95:8) – *Unknown; somewhere in Sinai.*

Masuate – 132

Mattanah – Israelite campsite on journey to the plains of Moab (Num 21:18–19) – *Uncertain; probably in Jordan, E of Dead Sea and N of Arnon Gorge.*

Mauretania – 163, 187

Mayan Barukh – 78

Mecca – 22, 51, **58**, 60

Meconah – Town settled by Jews after the Exile (Neh 11:28) – *Uncertain; possibly in NW Negev or Shephelah of Judah* – 146

Medeba – Moabite town captured from Sihon (Num 21:30) and allotted to Reuben (Josh 13:9, 16). Joab captured it (1 Chron 19:7). Mentioned in oracle against Moab (Isa 15:2). Fought over by Moab and Israel on number of occasions – *Madeba (225124), in Jordan, 20 mi. S of Amman, 12.5 mi. E of Dead Sea* – **17**, 23, 52, **53**, 55, **56**, **101**, **117**, 118, **119**, 125, 127, **132**, **157**, 158, **161**, **170**

Medes – 142

Media – Ancient homeland of Medes, SW of Caspian Sea but NE of Zagros Mountains. Media/Medes/Mede are mentioned 20 times in OT, exclusively at end of OT period. Persians took control of Medes; their king was called "king of the Medes and Persians" – 130, 133, 137, 142, **143**, 153, **175**

Medina – 51, 58

Mediterranean Sea – 12, **13**, 16, **17**, 18, **18**, 21, 23–26, **28**, **31**, 32, 33, **33**, 37–40, **38**, 42, 44, 46, **46**, 49, **49**, 51, 56, 57, **58**, 59, 60, **60**, 62, **62**, 63, 64, 65, **72**, 75, **75**, **78**, **80–82**, 83, 84, 88, **88–90**, 91, **91**, **92**, 94, 96, 97, 98, 99, 100, **100**, **102**, **103** 105, **107**, 109, 111, 114, **117**, 119, 120, 121, 122, **123**, 124, **125**, 130 **128–32**, **134**, 135, **137**, **138**, **141–45**, **147–51**, 148, 150, 151, 152, **157**, 159, 160, 161, **161**, 162, 163, **163**, **164**, **167**, **168**, 169, **170**, 175, **176–78**, 180 181, **182**, 184, 187, **185–87**, 202

Megiddo – Major Canaanite city captured by Joshua (12:21) and allotted to Manasseh (17:11; 1 Chron 7:29), who was not able to take possession of it (Judges 1:27). Evidently came under Israelite control under David, for it was a district capital of Solomon (1 Kings 4:12), who fortified it (9:15). Ahaziah of Judah died here (2 Kings 9:27) as did King Josiah (23:29, 30; 2 Chron 35:22). Mentioned in an oracle of Zechariah (12:11) – *T. el-Mutesellim/T. Megiddo (167221), on SW edge of Jezreel Valley, guarding important pass through Carmel Range* – 13, 21, 27, 28, **28**, **31**, **33**, 36, 37, 38, 61, **72**, 74, 75, **75**, **78**, **80**, **82**, 83, 87, **88**, **90**, **91**, 95, 97, 98, 99, **99**, **103**, 105, **105**, 107, **107**, 109, **114**, 116, **117**, 119, **120**, 121, 122, **123**, 125, 126, **129**, 132, **137**, 138, **138**, 145, **145**, 206

Megiddo, mountain of – See Armegeddon – 36

Megiddo, waters of – Wadi in vicinity of Megiddo and Taanach where Canaanite kings traditionally divided spoils of war (Judges 5:19).

Me Jarkon – "Waters of the Jarkon." Place allotted to Dan (Josh 19:46) – *Uncertain, and text is difficult. May refer to Nahr el-Auja/N. Yarkon, which flows from near Aphek W to Mediterranean at N Tel Aviv* – 100, **100**

Melos – 175

Memphis – Capital of Egypt during Old Kingdom (third millennium B.C.); important city and burial grounds during most periods. Mentioned in prophetic literature of the OT, usually in negative light (Isa 19:13; Jer 2:16; 46:14; Ezek 30:13, 16). Some exiles from Judah settled there (Jer 44:1) – *Area in and around Mit Rahinah on W bank of Nile, 13 mi. S of Cairo* – **13**, **72**, 73, 74, 79, **80**, 86, 89, 136, **137**, 141, **141**, **142**, 147, 148, 175

Menahemya – 78

Mephaath – Transjordanian town allotted to Reuben (Josh 13:18). Levitical city (21:37; 1 Chron 6:79). Mentioned in oracle against Moab (Jer 48:21) – *Uncertain; possibly T. Jawah (239140), 7 mi. S of Amman in Jordan* – 101, 102

Merathaim, land of – Symbolic name for Babylonia (Jer 50:21) meaning "double rebellion." Name seems to be wordplay on Babylonian "bitter river."

Meribah – Place near rock at Horeb (= Sinai?) where Israelites grumbled and Moses struck the rock so that water came out (Exod 17:7; Ps 95:8) – *Unknown; in Sinai, E of Red Sea.*

Meribah, waters of – Place near Kadesh Barnea where Moses struck the rock rather than speaking to it as God had commanded (Num 20:13, 24; 27:14; Deut 33:8; Ps 81:7; 106:32) – *In vicinity of Kadesh Barnea.*

Meribah Kadesh – Alternate name for "waters of Meribah" (Deut 32:51; Ezek 47:19; 48:28) – **104**

Merom, Waters of – Place in (Upper?) Galilee where Joshua defeated Canaanite forces led by king of Hazor (Josh 11:5, 7) – *Uncertain; possibly T. el-Khirbeh (190275), in S Lebanon, 19 mi. SE of Tyre, but Qarn Hattin/H. Qarne Hittim (193245), 10 mi. ENE of Nazareth, seems more probable* – **95, 95, 132**

Meron – **78**

Meron, Mount – **18, 25, 31, 32, 168, 171**

Meronoth – Town from which Jadon came to help Nehemiah build wall of Jerusalem (Neh 3:7). One of David's servants was evidently from here as well (1 Chron 27:30) – *Uncertain; probably near Gibeah, N of Jerusalem in Benjamin.*

Meroth – **164**

Meroz – Village cursed because of failure to assist forces of Deborah against Canaanites (Judges 5:23) – *Uncertain; probably in vicinity of Jezreel Valley.*

Mesad Hasidim – **170**

Mesha – One of the limits (town? country? region?) of area where descendants of Joktan lived (Gen 10:30) – *Unknown; possibly in Arabia.*

Meshech – Person and tribal name of group that settled in mountainous area SE of Black Sea. Known in biblical text as remote and barbaric (Ps 120:5; Ezek 27:13; 32:26; 38:2; 39:1) – **71**

Meshed – **75, 143**

Mesopotamia – **14, 62, 65–68, 65, 70, 72, 72, 73, 75, 76, 84, 85, 87, 106, 121, 136, 140, 141, 142, 149, 150, 175, 180, 181, 186, 203**

Metheg Ammah – "Bridle of the mother city." Taken by David from Philistines (2 Sam 8:1). Parallel passage (1 Chron 18:1) has Gath – *Unknown if not an alternate name for Gath.*

Metulla – **95**

Me Yarkon – **100**

Mezad Zohar – **43, 44**

Micmash – Village in tribal territory of Benjamin where Philistines mustered their troops against Israel. Jonathan and armor bearer attacked Philistine camp here (1 Sam 13–14; mentioned 7 times). Along traditional N invasion route to Jerusalem near Mukhmas (Isa 10:28). Jews returning from exile settled here (Ezra 2:27; Neh 7:31; 11:31) – *Kh. el-Hara el-Fawqa (176142), 7.5 mi. NNE of Jerusalem* – **18, 28, 43, 43, 111, 112, 112, 126, 134, 144, 154, 155, 204**

Micmethath – Town on boundary between Ephraim and Manasseh (Josh 16:6; 17:7) – *Uncertain; possibly Kh. Makhneh el-Foqa (175176), 2.5 mi. SSW of Shechem* – **38, 98**

Middin – Town/fort in Wilderness of Judah (Josh 15:61) – *Uncertain; possibly Kh. Abu Tabaq (188127), 10.5 mi. ESE of Jerusalem* – **97, 134**

Midian – Descendant of Abraham and Keturah and ancestor of Arabian tribe that bore his name. Midian/Midianite(s) mentioned 57 times in OT, once in NT (Acts 7:29). This nomadic people seems to have had its center in NW Arabia, E of Gulf of Aqaba/Elath, but at times entered Jezreel Valley (story of Gideon), S Transjordan, and maybe even Negev and N Sinai – **58, 60, 60, 88, 89, 90, 118**

Migdal Eder – Place S of Bethlehem but N of Hebron where Jacob/Israel camped (Gen 35:21) – *Unknown.*

Migdal El – Town allotted to Naphtali (Josh 19:38) – *Unknown; probably in Upper Galilee.*

Migdal Gad – Shephelah town allotted to Judah (Josh 15:37) – *Uncertain; possibly Kh. el-Mejdeleh/H. Migdal Gad (140105), 12 mi. W of Hebron* – **97, 134**

Migdol – Town in Lower Egypt where Jews lived (Jer 44:1; 46:14). Ezekiel refers to it as the N(E) extremity of Egypt (Ezek 29:10; 30:6) – *Site 0.6 mi. N of Tell el-Her, ca. 12.5 mi. NE of Qantar, E of Suez Canal in NW Sinai.*

Migdol (Exodus) – "Fort." Place near which Israelites camped when fleeing Egypt (Exod 14:2; Num 33:7) – *Uncertain; there were numerous "forts" along Egypt's NE frontier* – **89, 130, 141**

Migron – Place N of Jerusalem where Saul camped with his men, possibly near Gibeah (1 Sam 14:2). Also mentioned as being on invasion route from N into Jerusalem, but it seems to be N of Micmash (Isa 10:28) – *Unknown; there may have actually been two Migrons.*

Miletus – Prominent harbor city in SW Asia Minor where Paul stopped on third journey on way to Jerusalem and met with elders from Ephesus (Acts 20:15, 17; also 2 Tim 4:20) – *Site on coast of SW Turkey now partially occupied by town of Palatia* – **13, 143, 143, 181, 185, 185, 186**

Minnith – The judge Jephthah captured 20 cities in its vicinity as he subdued the Ammonites (Judges 11:33). Famous for its wheat (Ezek 27:17) – *Unknown; in Transjordan* – **108**

Mishal – Town allotted to Asher (Josh 19:26). Levitical city (Josh 21:30; called "Mashal" in 1 Chron 6:74) – *Uncertain; possibly T. Kisah/T. Kison (164253), 5 mi. SE of Acco* – **99, 102**

Mishor – See Moab, Tableland of – **17, 18, 23, 53, 55, 56, 101, 107, 108, 128, 128**

Misrephoth Maim – Joshua pursued defeated Canaanites in this direction (Josh 11:8) and extended Israelite control N to this point (13:6) – *Uncertain; N of Galilee in vicinity of Sidon; possibly in area of Litani River (Lebanon)* – **95, 95**

Mitanni – **87, 88, 105**

Mithcah – Israelite campsite during wilderness wanderings, between Terah and Hashmonah (Num 33:28–29) – *Unknown.*

Mitla Pass – **60**

Mit Rahina – **81, 86**

Mitylene – Port on Greek island of Lesbos where Paul's ship spent night on way to Jerusalem at end of third journey (Acts 20:14) – *Mytilene, on E shore of Lesbos, off W coast of Turkey* – **185, 185**

Mizar, Mount – Mountain mentioned in connection with Mt. Hermon in Ps 42:6 – *Uncertain; possibly in region of Mt. Hermon, although some think it may be reference to the "littleness" of Mt. Zion in contrast to the massiveness of Mt. Hermon.*

Mizpah (Benjamin) – Town allotted to Benjamin (Josh 18:26). Here Israelites gathered in preparation for war against Benjamin after incident with Levite's concubine (Judges 20–21). Important cult center during days of Samuel (1 Samuel 7; 10:17). Fortified by Asa of Judah (1 Kings 15:22; 2 Chron 16:6). Later became administrative center of Gedaliah, governor of defeated Judah for Babylonians (2 Kings 25:23, 25; Jer 40–41). Men from Mizpah helped Nehemiah rebuild wall of Jerusalem (Neh 3) – *T. en-Nasbeh (170143), 7.5 mi. NNW of Jerusalem* – **41, 43, 98, 105, 107, 110, 111, 111, 112, 126, 127, 134, 140, 141, 144, 146, 154, 154, 189**

Mizpah (Gilead) – Home of the judge Jephthah and place where Israel assembled before battle with Ammonites (Judges 10:17; 11:11, 29, 34). Also mentioned in Hosea 5:1 – *Uncertain; possibly Kh. Jalad (223169), 15 mi. NW of Amman in Jordan, 14 mi. S of Jabbok in Gilead* – **107, 108**

Mizpah (Jacob) – Place in Gilead where Jacob and Laban sealed covenant of friendship (Gen 31:49) – *Unknown; probably N of Jabbok River.*

Mizpah (Judah) – Village allotted to Judah (Josh 15:38) – *Unknown; in Judean Shephelah, probably near Lachish.*

Mizpah (Moab) – Place of refuge where David sent his father and mother (1 Sam 22:3) – *Unknown; E of Dead Sea in Moab.*

Mizpah, region/Valley of – Hivites from this region fought against Joshua (11:3), who defeated them and pursued them N in this direction (v. 8) – *Uncertain; near foot of Mt. Hermon; possibly in Marj Ayyun region of S Lebanon* – **95, 95**

Mizraim – See Egypt – **71, 72**

Moab – Personal, tribal, and geographical name used (in various forms) 194 times in OT. Heartland of Moab was E of Dead Sea between Zered and Arnon Rivers. At times expanded N into plateau region N of Arnon – **17, 18, 23, 28, 43, 43, 44, 52, 53, 55, 56, 81, 92, 92, 97, 104, 106, 107, 108, 113, 114, 117, 118, 120, 121, 125, 126, 127, 128, 132, 137, 138, 140, 141, 142, 144**

Moab, Mountains of – **44**

Moab, Plains of – **92, 92, 94**

Moab, Tableland of (Mishor) – Area in N Moab stretching from Arnon Gorge in S to Heshbon in N; called the "plateau" in the NIV (Deut 3:10; 4:43; Josh 13:9, 16–17, 21; 20:8; Jer 48:8, 21); called the "Mishor" in Hebrew – **101, 103, 104, 107, 108**

Moabitis – **150, 151, 152, 157**

Modiin – **153, 154, 155**

Moladah – Negev village allotted to Judah (Josh 15:26) as well as to Simeon (19:2; 1 Chron 4:28). After exile Jews lived here (Neh 11:26) – *Uncertain; possibly Kh. el-Waten/H. Yittan (142074), 5 mi. E of Beersheba* – **97, 134, 144, 146**

Monastery of St. Catherine – See Saint Catherine's Monastery – **60, 90**

Moreh – Site of a great oak tree near Shechem where Abram camped when he first entered Canaan (Gen 12:6). Near here the Israelites were to read the blessings and the curses (Deut 11:30). Possibly the "oak at Shechem" where Jacob hid the teraphim is the same place (Gen 35:4) – *Unknown; near Shechem.* **77, 77**

Moreh, hill of – Gideon attacked Midianites who were camped near hill of Moreh (Judges 7:1) – *Jebel Nabi Dahi/Mt. Moreh, at E end of Jezreel Valley* – **34, 107, 107, 114, 115**

Moresheth – Home of Micah the prophet (Mic 1:1; Jer 26:18). See Moresheth Gath – **48, 125**

Moresheth Gath – Full name of home of Micah the prophet (Mic 1:14) – *Uncertain; possibly T. el-Judeideh/T. Goded (141115), in Shephelah, 6 mi. NE of Lachish* – **43, 36**

Moriah – Abraham took Isaac to "region of Moriah" to sacrifice him (Gen 22:2). Solomon built temple on Mt. Moriah (2 Chron 3:1) – *Temple mount in Jerusalem now occupied by* the Dome of the Rock (172131) – 80, **84**, 189, 190, **190, 191**

Moserah – Place where Aaron died (Deut 10:6). Evidently near or identical to Mt. Hor (Num 20 passim).

Moseroth – Israelite campsite between Hashmonah and Bene Jaakan (Num 33:30–31) – *Unknown; in Sinai or S Negev. Some suggest identical to Moserah.*

Mozah – Town allotted to Benjamin (Josh 18:26) – *Qalunyah/Mevasseret Ziyyon (165134), 5 mi. WNW of Jerusalem* – **98, 134**

Murat – 70

Mycenae – 13

Myra – City near S coast of Turkey where Paul and escorts transferred to Alexandrian ship bound for Italy (Acts 27:5) – 186, **186**

Mysia – Paul passed through Mysia on way to Troas on second journey (Acts 16:7–8) – *Territory in NW Turkey stretching to Aegean Sea, Hellespont, and Propontis* – 147, 148, **182, 183**

Naamah – Town allotted to Judah in the Shephelah (Josh 15:41) – *Unknown.*

Naarah – Town on SE border of Ephraim between Ataroth and Jericho (Josh 16:7). Called Naaran in 1 Chron 7:28 and said to be in Ephraim – *T. el-Jisr (190144), 1.8 mi. NW of Jericho.*

Naaran – See Naarah – **98, 126**

Nabatean Kingdom/Nabateans – 149, 161, 164, 167

Nablus – See Neapolis – 205

Nacon, threshing floor of – See Kidon, threshing floor of.

Nafud Desert – 12, 13

Nahala – 102

Nahal Aijalon – See Aijalon, Valley of – **38**, 47

Nahalal – Town allotted to Zebulun (Josh 19:15). Levitical city (21:35). Called Nahalol in Judges 1:30 – *Unknown; in or just N of Jezreel Valley* – 99

Nahal Arnon – 43

Nahal Arugot – 43, 44, 128, **128**

Nahal Beersheba – 49, 50

Nahal Besor – See Besor Ravine – 16, **17, 18, 28**, 46, **46**, 47, 49, **49**

Nahal Gerar – See Gerar, Valley of – 46, **46**, 47, 78

Nahal Harod – 33

Nahal Hebron – 50

Nahaliel – One of last campsites of Israelites, N of Arnon Gorge, E of Dead Sea, S of Bamoth (Num 21:19) – *Unknown.*

Nahal Jabneel – See Jabneel Valley – 33, 34, **34**

Nahal Kanah – 38

Nahal Kesalon – 113

Nahal Kishon – 33

Nahal Lachish – 46, 48, **100**, 113

Nahal Litani – See also Litani River – 28

Nahalol – See Nahalal – 99

Nahal Paran – 89

Nahal Pattish – 46

Nahal Raqqad – See Raqqad – 27, 29, **29**, 30, 31

Nahal Shechem – 38, 40, 127

Nahal Shiloh – 38

Nahal Shiqma – **46**, 78

Nahal Sorek – See Sorek – **46**, 96, 113

Nahal Tabor – 33, 34

Nahal Tanninim – 16, **17, 18, 38, 38**

Nahal Yarkon – See Jarkon River and Me Jarkon – 16, **17, 18**, 47, **100, 111**

Nahal Zered – See Zered Valley/River – 23, 55

Nahal Zin – **18, 28, 48**, 51

Nahal Zohar – 44

Naharin – 87

Nahariya – 82

Nahor, town of – Could merely be town in which Abraham's brother Nahor lived (Gen 24:10), but a town named Nahor, near Habor River in N Syria, is mentioned in Ebla and Mari texts – *Unknown.* 65

Nahr Kabir – 63, 64

Nain – Town where Jesus raised son of widow from the dead (Luke 7:11) – *Nein (183226), 6 mi. SE of Nazareth on lower N slope of Mt. Moreh* – 33, 34, 168

Naioth – Settlement in or near Ramah where Samuel was located, to which David fled, and where Saul prophesied (1 Sam 19:18–19, 22–23; 20:1) – *Uncertain; near Ramah* – 113

Naphoth – Mentioned in connection with Manasseh's tribal allotment, possibly referring back to "Dor," which is "third in the list" (Josh 17:11). See Naphoth Dor.

Naphoth Dor – Possible translation: "Forest in the plain of Dor." Thus descriptive of region around coastal city of Dor. King fought against Joshua (11:2; 12:23). Was 4th Solomonic district (1 Kings 4:11) – *Narrow coastal strip E of Dor, between Mediterranean and Mt. Carmel.*

Naphtali – Son of Jacob and name of tribe; mentioned 50 times in OT, 3 times in NT. On occasion designates tribal territory, W and NW of the Sea of Galilee – 32, 34, 35, 96, 99, **99**, 100, **102**, 106, 107, 122, 133, 136

Naphtali, Hill Country of – Hilly/mountainous territory of Galilee where tribe of Naphtali settled and where Kedesh in Galilee was located (Josh 20:7).

Naqb Ishtar – 55, 56

Narbonenis – 163, 187

Nazareth – Small, insignificant town (John 1:46) in Lower Galilee where Gabriel appeared to Mary (Luke 1:26). Mary and Joseph traveled from here to Bethlehem (Luke 2:4) where Jesus was born. After flight into Egypt they returned to Nazareth to live (Matt 2:23; Luke 2:4, 39, 51). Jesus eventually left the city for a wider ministry (Matt 4:13; Mark 1:9) but at one point he was rejected by the inhabitants of the town (Luke 4:16). He was called a "prophet from Nazareth in Galilee" (Matt 21:11); the phrase "Jesus (Christ) of Nazareth" is used 17 times in the NT – *En-Nasira/Nasrat (178234), today a large Arab city on S edge of Lower Galilee, 16 mi. W of S tip of Sea of Galilee* – 18, 21, 31, 33, **33**, 34, 36, 78, 166, 167, **167, 168**, 170, 176

Neah – Town on N border of Zebulun between Rimmon and Hannathon (Josh 19:13) – *Unknown.*

Neapolis (Greece) – Aegean seaport of Philippi where Paul first set foot on European soil on second journey (Acts 16:11). He probably passed through it twice on third journey (20:1, 6). – *Kavalla, in N Greece, 10 mi. SE of Philippi* – 175, 176, **182, 183, 187**

Neapolis – See Nablus and Shechem – 205

Neara – 166, **167**

Neballat – Town near E edge of coastal plain where Benjamites settled after the Exile (Neh 11:34) – *Beit Nabala/H. Nevallat (146154), 13 mi. ESE of Joppa* – 144

Nebi Samwil – See Gibeah of God and Gibeon, high place at – 111

Nebo (of Judah?) – Residents of this town participated in first return from the Exile

(Ezra 2:29; Neh 7:33); some later repented of the sin of intermarriage (Ezra 10:43) – *Uncertain; possibly Nuba (153112), 7 mi. NW of Hebron in Shephelah* – 144

Nebo (Moab) – Transjordanian town allotted to Reuben (Num 32:3, 38: 33:47; 1 Chron 5:8). Later under control of Moabites and mentioned in prophetic oracles (Isa 15:2; Jer 48:1, 22) – *Kh. Ayun Musa (220131), 9 mi. E of N end of Dead Sea* – 92, 127

Nebo, Mount – "Mount" near Nebo where Moses died (Deut 32:49; 34:1) – *Ras es-Saighah (220130), 10 mi. E of N end of Dead Sea. See also Pisgah* – 18, 92, **92, 94**

Negev – geographical region on S boundary of Judah, shaped somewhat like hourglass on its side, with center at Beersheba. Mentioned 38 times in OT. Some of its subdistricts are also mentioned: Negev of Jerahmeel, Negev of the Kenites, Negev of Judah (1 Sam 27:10), Negev of the Kerethites, and the Negev of Caleb (1 Sam 30:14). Agriculturally marginal because of low amounts of rainfall (8 to 12 in.) – 12, 18, 22, 28, 42, 46, **46**, 47, 49, 50, 51, 59, **60**, 77–81, **77, 84**, 88, 91, 96, **97**, 98, 115, 119, **120**, 121, 124, 128, 131, **134**, 146, 172, 203

Negev Basin – 17, 18, **18**, 42, **43**, 49, **49**

Negev Highlands – 18, **18**, 22, **49**, 50, 51, 78, **78**, 79, 81, 92, **92**, 121

Negev of Caleb – Area of Negev where Calebites lived and which was raided by Amalekites (1 Sam 30:14). – *In Hill Country of Judah, S of Hebron but NE of Beersheba* – 114, 115

Negev of Jerahmeel – Area of Negev where Jerahmeelites lived and which was defended by David (1 Sam 27:10). – *Probably in S Judah, in E Negev Basin* – 114, 115

Negev of Judah – Area of Negev defended by David (1 Sam 27:10) and where Joab completed the census (2 Sam 24:7) – *In S Judah, in vicinity of Beersheba* – 114, 119

Negev of the Kenites – Area of Negev where Kenites lived which was defended by David (1 Sam 27:10) – *Probably in NE Negev Basin, near Arad* – 114

Negev of the Kerethites – Area in W Negev raided by Amalekites (1 Sam 30:14). Kerethites were evidently an Aegean people who settled there (cf. Zeph 2:6) – *Probably S Philistine Plain area and W Negev region E and NE of Gaza* – 114, 115

Nehardea – 175

Neiel – Town allotted to Asher (Josh 19:27) – *Kh. Yanin/H. Yaanin (171255), 8.5 ESE of Acco* – 99

Nephtoah, Waters of – Site on border between Judah and Benjamin (Josh 15:9; 18:15) – *Lifta/Me-Neftoah (168133), 3 mi. NW of Jerusalem* – 41, 43

Netaim – Settlement where royal Judean potters lived (1 Chron 4:23) – *Unknown.*

Netophah – Inhabitants of town participated in first return from the Exile (Ezra 2:22; Neh 7:26). A number of people are called "Netophathite(s)" (11 times in OT) – *Uncertain; possibly Kh. Bedd Faluh (171119), 8 mi. S of Jerusalem* – 144

Nezib – Town allotted to Judah in a Shephelah district (Josh 15:43) – *Kh. Beit Nesib esh-Sharqiyeh (151110), 7 mi. NW of Hebron* – **97, 134**

Nibshan – Town in wilderness district of Judah (Josh 15:62) – *Uncertain; possibly Kh. el-Maqari (186123), 10 mi. SE of Jerusalem* – **97, 134**

Nicaea – 182, 183

Nicomedia – 187

Nicopolis – Paul intended to spend winter here (Titus 3:12). Several cities have this name; here Nicopolis in Epirus seems to be meant.

See also Emmaus – *Nikopolis, NNE of Preveza in W Greece* – **167**, 173, **187**

Nile – River that begins in Central Africa and flows N through Egypt; 4,145 mi. long. Mentioned 31 times in OT, especially in connection with Israelites in Egypt and in prophetic oracles (Isa, Jer, Ezek, Amos, Nahum, Zech) – 12, **13**, 57, **58**, 59, **72**, 73, 74, 79, **80**, **81**, 83, 84, **86**, 87, 90, 118, **123**, **130**, **137**, 140, **141–43**, 143, 148, 160

Nimrah – See Beth Nimrah.

Nimrim, waters of – Place mentioned in oracles against Moab (Isa 15:6; Jer 48:34) – *Uncertain; possibly Wadi Gadira, which flows into Ghor Numera E of Dead Sea.*

Nimrod, land of – Land associated with heroic figure Nimrod (Mic 5:6; cf. Gen 10:8–11) – *Evidently area of ancient Babylonia and Assyria (in modern Iraq).*

Nimrud – 65

Nineveh – Great administrative center in Assyria, mentioned 20 times in OT. Jonah prophesied to its inhabitants (Jonah passim). Prominent in oracles of Nahum (passim) and in Zeph 2:13. Jesus referred to its inhabitants who responded to Jonah (Matt 12:41; Luke 11:32) – *Mounds of Quyunjiq and Nebi Yunus, on bank of Tigris River, opposite modern Mosul, in N Iraq* – **13**, 65, 66, 67, **77**, **78**, **80**, **123**, **130**, 135, 136, **137**, **142**

Nippur – 65, **72**, 73, 76, **77**, **78**, **137**, 141, **142**, **175**

Nisbis – **130**, 148

No-Amon – **130**, 136

Nob – Town to which David fled from Saul (1 Sam 21:1). Evidently the tabernacle, but not the ark, was here at the time. Saul slaughtered the priests that served here in revenge for assistance given to David (1 Sam 22:9, 11, 19). Attackers of Jerusalem approaching from the N passed here (Isa 10:32). Jews settled here after the Exile (Neh 11:32) – *Uncertain; possibly el-Isawiyah (173134), 1.5 mi. NE of Jerusalem* – 113, **114**, **134**, 144

Nobah – Nobah captured Kenath and renamed it after himself (Num 32:42). Mentioned in connection with Gideon's pursuit of Midianites (Judges 8:11). See Kenath – 108

Noph – **123**, **130**, 141

Nophah – Town captured by Israelites (Num 21:30; text is difficult) – *Unknown; evidently in Moabite Plateau E of N end of Dead Sea.*

Northern Kingdom – See Israel – 27, 40, 98, **126**, 127, 131, 133–36, 194

North Syrian Plain – 65

Nubia – 57, **58**, **72**, 74, 82, 83, 87

Numeira – **43**, 45, **56**, **75**, **78**, 81

Numidia – **163**, **187**

Nuseiriyeh Mountains – 62, 64

Nuweiba – 60

Nuzi – **13**, **72**, **77**, **80**

Oboth – Campsite of Israelites on trek to Canaan (Num 21:10–11). Evidently between Punon and Iye Abarim (33:43–44) – *Uncertain; E of S end of Dead Sea, but identifications of Punon and Iye Abarim are also uncertain* – 92

Oceanus Atlanticus – See Atlantic Ocean.

Odollam – OT Adullam – 154, **154**

Offense, Mount of – **190**

Olives, Mount of – Hill E of Jerusalem. David crossed it as he fled E from Absalom (2 Sam 15:30). Referred to in oracle of Zechariah (14:4) in connection with appearance of Yahweh. Woman caught in adultery was brought to Jesus here (John 8:1). Mentioned frequently in connection with last week of Jesus' life: Jesus passed over it as he triumphantly en-

tered Jerusalem (Matt 21:1; Mark 11:1; Luke 19:29, 37); later he taught his disciples here (Matt 24:3; Mark 13:3); and he took his disciples on the night he was betrayed (Matt 26:30; Mark 14:26; Luke 21:37; 22:39). Forty days after his resurrection Jesus ascended from here in the presence of his disciples (Acts 1:12) – *N-S range just E of Jerusalem that includes, from S to N, Jebel Batn el-Hawa, Jebel et-Tur, and Ras Abu Kharnub* – 119, 172, 173, **189**, 190, 193, 194, 197, 199, 200

Ombos – 86

On – Joseph married daughter of Potiphera, priest of On (Gen 41:45, 50; 46:20). See Heliopolis – **13**, **130**

Ono – Built by Benjamite (1 Chron 8:12). Jews lived here at time of return from the Exile (Ezra 2:33; Neh 7:37; 11:35). Sanballat and Geshem attempted to lure Nehemiah to the plain there (Neh 6:2), but he refused to come – *Kafr Ana/Ono (137159), 7.5 mi. E of Joppa* – 46, 47, **144**, 146

Ono, Plain of – See Ono – 144

Ophir – Country or region from which David and Solomon obtained fine gold and other exotic products (1 Kings 9:28; 10:11; 1 Chron 29:4; 2 Chron 8:18; 9:10); Jehoshaphat's attempt to do the same failed (1 Kings 22:48). Gold of Ophir also mentioned in poetic and prophetic literature of OT (Job 22:24; 28:16; Ps 45:9; Isa 13:12) – *Uncertain; possibly in S or SW portion of Arabian peninsula* – 22, **71**, 128

Ophni – Town allotted to Benjamin (Josh 18:24) – *Unknown; possibly located in Benjamin plateau, but E of watershed.*

Ophrah (Benjamin) – Town allotted to Benjamin (Josh 18:23) toward which Philistine raiding party advanced (1 Sam 13:17) – *Et-Taiyibeh (178151), 13 mi. NNE of Jerusalem* – **98**, 105, 112, **126**, 170, 172

Ophrah (Manasseh) – Village of Manasseh from which Gideon came and where the angel of the Lord appeared to him and he set up an altar for Yahweh (Judges 6:11, 24). Later, an "ephod" was worshiped at Ophrah (8:27, 32), and Abimelech killed 70 of his brothers there (9:5) – *Kh. Taiyibeh (167213), 5 mi. S of Megiddo* – 107, **107**, 108

Opis – 141, **142**

Orda – 157

Orhesa – 161, **164**

Orontes (River) – **62**, 64, **80**, 84, 87, **88**, **105**, 106, 127, 142, **149**, 150, 180, **181**

Orthosia – 149

Ostia – 187

Otrus – 187

Oxus River – 141, **143**, 148, 149

Oxyrrhynchus – 175

Paddan – Shortened form of Paddan Aram (Gen 48:7).

Paddan Aram – Place from which Isaac's wife Rebekah came (Gen 25:20). Later Jacob fled there and lived with his uncle Laban for 20 years. Here he married, raised his family, and accumulated great wealth (28:2, 5–7; 31:18; 33:18; 35:9, 26; 46:15; 48:7) – *Region in NW Mesopotamia, N of Euphrates, near Habur and Balik rivers* – 77, 84, **84**

Pakistan – 149

Palestine – 47, 62, 73–75, **75**, 78, **78**, 79, 82, 140, **149**, 150–52, 160, 162, 175, **175**, **176**, 179, **181**, 182, 185, 186, 196

Palmahim – 78

Palms, City of – Evidently another name for Jericho. Mentioned in connection with Moses' viewing the land (Deut 34:3) and Kenites entering it with Judah (Judges 1:16). Eglon captured it (3:13). Much later, Judean pris-

oners were released here (2 Chron 28:15) – *T. es-Sultan (192142), 14 mi. ENE of Jerusalem in Rift Valley.*

Palmyra – 63, 175

Pamphylia – Roman province bounded by Lycia on SW, Pidia on N, and Cilicia on E. Jews from Pamphylia were in Jerusalem on Day of Pentecost (Acts 2:10). Paul and Barnabas passed through twice on first journey; here John Mark abandoned them (13:13; 14:24; 15:38). Paul's ship passed by its coast on journey to Rome (27:5) – *Small lowland area along S-central coast of Turkey* – 147, 148, **163**, 175, 180, 181, **181**, **182**, **185**, 186

Panias – See Caesarea Philippi – **151**, 152, **157**, 160, **161**, 163, **164**

Pannonia – **163**, **187**

Paphos – Capital of island of Cyprus. Here Governor Sergius Paulus was converted by Paul on first journey (Acts 13:6) – *Baffa, 10 mi. NW of Kouklia on SW edge of Cyprus* – **175**, 180, **181**, **185**

Parah – Town allotted to Benjamin (Josh 18:23) – *Kh. Abu Musarrah (177137), 4.7 mi. NE of Jerusalem.*

Paralia – **151**, 152

Paran – Shortened form (Deut 1:1; 1 Kings 11:18) of Desert of Paran – 49, 51, 81, 91, **98**, 114, 118

Paran, Desert of – Ishmaelites settled here (Gen 21:21). Israelites passed through it on way to Canaan (Num 10:12; 12:16; Deut 1:1). From here spies were sent into Canaan; they returned to Israelite camp at Kadesh (Num 13:3, 26). Hadad the Edomite passed through it as he fled to Egypt from Solomon (1 Kings 11:18) – *Uncertain; seems to refer to a large amorphous desert area in central Sinai. Kadesh Barnea and SE Judah (see NIV footnote "Hebrew Paran" of 1 Sam 25:1) seem to border it on the N and the Desert of Shur on the W* – 49, **84**, **89**, 91

Paran, Mount – Poetic name for Mt. Sinai (Deut 33:2; Hab 3:3), which was in or near the Desert of Paran.

Parium – 187

Paros – 175

Parthia – 142, **143**, 153, **161**, **163**, 175, 180

Parvaim – Region from which a special type (reddish?) gold was obtained (2 Chron 3:6) – *Uncertain; possibly in Arabian peninsula.*

Pasargadae – 143, **148**

Pas Dammim – Alternate form for Ephes Dammim where David fought Philistines (2 Sam 23:9; 1 Chron 11:13).

Patala – 143, **148**

Patara – On return from third journey Paul changed ships here (Acts 21:1) – *In Lycia, in SW Asia Minor opposite Rhodes* – **185**, 186

Pathros – Area of Egypt mentioned in prophetic oracles against that country (Ezek 29:14; 30:14). Translated as "Upper Egypt" by NIV in Isa 11:11 and Jer 44:1–15 – *Area in Egypt along Nile from Cairo S to Aswan.*

Patmos, Island of – Island where John received divine revelation (Rev 1:9) – *Greek island of Patmos, W of SW coast of Turkey in Aegean Sea, ca. 35 mi. WSW of Miletus* – **184**

Pau – Town of Edomite chief Hadad (Gen 36:39; 1 Chron 1:50) – *Unknown; in Edom.*

Pehel – See Pella – **33**, 38, **54**, **75**, 82, 90, **105**, 105, 106, **107**, 151

Pekod – Region in S Babylonia where Aramean tribe of same name was centered. Mentioned in prophetic oracles (Jer 50:21; Ezek 23:23). Probably also a wordplay on Babylonian "[land of] punishment."

Pella – OT Pehel – **147**, **148**, 151, 151, **157**, 160, **161**, **164**, **167**, **168**, **170**, 171

Peloponnese – **182**, 184, 186, **186**

Pelusium – Egyptian fortress mentioned in oracle of Ezekiel (30:15–16) – *Tell Farama, 13 mi. E of Suez Canal, 1.8 mi. from Mediterranean Sea* – 141, **141–43**, **148**, **149**, 160, **163**, **175**

Penuel/Peniel – Place near Jabbok River where Jacob wrestled with a man (angel of God; Gen 32:30–31; cf. Hos 12:4). Inhabitants refused to help Gideon against fleeing Midianites; later Gideon punished it (Judges 8:8–9, 17). Fortified by Jeroboam I (1 Kings 12:25) – *T. edh-Dhahab esh-Sherqiyeh (215176), 8 mi. E of Jordan River* – 52, **54**, **84**, 107, **107**, 124, **125**, **126**, 127, **129**

Peor (Judah) – Town allotted to Judah (Josh 15:59b; LXX) – *Kh. Zakandah (164119), 9.5 mi. SW of Jerusalem* – 97, **134**

Peor (Moab) – High point in Moab where Balak took Balaam to curse Israel (Num 23:28). Later, Israelites worshiped Baal of Peor (Num 25:3, 5, 18; 31:16; Deut 4:3; Josh 22:17; Ps 106:28) – *Uncertain; possibly near Mt. Nebo, E of N end of Dead Sea.*

Perath – Place, mentioned in oracle of Jeremiah, where he hid a belt (13:4–7) – *Often identified with Euphrates, but more probably a valley close to Parah (see there).*

Perazim, Mount – Mentioned in oracle of Isaiah against rulers of Jerusalem (28:21). May be reference to previous judgment against Philistines at Baal Perazim (2 Sam 5:20; 1 Chron 14:11). See Baal Perazim.

Perea – Jewish Transjordanian district ruled by Herod the Great and during days of Jesus by Herod Antipas. Stretched from Machaerus in S to Pella in the N. Not specifically mentioned in NT, but note phrases "region across the Jordan," "on the other side of the Jordan," etc. – 43, **53**, **150**, 151, 152, **157**, 160, **161**, 163, **164**, 166, **167**, **168**, **170**, 171, 172, 174, **175–78**, 177

Perez Uzzah – Place, W of Jerusalem but E of Kiriath Jearim, where Uzzah was struck dead for touching the ark (2 Sam 6:8; 1 Chron 13:11) – *Unknown.*

Perga – Major city of Pamphylia through which Paul and Barnabas passed going into and out of Pamphylia and Pisidia (Acts 13:13–14; 14:25) – *Ruins near Murtana in S Turkey, ca. 8 mi. inland from Mediterranean* – **175**, 180, **181**, **187**

Pergamum – One of the seven churches of Revelation (Rev 1:11; 2:12) – *Bergama in W Turkey, 15 mi. inland (E) from Aegean coast; ca. 80 mi. N of Ephesus* – 152, 160, **163**, **175**, **181**, 185, **185**, **187**

Persepolis – 143, **143**, 146, 148

Persia – Kingdom mentioned 29 times in OT (2 Chron; Ezra; Esth; Ezek; Dan), sometimes in connection with Media – *Heartland in SW Iran but also used with reference to the extensive Persian Empire* – 62, 67, 141, 143, **143**, 146, 149, 150, 151, 153, 155

Persian Gulf – 12, **13**, 65–67, **65**, 72, 80, 130, 137, **142**, **143**, 148, **175**

Pethor – Place from which Balaam the prophet came (Num 22:5; Deut 23:4) – *Uncertain; possibly Tell el-Ahmar, 12 mi. S of Carchemish on W bank of Upper Euphrates River.*

Petra – **17**, 18, 23, **28**, **49**, 51, 55, 56, **56**, **60**, **149**, **157**, 159

Phaistos – 13

Pharathon – 155

Pharpar – One of the rivers of Damascus which Naaman preferred over the Jordan (2 Kings 5:12) – *Uncertain; possibly the el-Awaj, which flows through the plain a few mi. S of Damascus.*

Phasaelis – **164**, **170**, 172

Phasis – 143

Philadelphia (Asia Minor) – One of the seven churches addressed in book of Revelation (Rev 1:11; 3:7) – *Alashir in W Turkey along banks of Cogmaus River, ca. 75 mi. inland, E of Smyrna* – 185, **185**

Philadelphia (Decapolis) OT Rabbah of the Ammonites – **149**, **150**, 151, **151**, **157**, 158, **161**, **164**, **167**, **170**, 171, **175–77**

Philippi – One of the chief cities of Macedonia visited by Paul on his second (Acts 16:12; 20:6; 1 Thess 2:2) and probably third journeys. Letter to the Philippians addressed to the church here – *Philippi, ca. 9 mi. N of Aegean coastline near River Gangites* – 30, **171**, **175**, **182**, 183, 185, **185**, **187**

Philistia/Philistines, land of the – Coastal plain area settled by the Philistines, from the Nahal Besor in the S to the Yarkon River in the N. Philistia is mentioned only 7 times in OT (Exod 15:14; Pss 60:8; 83:7; 87:4; Isa 11:4; Joel 3:4; Amos 6:2), although the term "Philistine(s)" occurs 276 times – 14, 46, 47, **71**, 122, **125**, 135, 136, 156, **157**, 162

Philistine Plain – See Philistia – 16, **17**, 27, 46, **46**, 47, 96, 106, **114**, 115, 129, 131, 136, 146, 151, 156, 174

Philistines, Sea of – Exod 21:31. Name for Mediterranean Sea.

Philomenian – 187

Philoteria – **151**, **157**, **161**, **168**, 178

Phoenicia – Jesus healed daughter of Greek woman from this area (Mark 7:26). Christians came to area due to persecutions (Acts 11:19). Paul and Barnabas passed through Phoenicia on way to Jerusalem conference (15:3). At end of third journey, Paul boarded a ship headed for Phoenicia at Patara (21:2). "Phoenicia" of Isa 23:11 should be translated "Canaan" (NIV footnote) – *Narrow region along Mediterranean coast stretching ca. 185 mi. from Mt. Carmel in S to Mt. Cassius in N. In modern Lebanon and Syria* – 16, 63, 99, 123, **125**, 127, 150, **150**, 151, **151**, 152, **157**, **161**, 162, **163**, 164, **175**, 177, 178, **181**, **182**, **185**, 186, **186**

Phoenix – Place where captain of Paul's ship hoped to harbor for winter but due to storm they were blown past and shipwrecked on Malta (Acts 27:12) – *Bay on W side of Cape Mouros, on S side of island of Crete* – 186, **186**

Phrygia – In Hellenistic times a distinct district, during NT times divided between the Roman provinces of Asia and Galatia. Jews from Phrygia were in Jerusalem on Day of Pentecost (Acts 2:10). Paul visited Galatian Phrygia on all three missionary journeys; Antioch and Iconium were located here (16:6; 18:23) – *Indeterminate area in and near W edge of Anatolian plateau in Turkey* – **147**, 148, **175**, 180, 181, **181**, **182**, 183, 184, **185**

Pi Hahiroth – Place near which Israelites camped after leaving Etham, immediately before crossing the Red (Reed) Sea (Exod 14:2, 9; Num 33:7–8) – *Uncertain; possibly the low ground near Jebel Geneife, W of Suez Canal near Bitter Lakes* – 89

Pirathon – Home and burial place of the judge Abdon (Judges 12:13, 15). Home of Benaiah, one of David's warriors (2 Sam 23:30; 1 Chron 11:31; 27:14) – *Farata (165177), 7 mi. WSW of Shechem in Hill Country of Ephraim* – **38**, **98**, **107**, 108

Piraeus – 165

Pisgah – Hilltop or range near which Israel camped (Num 21:20). Balaam was taken here to curse Israel (23:14). From here Moses surveyed Canaan prior to his death (Deut 3:17, 27; 34:1). Area had been ruled by Sihon (Deut 4:49; Josh 12:3); allotted to Reuben

(Josh 13:20) – *Uncertain; probably near Mt. Nebo, ca. 9 mi. E of N end of Dead Sea.*

Pishon – One of the rivers of Eden (Gen 2:11) – *Unknown* – 70, 71

Pisidia – Region through which Paul passed on his first journey as he traveled from Pamphylia to Pisidian Antioch and back (Acts 13:14; 14:24) – *Mountainous district at W end of Taurus range in S central Turkey; in Paul's day part of province of Galatia* – 180, 181, **181**

Pisidian Antioch – See Antioch (Pisidian) – 180, 181, **181**, **182**, 183, 184, **185**

Pithom – One of the two "store cities" built by Israelites in Egypt (Exod 1:11) – *Uncertain; possibly Tell el-Maskhuta, 9 mi. W of Ismailia, or Tell er-Retabah, 9 mi. W of Tell el-Maskhuta; both in Wadi Tumilat in NE Egypt* – 88

Plain, Cities of the – Included Sodom, Gomorrah, Admah, Zeboiim, and Bela (Zoar). Lot chose to live in area (Gen 13:12); God destroyed some of them (19:29) – *Uncertain; possibly SE of the Dead Sea.*

Plateau – See Moab, Tableland of.

Pompeii – 175

Pontus – Jews from Pontus were in Jerusalem on Day of Pentecost (Acts 2:9). Apollos was from here (18:2). Peter addressed letter to Christians in area (1 Peter 1:1) – *Roman province along E portion of S shore of Black Sea (in Turkey), bounded by Halys River on W, Galatia and Cappadocia on S, and Armenia on E. In Paul's day combined with Bithynia into a single province* – **175**, **181**, **182**, **185**, 186

Pontus Euxinus – See Black Sea.

Port Said – 58, 59, 82

Prusa – 82, **182**, 183

Ptolemais – Greco-Roman name for Acco, one of the chief ports of Palestine. Paul stopped here on return from third journey (Acts 21:7) – *Acre/Akko (157258)* – 30, **31**, 32–34, **33**, **149**, **150**, 151, 152, 156, **157**, **161**, 162, **164**, 165, 166, **167**, **170**, **175**, **176**, 177, **177**, 178, **185**, 186, **187**

Pumbeditha – 175

Punon – Israelite campsite in wilderness between Zalmonah and Oboth (Num 33:42–43) – *Uncertain; possibly at Feinan (197004), in Jordan, 32 mi. S of Dead Sea* – 49, 51, 55, 56, **56**, **60**, 92

Pura – 143

Purushkhanda – 73

Put – Descendant of Ham (Gen 10:6; 1 Chron 1:8); more commonly country or people mentioned in prophetic oracles (Jer 46:9; Ezek 27:10; 30:5; Nah 3:9; and possibly Isa 66:19, NIV "Libyans" but LXX "Put") – *Uncertain; probably all or part of Libya in N Africa* – **71**, 72

Puteoli – Important port of Rome where Paul landed and stayed for seven days before proceeding by road to Rome, ca. 145 mi. distant (Acts 28:13) – *Puzzuoli, W of Naples* – **175**, **186**, 187

Puzzuoli – See Puteoli – 187

Pylos – 13

Qaloniya – See Emmaus – 173

Qantir – **81**, 88

Qarat ed-Dahr – **86**

Qarqar – 127, **130**, 131

Qatna – **13**, 80, 84, 105, 142

Qattara – 20, 54

Qedar – 146

Qedem – 83

Qeisarieh – See Caearea – 204

Qumran – 43, **43**, 45, **49**, 170

Quneitra – **31**

Qurna – 65, 66

Raamah – Personal and tribal name (Gen 10:7; 1 Chron 1:9; Ezek 27:22) – *Uncertain; probably located in Arabia, but exact location disputed* – 71

Rabbah (Judah) – Town in hill country allotted to Judah (Josh 15:6). Mentioned in extrabiblical sources – *Kh. Hamideh (149137), 15 mi. WNW of Jerusalem near the hill country.*

Rabbah (of the Ammonites) – Major Transjordanian town where Og's gigantic bed was kept (Deut 3:11). City was excluded from the tribal allotments (Josh 13:25), yet later Joab and David captured it for Israel (2 Sam 11:1; 12:26–27, 29; 1 Chron 20:1). Its king assisted David as he fled from Absalom (2 Sam 17:27). This capital of the Ammonites is mentioned in later prophetic oracles (Amos 1:14; Jer 49:2, 3; Ezek 21:20; 25:5). In NT times it was called Philadelphia – *Amman (238151), now capital of Jordan, 24 mi. E of Jordan River* – 17, 18, 23, 28, **28**, 52, **53**, 55, **92**, 94, 97, 101, **101**, 112, 117, 118, 119, **119**, 120, 122, 126, **130**, 132, 134, **137**, 142, 151

Rabbith – Town allotted to Issachar (Josh 19:20). Possibly a variant of Daberath, a Levitical town in Issachar (21:28; 1 Chron 6:72) not mentioned in city list of Josh 19.

Racal – Town in S Judah to which David sent booty taken from Amalekites (1 Sam 30:29) – *Uncertain; possibly textual error for Carmel, which is missing from list and is near Eshtemoa.*

Raetia Noricum – 163, 187

Rafia – See Raphia.

Rakkath – Town allotted to Naphtali, between Hammath and Kinnereth (Josh 19:35), both on W shore of Sea of Galilee – *Kh. el-Quneitireh/T. Raqqat (199245), 2.5 mi. NW of Tiberias* – 99

Rakkon – Town allotted to Dan (Josh 19:46) – *Unknown; if a town, then in vicinity of Joppa, but Hebrew text is difficult.*

Ramah (Asher) – Town on N border of Asher in vicinity of Tyre and Sidon (Josh 19:29) – *Unknown.*

Ramah (Benjamin) – Town allotted to Benjamin (Josh 18:25). Deborah judged Israel in vicinity (Judges 4:5); evidently located N of Gibeah (19:13). Home of Samuel (1 Sam 1:19; 2:11; also called Ramathaim [1:1]), from where he went on his circuit (7:15–17). Mentioned frequently in connection with the stories of Saul and David (1 Sam 1:1). Baashah of Israel fortified it (1 Kings 15:17; 2 Chron 16:1) but Asa removed fortifications (1 Kings 15:21–22; 2 Chron 16:5–6). Mentioned as being along traditional N invasion route toward Jerusalem (Isa 10:29) and in prophetic oracles (Hos 5:8; Jer 31:15; Matt 2:18). Jeremiah was released by the Babylonians at Ramah (Jer 40:1), and after the Exile, Jews settled there (Ezra 2:26; Neh 7:30; 11:33) – *Er-Ram (172140), 5 mi. N of Jerusalem* – 18, **18**, 28, **28**, 41, **43**, 46, 98, 104, **105**, 107, **107**, 110, 111, **111**, 112, 113, **114**, 124, **126**, 134, 144, 188, **189**

Ramah (Naphtali) – Town allotted to Naphtali on boundary between Lower and Upper Galilee (Josh 19:36) – *Kh. Zeitun er-Rameh (187259), 19 mi. E of Acco* – **33**, 99, 100

Ramah in the Negev – Town on border of Simeon (Josh 19:8) – *Uncertain; possibly Kh. Ghazzah/H. Uza (165068), 20 mi. ESE of Beersheba. Possibly same as Ramoth Negev (1 Sam 30:27)* – 97

Ramathaim – See Ramah (Benjamin) – 110

Ramath Lehi – Place near which Samson routed Philistines (Judges 15:17). See Lehi – 109

Ramath Mizpah – Town allotted to Gad (Josh 13:26) – *Uncertain; possibly Iraq el-Emir (221147), 11 mi. WSW of Amman* – 101

Rameses – One of the store cities the Israelites built in Egypt (Exod 1:11). At time of Exodus they traveled from here to Succoth (12:37; Num 33:3, 5) – *Uncertain; possibly Tell el-Daba, ca. 62 mi. NE of Cairo* – 88

Rameses, district of – Region in NE Nile Delta where Jacob and his descendants settled (Gen 47:11). More commonly called (the land of) Goshen.

Ramoth (Gilead) – Also called Ramoth (2 Kings 8:29; 2 Chron 22:6) and Ramoth in Gilead (Deut 4:43; Josh 20:8; 21:38; 1 Chron 6:80). Levitical city of refuge allotted to Gad (Deut 4:43; Josh 20:8; 21:38; 1 Chron 6:80). Headquarters of Ben-Geber in a Solomonic district (1 Kings 4:13). Here Ahab and Jehoshaphat fought against the Arameans (1 Kings 22; 2 Chron 18 passim) as did Joram (2 Kings 8:28; 2 Chron 22:5). Jehu was anointed king here (2 Kings 9 passim) – *T. Ramith (244210), 36 mi. N of Amman in Jordan* – 13, 18, 23, 25, 27, 28, **28**, 36, 52, **53**, 77, **77**, **93**, 102, 103, 117, **119**, 120, 122, **125**, 126, 127, 128, **129**, 131, 132

Ramoth (Issachar) – Levitical town in Issachar (1 Chron 6:73). Because of position in list, probably same as Jarmuth (Josh 21:29) and Remeth (19:21).

Ramoth Negev – Place to which David sent spoils (1 Sam 30:27) – *Uncertain; possibly Kh. Ghazzah/H. Uza (165068), 20 mi. ESE of Beersheba. Possibly same as Ramah in the Negev (Josh 19:8)* – **128**

Raphana – 30, **167**, 170, 171

Raphia – 28, **49**, 59, 60, 125, 132, 149, 151, **157**, 160, **161**

Raphon – 154

Raqqad River/Valley – See Nahal Raqqad.

Ras Ali – 75

Ras el-Jeifa – 89

Ras en-Naqb – 55, 56

Ravine of the Poplars – Valley crossed by fleeing Moabites (Isa 15:7) – *Uncertain; possibly Wadi el-Hasa or Sel Esal, E of S end of Dead Sea.*

Recah – Unknown city in Judah (1 Chron 4:12).

Red Sea – "Red Sea" comes from LXX translation of Hebrew "Reed Sea" – (1) Sea Israel crossed at time of the Exodus and in which Pharaoh's troops perished. Mentioned 14 times in OT and in Acts 7:36 and Heb 11:29 – *Uncertain; possibly in Bitter Lakes area, but there are many other proposals.* – (2) Name for Gulf of Suez area to which locusts were blown after 8th plague (Exod 10:19) and near which Israel camped before going to Desert of Sin (Num 33:10–11) – *Gulf of Suez.* – (3) Sea at SE border of Promised Land (Exod 23:31). Israel traveled toward it from Kadesh Barnea as they went around Edom (Num 14:25; 21:4; Deut 1:40; 2:1 and possibly 1:40). Ezion Geber was on its shore (1 Kings 9:26) as was Edom (Jer 49:21) – *Gulf of Aqaba/Elath.* – 13, 16, 17, 18, 22, 42, 44, 51, 56, **56**, 57, **58**, **72**, **81**, 88, 89, 91–93, **92**, 121, 122, **123**, 128, 130, **130**, **141**, **142**, 143, 146, **148**, 175, **187**, 202

Reed Sea – See Red Sea – 88, 89

Rehob (Beth Rehob) – Israelite spies traveled N to it (Num 13:21), and troops from here fought David's army (2 Sam 10:8). Shortened form of Beth Rehob, Aramean principality N of Israel. See also Beth Rehob – 91, 118

Rehob (Jordan Valley) – 38, 83, 90, 107, 125, 126

Rehob (northern Asher) – Town on N (NE?) border of Asher (Josh 19:28) – *Uncertain; possibly T. el-Balat (177280), 12 mi. SE of Tyre in Lebanon.*

Rehob (southern Asher) – Town allotted to Asher (Josh 19:30), who was unable to drive out Canaanites (Judges 1:31). Levitical city (21:31; 1 Chron 6:75) – *Uncertain; possibly T. el-Bir el-Gharbi/T. Bira (166256), 5 mi. ESE of Acco* – **33**, 99, **99**, 102, 103

Rehoboth (Negev) – Name of well Isaac dug in the Negev (Gen 26:22) – *Uncertain; possibly Kh. Ruheibe/H. Rehovot (108048), 22 mi. SW of Beersheba, but a site farther N, between Gerar and Beersheba seems more probable.*

Rehoboth (Edom) – Place from which Edomite ruler Shaul came (Gen 36:37; 1 Chron 1:48) – *Unknown; in Edom, not along Euphrates as some suggest.*

Rehoboth Ir – Probably not a town but reference to squares or suburbs of Nineveh or Calah (Gen 10:11) – *In N Iraq, in/near Nineveh/Calah.*

Rekem – Town allotted to Benjamin (Josh 18:27) – *Unknown; probably W of watershed* – 125, **128**

Remeth – Town allotted to Issachar (Josh 19:21). Probably same as Ramoth (1 Chron 6:73) and Jarmuth (Josh 21:29) – 99

Rephaim, Valley of – Valley/plain area WSW of Jerusalem on border between Judah and Benjamin (Josh 15:8; 18:16). On several occasions Philistines camped in valley as they attempted to invade Judah/Israel (2 Sam 5:18, 22; 1 Chron 11:15; 14:9). This relatively flat area served as breadbasket of Jerusalem (Isa 17:5) – *The broad "Baqa" area WSW of Jerusalem (now occupied by several Jerusalem neighborhoods) through which railroad runs W before entering narrow valley farther W* – 114, 116, 189, **190**

Rephidim – Campsite of Israelites prior to Mt. Sinai where water was obtained from the rock and where Amalekites attacked Israel (Exod 17:1, 8; 19:2; Num 33:14–15) – *Uncertain; some place it at Feiran Oasis in SW Sinai, but location is also dependent upon where Mt. Sinai is placed.*

Resen – Place mentioned in connection with Nineveh and Calah (Gen 10:12) – *Unknown; possibly reference is to large water installation associated with area.*

Retenu (Upper and Lower) – 80, 83

Reuben – Eldest son of Jacob and name of tribe that descended from him. Territorial allotment E and NE of N end of Dead Sea – **53**, 101, 102, 118, 122, 131

Rezeph – Sennacherib in message to Hezekiah mentions how he has captured the gods of Rezeph (2 Kings 19:12; Isa 37:12) – *Uncertain; possibly modern Risafa, 15 mi. S of Euphrates near Sura in Syria, or a Rezeph closer to Jebel Sinjar in N Iraq* – 130, 137

Rhagae – 148

Rhegium – Paul's ship stopped here on journey from Malta to Puteoli (Acts 28:13) – *Reggio at S tip of Italy, opposite Sicily* – **186**, 187

Rhinocorura – 149, 157, 159

Rhodes – Inhabitants of Rhodes traded with Tyre (Ezek 27:15; NIV follows LXX rather than Heb. Dedan). Paul's ship stopped here on return voyage of third journey (Acts 21:1) – *Rhodhos, Greek island, the second largest in Aegean Sea (ca. 45 mi. by 22 mi.) ca. 12 mi. off SW coast of Turkey* – 13, 72, 156, **175**, 181, 182, 185, 186

Riblah – City N of Israel on Orontes River, where Pharaoh Neco put Jehoahaz in chains (2 Kings 23:33). Here Nebuchadnezzar of Babylon set up major camp in campaign against states of S Levant and Egypt. Here Zedekiah, last king of Judah, was executed, as were other political and religious leaders (2 Kings 25:6, 20–21; Jer 39:5, 6; 52:9–10, 26–27). Probably Diblah of Ezek 6:14 refers to the same place – *Ribleh (296427), in Syria,*

65 mi. NNE of Damascus – **62, 137,** 138, 139, **142**

Riblah – Site along NE boundary of Canaan (Num 34:11) – *Unknown; probably E or NE of Sea of Galilee.*

Ridge Route – 28, 40–42, 78, 91, 104, 110, **111,** 112, 124, 172, 188

Rift Valley – 16, **17,** 18–20, **18,** 22, 25, 29, **29,** 31, 33–35, **34, 38,** 40–44, 49, 51, 52, **53, 54,** 55, 95, 98, 106, 127, 164, 166, 171, 188, **189**

Rimmon – Town in Negev allotted to Judah (Josh 15:32) and Simeon (19:7; 1 Chron 4:32). Zech 14:10 also seems to place it in S Judah – *Uncertain; possibly Tell Khuweilifeh/Tel Halif (137087), 9.5 mi. NNE of Beersheba, but cf. Hormah* – **134**

Rimmon, rock of – Place to which 600 Benjamites fled after being defeated by the rest of Israel (Judges 20:45, 47; 21:31) – *Uncertain; possibly in area of Rammun (178148), 11 mi. NE of Jerusalem* – **105**

Rimmon (Zebulun) – Town on NE border of Zebulun (Josh 19:13); Levitical city (= Dimnah of Josh 21:35; = Rimmon of 1 Chron 6:77) – *Rummaneh/H. Rimona (179243) or possibly nearby site at 177243, 6 mi. NNE of Nazareth* – **98,** 99, **99**

Rimmono – Alternate form of Rimmon (Zebulun) (1 Chron 6:77).

Rimmon Perez – Israelite campsite between Rithmah and Libnah (Num 33:19–20) – *Unknown.*

Rissah – Israelite campsite between Libnah and Kehelathah (Num 33:21–22) – *Unknown.*

Rithmah – Israelite campsite between Hazeroth and Rimmon Perez (Num 33:18–19) – *Unknown.*

Rodanim – **71**

Rogelim – Home of Barzillai of Gilead who aided David in his flight from Absalom (2 Sam 17:27; 19:31) – *Uncertain; possibly Bersinya (223215), 16.5 mi. SE of Sea of Galilee, or nearby Dhaharat Soqa* – 119, **119**

Rome – Capital of Roman Empire. Jews from Rome were present in Jerusalem on Day of Pentecost (Acts 2:10). Claudius had expelled some Jews from Rome (18:2). Paul wanted to visit it (19:21) and wrote a letter to the Christian community there (Rom 1:7, 15). He finally visited Rome, but as a prisoner (Acts 23:11; 25:25; 28:14, 16; 2 Tim 1:17) – *Rome in W-central Italy* – 152, 153, 155, 158–62, **163,** 165, 166, **175,** 176, 177, 179, 180, 183, 185–87, **186, 187,** 197

Rosh HaNiqra/Haniqra – See Ladder of Tyre – 16, **17, 18, 31, 32,** 78

Route of the Patriarchs – 28, 78

Royal Road – 143

Ruba al-Khali – 12

Rubicon – 160, 163

Rubute (Khirbet Hamida) – See Rabbah (Judah) – 105

Rumah – Home of Zebidah daughter of Pedaiah, mother of Jehoiakim (2 Kings 23:36) – *Kh. er-Rumeh/H. Ruma (177243), 6 mi. N of Nazareth.*

Ruweisat el-Ahdar – **89**

Saba – 72

Sabta(h) – Third son of Cush (Gen 10:7; 1 Chron 1:9) – *Possibly locality in Arabia or Nubia.* **71**

Sabteca(h) – Fifth son of Cush (Gen 10:7; 1 Chron 1:9) – *Possibly locality in south Arabia.*

Sa el-Hafar – **86**

Safed – 33, 78

Saft el-Hinna – **86**

Sagarita – 143

Sahara Desert – 57, 58

Saint Catherine's Monastery – **60**

Sais – 143

Sakha – 81

Salamis – First stop on Paul's first journey where he and Barnabas and John Mark preached in the synagogues (Acts 13:5) – *NE portion of Cyprus, along S coast, just N of Famagusta* – 143, 147, **147, 149,** 175, 180, **181**

Salecah – Town on E edge of Bashan, once controlled by Og (Deut 3:10; Josh 12:5). Allotted to Manasseh (Josh 13:11; cf. 13:30–31), but Gadites settled region (1 Chron 5:11) – *Salkhad (311212), in Jordan, ca 62 mi. ESE of S end of Sea of Galilee and 8 mi. S of Jebel Druze* – 30

Salem – Home of Melchizedek to whom Abraham paid tithe (Gen 14:18; Heb 7:1–2). Associated with Zion in Ps 76:2 – *Alternate form for Jerusalem, although other interpretations have been proposed* – 75, **77,** 81, 146, 189

Salim – Prominent site used to locate Aenon, where John was baptizing (John 3:23) – *Probably T. er-Radgha/T. Shalem (199200), 7.5 mi. SSE of Scythopolis (OT Beth Shan). See also Aenon* – **170,** 171

Salima Oasis – 58

Salmone – Prominent landmark of E-most portion of Crete. Paul's ship sailed S of it going from Cnidus to Fair Havens (Acts 27:7) – *Cape Sidero, E tip of Crete* – **186**

Salona – 187

Salt, City of – Town in the desert/wilderness district allotted to Judah (Josh 15:62) – *Uncertain; possibly Kh. Qumran (193127), at NW corner of Dead Sea* – 98

Salt, Valley of – Place where David and his warriors defeated Edomites (2 Sam 8:13; 1 Chron 18:12; Ps 60, title), as did later Amaziah of Judah (2 Kings 14:7; 2 Chron 25:11) – *Uncertain; possibly the es-Sebkha region, S of the Dead Sea although the Wadi el-Milh, E of Beersheba has also been suggested* – **43, 44,** 117, 118

Salt Sea – Common biblical name for Dead Sea (Gen 14:3; Num 34:3, 12; Deut 3:17; Josh 3:16; 12:3; 15:2, 5; 18:19). Also called "Sea of the Arabah" and "Eastern Sea"; see Dead Sea – 20, 45, **60,** 78, 91–93, **91, 92, 94, 97, 98, 101–3, 111,** 114, **114,** 128, **128,** 132, 201

Samaga – 157, 158

Samaria (city) – Capital city of N Kingdom of Israel. Founded by Omri (885–874 B.C.; 1 Kings 16:24), developed by later Israelite kings. Mentioned 109 times in OT and 10 times in NT. Its capture by Assyrians ended N Kingdom. Subsequently, district around it became known as Samaria, its inhabitants as Samaritans. Renamed Sebaste during days of Herod the Great (37–4 B.C.) – *Sebastiyeh (168187), 7 mi. NW of Shechem* – 27, **28, 38,** 40, **125, 126,** 127, **129–32,** 131–33, **137, 138,** 140, **142, 144, 145, 147,** 149, **149–51,** 151, 152, 154, **157,** 158, **161,** 165, 171, 174, **177,** 203

Samaria (district) – 132, **132, 138, 144,** 145, **145,** 146, 150, 151, **151,** 152, 154, 155, 156, **157,** 158, 162, 163, **164,** 166, **167, 168,** 170, 172, **175, 176,** 177, **178,** 180

Samarra – 65, 66

Samos – Ionian island Paul's ship passed on return voyage of third journey (Acts 20:15) – *Greek island of Samos, 1 mi. W of Turkish coast opposite Ephesus* – 175, 185, **185**

Samosata – 162

Samothrace – Island in NE Aegean which Paul passed traveling from Asia Minor to Europe on his second (Acts 16:11) and probably third (20:6) journeys – *Samothrace* – 182, 183

San el-Hagar (Tanis) – **86**

Sansannah – Town in Negev allotted to Judah (Josh 15:31) – *Kh. esh-Shamsaniyat/H. Sansanna (140083), 8 mi. NE of Beersheba* – **97,** 134

Saqqara – 58, 72, 73, 74, **81,** 86, 87

Sardinia – 163

Sardis – One of the seven churches of Revelation (1:11; 3:1, 4). Ancient capital of Lydia. On major highway into interior of Asia – *Ruins just S of Turkish village of Sart, 48 mi. E of Smyrna (Izmir)* – 141, **142,** 143, **143,** 147, 148, **148, 175, 181,** 185, **185, 187**

Sarid – Town on S boundary of Zebulun; from here boundary ran W (Josh 19:10) and E (19:12) – *T. Shadud (172229), 6 mi. NE of Megiddo on N edge of Jezreel Valley* – 99, **99**

Saronic Gulf – 182, 184

Saudi Arabia – 12, **13,** 23, 55, 56, 60, 88

Scorpion Pass – On SE portion of the boundary of Canaan (Num 34:4) and of territory of Judah (Josh 15:3). Also served as border point of Amorite territory (Judges 1:36) – *Uncertain; possibly Naqb es-Safa/Maale Aqrabbim (near 162035), 20 mi. SW of S tip of Dead Sea.*

Scythopolis – OT Beth Shan – **149, 150,** 151, 154, 156, **157,** 160, **161,** 164, 167, 168, 170, 171, 172, **175–78,** 205

Seba – Land associated with Egypt and Cush (Gen 10:7; 1 Chron 1:9; Isa 43:3) and with Sheba (Ps 72:10) – *Uncertain; possibly area of Ethiopia, although some tribal members may have moved E across strait of Bab el-Mandeb and roamed in NW Arabia (cf. Sabeans in Job 1:15; Ezek 23:42; Joel 3:8), but Isa 45:14 associates some Sabeans with Egypt and Cush.* 71

Sebam – Alternate form of Sibmah (Num 32:3).

Sebaste – OT Samaria – **164,** 165, **167,** 170, 172, 174, **175–78**

Sebkha – **49,** 51, 56

Secacah – Town in desert district allotted to Judah (Josh 15:61) – *Uncertain; possibly Kh. es-Samrah (187125), 10 mi. SE of Jerusalem* – **97,** 134

Secu – Place in Benjamin to which Saul went to gather information about Samuel and David (1 Sam 19:22) – *Unknown; probably in Gibeah and Ramah region N of Jerusalem.*

Seir – Name of eponymous ancestor of group of Horites (Gen 36:20–30) who were displaced by Edomites (Deut 2:12). Seir is used 38 times in OT (7 in conjunction with "hill country of," 2 "land of," 8 "Mount Seir") – *Usually identified with the mountains in Jordan, E of Arabah Valley, stretching from Zered in N to Aqaba in S; but numerous biblical texts indicate it was also used to refer to territory W of Arabah (e.g., Deut 1:2, 44; 33:2; Josh 11:17; 12:7; 1 Chron 4:42–43; et al.). Sometimes used as a synonym for land of Edom (e.g., Gen 32:3)* – 23, 55, 56, 81, **92,** 98, 128, 159

Seir, Mount (Judah) – Geographical marker on N boundary of Judah (Josh 15:10) – *Uncertain; possibly ridge W of Kiriath Jearim and N of Kesalon, ca. 11 mi. W of Jerusalem* – **17, 18,** 23, **56,** 78, 81, 128, **128,** 159

Seirah – Place to which Ehud escaped after killing Eglon (Judges 3:26) – *Unknown; probably W or NW of Jericho; could be town or forested region* – 106

Sela – Edomite fortress captured by Amaziah who renamed it Joktheel (2 Kings 14:7). Mentioned in oracle concerning Moab (Isa 16:1) and in Isa 42:11. The marker of Amorite territory may or may not be same place (Judges 1:36) – *Uncertain; possibly es-Sela (205020), 23 mi. SE of S tip of Dead Sea in Jordan. Umm el-Bayyara (192971) seems to be too far S for the Moabite associations with this place* – **56, 125, 128,** 129, **130**

Sela Hammahlekoth – Saul abandoned pursuit of David here ("rock of parting"; 1 Sam 23:28) – *Unknown; probably E or SE of Maon (23:25).*

Seleucia – Port city of Syrian Antioch (ca. 16 mi. E) from which Paul and Barnabas set sail on first journey (Acts 13:4) – *Site near Samandag in Turkey, in NE corner of Mediterranean, a few mi. N of present course of Orontes River* – 149, 150, 151, **151**, 152, **157**, 175, 180, **182**, 186

Seleucia (Mesopotamia) – 65, 148

Seleucia Pieria – 181

Semechonitis, Lake – 20, 31, **31**, 160, 161

Senaah – Some inhabitants of this town returned from exile with Zerubbabel (Ezra 2:35; Neh 7:38) – *Unknown* – **144**

Seneh – Cliff or other geographical feature near Philistine camp captured by Jonathan (1 Sam 14:4) – *Possibly a cliff on rim of Wadi Suweinit (ca. 176141), 7 mi. NNW of Jerusalem, near Micmash* – 112, **112**

Senir – Amorite name for Mt. Hermon (Deut 3:9), although some passages seem to distinguish it from Mt. Hermon (1 Chron 5:23; SS 4:8; Ezek 27:5) – *Mt. Hermon in N Israel/SW Syria, or one of its prominent peaks* – **29**, 30

Sennabris – 168

Sephar – Locality on border of lands of Joktan (Gen 10:30) – *Uncertain; probably in S Arabia.*

Sepharad – Obadiah (v. 20) refers to exiles from Jerusalem living here – *Uncertain; possibly near Lower Zab River in NE Iraq; some suggest Sardis in W Turkey.*

Sepharvaim – People from here were settled in N Israel by Assyrians (2 Kings 17:24, 31). The conquest of the city and its gods became proverbial (18:34; 19:13; Isa 36:19; 37:13) – *Unknown; probably in Syria, but numerous proposals* – 133

Sepphoris – 33, 34, **157**, 160, **161**, 162, **164**, 166, 167, **167**, 168, **170**, 175, 177, **177**, 178

Serabit el-Khadim – 60, 61, **81**, 89

Shaaalabbin – Town allotted to Dan (Josh 19:42) – *Probably variant of Shaalbim* – 100

Shaalbim – Place where Amorites maintained themselves after conquest (Judges 1:35). Solomon later placed Ben-Deker in charge of this Danite district (1 Kings 4:9) – *Selbit/T. Shaalevim (148141), 19 mi. SE of Joppa* – **103**, 104, **122**

Shaalim, district of – Area where Saul searched for lost donkeys (1 Sam 9:4) – *Uncertain; possibly in Benjamin, N of Jerusalem* – 111

Shaaraim – Town in Shephelah allotted to Judah (Josh 15:36). Mentioned as point of reference in story of David and Goliath (1 Sam 17:52) – *Uncertain; possibly Kh. Sairah (152127), in N Shephelah near Azekah, 10.5 mi. NE of Lachish* – 97, 113, **113**

Shaar HaGay – 25

Shaaraim (Simeon) – Town allotted to Simeon (1 Chron 4:31) – *Unknown; probably in S Shephelah or Negev.*

Shaar Hagolan – 78

Shahal – 75

Shahazumah – Place on N border of Issachar (Josh 19:22) – *Unknown; probably between Mt. Tabor and Jordan River.*

Shalisha – Area through which Saul passed looking for his donkeys (1 Sam 9:4) – *Uncertain; possibly in vicinity of Baal Shalisha, 16 mi. NE of Jerusalem* – 111, **111**

Shamir (Ephraim) – Home and burial place of the judge Tola in Hill Country of Ephraim (Judges 10:1–2) – *Unknown* – **107**, 108

Shamir (Judah) – Hill country town allotted to Judah (Josh 15:48) – *Unknown; probably S of Hebron.*

Shaphir – Town, probably in Shephelah, mentioned by Micah (1:11) – *Unknown.*

Sharm esh-Sheikh – 58, 59, 60

Sharon (Plain) – Region of Coastal Plain N of Yarkon River and S of Mt. Carmel. Here cattle were pastured (1 Chron 27:29) in David's day. Its fertility could be a symbol of divine approval (Isa 35:2), its desolation, of disapproval (33:9). Some inhabitants were influenced by healing of Aeneas in Lydda (Acts 9:35) – 16, **17**, 27, **33**, 37–40, **38**, 46, 47, 105, 115, **115**, 119, **119**, 122, 124, 127, 131, 146, 151, 154

Sharon (Transjordan) – Called a Gadite pastureland in Transjordan (1 Chron 5:16; also Moabite Stone, line 13) – *Unknown; E of Jordan River/Dead Sea* – 55

Sharuhen – Town in W Negev allotted to Simeon (Josh 19:6); called Shilhim in Josh 15:32 – *Probably T. el-Ajjul (093097), 4 mi. SW of Gaza, although other proposals have been made* – 85, **86**, 87, **88**, 90, **97**, 125

Shatt al-Arab – 65, 66

Shaubak – 25

Shaveh, Valley of – Place where Abram met king of Sodom after defeating Kedorlaomer (Gen 14:17). See King's Valley – 81, 189

Shaveh Kiriathaim – Transjordanian site where Kedorlaomer defeated Emites (Gen 14:5) – *Unknown.*

Sheba (Arabia) – Queen of this country visited Solomon (1 Kings 10; 2 Chron 9; "Queen of the South" Matt 12:42; Luke 11:31). Famous for its merchants, gold, incense, etc. (Job 6:19; Ps 72:10, 15; Isa 60:6; Jer 6:20; Ezek 27:22–23; 38:13) – *Uncertain; possibly in SW Arabian peninsula in vicinity of modern Yemen, although some suggest the horn of Africa, near modern Djibouti.* – 22, 44, **71**, 121

Sheba (Simeon) – Probably alternate name for Beersheba (Josh 19:2) but possibly variant of Shema (15:26).

Shebarim – Place toward which inhabitants of Ai chased Israel (Josh 7:5, see NIV fn.) – *Unknown; probably E of Ai.*

Shechem – Mentioned close to 60 times in the Bible. Important non-Israelite center prominent in stories of Abraham, Jacob, and later Abimelech (Judges 9). Seems to have served as Israelite tribal and religious center during days of Joshua. On boundary between Manasseh and Ephraim (Josh 17:2, 7). Levitical city and city of refuge (20:7; 21:21; 1 Chron 6:66–67). Served briefly as first capital of N Kingdom; replaced by Tirzah and then Samaria. Called Neapolis during Greco-Roman period – *T. Balatah (176179), 30 mi. N of Jerusalem, on E side of Nablus* – 17, 18, **18**, 21, 25, 28, **28**, 38, 40–42, 52, **53**, 77, **77**, **78**, 79, 80, **82**–**84**, 83, 90–92, 94, **94**, 98, 102, 103–5, **105**, 107, 108, **112**, 114, 117, 119, 120, 122, 124, **125**, **126**, 127, **129**, 140, **142**, 144, 157, 159, **161**, 170, 172, **189**, 205

Shem – 71

Shema – Town in Negev district allotted to Judah (Josh 15:26) – *Unknown.*

Shemer, Hill of – See Samaria – 127

Shen – Samuel set up marker at Ebenezer, between Mizpah and Shen, to commemorate victory over Philistines (1 Sam 7:12) – *Uncertain; possibly variant of Jeshanah* – 111

Shepham – Place on NE boundary of Canaan (Num 34:10–11) – *Unknown; E or NE of Sea of Galilee.*

Shephelah (of Judah) – Geographical term for the low hills W of Hill Country of Judah but E of Philistine plain (save in Josh 11:2, 16b). Used 20 times in Bible, but NIV translates as "(western) foothills" – 33, 37, 42, **43**, 46–48, **46**, **94**, 95, 96, 98, 105, 109, 113, **113**, 119, **119**, 124, 128, 131, 135, 138, 146, 151, 154, 174, 177, 188, **189**, 202

Shephelah (foothill) of Carmel – 33, 37, 43

Shepher, Mount – Israelite campsite between Kehelathah and Haradah (Num 33:23–24) – *Unknown.*

Shibah – Name of well dug by Isaac in Negev, later called Beersheba (Gen 26:33).

Shihor (River) – Water course on the E of Egypt that marked SW limits of the land that remained to be conquered (Josh 13:3) and limit of David's influence (1 Chron 13:5). Also mentioned in Isa 23:3 and Jer 2:18 – *NE portion of Pelusaic branch of Nile in E delta of Egypt, or the frontier canal in far E delta* – 118

Shihor Libnath – Point (town? stream/wadi named after a town?) on S boundary of Asher in Mt. Carmel area (Josh 19:26) – *Uncertain; possibly Libnath is T. Abu Huwam (152245), 9 mi. SSW of Acco in modern Haifa.*

Shikkeron – Town on W portion of N boundary of Judah between Ekron on E and Mount Baalah on W (Josh 15:11) – *T. el-Ful (132136), 17 mi. SE of Joppa* – 97

Shilhim – Town in Negev allotted to Judah (Josh 15:32) – *Unknown; but see Sharuhen.*

Shiloh – Religious center in Hill Country of Ephraim where some of the tribal allotments were made, the tabernacle was set up, and Eli and Samuel ministered. Mentioned 32 times in OT, mostly in Josh, Judges, and 1 Sam, but also prominent in sermons of Jeremiah (7:12, 14; 26:6, 9) – *Kh. Seilun (177162), 20 mi. NNE of Jerusalem, E of ancient road from Bethel to Shechem, S of Lebonah (Judges 21:19)* – 18, **18**, 28, **28**, 38, 40, 82, 90, 94, 98, **98**, 102, 104, **105**, 110, **111**, 131, 140, 144, 190, 192, 194

Shimon – See Shimron – 90

Shimron – Canaanite town whose king fought against Israel (Josh 11:1). Allotted to Zebulun (19:15). Possibly same as Simeon (2 Chron 34:6) – *Kh. Sammuniyeh/T. Shimron (170234), 9 mi. NNE of Megiddo* – 31, 33, 36, 95, **95**, 99, **99**, 105

Shimron Meron – One of 31 towns vanquished by Israelites (Josh 12:20). Possibly fuller designation of Shimron, unless the LXX is correct in reading two towns: Shimron and Meron.

Shinar – Hebrew name for Babylonia: land that included cities of Erech, Akkad, and Calneh (Gen 10:10) and where Babel was located (11:2). Amraphel was king of Shinar (14:1, 9). Achan stole a "robe from Babylonia" (Josh 7:21; Heb. "Shinar"; see NIV fn.). Also mentioned in Hebrew text of Isa 11:11; Dan 1:2; and Zech 5:11 (see NIV fns.) – *In S Iraq* – 72, **78**, 81

Shion – Town allotted to Issachar (Josh 19:19) – *Uncertain; possibly Kh. Mugheir (183232), 4 mi. SE of Nazareth.*

Shittim – Last campsite of Israel before crossing the Jordan under Joshua (Num 25:1; Josh 2:1; Mic 6:5). From here spies were sent to Jericho (Josh 3:1). See Abel Shittim – *T. el-Hammam (214138), in Plains of Moab, E of Jordan River, NE of Dead Sea.*

Shual – Philistine raiding party turned toward Ophrah in vicinity of Shual (1 Sam 13:17) – *Uncertain; see Ophrah.*

Shubat-Enlil – 67

Shunem – Town allotted to Issachar (Josh 19:18) near which Philistines camped in preparation for battle with Saul (1 Sam 28:4). Abishag, who served David (1 Kings 1–2), was from here. A woman of Shunem assisted Elisha

251

(2 Kings 4) – *Solem (181223), 9 mi. E of Megiddo, at S foot of Mt. Moreh* – **33**, **34**, **99**, **114**, 115, **125**, **131**

Shur – Israelites wandered in Desert of Shur after crossing Red Sea (Exod 15:22). In a number of passages it serves as a marker (Gen 16:7; 20:1; 25:18; 1 Sam 15:7; 27:8) – *Uncertain; possibly a line of Egyptian forts near, or E of, present-day Suez Canal* – 60, 79, 112, 115

Shushan – 143

Siannu – 130

Sibmah – Town allotted to Reuben from domain of Sihon (Num 32:38; Josh 13:19). Passed into Moabite hands. Famous for its vineyards (Isa 16:8–9; Jer 48:32) – *Unknown.*

Sibraim – Site on N border of Israel between Damascus and Hamath (Ezek 47:16) – *Unknown; N of Damascus.*

Sicily – **186**, 187

Siddim, Valley of – Place where four kings of the N met with kings of cities of the plain (Gen 14:3, 8, 10) – *Uncertain; possibly S end of Dead Sea, or es-Sebkah region S of it* – **43**, 44, 45, 81, 201

Side – 175

Sidon (region) – A principal city of Phoenicia, mentioned 34 times in Bible. On NW border of Israelite settlement (Josh 11:8; 19:28; 2 Sam 24:6). Frequently mentioned in the Bible in connection with Tyre, especially in the prophetic literature. Jesus visited region (Matt 15:21; Mark 7:31) and mentioned it in cursing Korazin and Bethsaida (Matt 11:21–22; Luke 10:13–14). People of Sidon were present when Herod Agrippa I was struck with a disease (Acts 12:20). Paul's ship stopped here at beginning of journey to Rome (27:3) – *Saida (184329), 24 mi. SSW of Beirut on Lebanese coast* – **13**, 18, 27, **28**, 32, 36, **62**, 64, **84**, **94**, 95, **95**, 99, **100**, **105**, 117, 119, **119**, **125**, **126**, 127, **129–32**, 131, 135, 138, **142**, 146, **147**, 148, **149**, **150**, 151, 152, **157**, 162, **164**, **167**, **170**, 171, **175**, **177**, **182**, 186, **186**, **187**

Sile – 87, 88, **89**, **107**

Silwan – 193

Simeon – Second son of Jacob, ancestor of Israelite tribe. Mentioned 43 times in Bible. Tribal allotment (Josh 19:2–7; 1 Chron 4:28–32) in the S, within Negev district of Judah (cf. Josh 15:21–32). Simeonites seemed to have migrated to various regions in and around Israel (cf. 1 Chron 4:39–43; 2 Chron 15:9; 34:6) – 97, 98, **102**, 136, 202

Simonias – 168

Sin, Desert of – Area Israel passed through after Elim but before Rephidim (Exod 16:1; 17:1). Here manna began to be provided, as were quail – *Uncertain; depends upon location of Mt. Sinai. Probably in W or NW Sinai, E or SE of Suez.*

Sinai (Desert of, Mount) – The term Sinai is used 35 times in OT (all but 4 in Pentateuch) and 4 times in NT. Mt. Sinai (17 of 35 references) seems to be a specific peak in larger area called Desert of Sinai (13 of 35 references). The latter sometimes referred to as Horeb (17 times OT), but only once is the mountain specifically referred to as Mt. Horeb (Exod 33:6). All biblical references are associated with Moses and the giving of the law (Exod 19:2; Num 10:12), save for Elijah's flight to Horeb (1 Kings 19:8) – *Many proposals, but traditionally at Jebel Musa in central portion of S Sinai, although Jebel Sin Bisher (W portion of central Sinai) seems to be a viable alternative* – 12, **13**, 14, 27, 28, 42, 49, **49**, 51, 57, 59–61, **58**, **60**, 71, **72**, 75, 79, **80**, 81, 86–92, **86**, **89**, 115, 118, 136, 141, 142, 146, **147**, 148, 172, 174, 204

Sinim – Used as figurative reference to the S in prophetic oracle of restoration (Isa 49:12;

Hebrew form also used in Ezek 29:10 and 30:6 where NIV translates "Aswan") – *Aswan, on E bank of Nile in S Egypt.*

Sinope – 143, 175, 187

Siphmoth – One of a number of villages to which David sent gifts (1 Sam 30:28) – *Unknown; in S Hill Country of Judah or Negev.*

Sippar – 67, 137, 143

Sirah, well of – Well (or cistern) of Sirah at which Abner received Joab's summons to Hebron (2 Sam 3:26) – *Unknown.*

Sirion – Sidonian name for Mt. Hermon (Deut 3:9), but parallel to "Lebanon" in Ps 29:6. NIV of Deut 4:48 reads "Mount Siyon" – *Sirion may refer to whole Anti-Lebanon range of which Mt. Hermon is a part; E Lebanon* – 29, 30

Sitah – Name of second of three wells dug by Isaac's servants (Gen 26:21) – *Uncertain; probably in one of the valleys between Gerar and Beersheba.*

Siyon, Mount – Alternate name for Mt. Hermon (Deut 4:48). Possibly variant of Sirion.

Smyrna – One of the seven churches of Rev (1:11; 2:8). Prominent Roman city, famous for emperor worship – *Izmir on central portion of W coast of Turkey* – 185, **185**, 187

Soco – See Socoh.

Soco/Socoh (Hill Country of Judah) – Town in hill country allotted to Judah (Josh 15:48; cf. 1 Chron 4:18, "Soco") – *Kh. Shuweikeh (150090), 10 mi. SW of Hebron* – 134

Soco/Socoh (Sharon Plain) – Town in Solomon's third administrative district (1 Kings 4:10) associated with Arubboth and land of Hepher – *Kh. Shuweiket er-Ras (153194) on E edge of Sharon Plain, 26 mi. NNE of Joppa* – 33, 38, **38**, **98**, 122, **126**, 129

Soco/Socoh (Shephelah) – Town in N Shephelah district allotted to Judah (Josh 15:35). David fought Goliath near it (1 Sam 17:1). Fortified by Rehoboam for Judah (2 Chron 11:7, "Soco"). Taken by Philistines during reign of Ahaz (28:18, "Soco") – *Kh. Abbad/H. Sokho (147121), 17 mi. WSW from Jerusalem* – 46, 48, 97, 113, **113**, 125, 134

Sodom – City on SE boundary of Canaan (Gen 10:19) where Lot settled (Gen 13). Fought against kings of the N (Gen 14). Destroyed because of its wickedness (Gen 18, 19). It and Gomorrah became symbols of wickedness and of God's judgment. Mentioned 47 times in Bible – *Unknown; possibly one of the Early Bronze III sites E and SE of Dead Sea in Jordan* – **25**, 44, 45, 75, 81

Sodom, Mount – 43, 44, 45

Sogdiana – 143

Sorek, Valley of – Place where Samson fell in love with Delilah (Judges 6:4) – *Wadi es-Sarar/Nahal Soreq, W of Beth Shemesh (area around Timnah [141132] in NW Shephelah, 21 mi. SE of Joppa* – 47, 100, **100**, 109, 110, **111**, 135

Spain – Paul wanted to minister here (Rom 15:24, 28); some early Christian traditions suggest he eventually went – *Modern Spain* – 12, 187, **187**

Sparta – 13, 143, 146, 175

Strato's Tower/Tower of Strato – See Caesarea – **38**, 39, **150**, 151, **157**, **161**, 163, **164**, 165

Subite – 132, 145, **145**

Succoth (Egypt) – Site to which Israel traveled after leaving Rameses but before arriving at Etham (Exod 12:37; 13:20; Num 33:5–6) – *Uncertain; possibly Tell el-Maskhuta in Wadi Tumilat, 9 mi. W of Ismailia, in NE Egypt* – 88, **89**

Succoth (Transjordan) – Place where Jacob camped after encounter with angel of the Lord

---

(Gen 33:17). Allotted to Gad (Josh 13:27), Gideon punished its leaders after they refused to help him against the Midianites (Judges 8). Solomon cast bronze vessels for the temple in the area (1 Kings 7:46; 2 Chron 4:17), and the Valley of Succoth is referred to in the Psalms (60:6; 108:7) – *T. Deir Alla (208178), 22 mi. SSE of Beth Shan, E of Jordan near Jabbok* – **38**, **52**, **53**, **54**, 77, **77**, 78, **84**, **90**, **101**, 107, **107**, **120**, **126**, 132

Succoth, Plain of – 52

Suez – 51, 57, **58**, 60, 87–89, 118, 143

Suez, Gulf of – 57, **58**, 59, 60, **60**, 86, 88, **89**, 143

Sultan, Way of the – 51

Sumer – 66, 72, 73, **77**, 80, 105

Sumur – 62, 64, 87, 130

Suph – Place mentioned to localize setting of Moses' address to Israel (Deut 1:1) – *Unknown.*

Suphah – Mentioned in the difficult phrase "Waheb in Suphah" (Num 21:14) – *If a place, then in Moab, probably near Arnon Gorge.*

Susa – One of the capitals of the Achaemenian kings. Mentioned in Ezra 4:9 and Dan 8:2. The city/court of King Xerxes are setting for story of Esther (mentioned 19 times). Here Nehemiah served King Artaxerxes I – *Shush, 65 mi. NE of Tigris River, ca. 200 mi. WSW of Esfahan; in Iran* – **13**, **65**, 137, 142, 143, **143**, 148, 175

Sychar – Town in Samaria where Jesus met woman at well (John 4:5) – *Uncertain; probably at Askar (177180), 1 mi. NE of Shechem, if not at Shechem itself* – **170**, 172

Syene – 58

Syracuse – Port city where Paul stayed for 3 days when traveling from Malta to Puteoli on voyage to Rome (Acts 28:12) – *Syracuse on SE coast of Sicily* – **186**, 187

Syria – Large Roman province at E end of Mediterranean. OT Aram. Mentioned 8 times in NT, at times in connection with Cilicia (Acts 15:41; Gal 1:21) – *Area included much of modern states of Syria and Lebanon, as well as SE Turkey* – 12, **13**, 14, 16, 22, 27, 30, 62, **62**, 63, 65, 68, 84, 87, 88, 91, 108, 121, 140, 142, **142**, 146, 149, **149**, 150, 152, 155, 156, 160, 161, **163**, **164**, 166, **170**, 174, **175–78**, 176, 180, 181, **181**, **182**, **185–87**, 193, 200, 201

Syrian Desert – 12, 62, **62**, 63, **148**

Syrian Gates – **147**, 148

Syro-Arabian Desert – 65, 68

Syrtis/Gulf of Syrtis – Shallow area off N coast of Libya that Paul's ship tried to avoid (Acts 27:17) – *Gulf of Sidra on N coast of Libya* – 187

Taanach – Town conquered by Israelites (Josh 12:21), settled by Manasseh (1 Chron 7:29; Judges 1:27. Said to be "within" Issachar [Josh 17:11], but probably "beside" or "on the border of" Issachar is a better translation). Levitical city (Josh 17:11). Canaanites lived here (Judges 1:27) and traditionally divided war booty in its vicinity (5:19). In 5th Solomonic district (1 Kings 4:12) – *T. Tinnik (171214), 4 mi. SE of Megiddo* – 33, 36, 37, **38**, 78, 82, 87, **88**, **90**, 97, **98**, 99, **102**, 103, 105, 107, **107**, **109**, 116, **117**, 122, **125**, **126**, 203

Taanath Shiloh – Town on NE border of Ephraim (Josh 16:6) – *Kh. Tana el-Foqa (185175), 4.5 mi. SE of Shechem* – 98

Taba – 49, 60

Tabariyeh – See Tiberias – 205

Tabbath – Place toward which Gideon pursued Midianites (Judges 7:22) – *Unknown; probably E of Jordan River* – 107

Taberah – Place in wilderness where "fire from the Lord burned" among Israelites as punishment (Num 11:3; Deut 9:22) – *Unknown* – 91

Tabgha – See Heptapegon – 169

Tabor – Levitical town in Zebulun (1 Chron 6:77) – *Unknown.*

Tabor, (Mount) – On NW boundary of Issachar (Josh 19:22). Only in story of Deborah and Barak is Mt. Tabor referred to (Judges 4:6, 12, 14). Zebah and Zalmunna killed Gideon's brothers nearby (8:18). Mentioned in poetic (Ps 89:12) and prophetic literature (Jer 46:18; Hos 5:1) – *Jebel et-Tur/Har Tavor (186232), 4.5 mi. ESE of Nazareth* – 28, **31**, 33, **33**, 34, 36, 95, 99, **99**, 100, 107, **107**, 151, **168**, **170**, 171, **176**, 203

Tadmor – Large oasis and caravan stop in N Syrian desert, controlled by Solomon (2 Chron 8:4; cf. 1 Kings 9:18, NIV Tadmor, but Heb. Tamar) – *Palmyra, 130 mi. NE of Damascus in Syria* – 13, 14, **62**, 63, 64, 67, **80**, 121, **123**, **130**, **137**, **142**, 143

Tahath – Israelite wilderness campsite after Makheloth but before Terah (Num 33:26–27) – *Unknown.*

Tahpanhes – Egyptian town mentioned in late prophetic literature (Jer 2:16; Ezek 30:18), especially in connection with Jeremiah's forced exile to Egypt and his prophecy concerning Nebuchadnezzar (Jer 43:7–9; 44:1; 46:14) – *Tell Defenneh, in NE Egypt, on Pelusaic branch of Nile, 27 mi. SSW of Port Said, 8 mi. W of el-Qantara* – **141**

Tahtim Hodshi, region of – Region or town in a region through which Joab passed while taking the census for David (2 Sam 24:6) – *Unknown; seems to be located between Gilead and Dan.*

Tamar – Site mentioned by Ezekiel as being on SE boundary of a restored Israel (Ezek 47:18–19; 48:28); also mentioned in Heb. text of 1 Kings 9:18 as having been built by Solomon – *Uncertain; possibly Ein Husb/Hazeva (173024), 23 mi. SW of S tip of Dead Sea* – 28, 49, 51, **56**, 60, 63, 81, **92**, **120**, 121, **125**, 128, **128**, 145

Tanis – See San el-Hagar – 88, **130**

Tappuah (Ephraim) – Town conquered by Israel (Josh 12:17), on border between Ephraim and Manasseh. Allotted to Ephraim (17:18), but land around it to Manasseh (16:8; 17:8) – *Sheikh Abu Zarad (172168), 8 mi. SW of Shechem* – 38

Tappuah (Judah) – Town in N Shephelah allotted to Judah (Josh 15:34) – *Unknown.*

Taralah – Town allotted to Benjamin (Josh 18:27) – *Unknown; probably in W Benjamin plateau, NW of Jerusalem.*

Taricheae – 34, 35, **157**, 166, **167**, 168, **168**, 171, 177, **178**

Tarraconensis – **163**

Tarshish (southeast) – Place mentioned in association with Sheba, Seba, and Dedan (Arabian places/tribes; Ps 72:10; Isa 60:9). Solomon sent ships there and Jehoshaphat attempted to do so (1 Kings 10:22; 2 Chron 20:36; see NIV fns. in each case) – *Unknown; possibly in Arabia or E Africa* – **71**, **128**

Tarshish (Mediterranean) – Place (town? region?) along shores of Mediterranean (Isa 66:19) W of Levant with which the Levantine countries traded (Jer 10:6; Ezek 27:12). Jonah attempted to flee there (1:3; 4:2) – *Uncertain; possibly in Spain, North Africa, Sicily, etc.*

Tarsus – City where Paul was born (Acts 9:11; 21:39; 22:3) and to which he returned after his conversion (9:30; 11:25). Major trading and university city in Paul's day – *Tarsus, in S Turkey, in NE corner of Mediterranean, 10 mi. inland from the coast* – 13, **137**, **143**, **147**, 148, **175**, 180, 181, **181**, **182**, 183, **185**, **187**

Taurus Mountains – 67, **72**, **77**, **80**, 152, 180, 181, **181**, **182**, 183

Tatam – Hill country town allotted to Judah (Josh 15:59b; LXX only) – *Unknown.*

Taxila – **143**, 148

Tebah – Town of Hadadezer from which David took quantities of bronze (2 Sam 8:8 [Heb. "Betah"]; 1 Chron 18:8 [Heb. "Tibhath"]). Probably "Tibhath" would be a better translation in both instances – *Unknown; N of Israel* – 118

Tebtynis – 175

Tekoa – Hill country town allotted to Judah (Josh 15:59b; LXX only). One of David's mighty men was from here (2 Sam 23:26; 1 Chron 11:28; 27:9). A woman from Tekoa was brought to David to plead for Absalom (2 Sam 14:2, 4, 9). Amos was from here (1:1), and Jeremiah mentions it in an oracle (6:1). Men of Tekoa helped rebuild wall of Jerusalem (Neh 3:5, 27) – *Kh. Tequ (170115), 10 mi. SSW of Jerusalem* – 42, **43**, 44, **87**, **119**, **125**, **131**, **134**, **144**, 146, **154**, 155, 161, **164**

Tekoa, Desert/Wilderness of – Wilderness area E of Tekoa into which Jehoshaphat led his troops (2 Chron 20:20) – 155

Tel: see also under Tell.

Tel Agrah – 75

Telaim – Locality in S Judah where Saul mustered his troops prior to battle with Amalekites (1 Sam 15:4) – *Unknown* – 112

Tel Anafa – 75

Tel Aphek – See Aphek (Sharon) – 75, **109**

Tel Arad – See Arad – **72**, **73**

Tel Ashir – 78

Tel Assar – Town conquered by Assyrians (2 Kings 19:21; Isa 37:12) – *Unknown; possibly in NE Syria or NW Iraq.*

Tel Aviv – Settlement in Babylonia where Ezekiel met Jewish exiles (3:15) – *Unknown; on the Kebar River in S Iraq.*

Tel Bira – 78, **82**

Tel Dalit – 75

Tel Dan – See Dan – 75

Tel Dothan – See Dothan – 75

Teleilat el-Ghassul – 75

Tel Ektenu – 78

Telem – Negev town allotted to Judah (Josh 15:24). Some suggest it is alternate form of Telaim, but Heb. roots are different – *Unknown, although both T. el-Milh/Tel Malhata (1520690, 11 mi. E of Beersheba and Kh. el-Meshash/T. Masos (146069), 8 mi. ESE of Beersheba have recently been suggested. But see Arad; Hormah* – 112

Tel Erani – 46, 47, 73, 75

Tel Eton – See Eglon – 90, **109**

Tel Gamma – See Yurza – 90

Tel Gerisa – See Gath Rimmon – 75, **82**, 90

Tel Halif – See Rimmon – 75, **78**

Tel Haror – See Gerar – 82

Tel Harsha – Jewish settlement in Babylonia from which Jews returned to Judea (Ezra 2:59; Neh 7:61) – *Unknown; in S Iraq.*

Tel Hefer – 75

Tel Jemmeh – 82

Tel Kabri – 75, **82**

Tel Keison – 75

Tel Kison – 82

Tel Kurdani – 82

Tell: see also under Tel.

Tell Abu Huwam – See Shihor Libnath – 33

Tell Abu Seifa (Sile) – 86

Tell Atrib – 81

Tell Balatah – See Shechem – 77

Tell Basta – 81, 86

Tell Beit Mirsim – 46

Tell Defenneh – 60

Tell ed-Dab'a/Tell el-Dab'a – See Rameses – 80, 81, 85, 86, 88, 89

Tell el-Ajjul – See Sharuhen – 46

Tell el-Dab'a See Tell ed-Dab'a

Tell el-Farah (N) See Tirzah – 75, 82

Tell el-Farah (S) – 46, 49

Tell el-Farama – See Pelusium – 60, 89

Tell el-Ful – See Gibeah (in/of Benjamin) and Gibeah (of Saul) – 111

Tell el-Heir – 60

Tell el-Hesi – 46, 75, 90, 203

Tell el-Maskhuta – See Succoth (Egypt) – 81, 86, 88, 89, 146

Tell el-Yahudiya – 81, 86, 89

Tell er-Retabah – See Pithom – 60, 86, 88, 89, 141

Tell er-Ruweisa – 82

Tell esh-Sheikh Ahmad el-Areini – 207

Tell es-Sahaba – 81

Tell es-Saidiya – See Zaphon (Gad) – 90

Tell es-Samak – 33, 39

Tell es-Sultan – See Jericho – 82, 93, 204

Tell Mardikh – See Ebla – 64, 74, 203

Tell Marjame – See Baal Shalishah – 82

Tell Mugdam – 86

Tell Nabasha – 86

Tell Tayinat – 121

Tell Umm Hagar – 60

Tell Umm Hamud – 78

Tel Mahfar – 75

Tel Malhata – See Arad and Telem – 75, 82

Tel Masos – See Amalek, city of, Hormah, and Telem for various proposals – 82, 112

Tel Melah – Jewish settlement in Babylonia from which Jews returned to Judea (Ezra 2:59; Neh 7:61) – *Unknown; in S Iraq.*

Tel Mevorach – 38, 39, 82

Tel Mikhal – 38, 39

Tel Mor – 82, 90

Tel Nagila – 75, 82

Tel Obeid – 65

Tel Poran – 75

Tel Qadesh – 75, 82

Tel Qashish – 82, 90

Tel Qasile – 38, 78, 109, 120

Tel Qiri – 109

Tel Qishyon – See Kishion – 75

Tel Raqat – See Rakkath – 75

Tel Regev – 78

Tel Rehov – See Rehob (Jordan Valley) – 75

Tel Rekhesh – 75, 82

Tel Ridan – 82

Tel Safit – 75

Tel Sarid – See Sarid – 75

Tel Sera – See Ziklag – 90

Tel Shimron – See Shimron – 75, 82

Tel Shiqmona – 90

Tel Yarmuth – See Jarmut (Judah) – 75, 82, 90

Tel Yinam – 82

Tel Yosef – 78

Tel Zafit – See Gath (Philistine) – 82

Tel Zeror – 82, 90

Tel Zippor – 78, 90

Tema – Desert oasis mentioned in connection with caravan trade in Job (6:19) and Isa (21:14). Jeremiah seems to locate it in N Arabia (25:23) – *Teima (Tayma), 250 mi. SE of Aqaba/Elath in Saudi Arabia; 200 mi. NNE of Medina* – 13, 123, 130, 137, 140, **142**, **143**

Teman – Edomite town mentioned in prophetic oracles (Amos 1:12; Obad 9; Hab 3:3; Jer 49:20). Famous for wisdom (Jer 49:7). Eliphaz, one of Job's "comforters," was from here – *Uncertain; possibly Tawilan (197971), in S Jordan, 3 mi. E of Petra, 53 mi. S of S end of Dead Sea* – 56, 125, 128

Tepe Gawra – 65

Tephon – 154

Terah – Israelite campsite during wilderness wanderings between Tahath and Mithcah (Num 33:27–28) – *Unknown.*

Terqa – 80, 130

Tesmes – 143

Thamna – 154, 155, 160, **161**, 176, **176**

Thapsacus – 143, 148

Tharthar depression – 66

Thebes – One-time Egyptian capital city mentioned in prophetic oracles (Jer 46:25; Ezek 30:14–16; Nah 3:8) – *Luxor and area N of it, in S Egypt on E bank of Nile, ca. 400 mi. S of Cairo* – 13, 14, 57, **58**, 72, 73, 79, **80, 81**, 85, **86**, 136, **137**, 141, **143**, 148

Thebez – Town where Gideon's son Abimelech was killed by millstone (Judges 9:50; 2 Sam 11:21) – *Unknown; in Shechem area, although some identify it with Tubas (185192)* – 108

Thella – 166, 167, 168

Therma – 183

Thermaic Gulf – **182**, 183

Thermopylae – 143, **143**, 148, 152

Thessalia – 182

Thessalonica – Capital of Macedonia. Visited by Paul on second journey (Acts 17:1, 13) and probably also later (third journey and Phil 4:16). Aristarchus from Thessalonica accompanied Paul to Jerusalem (Acts 20:4) and to Rome (27:2). Demas deserted him and went here (2 Tim 4:10). Paul wrote two letters to the church here – *Thessaloniki, in N Greece on N end of Gulf of Salonika* – 175, **182**, 183–85, **185**, **187**

Thrace – 143, **143**, 148, 149, 163, 180, 181, 182, 185–87

Three Taverns – Stopping point on Appian Way, about a day's journey S of Rome (i.e., ca. 33 mi. S). Here Christians from Rome met Paul (Acts 28:15) – *Near modern Cisterna* – **186**, 187

Thuburba – 187

Thyatira – City in W Asia Minor, one of those addressed in Revelation (1:11; 2:18, 24). Lydia was from here (Acts 16:4) – *Akhisar in W Turkey, 50 mi. NE of Izmir, 33 mi. NNW of ancient Sardis* – **182**, 183, 185, **185**, 187

Tiberias – Capital of Galilee and Perea in days of Jesus. No evidence Jesus visited here, but boats from here are mentioned in John 6:23 – *Tabariyeh/Teverya (201242) on W shore of Sea of Galilee* – 25, **31**, 33, **34**, 35, 164, 166–68, **167**, **168**, **170**, 171, 175, 176, 177, **177**, 178, 204, 205

Tiberias, Sea of – Alternate name for Sea of Galilee (John 6:1; 21:1) – 35

Tiber River – 187

Tibnine – 31, 32

Tigris – One of the four rivers associated with Garden of Eden (Gen 2:14). On its banks Daniel received a divine revelation (10:4) – *Tigris River that flows through E Iraq* – 12, **13**, 65–67, **65**, 70–73, **72**, 77, 78, 80, 123, 130, 137, 141, **142, 143**, 148, 149

Tilmun – 73

Timna(h) (copper mines) – **49**, 51, **58**, 60, **60**, 61, 89, **92**, 121

Timnah – Town on NW border of Judah (Josh 15:10), but allotted to Dan (19:43). Occupied by Philistines in Samson's day (Judges 14 passim). Passed into and out of Philistine and Israelite hands (2 Chron 28:18; cf. 26:6). Conquered by Sennacherib in 701 B.C. May also have been scene of Judah's encounter with Tamar (Gen 38) – *T. el-Batashi/T. Batash (141132), 21 mi. SE of Joppa* – 46, 47, **84**, 90, 97, **100, 107**, 109, **109**, 113, **128**, 131, **134**, 135

Timnah (Judah) – Town in hill country allotted to Judah (Josh 15:57) – *Unknown; probably S or SE of Hebron.*

Timnah Heres – Place where Joshua was buried (Judges 2:9). Alternate form for Timnath Serah.

Timnath Serah – Town allotted to Joshua (Josh 19:50) and place where he was buried (24:30; cf. Judges 2:9) – *Kh. Tibnah (160157), 18 mi. NW of Jerusalem near W edge of Hill Country of Ephraim* – **38**, 98, 112, **112**

Timsah, Lake – 50

Tiphsah – Town attacked by Menahem (2 Kings 15:16) – *Unknown; possibly textual corruption for Tappuah or Tirzah.*

Tiphsah (Euphrates) – Town on NE limit of Solomon's territory (1 Kings 4:24) – *Dibseh (Syria), 55 mi. ESE of Aleppo, on W bank of Euphrates at the great bend* – 62, **62**, 121, **123, 130**

Tiras – 71

Tirqa – 62

Tirzah – Town conquered by Joshua (Josh 12:24) and possibly settled by descendants of Tirzah, a daughter of Zelophehad (17:3). Capital of Israel from the days of Jeroboam I (1 Kings 14:17). Omri moved capital to Samaria (16:23; cf. 15:21, 33; 16:6, 8–9, 15, 17). Menahem, one of last Israelite kings, served as governor here (2 Kings 15:14, 16). Famous for its beauty (SS 6:4) – *T. el-Farah (182188), 6 mi. NE of Shechem at head of Wadi Faria* – 28, **38**, 40, **40**, 82, 90, 98, 124, **126**, 127, **129**, 171

Tishbe – Evidently the home of Elijah (1 Kings 17:1) the "Tishbite" (6 times) – *Unknown; probably in Gilead* – 131

Tob – Town and district that served as place of refuge for the judge Jephthah (Judges 11:3, 5) and supplied troops to fight against David (2 Sam 10:6, 8) – *Et-Taiyibeh (266218), 45 mi. NE of Amman Jordan* – 117, 118

Togarmah – See Beth Togarmah – 71, 130

Token – Town allotted to Simeon (1 Chron 4:32). Parallel lists in Josh 19:7 and Josh 15:42 have Ether – *Unknown; probably in S Shephelah or N Negev.*

Tolad – Town allotted to Simeon (1 Chron 4:29). Variant of Eltolad.

Tophel – One of six places mentioned to localize where Moses spoke to Israel (Deut 1:1) – *Unknown, although et-Tafileh (208027), 20 mi. SE of S end of Dead Sea, has been suggested.*

Tower of Strato – See Strato's Tower.

Traconitis/Trachonitis – One of the areas included in tetrarchy of Herod Philip (Luke 3:1) – *Volcanic region known as el-Leja (ca. 300 sq. mi. area), which begins 22 mi. SSE of*

Damascus; *in Syria* – **29**, 150, 151, 163, **164**, 165, **167**, 169, **170**, 174, 176, **175–77**

Tralles – 187

Trans-Euphrates – Persian administrative unit; later separate satrapy. Mentioned 14 times in Ezra, 3 times in Nehemiah. Translated "the province Beyond the River [Euphrates]" in RSV – *Area stretching form Upper Euphrates-Orontes region S through Lebanon, Syria, and Palestine into N Sinai* – 142, **143**, 144

Transjordan – 20, 22, 24, 28, 32, **38**, 43, 50, 51, 77–79, 87, 88, 91, 92, 98, 100, 101, 102, 104, 105, 106, 108, 116, 119, 124, 127, 128, 130, 131, 133, 140, 146, 150, 151, 152, 154, 158, 169, 172, 175

Transjordanian Highway – 23, 27, 28, 30, 36, 51, 52, 55, 56, 81, 87, **88**, 92, 102, 158, 159, 160, 188

Transjordanian Mountains – 16, **17**, **18**, 22, 23, 28, 51, 91

Transversal Valley – 189, **190**

Trapezus – 1143

Tree of Moreh – See Moreh – 77

Tripoli(s) – 62, 64, 155, 175, 187

Troas – Gateway to Macedonia. Visited by Paul on second (Acts 16:8, 11) and third journeys (20:5–6). Here he preached (2 Cor 2:12) and left a cloak with Carpus (2 Tim 4:13) – *(Alexandrian) Troas, Eskistanbul, in NW Turkey, on coast, 15 mi. S of ancient Troy* – 181, **182**, 183, 185, **185**

Tubal – Region in E-central Turkey mentioned in prophetic literature (Isa 66:19), especially in connection with Meshech (Ezek 27:13; 32:26; 38:2–3; 39:1) – *Region in and N of Taurus Mountains in Turkey, E of modern Kayseri* – **71**, 130

Turan, Mount – 18

Turkey – **13**, 20, 27, 62, 65, 70, 74, 140, 150, 162, 175, 180, 186

Tyre – Phoenician city located on an island until Alexander connected it to the mainland by a mole (332 B.C.). Famous for maritime activities and trade. Mentioned 48 times in OT, 12 times in NT (9 in Gospels, 3 in Acts). On border of Asher (Josh 19:29), but probably never controlled by Israel. Hiram, its king, assisted David and Solomon in building projects and maritime activities. Mentioned frequently in prophetic literature, especially Ezek 26–28 – *es-Sur (168297), in Lebanon, 46 mi. SSW of Beirut, 12 mi. N of Israeli/Lebanese border* – 13, **17**, 18, **18**, 21, 27, **28**, **29, 31**, 32, 36, 62, 64, 80, **84**, 95, **99**, 100, **103**, 105, 107, 109, **117**, 119, 120, 121, 122, **122, 123, 125, 126**, 127, **129–32**, 131, 136, **137**, 138, **138**, 140, **142**, 143, 146, 147, 148, **149**, 150, 151, 152, **157**, 161, 162, **164**, 166, **167, 168, 170**, 171, **175–77**, 178, **182, 185**, 187

Tyre of Transjordan – 144

Tyropoeon Valley – 199, 189, **190**, 195

Ugarit – 13, 62, 64, 72, 77, 80, 108, 109

Ulai (Canal) – Stream or irrigation canal near Pesian capital of Susa where Daniel received vision of ram and goat (Dan 8:2, 16) – *In Susa region, possibly joining Kerkha and Karun Rivers.*

Ulatha – 163, **164**, 167, 168, 169, **170**

Ullaza – 105

Ullisu – **72**, 73

Umma – 76, 78

Ummah – Town allotted to Asher (Josh 19:30) – *Unknown; in Plain of Acco region; some LXX manuscripts suggest Acco.*

Umm el-Fahm – 33, 37, **38**

Umm el-Hawa – 75

254

Umm Qeis – See Gadara – 171

Uphaz – If a locality (Jer 10:9), it was known for its "fine gold" (as "Uphaz" is translated in Dan 10:5).

Upper Egypt – See Pathros – 57, **58**, 59, 61, **72**, 73, 74, 82, 85, 136

Ur – Birthplace and original home of Abram (Gen 11:28, 31; 15:7; Neh 9:7) – *Probably Tell el-Muqayyar, 190 mi. SE of Baghdad in SE Iraq, although alternate sites such as Urfa (SE Turkey) and Lake Van region (E Turkey) have been suggested* – 13, 14, 66, **72**, 73, 76, **77**, **78**, 80, 130, 137, 142, 143

Urartu – 130, 137, 142

Urmia, Lake – 130

Uruk – 72, 73, 143

Urusalima/Urusalimum – See Jerusalem – 75, 190

USSR – 13

Uthina – 187

Uvdah Valley – 78

Uz – Land where Job lived (Job 1:1). Jeremiah seems to place it E of Edom (25:2; Lam 4:21) – *Uncertain; E of Edom on edge of Arabian desert, possibly in Wadi Sirhan area, which begins ca. 50 mi. ESE of Amman.*

Uzal – Place mentioned in connection with trading Danites and Greeks (Ezek 27:19) – *Unknown, although Sanaa, the capital of Yemen in Arabia, and other places have been suggested.*

Uzu – 135

Uzzen Sheerah – Town (re)built by Sheerah, a daughter of Ephraim (1 Chron 7:24) – *Unknown; but evidently in vicinity of Upper Beth Horon.*

Van, Lake – 130

Venetia – 163

Verria – See Bered – 183

Via Maris – 27

Vienne – 187

Wadi Ahdar – 89

Wadi Auja – 42, 43, **43**, **53**, 54

Wadi Beersheba – 163

Wadi Doubbe – **31**, 32

Wadi el-Aqaba – 89

Wadi el-Arish – See also El-Arish and Egypt, Wadi of – **49**, 60, **60**, 89, 91, **91**, 159

Wadi el-Bir – 75

Wadi el-Kharrar – See Bethany, on the other side of the Jordan – 171

Wadi el-Malik – 99

Wadi esh-Sheikh – 89

Wadi Faria – See also Faria – **38**, 40, 52, **53**, 54, **54**, 77, **77**, 78, **78**, 84, 124, 127, 170, 171, 177

Wadi Feiran – 60

Wadi Fidan – 56, **56**

Wadi Firan – 89

Wadi Gharandal – 60, 89

Wadi Hammamat – 57

Wadi Hisma – 55, **56**

Wadi Jabbok – See Jabbok River – 77, **77**

Wadi Maghara – 61

Wadi Musa – 56, **56**

Wadi Musrarah – 99

Wadi of Egypt – See Egypt, Wadi/Brook of.

Wadi Qilt – 43, **43**

Wadi Sidri – 89

Wadi Sirhan – 108

Wadi Suder – 60

Wadi Suweinit – 112

Wadi Tharthar – 65

Wadi Tumilat – 88, 89

Wadi Yabis – 204

Waheb – Mentioned in the difficult phrase "Waheb in Suphah" (Num 21:14) – *If a place, then in Moab, probably near Arnon Gorge.*

Way of Edom – 131

(Western) Foothills – See Shephelah.

White Nile – 57, 58

Wild Goats, Crags of the – Area where Saul looked for David (1 Sam 24:2) – *Wilderness area W of En Gedi, if not the En Gedi oasis itself.*

Xanthus – 143

Yaar Hadera – 78

Yaham – 27, 38, **38**, 87

Yanoam/Yenoam – 105, 106, 107

Yarkon River – See Jarkon River; Nahal Yarkon – **38**, 46

Yarmuk River – 17, 18, 20, 23, 27–30, **28**, **29**, 31, 34, 44, 52, **53**, 54, **54**, 102, 103, 108, 126

Yarmuta, Mount 106

Yarmuth – 95

Yathrib – 140, 142, 143

Yaudi – Country that at one time controlled both Damascus and Hamath (2 Kings 14:28) – *Uncertain; some reference to be to Judah (of days of David and Solomon), while others suggest principality, called Yaudi in Assyrian and other inscriptions, located near Zenjirli in SE Turkey.*

Yavneh – See Janeel (Judah) – 78

Yavneh Yam – 82

Yemen – 51

Yeroham – 78

Yodefat Range – 34

Yurza – See T. Gamma – **28**, 46, 105

Zaanan – Town mentioned in Micah's lament for settlements in Shephelah (1:1) – *Unknown; possibly same as Zenan (Josh 15:37).*

Zaanannim – Place along S border of Naphtali famous for a large tree (oak; Josh 19:33). Also site where Heber the Kenite camped (Judges 4:11) near Kedesh (Naphtali) – *Uncertain; possibly Shajarat el-Kalb/Hurshat Yaala (200232), 3 mi. SW of S tip of Sea of Galilee* – 99, 100

Zab (River), Greater/Lesser – 66, 65, **72**, 137

Zadrakarta – 143, 148

Zagros Mountains – 12, 13, 65, **65**, 67, 68, **72**, 80

Zahar – Place famous for wool (Ezek 27:18) – *Some identify it with Sahra, NW of Damascus, but RSV translates "white wool."*

Zair – Place where Jehoram/Joram fought Edomites (2 Kings 8:21) – *Uncertain; possibly in Edom. Parallel text (2 Chron 21:9) has "with his officers."*

Zalmon – Snow on Zalmon is mentioned in Psalm 68:14 – *Uncertain; context seems to point to Bashan region; possibly area of Jebel Druze, ca 60 mi. SE of Damascus.*

Zalmon, Mount – Mountain near Shechem where Abimelech and his men cut wood to burn the stronghold of Shechem (Judges 9:48) – *Uncertain; possibly Mt. Gerizim, Mt. Ebal, or Jebel el-Kabir (NE of Shechem)* – 108

Zalmonah – Israelite campsite after Mt. Hor but before Punon (Num 33:41–42) – *Unknown, although es-Salmaneh (188021), 22 mi. W of Dead Sea, has been suggested, among other sites* – 92

Zanoah (Hill Country) – Town allotted to Judah (Josh 15:56) – *Unknown; probably S or SE of Hebron.*

Zanoah (Shephelah) – Town in N Shephelah allotted to Judah (Josh 15:34) and settled after exile (Neh 3:13; 11:30) – *Kh. Zanu/H. Zanoah (150125), 14.5 mi. WSW of Jerusalem* – **97**, 113, 134, 144, 146

Zaphon (Gad) – Town allotted to Gad (Josh 13:27) where Ephraimites met with Jephthah (Judges 12:1) – *Uncertain; possibly T. es-Saidiyeh (204186), 17 mi. SSE of Beth Shan, just E of Jordan River* – **54**, 101, 107, 108, 126, 129

Zaphon (mountain) – Mountain sacred to Canaanites with which Zion is compared (Ps 48:2) – *Mt. Casius (Jebel el-Aqra), 70 mi. WSW of Aleppo in Turkey, on border with Syria on Mediterranean coast.*

Zarephath – Sidonian town to which Elijah went during famine in Israel (1 Kings 17:9–10) and stayed with a widow (cf. Luke 4:26). Obadiah locates it on N boundary of Israel (20) – *Sarafand (176316), 13 mi. NNE of Tyre on Lebanese coast* – 62, 131

Zarethan – Place in central Jordan Valley where waters piled up as Israelites crossed Jordan (Josh 3:16). In 4th Solomonic district (1 Kings 4:12). Nearby bronze implements for the temple were cast (1 Kings 7:46; 2 Chron 4:17, Heb. "Zeredatha") – *Uncertain; possibly T. Umm Hamad (205172), 21 mi. NE of Jericho on E side of Jordan and N side of Jabbok. T. es-Saidiyeh has also been suggested (see Zaphon)* – 91, 94, 120

Zeboiim – City on SE border of Canaan (Gen 10:19). One of the five cities of the plain (Gen 14:2, 8). Evidently destroyed with Sodom and Gomorrah (Hos 11:8) – *Probably E or SE of Dead Sea* – 75, 81

Zeboim – Benjamite settlement in postexilic period (Neh 11:34) – *Unknown; probably in or near coastal plain near Hadid and Neballat, ca. 13 mi. SE of Joppa.*

Zeboim, Valley of – Philistine raiding party was sent toward it (1 Sam 13:18) – *Uncertain; probably E or SE of Micmash* – 112

Zebulun – Son of Jacob and tribe of Israel, mentioned 49 times in Bible. Settled in Lower Galilee, just N of Jezreel Valley – 34, 97–100, **99**, 102, 107, 108, 122, 135, 202

Zedad – Town on N boundary of Canaan, E of Lebo Hamath (Num 34:8; Ezek 47:15) – *Sadad (330420), 67 mi. NE of Damascus* – 145

Zela/Zelah – Town allotted to Benjamin (Josh 18:28). Here David buried bones of Saul and Jonathan (2 Sam 21:14) – *Unknown; in W Benjamin plateau, NNW of Jerusalem.*

Zelzah – Place on border of Benjamin where Rachel's tomb was located (1 Sam 10:2) – *Unknown* – 111

Zemaraim – Town allotted to Benjamin (Josh 18:22). The mountain associated with it figures in war between Abijah and Jeroboam I (2 Chron 13:4) – *Uncertain; possibly Ras et-Tahuneh (170147), 9 mi. N of Jerusalem* – 126

Zemaraim, Mount – See Zemaraim – 126

Zenan – Town in S Shephelah allotted to Judah (Josh 15:37) – *Unknown.*

Zenifim – 51

Zephath (in Negev) – Canaanite town destroyed by Judah and Simeon and renamed Hormah (Judges 1:17).

Zephath (in Sharon) – 33, 87, 88

Zephathah, Valley of – Valley near (N of?) Mareshah where Asa defeated Zerah the Ethiopian (2 Chron 14:10) – *Uncertain; probably in Mareshah region. LXX suggests "val-*

ley N of Marisa," implying the Valley of Elah – 128

Zer – Town allotted to Naphtali (Josh 19:35) – *Unknown; probably S or W of Hammath.*

Zeredah – Birthplace and home of Jeroboam I before his revolt against Solomon (1 Kings 11:26) – *Uncertain; possibly Deir Ghassaneh (159161), 16 mi. SW of Shechem, in Hill Country of Ephraim.*

Zered Valley/River – Israel stayed here just before camping at the Arnon Gorge (Num 21:12; Deut 2:13–14) on their approach to the Plains of Moab – *Wadi el-Hesa, which flows from ESE to WNW toward the SE corner of the Dead Sea* – 17, 18, 22, 23, 28, **28**, 55, **56**, **91**

Zererah – Place along SE path of Midianites fleeing from Gideon (Judges 7:22) – *Unknown; possibly Zarethan is meant* – 107

Zereth Shahar – Town allotted to Reuben (Josh 13:19) – *Uncertain; possibly ez-Zarat (203111), on E shore of Dead Sea* – 101

Ziddim – Town allotted to Naphtali (Josh 19:35) – *Unknown; probably W of Sea of Galilee.*

Ziklag – Town allotted to both Judah (Josh 15:31) and Simeon (19:5; 1 Chron 4:30). After fleeing from Saul to Achish, David was settled in this town to protect the Philistines' S flank, but he protected the Judeans as well (1 Sam 27:6; 30 passim; 2 Sam 1:1; 4:10; 1 Chron 12:1, 20). Jews settled here after the Exile (Neh 11:28) – *Uncertain; possibly T. esh-Shariah/T. Sera (119088), 15 mi. ESE of Gaza* – **46**, 97, 114–16, **114**, **117**, **134**, **144**, 146

Zin, Desert of – From here Moses sent spies into Canaan (Num 13:21). Kadesh (Barnea) was in or beside the Desert of Zin (Num 20:1; 27:14; 33:36; Deut 32:51). Part of S boundary of Canaan (Num 34:3–4) and of Judah (Josh 15:1, 3) – *Uncertain; located W of Rift, SW of Dead Sea, NW of Elath/Aqaba* – 16, 17, 18, 49, **89**, 91, 97

Zion – Ancient name for Jerusalem appearing 158 times in OT and 7 times in NT (NIV); primarily in poetic and prophetic passages, especially in Ps, Isa, Jer, and Lament; only 6 times in historical books. Can refer to the city (SE hill), the ancient citadel, or the temple mount, and by extension to Judah – 189, 192, **195**

Zior – Hill country town allotted to Judah (Josh 15:54) – *Unknown; probably located to S or SW of Hebron.*

Ziph – Negev town allotted to Judah (Josh 15:24) – *Uncertain; possibly Kh. ez-Zeifeh (148047), 18 mi. SE of Beersheba* – **43**

Ziph (Hill Country) – Allotted to Judah (Josh 15:55). David fled there from Saul (1 Sam 23:24; Ps 54, title). Fortified by Rehoboam (2 Chron 11:8). Calebites may have settled in region (1 Chron 2:42; 4:16) – *T. Zif (162098), 4 mi. SE of Hebron.* 44, 97, 114, **114**, **125**, **134**, 135

Ziph, Desert/Wilderness of – Area E of Ziph (hill country) where Saul pursued David (1 Sam 23:14–15; 26:2) – **114**

Ziphon – Town on N boundary of Canaan, between Zedad and Hazar Enan (Num 34:9) – *Uncertain; possibly Hawwarin (347407), 75 mi. NE of Damascus.*

Ziz, Pass/Ascent of – Ascent in En Gedi area via which Ammonites, Moabites, and Meunites invaded Judah in days of Jehoshaphat (2 Chron 20:16) – *Uncertain; possibly Wadi Hasasa N of En Gedi on W shore of Dead Sea* – 44, **128**

Zoan – City mentioned in date formula for founding of Hebron (Num 13:22). Plagues preceding the Exodus occurred in vicinity (Ps 78:12, 43). Mentioned in prophetic oracles of Isaiah (19:11, 13; 30:4) and Ezekiel (30:14) – *San el-Hagar, in E Delta, 82 mi. NE of Cairo* – **13**, 107

Zoar – One of the five cities of the plain attacked by kings of the N (Gen 14:2, 8). Lot escaped to it as Sodom and Gomorrah were being destroyed (Gen 19). Mentioned in description of Moses' survey of Promised Land (Deut 34:3) and with Moabite towns in prophetic oracles (Isa 15:5; Jer 48:34) – *Uncertain; possibly es-Safi (194049), 5 mi. S of S end of Dead Sea or one of the antiquity sites in vicinity (Hirbat ash-Sheh Isa? or Tawahin as-Sukkar?)* – **17**, 18, 22, **28**, **43**, 45, **49**, **56**, **60**, **75**, **77**, **78**, 81, **128**, **132**, 20a

Zobah – Aramean city-state N of Israel that was defeated by Saul (1 Sam 14:47). Hadadezer, its king, supplied troops to assist Ammonites against David and Joab, but they were routed and Zobah eventually fell to David (2 Sam 8, 10 passim; 1 Chron 18–19 passim; Ps 60, title). Also mentioned in connection with the rebel Rezon (1 Kings 11:23–24) – *Heartland was central Beqa Valley region in Lebanon* – 113, **117**, 118, 121, 123, **134**

Zohar – 44, 45

Zophim, field of – "Field of the watchers." Place to which Balak took Balaam to curse Israel (Num 23:14) – *Uncertain; on top of Pisgah.*

Zor – 20, 52, 54

Zorah – Town in N Shephelah allotted to Judah (Josh 15:33) as well as to Dan (19:41). Some Danites migrated from area to Laish in the N (Judges 18:2, 8, 11). Manoah, Samson's father and a Danite, was from Zorah (13:2). Samson was active in area (13:25) and was buried in vicinity (16:31). Rehoboam fortified it (2 Chron 11:10), and Jews settled here after the Exile (Neh 11:29) – *Sarah/T. Zora (148131), 15 mi. W of Jerusalem* – 97, 100, **100**, 107, 109, 113, **125**, **134**, **144**, 146

Zuph, district of – Area where Saul searched for lost donkeys (1 Sam 9:5) – *Uncertain; probably named after Zuphite clan and located in territory of Benjamin, possibly in area of Ramah.* 111

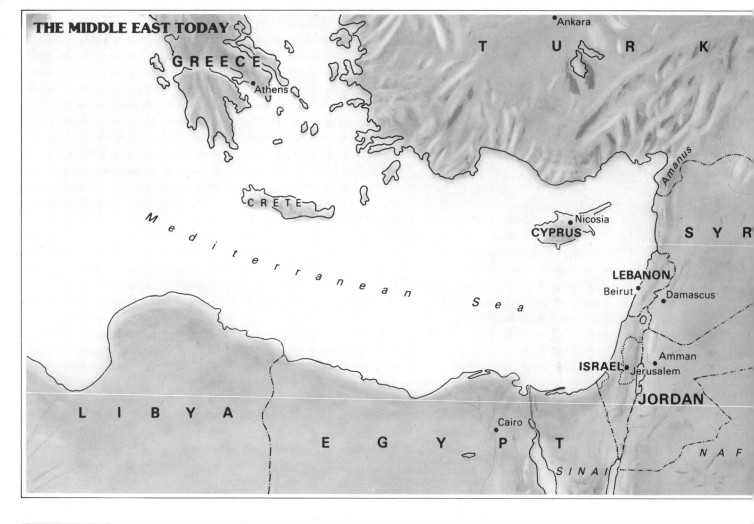

THE MIDDLE EAST TODAY

GREECE

Ankara

T U R K

Athens

C R E T E

Mediterranean Sea

Nicosia

CYPRUS

S Y R

LEBANON

Beirut

Damascus

ISRAEL

Amman

Jerusalem

JORDAN

LIBYA

Cairo

E G Y P T

SINAI

N A F

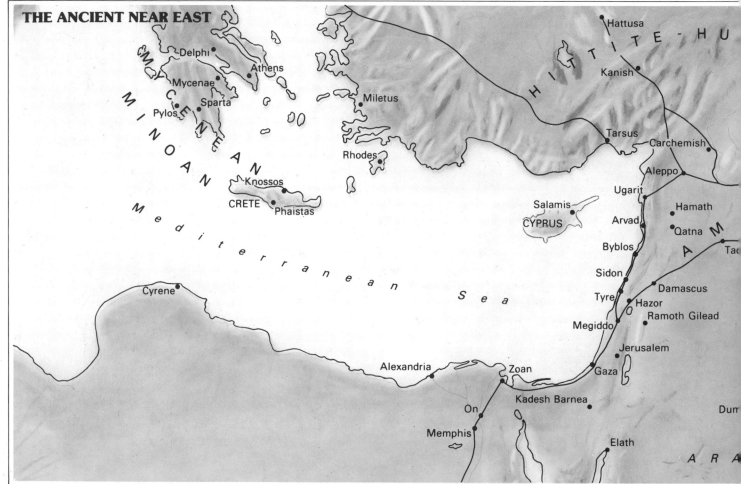

THE ANCIENT NEAR EAST

Hattusa

HITTITE-HU

Delphi

Athens

Kanish

Mycenae

Sparta

MINOAN

MYCENEAN

Pylos

Miletus

Tarsus

Carchemish

Rhodes

Aleppo

Knossos

Ugarit

CRETE

Phaistas

Salamis

CYPRUS

Hamath

Arvad

Qatna

M

Byblos

A

Tad

Sidon

Tyre

Damascus

Hazor

Ramoth Gilead

Megiddo

Cyrene

Mediterranean Sea

Jerusalem

Alexandria

Zoan

Gaza

On

Kadesh Barnea

Dum

Memphis

Elath

A R A